Lucio Tommaso De Paolis · Pasquale Arpaia ·
Marco Sacco
Editors

Extended Reality

International Conference, XR Salento 2023
Lecce, Italy, September 6–9, 2023
Proceedings, Part I

 Springer

Editors
Lucio Tommaso De Paolis ⓘ
University of Salento
Lecce, Italy

Pasquale Arpaia ⓘ
University of Naples Federico II
Naples, Italy

Marco Sacco ⓘ
CNR-STIIMA
Lecco, Italy

ISSN 0302-9743   ISSN 1611-3349 (electronic)
Lecture Notes in Computer Science
ISBN 978-3-031-43400-6   ISBN 978-3-031-43401-3 (eBook)
https://doi.org/10.1007/978-3-031-43401-3

This Springer imprint is published by the registered company Springer Nature Switzerland AG
The registered company address is: Gewerbestrasse 11, 6330 Cham, Switzerland

Paper in this product is recyclable.

Preface

In recent years, there has been a huge research interest in Virtual Reality (VR), Augmented Reality (AR), and Mixed Reality (MR) technologies that now play a very important role in various fields of application such as medicine, industry, cultural heritage, and education. The boundary between the virtual and real worlds continues to blur, and the constant and rapid spread of applications of these technologies makes it possible to create shortcuts that facilitate the interaction between humans and their environment and to encourage and facilitate the process of recognition and learning.

Virtual Reality technology enables the creation of realistic-looking worlds and enables the user to completely isolate himself from the reality around him, entering a new digitally created world. User inputs are used to modify the digital environment in real time and this interactivity contributes to the feeling of being part of the virtual world. Augmented Reality and Mixed Reality technologies, on the other hand, allow the real-time fusion of digital content into the real world to enhance perception by visualizing information that the user cannot directly detect with his/her senses. Applications of AR and MR technologies complement reality rather than replacing it completely and the user has the impression that virtual and real objects coexist in the same space.

eXtended Reality (XR) is an umbrella term encapsulating Virtual Reality, Augmented Reality, and Mixed Reality technologies.

Thanks to the increase in features that allow us to extend our real world and combine it with virtual elements, eXtended Reality is progressively expanding the boundaries of how we live, work, and relate.

The potential of XR technology is amazing and can transform consumers' everyday experiences and generate benefits in many market sectors, from industrial manufacturing to healthcare, education, cultural heritage, and retail.

This book contains the contributions to the International Conference on eXtended Reality (XR SALENTO 2023) held on 6–9 September 2023 in Lecce (Italy) and organized by the Augmented and Virtual Reality Laboratory (AVR Lab) at University of Salento (Italy). To accommodate many situations, XR Salento 2023 has been scheduled as a hybrid conference with the option of attending and presenting the paper in-person or following the scheduled activities remotely.

The goal of XR SALENTO 2023 is to create a unique opportunity for discussion and debate among scientists, engineers, educators, and students and allows them to connect with fellow entrepreneurs and companies operating in the same sector, thus experiencing applications of these emerging technologies.

XR SALENTO is an evolution of previous editions of the International Conference on Augmented Reality, Virtual Reality and Computer Graphics (SALENTO AVR), which had united the AR/VR community since 2014.

To cope with the growing demand for applications of eXtended Reality combined with other technologies, XR SALENTO 2023 also considered applications based on Digital Twins, Artificial Intelligence, and Data Mining technologies and realized to create a digital representation, collect and store data in real time, simulate the future state, and facilitate optimization.

We would like to sincerely thank the keynote speakers who gladly accepted our invitation and shared their expertise through enlightening speeches, helping us to fully meet the conference objectives. We were honored to have the following invited speakers:

- **Mariano Luis Alcañiz Raya** - Universitat Politècnica de València, Spain
- **Antonella Guidazzoli** - CINECA, Italy
- **Fabrizio Lamberti** - Politecnico di Torino, Italy

We cordially invite you to visit the XR SALENTO 2023 website (www.xrsalento.it) where you can find all relevant information about this event.

We are very grateful to the members of the Program Committee for their support and time spent in reviewing and discussing the submitted papers and doing so in a timely and professional manner. The received submissions were reviewed considering originality, significance, technical soundness, and clarity of exposition.

Based on the reviewing scores and critiques, 70 papers were selected for oral and poster presentation and publication in these proceedings.

We hope the readers will find in these pages interesting material and fruitful ideas for their future work.

July 2023   Lucio Tommaso De Paolis
                                                             Pasquale Arpaia
                                                             Marco Sacco

Organization

Conference Chair

Lucio Tommaso De Paolis   University of Salento, Italy

General Chairs

Pasquale Arpaia   University of Naples Federico II, Italy
Marco Sacco   STIIMA-CNR, Italy

Steering Committee

Andres Bustillo   University of Burgos, Spain
Antonio Lanzotti   University of Naples Federico II, Italy
Salvatore Livatino   University of Hertfordshire, UK
Roberto Pierdicca   Polytechnic University of Marche, Italy
Paolo Proietti   Leonardo SpA, Italy
Antonio Emmanuele Uva   Polytechnic University of Bari, Italy

Scientific Program Committee

Andrea Francesco Abate   University of Salerno, Italy
Sara Arlati   STIIMA-CNR, Italy
Álvar Arnaiz-González   Universidad de Burgos, Spain
Selim Balcisoy   Sabancı University, Turkey
Fabio Bello   Leonardo SpA, Italy
Marco Biagini   Italian Ministry of Defence, Italy
Monica Bordegoni   Polytechnic University of Milan, Italy
Davide Borra   No Real Interactive, Italy
Andrea Bottino   Polytechnic University of Turin, Italy
Andres Bustillo   University of Burgos, Spain
Massimo Cafaro   University of Salento, Italy
Maria Concetta Carruba   Università Telematica Pegaso, Italy
Marina Carulli   Politecnico di Milano, Italy
Laura Cercenelli   University of Bologna, Italy

Umberto Cesaro   University of Naples Federico II, Italy
Sofia Chiarello   University of Salento, Italy
Federica Faggiano   University of Salento, Italy
Benito Luigi Nuzzo   University of Salento, Italy
Giovanna Ilenia Paladini   University of Salento, Italy
Ileana Riera Panaro   University of Salento, Italy
Giada Sumerano   University of Salento, Italy

Keynote Speakers

From Reality to Extended-Social Reality: Conceptualizing XR As a Bridge Between Mirror Worlds

Mariano Alcañiz

Polytechnic University of Valencia, Spain

Mariano Alcañiz, Ph.D., is the founding director of the Immersive Neurotechnologies Lab (LabLENI) at UPV and a Full Professor of Biomedical Engineering at the Polytechnic University of Valencia. His general research interests hover around a better understanding and enhancement of human cognition, combining insights and methods from computer science, psychology, and neuroscience. His work is centered on using empirical, behavioral science methodologies to explore people as they interact in these digital worlds. Still, he also researches to develop new ways to produce Extended Reality (XR) simulations. Towards this end, he has been involved in clinical psychology, neurodevelopmental disorders, consumer neuroscience, organizational neuroscience, education and training projects.

He has published more than 350 academic papers in interdisciplinary journals such as Scientific Reports and PLoS One and domain-specific journals in biomedical engineering, computer science, psychology, marketing, management, psychology, and education. The Spanish Research Agency and the European Commission have continuously funded his work for 30 years.

He is the coordinator of several national and European R&D programs of excellence. He has been the National Program Coordinator of the Information Society Technology (IST) of the Ministry of Science and Innovation of Spain (2015–2019) and the Spanish representative for ICT area at the Horizon 2020 European Research Program Committee. He is also Vice-President for Academic and Scientific Issues of the European Association for Extended Reality (EURO-XR).

Transforming Cultural Heritage Preservation and Valorization: The Contribution of Supercomputing, Artificial Intelligence, and the Digital Twin Paradigm

Antonella Guidazzoli

CINECA, Italy

Antonella Guidazzoli graduated with honors in Electronics and History from the University of Bologna. Since 2007, she has been the head of the Visual Information Technology Laboratory (VISIT Lab - http://visitlab.cineca.it) at CINECA (www.cineca.it/en), one of the most important Supercomputing centers internationally. The Visit Lab is responsible for activities on advanced visualization methods ranging from scientific visualization to real-time 3D graphics and XR applications.

She is also a lecturer and course director of the CINECA Summer School on Computer Graphics for Cultural Heritage. Antonella has published several papers in major international conferences such as the ACM SIGGRAPH conference and won awards for projects in the field of e-Culture and Digital Heritage. In addition, Antonella is an evangelist of Quantum computing.

eXtended Reality for Education and Training

Fabrizio Lamberti

Politecnico di Torino, Italy

Fabrizio Lamberti received his MSc and PhD degrees in Computer Engineering from Politecnico di Torino, Italy in 2000 and 2005 respectively. Currently, he is a Full Professor at the Department of Control and Computer Engineering, Politecnico di Torino, where he leads the "Graphics and Intelligent Systems" research laboratory and is responsible for the hub of VR@POLITO, the "Virtual Reality" initiative of Politecnico di Torino. Since October 2021, he is the Chair of the PhD Programme of Politecnico di Torino in "Computer and Control Engineering". Fabrizio Lamberti has authored/co-authored more than 250 technical papers in the areas of computer graphics and vision, human-machine interaction, intelligent computing, and educational technologies. Since 2002, he is a Senior Member of IEEE. He is currently a Member of the Board of Governors (Elected Member at Large 2021–2023) of IEEE Consumer Technology Society (CTSoc). He also serves as Vice President for Technical Activities of CTSoc. He currently serves as an Associate Editor for IEEE Transactions on Computers, IEEE Transactions on Learning Technologies, IEEE Transactions on Consumer Electronics, and IEEE Consumer Electronics Magazine.

Contents – Part I

Digital Twin

Artificial Intelligence

User Experience in eXtended Reality

**Virtual Reality for Neurofeedback, Biofeedback and Emotion
Recognition**

Contents – Part II

eXtended Reality in Health and Medicine

eXtended Reality in Industrial Field

eXtended Reality

Passive Haptic Feedback for More Realistic and Efficient Grasping Movements in Virtual Environments

Lorenzo Gerini[✉], Fabio Solari, and Manuela Chessa

Department of Informatics, Bioengineering, Robotics, and Systems Engineering,
University of Genoa, Genoa, Italy
lorenzo.gerini@edu.unige.it

Abstract. Achieving natural interaction in virtual environments is essential to create realistic simulations in various fields, including healthcare and education. The ability to interact in Virtual Reality (VR) in a natural way, through a combination of visual and physical feedback can greatly enhance the experience and effectiveness of these simulations. Recent works have shown that the lack of haptic and tactile feedback produces significant differences in grasping actions performed in immersive VR, with respect to the same actions performed in the real world. The passive haptics approach, which relies on physical proxies to introduce tactile feedback in VR, has been explored to address this issue. This work focuses on a specific interaction task that involves both hand movements and grasping: pouring coffee into a cup and mimicking the action of drinking it. We take into account three different scenarios: a traditional VR environment where virtual objects don't have any real counterparts; an MR environment that uses an ecological object substitution technique where the user can interact with real objects that are tracked in real-time and see a virtual counterpart; and the corresponding real scenario. We compute the Minimum Jerk Cost and the Dynamic Time Warping distance between trajectories as metrics to compare movements in the different modalities in terms of their smoothness and trajectory shape, respectively. Our results show that movements in MR environments are smoother and produce more similar trajectories to real-world movements compared to classical VR environments. This indicates that MR with passive haptic feedback could produce more realistic and efficient human movements in virtual environments.

Keywords: Virtual Reality · Mixed Reality · Human-Computer Interaction

1 Introduction

A critical milestone in realizing a fully immersive virtual experience is the ability to enable users to freely explore, interact with, and manipulate virtual objects in a manner that closely resembles real-world interactions.

L. T. De Paolis et al. (Eds.): XR Salento 2023, LNCS 14218, pp. 3–22, 2023.
https://doi.org/10.1007/978-3-031-43401-3_1

Interacting with objects is a fundamental aspect of everyday human life, and replicating this interaction in virtual environments presents a significant challenge. While modern Virtual Reality (VR) systems offer high-quality visual and auditory stimuli, providing realistic haptic feedback that allows users to freely interact and perceive through the sense of touch, just as they do in the real world, remains a significant obstacle.

Most VR devices feature handheld controllers that facilitate basic interaction tasks such as object grasping and manipulation. However, these interactions often suffer from a notable limitation - a lack of authentic tactile feedback, which hampers the accurate replication of the sensations experienced during real-world interactions with physical objects. Controllers cannot provide users with the tactile experience of grasping a cube and perceiving the sharpness of its edges or the texture of its material. The use of hands as a natural and intuitive means of interacting with 3D objects has garnered attention as VR environments become more realistic [2]. Nevertheless, the absence of realistic haptic feedback in VR remains a primary barrier to achieving authentic object manipulation experiences [22].

In this context, integrating virtual and real elements to leverage passive haptics [10], could be a promising solution. Passive haptics involves receiving feedback from touching a physical object registered to a virtual object. When users touch or manipulate an object in the virtual world, they simultaneously touch or manipulate a corresponding object in the physical world. This element enables users to interact with the environment almost as naturally as they would in the real world.

Taking into account the definition presented in [23], which is based on the concepts and constructs introduced by Milgram and Kishino [15], we consider such an environment as a Mixed Reality (MR) environment. As the authors stated, "a MR environment is one in which real world and virtual world objects and stimuli are presented together within a single percept. That is, when a user simultaneously perceives both real and virtual content, including across different senses, that user is experiencing Mixed Reality".

MR has been recently explored in healthcare simulation [9,26] and other fields, where researchers are exploring hybrid approaches that combine physical and virtual simulations. MR systems retain the natural haptic feedback of physical simulations and the performance evaluation tools typically used in VR simulations. Several works have explored different approaches to introduce haptic feedback in VR. Huard et al. [11] developed a system based on passive haptics that allows remote participants to play cards together in a virtual environment by tracking an entire deck of cards, individually represented in the virtual world. Clarence et al. [5] employed a technique called *haptic retargeting* to map multiple virtual objects onto a single physical proxy, and identified an overall haptic retargeting limit through experimental sessions. Yu et al. [27] presented a prototype that uses origami carried by a drone to provide haptic feedback in VR, delivering the origami to the user's hand just as they are about to touch a virtual object, offering a novel and customizable approach termed as *encountered-type haptic*.

This paper extends the preliminary results shown in [7]. We present a MR system that leverages tangible, physical objects whose 6DOF pose is tracked in real-time to build a virtual representation of them. This approach exploits passive haptic feedback to enable interactions such as grasping and picking up actions on physical objects. At the same time, users perceive virtual shapes consistent in size and orientation with their physical counterparts. This integration of physical and virtual elements aims to provide a seamless and immersive experience where users can interact with the virtual environment through tangible objects naturally and intuitively. In particular, we consider two configurations:

- Physical objects are simple 3D shapes, i.e., prisms, onto which we map more complex virtual objects having the same spatial occupancy.
- Physical objects are complex 3D shapes, similar to the virtual ones, so only the visual appearance changes in the mixed visualization.

We aim to investigate the similarity between interaction movements, such as grasping, picking up, and placing, in MR and the real world. To achieve our goal, we examine hand movements during a simple task, such as picking up a moka coffee maker, pouring the coffee, and mimicking the action of drinking it, in three scenarios ranging from virtual to real. We compute the 3D position of the hands and analyze the movements in terms of jerk, following the minimum jerk theory [6, 19] (preliminary results of this already shown in [7]). Moreover, we assess the similarity between movement trajectories in the various conditions by computing the Dynamic Time Warping distance for time-series analysis [18, 20]. To further characterize the movements, we also calculate the average speed, average completion time, and estimate the number of direction changes.

The following hypotheses are formulated:

H1. MR with passive haptics allows users to perform tasks more smoothly than VR.

H2. MR with simple placeholders, i.e., tracking simple 3D prisms, allows us to obtain smooth movements without the need to track complex shapes.

H3. Movements' trajectories in the real world exhibit greater similarity to those obtained in MR compared to VR.

The rest of the paper is structured as follows. In Sect. 2, we describe how we have implemented the MR, passive haptic, environments, the metrics used to analyze the hand movements, and the experimental protocol. In Sect. 3, we present the results. In Sect. 4, we discuss the obtained results and future directions.

2   Materials and Methods

2.1   Hardware Setup

The hardware setup consists of three components: (i) an Oculus Rift CV1 head-mounted display, (ii) a Leap Motion Controller that tracks users' hands at a frequency of 120 Hz in both VR and MR environments, and also in the real environment; it is attached to the headset in VR and MR, and on a headband in the real scenario, and (iii) a consumer PC webcam that serves as input to the object tracking system. The webcam has a 1080p resolution and a 105° field of view. It is positioned in front of the user, at a distance of 69.5 cm from the table edge where the user is sitting, and is mounted on a tripod that is 10 cm high.

2.2 System Implementation

Virtual Environments. The VR and MR environments are developed using Unity. They consist of a simple room with a table aligned with the real table in front of the user. We utilize Leap Motion tracking data to calibrate the virtual table offline to ensure alignment. This involves placing the hands on the real table and acquiring palm positions for both hands, which are then used to position the virtual table accordingly.

6DOF Object Tracking. To interact with real objects in virtual environments, we must track their 6DOF pose in real-time. We developed a vision-based approach using Vuforia Engine 10.6 to avoid using physical trackers, which can be expensive and obtrusive when interacting with small objects. Vuforia offers different functionalities for tracking object or image targets in real-time, including Object Targets and Model Targets, which estimate the objects' pose based on texture features and 3D models. The Model Targets functionality is significantly more robust than the discontinued Object Targets, providing more accurate results. However, it should be noted that tracking multiple Model Targets simultaneously is not currently supported. Therefore, in our implementation, we utilize both Model Targets and Object Targets to overcome this limitation. The 3D models of the real objects are obtained through photogrammetry using 3DF Zephyr[1] and Autodesk ReCap Photo[2].

In our experiments, we tested two tracking configurations that involved tracking the 6DOF pose of two objects. A prism and a coffee cup are tracked in the first configuration, while a Moka coffee maker and a coffee cup are tracked in the second configuration. The Moka coffee maker had a texture that lacked detail, so we attached three fiducial markers with recognizable features to its sides to improve tracking performance.

After setting up Vuforia's targets in Unity, we use the estimated 6DOF pose of real objects from Vuforia to map them in real-time with a 3D model. In the first configuration, we track a simple physical prism and we map a CAD model of a Moka coffee maker onto it. In the second configuration, we track a Moka coffee maker and we map it with its own 3D model. In both configurations, the coffee cup was mapped with its own 3D model.

---

[1] 3DF Zephyr, https://www.3dflow.net/3df-zephyr-photogrammetry-software/.
[2] Autodesk ReCap Photo, https://www.autodesk.it/products/recap/.

Figure 1 illustrates the complete process, starting from the inputs to the object tracking system and leading to the visualization of the virtual counterpart of the tracked real object.

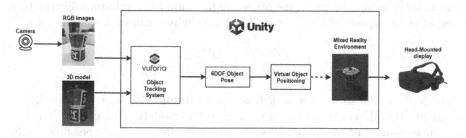

Fig. 1. Object tracking process: real object's 3D model and RGB images acquired by the Camera serve as input to the Vuforia-based Object Tracking System, which provides the 6DOF object pose for virtual object positioning in the MR environment.

Reference Frames Alignment. Vuforia estimates and tracks the 6DOF object pose relative to the camera. To display objects from the user's point of view in the HMD, it's necessary to align the camera's reference frame with that of the HMD - the Oculus reference frame. To achieve this alignment, a marker is placed on the front plate of the HMD. The Vuforia Engine's image-tracking functionality is then used to detect the marker, allowing for the estimation of the HMD pose in the camera reference frame. With the HMD pose in the Oculus reference frame, we calculate the rigid transformation between the two reference frames. Since the camera position is fixed, this stage can be performed offline. The computed transformation is then applied online to align the reference frames, enabling us to display objects in the HMD from the user's point of view.

2.3   Movement Analysis

In this study, we focus on the analysis of hands movements while performing a given interaction task. The analysis relies on several measures, including the Minimum Jerk Cost and Dynamic Time Warping, which allow us to evaluate the smoothness and similarity of trajectories between different conditions. Moreover, we compute the average speed and completion time and estimate the number of direction changes to compare the experimental conditions further.

Minimum Jerk Cost. Spatio-temporal invariance is a characteristic of human motion; in reaching movements, trajectories are straight with a bell-shaped speed profile. Additionally, movements are typically performed gracefully and fluidly, and the overall objective is to execute the smoothest movement possible that moves the hand from one equilibrium position to another [16]. The two main hypotheses that have been used to describe human arm movement planning are the optimization of smoothness-based or energy consumption-based cost functions and the two-thirds power law between curvature and velocity [17].

Regarding the first method, one strategy is to minimize the kinematically dependent quantities, such as the displacement and its derivatives in task-space coordinates (or angles and their derivatives in joint coordinates). The minimum jerk model [6] can be found in this category. To describe a point-to-point movement in a given time frame t_f, the objective function to be minimized is the time integral of the square of the magnitude of jerk, which can be formulated as:

$$MJC = \frac{1}{2} \int_0^{t_f} \left(\frac{d^3 x}{dt^3}\right)^2 + \left(\frac{d^3 y}{dt^3}\right)^2 + \left(\frac{d^3 z}{dt^3}\right)^2 \, dt \tag{1}$$

where MJC is the Minimum Jerk Cost to be minimized, and $(x(t), y(t), z(t))$ represents the 3D trajectory in time. The jerk is widely used in the literature as a measurement of the movements' smoothness, also for the upper limbs [6,8]. We compute the 3D trajectories and then the MJC for the left and right index, thumb, and palm. We then average these MJC values, thus obtaining a single cost which we use to measure the smoothness of the movements.

Dynamic Time Warping. Dynamic time warping (DTW) is a commonly used algorithm in time series analysis that can be used to compare two temporal sequences with different lengths or rates of change [20]. It has applications in a variety of fields, ranging from speech recognition and handwriting recognition to gesture recognition [18], where it has been utilized for evaluating physical rehabilitation exercises [28] or for the recognition of sign language [14].

DTW considers the temporal aspect by aligning sequences in time to find the best match between them. It is particularly useful for comparing sequences with similar shapes but different temporal profiles. For instance, if one trajectory is faster than another, DTW can align the trajectories in time so that corresponding points are compared, even if they occur at different times in the sequences. This makes it useful for comparing trajectories in different scenarios where the temporal dynamics of the trajectories may vary.

Let S_1 and S_2 be two sequences of length N and M, respectively. The algorithm begins by initializing a distance matrix, D, which is an $N \times M$ matrix where $D(i, j)$ represents the distance between the i-th point in sequence S_1 and the j-th point in sequence S_2, calculated using a distance metric such as Euclidean or Manhattan distance.

The Cumulative Distance Matrix C, which stores the accumulated cost of matching each point in one sequence to each point in the other sequence up to a given point in time, is then computed [3]. Specifically, C is a $(N + 1) \times (M + 1)$ matrix where each entry represents the accumulated cost of the best alignment between the first i points of the first sequence and the first j points of the second sequence, denoted as $C(i, j)$. The initialization of the first row and column of the Cumulative Distance Matrix C is as follows:

$$\begin{aligned} &C(0,0) = 0 \\ &C(i,0) = \infty \; \forall \, i = 1, \ldots, N \\ &C(0,j) = \infty \; \forall \, j = 1, \ldots, M \end{aligned} \tag{2}$$

The remaining elements are calculated recursively as follows:

$$C(i,j) = D(i,j) + \min(C(i-1,j), C(i,j-1), C(i-1,j-1))$$
$$\forall\, i = 1,\ldots,N \ and \ \forall\, j = 1,\ldots,M \tag{3}$$

After computing the Cumulative Distance Matrix, the next step is to find the optimal or warping path that minimizes the total distance between the sequences. This involves starting at the bottom-right corner of the matrix and recursively following the path of the minimum cost back to the top-left corner. The optimal path is represented as a set of pairs of indices (i,j) corresponding to the aligned points in sequences S_1 and S_2.

Finally, the DTW distance between two sequences S_1 and S_2 can be computed as follows:

$$DTW(S_1, S_2) = \frac{1}{L} \sum_{(i,j) \in P} D(i,j) \tag{4}$$

where $D(i,j)$ is the distance between the aligned points at indices (i,j) along the optimal path P, and L is a normalization term that is usually set equal to the length of the optimal path, the length of the longest sequence, or the diagonal length of the cost matrix [13, 20].

The DTW distance measures the similarity between the two sequences. A smaller DTW distance indicates a higher degree of similarity between the sequences, while a larger DTW distance indicates a lower degree of similarity.

Change of Direction Detection. Direction changes in hands' trajectories are detected with a curvature-based approach. To determine the number of direction changes in a given hand trajectory, the curvature is computed for each point along the trajectory as follows:

$$k(t) = \frac{\|\boldsymbol{v}(t) \times \boldsymbol{a}(t)\|}{\|\boldsymbol{v}(t)\|^3} \tag{5}$$

where $\boldsymbol{v}$ and $\boldsymbol{a}$ are the speed and acceleration vectors of the 3D trajectory $(x(t), y(t), z(t))$.

The points where the curvature exceeds a certain threshold are identified as the ones indicating a change in direction. The threshold value was determined through an iterative process of testing multiple threshold values and evaluating the results.

When multiple points in the hand trajectory exceed the curvature threshold and are located close to each other, to avoid counting multiple direction changes in the same motion segment, the point with the highest curvature value was selected as the representative for that motion segment. We consider two points belonging to the same motion segment if their Euclidean distance equals or exceeds a threshold (experimentally set to 4.5 cm). This is based on the assumption that the point of maximum curvature represents the most significant change in direction. The number of direction changes for a given trajectory is then counted by summing the selected points where the curvature exceeds the threshold.

2.4   Experiment

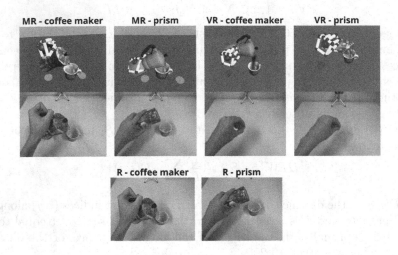

Fig. 2. The 6 conditions considered for the experiment

The users are seated in front of a table. They see a Moka coffee maker and a cup in all the conditions. They are asked to pick up the coffee maker, pour the coffee, and mimic the action of drinking it. The following 6 conditions are considered (see Fig. 2):

MR - prism. The real scene consists of a prism and a cup. Their 6DOF poses are estimated and augmented with a virtual moka coffee maker and a virtual cup.

MR - coffee maker. The real scene consists of a moka coffee maker and a cup. Their 6DOF poses are estimated and augmented with a virtual moka coffee maker and a virtual cup that resemble the real objects.

VR - prism. The user interacts within an immersive virtual scenario. The virtual environment includes a virtual prism and a virtual cup.

VR - coffee maker. The user interacts solely within an immersive virtual scenario. The virtual environment includes a virtual coffee maker and a virtual cup.

R - prism. The real scene consists of a prism and a cup, the ones used in the MR - prism condition.

R - coffee maker. The real scene consists of a moka coffee maker and a cup, the ones used in the MR - coffee maker condition.

The experiment has a within-subjects design, with each subject testing the 6 experimental conditions in a pseudo-random order to eliminate possible learning effects. The conditions were tested in pairs, with MR conditions, VR conditions, and R conditions tested together, respectively. Each condition was repeated 7 times. 15 right-handed subjects (age 26.2 ± 1.87) participated in the experiment. They all had normal or corrected-to-normal sight and were new to the experiment. Before the experiment, they were instructed about the task they had to accomplish. The task was unconstrained, and they were free to perform it as they preferred.

After each pair of conditions, participants were administered two questionnaires, the System Usability Scale (SUS) questionnaire [1] and the Slater-Usoh-Steed questionnaire [24, 25], to gather subjective feedback on system usability and *sense of presence*, respectively.

3   Results

3.1   Data Processing and Visualization

The raw data of the 3D positions of the left and right thumb, index, and palm are processed using a median filter with a window size of 5 samples. This filtering technique is applied to smooth the measurements and remove noise that may arise from the acquisition system.

In Fig. 3, the resulting 3D trajectories of the left and right palms for 7 out of the 15 subjects are visualized on XZ and YZ planes for the 6 conditions to examine their spatial distribution.

3.2   Movements' Smoothness: Minimum Jerk Cost

The Minimum Jerk Cost (MJC) is computed using Eq. 1, integrating from the beginning to the end of each repetition. The MJC values for the index, thumb, and palm are then averaged to obtain a single measurement representing the smoothness of the movement for each subject, experimental condition, and trial. Figure 4 shows the averaged MJC values across subjects for the 6 experimental conditions and 7 trials. The costs are different for VR (yellow), MR (green), and R (violet) conditions, considering both the prism (dotted line) and the coffee maker (dashed line) conditions. Solid lines represent the mean values of the coffee maker and prism conditions. The plots do not reveal appreciable differences among trials.

Table 1 presents the mean values and standard deviations, computed by averaging across subjects and trials. The table also includes the mean values of the prism and coffee maker conditions combined, reported in the MR, VR, and R rows. The costs for VR conditions are higher compared to MR conditions, and costs in real conditions are the lowest. This finding confirms our H1 hypothesis that movements in MR are smoother compared to VR.

For this and all subsequent analyses, the ANOVA test and Tukey-Kramer post-hoc test were performed to examine whether there were differences among the six experimental conditions. Prior to the analysis, checks for normality assumptions were conducted using the Anderson-Darling test. All seven trajectories for each subject and condition were included in the analyses. The results

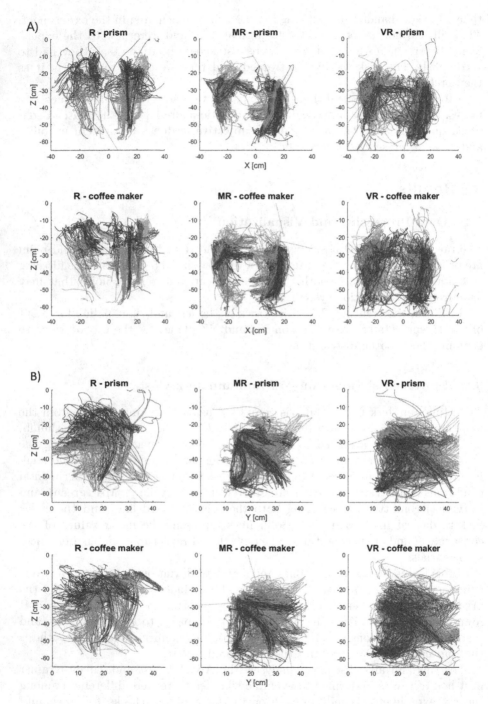

Fig. 3. Palm trajectories (color-coded according to the subject) for left and right hands and the 6 experimental conditions on planes XZ (A) and YZ (B).

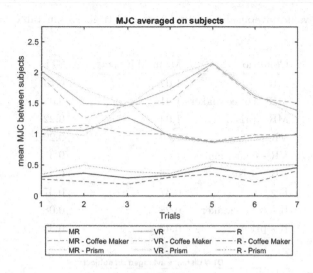

Fig. 4. Minimum Jerk Cost averaged across subjects. Solid lines represent the mean values of the coffee maker and prism conditions. (Color figure online)

showed a statistically significant difference in means, with $F(5,36) = 55.24$, and $p < 0.01$. Specifically, there was a significant difference among the MR, VR, and R groups, but no differences between the coffee maker and prism conditions within each MR, VR, and R modality. In particular, the cost for MR - prism was significantly ($p < 0.01$) lower than the costs in any VR conditions. This finding confirms our H2 hypothesis, suggesting that tracking a simple 3D object like a prism can improve movement smoothness without the need to track a complex 3D shape.

3.3   Trajectories Similarity: Dynamic Time Warping

To compare hand trajectories obtained under different experimental conditions, the following pairs of corresponding conditions are considered:

- VR prism vs. R prism
- MR prism vs. R prism
- VR prism vs. MR prism
- VR coffee maker vs. R coffee maker
- MR coffee maker vs. R coffee maker
- VR coffee maker vs. MR coffee maker

The DTW distance between the trajectories of corresponding trials is computed for each subject and pair of conditions. These DTW distances are then averaged across all subjects for each trial to obtain a global DTW distance for each pair of conditions. This process is repeated for each hand, and the final results are averaged across both hands to obtain an overall measure of DTW distance. Figure 5 shows the averaged DTW distances across subjects for the 6 pairs of experimental conditions and 7 trials.

Table 1. MJC values averaged across subjects and trials (mean values and standard deviations).

Condition	Mean MJC (m^2/s^5)	STD
MR	1.02	0.13
MR - coffee maker	1.01	0.08
MR - prism	1.04	0.22
VR	1.69	0.29
VR - coffee maker	1.63	0.3
VR - prism	1.76	0.33
R	0.37	0.07
R - coffee maker	0.28	0.08
R - prism	0.45	0.33

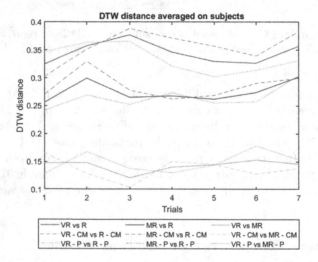

Fig. 5. DTW distances averaged across subjects. Solid lines represent the mean values of the coffee maker and prism conditions.

Table 2 presents the mean values and standard deviations computed by averaging across subjects and trials. The DTW distances between R and MR conditions are lower than those between R and VR conditions. This indicates a higher similarity between R and MR, as opposed to R and VR, confirming our H3 hypothesis. However, the lowest DTW distances are observed between VR and MR conditions.

The ANOVA test and post-hoc test conducted revealed a statistically significant difference in means, with F(5,36) = 113.27 and p < 0.01. Consistent with the MJC analysis, there is a significant difference observed among the MR, VR, and R groups, while no significant differences are found between the coffee maker and prism conditions within each MR, VR, and R modality.

Table 2. DTW distances averaged across subjects and trials (mean values and standard deviations).

Condition	Mean DTW distance	STD
MR vs R	0.275	0.018
MR vs R - coffee maker	0.286	0.023
MR vs R - prism	0.265	0.02
VR vs R	0.345	0.019
VR vs R - coffee maker	0.356	0.029
VR vs R - prism	0.335	0.024
VR vs MR	0.143	0.01
VR vs MR - coffee maker	0.137	0.02
VR vs MR - prism	0.149	0.019

3.4   Number of Direction Changes in Trajectories

The number of direction changes is computed for each trial, and an average value is obtained for each experimental condition and subject. The final results are then averaged across all subjects to obtain a global result for each condition. Table 3 presents the mean values and standard deviations computed by averaging across subjects and trials.

Although visual inspection of the results revealed the presence of some false positives and false negatives, the obtained results in the R - coffee maker and R - prism conditions appear reasonable considering the expected hand movements involved in the task performed by the subjects. The movements typically performed with the right hand include moving the hand towards the cup, picking up the cup and moving it closer to the coffee maker to pour the coffee, moving the cup to simulate the action of drinking, placing the cup back on the table, and pressing the button to conclude the trial. Indeed, for the R conditions, it is expected that at least four or five direction changes would occur during the task.

Figure 6 visualizes a sample trajectory for the R - coffee maker condition, with detected changes in direction highlighted using black circles.

The ANOVA test conducted revealed a statistically significant difference in means, with $F(5,84) = 11.57$ and $p < 0.01$. Although the post-hoc test showed that there is no significant difference in means between the R and MR groups, there is a significant difference between the VR group and the MR and R groups. No differences between the coffee maker and prism conditions within each MR, VR, and R modality emerged.

Table 3. Average number of direction changes (mean values and standard deviations).

Condition	Mean Nr. of direction changes	STD
MR	7.80	1.68
MR - coffee maker	8.62	2.62
MR - prism	6.97	1.39
VR	11.53	3.59
VR - coffee maker	11.80	3.73
VR - prism	11.26	4.19
R	6.60	1.29
R - coffee maker	7.30	1.69
R - prism	5.89	1.38

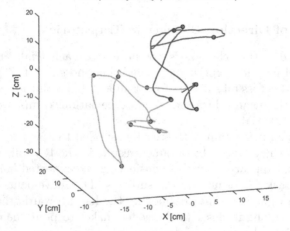

Fig. 6. Direction changes detection results for a sample trajectory, for right (blue) and left (yellow) hands, in R - coffee maker conditions. (Color figure online)

3.5   Average Speed and Time to Complete the Task

Table 4 presents the mean speed values and standard deviations computed by averaging across subjects and trials. It is observed that the mean speed in R and MR conditions is lower compared to the mean speed in VR conditions. This difference in speed could be attributed to the repetitive and rapid movements made by subjects when attempting to grasp virtual objects in bare-hand interactions. However, the results of the ANOVA test and post-hoc test indicated that there is no statistically significant difference in means, with $F(5,84) = 2.02$ and $p = 0.084$.

Table 4. Average speed (mean values and standard deviations).

Condition	Mean Speed (cm/s)	STD
MR	13.68	3.67
MR - coffee maker	14.30	3.80
MR - prism	13.06	4.63
VR	16.73	3.97
VR - coffee maker	16.41	4.52
VR - prism	17.06	4.00
R	13.82	5.04
R - coffee maker	12.94	5.13
R - prism	14.70	5.46

Table 5 presents the mean completion time and standard deviations computed by averaging across subjects and trials. The VR conditions exhibit higher completion time compared to the R and MR conditions. The MR - coffee maker condition shows a higher standard deviation compared to the MR - prism condition. This could be attributed to the higher occurrence of object tracking failures in the MR - coffee maker condition due to the complexity of the coffee maker object, while the MR - prism condition involves a simpler prism object, making tracking relatively easier.

Table 5. Average completion time (mean values and standard deviations).

Condition	Mean completion time (s)	STD
MR	11.64	4.62
MR - coffee maker	13.35	7.16
MR - prism	9.94	2.47
VR	14.72	5.85
VR - coffee maker	15.82	6.22
VR - prism	13.63	5.73
R	9.91	2.48
R - coffee maker	11.66	3.72
R - prism	8.16	2.01

The ANOVA test conducted revealed a statistically significant difference in means, with $F(5,84) = 4.67$ and $p = 0.0008$. However, post-hoc test revealed a significant difference in means only between R - prism and both VR conditions and between MR - prism and VR - coffee maker conditions.

3.6   System Usability and Sense of Presence Assessment

System Usability. The SUS score was obtained for each subject, and then a global SUS score was calculated by averaging the scores across all subjects. Results are shown in Table 6 (mean SUS scores and standard deviations for each modality (MR, VR, R)). The SUS score obtained for the VR conditions is lower than the one obtained in the MR conditions. The ANOVA test conducted revealed a statistically significant difference in means, with $F(2,42) = 28.93$ and $p < 0.01$. In particular, there is a significant difference between MR and VR means.

Sense of Presence. The Presence score for each subject is obtained by averaging the subject answers (range 1–7). The resulting scores were then averaged across all subjects to obtain a global Presence score for each modality. The global Presence score for each modality and standard deviation are shown in Table 7. The Presence score obtained for the VR conditions is lower than the one obtained in the MR conditions. The ANOVA test conducted revealed a statistically significant difference in means, with $F(2,15) = 52.65$ and $p < 0.01$. Post-hoc test revealed significant differences in means among all groups.

Table 6. Mean and standard deviation of SUS score values averaged across all subjects.

Modality	Mean SUS score	STD
MR	78.17	16.35
VR	51.67	16.30
R	90	8.13

Table 7. Mean and standard deviation of Presence score values averaged across all subjects.

Modality	Mean Presence score	STD
MR	5.47	0.93
VR	4.65	1.37
R	6.58	0.52

4   Conclusion and Discussion

In this paper, we have analyzed the smoothness and trajectory similarity of simple hand movements in MR and VR compared to the real world. As a metric to evaluate smoothness, we have followed the Minimum Jerk Cost theory [6,19], while the Dynamic Time Warping algorithm [18,28] was utilized to evaluate the similarity between trajectories in different conditions. We also characterized hand movements by computing the average speed, completion time, and estimation of the number of direction changes for each experimental condition.

Our research focused on bare hands objects manipulation, specifically on a simple task that is commonly performed in everyday life. This task involved grasping a moka coffee maker, pouring coffee into a cup, and bringing the cup to the mouth, mimicking the action of drinking the coffee.

Our main research hypothesis is that MR with passive haptics allows users to perform tasks more smoothly than VR, which lacks haptic and friction feedback (H1). Our results confirm this hypothesis, as we found that MR conditions had a Minimum Jerk Cost (MJC) 2.7 times higher than the corresponding real-world (R) conditions. On the other hand, the MJC for VR conditions was 4.6 times higher than that of the real-world conditions, indicating significantly less smoothness. These results confirm the preliminary data presented in [7]. In VR conditions, it can be more difficult to complete the task because of noisy and unstable tracking of the users' hands, which often makes grasping virtual objects difficult. In MR conditions, users can maintain their grasp of physical objects even when hand tracking is temporarily lost. This enables users to perform movements that are smoother and more similar, in terms of trajectory shape, to those performed in the real world. Indeed, the Dynamic Time Warping (DTW) distance is higher between VR and R conditions (0.34) than the one between MR and R conditions (0.27), confirming our hypothesis (H3) that movements' trajectories in the real world show greater similarity to those obtained in MR compared to VR.

However, we can not ignore that the lowest DTW distance is obtained between VR and MR conditions (0.14). Like hand tracking in VR, object tracking in MR is affected by noise and susceptible to tracking failures. During the experiments in MR conditions, subjects tended to avoid fast movements to maintain tracking stability, as shown by the average speed in MR conditions which is slightly lower than in R conditions. The average completion time is higher in both VR and MR conditions compared to the R conditions, possibly due to tracking failures in both cases, hands tracking in VR, and object tracking in MR. These tracking issues could also be the cause that led to the low DTW distance observed between VR and MR conditions. Additionally, we wanted to find out whether implementing MR by tracking (and grasping) a simple 3D shape, such as a prism, on which a more complex 3D object is displayed, in our case, a coffee maker, could be sufficient to provide haptic and friction feedback and enhance the smoothness of the movements in comparison to VR (H2). The results obtained from our experiment confirm the H2 hypothesis, too. Indeed there are no significant differences between the MJC costs in the MR - prism, and MR - coffee maker conditions.

The MR - prism condition is also characterized by a lower average number of direction changes, which is closer to the one obtained in R conditions, compared to the MR - coffee maker condition. The same trend is observed for the average speed and completion time parameters. This could be attributed to the fact that the prism has a simple 3D shape, making it easier to grasp and reducing the time between grasping and performing the pouring action, compared to the coffee maker. Additionally, tracking a simple 3D shape is generally easier than tracking a complex 3D shape. Considering this, the MR - prism condition is more stable and allows a better interaction. These findings further support the idea that implementing MR with passive haptics feedback could be a promising solution to overcome bare hands manipulation, combining the possibility of touching and grasping physical objects with the possibility of enhancing them in VR.

Mixed Reality   **Virtual Reality**

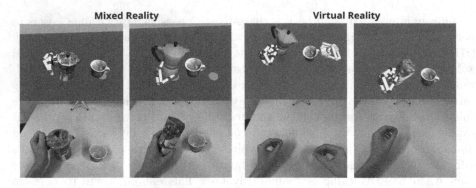

Fig. 7. Snapshots of the fingers' positions in MR (left) and VR (right).

The SUS questionnaire showed a preference for MR conditions over VR conditions in terms of usability. Subjects faced challenges in completing the interaction task in VR due to the lack of physicality, hand tracking issues, and unintentional drops of virtual objects. In contrast, MR conditions provided haptic and friction feedback from real objects, aiding successful task completion despite occasional object tracking failures.

The Slate-Usoh-Steed questionnaire found higher scores for MR conditions than VR conditions, indicating a stronger sense of presence. Haptic and friction feedback likely contributed to this result. One subject noted that *"hand tracking is not essential for the task, it comes naturally to think that the hand is visible when you pick up the object"*, even when the virtual hand is not visualized due to tracking failures. Another subject expressed concern about spilling coffee and made efforts to improve accuracy. These behaviors suggest that the MR environment fosters a greater sense of presence.

4.1   Future Works

Possible areas of improvement for this study could include enhancing the object-tracking system's stability and accuracy. Despite the previously mentioned tracking failures, misalignment between the real and virtual objects was observed depending on the position of the real object in relation to the camera. However, there is a point where real and virtual objects align perfectly. This effect was partially reduced with the calibration of the camera and correction of intrinsic distortion introduced by the lens, performed as preprocessing steps before feeding frames to the object-tracking systems. The same issue was identified in [21], where a comparable setup utilizing Vuforia and an external camera was employed for object tracking and augmentation. In that study, the offset error was considered to be a scaling error.

Results obtained from the experiment presented in this paper could lead to further discussions on the analysis of pick and place actions and finger configurations during grasping [4,12]. Figure 7 shows the finger positions on virtual objects in both MR (left) and VR (right) conditions. In MR, the finger positions closely resemble real grasps of physical objects, as observed in previous studies [12]. However, in VR, users tend to close their hands in unrealistic configurations, as reported in other studies [4]. Also, using a simple 3D placeholder in MR can lead to inconsistent finger positions in relation to virtual objects, as shown in the second column of Fig. 7, where an implausible grasp of the moka coffee maker is observed. This issue was also reported by certain users during the experiments.

Future works could also explore the application of Mixed Reality environments with passive haptic feedback to more complex tasks that require higher levels of dexterity and precision. For instance, activities involving spatial reasoning or decision-making, which could be beneficial for training and rehabilitative purposes, could be examined to evaluate the efficacy of the suggested system in more challenging scenarios.

References

1. Brooke, J.: Sus: a quick and dirty usability scale. Usabil. Eval. Ind. **189** (1995)
2. Buckingham, G.: Hand tracking for immersive virtual reality: opportunities and challenges (2021)
3. Candelieri, A., Fedorov, S., Messina, V.: Efficient kernel-based subsequence search for enabling health monitoring services in IoT-based home setting. Sensors **19**, 5192 (2019)
4. Chessa, M., Maiello, G., Klein, L.K., Paulun, V.C., Solari, F.: Grasping objects in immersive virtual reality. In: IEEE VR, pp. 1749–1754 (2019)
5. Clarence, A., Knibbe, J., Cordeil, M., Wybrow, M.: Investigating the effect of direction on the limits of haptic retargeting. In: 2022 IEEE International Symposium on Mixed and Augmented Reality (ISMAR), pp. 612–621 (2022)
6. Fligge, N., McIntyre, J., van der Smagt, P.: Minimum jerk for human catching movements in 3D. In: IEEE RAS and EMBS BioRob, pp. 581–586 (2012)
7. Gerini, L., Solari, F., Chessa, M.: A cup of coffee in mixed reality: analysis of movements' smoothness from real to virtual. In: 2022 IEEE International Symposium on Mixed and Augmented Reality Adjunct (ISMAR-Adjunct), pp. 566–569. IEEE (2022)
8. Ghasemloonia, A., Maddahi, Y., Zareinia, K., Lama, S., Dort, J.C., Sutherland, G.R.: Surgical skill assessment using motion quality and smoothness. J. Surg. Educ. **74**(2), 295–305 (2017)
9. Girau, E., et al.: A mixed reality system for the simulation of emergency and first-aid scenarios. In: IEEE EMBC, pp. 5690–5695 (2019)
10. Hoffman, H.: Physically touching virtual objects using tactile augmentation enhances the realism of virtual environments. In: Proceedings. IEEE 1998 Virtual Reality Annual International Symposium (Cat. No. 98CB3618, pp. 59–63 (1998). https://doi.org/10.1109/VRAIS.1998.658423
11. Huard, A., Chen, M., Sra, M.: CardsVR: a two-person VR experience with passive haptic feedback from a deck of playing cards. In: 2022 IEEE International Symposium on Mixed and Augmented Reality (ISMAR). IEEE, October 2022
12. Klein, L.K., Maiello, G., Paulun, V.C., Fleming, R.W.: Predicting precision grip grasp locations on three-dimensional objects. PLoS Comput. Biol. **16**(8), e1008081 (2020)

13. Lee, H.S.: Normalization and possibility of classification analysis using the optimal warping paths of dynamic time warping in gait analysis. J. Exerc. Rehabil. **19**(1), 85–91 (2023)
14. Li, W., Luo, Z., Xi, X.: Movement trajectory recognition of sign language based on optimized dynamic time warping. Electronics **9**(9) (2020)
15. Milgram, P., Kishino, F.: A taxonomy of mixed reality visual displays. IEICE Trans. Inf. Syst. **77**(12), 1321–1329 (1994)
16. Morasso, P.: Spatial control of arm movements. Exp. Brain Res. **42**(2), 223–227 (1981)
17. Richardson, M.J., Flash, T.: Comparing smooth arm movements with the two-thirds power law and the related segmented-control hypothesis. J. Neurosci. **22**(18), 8201–8211 (2002)
18. Riofrio, S., Pozo, D., Rosero, J., Vasquez, J.: Gesture recognition using dynamic time warping and kinect: a practical approach, pp. 302–308 (11 2017). https://doi.org/10.1109/INCISCOS.2017.36
19. Roren, A., et al.: Assessing smoothness of arm movements with jerk: a comparison of laterality, contraction mode and plane of elevation. A pilot study. Front. Bioeng. Biotechnol. **9** (2021)
20. Sakoe, H., Chiba, S.: Dynamic programming algorithm optimization for spoken word recognition. **26**, 43–49 (1978)
21. Schott, D., Heinrich, F., Stallmeister, L., Hansen, C.: Exploring object and multi-target instrument tracking for AR-guided interventions. Curr. Direct. Biomed. Eng. **8**(1), 74–77 (2022). https://doi.org/10.1515/cdbme-2022-0019
22. Sirizzotti, M., Guercio, S., Lampus, F., Marti, P., Lusuardi, L., Innocenti, A.: Tangible interactions in virtual reality environments. In: ETIS (2020)
23. Skarbez, R., Smith, M., Whitton, M.C.: Revisiting milgram and Kishino's reality-virtuality continuum. Front. Virtual Real. **2**, 647997 (2021)
24. Slater, M., Steed, A., McCarthy, J., Maringelli, F.: The influence of body movement on subjective presence in virtual environments. Hum. Factors **40**(3), 469–477 (1998). https://doi.org/10.1518/001872098779591368, pMID: 9849105
25. Usoh, M., et al.: Walking >walking-in-place> flying, in virtual environments. In: Proceedings of the 26th Annual Conference on Computer Graphics and Interactive Techniques. SIGGRAPH '99, pp. 359–364. ACM Press/Addison-Wesley Publishing Co., USA (1999)
26. Viglialoro, R.M., Condino, S., Turini, G., Carbone, M., Ferrari, V., Gesi, M.: Augmented reality, mixed reality, and hybrid approach in healthcare simulation: a systematic review. Appl. Sci. **11**(5), 2338 (2021)
27. Yu, D., et al.: Haptics in VR using origami-augmented drones. In: 2022 IEEE International Symposium on Mixed and Augmented Reality Adjunct (ISMAR-Adjunct), pp. 905–906 (2022)
28. Yu, X., Xiong, S.: A dynamic time warping based algorithm to evaluate kinect-enabled home-based physical rehabilitation exercises for older people. Sensors **19**(13) (2019)

Virtual 3D System of Two Interconnected Tanks for Level Control Using the Hardware in the Loop Technique

Alexis S. Zambrano, Edwin P. Pruna$^{(\boxtimes)}$, Marco A. Pilatásig, and Ivón P. Escobar

Universidad de las Fuerzas Armadas ESPE, Sangolquí, Ecuador
{aszambrano2,eppruna,mapilatagsig,ipescobar}@espe.edu.ec

Abstract. This article presents the design and simulation of the control of a system of two interconnected tanks using the Hardware in the Loop technique. An industrial process is implemented in a virtualised environment with characteristics approximating those of a real plant with the help of the Unity graphics engine, with the purpose of having the behaviour of the two-tank system in a simulation loop; which allows the behaviour of the process to be evaluated and a control law corresponding to the system to be implemented using a physical PLC and communicating it with the virtual environment with industrial protocols. Achieving an interactive and immersive virtual environment for the user, which allows visualising and navigating in the application as if it were a real process.

Keywords: HIL Simulation · Virtual Environment · Tank Level Control

1 Introduction

The basic idea of simulation in HIL is to include a part of the real hardware in the simulation loop during the development of the system [1, 2]. Instead of evaluating the control algorithm on a purely mathematical model of the system, real hardware (if available) can be used in the simulation loop. For the industrial process to respond correctly, a mathematical model is required, which must provide all the process signals in real time that are then converted by the D/A modules and supplied to the controller as voltages [3]. In a HIL simulation, the interactions between the system under test and the real-world environment are usually modelled as a continuous system defined by a set of non-linear differential equations [4].

Employing this technique has many benefits such as: the design and testing of control hardware and software without the need to operate the actual process [5]; HIL simulation requires less hardware than physical prototyping and therefore costs less. It allows to reduce the costs that would be involved in a real process by the simple fact that the availability of personal computers facilitates the use of different programming and simulation techniques [6]. The HIL technique has many advantages which are used in industry and in education for the teaching of process control.

L. T. De Paolis et al. (Eds.): XR Salento 2023, LNCS 14218, pp. 23–35, 2023.
https://doi.org/10.1007/978-3-031-43401-3_2

HIL simulation is combined with virtual reality, which is defined as a set of merged technologies developed to integrate the user with virtually designed environments [7]. We speak of e-learning, i.e., learning generated or mediated by different technologies based in one way or another on electronic media to carry out all or part of the training process. There are definitions that assimilate it to any educational process related to technologies [8]. Virtual learning consists of students interacting with the virtual world to perform simulated experiments and visualise the effects of the experiment in a 3D environment [9].

In this context, there is a lot of research using the HIL technique, for example: in [10] the work was carried out in 2004, the authors noted the potential as the technique matures and the professions work to develop procedures that allow for rigorous and systematic evaluation of alternative control algorithms. In [11] the authors analyse a flow plant and achieve an animation of performance similar to a real one and whose responses to the implemented controllers are in real time, and conclude that it is a low-cost approach to teaching process control. In [12] a neural simulation based on HIL is performed to test the engine control system in gas turbines, where the authors conclude that they have managed to decrease the average error of their process, however, the computational load of the microcontroller increased, so they recommend that there are limitations in the computational complexity. The authors in [13] highlight that their main technical challenges in designing the HIL test system were the need to test several devices at the same time and the real-time requirements, due to the need to simulate millisecond-scale fault currents. By analysing the different projects of different authors applying the HIL technique both their fruitful results and feedbacks can be useful in the development of the present work. Furthermore, each of the project analysed dealt with e-learning, but if developed in a more professional way, it can be used in the training o operators in industrial plants.

This paper focuses on the level variable because level and flow control between tanks is a control problem in industrial processes and engineering applications [14, 15], often tanks are coupled and the levels interact with each other, and this also has to be controlled. In most applications a PID controller is used for liquid level control in tanks [16, 17], consequently, it has been chosen as the main one for the respective total control of the interconnected two-tank system.

This article is focused on the implementation of an industrial process, specifically the level control of two interconnected tanks, using the Hardware in the Loop technique in an interactive way with the user. All the components of the plant are designed from a P&ID diagram, as shown in Fig. 1, which is taken as a reference for the creation of the 3D plant, including the process, sensors and actuators. The Unity graphics engine is used to create the complete animation of the plant, approximating reality by using the mathematical model, while the process controller is implemented in a physical PLC, which allows the system to be controlled in real time. Finally, the operation of the process is shown, allowing the user to observe the behaviour and interact with the plant.

2 Structured System

The present research is based on the level control of a system of two interconnected tanks, because level control between tanks is a frequent control problem in industrial processes.

2.1 Mathematical Model

A schematic diagram is made (Fig. 1), where all the variables are related in order to obtain the mathematical model of the interconnected tank system. The process is a MIMO system, whose inputs are the flow variations (Q_1 y Q_2) entering the tanks through the opening variation of solenoid valves 1 and 2. The outputs are the height variations of each of the tanks h_1 y h_2. It is important to emphasize that the height of tank 1 must be higher than tank 2. The two tanks are interconnected by a shut-off valve, in which a flow rate Q_{12} flows and finally the flow output of the whole process Q_{out} is constant.

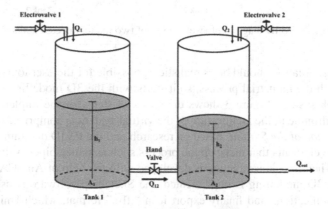

Fig. 1. Schematic Diagram of Coupled Tanks.

Then, the mathematical models representing the dynamic behaviour of the process have been obtained for its implementation in the virtual environment. The equations are denoted in (1) and (2).

$$A\frac{dh_1}{dt} = k_1a_1 - s_1\sqrt{2g(h_1 - h_2)} \tag{1}$$

$$A\frac{dh_2}{dt} = k_2a_2 + s_1\sqrt{2g(h_1 - h_2)} - s_2\sqrt{2gh_2} \tag{2}$$

The mathematical models obtained are non-linear equations. Where h_1 and h_2 are the heights of tank 1 and tank 2 respectively; k_1 and k_2 are the flow rate constants; a_1 and a_2 the valve openings; s_1 and s_2 the pipe cross sections; A is the internal area of the tanks, both tanks are assumed to have the same characteristics; and g is gravity.

2.2 3D Virtual System Design

Based on the schematic diagram, ISA standards 5.1 and 5.3 are used to make the P&ID diagram of the plant, Fig. 2, which provides relevant information on the physical and instrumentation composition of the system.

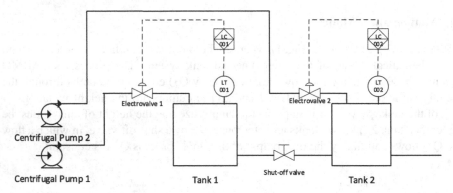

Fig. 2. P&ID diagram of level control of two interconnected tanks.

The plant simulation should be as realistic as possible for the user to have a greater interaction with the industrial process, so it starts with the 3D modelling of the inter-connected tank system. Figure 3 shows the series of steps for the implementation of the virtual environment, the architecture of the virtual system is comprised of two main stages: *i) Creation of the Station:* based on research and the P&ID diagram, the dimensions of all the elements that make up the process such as tanks, pipes, valves, etc. can be obtained. Then the plant structure is developed with the help of AutoCAD software and when the 3D modelling is implemented, the SketchUp software is used to make additional modifications and finally export it in ".fbx" format, which Unity supports these types of files for 3D modelling applications; and *ii) Virtual Environment:* where the fbx format file is imported into the Unity, in order to make the final modifications and provide more realism to the modelling and therefore carry out animation strategies with the help of the mathematical models of the dynamic system to animate the evolution of the plant with respect to time.

The operating loop was performed in 3 main stages: Controller, Scripts and Virtual Scene (Fig. 4).

The "Virtual Scene" stage consists of animation modules of the virtual environment in the Unity, allowing for more interaction with the plant, observation of the correspond-ing animations and the results of the evolution of the process over time. This stage is subdivided as: *(i) Avatar*, navigates through the virtual environment in third person, thus allowing the user to have a better visibility and interaction with the plant; *(ii) Control Panel*, the user can start the process, manipulate the desired values, choose the type of control desired, either automatic or manual control with its respective pilot lights and has an emergency stop button; *(iii) Shut-off Valve*, the user can manipulate the opening of the shut-off valve at the interconnection of the tanks; *(iv) System Graphics*, consists of

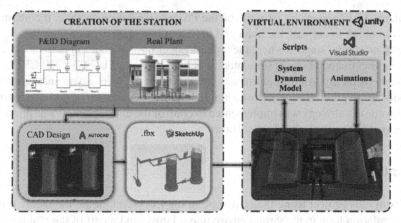

Fig. 3. 3D Object Construction Diagram.

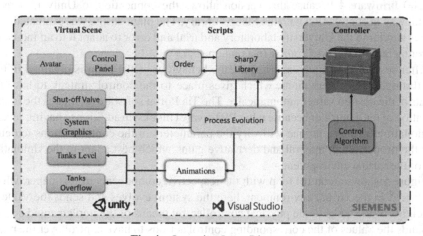

Fig. 4. Operating Loop Diagram.

computational modules showing the plant response curve as process values in conjunction with desired values, control values and control errors; *(v) Tanks Level*, the height of the interconnected tank system varies with respect to the evolution of the process over time; *(vi) Tanks Overflow*, an animation that is triggered when the liquid level in the tanks exceeds their maximum capacity.

The "Scripts" stage has the programming codes implemented in Visual Studio software for the correct functioning of the virtual environment. They consist of: *(i) Sharp7 Library*, is a driver to communicate with the Siemens PLC S7, here the corresponding variables are sent to have a complete control of the industrial process.; *(ii) Order:* receive the control panel command from the user from Unity and send the corresponding variables for the respective action.; *(iii) Process Evolution*: is the mathematical model of the interconnected tank system, where the level evolves with respect to the simulation time. It is the heart of the application environment because it represents the operation of the entire plant.; *(iv) Animations*: depends on the Process Evolution module, it contains the respective coding to animate the plant and to have a better interaction with it.

The "Controller" stage is where the only physical implementation is found, because everything mentioned above is simulated. It is made up of a PLC S7-1200 CPU 1214c of the Siemens family. All the control was carried out at tag level, so no analogue inputs or outputs are required. It consists of a single module, which is: *(i) Control Algorithm*, where the control strategy was implemented to control the entire plant. It was previously programmed in the Tia Portal V16 software.

3   Control Scheme

By realising this project using the Hardware in the Loop technique, the whole process is in a simulation loop in the virtual environment Unity, and a part of the real hardware is included, which is the plant controller (PLC). In this case, the PLC chosen was the S7-1200 firmware 4 because this version allows the connection to Unity in a more optimal way in conjunction with the Sharp7 library. The plant design was evaluated with devices similar to the University laboratory and trial and error to adapt it to an industrial environment with features similar to a real one.

After several open-loop experiments, the behaviour of the plant is obtained in real time through manual variations, which gives place to the control strategy to have the heights at the desired values automatically. The Tia Portal software facilitates the implementation of the controller because it has PID control blocks, in addition to having several functionalities. This technique will vary the parameters of the control actions to determine the proportional, integral and derivative gains which best adapt to the simulation loop of the virtual environment.

Figure 5 shows a control loop with the respective components of this paper, where the plant is in the virtual environment, here the system evolves and sends the value of the heights of the tanks to the physical controller, by means of the implemented control law sends the values of the corresponding control actions to have control over the plant.

4   Tests and Results

This section shows the full implementation of the virtual environment in the industrial environment, specifically in the level control of two interconnected tanks. Figure 6 shows the entire infrastructure that makes up the virtual environment that was implemented in this work, where the most important elements are detailed.

An avatar (Fig. 7) is placed in order for the user to have more interaction with the virtual environment, by controlling it like a video game, he has the possibility of moving around the available space, controlling it as an operator in the industry would do and at the same time observing the behaviour of the industrial process by means of animations.

Figure 8 shows the implemented animations of the liquid level variations inside the tanks. These animations change with respect to the evolution of the mathematical models. The approximate level of the tanks can be observed with the bar at the front of each tank. In addition, there is an animation of the flow entering the tanks, these

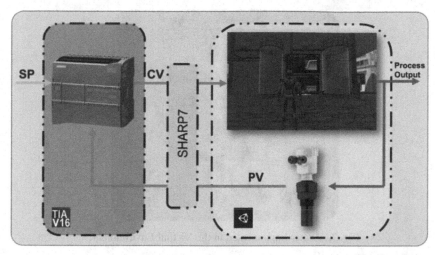

Fig. 5. Interconnected Tank System Control Diagram.

Fig. 6. Virtual Environment Implemented.

animations vary with respect to the control actions (opening of the control valves) sent from the PLC.

The response curves were implemented by computational modules, including the value of the heights, control signals and control errors, as shown in Fig. 9.

And also, for the user to interact with electrical signals, manual control has been implemented. These signals are received by the analogue inputs of the PLC through voltage variations from 0 to 10 V (Fig. 10), in this way the user can manipulate the openings of the electrovalves.

Table 1 shows the PID controller constants which were obtained through the auto tuning of the PLC S7 1200 and improving the response curve by trial and error.

Below are the images of the correct, real-time operation of the interconnected tank system.

Fig. 7. Avatar Implemented in the Virtual Environment.

Fig. 8. Animations of Tank Level Variations.

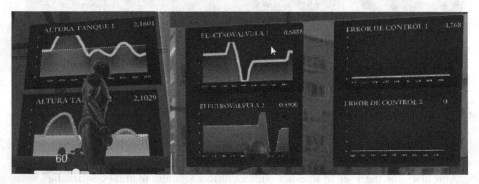

Fig. 9. Computational Modules.

At first, the process is stopped. At this point, the simulation is waiting for the user's instruction to start (Fig. 11).

Once started, the controller begins to bring the variables to the desired value assigned at the start of the application. And at the same time, the control actions can be observed to vary with respect to time, making it possible to control the process variables (Fig. 12).

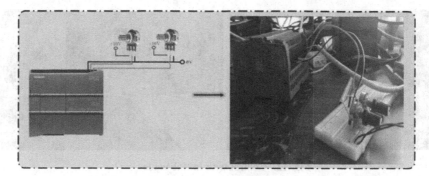

Fig. 10. Manual Control by Analogue Inputs.

Table 1. PID Constants Resulting from Autotuning.

System	Kp	Ti (s)	Td (s)
Tank 1	21.55177	1.23018	3.115516×10^{-1}
Tank 2	9.63805	1.018066	$2.556272 \times 10–1$

Fig. 11. Virtual Environment in its Initial Presentation.

To verify the robustness of the controller, the Set Point of the first tank is changed and it is observed how the whole process evolves. We can see that the level of tank 1 is controlled, and in the course of the control we can also observe a small perturbation in the level of tank 2, but it is not such a pronounced variation. Similarly, the control actions can be observed how they respond to the change made by the user to bring the levels of the tanks to the desired value (Fig. 13).

Fig. 12. Control with Initial Values.

Fig. 13. Change of Set Point Tank 1.

The load value is now varied by closing the valve up to 20%. This will serve as a perturbation to the interconnected tank system and verify the robustness of the controller. It can be observed that in both levels there are small variations, despite the variation of the disturbance (hand valve), the controller keeps them at the desired value. It can be observed in the change of the control actions, the necessary changes made by the controller to maintain the level variables at their desired value (Fig. 14).

Fig. 14. Change in Perturbation Value (20%).

Similarly, maintaining the same Set Point values, the hand valve is varied, in this case opening it up to 90%, and the evolution of the process and the controller is monitored. As in the previous case, variations can be appreciated in the evolution of the level variables, however, the same Set Point is maintained. In the control action graphs, it can be noticed how these variables change in order to maintain the tank level at the desired value (Fig. 15).

Fig. 15. Change in Perturbation Value (90%).

Now, keeping the disturbance value, the Set Points of the 2 tanks are varied to observe how the controller performs. By changing these Set Point values, the controller is robust and reliable. Similarly, the control actions vary according to the control law. It can be observed that the control action of the first electrovalve is at its maximum value (Fig. 16).

Fig. 16. Change of Set Point in Tank 1 and 2.

The response graphs of the evolution of the implemented controllers are presented below (Fig. 17).

Table 2 presents the response times of the controllers that were implemented in the 2 tanks. It shows that their response times are acceptable for optimal control and their errors are within an acceptable range.

After testing, the mathematical model is shown to work correctly and works in a similar way to a real process. These were validated by the response curves of the controls with the interaction with the virtual environment. The response curves are first order, similar to some real industrial process references. The correlation between the two tanks has also been proven, demonstrating the dependence of one level on the other and the interconnection of the tanks.

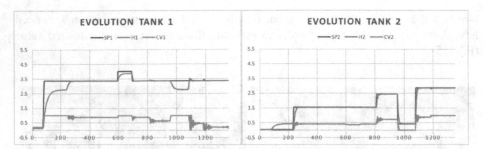

Fig. 17. Evolution of the Interconnected Tank System.

Table 2. Analysis of the Response Times of the Implemented Controllers.

System	Rise Time (s)	Stabilisation Time (s)	Maximum overshoot percentage (%)	Controller Error Time (s)	Error (%)
Tank 1	111.5	144.2	No overshoot	147.8	0.6878
Tank 2	112.15	137.7	No overshoot	143.9	2.75

5 Conclusions

The virtualisation of a system of two interconnected tanks with characteristics similar to those of a real process, allows the user to become familiar with this type of industrial environment where they work with level control in a tank system, because it is the variable that is most controlled in industrial processes, and in this form they can carry out training or use it in the field of teaching-learning, without the need to manipulate a real industrial process, only using the executable application in the medium-high quality computer with current technology and a physical controller (PLC).

The present work presents a low-cost solution, which greatly reduces the risk to personnel and material losses by interacting with real processes of inexperienced people.

Acknowledgements. The authors would like to thank the Universidad de las Fuerzas Armadas ESPE for the support for the development of this work, especially the project 2020-PIC-017-CTE "Simulación de proceso industriales, mediante la técnica Hardware in the Loop, para el desarrollo de prácticas en Automatización Industrial".

References

1. Bacic, M.: On hardware-in-the-loop simulation, December 2005
2. Fathy, H.K., Filipi, Z.S., Hagena, J., Stein, J.L.: Review of hardware-in-the-loop simulation and its prospects in the automotive area. Model. Simul. Mil. Appl. **6228**, 62280E (2006). SPIE. https://doi.org/10.1117/12.667794
3. Grega, W.: Hardware-in-the-loop simulation and its application in control education, February 1999
4. Ledin, J.A.: Hardware-in-the-loop simulation. In: Embedded Systems Programming, pp. 42–62 (1999)
5. Isermann, R., Schaffnit, J., Sinsel, S.: Hardware-in-the-loop simulation for the design and testing of engine-control systems, Darmstadt (1999)
6. Gomez, M.: Hardware-in-the-Loop Simulation, November 2001. http://www.embedded.com/showArticle.jhtml?articleID=15201692. Accessed 27 Feb 2022
7. Ibáñez Jácome, P.F.: Desarrollo de un entorno virtual 3D que simule un proceso industrial de nivel, orientado al entrenamiento para la calibración de una válvula de control, Latacunga (2021)
8. Silva Quiroz, J.: Diseño y moderación de entornos virtuales de aprendizaje (EVA). Santiago de Chile: Editorial UOC (2011)
9. Bogusevschi, D., Muntean, C.H., Muntean, G.-M.: Teaching and learning physics using 3D virtual learning environment: a case study of combined virtual reality and virtual laboratory in secondary school. J. Comput. Math. Sci. Teach. **39**(1), 5–18 (2020)
10. Bullock, D., Johnson, B., Wells, R.B., Kyte, M., Li, Z.: Hardware-in-the-loop simulation. Transp. Res. Part C Emerg. Technol. **12**(1), 73–89 (2004). https://doi.org/10.1016/j.trc.2002.10.002
11. Pruna, E., Jimenez, I., Escobar, I.: Hardware-in-the-loop of a flow plant embedded in FPGA, for process control. Intell. Manuf. Energy Sustain., 181–189 (2020)
12. Kumarin, A., Kuznetsov, A., Makaryants, G.: Hardware-in-the-loop neuro-based simulation for testing gas turbine engine control system. In: Global Fluid Power Society PhD Symposium (GFPS), pp. 1–5, July 2018
13. Bertoletti, L., Ragaini, E., Liu, J.: Hardware-in-the-loop simulation for testing low voltage circuit breakers selectivity. In: 2017 IEEE International Conference on Environment and Electrical Engineering and 2017 IEEE Industrial and Commercial Power Systems Europe (EEEIC/I&CPS Europe), pp. 1–5, June 2017
14. Mogrovejo Merchán, D.G.: Diseño e implantación de un sistema de cuatro tanques interconectados con control PID robusto multivariable, Cuenca (2017)
15. Cartes, D., Wu, L.: Experimental evaluation of adaptive three-tank level control (2005)
16. Rosander, P.: Averaging level control in the presence of frequent inlet flow upsets, Linköping (2012)
17. Dukelow, S.G.: The Control of Boilers, 2nd edn. Instrument Society of America (1991)

Virtual Environment for the Control of a Temperature Process Based on Hardware-in-the-Loop

Byron P. Corrales[1,2], Edwin P. Pruna[1(✉)], Ivón P. Escobar[1], and Luigi O. Freire[1,2]

[1] Universidad de las Fuerzas Armadas ESPE, Sangolquí, Ecuador
{bpcorrales,eppruna,ipescobar,lofreire}@espe.edu.ec
[2] Universidad Técnica de Cotopaxi, Latacunga, Ecuador
{byron.corrales,luigi.freire}@utc.edu.ec

Abstract. In this work a virtual temperature environment is developed for the Automatic Control training, which meets the characteristics of a real system of oven painting for automobiles. The process was designed using Blender and the Unity3D graphic engine was used in order to achieve a high level of realism in the simulated environment. In addition, it is based on the Hardware-In-the-Loop (HIL) technique, through which aspects of the process can be considered, such as the behavior of sensors and actuators that generate electrical signals, which allows the interaction between the virtual environment and the controller that is implemented, for which by means of a survey the degree of familiarization that the students had was evaluated, giving 90.5% of acceptance focused on the understanding of the handling of the system.

Keywords: Unity3D · 3D virtual environment · Hardware-in-the-Loop · virtual temperature process

1 Introduction

Technological advances have caused virtual reality oriented applications to become more and more popular not only in the field of entertainment but also in other areas such as: education, medicine, control systems, among others. These advances allow users to experiment with complex processes in a practical way without having to be in person in front of them, but can interact within the simulation environment [1].

To achieve learning, the engineering student must accumulate both theoretical and practical knowledge. In a globalized scenario such as the one we live in today, academic preparation in certain areas is complex and, in many cases, unattainable, especially due to economic aspects, equipment handling and even the risk of using them due to lack of knowledge. Among the possible solutions to help address this problem are virtual reality scenarios because in a simulation environment there are no difficulties mentioned above, rather they can be an alternative for the user to become familiar with a real environment, apply learned theories, experiment with connections, perform actions, make decisions

L. T. De Paolis et al. (Eds.): XR Salento 2023, LNCS 14218, pp. 36–51, 2023.
https://doi.org/10.1007/978-3-031-43401-3_3

and even have failures, solve them and try again as many times as necessary, seeking to consolidate the knowledge [2–4].

The analysis of the performance of industrial processes and the implementation of control strategies in them until a few years ago was complicated due to several factors including excessive time in their analysis, the impact on production due to direct intervention in the process, excessive calculations, among others. That is where through technological progress has been able to give greater emphasis on mathematical modeling that helps characterize a system in a set of equations within which have all the peculiarities of the process to be subsequently executed in a virtual reality software, thereby it is possible to represent its operation and simulate the performance in real time evaluating different critical situations [5–7].

In the study of engineering learning is a systematic process that goes from the analysis of the different principles and is complemented with experimental practice, in this sense the area of Control and Industrial Automation is not left behind, under this concept the importance of laboratories is established. In this area the availability of an environment that meets the basic characteristics so that the student can know and learn through practice is complicated due to the high cost of installation and then the constant maintenance to which they must be subjected. That is the importance of virtual laboratories, which are those that practically simulate a real scenario while preserving its characteristics and functions, in addition, there are also remote laboratories that basically have the possibility of being remotely controlled [8–10].

Nowadays, the development of virtual applications is widely used, due to its many advantages, among which stand out the time saving and cost reduction in implementation and considering the almost total absence of maintenance. It is necessary to have the mathematical model itself that will serve to simulate the operation of each element of the system. The Hardware-In-the-Loop (HIL) technique is the one that allows the interaction between virtual systems with physical elements, in this case a controller [11, 12].

In the industrial field, temperature is one of the variables most involved in the processes, thus the importance of knowing how to control it and knowing the techniques for its treatment. Applying advanced control techniques in processes involving temperature can ensure that certain aspects such as quality, efficiency and energy consumption are improved at the time of making a product [13]. To evaluate the performance of a control system applied to a real or virtual process involves analyzing the characteristic parameters in its performance of the transient response it presents when the input is modified, in addition to the presence of external disturbances to the process [13, 14].

According to what was established in the introduction, this article shows a temperature environment based on the application of an oven painting process for automobiles, using Hardware-In-the-Loop simulation with the purpose of linking controllers so that they can be tested and validated focused on their training. When performing a virtualization of the system, all the dynamic response characteristics are contemplated as design details, for which Blender is used in the design of materials and characterization of components, while Unity3D is used as the graphic engine of the application.

This article is organized in 5 sections which include the Introduction. Section 2 shows the structure of the system being virtualized. The next section deals with the details of the development of the system, starting from the particular aspects such as the operation diagram to the description of the elements that make up the virtual environment. Section 4 deals with the results of the project, focusing on the comparison with real processes. Finally, Sect. 5 shows the conclusions generated by the work.

2 System Structure

For the implementation of the system, HIL simulation is used, which uses specific hardware and software, which are linked and allow to generate a process with a high degree of realism and impact. Figure 1-a shows the real oven painting process, which includes a set of electrical resistors, which are used to heat the cabin generally at a temperature ranging between 60 to 80 °C for a period of approximately 45 min, this is done in order to give a quality finish, durable and in a short time to the car's paint. Figure 1-b shows the virtualization of the process where the elements that can be found in a workshop for this purpose have been taken into consideration.

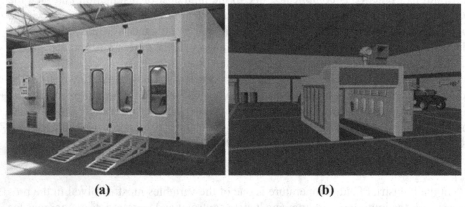

(a)   **(b)**

Fig. 1. a) Real Process b) Virtual Process

Figure 2 shows the system structure and describes the interaction between the virtual environment and the electronic devices used. Serial communication between the Arduino Uno board and Unity is used by means of C# programming in order to be able to perform the data exchange between the real and virtual world and its subsequent application to the controller.

In the first instance, the process of oven painting for automobiles is simulated, which is implemented in a computational system that uses the Unity3D graphics engine. For this, a mathematical model is required, this mathematical equation was obtained experimentally from a real temperature process. When simulating the operation, the system contemplates all the characteristics of the real process, this is of great help and is taken advantage of since it allows in the end to carry out different experiments and to evaluate situations that in a real scenario would be complicated to do it.

To achieve this, the simulation of a car entering the paint booth was implemented, allowing the possibility of interacting with the process and simulating the gradual

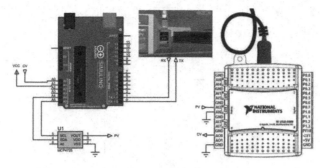

Fig. 2. System structure

increase in temperature visualized in the change of color inside the oven and later the presence of smoke in the oven's chimney.

The next stage of the system consists of data acquisition, for which the Arduino Uno development board is used, which receives the electrical signals from the controller and enters them into the virtual process, and then the data returned by the system transforms them back into electrical signals to be analyzed and processed by the controller, which means that this board acts as a gateway for electrical signals and data between the controller and the virtual environment. The use of the Arduino Uno board is ideal for this type of project because it is a low cost element, it is easy to communicate with the computer system and its programming is simple.

It also highlights the existence of the signal conditioning stage, which allows the signals to be standardized so that the system can be used in any type of industrial controllers, allowing the verification of different proposed algorithms.

3 Application Development

3.1 Virtual Environment

The system has been chosen because temperature processes are the most common in the industry, being important its study and analysis in the educational field, besides the variables that compose it allow to analyze different techniques for its control and stabilization. Figure 3 shows the P&ID diagram of the system.

The design of the virtual environment contemplates a temperature oven, which works based on electrical resistors. For temperature measurement the system uses as primary element a PT-100 type RTD coupled to an intelligent transmitter that is capable of configuring its measurement ranges with an electrical output from 4 mA to 20 mA. In addition, there is a final control element based on a phase control system based on SCRs.

The development of the virtual environment has been carried out using various software, as shown in Fig. 4. The Process Design section details the use of Blender as well as Unity 3D in the process.

Process Design
The 3D modeling of the process is performed entirely using Blender, which has the

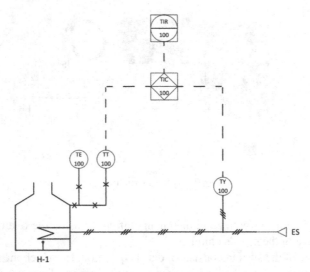

Fig. 3. P&ID diagram of a temperature process

appropriate tools for the design generating a high degree of detail and realism. Considering the P&ID diagram of the plant, the equipment and instruments are created and properly placed within the scenario, here the different materials are created, distributed and modeled so that in a next phase they are animated with the help of Unity3D. Blender has the characteristic of being a free access software, has several libraries, allows the import of elements and it is here where you can eliminate duplicated elements in the meshes, which generates more realism to the design. The help of this software in achieving highly detailed designs allows the simulation of all the scenarios proposed with the greatest possible realism. Figure 5 shows the model designed in Blender.

Figure 6 shows the design of the fans, here it is necessary to be able to simulate the rotation of the blades, for this a central point should be located where you can get this rotation with high realism. These fans are used to simulate the cooling of the interior of the cabin, it should be noted that these fans are used at the didactic level to give a disturbance to the system where the student must test their controllers and verify the response of the process always trying to maintain the temperature at which it was previously set.

Characterization, Animation and Simulation

Once the development phase of the virtual environment in Blender is finished, it is exported in FBX format to be imported into Unity3D in order to configure the textures, sounds, lighting, camera management, materials, rotation points, animations and especially the serial communication with the Arduino Uno data acquisition board. Unity3D version 2019.3.5f1 was used for this purpose. Figure 7 shows the realism of the scene achieved.

Unity3D has the great potential to develop animations and movements necessary for the virtual environment to be similar to the reality. For this project we animated character movements, heating effects, and also the numerical display and trends in the HMI.

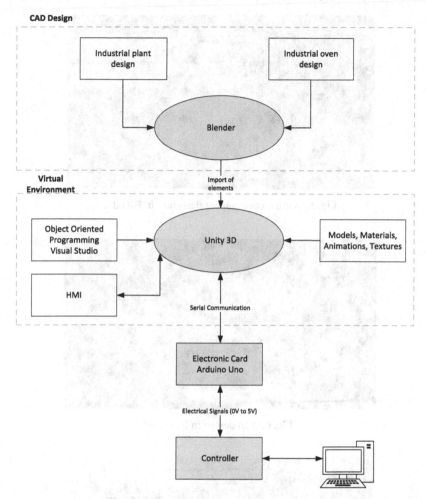

Fig. 4. Virtual environment design structure

For the communication between Unity3D and the Arduino Uno board, a COM port availability validation process is performed, where the analysis of the available ports is established and displayed in the form of a list, after which the user must select the one assigned to his board. This step is essential to enter the simulation environment as shown in Fig. 8.

It is important to consider that if the communication port is not properly established, the option to enter the process will not be enabled. See Fig. 9.

For the visualization of the temperature performance inside the cabin, an interface has been created where the user receives values of the expected temperature and its actual value, as shown in Fig. 10.

As previously mentioned, the process is based on the simulation of the operation of electrical resistors, which will generate the temperature increase in the oven, for which there is a module for activating the thyristors, as shown in Fig. 11.

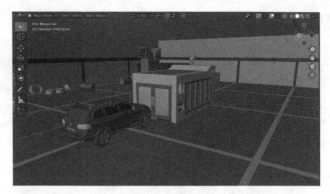

Fig. 5. Virtual environment designed in Blender

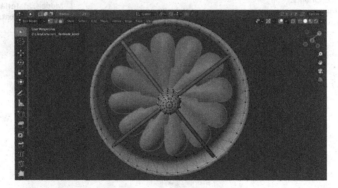

Fig. 6. Fan design in Blender

Fig. 7. Application developed in Unity3D

Once the car enters the cabin the process begins to increase the temperature, this can be seen in the simulation as internally the resistors begin to gradually become reddish in color due to the heating effect, in addition to the chimney there is a gradual presence of smoke, effects that go hand in hand with the temperature trends, see Fig. 12.

Through programming in C# the mathematical model that will govern the simulation can be introduced, in this way the system function is expressed by Eq. 1, which is

Fig. 8. Serial port selection stage

Fig. 9. Enabling the process

expressed in the frequency domain, and must be programmed transforming it to the time domain. This equation was obtained experimentally from a laboratory furnace which has as heating element a tubular resistance of 1100 W at 120V/60 Hz and a resistance of 12.5 Ω, the initial temperature for the modeling of the process was 8 °C.

$$P(s) = \frac{1.58}{1 + 836\,s}e^{-110\,s} \tag{1}$$

Inside the process there is a touch screen of type Simatic HMI KTP700 Basic Panel, where relevant system information such as the P&ID diagram, the controls used for system operation and the relevant system values used to be applied to the external controller are available. This can be noted in Fig. 13.

After having defined all the characteristics that contemplate the oven, we proceed to use different scripts, which in turn are the programming codes necessary to simulate the system response. For this purpose, the transfer function previously established in the

Fig. 10. System trends in Unity3D

Fig. 11. Electrical resistors activation module

time domain is used. As a result of the implemented equation a value will be obtained which is displayed in the temperature transmitter as in the process trend curve, Fig. 14.

3.2 Reading and Writing of Information

For the transfer of information between the Arduino Uno board and the simulation environment in Unity3D, the Serial Communication is used at a speed of 9600 bps. The signals received by the controller are conditioned to standard values between 1 V to 5 V and when entering the board are converted into digital data which will be the values used in the mathematical model for the respective simulation. The diagram of flow is shown in Fig. 15, where once the serial port is initialized and selected, it is passed to the reading stage, it is identified if there is any change in the input signal, by comparing

Fig. 12. Cabin temperature increase

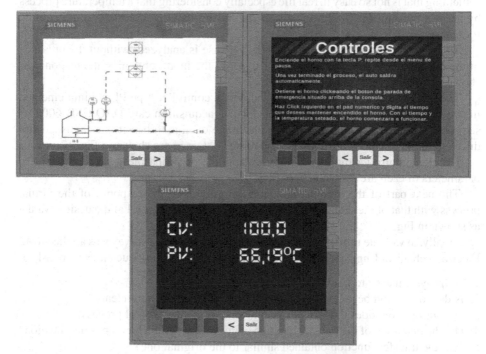

Fig. 13. Information on HMI KTP700 display

it at each instant of time with the previous signal, then it is analyzed if there is the activation of the disturbance by activating the fans, With this analysis is entered to the function of calculating the value of the current temperature by the mathematical model implemented, this value is recorded in the trend and then sent through the serial port to the Arduino Uno card, the signal is converted into an analog data by implementing the MCP4725 module, which is a digital - analog converter with 12-bit resolution.

Fig. 14. Temperature display on transmitter

4   Results

The development of the system is designed to be applied in the training and validation of controllers using a temperature process. The availability of a simulated environment that responds with the characteristics of a real process allows to make several experiments something that is not so easy in real life especially considering that a temperature process by its own dynamics is of slow characteristic having its great notoriety in the cooling for a new start.

To analyze its operation, the open-loop response is analyzed, without the presence of the controller, only with an excitation signal at the input, obtaining the response as shown in Fig. 16.

Then the virtual environment is applied with a controller type PI and implemented in two devices such as a PLC S7-1200 and a data acquisition card DAQ USB-6009. A setpoint value at which the temperature inside the oven is to be set is established and different tuning methods are applied. The results obtained are shown in Fig. 17.

Different controller tuning methods are applied, of which the main representative parameters of each are shown in Table 1.

The next part of the system validation is to compare the response of the virtual process with that of the real process, achieving temperature control at the desired value, as shown in Fig. 18.

Finally, to validate the degree of acceptance of the system, a survey was applied to 42 Electromechanical Engineering students, in which the following questions were asked:

1. Is the system easy to use?
2. Is the connection between the virtual process and the hardware clear?
3. In your opinion, does the virtual system work similar to the real process?
4. Did the obtaining of the transfer function of the virtual system have any complication?
5. Was the transfer function obtained similar to the original one?
6. Does the design of the virtual system present realism?

Figure 19 shows the results of the survey.

From the analysis of the results, it is possible to identify a high acceptance in reference to the handling of the system, in addition the interaction between hardware and software is simple which does not generate complications. In obtaining the transfer function of the virtual system and its comparison with the original mathematical model there is an acceptance of more than 90% of the surveyed students. In conclusion, the system presents a high realism compared to the process available in the laboratories.

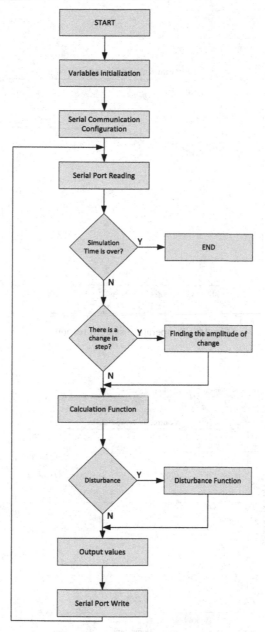

Fig. 15. Process flow diagram

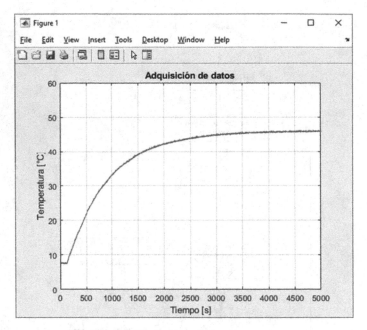

Fig. 16. Temperature system response

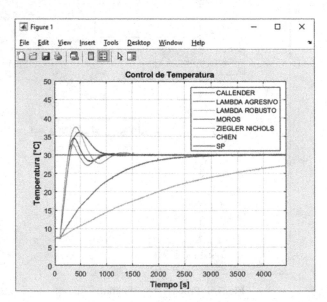

Fig. 17. Response to a PI controller

Table 1. PI Controller performance parameters

METHOD	SP	T_{max} [^oC]	K_C	T_i [min]	PEM [%]	T_S [s]
Ziegler Nichols	30,00	32,93	5,017	5,627	9,77%	1407
Lambda Agresivo	30,00	30,28	0,660	12,697	0,93%	3422
Lambda Robusto	30,00	27,33	0,239	12,697	–	>5000
Callender	30,00	36,24	3,166	6,206	20,80%	1300
Chien	30,00	37,62	3,902	3,973	25,40%	1591
Moros	30,00	34,61	4,460	5,115	15,37%	1263

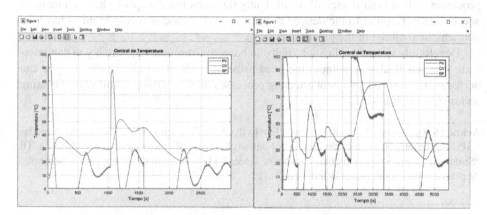

Fig. 18. Response of the process a) real b) simulated

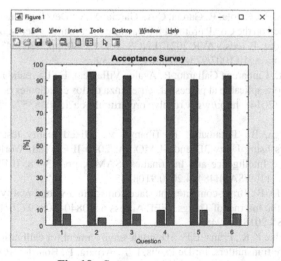

Fig. 19. System acceptance survey

5 Conclusions

By using the virtual application, the implementation of controllers can be evaluated thanks to the use of the Hardware-In-the-Loop technique, with which external signals enter the simulation environment and are transformed into temperature values responding to a mathematical equation that represents the performance of the process, and on the other hand the values of the virtual application are returned to the controller in the form of electrical signals to be analyzed by the controller. This feature allows it to be tested with several controllers and different tuning techniques, all this focused on the training of its use in automation.

The use of design software such as Blender helps to give a realistic touch to the processes with a high degree of detail. Unity3D helps the designs to have animations and basically respond to the desired dynamics, in this case it is important to have the mathematical model of the process.

Developing virtual applications helps to have environments in which you can intervene in a practical way without the need to be in front of a real process, so you can perform different tasks without affecting processes and with the possibility of repeating and making changes.

Acknowledgements. The authors would like to thank the Universidad de las Fuerzas Armadas ESPE for the support for the development of this work, especially the project 2020-PIC-017-CTE "Simulación de proceso industriales, mediante la técnica Hardware in the Loop, para el desarrollo de prácticas en Automatización Industrial".

References

1. Montalvo-Lopez, W., Catota, P., Garcia, C.A., Garcia, M.V.: Development of a virtual reality environment based on the CoAP protocol for teaching pneumatic systems. In: De Paolis, L.T., Arpaia, P., Bourdot, P. (eds.) AVR 2021. LNCS, vol. 12980, pp. 528–543. Springer, Cham (2021). https://doi.org/10.1007/978-3-030-87595-4_39
2. Flores Cruz, J.A., Camarena Gallardo, P., Avalos Villarreal, E.: La realidad virtual, una tecnología innovadora aplicable al proceso de enseñanza de los estudiantes de ingeniería. Apertura **6**(2), 1–10 (2014). http://www.redalyc.org/articulo.oa?id=68835725008. Accessed 05 Apr 2023
3. Szalai, M., Varga, B., Tettamanti, T., Tihanyi, V.: Mixed reality test environment for autonomous cars using Unity 3D and SUMO. In: 2020 IEEE 18th World Symposium on Applied Machine Intelligence and Informatics (SAMI), pp. 73–78. IEEE, January 2020. https://doi.org/10.1109/SAMI48414.2020.9108745
4. Coogan, C.G., He, B.: Brain-computer interface control in a virtual reality environment and applications for the Internet of Things. IEEE Access **6**, 10840–10849 (2018). https://doi.org/10.1109/ACCESS.2018.2809453
5. Rocha, V.I., Rocha, K.R., Pruna, E.P.: 3D virtual environment for calibration and adjustment of smart pressure transmitters. In: De Paolis, L.T., Arpaia, P., Bourdot, P. (eds.) AVR 2021. LNCS, vol. 12980, pp. 639–654. Springer, Cham (2021). https://doi.org/10.1007/978-3-030-87595-4_46

6. Alpúsig, S., Pruna, E., Escobar, I.: Virtual environment for control strategies testing: a hardware-in-the-loop approach. In: De Paolis, L.T., Arpaia, P., Bourdot, P. (eds.) AVR 2021. LNCS, vol. 12980, pp. 588–602. Springer, Cham (2021). https://doi.org/10.1007/978-3-030-87595-4_43

7. Ibáñez, P., Pruna, E., Escobar, I., Ávila, G.: 3D virtual system for control valve calibration. In: De Paolis, L.T., Arpaia, P., Bourdot, P. (eds.) AVR 2021. LNCS, vol. 12980, pp. 560–572. Springer, Cham (2021). https://doi.org/10.1007/978-3-030-87595-4_41

8. Ipanaqué, W., Belupú, I., Valdiviezo, J., Vásquez, G.: Memorias del XVI Congreso Latinoamericano de Control Automático (2014)

9. Kucera, E., Haffner, O., Leskovsky, R.: Interactive and virtual/mixed reality applications for mechatronics education developed in unity engine. In: 2018 Cybernetics & Informatics (K&I), pp. 1–5. IEEE, January 2018. https://doi.org/10.1109/CYBERI.2018.8337533

10. Goodwin, G.C., Medioli, A.M., Sher, W., Vlacic, L.B., Welsh, J.S.: Emulation-based virtual laboratories: a low-cost alternative to physical experiments in control engineering education. IEEE Trans. Educ. **54**(1), 48–55 (2011). https://doi.org/10.1109/TE.2010.2043434

11. Hernandez-Oliva, N., Calva-Yanez, M.B., Sepulveda-Cervantes, G., Portilla-Flores, E.A., Ardul Munoz-Hernandez, G., Suarez-Santillan, R.A.: A pendulum path tracking implemented in Hardware-in-the-Loop. In: 2019 International Conference on Electronics, Communications and Computers (CONIELECOMP), pp. 81–87. IEEE, February 2019. https://doi.org/10.1109/CONIELECOMP.2019.8673247

12. Zhang, Z., Zhang, M., Chang, Y., Aziz, E.-S., Esche, S.K., Chassapis, C.: Collaborative virtual laboratory environments with Hardware in the Loop. In: Auer, M., Azad, A., Edwards, A., de Jong, T. (eds.) Cyber-Physical Laboratories in Engineering and Science Education, pp. 363–402. Springer, Cham (2018). https://doi.org/10.1007/978-3-319-76935-6_15

13. Yang, Z., Sun, B., Li, F., Zhang, L.: A temperature optimal control method of temperature control system considering thermal inertia. In: 2019 Chinese Control Conference (CCC), pp. 5226–5231. IEEE, July 2019. https://doi.org/10.23919/ChiCC.2019.8865163

14. Guambo, W., Corrales, B.P., Freire, L.O., Albarracin, M.D.: Performance evaluation of a predictive and PID control applied to a didactic flow regulation process. In: Reddy, A.N.R., Marla, D., Favorskaya, M.N., Satapathy, S.C. (eds.) Intelligent Manufacturing and Energy Sustainability. SIST, vol. 265, pp. 559–570. Springer, Singapore (2022). https://doi.org/10.1007/978-981-16-6482-3_55

Visualization of Large Datasets in Virtual Reality Systems

Bruno Ježek[ID], Ondřej Šimeček[ID], Martin Konvička[(✉)][ID], and Antonín Slabý[ID]

University of Hradec Kralove, Rokitanskeho 62, 50002 Hradec Kralove, Czech Republic
{bruno.jezek,ondrej.simecek,martin.konvicka,
antonin.slaby}@uhk.cz

Abstract. This article explores the technology of large data files and the possibilities of their visualization in virtual reality. The three-dimensional unlimited scene, perception of perspective, freedom of movement, and interaction using natural gestures are all unique properties of virtual reality that can significantly change the way we receive, control, and evaluate visualization. Individual elements are discussed in detail, and their positive and negative aspects are described along with the potential applications. The knowledge gained from exploring extensive data files and virtual reality is used to develop two interactive demonstrations. The first virtual scene deals with the visualization of data from the smart city of Aarhus. The second demonstration works with the statistical data pertaining to the Czech Republic. The benefits and findings are then evaluated and summarized. The work also describes other possible uses of this technology and directions for further development.

Keywords: data visualization · information visualization · virtual reality · interaction

1 Introduction

The goal of the publication is to explore extensive data sets along with some ways of visualizing them. Furthermore, the benefits of virtual reality and its ability to display data will be evaluated. After a separate evaluation of these areas, the possibility of using virtual reality to visualize large data files will be verified. Attention is focused on both the software solutions with their associated obstacles as well as the hardware technologies. The availability of the data appropriate for visualization and the process of selection will also be examined. The publication aims to answer the following questions: Is it possible to effectively visualize large data files in virtual reality? Are software and hardware technologies at such a level of development that it is possible to create visualizations without significant obstacles? Are the benefits of visualization great enough to outweigh its negative side effects? Could it be possible to use the visualization of extensive data files in virtual reality in the academic or commercial sphere? The publication is organized as follows: Firstly, information about large data files and virtual reality technologies is summarized. Then, the principles of visualization and the possibility of displaying data

L. T. De Paolis et al. (Eds.): XR Salento 2023, LNCS 14218, pp. 52–68, 2023.
https://doi.org/10.1007/978-3-031-43401-3_4

in a virtual scene is explored. Finally, all findings, concepts, and claims will be verified through the documentation of two practical applications, which contain simplified proposals for the use of virtual reality to visualize large data files.

2   Virtual Analysis in Visualization - Benefits and Deficiencies

2.1   Strengths and Benefits of Virtual Reality

The strengths of virtual reality lie mainly in spatial freedom, the ability to draw users in and allow them to perceive space, movement, interaction approaching the real use of hands, and the possibility to capture size, speed, and volume in a more visceral way. Future visualizations should exploit as many of these advantages as possible and thus provide an experience that will outweigh the current shortcomings of the technology. Our first publication [1] was devoted to this problem. Here, we merely summarize the key findings.

Perception of space: The use of advanced algorithms and 3D visualization techniques regularly employed in virtual reality is already a great benefit in itself. The emphasis on realism is the main reason why the development of imaging technologies is leading to ever-better mediation of spatial perception. Included graphical cues are becoming more realistic, especially through improved technologies for rendering, working with light, shading, and the like. The closer the simulated environment is to the real one, the less confusing it is for the human mind, which makes it easier to focus on the perception of the data contained rather than the way they are displayed. The quality of the mediation of spatial perception is a key component in many technical fields. This fact is evident in a number of types of software with applications in the field of technical design. Thanks to virtual reality, a high degree of imagination is no longer required for many technical professions. The perception of space mediates the natural perception of object size, symmetry, perspective, and other key factors.

Perception of movement: Virtual reality partly allows the use of moving parts of the virtual scene. The scene can evolve and become very dynamic. The human mind is used to a naturally changing environment and can perceive it well. As long as the scene contains a certain number of fixed points, such as the floor where the user stands [1], there are no problems perceiving movement. Movement can also be effectively used to improve visualizations. This makes it easier to notice changes in the data frequency, expansion/shrinking speed, or rate of growth. Supplemented by a suitable control, the user can get a better idea about the real trends hidden in the data by investigating.

Perception of interaction: Interaction is a very important element of visualization that is often overlooked. The combination of mouse and keyboard has been a proven technology for decades and is optimized for full use of the computer's capabilities. Virtual reality is a concept that replaces the whole old system. Special drivers try to move the principles of interaction closer to the real movement of the hands. The buttons are placed so that the user does not have to think about them. If he wants to pick up an object in virtual reality, he presses a combination of buttons that resembles the grip of the palm. This makes the interaction with the environment and visualizations much more natural and smoother. The user also usually does not have to learn controls and needs just a short test and a demonstration of use. Newer virtual reality systems contain cameras to monitor the space in front of the user. As a result, systems have begun to detect hands and fingers using computer vision. It is therefore possible that in the next generation of VR technologies, they will no longer be part of a special driver, but the user will interact directly with the visualization with their hands. Simple and intuitive control offered by virtual reality can help fuel the boom of this technology.

The ability to grab the user's attention: Virtual reality has the propensity to draw, attract, and motivate the user to concentrate and remember as much information as possible. Thanks to the aforementioned unlimited virtual scene, realistic graphics, and an extensive living environment, the user is naturally motivated to explore and spend as much time as possible inside the visualization.

Other special benefits are tied to certain application areas. Innovations in the area of more pleasant and intensified virtual teaching and virtual meetings are certainly worth mentioning. Another benefit of virtual reality is the possibility of enabling users to experience crisis situations, control dangerous techniques, perform demanding simulations, and test other scenarios that could be dangerous or risky in the real world. This feature has already been tested in the training of people in many professions.

2.2 Deficiencies of Virtual Reality

Virtual reality and the technologies associated with it are still relatively new, and the systems are constantly developing and improving. Naturally, shortcomings are not yet fully eliminated. Both the creator and the user of a visualization in virtual reality should be aware of them and take action to avoid them or reduce their adverse effects.

Technological restrictions: These are associated with specific technical equipment and its parameters. Among many such parameters could be the proximity of glasses to the eye of the observer, influencing the overall quality, the way of connecting to the computer, weight, heating, and the resulting user restrictions.

Psychological restrictions: All negative effects of virtual reality are not limited to just technical problems. Given that the user is cut off from the real world and receives all information only from the VR device, problems associated with the natural human perception of the environment are not uncommon.

Nausea was one of the problems that was very significant, especially in the early days of virtual reality. The inner ear is highly sensitive to even slight discrepancies between the visual input received by the eyes and the corresponding sensory input received by the ear. Therefore, it is crucial for any system to detect the user's movements accurately and redraw the displayed information instantaneously to prevent any disruption in the sensory feedback loop.

Therefore, several methods have been developed to help eliminate this problem. They are now a standard part of most frameworks for developing virtual reality applications.

When using and developing visualizations for virtual reality, it is also necessary to remember the psychological perception of the surroundings. A cramped or dark virtual environment can evoke anxiety or claustrophobic feelings. A suitable visualization should therefore contain an environment that provides a pleasant and convenient experience for the widest range of users.

3 Extensive Data Files (Big Data)

This part of the article will be devoted to extensive data files, especially in connection with the issue of their visualization using virtual reality. We will mention the basics of filtration, storage, and analysis of "big data", because certain aspects of visualization must take these areas into account or are limited by them. Due to the size and complexity of extensive data files, the term "big data" is also commonly used. Preprocessing and quality analysis of this data can bring many benefits. Therefore, some methods for their sorting, filtration, storage, and processing have been developed and standardized.

Creating and Collecting Data. For a proper understanding of extensive data files, it is essential to delve into the process of how the data is generated and gathered, as well as the potential variations that may exist. The generally accepted concept to define the basic properties of large data files is referred to as 3 V - Velocity, Volume and Variety. Within this subchapter, these three terms or properties will be defined and described [2].

Data timeframe: The reliance on time can both pose a significant limitation and represent a crucial characteristic when dealing with vast data sets. In this context, it may be useful to differentiate between data that is acquired and processed in real-time and data that can be processed at a later stage.

Data size: The exact amount of data needed to consider the use of the term "Big Data" is not well defined. Higher units of terabytes (TB) or petabytes (PB) are often mentioned. This data is difficult or even impossible to process with standard tools, which leads to the use of specialized hardware (a server instead of a personal computer). Extensive data files tend to be generated by systems with millions of users, such as systems of multinational corporations or governments, IoT systems (Internet of Things), or smart factories. The total size of the data corresponds to the extensiveness of these systems [3]. The difficult part of data processing is storing a large amount of data while maintaining easy availability of specific information and the possibility to perform operations on the largest part of the data at the same time. Over time, several hardware and software methods have been developed to help store data in the necessary form and with high availability.

Data diversity: When it comes to smaller systems, it is relatively straightforward to standardize well-processed data. However, "Big Data" systems typically generate vast amounts of heterogeneous data, which may not conform to any standard format or structure. Such data is often user-generated and can include things like social media content, audio, or video files.

Data Filtration and Sorting. Filtering and sorting are two crucial steps in processing large data files. Because of the limited time available, only relevant data should be forwarded to the next processing phase. Filtering and classification help to select those parts of the data that can yield a quality result. A robust filtering system is necessary, especially when dealing with highly diverse data. Before processing, the system needs to "understand" the data by analyzing its structure, evaluating it, and visualizing the results. In recent years, neural networks and machine learning have become increasingly popular for automatic data processing. These techniques can perform high-quality filtering and sorting without requiring the system to define accurate decision-making parameters in advance.

Data integration can also have the potential to improve system functionality. However, since the format and structure of data can vary widely, it is crucial to establish an appropriate setup for data fusion. The complexity of the system may also lead to variations in the importance of different data sources or the presence of missing information.

Data Analysis. The data analysis phase is the most critical stage of processing large data files. Although the objectives of the analysis may vary, it is possible to find standard methods that can be freely used in almost any "Big Data" analysis. Sometimes these methods can overlap or supplement each other to achieve a better result [4]. The most important are the statistical analysis and methods of machine learning, which also include genetic and evolutionary algorithms, decision trees, or targeted techniques for network data, social data, text analysis, and multimedia analysis [5].

Statistical methods and the algorithms used to implement them have been evolving for centuries, making them well-proven, thoroughly explored, and standardized. Most analytical tools contain basic statistical methods, such as investigating correlation, regression analysis, or verifying hypotheses by distribution. These methods allow us to explore the fundamental data and identify essential indicators for further decision-making. One advantage of this analysis is its speed, as the algorithms used are highly optimized and efficient. However, the rigidity of standard statistical procedures can be a disadvantage, particularly when dealing with heterogeneous and unstructured data [5]. It may be difficult to apply these methods to such data types, and they may not yield the most accurate results.

Recent advancements in server and computer performance have led to the increased use and deployment of machine learning methods. With technologies such as neural networks, computers can process vast amounts of data and identify hidden connections. Large data files can be directly used to train the system and improve results. Machine learning can be divided into several main directions. Supervised learning works on the principle of learning a mapping from training data to a desired output, which is known during training. Unsupervised learning, where the desired output is not given for the input data, often produces data clusters or searches for significant variables or anomalies. The third and final type is reinforcement learning, where the system can register feedback in the form of rewards for correct behavior and punishment for behavior that does not lead to the desired goal.

The machine learning methods mentioned above can greatly simplify the development of data analysis systems, especially when dealing with large amounts of data that cannot be easily analyzed using standard methods due to inconsistencies or structural issues. To handle "big data," frameworks are often combined, integrating multiple approaches and techniques along with optional storage management systems, data source connection tools, and filtering tools. Organizations can choose between complete packages of services to manage their data [6]. Apache Hadoop is one of the most popular open-source tools for processing large data files, while MapReduce is another significant framework focused on efficient "Big Data" processing. Spark is an open-source framework developed as a successor to Hadoop. It is worth mentioning SAS in this area, even though it is not a specific framework or technology, as it is an important company in the field.

4   Visualization Principles for Extensive Data Files

In this part of the article, we will list the fundamental principles of visualization and the possibility of its use in virtual reality. In addition to general visualization principles, it is advisable to mention some principles that are necessary or strongly recommended to use due to the size or diversity of data in extensive data files.

Real time interaction: Real-time interaction is crucial for systems processing large data files, as even a slight delay in interaction could discourage users from using the system [7]. Therefore, it is important for the system to maintain interaction with minimal delay, even when working with millions of objects.

Abstraction and data reduction: Another important aspect to consider when visualizing extensive data files is abstraction and data reduction. If a large amount of data cannot be displayed in a simple form, it may not be suitable for visualization. This is because the user may be overwhelmed and find it difficult to process the information. Therefore, it is essential to apply abstraction and data reduction techniques to simplify the representation of the data, particularly when working with extensive data files.

Continuous results: In certain scenarios, displaying the results of analysis immediately may not be feasible due to hardware limitations or technical difficulties. In such cases, the visualization system should at least enable the display of ongoing partial results. This can assist the user in making timely adjustments or interrupting the whole process without needing to wait for undesired results to be computed, which can be wasteful in terms of time and resources. Parallel computation support in most systems facilitates the acquisition and display of basic information about the process. Some systems use incremental techniques, enabling data retrieval from a specific sample without having to load the entire large data file. To reduce data flow and enable faster interaction, systems should utilize caching and pre-fetching mechanisms to visualize large data files. This enables faster display of previously loaded data and quicker loading of minor changes. Smart pre-caching mechanisms can substantially enhance user-friendliness and reduce loading time for new results [7].

System adaptability: The visualization of "Big Data" should be flexible enough to adapt to specific use cases. This element is crucial for commercial systems catering to diverse customers from varied domains. Each domain may necessitate its own data previews, and hence, the visualization should cater to the user's most pressing needs. These could entail hiding or displaying panels, advanced filtering, selection of visualization type and graphical representation, and other customizations.

5   Practical Demonstrations of Visualization and Their Goals

Two interactive visualizations will now be demonstrated to verify the concepts and answer questions. The following two samples will use the theoretical knowledge obtained in order to create a clear and high-quality data display. In addition to visualizing selected data, emphasis will also be placed on the virtual scene and additional visualizations so that they do not induce negative feelings in the user but rather support the transmission of key information.

5.1 Interactive Sample - Smart City

The Smart City visualization is designed to showcase data collected from a smart city's real-world environment. It serves as a practical demonstration that can be modified and reused to present results related to land-use planning or investment evaluation. This visualization enables the extraction of commercially valuable insights from the data. Similar IoT-based smart city systems involving networks of sensors, large-scale data collection, and public dissemination of data are being planned in various locations. Thus, similar visualizations could serve as an initial step in further analysis or as a standardized analytical tool for the automated presentation of this data to the general public.

Motivation. The smart city principle is based on a network of sensors that measure various basic parameters such as temperature, air quality, traffic density, noise, and more. These sensors are typically located in strategic areas like intersections or residential areas, mounted on street lamps or other urban fixtures. Data is collected at regular intervals, often every five minutes. However, monitoring a city using these sensors can generate gigabytes of data every day, which can be challenging to visualize effectively. For instance, while a line chart can show the temperature at a specific location during the day, it becomes difficult to scale this solution to several hundred locations throughout the city. A possible solution is to use a map for visualization, but that can lead to information overload with too many layers of data or specific values. Currently, there is no comprehensive, standardized system available to present data coming from smart cities in a clear and concise manner. Therefore, it is essential to consider factors like the enormity of the data, the complexity of the sensor information structure, the visualization potential, and the multi-dimensional nature of the data to create a suitable virtual reality visualization system and evaluate its benefits.

Obtaining Data. To create the visualization, it was essential to obtain data that matched the complexity, size, and multidimensional nature required for the project. Additionally, the data needed to be connected to a real city to provide context and enhance the visualization. The Citypulse Smart City datasets provided by the University of Surrey [8] were deemed appropriate due to their comprehensive nature, containing information from Aarhus cities in Denmark, Brasov in Romania, and Surrey in the UK. Aarhus was ultimately chosen for visualization as it contained road traffic data, weather information, cultural and book events, and parking occupancy data, all of which were generated by the Dataset of Air Quality and Pollution. The data provided was from various monthly intervals in 2014. However, weather data concerning clouds was not available in the Citypulse dataset, so it was necessary to use the VisualCrossing API [9] to obtain that information. To provide a more complete picture of the city's functioning over time, information about the approximate sunrise and sunset during the measured period was obtained from publicly available astronomical data. The Aarhus data was collected from 449 sensors, and the uncompressed data from August to September 2014 in CSV and JSON formats was approximately 953 MB.

Creation Process. In creating the visualization, a key priority was given to ensuring its reusability. The various components were designed to be adaptable for use in other projects and with different datasets. The system was developed to use an online API or data that supports the API connection format, allowing for flexibility in its usage. This means that the system is not limited to Aarhus and can be adapted for other smart cities without significant modifications. Additionally, real-time data could be integrated into the system to display current visualizations. The majority of the system's functions rely on automated data generation, with only a few manual components.

Map and Terrain Creation. As we are dealing with geographical data, the first step was to create a map and terrain on which the data would be visualized. The coordinates of each sensor were obtained from the dataset. A simple script was used to calculate the maximum and minimum latitude and longitude, which created a rectangle that could be cut out of the map to reliably include all the data. To ensure that some data was not too close to the edge of the map, the coordinates were slightly extended.

To obtain the background map, OpenStreetMap [10] was used, which allows for the export of a selected area in PNG format. However, a flat display of the map would not differ much from the standard 2D display on a computer monitor. To utilize the potential of virtual reality, the map needed to be represented in 3D. Here, the modeling tool Blender or commercial geographic 3D models could be used, but as stated, the aim of this work was to create a reusable system. Therefore, a system for plastic terrain generation was created.

The terrain elevation map was obtained from the GMTED2010 model [11], from which data can be extracted using the EarthExplorer tool. The elevation map is a black-and-white image where fully black represents the lowest altitude and fully white represents the highest altitude. First, a regular mesh with vertex arrangement in a grid shape was generated. To achieve optimal rendering performance and a sufficiently detailed mesh, a grid resolution of 80x80 points was chosen. The positions of the vertices of this mesh were then shifted along the Y-axis (upward axis) according to the color of the pixel at the given coordinate. Aarhus is a port city, so the highest point in the visualization area is 100 m above sea level. Thus, the terrain is milder, but a 3D terrain model is beneficial for better rendering of the city and understanding its layout. A layer of a standard map was applied to the created mesh. However, the resulting model appeared unremarkable in the scene. Therefore, the mesh was modified to generate vertical edges of the map. This makes the model look like a cutout from a solid object.

City Generation. The plastic terrain with a texture map applied did not yet sufficiently resemble the visualization of the city. Buildings are a significant part of the city, especially skyscrapers or other large structures. Therefore, creating models of buildings was another part of the visualization process. The OpenStreetMap system contains data about streets, buildings, intersections, companies, and other parts of the map. The data for the entire planet in XML format was 118 GB. If the visualization were to offer the generation of any location on Earth, it would be necessary to create a system to process such massive data. To simplify this process, there are web projects that offer only specific regions or cities exported, so it was not necessary to process the data for the entire planet. As one of the larger cities, complete OSM data in Aarhus's format is available using the BBBike web system. The file size is approximately 192 MB. To optimize loading and processing, all unnecessary information, such as streets or company data, could be removed from the data. The osmfilter command-line tool can extract only certain parts of the data. This made it possible to reduce the size of the processed file to just under 100 MB.

The OSM file format is based on the XML structure, so it is possible to process it with the built-in C# language libraries, which are used in Unity for creating scripts. Individual points on the map form the "node" tag and have parameters such as id, geographic coordinates, and other details. Buildings have a paired "way" tag of a specific type and contain references to "nodes" that make them up. By loading these values, it is possible to generate an outline of a building. Most buildings also have parameters indicating the number of floors, allowing for an estimate of their height. This data was sufficient to create a script that generated a simple mesh of buildings. During generation, the height map must also be taken into account so that the buildings correspond to the terrain of the model. In Aarhus and its surroundings, there are over 100,000 buildings, so generating them takes several seconds. Therefore, this process must be performed during visualization creation; otherwise, it would result in freezing. If the map change were to be a real-time part of the visualization, the generation would have to occur on a separate thread.

Although the generated buildings are simple shapes without details or textures, it is possible to better identify individual areas of the city immediately. Due to their height and shapes, it is easy to detect the center, industrial area, or housing estates with apartment buildings. This element significantly contributes to the clarity of the visualization.

The follow-up part of the process was the visualization of the CityPulse datasets into a 3D city model. Firstly, it was necessary to find the positions of the sensors and load and process the data. The sensor data contained information about latitude and longitude, so the same calculation used for generating the building positions could be used to ensure they were placed in the correct position on the map. A script was created to handle loading and visualizing one sensor. A different script then ensured the synchronization of all sensor times and overall visualization settings.

However, during the creation process, a performance issue arose. The CSV files with data for one sensor took up around 2 MB. Loading them into memory, traversing the data with a loop, and retrieving the desired value required a lot of memory and processing power. This process would have to be performed for more than 400 sensors in the scene at a rendering speed of 90 frames per second. As a result, the visualization appeared jerky, and the decrease in frame rate caused nausea. Therefore, similar to mesh generation, file processing had to be moved to the visualization creation phase. Instead of loading data from files, the required values were moved to data arrays. In this process, it was possible to remove indices, ID values, geographical coordinates, and other unnecessary data. This reduced the size of the stored information, which led to an increase in performance. There were no more problems with frame rate drops. This solution, however, had a negative impact on the scene's data size because all necessary data was stored directly in the sensors. The scene file is approximately 530 MB, which is noticeable when opening and loading this visualization for the first time. If the visualization were to be further expanded, an optimal solution would need to be found.

Another problem occurred during the synchronization of the sensor data timestamps. The information was stored at five-minute intervals. For some sensors, there were apparently outages, causing occasional missing values. This resulted in a problem with missing data and significant fluctuations in the visualization. This deficiency was solved by modifying the visualization script for the sensor. If the sensor received a command to retrieve a value for a specific time and no value existed for that time, it found the next closest timestamp and used it for visualization. Thanks to the short time intervals, this solution did not undermine the informational value of the visualization and effectively covered visible data gaps.

Once the performance issues were resolved, the focus shifted towards developing ways to display the data. Information about the traffic situation, specifically the current number of vehicles at the sensor location, was chosen as the first visualized value. This value is a whole number ranging within easily imaginable limits. The first visualization method used was displaying a hemisphere at the sensor's position. The hemisphere's diameter represented the current value, such that the more vehicles passing through the location, the larger the hemisphere. Even this simple visualization provided quality information about locations where traffic is more frequent. To highlight key values, color information was added to the visualization. The hemisphere was smoothly colored from green to red within the range of 0 to 15. Therefore, if 15 or more vehicles were passing through the location, the hemisphere would be colored deep red. It was now very easy to observe critical areas where concentrated traffic jams form during peak traffic (Fig. 1). In further iterations, the hemisphere was replaced by a cube, whose height had the same function as the hemisphere's diameter. This solution slightly increased clarity as it covered less surface area of the map, but otherwise the visualization effect was almost comparable. Other values from other datasets were also tried, but the informational value of the visualization remained the same.

Fig. 1. Visualization of data on the plastic model of the city. Left - morning rush hour. Right – transportation activity at night.

Extending the Visualization. Through visualization, it was possible to explore a selected value and its behavior within the city, but the display was still too static, and there was room for increasing the information density. The partial goal was therefore to add additional information that would expand and not overlap the key value. For this purpose, a dataset with meteorological data was suitable. The data were not recorded for each of the sensors but only for the entire city at once. Even so, it was sufficient information to improve the visualization. Using a particle system that is part of the Unity engine, a representation of the wind was created. The wind speed value influenced the speed of particles, the direction of the wind was shown in the direction in which the particles flew, and the color of the particles was interpolated from blue to red according to the current air temperature. Although this information probably does not affect, for example, the current traffic situation, it can be very valuable in combination with pollution. Another additional visualization was the display of current cloudiness. Again, a particle system with a graphical representation of clouds was used (Fig. 2). Cloudiness was not part of the meteorological dataset, so it was determined additionally using data from the API. It could range from clear, partially cloudy, cloudy, overcast to rainy. The representation of cloudiness is therefore more of a graphical representation of the current situation, but again, it can provide useful information in combination with appropriate data. The display of the sun's movement across the sky and thus the representation of the sunrise and sunset proved to be another very suitable addition to the visualization. The targeted effect was achieved using a yellow sphere representing the sun and a point light source that simulated the impact of sunlight on the terrain. A programming script ensured synchronization of the light with data visualization. Thanks to the rendering of shadows and plastic terrain, it was possible to very effectively depict the sunrise and sunset over the city. Some information from the datasets gained much higher informative value thanks to this addition. For example, it was possible to observe the morning rush hour much better when people hurry to work. In the afternoon, the reverse situation when people leave the workplace is clearly observable.

Fig. 2. A display visualizing additional information about the wind direction and cloudiness.

Acquired Knowledge. The development of visualization has demonstrated that the technical means for creating virtual reality applications that presents extensive data exist.

Although there has been a focus on open data in recent years, there are not many datasets available for smart cities. It is also necessary to programmatically process more extensive map data. APIs available in this area are either paid or limited. It is not a problem to obtain simpler information, such as historical meteorological or astronomical data.

The Unity engine can render millions of vertices and triangles. Technical limitations in terms of rendering are therefore very low, and they should not be a limiting factor on at least a moderately powerful device. However, it is not suitable to process and analyze data during visualization. For this task, it is advantageous to preprocess data or provide processing on an external server and only load the resulting data using APIs.

However, the main findings were related to the functioning of the visualization itself. The created demo showed that it is possible to connect large amounts of data with displays in virtual reality. The plastic 3D model of the city, including buildings, provided a better idea of the nature of the terrain and the functioning of the area. Displaying only one value on this model did not bring many advantages compared to a standard 2D map display, but if there are hundreds of values, it is easy to observe correlations. Another significant feature is the easier tracking of multidimensional data. Although cloudiness, wind conditions, time of day, and current traffic conditions are displayed in the demo, the elements do not obscure each other, and their combination makes it possible to understand broader contexts. In cases where there is no need to track specific numerical values but rather to see the extensive visualization as a whole, virtual reality is an excellent tool. Thanks to the floating control panel, the visualization can be adjusted and controlled without interruption. Although it may not be apparent at first glance, the visualization is very extensive, and it would be difficult to display the entire space on a standard monitor without zooming, which would hide detailed information. By using the wide field of view of virtual reality and the almost unlimited size of the scene, it is possible to view very complex and extensive visualizations containing small details.

5.2 Interactive Sample - Czech Republic

The second visualization focused on displaying data that are more general and not directly defined by location or precise time. This makes it a more abstract visualization than the Smart City demonstration and allows for the use of more general datasets and the creation of more creative displays with various dimensions of data. For this visualization, publicly available data measured by the Czech Statistical Office were used. The demonstration could serve as a visualization tool for datasets in various fields.

Motivation. There is a large amount of data related to geography that is not directly defined by position. Often, these include data from national, regional, or local government agencies. All of these institutions have an obligation to publish data, but they often only do so in the form of tables or textual descriptions. As a result, residents and businesses may find it difficult to evaluate the impact of such data on themselves or their activities. If they want to conduct, for example, a market survey, they often have to turn to experts who know how to work with the data. A publicly available tool for efficient visualization of such data could help with similar tasks.

Data Acquisition. The Czech Statistical Office (CSU) publishes dozens of different data sets [12]. Data are published in categories such as prices, transport, services, population, and others at regular intervals. Rapidly changing data, such as fuel prices, are updated weekly, while less volatile data are updated monthly, quarterly, or annually. With the web interface, data can be displayed using tables, line or column charts, or color maps. It is also possible to download data in XLSX, XML, and PDF formats. CSU does not provide an official API that would allow for filtering, paging, and other operations. It is necessary to download the entire files and process them directly in the visualization. Common statistics for visualization purposes were chosen, such as Deaths by Months and Age Groups, Number of Employees, and Average Gross Monthly Wages. The data were downloaded in XML format for the years 2011–2022, at monthly frequencies by regions. A standardized XML schema was used for the file structure, so it would be possible to use other CSU data with minimal adjustments.

Creation Process. When creating the interactive demo of the Czech Republic, the emphasis was not put on realism as much as it was with Smart City. Attention was rather focused on various ways to convey data and project their dimensions into visualization. A small part of the code was taken from the Smart City demonstration, but the majority of the code had to be custom-made for this demo as a different approach to generating terrain and displaying data was chosen. Once again, emphasis was placed on reusability, creation through data generation, and simplicity.

Map Creation. It was tempting to use a plastic 3D terrain model generated using OpenStreetMap again, but because the data only concerned the Czech Republic, a large part of it would be unused in the visualization. Also, the data was divided by regions, so that the emphasis was placed on highlighting the borders between regions. Finally, a different approach was chosen for creating the base map. The Czech Office of Surveying, Mapping, and Cadastre provides precisely defined region boundaries in SHP format for download on their portal, using geographic coordinates. With the help of a script, a mesh outline of the region was easily generated. The process of filling the region using triangulation came with some difficulties. It was not possible to simply connect individual vertices to a vertex in the middle, as some regions contain folds that would be covered in this way. Especially problematic is the drawing of the Central Bohemian region, which has the capital city of Prague in the middle, creating an opening. In the end, the TriangleNet library was used, which can triangulate the surface without covering folds or openings using an advanced algorithm. Vertical edges were added to the regions again, so that they were not just flat but looked plastic. The regions are not drawn close together but have a small space between them to highlight the borders. Using regions without texture was tested, but it did not improve the visualization; rather, it was more difficult to navigate in the model. Therefore, the texture obtained using OpenStreetMap was used again. The terrain was not height-deformed as in Smart City. Instead, in addition to the color texture, a texture for normal mapping was used. Thanks to this texture, it is possible to simulate the behavior of light as if the surface of the model had height details. Since the visualization is set up to have the model perpendicular to the user's view, most of the time they will not notice this technique, and the feeling of plasticity will be preserved. This solution is more optimal in terms of rendering performance, but it reaches its limits when there are too many differences in the surface of the model.

Data Visualization. The first dataset to be visualized captured the number of deaths by months and age groups. Similar to the first example, a script that maintained all the data and ensured the rendering was created for the region. For initial testing, a number of cubes were randomly placed over the region that corresponded to the number of deaths in the region. The problem was that, using random generation, the cubes were being created in a square on the plane, overreaching into spaces where the region did not exist. It was necessary to ensure that they were generated only on the plane of the region, which in some cases had a very complex shape. Testing using our calculations would be too demanding and would probably involve an approximation. The solution was to create a simple physical test using a raycast. When a random position was generated, a test was performed. If it passed, a cube was placed there; otherwise, a new random position was generated. Although this solution is not optimal, it ensures the correct placement of cubes and is performance-sufficient even for thousands of generated positions.

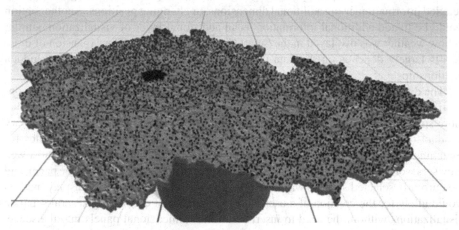

Fig. 3. Model of the Czech Republic containing pictograms of persons according to the number of deceased in the region

In the next phase, the blocks were replaced with pictograms of people, which made it possible to clearly identify that the visualization represents the number of individuals. This simple visualization was sufficient for estimating population density and recognizing fluctuations in the data (Fig. 3). The problematic part of this visualization is the capital city of Prague. Due to the high population density, it is almost impossible to recognize the differences and the number of pictograms. One possible solution would be to reduce the size of the pictograms, but this would result in poor readability in other parts of the country. A better way to optimize this problem might be to allocate this region to a separate or complementary visualization where the region could be seen on a larger scale and smaller details could be recognized.

The second dataset visualized captured the number of employees and the average gross monthly salary. It differed from the previous dataset in that it was 2-dimensional. Also, the number of employees was not in units of population but in thousands. The average gross monthly salary was given in Czech crowns. The same system used to display the number of deaths was used for the visualization of the number of employees, where one person pictogram represented a thousand persons in a given region. The goal was to add salaries to this visualization to track the connection between the two data sets. One option was to display a money pictogram whose size would represent the state of the monthly salary in the region. However, this option obscured the pictograms of persons, observation based on size was not precise, and differences between regions were difficult to determine. The highest-quality solution was obtained using the scaling of the given region's height. The standard height of a plastic model was 0.1 units, and the resulting height was calculated by multiplying this base by the gross monthly salary converted to ten thousand units (salary/10 000). As a result, the changes were sufficiently significant while remaining within the required threshold for observation. Additionally, this visualization technique did not interfere with the display of pictograms.

In a similar way, it would be possible to expand the display to include other dimensions of data. For example, by coloring regions, showing districts in regions, adding detailed information, using additional dimensions, or changing positions. Another option would be to add additional information as an additional layer of visualization, similar to how weather was displayed in the Smart City demonstration. The expansion of more details largely depends on the data used and whether it is necessary to find hidden relationships.

The display system using a floating panel was adopted from the Smart City demonstration (Fig. 4). In the case of visualizing the Czech Republic, the goal was to display more specific values and provide the user with precise numbers. It was also necessary to adapt the user interface to support a larger number of unrelated datasets. Tabs for switching between different statistics were introduced, closely modeling how most web browsers work. The names of available datasets were displayed at the top of the panel, and the currently selected statistic was highlighted in color. Expanding this display method would allow for the creation of a user interface capable of controlling several separate visualizations without the need to insert additional dimensional panels into the scene. At the same time, the user always sees only the visualization settings they are currently working with, so their attention is not distracted.

One element that was not part of the Smart City visualization was contextual indicators located directly in the displayed model. To easily track the differences between regions and compare their numerical data, a simple flat text panel was added to each region. This table was displayed when the controller pointer focused on a specific area. To be able to move around the scene and still have the ability to display this additional information, the panel is always facing the player. As the system contained two controllers, it was possible to display contextual data for two different regions and compare their values in this way.

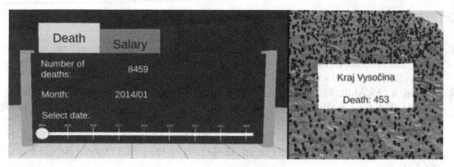

Fig. 4. On the left - virtual panel extended with tabs located on the upper edge. Right - Auxiliary context visualization showing values for the selected region.

6 Conclusions

The main contribution from a theoretical and practical standpoint was to demonstrate the feasibility of creating virtual reality visualizations of large data files. Adequate software and hardware technologies were found to be available for development, and storage and data processing standards make the necessary display creation relatively easy. The recommended approach is to use established software tools, such as the Unity game engine or publicly available sources like OpenStreetMap, to accelerate development and ensure the system's compatibility with other tools. Given that virtual reality visualization is still an emerging field, it is important to establish standards and recommended practices instead of fragmenting the system.

Interactive demonstrations have proven that virtual reality can effectively display multi-dimensional data and present information in a comprehensible way. Created visualizations further validated the unique benefits of virtual reality, such as the perception of a three-dimensional virtual scene, freedom of movement, and natural interaction through hands and gestures. However, the negative aspects of virtual reality, such as the high cost of devices, the need for free space, and user discomfort, must be taken into account. Much consideration must be put into the creation of visualizations in virtual reality. Otherwise, the negative effects could outweigh the benefits. Visualization in virtual reality should therefore be aimed at maximizing the advantages of this technology rather than competing with desktop computer visualization and presentation tools.

Current options for visualizing large data files in virtual reality are suitable for both commercial and academic use. The technology can be beneficial in areas such as architecture, design, marketing, research, training, and more, with ample room for further independent research and user testing to improve presentation and perception.

Acknowledgments. This work and the contribution were supported by a project of Students Grant Agency (SPEV 2023) - FIM, University of Hradec Kralove, Czech Republic.

References

1. Ježek, B., Šimeček, O., Slabý, A.: Virtual scene components for data visualization. In: De Paolis, L.T., Arpaia, P., Bourdot, P. (eds.) AVR 2021. LNCS, vol. 12980, pp. 3–16. Springer, Cham (2021). https://doi.org/10.1007/978-3-030-87595-4_1
2. Kitchin, R., McArdle, G.: What makes big data, big data? Exploring the ontological characteristics of 26 datasets. Big Data Soc. **3**, 2053951716631130 (2016). https://doi.org/10.1177/2053951716631130
3. Sagiroglu, S., Sinanc, D.: Big data: a review. In: 2013 International Conference on Collaboration Technologies and Systems (CTS), pp. 42–47 (2013). https://doi.org/10.1109/CTS.2013.6567202
4. Silva, B.N., Diyan, M., Han, K.: Big data analytics. In: Khan, M., Jan, B., Farman, H. (eds.) Deep Learning: Convergence to Big Data Analytics, pp. 13–30. Springer, Singapore (2019). https://doi.org/10.1007/978-981-13-3459-7_2
5. Choi, T.-M., Wallace, S.W., Wang, Y.: Big data analytics in operations management. Prod. Oper. Manag. **27**, 1868–1883 (2018). https://doi.org/10.1111/poms.12838
6. Arfat, Y., Usman, S., Mehmood, R., Katib, I.: Big data tools, technologies, and applications: a survey. In: Mehmood, R., See, S., Katib, I., Chlamtac, I. (eds.) Smart Infrastructure and Applications. EAISICC, pp. 453–490. Springer, Cham (2020). https://doi.org/10.1007/978-3-030-13705-2_19
7. Bikakis, N.: Big Data Visualization Tools (2018). http://arxiv.org/abs/1801.08336. https://doi.org/10.48550/arXiv.1801.08336
8. CityPulse Smart City Datasets – Datasets. http://iot.ee.surrey.ac.uk:8080/datasets.html. Accessed 29 Apr 2023
9. Weather Data & Weather API | Visual Crossing. https://www.visualcrossing.com/. Accessed 29 Apr 2023
10. OpenStreetMap. https://www.openstreetmap.org/. Accessed 29 Apr 2023
11. Earth Resources Observation And Science (EROS) Center: Global Multi-resolution Terrain Elevation Data 2010 (GMTED2010) (2017). https://www.usgs.gov/centers/eros/science/usgs-eros-archive-digital-elevation-global-multi-resolution-terrain-elevation. https://doi.org/10.5066/F7J38R2N
12. Statistiky VDB. https://vdb.czso.cz/vdbvo2/faces/cs/index.jsf?page=statistiky. Accessed 29 Apr 2023

A Framework for Animating Customized Avatars from Monocular Videos in Virtual Try-On Applications

Alberto Cannavò[1]([✉])(iD), Roberto Pesando[2], and Fabrizio Lamberti[1](iD)

[1] Department of Control and Computer Engineering,
Politecnico di Torino, Turin, Italy
{alberto.cannavo,fabrizio.lamberti}@polito.it
[2] Protocube Reply, Turin, Italy
r.pesando@reply.it

Abstract. Generating real-time animations for customized avatars is becoming of paramount importance, especially in Virtual Try-On applications. This technology allows customers to explore or "try on" products virtually. Despite the numerous benefits of this technology, there are some aspects that prevent its applicability in real scenarios. The first limitation regards the difficulties in generating expressive avatar animations. Moreover, potential customers usually expressed concerns regarding the fidelity of the animations. To overcome these two limitations, the current paper is aimed at presenting a framework for animating customized avatars based on state-of-the-art techniques. The focus of the proposed work mainly relies on aspects regarding the animation of the customized avatars. More specifically, the framework encompasses two components. The first one automatizes the operations needed for generating the data structures used for the avatar animation. This component assumes that the mesh of the avatar is described through the Sparse Unified Part-Based Human Representation (SUPR). The second component of the framework is designed to animate the avatar through motion capture by making use of the MediaPipe Holistic pipeline. Experimental evaluations were carried out aimed at assessing the solutions proposed for pose beautification and joint estimations. Results demonstrated improvements in the quality of the reconstructed animation from both an objective and subjective point of view.

Keywords: Animating customized avatar · MediaPipe holistic pipeline · SUPR · Pose beautification

1 Introduction

The possibility to animate in real-time avatars is becoming of paramount importance in different fields, ranging from entertainment and 3D game production to virtual heritage applications [36]. Among the others, online shopping is attracting

L. T. De Paolis et al. (Eds.): XR Salento 2023, LNCS 14218, pp. 69–88, 2023.
https://doi.org/10.1007/978-3-031-43401-3_5

more and more the attention of researchers and practionaries. In fact, according to the statistics reported in Statista[1], in 2022, online sales amounted to around 800 billion dollars and it is expected that in 2025 they may even exceed 1.2 trillion. In this context, animated avatars started to be widely adopted as virtual characters in virtual try-on (VTO) and virtual fitting room (VFR) applications [21]. These technologies support customers in the choice of the most appropriate fitting garment given their body shapes and measurements [5]. In fact, VTO applications provide potential customers with the possibility to virtually try on products [19], even broader collection and inventories [33], without the need to produce the real objects or ask the customers to physically move in the store. These benefits also represent a good opportunity to implement sustainable behavior as it reduces the production of waste and pollution [34]. Although VTO applications have technically been available for a while, it is worth observing that their usage remains still limited [20]. Reasons can be found mainly in the difficulties of generating expressive avatar animations and concerns expressed by potential customers about the fidelity of the simulation.

For what it concerns the first aspect, in order to animate avatars, it is possible to look at traditional graphics suites such as Blender[2] or Autodesk Maya[3]. However, generating virtual character animations through traditional tools has been proven to be a time-consuming and skill-intensive task. For this reason, alternative interfaces based, e.g., on virtual reality (VR) and 3D user interfaces have been presented in the literature, e.g., in [2,6]. To overcome the difficulties of the traditional animation approach, alternative techniques were made available to capture the movements of a user and transfer his or her gestures to an avatar. These techniques include the use of sensors for facial tracking [8], 3D scanners [10], multiple camera settings [43], wearable IMUs [7], and depth cameras [41].

Although the methodologies presented above accurately capture the movements of the users they also require expensive instruments, complex environment setups, and/or time-consuming operations, e.g., to fix reconstruction issues or filter noise signals [35]. All these factors could prevent the applicability of such solutions in the fashion industry for VTO applications, since virtual shopping should be characterized by simple and fast experiences to solicit potential customers [20]. Considering these limitations, monocular video-driven motion capture could represent a valid solution for tracking the motion of customers and animating high-fidelity avatars, as videos can be easily retrieved from personal devices (such as smartphones).

As mentioned, another aspect that still limits the widespread of VTO applications is represented by the concerns expressed by potential customers regarding the low accuracy of the simulation and poor representation of the customer's body and face. These factors cause dissatisfaction with the fitting results [12]. To

---

[1] Statistics on online sales: https://tinyurl.com/fashion-ecommerce-value.
[2] Blender: https://www.blender.org/.
[3] Autodesk Maya: https://tinyurl.com/bda6pcwa.

satisfy customers' expectations, high-fidelity simulations, as well as customizable avatars, are needed. Avatars should rely on a high-quality human model reconstruction and should be reconfigurable in order to fit the shape and pose of the customers [35].

Moving from these considerations, the proposed work presents a framework to support the generation of avatar animations for VTO applications. More specifically, the goal of this work is not to present just another VPO application but rather focus on aspects regarding the avatar animation, disregarding factors such as how the avatar is modeled, how clothes are simulated, tools for testing different garment sizes, etc.

To achieve this goal, the framework considered state-of-the-art techniques with the aim to obtain an accurate reconstruction of the customers' avatars and high-fidelity simulations. More specifically, the Sparse Unified Part-Based Human Representation (SUPR) [28] is used as a parametric model to generate and animate the 3D avatar of the customers. This choice was taken after observing that with respect to other models, such as GHUM [39], Sparse Trained Articulated Human Body (STAR) [27], SMPL eXpressive (SMPL-X) [31] and Skinned Multi-Person Linear Model (SMPL) [22], the SUPR parametric model can achieve better reconstruction performance [28]. This is made possible through the expressiveness of this model and its parameters that have been trained with the use of the largest dataset with respect to the other models, thus making this solution able to model complex body shapes and robust to possible lacking data. The MediaPipe framework[4] was adopted for holistic landmark detection and tracking of the human body [23]. These state-of-the-art tools were integrated into the framework by developing an add-on, named Rig-SUPR, for a common graphics suite (i.e., Blender). The Rig-SUPR add-on is able to create the animation data structure needed for animating a customized avatar. Moreover, the framework envisages an animation system to enable motion capture from monocular images. The devised animation system features techniques for joint estimation and poses beautification with the aim of fixing tracking errors and making the animation smooth.

2   Related Work

As mentioned, the framework includes the Rig-SUPR add-on designed for the automatic generation of the animation data structure and an animation system that enables motion capture through monocular images. For this reason, the current section reviewed works related to both topics. Finally, the last paragraph reviewed relevant works presenting frameworks for the generating and animating custom avatars.

---

[4] Holistic landmarks detection: https://tinyurl.com/yc3m6b9v.

2.1 Generating Animation Data Structure

Operations to be tackled when preparing arbitrarily shaped avatars for the animation process include the rigging and skinning process as well as the generation of supporting data structures (i.e., blenshapes).

During the rigging process, a hierarchical structure of bones, referred to as a skeleton, is generated and embedded in the mesh of the avatar [3]. Nowadays, different approaches are available for rigging a mesh and making it ready for a game engine. Among the others, it is possible to mention the use of tools such as Mixamo[5]. This tool simplifies the rigging and the generation of animations for both artists and developers by providing simplified functionalities for animating avatars. More specifically, for what it concerns the rigging, users can simply upload a character's mesh and then place the so-called *joint locators* (e.g., wrists, elbows, knees, and hip) on the mesh to obtain its rigged version.

Another approach involves importing the mesh into 3D graphics software such as Blender or Maya. In this case, rigging can be done both manually or using specific add-ons to automatize some steps of the process. As a matter of example, Auto-Rig Pro[6], is an add-on for Blender that allows for both manual creation of custom rigs and automatic bone placement. The automatic placement of the bones is achieved by adding green markers to nine specific key points. This add-on is also able to generate a rig that can be used in game engines such as Unreal or Unity. Rigify[7] is a modular rigging system developed as an add-on for Blender. Users can either make use of default rigs provided by the add-on or create new ones. The created rigs can be saved for future use. This tool supports only manual bone placement, so new skeletons can be assembled only by manually positioning bones within the mesh.

The work described in [40] proposed a full automatic rigging tool. More specifically, given a 3D model provided as input to the system, it predicts a skeleton that matches the animator's expectations in terms of joint placement and topology. The method works both for humanoid and not human characters. Besides supporting the avatars rigging, the system is also able to perform skinning, i.e., the process that binds the 3D mesh to the skeleton by setting up the influence that each bone has on the surrounding vertices of the mesh, causing them to move accordingly [15]. The method for computing the skin weights is based on a deep neural network that operates directly on the mesh representation without making assumptions about the class and topology of the shape. The neural network has been trained with a large and diversified dataset containing 3D models, their skeletons, and the corresponding vertex weights.

2.2 Motion Capture

Several techniques are also available to support motion capture, that differ in terms of setup complexity and tracking accuracy. For this paper, it has been

---

[5] Mixamo: https://www.mixamo.com/#/.
[6] Auto-Rig Pro: https://blendermarket.com/products/auto-rig-pro.
[7] Rigify: https://tinyurl.com/rigify.

chosen to focus on the optical markerless techniques based on monocular videos, which typically are affordable solutions characterized by acceptable tracking accuracy [35]. As a matter of example, the work in [38] presented DeepPose, a deep neural network developed by Google for 2D pose estimation. In this work, the detection of the 2D joints' positions was translated into a regression problem. The model implements a multi-layer network to improve prediction accuracy and leverages a holistic approach, hence the network was not focused on a single joint but on a set of them. In this way, it is possible to make predictions also in those cases in which joints are occluded.

Another approach is based on the use of heatmaps, i.e., an image that contains information regarding the probability to find a given joint in the considered frame. For instance, the work in [37] presents ConvNet Pose, an architecture based on convolutional networks and heatmaps that envisages an effective "position refinement" model designed to accurately predict the position of the joints within a localized region of an image.

The work in [9] presents OpenPose, i.e., an open-source real-time system for detecting multiple persons (including body, foot hand, and facial key points) from 2D images. The methodology leverages a non-parametric representation, called Part Affinity Fields (PAFs), to learn the association between body parts and individuals in the image. This approach that starts from individual parts of the body to detect human poses is usually indicated as the bottom-up approach. The results demonstrated that this approach is able to achieve high accuracy and real-time performance, regardless of the number of subjects in the image. Conversely, in [11] a top-down approach is used. With this approach, the system first identifies people in the given input frame (human detection phase), and then it recognizes the poses of each person (pose detection phase). More specifically, the authors in [11] moved from the observation that the accuracy of such kind of top-down methods mainly relies on the accuracy of the human detector, as any errors are automatically propagated to the pose detector. For this reason, the work in [11] proposed a two-step framework named AlphaPose. In the first step, the system leverages a top-down approach for reconstructing individual poses, which may be redundant or inaccurate. In the second step, these issues are addressed by applying a regional multi-person pose estimation method.

The work described in [25] is able to merge the advantages of both the top-down and bottom-up approaches by proposing a solution based on the popular YOLO framework. More specifically, the proposed model learns simultaneously how to detect the bounding boxes of multiple subjects and their corresponding 2D poses in a single pass. This eliminates the need for post-processing in bottom-up approaches to group detected key points into a skeleton because each bounding box is associated with a pose. Differently than top-down approaches, there is no need for multiple passes as all individuals are localized along with their poses in a single inference.

Finally, the work in [23] presented the MediaPipe framework. Differently than previous works, MediaPipe can be regarded as a set of models specialized for different tasks, e.g., image classification and segmentation, gesture recognition, and text or audio classification. In particular, the current work takes advantage of the

MediaPipe Holistic pipeline, i.e., a set of models for pose, face, and hand detection, each specialized in its domain. The functioning of the MediaPipe Holistic pipeline moves from the observation that each model should receive a different input, depending on the region it is specialized. For this reason, the pipeline first estimates the human pose by making use of BlazePose, i.e., a lightweight convolutional neural network architecture able to detect 33 body key points ensuring a high frame rate also on mobile devices [4]. Afterward, three regions of interest (ROIs) crops were derived for each hand and for the face. Re-crop models are then applied to improve the ROI and obtained high-resolution ROIs. Successively, the cropped images are provided as input to ask-specific face and hand models to estimate their corresponding landmarks. More specifically, the MediaPipe Face Mesh [13] is a real-time solution for estimating 468 3D face landmarks, even on mobile devices. This solution is able to infer the 3D surface of the face using only a single camera input, thus eliminating the requirement for dedicated depth sensors. The MediaPipe hands model [42] leverages machine learning to detect from a single frame the 21 landmarks of each hand. Studies, such as [18], demonstrated that MediaPipe solutions are able to achieve better performance in terms of pose accuracy and computing resources for real-time applications.

2.3   Generating and Animating Custom Avatars

The literature has already proposed a number of frameworks devoted to the generation and animation of custom avatars. For instance, the work in [26] describes a framework for creating interactive avatars. The proposed pipeline assembles different freely available or open-source software, e.g., MD-Lab and Blender to support the overall process. Moreover, the generated avatars can be deployed on several game engines and it has been proven to be used in different application scenarios [26]. However, the use of MB-Lab as a tool for generating avatars could represent a limitation in the application scenario of the current paper, i.e., VTO applications, since the use of a reduced set of sliders to define the body shape could limit the expressiveness of the avatar. Differently than [26], the current work only assumes that the mesh of the avatar is described with the SUPR parametric model, thus making it possible to leverage machine learning algorithms for the automatic generation of avatars.

Another example is reported in [17] which presents an approach for creating and animating avatars for real-time rendering applications based on a workflow that combines and incorporates commercial tools. Similarly to the previous work, the software named Curious Lab's Poser was leveraged to model the avatar. Besides the limitation regarding the expressiveness of the avatar (as discussed above), the work proposed in [17] also introduced limitations regarding the avatar animations. In fact, the animations can only be activated from a pre-recorded library of animations generated with the software. The only movements that can be directly controlled are the pointing and "look at" gestures (controlled through an inverse kinematic approach) as well as the walking movement (implemented by leveraging the algorithm proposed in [29]).

Finally, the work in [1] describes a pipeline for creating realistic ready-to-animate virtual avatars. In this case, the modeling of the avatar is based on fitting 3D scans to the template model of Autodesk's Character Generator. The template model already contains a complex skeleton structure, skin weights, blendshapes, and the controller for eyes and teeth. In this way, the generated avatar obtained by the fitting of 3D scans with the template is ready to be animated. A limitation of this approach is related to the high complexity of the hardware used for 3D scanning, as it relies on a custom-built camera rig composed of more than 40 cameras. This limitation could prevents its application in the considered usage case scenario as VTO applications designed for on-site stores requires simple and cheap solutions [35].

3   Methodology

In order to animate in real-time customized avatars, a number of steps are necessary, which include rigging, skinning, operations to import the avatar into Unity Game Engine[8], retargeting of the animation data between different skeletons and motion capture. To this aim, the framework envisages a number of components that have been designed to execute the above operations.

3.1   Rig-SUPR Add-On

This component is in charge of executing the rigging, skinning of the mesh, generating the data structures needed for the animation of the avatar, and making it usable in a game engine such as Unity. To this aim, the add-on named Rig-SUPR was developed for Blender (written in Python). The Rig-SUPR is able to automatically compute a rig for the avatar that is compliant with the SUPR definition. Before rigging and skinning, the user is requested to import the mesh of the avatar to be animated as .obj file. Generating the mesh of the avatar is out of the scope of this work, but it can be easily accomplished by using existing tools available in the literature or in the market (e.g., a Blender add-on for generating SMPL-X avatar can be downloaded at https://smpl-x.is.tue.mpg.de/index.html).

Then the mesh is provided with a skeleton. To generate the skeleton the Rigify add-on was leveraged. More specifically, the add-on provides common building blocks that can be arranged (and saved for further use) to form the SUPR skeleton described in [28].

Once the SUPR skeleton has been manually generated the first time, the lines of codes to recreate the skeleton are generated by using a built-in function of the Rigify add-on. More specifically, the rig is saved as a python (.py) file that can be launched in Blender to recreate the exact skeleton structure. In this way, the Rig-SUPR add-on can take advantage of this skeleton to rig every avatar without asking users to manually recreate it every time

---

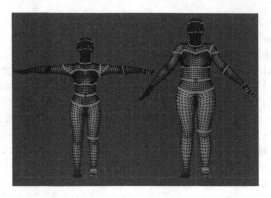

Fig. 1. Example of vertex groups identified for different body shapes.

Once the skeleton is inserted, the mesh of the avatar is associated with it (completing the rigging process), and the influence of the bones on the vertices is computed by transferring the values from a template (thus achieving the skinning process). More specifically, in order to accommodate different body shapes of the avatars it was necessary to design and develop a methodology able to adapt the pre-computed skeleton to different avatar topologies. This operation takes place by first identifying a set of vertex groups, i.e., a list of vertices belonging to the mesh, that represent the borders of the segmented mesh (e.g., arms, foot, hip, etc.). In other words, fifty vertex groups are identified that enclose the areas in which the conjunctions of the joints are found. Figure 1 shows the vertex groups used for this purpose. The identification of the vertex groups for different body shapes (as illustrated in Fig. 1) is made possible under the hypothesis that all the meshes of the avatars to be animated are compliant with the SUPR definition. Therefore all the meshes contain exactly the same number of vertices and the same vertex can be identified in different meshes by using the same index. In this way, once identified the indices of the vertices needed for creating the vertex group the first time, the Rig-SUPR add-on is able to automatically recreate the vertex group for different avatars. Once the vertex groups are identified, their centroids are computed to obtain the position in which the bones of the pre-computed skeleton have to be placed. Bones are placed and/or transformed (i.e., translated, rotated, scaled) to fit as much as possible the target positions identified by the centroids.

As anticipated the skinning, i.e., the definition of the influence that bones of the skeleton have on the vertices of the mesh, is performed by transferring the weights from a template under the same hypothesis that is possible to identify the same vertices between the template and the current mesh avatar by using the same index.

The last step for making the avatar compliant with the SUPR parametric model envisages the transferring of blendshapes from the template to the avatar. Blenshapes are defined in the SUPR parametric model to control the general shape of the avatar (300 blendshapes), facial expression (10 blendshapes) and corrective poses (400 blendshapes) (Fig. 2). The process adopted for activating the facial expression and corrective blenshapes is described in Sect. 3.2.

At the end of the execution of the Rig-SUPR add-on, a full animable avatar is obtained. That avatar can be animated in Blender by using traditional animation approaches or exported as .fbx to use the customized avatar in game engines such as Unity or Unreal.

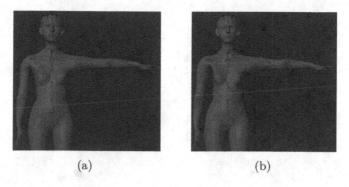

(a)   (b)

Fig. 2. Effects of the skin weight in the pose: a) correct skin weight and b) the incorrect one obtained with the default weights assignment.

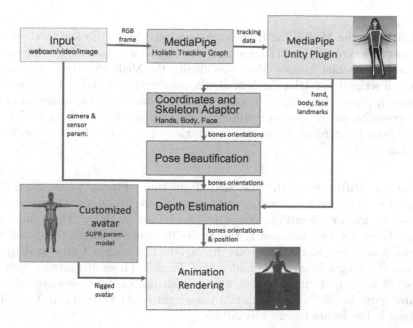

Fig. 3. Components of the animation system.

3.2   Animation System

Once the .fbx file containing the information of the avatar has been generated, it is possible to import it as an asset in the Unity Game engine. As anticipated, the monocular images extracted from static pictures, videos, or webcam streams are used as sources for motion capture. The main components of the animation system are depicted in Fig. 3.

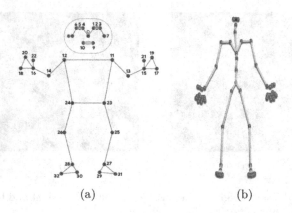

(a)   (b)

Fig. 4. Comparing the topologies of the two skeletons: a) MediaPipe and b) SUPR [28] skeleton.

MediaPipe. The MediaPipe framework (vers. 0.8.10) is the low-level component that is leveraged for 3D landmark detection and tracking of the human body from monocular images. More specifically, the MediaPipe Holistic pipeline has been leveraged to retrieve information regarding the hands (21 landmarks for each hand), pose (33 landmarks), and facial expressions (468 landmarks) of the user. Depending on the type of landmark, information retrieved from MediaPipe are interpreted according to the documentation[9] to extract the 3D coordinates of the landmarks.

MediaPipe Unity Plugin. The MediaPipe Unity Plugin[10] (version 0.10.1) acts as a bridge between Mediapipe and Unity. It makes it possible to manipulate the machine-learning solutions offered by MediaPipe in Unity. This plugin was mainly chosen for two reasons: i) the flexibility, since it offers the possibility to develop and test MediaPipe code directly in C# within Unity, and ii) the fact that the plugin is available under MIT license. These advantages come at the cost of lower performance when multiple MediaPipe functions are called in the same game loop. To cope with this issue lightweight custom script could be leveraged in the future to run MediaPipe.

---

[9] MediaPipe Guide: https://tinyurl.com/MediaPipe-Holistic.
[10] MediaPipeUnityPlugin   Public: https://github.com/homuler/MediaPipe Unity.

Coordinates and Skeleton Adaptor. The coordinates and skeleton adaptor is in charge of processing and converting the 3D positional coordinates of the face, body, and hands landmarks into positions and orientations of the joints to animate the avatar. More specifically, the adaptor first changes the coordinate system by passing from right- (used by MediaPipe to track the landmarks) to left-handed (leveraged in Unity) coordinate system. Afterward, a methodology is envisaged to retarget the animation data gathered by the MediaPipe pipeline (that referred to a given skeleton topology) into the one described in the SUPR parametric model. The differences between the two skeletons are illustrated in Fig. 4.

For the joints that are not co-located in the same portion of the body in both skeletons, the retargeting methodology estimates the missing joint information by averaging the 3D positions of a given constellation of landmarks and, for this point, it computes the normal to the plane containing the landmarks. In this way, the correspondence between a set of landmarks and a bone is established. For example, the information regarding the bone of the head in the SUPR skeleton is computed by considering the set of MediaPipe landmarks that includes the mouth, the left, and right eyes (the landmark number 2, 5, 9, 10 in Fig. 4a).

Once the mapping among the bones of the two skeletons has been identified, the final position and orientation expressed as quaternions are retrieved. In particular, the upward and forward direction of each bone is computed by considering the 3D positions of the corresponding pair of landmarks. Then the two vectors are used to retrieve the actual orientation of the bones. The orientation of each bone is also leveraged to activate the weight of the 400 corrective pose blendshapes of the SUPR parametric model. More specifically, the orientations expressed in quaternions are first converted into the axis-angle representation and then the Rodrigues' rotation formula is applied to compute the weights of the blendshapes.

As mentioned above, the SUPR parametric model also includes 10 blendshapes that can be leveraged for animating facial expressions. To this aim, the distance computed among a subset of the 468 facial landmarks tracked with MediaPipe is converted into weights for blendshape activation. As a matter of example, the distance between the landmarks 0 and 291 (i.e., the landmarks placed on the top and on the bottom right corner of the mouth[11]), is considered to activate the blend shape for smiling. The longer the distance, the greater the weight assigned to the corresponding blendshape.

Pose Beautification. Although MediaPipe achieves significant tracking performance, it also introduces errors in the prediction of the landmark. Comparing the pose extracted from a reference animation (as shown in Fig. 5a) with the landmark detected by Medipipe (Fig. 5b) it is possible to spot some errors, especially for bones that refer to the feet (always facing downwards), legs (positioned further back) and torso (to which a rotation to the intermediate bones

---

[11] Face landmark detection guide: https://tinyurl.com/3vx5fjv9.

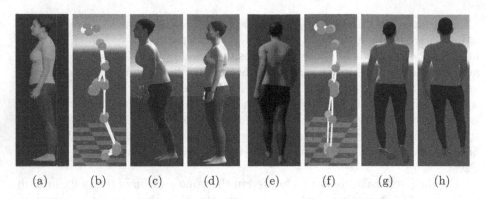

(a)   (b)   (c)   (d)   (e)   (f)   (g)   (h)

Fig. 5. Comparing the poses of the avatar: a,e) the reference animations b) landmark detection retrieved by MediaPipe, reconstructed animation c) without and, d) with pose beautification.

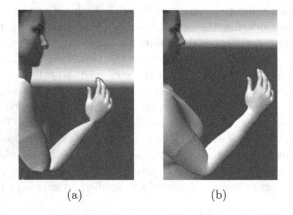

(a)   (b)

Fig. 6. Effect of the Candy-wrapper on the animation.

is applied). These errors become particularly evident when the system reconstructs the pose used to animate the avatar (as shown in Fig. 5c). To cope with this issue, a beautification process is introduced able to fix the pose (as shown in Fig. 5d). The beautification process makes use of bones' constraints and specific offset applied to the skeletons to bring the avatar's bones back to their desired positions.

Another aspect considered during the beautification process is the tracking issue observed when the subject is framed from the back (as shown in Fig. 5e and Fig. 5f). In fact, MediaPipe was no longer able to track the movement of the feet and ankles, resulting in unnatural movements of the avatar (Fig. 5g). To address this issue, ankle rotation constraints were imposed to avoid incorrect movements between the leg and foot joints. The result of this operation is shown in Fig. 5h. At current, the above offsets and constraints, have been obtained experimentally by retargeting the motion capture data into a number of avatars characterized by different sizes and shapes. In the future, a calibration procedure could be envisaged before the motion capture session that asks the users to assume a given set of poses. In this way, personalized offset and constraints could be computed for each avatar, thus improving the quality of the reconstructed animations.

In addition, the pose beautification is in charge of limiting the issue of the *candy wrapper*, i.e., an artifact due to the use of linear blend skinning (LBS) that is noticeable when large joint rotations are applied [32]. The artifact is also due to the possibility of representing the same orientation with different quaternions. An example showing the effect of the candy wrapper artifact on the elbow and wrist joints is depicted in Fig. 6a. To cope with the above issues, first, corrective blendshapes of the SUPR parametric model are leveraged (as described above), then, offsets are applied to the orientations of the bones (i.e., elbows and wrists) when high joint rotations are observed. The effect of the beautification process is depicted in Fig. 6b.

Finally, a Kalman and a Low-pass filter are applied to the tracking data with the aim of reducing the noise and smoothing the movements of each joint by weighing, with appropriate coefficients, the new position with respect to the previously assumed ones. The contribution of these two filters has made it possible to improve the naturalness of the movements.

Depth Estimation. By leveraging the raw positional data of the landmarks gathered by MediaPipe it is possible to create only in-place animations. This is due to the fact that tracking data are provided relative to the root of the skeleton, and the global position of the entire skeleton (or the root) is missing. To solve this issue, a methodology to estimate the 3D movements of the avatar is designed. More specifically, the horizontal and vertical movements of the avatar are obtained by transforming the position on the hip landmark from the screen space of the input video to a point in Unity world space belonging to an orthogonal plane in front of the Unity virtual camera. To retrieve the depth position, Eq. 1 is used:

$$depth = \frac{focal\_lenght \times avatar\_height \times image\_height}{mp\_height \times sensor\_height} \tag{1}$$

where *focal_length* is the focal length of the camera used to make the video, *avatar_height* is the real height of the person in the video, *image_height* is the vertical resolution of the image, *mp_height* is the height of the person detected by the MediaPipe and *sensor_height* the vertical size of the camera sensor.

Animation Rendering. This module is in charge of showing the generated animation (as shown in Fig. 7). A graphical user interface allows the user to select the source (i.e., image, video, or stream of the webcam) to be activated for the motion capture and start the tracking session. Once the animation has been generated, it can be recorded for further playback both inside Unity and outside (as a video).

Fig. 7. Animation rendering: 3D Unity scene (left) and a preview of the reconstructed animation overlaying the reference animation (right).

4   Experimental Evaluation

A user study was conducted to evaluate the effects of introducing the techniques for joint estimations and pose beautification described in Sect. 3.2. More specifically, both objective and subjective measurements were leveraged to estimate the accuracy and quality of the reconstructed animation. To this aim, synthetic animations were first generated by using Blender and motion capture data contained in the dataset Advanced Computing Center For The Art and Design (ACCAD) included in the Archive of Motion Capture As Surface Shapes (AMASS) dataset [24] (as previously done in work such as [16]). The animation data selected for this experiment mainly include walk cycles and hand gestures. The videos representing the moving avatar used as input for the animation system were rendered and recorded through Blender. It has been chosen to make use of synthetic animations so that it was possible to consider them as a ground truth from which it is possible to retrieve actual joint positions and orientations and compute objective metrics. Moreover, in this way, the exact camera parameters for depth estimation were made available to the animation system, without introducing additional bias.

4.1   Metrics

To assess the accuracy of the reconstructed animation two metrics, already proposed in [14], were considered as objective measurements: the Mean Per Joint Position Error (MPJPE) and Mean Per Joint Angular Error (MPJAE). The first metric evaluates the joint position error between the ground truth and the reconstructed animation. For a frame f and a skeleton S, the metric is computed as:

$$E_{MPJPE}(f, S) = \frac{1}{N_S} \sum_{i=1}^{N_S} \left\| m_{f,S}^{(f)}(i) - m_{gt,S}^{(f)}(i) \right\|_2 \qquad (2)$$

where N_S represents the number of joints in the skeleton S, and $m_{f,S}^{(f)}(i)$ and $m_{gt,S}^{(f)}(i)$ are the functions that return the 3D coordinates of the i-th joint of the skeleton S, at frame f, for the reconstructed and ground truth animation.

Similarly, the MPJAE evaluates the distance between the two animations by using the angles between the joints of the skeleton. This metric was computed as:

$$E_{MPJAE}(f, S) = \frac{1}{3N_S} \sum_{i=1}^{3N_S} \left| (m_{f,S}^{(f)}(i) - m_{gt,S}^{(f)}(i)) mod \pm 180 \right| \qquad (3)$$

where, in this case, the function $m_{f,S}^{(f)}(i)$ and $m_{gt,S}^{(f)}(i)$ returns the joints angles.

For what it concerns subjective measurements, participants were requested to fill in a post-test questionnaire aimed at evaluating the animation quality, appearance quality, overall rating, and perceived similarity with the ground truth based on the questionnaire proposed in [30]. Statements were rated in a 1-to-5 Likert scale, from strongly disagree to strongly agree. The questionnaire is available for download at https://tinyurl.com/446ja398.

4.2 Participants

Overall, 18 participants (five male and 13 female) were involved in the experiments. Participants were aged between 20 and 62 (M = 32.17, SD = 13.12). According to the demographics questionnaire completed before the experiment, participants were in general not familiar with technologies involved in the experiments, i.e., video games or 3D computer graphics, VTO applications, and motion capture systems.

4.3 Procedure

In the experiment, the following configurations were considered:

- *T1* (depth and joint estimation off): This configuration represents the pure use of MediaPipe without any improvements. In this scenario, also the avatars in the ground truth animations were maintained fixed in the origin of the reference system to make it comparable with the reconstructed animation.
- *T2* (depth off, joint on): It is used to evaluate the improvements regarding the joint estimation. Even in this case, the avatars in the ground truth animations were maintained fixed in the origin of the reference system.
- *T3* (depth on, joint off): It is used to obtain an animation comparable with the ground truth but without the beautification.
- *T4* (dept and joint on): It is used to evaluate all the improvements introduced in this work with respect to the ground truth.

Objective measurements were computed only for the T1, T2, and T4. Regarding the subjective evaluation, participants were first instructed about the overall procedure of the experiment. After completing the demographics questionnaire, they were requested to watch three videos showing the ground trust, as well as the T3 and T4 conditions. The videos used for the experiment are available for download at https://tinyurl.com/2akm542w. The order for showing T3 and T4 was randomly selected to avoid bias. Afterward, the participants fill in the post-test questionnaire to evaluate the quality of the watched animation. The steps including watching the three videos and filling in the questionnaire were repeated for all the six animations contained in the ACCAD dataset, for a total of 18 videos watched by each participant. General feedback and preferences were asked at the end of the experiment.

5   Results

Table 1 reports the values of the two metrics MPJPE and MPJAE for the considered configurations. Observing the overall accuracy, computed by averaging the values observed in the six considered animations, it can be observed that the use of the pose estimation module (T2) reduces both the positional (52.35%) and angular (6.45%) errors with respect to the pure use of MediaPipe (T1). The introduction of the depth estimation (T4), makes the system achieve an accuracy equal to $1.60m$ and $29.16°$. The error is particularly evident in those animations characterized by long displacements in depth (e.g., B11 and B15).

Table 1. Objective results in terms of MPJPE and MPJAE for the six animations.

		D3	B2	B10	B11	B16	B15	Overall
T1	MPJPE (m)	0.087	0.108	0.108	0.114	0.124	0.124	0.111
	MPJAE($degree$)	36	26	29	32	32	35	31.667
T2	MPJPE (m)	0.014	0.097	0.038	0.047	0.077	0.051	0.054
	MPJAE($degree$)	34	25	27	30	27	32	29.167
T4	MPJPE (m)	0.017	1.100	1.320	2.260	1.980	2.970	1.608
	MPJAE($degree$)	34	25	27	30	27	32	29.167

The statistical analysis was performed by using the Wilcoxon Signed-Rank Test for paired samples. Starting from the animation quality (shown in Fig. 8), it is possible to observe that participants recognized the improvements brought by the use of the pose estimation module (T4) as all the differences are statistically significant with respect to the T3 configuration. More specifically, participants, when watching the animations generated with the T4 configuration, judged the movements of the avatar more natural (2.69 vs 1.44, $p < .001$), and more smooth (2.45 vs 1.49, $p < .001$) than T3. Moreover, movements with T4 were perceived as characterized by lower robotic-like (3.54 vs 4.56, $p < .001$) and mechanical (3.09 vs 4.61, $p < .001$) gestures. Finally, with respect to T3 the movements of T4 were felt as less artificial (3.37 VS 4.54, $p < .001$), and the avatar was judged to be less stiff (3.33 VS 4.55, $p < .001$).

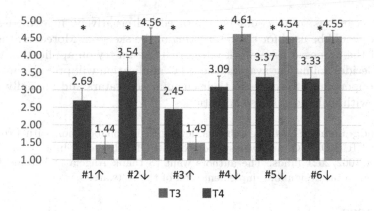

Fig. 8. Subjective results in terms of perceived animation quality.

Regarding appearance quality, statically significant differences were identified only for the statement related to the realism of the avatar, which looked more realistic with T4 than T3 (2.74 vs 1.47, $p < .001$).

Concerning the overall rating, participants judged the movements with T4 more plausible (3.17 vs 1.67, $p < .001$) and pleasant (2.74 vs 1.48, $p < .001$) than T3.

Finally, although the animations generated with T4 were considered to derive less than T3 with respect to the ground truth (2.91 vs 4.27, $p < .001$), it can be observed that the score is slightly lower than 3. This aspect means that more efforts should be devoted aimed at improving the similarity between the ground truth and the generated animations.

6   Conclusion and Future Work

This work presents a framework for animating customized avatars created through the SUPR parametric model. The framework includes two main components, i.e., the Rig-SUPR add-on for the automatic rigging, skinning, and generation of the animation data structure (e.g., blendshapes) and an animation system for animating the avatars with motion capture from monocular images. The animation system leverages the MediaPipe Holistic pipeline for pose estimation and supports the retargeting of the motion capture data gathered by MediPipe to the SUPR skeleton. Moreover, a pose beautification and dept estimation module have been integrated into the animation system with the aim of improving the animation quality. Experimental evaluations demonstrated improvements in the quality of the reconstructed animations both from an objective and subjective perspective.

As observed by analyzing the results, further efforts are required to improve the similarity between the reconstructed animations and the ground truth. To this aim, different retargeting, depth estimation, and pose beautification solutions will be investigated. For instance, to improve the depth estimation, a multiple cameras setup could be leveraged. Alternatively, machine-learning approaches could be used for the retargeting of the skeleton. Moreover, the integration of the proposed framework into a real virtual try-on application will be studied. Besides animating avatars, the VTO application will provide customers with the opportunity to re-create their customized avatars and virtually try on garments with realistic clothes simulation.

Acknowledgements. This research was developed in collaboration with Protocube Reply and VR@POLITO, and was supported by PON "Ricerca e Innovazione" 2014-2020 - DM 1062/2021 funds. The authors want to thank Angela D'Antonio for her contribution to the design and implementation of the software.

References

1. Achenbach, J., Waltemate, T., Latoschik, M.E., Botsch, M.: Fast generation of realistic virtual humans. In: Proceedings of the ACM Symposium on Virtual Reality Software and Technology, pp. 1–10 (2017)
2. Arora, R., Kazi, R.H., Kaufman, D.M., Li, W., Singh, K.: Magicalhands: mid-air hand gestures for animating in VR. In: Proceedings of the ACM Symposium on User Interface Software and Technology, pp. 463–477 (2019)
3. Baran, I., Popović, J.: Automatic rigging and animation of 3d characters. ACM Transa. Graph. **26**(3), 72-es (2007)
4. Bazarevsky, V., Grishchenko, I., Raveendran, K., Zhu, T., Zhang, F., Grundmann, M.: Blazepose: on-device real-time body pose tracking. arXiv preprint arXiv:2006.10204 (2020)
5. Blázquez, M.: Fashion shopping in multichannel retail: the role of technology in enhancing the customer experience. Int. J. Electron. Commer. **18**(4), 97–116 (2014)
6. Cannavò, A., Lamberti, F., et al.: A virtual character posing system based on reconfigurable tangible user interfaces and immersive virtual reality. In: Proceedings of the Smart Tools and Applications in Graphics, pp. 1–11. Eurographics (2018)
7. Cannavò, A., Pratticò, F.G., Ministeri, G., Lamberti, F.: A movement analysis system based on immersive virtual reality and wearable technology for sport training. In: Proceedings of the International Conference on Virtual Reality, pp. 26–31 (2018)
8. Cao, C., Weng, Y., Zhou, S., Tong, Y., Zhou, K.: Facewarehouse: a 3D facial expression database for visual computing. IEEE Trans. Vis. Comput. Graph. **20**(3), 413–425 (2013)
9. Cao, Z., Hidalgo, G., Simon, T., Wei, S.E., Sheikh, Y.: Openpose: realtime multiperson 2D pose estimation using part affinity fields. IEEE Trans. Pattern Anal. Mach. Intell. **43**(1), 172–186 (2021)
10. Cudeiro, D., Bolkart, T., Laidlaw, C., Ranjan, A., Black, M.J.: Capture, learning, and synthesis of 3D speaking styles. In: Proceedings of the IEEE/CVF Conference on Computer Vision and Pattern Recognition, pp. 10101–10111 (2019)
11. Fang, H.S., Xie, S., Tai, Y.W., Lu, C.: RMPE: regional multi-person pose estimation. In: Proceedings of the IEEE International Conference on Computer Vision. pp. 2334–2343 (2017)
12. Gao, Y., Petersson Brooks, E., Brooks, A.L.: The performance of self in the context of shopping in a virtual dressing room system. In: Nah, F.F.-H. (ed.) HCIB 2014. LNCS, vol. 8527, pp. 307–315. Springer, Cham (2014). https://doi.org/10.1007/978-3-319-07293-7_30

13. Hangaragi, S., Singh, T., Neelima, N.: Face detection and recognition using face mesh and deep neural network. Procedia Comput. Sci. **218**, 741–749 (2023)
14. Ionescu, C., Papava, D., Olaru, V., Sminchisescu, C.: Human3. 6m: large scale datasets and predictive methods for 3d human sensing in natural environments. IEEE Trans. Pattern Anal. Mach. Intell. **36**(7), 1325–1339 (2013)
15. James, D.L., Twigg, C.D.: Skinning mesh animations. ACM Trans. Graph. **24**(3), 399–407 (2005)
16. John, V., Trucco, E.: Charting-based subspace learning for video-based human action classification. Mach. Vis. Appl. **25**, 119–132 (2014)
17. Knöpfle, C., Jung, Y.: The virtual human platform: simplifying the use of virtual characters. Int. J. Virtual Reality **5**(2), 25–30 (2006)
18. Kulkarni, S., Deshmukh, S., Fernandes, F., Patil, A., Jabade, V.: Poseanalyser: a survey on human pose estimation. SN Comput. Sci. **4**(2), 136 (2023)
19. Lagė, A., Ancutienė, K.: Virtual try-on technologies in the clothing industry: basic block pattern modification. Int. J. Cloth. Sci. Technol. (2019)
20. Lee, H., Xu, Y.: Classification of virtual fitting room technologies in the fashion industry: from the perspective of consumer experience. Int. J. Fashion Des. Technol. Educ. **13**(1), 1–10 (2020)
21. Liu, Y., Liu, Y., Xu, S., Cheng, K., Masuko, S., Tanaka, J.: Comparing VR-and AR-based try-on systems using personalized avatars. Electronics **9**(11), 1814 (2020)
22. Loper, M., Mahmood, N., Romero, J., Pons-Moll, G., Black, M.J.: SMPL: a skinned multi-person linear model. ACM Trans. Graph. **34**(6), 1–16 (2015)
23. Lugaresi, C., et al.: Mediapipe: a framework for building perception pipelines. arXiv preprint arXiv:1906.08172 (2019)
24. Mahmood, N., Ghorbani, N., Troje, N.F., Pons-Moll, G., Black, M.J.: Amass: archive of motion capture as surface shapes. In: Proceedings of the IEEE/CVF International Conference on Computer Vision, pp. 5442–5451 (2019)
25. Maji, D., Nagori, S., Mathew, M., Poddar, D.: Yolo-pose: enhancing yolo for multi person pose estimation using object keypoint similarity loss. In: Proceedings of the IEEE/CVF Conference on Computer Vision and Pattern Recognition, pp. 2637–2646 (2022)
26. Nunnari, F., Heloir, A.: Yet another low-level agent handler. Comput. Animat. Virtual Worlds **30**(3–4), e1891 (2019). https://doi.org/10.1002/cav.1891, https://onlinelibrary.wiley.com/doi/abs/10.1002/cav.1891
27. Osman, A.A.A., Bolkart, T., Black, M.J.: STAR: sparse trained articulated human body regressor. In: Vedaldi, A., Bischof, H., Brox, T., Frahm, J.-M. (eds.) ECCV 2020. LNCS, vol. 12351, pp. 598–613. Springer, Cham (2020). https://doi.org/10.1007/978-3-030-58539-6_36
28. Osman, A.A., Bolkart, T., Tzionas, D., Black, M.J.: SUPR: a sparse unified part-based human representation. In: Avidan, S., Brostow, G., Cissé, M., Farinella, G.M., Hassner, T. (eds.) ECCV 2022. Lecture Notes in Computer Science, vol. 13662, pp. 568–585. Springer, Cham (2022). https://doi.org/10.1007/978-3-031-20086-1_33
29. Park, S.I., Shin, H.J., Kim, T.H., Shin, S.Y.: On-line motion blending for real-time locomotion generation. Comput. Animat. Virtual Worlds **15**(3–4), 125–138 (2004)
30. Parmar, D., Olafsson, S., Utami, D., Murali, P., Bickmore, T.: Designing empathic virtual agents: manipulating animation, voice, rendering, and empathy to create persuasive agents. Auton. Agent. Multi-Agent Syst. **36**(1), 17 (2022)
31. Pavlakos, G., et al.: Expressive body capture: 3D hands, face, and body from a single image. In: Proceedings of the IEEE/CVF Conference on Computer Vision and Pattern Recognition, pp. 10975–10985 (2019)

32. Rumman, N.A., Fratarcangeli, M.: Skin deformation methods for interactive character animation. In: Braz, J., et al. (eds.) VISIGRAPP 2016. CCIS, vol. 693, pp. 153–174. Springer, Cham (2017). https://doi.org/10.1007/978-3-319-64870-5_8

33. Savastano, M., Barnabei, R., Ricotta, F.: Going online while purchasing offline: an explorative analysis of omnichannel shopping behaviour in retail settings. In: Proceedings of the International Marketing Trends Conference, vol. 1, p. 22 (2016)

34. Scurati, G.W., Bertoni, M., Graziosi, S., Ferrise, F.: Exploring the use of virtual reality to support environmentally sustainable behavior: A framework to design experiences. Sustainability **13**(2), 943 (2021)

35. Song, W., Wang, X., Gao, Y., Hao, A., Hou, X.: Real-time expressive avatar animation generation based on monocular videos. In: Proceedigns of the IEEE International Symposium on Mixed and Augmented Reality Adjunct, pp. 429–434. IEEE (2022)

36. Tang, M.T., Zhu, V.L., Popescu, V.: Alterecho: loose avatar-streamer coupling for expressive vtubing. In: Proceedings of the IEEE International Symposium on Mixed and Augmented Reality, pp. 128–137. IEEE (2021)

37. Tompson, J., Goroshin, R., Jain, A., LeCun, Y., Bregler, C.: Efficient object localization using convolutional networks. In: Proceedings of the IEEE Conference on Computer Vision and Pattern Recognition, pp. 648–656 (2015)

38. Toshev, A., Szegedy, C.: Deeppose: Human pose estimation via deep neural networks. In: Proceedings of the IEEE conference on Computer Vision and Pattern Recognition, pp. 1653–1660 (2014)

39. Xu, H., Bazavan, E.G., Zanfir, A., Freeman, W.T., Sukthankar, R., Sminchisescu, C.: GHUM & GHUML: generative 3D human shape and articulated pose models. In: Proceedings of the IEEE/CVF Conference on Computer Vision and Pattern Recognition, pp. 6184–6193 (2020)

40. Xu, Z., Zhou, Y., Kalogerakis, E., Landreth, C., Singh, K.: Rignet: neural rigging for articulated characters. ACM Trans. Graph. **39** (2020)

41. Yu, T., Zheng, Z., Guo, K., Liu, P., Dai, Q., Liu, Y.: Function4d: real-time human volumetric capture from very sparse consumer RGBD sensors. In: Proceedings of the IEEE/CVF Conference on Computer Vision and Pattern Recognition, pp. 5746–5756 (2021)

42. Zhang, F., et al.: Mediapipe hands: on-device real-time hand tracking. arXiv preprint arXiv:2006.10214 (2020)

43. Zhang, Y., Li, Z., An, L., Li, M., Yu, T., Liu, Y.: Lightweight multi-person total motion capture using sparse multi-view cameras. In: Proceedings of the IEEE/CVF International Conference on Computer Vision, pp. 5560–5569 (2021)

A Framework for Developing Multi-user Immersive Virtual Reality Learning Environments

David Checa(✉) , Bruno Rodriguez-Garcia, Henar Guillen-Sanz,
and Ines Miguel-Alonso

Department of Computer Engineering, University of Burgos, Burgos, Spain
{dcheca,brunorg,hguillen,imalonso}@ubu.es

Abstract. Multi-user immersive Virtual Reality (iVR) environments have gained attention for their potential to facilitate collaborative learning experiences. These environments offer ideal settings for social interaction, collaborative learning, and experiential learning. However, the development of these immersive environments can be time-consuming, and existing options often have limitations that hinder widespread adoption in educational settings. The framework aims to address these challenges by providing a structured approach to design and development multi-user immersive virtual reality environments. The proposed framework integrates key components such as user interaction, data tracking, and visualization functionalities, with a focus on enhancing learning outcomes and promoting collaborative experiences. Through the utilization of the framework, developers can create interactive iVR learning environments that facilitate meaningful engagement and knowledge acquisition. To illustrate its functionality, a case study is presented, showcasing a multi-user virtual reconstruction of San Juan de Arce, La Rioja (Spain) for cultural heritage learning. The results demonstrate the potential of the framework in creating engaging and educational experiences while reducing dependence on external tools. Future research directions emphasize the continuous improvement and adaptability of the framework to meet diverse educational needs.

Keywords: Virtual Reality · Learning · Multi-user · Framework

1 Introduction

Education is often slow to adopt technological improvements [1]. In the last decade, the democratization of immersive Virtual Reality (iVR) technologies has allowed their growing use in educational contexts. While iVR is costly, what are its benefits compared to traditional education? iVR is thus one step ahead in the incorporation of technology in the classroom (as was previously the case with videos, computers...). Its effectiveness has been evidenced in repeated analyses, highlighting the substantial improvement in student engagement and interest in these environments [2]. The immersive nature of iVR allows learners to actively participate and interact with the virtual world, leading

© The Author(s), under exclusive license to Springer Nature Switzerland AG 2023
L. T. De Paolis et al. (Eds.): XR Salento 2023, LNCS 14218, pp. 89–103, 2023.
https://doi.org/10.1007/978-3-031-43401-3_6

to heightened levels of engagement and motivation. Moreover, iVR has demonstrated its potential to facilitate the understanding of complex concepts by providing interactive and experiential learning experiences [3]. By simulating realistic scenarios and environments, iVR enables learners to visualize abstract ideas and concepts, leading to enhanced comprehension and knowledge retention [4].

In recent years, multi-user iVR environments have gained significant attention for their potential to facilitate collaborative learning experiences [5]. These environments provide ideal settings for social and collaborative learning, as well as for experiencing situated and experiential learning. It is also evident that the creation of these immersive Virtual Reality Environments (iVREs) is a very time-consuming activity [6]. For that reason, some researchers or professors use iVREs based on pre-created applications. However, publicly available options for multi-user iVR learning environments often come with limitations that hinder their widespread adoption in educational settings. These limitations include heavy reliance on proprietary tools provided by developers and the uncertainty of ongoing support and updates. Additionally, existing multi-user iVR environments are not specifically designed solely for educational purposes; instead, they often require adaptation to be effectively utilized for learning experiences.

Addressing these challenges, this paper presents a framework for developing multi-user iVR learning environments. The framework provides a structured approach to design and development, empowering educators, and developers to create immersive and interactive iVR learning experiences independently. By integrating key components such as user interaction, data tracking, and visualization functionalities, the framework aims to enhance learning outcomes and promote collaborative experiences.

To illustrate the functionality and potential of the framework, a case study is presented in this paper. We showcase a multi-user virtual reconstruction of San Juan de Arce, a historical site located in La Rioja, Spain, for cultural heritage learning. Through this case study, we demonstrate how the framework can be applied to create engaging and educational experiences that immerse learners in the exploration of cultural heritage, reducing reliance on external tools, and fostering meaningful engagement and knowledge acquisition.

This paper is structured as follows: in Sect. 2 the state of the art is exposed. Then Sect. 3 covers how a multiplayer iVR application was designed and developed, which was used for the case study, described in Sect. 4. Finally, the conclusions summarize and analyze this research in Sect. 5.

2 State of the Art

iVR learning experiences have the potential to achieve learning objectives across cognitive processes and knowledge dimensions. Different key features have been identified in these works as advantages of iVR for learning enhancement. In first place the motivation and engagement. Maintaining learner interest and motivation is a challenge for any educator. A motivated learner will be more engaged and more determined to try to understand the learning material, as well as more resilient to potential obstacles to its understanding [10]. Most investigations measure motivation and engagement and conclude that the use of iVR leads to increased interest and engagement when compared to conventional learning environments or other 2D multimedia systems [3, 11]. Secondly, iVR provides higher levels of interaction than conventional educational methodologies, that are usually language-based, conceptual and abstract; characteristics that compromise the implementation of practical learning. iVR supports 'doing' rather than only observing, which leads to a constructivist approach, where students learn through interaction and even collaborate with other students. In this way, students can experiment, investigate and obtain instant feedback in a personalized experience that can improve learning [12]. They can learn experientially and proceed at their own pace. iVR offers enhanced learning through active participation, in which learners create their knowledge through practice, using motor and cognitive skills and receiving frequent feedback. This makes learning content easier to connect to the real-world context [13]. Thirdly, iVR can also create a window to another place and time, so that students can discover places and sites that are far away, inaccessible or no longer exist today. Likewise, iVR also can be used for empathy training, enabling students to empathize with others and to broaden their range of perspectives and experiences beyond their normal spheres of interaction. Finally, as the COVID-19 pandemic has highlighted, there is a need for tools that facilitating e-learning and iVR has been shown to be effective in distance learning processes [14]. The immersive nature of iVR helps block out other distractions, making students more focused and concentrated on learning objectives [15].

It is very difficult to find suitable learning content or content with the potential to be applied if a classroom. Commercial solutions usually have to be found in game software engines, usually with poor labeling and a very large catalog. Likewise, it is common to find iVR applications with an absence of learning theories, designed without taking into account either the rationality of the design or the user experience [9]. A prerequisite for an effective iVR educational application is its pedagogical approach and the learning theory it applies [7]. This learning theories can be categorized according to how learners assimilate, process and retain the information they have learned [8]. The promotion of iVR-based learning is linked to a fusion of principles from multiple pedagogical perspectives. Regardless of which learning theories under each paradigm are used, it is crucial for the development of iVR applications to be firmly grounded in existing learning theories, because these theories offer guidelines on the motivations, learning process and learning outcomes of the learners.

Researchers also face additional challenges when it comes to determining which application to use, as there are several categories of iVR experiences. According to the technical characteristic of interactivity can be categorized into four classes: explorative interaction, explorative, interactive and passive. First, *explorative interaction* experiences are those experiences that allow the user to explore and to interact freely with the virtual environment. They allow users to move freely through space and interact with most of the objects involved in the simulation. Second, *explorative* experiences are more restricted solutions, which allow free exploration of the virtual environment, although no direct interaction. It is possible for the operator to navigate freely but the user has almost no direct interaction capabilities with the objects present in the simulation. Third, *interactive* experiences permit user interaction with the environment, but no free movement through it. Generally, users can interact with any nearby objects. However, they do not have the ability to move around the virtual environment, beyond a very limited surrounding area. Finally, *passive* experiences are the most restricted solution in which user interactivity and movement are very limited. The use of passive experiences is clearly related to the use of 3DoF devices, due to their technical limitations affecting movement and interaction.

In addition to these categories, there are also those inherent to multi-user experiences. Multi-user iVR refers to experiences that allow multiple participants to access shared virtual spaces, events, and experiences simultaneously. Multi-user iVR environments designed for learning purposes should possess certain common affordances that contribute to their effectiveness. It should provide a sense of *social presence*, allowing participants to feel connected and engaged with others. This sense of presence enhances collaboration, communication, and a feeling of being part of a shared learning community. Within these immersive environments, participants are represented by avatars, enabling them to interact and engage with one another in real time. Should strive to replicate real-world *social interactions* and dynamics as closely as possible. By simulating realistic social cues, gestures, and communication mechanisms, participants can engage in authentic and meaningful social interactions, fostering deeper engagement and immersion. The new Head Mounted Displays (HMDs) integrates eye gaze and gesture tracking systems, which achieves a significant improvement in this aspect. Also, these environments should *facilitate immediate and seamless communication* among participants. This allows for real-time interactions, discussions, and exchanges of ideas, enhancing collaborative learning experiences and promoting active engagement.

In a review of the tools available, there is a wide variety of multi-user iVR learning environments on the market, which can be classified into social, collaborative, experimental development, and exhibition multi-user virtual reality learning environments. *Social*, refers to the interactive and collaborative multi-user iVR learning environments, where participants can engage with one another, communicate, and interact in real-time. It involves fostering connections, promoting social interactions. *Collaboration* refers to the cooperative and collective efforts of participants to work together towards a common goal or task in a collaborative multi-user virtual reality learning environment. It involves sharing ideas, resources, and knowledge, as well as engaging in joint problem-solving, group discussions, and teamwork. Collaboration fosters active learning, mutual support, and the exchange of diverse perspectives. *Experimental Development* refers to the iterative and exploratory process of designing, testing, and refining new approaches, techniques, or tools. It involves experimenting with different features, functionalities, and instructional strategies within the virtual environment to enhance the learning experience. Experimental development allows for innovation, adaptation, and continuous improvement in iVR learning environments. Finally, *exhibition* refers to presentation of educational content or experience. It involves showcasing educational materials, virtual replicas of real-world objects, interactive simulations, or multimedia presentations to engage learners and provide them with immersive learning experiences. Exhibitions in iVR environments offer learners the opportunity to explore, interact with, and gain knowledge about specific subjects or themes in a visually rich and immersive manner. Table 1 shows the commercial multi-user iVR learning environments found in each category. Most of these multi-user environments could be classified in several categories but they were grouped in the one with the most shared attributes or in the one that most corresponded to their main purpose.

Table 1. Applications available in each multi-user iVR learning environment category.

Social	Collaboration	Experimental Development	Exhibition
VR Chat	Immersed	Noda	Spatial
Rec Room	vSpatial	SculptrVR	Engage
Sense Tower	Stellarx	Multibrush	Museum of Other Realities
Big Screen	Wooorld	Gravity Sketch	Rooom
Let's Connect VR	VRedu	Quadrobee	
Paire		BaselineZ	
Venu			

As can be seen, there is a wide variety of multi-user content with the potential to be used for learning purposes. This diversity of options is also a challenge for educators and developers. The challenge lies in selecting the right multi-user content that aligns with educational objectives, promotes effective learning outcomes, and maximizes learner engagement. Added to this is the continuous development and evolution of multi-user content, which adds even more complexity to the selection process. Educators and developers must stay informed about emerging technologies, advancements in iVR, and updates to existing multi-user platforms. This dynamic landscape demands ongoing research, exploration, and evaluation to ensure that the chosen multi-user content remains relevant, effective, and up to date.

For instance, educators may invest significant effort in creating their educational experiences within existing multi-user platforms, only to face the risk of sudden closure or discontinuation, as exemplified by the case of Altspace VR. Such drawbacks highlight the dependency on external platforms and the potential disruption it can cause to educational endeavors.

To overcome these challenges, educators and developers have increasingly adopted the creation of custom iVR learning environments. This approach enables them to exert greater control over the content, functionalities, and longevity of their educational experiences. By tailoring the virtual environment to their specific needs, they ensure continuity and circumvent the limitations and uncertainties associated with relying on third-party platforms. Creating a self-contained environment provides educators and developers with the freedom to design and curate their content, incorporate relevant pedagogical strategies, and implement the desired features and interactions. It grants them the autonomy to adapt and iterate their virtual reality learning environment as educational needs evolve, without being reliant on external parties for ongoing support or updates. This approach fosters stability, consistency, and the ability to align the virtual environment closely with the intended educational goals and objectives.

3 Development of a Multiplayer iVR Application

3.1 Design Procedure of Multi-user iVR Educational Experiences

The use of iVR by itself does not automatically improve learning, even when learners report very high satisfaction rates [16]. Most research gives no consideration to nor explains how the Immersive Virtual Reality Learning Environments (iVRLEs) are designed and used to enhance learning. However, as already mentioned, there are many ready-to-use solutions, but on the other hand, we must adapt to what they already offer.

Nowadays, developing an iVR application is expensive (in terms of time and money) and needs a multidisciplinary team. This section presents some of the key features needed for the design and successful use of an iVRLE in education. Three stages are followed for the development of an educational application in iVR: pre-design, design and evaluation.

In the first stage, the pre-design, a breakdown of the requirements included the definition of the target audience and the application domain. The learning objective must be important and enhanced by the introduction of iVR technologies. For example, it can focus on difficult-to-understand problems or learning that has proven to be resistant to conventional pedagogy. In this initial phase, the iVR experience was defined by taking into account the four key objectives for an iVRLE: interaction, immersion, user involvement and, to a lesser extent, photorealism [17]. Depending on the target audience and the scope of application, each objective will play a different role. Finally, the educational objectives must also be defined. Learning goals must be well-established, so that the user will not become lost in the amusement of the iVRLE.

In the second phase, the design phase, it is best to raise some questions: *Which iVR technology is best suited for the proposed application?* As described above, there is a wide variety of devices with substantial differences in functionality, portability and price. The interaction interfaces are subdivided into: general, customized and automatic. The general ones include keyboards, mouse and iVR controllers that are normally included with each HMDs. The second group refers to interfaces customized by the application developer, usually found in educational experiences related to medical fields, which enhance the user's ability to learn specific tools. The third group includes all sensors that collect data automatically; they can be integrated into HMDs, such as accelerometers or eye-tracking sensors, or adapted to the user, such as biometric devices. These sensors are essential tools that provide insight into the user's performance and decision-making capabilities. It is also important to consider *which is the best game design for this application?* In the learning experience, the learner has to select, organize, and integrate information within a limited working memory, so the iVR learning environment should be directly designed to support these processes. For example, interactivity should be designed to be easy to use; a well-designed learning curve should be developed for novices to the iVR technology; and preferably a game structure that offers genuine game play, rather than quiz-like questions and answers, should be created. A balance between immersion, freedom and comfort must be sought in the design of an iVR experience. In addition, the design should take account of incorporating game-based learning elements that support the motivational needs of competence, autonomy and relatedness, so that the motivation and the engagement of the student is maintained. Finally, the application should be designed in such a way that it can be modified, customized and easily updated by the instructors, so they can fit the needs to their individual classes and students. An advanced graphical application programming interface (API) for game engines is usually employed. Unity 3D and Unreal Engine are the two most common game engines in iVR. These two engines include tools such as physical force simulators, graphics engines (responsible for generating 3D graphics using methods such as rasterization, ray tracing, etc.) and interaction modules to integrate devices such as iVR controllers, custom interfaces or sensors in a simple way in the experiences.

Finally, the third stage consists of the evaluation of the iVRLE. The evaluation should take into account which are the key factors to be evaluated and how are they can be better evaluated. If iVR is to gain wide-spread acceptance as a reliable pedagogical method, it must demonstrate that it can confer a tangible benefit in terms of learning outcomes over less immersive and traditional teaching methods [7]. It has been observed that most

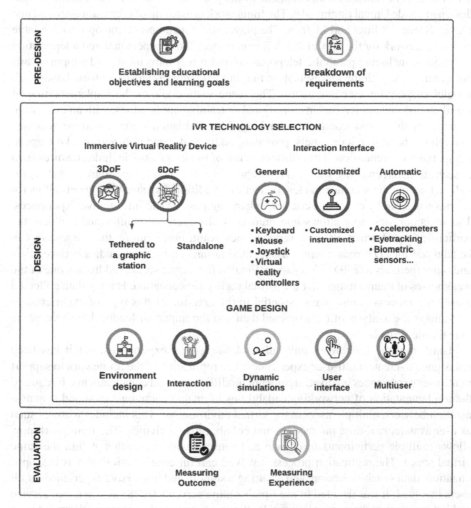

Fig. 1. Proposed process for the design and implementation of an iVRLE.

studies on iVR as a learning tool have no well-defined evaluation method or perform no comparison with other methods of education [3]. Most studies used only one of the following evaluation procedures: questionnaires, user interviews, data recording, and direct user observation. A combination of two of these procedures, especially questionnaires and indicators extracted from data recording, would also increase confidence in the results, especially if standardized questionnaires were used. This strategy would increase the validity and reliability of the conclusions, as previous studies have pointed out [18]. Figure 1 summarizes the flow chart for the design and implementation of an iVRLE.

3.2 Framework Development

This framework is based on an extension of the previous version [19] and also has been designed inside Unreal Engine 5™. The framework is made up of four main components: Player, Scene, Utilities and Metrics. The player section comprises the options available in the framework for the user of the iVR experience. It offers personalized teleportation techniques, including parabolic teleportation and direct movement, and supports various controllers, with the representation ranging from controllers to realistic hands with a watch/display for user interaction. The scene section allows the implementation of gamified tasks and objectives in educational or training applications, with an evaluation manager enabling task completion tracking. The evaluation manager can be accessed through the hand watch or panels, providing additional scene information like maps to aid spatial comprehension. The utilities section of the framework includes features such as scene transfer, enabling seamless level changes while preserving progress. It also provides a load menu for contextual level selection. Additionally, gaze view events allow for actions triggered by direct eye contact, enhancing passive and informative experiences. The spectator view tool allows non-immersed observers to monitor and evaluate the participant's performance from a separate viewpoint. Furthermore, the framework can be adjusted for 2D screen monitor usage, facilitating comparative studies between iVR and other methods like 2D video games. Finally, the metric section addresses one of the weaknesses of many studies that use virtual reality for education. Having data collected during the process is nowadays essential in the creation of this type of experience. It also allows the analysis of the extracted data and the import of feedback into the game in real time (Fig. 2).

Until now the framework only allowed single-user experiences, but it has been redesigned to create multi-user experiences. The replication of the framework to support multi-user experiences involved significant modifications and enhancements. It required the implementation of networking capabilities to enable communication and synchronization between multiple users in the virtual environment. This includes features such as user avatars, real-time interaction, and collaborative activities. The framework now allows multiple participants to engage and interact with each other within the same virtual space. The replication process involved careful consideration of network optimization, data synchronization, and ensuring a smooth and immersive experience for all users involved. It was decided to use Epic's online services (EOS) as it is a free service and independent of the game platform. It allows you to launch, operate and expand your game, whatever the gaming platform on which the clients are running. Also implement

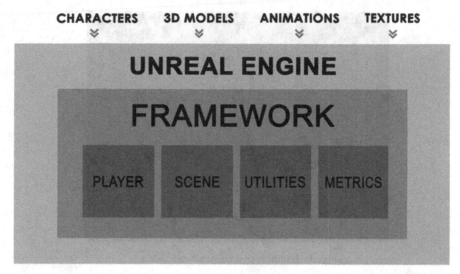

Fig. 2. Diagram of the framework and pipeline of the creation of experiences.

functionality like authentication, player progression tracking, matchmaking, voice chat and statistics.

Several adjustments were made to the player section of the framework to support multi-user experiences. Instead of a single player character, the framework now allows for the creation and control of individual avatars for each participant, providing a unique identity and presence within the virtual environment. Ready Player Me, a platform that allows avatar customization, was implemented. In this way, participants in the virtual environment were able to personalize their avatars with unique appearances, including various clothing options, hairstyles, and facial features as seen in Fig. 1. This level of customization helped to foster a sense of individuality and personalization for each user. Additionally, the player component incorporates features for real-time communication and collaboration among users. This includes voice chat communication channels, enabling participants to interact, exchange information, and coordinate their actions within the shared virtual space. To facilitate user interactions and enhance immersion, the player component was enhanced with synchronized hand movements and gestures. This allows users to engage in gestures and hand-based interactions with virtual objects and environments, fostering a sense of presence and natural interaction within the multi-user experience. Moreover, the player component integrates mechanisms for spatial awareness and collision detection to ensure that users can navigate and move within the virtual environment without interfering with each other's movements. This involves implementing techniques such as collision avoidance, user tracking, and positional tracking to maintain a smooth and seamless experience for all participants (Fig. 3).

Likewise, several adjustments were made to the *scene* component of the framework to support multi-user experiences. Mechanisms for synchronized and replicate events and activities, were developed to ensure that all participants experienced the same sequence of events and had equal opportunities to engage with the learning content. This synchronization was crucial for maintaining coherence and consistency within the multi-user

Fig. 3. Example of a personalized avatar.

experience. Furthermore, specific menus were created and made accessible through the user's wristwatch interface. These menus provided convenient control and customization options for interacting with fellow participants. For example, users could mute or unmute their colleagues' audio, allowing them to selectively listen to specific individuals or maintain silence when needed. In addition, the wristwatch interface offered additional scene information and functionalities to enhance navigation and collaboration. Users could access 3D maps displaying the virtual environment and real-time location markers of other participants. This feature enabled users to locate and track the movements of their peers, promoting better coordination and communication within the shared space. The wristwatch interface served as a central hub for users, providing quick and easy access to various scene-related features and interactions. By incorporating these menus into the wristwatch interface, the framework facilitated seamless control over social interactions and access to scene-related information, ultimately enhancing the overall user experience in multi-user iVR environments.

Within the *Utilities* section of the framework, a significant adjustment was made to introduce a tool that allows users to point and highlight specific objects or locations within the virtual environment, making it visible to all participants. This feature, known as the "pointing tool," enhances communication and collaboration by enabling users to draw attention to specific elements and facilitate shared focus. By activating the pointing tool, users can extend a virtual pointer or laser-like beam from their hand or controller to highlight an object or designate a specific area of interest. The beam is visible to all participants in the multi-user experience, making it easier for everyone to follow and understand the direction of attention. This tool proves particularly useful during discussions, presentations, or group activities where visual cues are essential for effective communication. The pointing tool enhances the social dynamics and engagement within the virtual environment by promoting shared attention and facilitating discussions around specific objects or locations. It serves as a powerful communication tool, allowing users to direct focus and guide the collective exploration and interaction within the multi-user experience.

Under the *Metrics* section of the framework, significant adjustments were made to enhance the data collection and analysis capabilities. Now, all participant data is stored and can be analyzed later, providing valuable insights into user behavior and performance within the virtual environment. The framework includes a comprehensive data logging system that captures various metrics, such as movement patterns, interaction events, task completion times, and user interactions with objects and elements within the virtual scene. This data is then stored in a structured format, allowing for in-depth analysis and evaluation.

In addition to real-time data analysis, the framework also enables the playback of recorded sessions, allowing researchers or educators to review and analyze user interactions from a third-person perspective. This feature is particularly valuable for post-experience evaluation and gaining insights into the overall user experience and learning outcomes. Furthermore, this replay can generate heatmaps based on user interactions and movements. These heatmaps visually represent the frequency and intensity of user activity within specific areas of the virtual environment as can be seen in Fig. 4. They provide a powerful tool for identifying points of interest, areas of high engagement, or potential bottlenecks in the user experience. Furthermore, the framework allows for the identification of outliers or unusual behavior patterns among participants. By analyzing the collected data, it becomes possible to detect outliers, anomalies, or unexpected user actions that may warrant further investigation or adjustments in the virtual environment design. By incorporating these adjustments to the Metrics section, the framework provides a robust foundation for data-driven analysis and evaluation of user behavior and performance within the iVRLE. It empowers researchers and educators to gain valuable insights, identify areas for improvement, and make informed decisions based on the collected data.

Fig. 4. Example of a generated heatmap based on the user interactions and movements.

4 Case Study: San Juan de Arce, La Rioja (Spain)

This framework has been implemented in a case study for its validation. The aim of this implementations is to demonstrate its capabilities in the field of creating multi-user iVR experiences focused on cultural heritage.

The Pilgrims' Hospital of San Juan de Arce in Navarrete has been recreated virtually because only the ruins of the floor plan of the chapel, the doorway and the windows are preserved, which were moved to the local cemetery. Through this virtual reconstruction, it has been possible to recreate the appearance and distribution of the hospital in the 14th century. Visitors have the opportunity to explore the inner courtyard and enter the hospital's rooms. In addition, they will be able to appreciate and examine objects related to the pilgrims, providing a more immersive and detailed experience of what life was like in the hospital and the care provided to pilgrims on the Camino de Santiago who passed through. It is important to note that this virtual reconstruction has been created to provide a historical representation of the Pilgrims' Hospital of San Juan de Arce in the 14th century. It seeks to provide a visual and interactive experience to better understand the importance of this place for the pilgrims of yesteryear.

The educational multi-user visit, as seen in Fig. 5, is a directed tour where a guide provides detailed explanations about each part of the virtual reconstruction. Thanks to the tools provided by the framework, the guide has the ability to point out specific points in the virtual space and provide references to them. Additionally, the framework enables interactive features, allowing visitors to participate by speaking or muting them all, creating a collaborative and engaging experience.

Fig. 5. Visitors on a guided tour of the Pilgrims' Hospital of San Juan de Arce in the 14th century.

During the tour, the guide can utilize the virtual environment to enhance the explanations and create an immersive learning experience. They can highlight important features, artifacts, or architectural details by pointing directly at them in the virtual space as seen in Fig. 6. This visual aid helps to enrich the understanding of the visitors and fosters a more interactive and dynamic tour. Moreover, the framework allows for two-way communication, enabling visitors to ask questions, share their insights, or engage in discussions with the guide and other participants. The guide has the ability to manage the audio settings, muting or unmuting visitors when necessary to maintain a smooth and organized tour.

Fig. 6. Example of the guide highlighting important architectural details by pointing them out directly in the virtual space.

Additionally, each user is equipped with a wristwatch that displays a mini-map for orientation purposes as seen in Fig. 7. This mini-map provides a visual representation of the virtual environment, allowing users to navigate and understand their location within the reconstruction. Users can easily identify different areas, landmarks, and points of interest. Furthermore, the wristwatch also displays volume indicators, indicating the proximity and direction of sounds within the virtual space. This feature helps users to identify audio cues and enhances the overall immersive experience. By following the volume indicators, users can locate specific audio sources or engage in conversations with fellow participants or the guide. Finally, the wristwatch facilitates social interaction by showing the presence and positions of other users within the virtual experience. Users can easily identify and locate their companions, enabling them to collaborate, discuss, or simply observe the actions and movements of others.

Fig. 7. Wristwatch showing to the user the 3d view of the reconstruction.

5 Conclusions

The present work represents the collaborative efforts of a multidisciplinary team, resulting in the development of a versatile framework tailored for multi-user educational experiences in virtual reality. iVR brings several advantages compared to traditional education, including improved student engagement, interest, and motivation. It enables active participation and interaction with the virtual world, leading to enhanced comprehension and knowledge retention. Multi-user iVR environments have gained attention for facilitating collaborative learning experiences and providing opportunities for social and experiential learning. The main drawback is that developing iVR learning environments is a time-consuming activity, and existing publicly available options often come with limitations, such as reliance on proprietary tools and lack of ongoing support and updates.

To address these challenges, the framework presented here takes into account the importance of the design of Immersive Virtual Reality Learning Environments (iVR-LEs). The use of iVR by itself does not automatically improve learning, even when learners report very high satisfaction rates. By considering the design and evaluation aspects described above, the framework aims to offer educators and developers the autonomy to create engaging and educational iVR experiences. It empowers educators and developers to create interactive iVR learning experiences independently, integrating key components such as user interaction, data tracking, and visualization functionalities. Finally, a case study of a multi-user virtual reconstruction of a historical site demonstrates the functionality and potential of the framework in creating engaging and educational experiences that immerse learners in cultural heritage learning. Special attention has been given to the development of comprehensive metrics to extract meaningful results for the final validation with students. This addresses a common weakness observed in the validation of educational iVR experiences, and the framework aims to overcome this limitation. As the ongoing efforts continue to validate and integrate the framework into different types of experiences, it holds promise to become a reliable and effective tool for educational and training purposes in iVR, benefiting both researchers and educators.

Acknowledgments. This work was partially supported by the ACIS project (Reference Number INVESTUN/21/BU/0002) of the Consejeria de Empleo e Industria of the Junta de Castilla y León (Spain), the Erasmus+ RISKREAL Project (Reference Number 2020-1-ES01-KA204-081847) of the European Commission and the FLEXIMEC20 project (Reference Number 10/18/BU/0012 of the Planes Estrategicos de I+D) of the Instituto para la Competitividad Empresarial de Castilla y León (Spain) cofinanced with European Union FEDER funds.

References

1. Selwyn, N.: Education & Technology. Key Issues & Debates (2011). https://doi.org/10.1007/s11159-022-09971-9
2. Checa, D., Bustillo, A.: A review of immersive virtual reality serious games to enhance learning and training. Multimed Tools Appl. **79**, 5501–5527 (2020). https://doi.org/10.1007/s11042-019-08348-9

3. Radianti, J., Majchrzak, T.A., Fromm, J., Wohlgenannt, I.: A systematic review of immersive virtual reality applications for higher education: design elements, lessons learned, and research agenda. Comput. Educ. **147** (2020). https://doi.org/10.1016/j.compedu.2019.103778

4. Checa, D., Miguel-Alonso, I., Bustillo, A.: Immersive virtual-reality computer-assembly serious game to enhance autonomous learning. Virtual Real. (2021). https://doi.org/10.1007/s10055-021-00607-1

5. Dieterle, E.: Multi-user virtual environments for teaching and learning. In: Encyclopedia of Multimedia Technology and Networking, 2nd edn. (2011). https://doi.org/10.4018/978-1-60566-014-1.ch139

6. Checa, D., Alaguero, M., Arnaiz, M.A., Bustillo, A.: Briviesca in the 15th c.: a virtual reality environment for teaching purposes. In: De Paolis, L., Mongelli, A. (eds.) AVR 2016. LNCS, vol. 9769, pp. 126–138. Springer, Cham (2016). https://doi.org/10.1007/978-3-319-40651-0_11

7. Mikropoulos, T.A., Natsis, A.: Educational virtual environments: a ten-year review of empirical research (1999–2009). Comput. Educ. **56**, 769–780 (2011). https://doi.org/10.1016/j.compedu.2010.10.020

8. Pritchard, A.: Ways of Learning: Learning Theories for the Classroom. Routledge (2017)

9. Fowler, C.: Virtual reality and learning: where is the pedagogy? Br. J. Edu. Technol. (2015). https://doi.org/10.1111/bjet.12135

10. Parong, J., Mayer, R.E.: Learning science in immersive virtual reality. J. Educ. Psychol. **110** (2018). https://doi.org/10.1037/edu0000241

11. Makransky, G., Borre-Gude, S., Mayer, R.E.: Motivational and cognitive benefits of training in immersive virtual reality based on multiple assessments. J. Comput. Assist. Learn. **35** (2019). https://doi.org/10.1111/jcal.12375

12. Roussou, M., Slater, M.: Comparison of the effect of interactive versus passive virtual reality learning activities in evoking and sustaining conceptual Change (2017). https://doi.org/10.1109/TETC.2017.2737983

13. Papanastasiou, G., Drigas, A., Skianis, C., Lytras, M., Papanastasiou, E.: Virtual and augmented reality effects on K-12, higher and tertiary education students' twenty-first century skills. Virtual Real. **23** (2019). https://doi.org/10.1007/s10055-018-0363-2

14. Urueta, S.H., Ogi, T.: A TEFL virtual reality system for high-presence distance learning. In: Advances in Intelligent Systems and Computing (2020). https://doi.org/10.1007/978-3-030-29029-0_33

15. Ibáñez, M.B., García, J.J., Galán, S., Maroto, D., Morillo, D., Kloos, C.D.: Design and implementation of a 3D multi-user virtual world for language learning. Educ. Technol. Soc. **14** (2011)

16. Makransky, G., Terkildsen, T.S., Mayer, R.E.: Adding immersive virtual reality to a science lab simulation causes more presence but less learning. Learn. Instr. **60**, 225–236 (2019). https://doi.org/10.1016/J.LEARNINSTRUC.2017.12.007

17. Roussos, M., Johnson, A., Moher, T., Leigh, J., Vasilakis, C., Barnes, C.: Learning and building together in an immersive virtual world. Presence Teleoper Virtual Environ. (1999). https://doi.org/10.1162/105474699566215

18. Petri, G., Gresse von Wangenheim, C.: How games for computing education are evaluated? A systematic literature review. Comput. Educ. (2017). https://doi.org/10.1016/j.compedu.2017.01.004

19. Checa, D., Gatto, C., Cisternino, D., De Paolis, L.T., Bustillo, A.: A framework for educational and training immersive virtual reality experiences. In: De Paolis, L., Bourdot, P. (eds.) AVR 2020. LNCS, vol. 12243, pp. 220–228. Springer, Cham (2020). https://doi.org/10.1007/978-3-030-58468-9_17

Embracing XR System Without Compromising on Security and Privacy

Rebecca Acheampong[1]([⊠]), Titus Constantin Balan[1], Dorin-Mircea Popovici[2],
and Alexandre Rekeraho[1]

[1] Transilvania University of Brasov, Brasov Memorandumului 43, Brasov, Romania
{rebecca.acheampong,titus.balan,alexandre.rekeraho}@unitbv.ro
[2] Ovidiu University of Constanta, 124 Mamaia Bd, 900527 Constanta, Romania
dmpopovici@univ-ovidius.ro

Abstract. Virtual, Augmented and Mixed Reality (VR/AR/MR) called together as Extended Reality (XR) have become increasingly popular in recent years, offering new opportunities for education, entertainment, and communication. However, the widespread adoption of XR systems has raised concerns about their security and privacy implications. Our work provides analysis of current security and privacy threats, existing mitigation solutions of other research papers and presents the results. We identified common and unique cybersecurity and privacy threats in XR and classified them under confidentiality, integrity and availability and proposed some mitigation considerations. We further explored the risks associated with users and organizations highlighting much on identity theft. In addition, we investigated the existing ethical policies and argued their implementation and proper security and privacy controls will contribute in mitigation of the cyber challenges in XR.

Keywords: Virtual Reality · Augmented Reality · Extended Reality · Privacy · Cybersecurity · Confidentiality · Integrity · Availability

1 Introduction

XR systems are becoming increasingly popular for creating immersive and interactive experiences [1]. Such experiences are generated by VR, AR, and MR technologies. XR is the generic term that is used to describe the combination of AR, VR, and MR [2, 3]. There is no doubt that XR is breaking grounds in health, education, industry, marketing manufacturing, architecture, and so many areas. As digital transformation is greatly being adopted in many areas of work, XR is not left out, bringing a vast innovation in the technologies used for XR. For example, with the use of Smart AR glasses, Boeing was able to convert from cross-checking approach to line-of-sight instructions which aided them to minimize the risk of errors and reducing production time by 25% [4].

Another ground breaking application of XR also in the area of collaboration where an automotive company called Mercedes-Benz integrated Microsoft HoloLens in conjunction with remote assistance to arm their technical specialist to provide maintenance and remote support services [5]. In the same area of collaboration, L'Oréal in

L. T. De Paolis et al. (Eds.): XR Salento 2023, LNCS 14218, pp. 104–120, 2023.
https://doi.org/10.1007/978-3-031-43401-3_7

the beauty industry has implemented the use of Microsoft HoloLens 2 and dynamics 365 remote assist to provide real time industrial equipment installation, audit and maintenance operations to augment performance whilst reducing time and cost [6].

However, with the increasing adoption of XR technologies, there is also a growing concern about the security of these systems. There have been a number of studies pointing out the security risks that are available in XR [7]. It is believed that XR communicate on the same protocol as the internet and so, the same attacks that have been seen over the years are likely to continue within the XR environment. Nonetheless, the uniqueness of XR might bring unique security attacks like deep fakes and fake identities [9], at the same time widening the scope of Identity Theft [10]. The good thing is that at the infancy and growing state of XR technology, academic researchers are raising the awareness of security risks that could discourage the usage of XR in the future. For instance, [2] conducted a research survey on security and privacy in VR. In their study, they conducted a review of the general security and privacy threats and with a later focus on authentication. On the other hand, some researchers also concentrated on threat analysis of metaverse and XR. This paper gives an overview of metaverse XR systems and discusses the privacy and security challenges [11]. Another study also focused on the taxonomy of the security challenges of VR. Their study comparatively categorized existing cybersecurity threats against existing cybersecurity defense in a single comparative matrix [12]. Now, as we know the metaverse is gaining grounds and it is perceived to become the future internet of 3D worlds [13] powered by the XR technologies, it is vital to invest in security and create the awareness in order to have a better and more secured metaverse future.

In view of this, S. Qamar et al. performed a systematic review of threat analysis in metaverse and XR. The paper discusses the flaws and vulnerabilities of XR systems, as well as the cybersecurity challenges and user safety concerns. While there are few survey studies in the area of cybersecurity and privacy that concentrate either on VR or AR, there remains S. Qamar et al. study that covers XR and extends to metaverse as well [11]. However, they identified impacts of risk only to human health, risk impact on organization or production of business processes were neglected.

The aim of our study is to explore and examine the unique security and privacy issues posed by XR systems, analyze and characterize them and to propose effective strategies and best practices to securely adopt and utilizes XR systems. The paper also seeks to review the current trends of XR and investigates the legal and ethical policies in place that governs the use of XR systems. For the purpose of our study, we limit XR to AR and VR.

During our study, we conducted an investigation and analysis of current literature related to security and privacy research for XR systems. We used a literature review approach [14] to gather information on the current state of cybersecurity and privacy in extended reality (XR) systems. Additionally, we reviewed books, published articles, conferences, web blogs, opinion of experts, invited presentations to identify security and privacy issues. We used research tools like Scopus and Litmap to collect papers for review. The table below shows the search queries used in Scopus (Table 1).

The papers were filtered using statistical methods to filter out the irrelevant cases that have no relevance to our study. After the analysis, papers with either security or privacy or with both were selected, 50 papers. The analysis of the papers shows a limited review

Table 1. Search queries for retrieving documents in Scopus.

Search Case	Query String	Year Range	Retrieved Papers
Q1 Security and Privacy in XR	("Cybersecurity " OR "Security" OR "Privacy" OR "vulnerab*") AND TITLE ("Extended reality" OR "Virtual Reality" OR "Augmented Reality")	2016–2023	117

study. As indicated in the section one, the reviews are mostly either for VR or AR. This becomes necessary for our paper to consider a study in a study in both AR and VR, and also explore the existing ethical and legal laws that protects user's privacy in XR usage (Fig. 1).

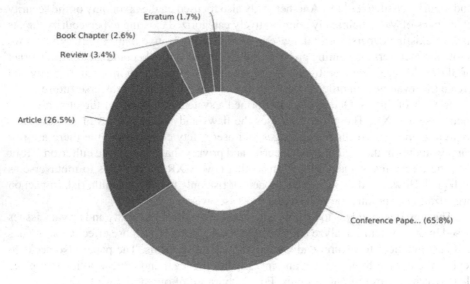

Fig. 1. A graphical representation of the papers by type

Our research paper is organized as follows. The next section presents background of the study, followed by section three which presents the identified threats, the next section four discusses the classification of risks. Section five presents the discussion of the results and section six concludes the study.

2 Background

2.1 XR System

XR is a term that describes the collection of technologies that allow people to interact with digital contents in a more immersive manner [1]. It includes, VR, AR and MR. VR is composed of interactive computer simulations giving the impression and a feeling of being immersed. A headset which is commonly known as HMD device is often used in VR systems to give users full immersion. The quality of VR experience is measured by the level of Immersion, Interactivity, and Presence – the feeling of being physically present in the virtual worlds [15]. Contrarily, AR systems typically use a smartphone, tablet, or special glasses to overlay digital content over the user's perspective of the real environment. AR could be marker-based or marker less/location based.

Fig. 2. An XR Environment

2.2 Current Trends

While research in XR advanced slowly, over the past ten years, we have seen incredible development in industry XR efforts, initially sparked by the widespread availability of smartphones and then the more ubiquitous the Headsets have become [16]. It is believed that the covid-19 pandemic has facilitated the adoption of the technology [17]. Organizations and governments are experimenting more and more ways to utilize the benefit of this technology [18]. Nonetheless, we cannot deny the fact that, improvements in processing, form factor, sensing, and cost of headsets [19] is contributing to the adoption (Fig. 3).

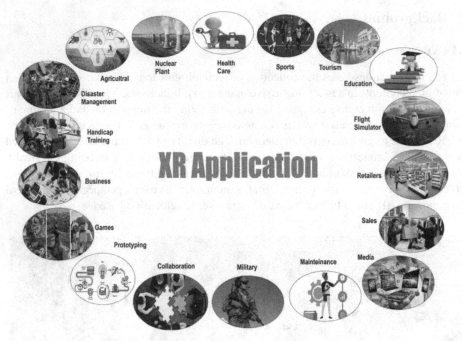

Fig. 3. XR applications (adapted from [11])

2.3 Applications of XR and Benefits

Overall, XR systems offer a more immersive and interactive way to experience digital content, which can be useful in a variety of industries such as gaming, education, healthcare, and engineering and a lot more. As indicated in Fig. 2 the benefits are much more as well as the security dangers. Talking about security issues, other studies are revealing how XR can be used to enhance cybersecurity. There is an AR application that is used for real time security surveillance [20]. Scientific academicians have defined effective learning as a process of active sense making and knowledge creation. In XR Learners engage in meaningful interactions and exploration in a range of formal and informal learning environments to have a meaningful experience [21].

3　Identified Threats

We begin by reviewing the works of the surveys that have been done so far. A study introduced the cybersecurity challenges associated with AR applications, specifically in the context of Telehealth and Emergency Medical Services (EMS). The paper emphasizes the necessity of protecting medical information and patient privacy in AR systems. The paper also examines AR use cases in the telemedicine and emergency medical services domains, stressing on the need of patient privacy [13]. Though the paper talked about the vulnerabilities that may be available there are no records of types of threats that can exploit the discussed vulnerabilities.

Another study explored in VR privacy and security, classifies potential issues and threats, and perform analysis of the causes and effects of the identified threats. Other studies in VR authentication and an overview of additional potential uses of VR in the area of cybersecurity, such as using VR to teach cybersecurity were also explored [2]. Though the study identified privacy issues like legal flaws, unclear policies, third party, etc., it is expected that detail discussion of ethical policies should be addressed of which the paper did not touch on that.

Again, a paper explores the cybersecurity issues that arise in VR environments as a result of the large attack surface given by the various system components. The paper provides a systematic classification of known VR cyber threats against existing defenses to assist researchers in identifying critical research areas for the future [10]. Their paper provided a good taxonomic presentation of cybersecurity issues but it is important to note that new threats may emerge over time that are not covered by this taxonomy presented in their paper.

A study also describes XR systems and the metaverse, and reviews XR system flaws and vulnerabilities, as well as cybersecurity challenges and user safety concerns. The paper suggests strategies for primary lines of defense and provides recommendations for safety measures to be implemented [11]. The paper gave a comprehensive overview of the cyber threats in XR and detailed the areas of applications of XR, but the paper focused on cyber-attack impacts on human health. No organizational or environmental impacts were considered having talked about various areas of applications of XR.

In addition, a study also, conducted a review of current works to analyze the potential of Social VR (SVR) to change social activity digitalization, particularly in the context of the COVID-19 epidemic. This was to addresses the issue of protecting users' identity and privacy in SVR, particularly in the context of digital bodies or avatars that may be personalized to look like individuals [14]. The study employed diversity of methods towards the literature, which could increase difficulty in conducting a comprehensive meta-analysis of them and may result in some individual characteristics not be effectively presented. The limitation of scope of concern to only digital bodies will cause other greatly relevant privacy issues in social VR discussed in selected literature to be overlooked.

3.1 Privacy Threats in XR Systems

XR devices are embedded with sensors that enable tracking of user behavior, movements, gaze and many more of their users and their surroundings [20]. Whiles this sensitive information gathered could be useful to render contents in XR and enrich the XR experience, they could be dangerous in the hand of threat actors. According to FPF's analysis, sensors that track physical body motions may also weaken user anonymity [22]. A group of researchers at Rutgers University demonstrated eavesdropping attack called face-mic to target XR Headset. In their study, they leveraged on the built in motion sensors of the well-known XR headsets to subtly record facial dynamics associated with speech. Talking in a virtual environment causes the XR headset to press on your cheekbones which can generate vibrations. Researchers of face-mic analyzed the vibrations to extract the quality information to understand the information recorded. They found out that the accelerometer and the gyroscope in popular XR headsets used requires no permission for access [23].

Privacy loss in XR may have a huge impact on the user because the information gathered by XR is more personal. Users may be or not be aware that such data is being collected by the XR environment under use. Critically, each XR data source has the likelihood to be exploited in a number of expected and unexpected ways [3].

Biometric data use in positional tracking helps to identify users. User anonymity is vital for users to hide what information is not for the public [14]. The biometric information needed for positional tracking could be used by third parties to reveal detail information on distinctive and protected traits to without user's knowledge which compromise on user anonymity. This could lead to blackmail possibilities if user's anonymous activity is linked to their real world identity.

XR sensed data makes it possible to understand user's behavior, their actions and intentions as well as their cognitive processes and many more biological data. Third parties can use this data to create a digital copy of a user. This offers them exclusive access to personal information about their lives, including their likes, opinions, and views. This erode also user's mental privacy. Bystanders within the proximity of the XR user is exposed to the same privacy risks as the user. The study raised concerns about the potential privacy risks connected with AR headsets. Such risks could be as result of volumetric capture, and biometric identification, which could expose bystanders to privacy infringement [20].

As part of perceptual computing [24], AR applications may record and send sensitive user data, including pictures and videos of the user's surroundings without the user's awareness or consent. The authors of [20] further argued that it is possible for AR applications to reveal sensitive information about the user to the public. XR data confidentiality is impacted by privacy threats. Attacks like eavesdropping provide an attacker access to private data through packet sniffing [25]. Through screen or hand movement monitoring in VR sessions, an attacker can also collect user authorization data by shoulder surfing.

3.2 Security Threats in XR Systems

HR headsets are simply another type of computer and could be grouped under IOT devices [18]. The level of device design has advanced quickly and there is the craving for more ubiquitous XR headset. Just like every connected device, XR is vulnerable to malicious attacks and hence need proper security controls [26]. According to [19] security of XR could be put into two main types. Namely product and protocol security. The author further described protocol security as data in transit and at rest must be encrypted. Physical risks to the user, as well as privacy and cybersecurity risks, distinguish XR security risks from traditional cybersecurity threats. Traditional cybersecurity threats primarily target computer systems and networks, whereas XR systems involves attacks on both physical and virtual worlds [17].

Peter Casey and colleagues focused on immersive attacks. Their study was named as Human Joystick attack. Human joystick attack is a VR system attack that includes transporting the user to a physical location without their awareness. The authors conducted a human participant deception investigation in this work to establish the success of this attack. By modifying the VR environment, they succeeded to transport the user to a new position in actual space without the user recognizing it. Evidence shows the researchers were able to block the users vision with overlay attack, remove user safety boundaries with chaperon attack and direct the user view with tracker attack [17, 20]. Such attacks can lead the user to become a victim of physical harm. More immersive attacks are likely to appear in the near future.

Attack like Man-in-the-room is possible. In a study posted by Bengali et al. from New Haven university, they discovered a vulnerability in BigScreen app and Unity3D to conduct a successful man-in-the-room attack. Though the BigScreen and Facebook claim to have patched the vulnerability, it looks quite freaky. Man-in-the-room attacks allow attacker to invisibly participate in a VR room, take control of users through their command and control server to manipulate users [21]. Unauthorized access might be used by an attacker to alter any sensitive data [14]. Security in XR must be taken serious and should not end only at authentication. Other security methods should be considered [27].

The section presents the unique privacy and security challenges discussed. As users immerse themselves in virtual environments or interact with digital overlays in the real world, their personal information and interactions become susceptible to various risks. Attacks that will arise from these security and privacy concerns could be threatening to human lives and the environment. These risks are crucial for ensuring user trust and maintaining the integrity of XR systems. Having the awareness of the privacy and security issues is the first step, and understanding them will help designers and security experts develop mitigation solutions.

4 Classification of Risks

Typically, XR applications gather more data about users and their activities than social media sites and other technology. It raises numerous privacy issues, including those involving hacking, the use and user information security and data security [11]. We therefore classify the identified threats as tabulated in the table below (Table 2).

4.1 Data Breach

Data breach in XR can happen without the user ever knowing that their data is compromised [11]. Data breach is a security violation and can compromise confidentiality, integrity and availability. Confidentiality is a security principle that ensures that data is accessible only by authorized user and so a breach of confidentiality is a privacy violation. Integrity of data ensure data is not altered [25] by third party while availability ensures data or XR assets are available when needed (Table 3).

4.2 Organizational Risks

Loss of confidentiality, integrity and availability when using XR have a great impact on users and the environment. Certain attacks like DOS can cause delay is synchronization in tracking which can cause dizziness or vomiting [11]. Attacks that results from chaperon

Table 2. Threats description.

Threats	Threat Description
Content Unawareness	Content awareness is a situation where a user is unaware of the real world because the level of user absorption in VE. Users actions could be monitored from the physical world. Users XR applications can capture the user's surroundings including standbys without his awareness [20]
Identity Theft/Impersonation	When a malicious actor steals users identify information to commit fraud. In XR, the sensitive information when falls in the hands of threat actors can lead to impersonation [14, 28, 29]
Unauthorized access	An access into vital information and users VE without in XR without permission [30]
Man-in-the-middle attack	Attackers can intercept and modify data transmitted between XR devices and servers [11]
Denial of service	DOS could be carried out in XR to crash sessions to cause them to fail [25]
Data-tampering	Manipulation of data with malicious intent to cause harm or commit a crime [31]

can cause physical injury. Attacks that compromise confidentiality of a firm could be access to the firms secrete code that competitors can use to collapse their business [37]. This will lead to financial loss to the company. Organization's reputation is at stake when integrity is compromised. Alteration of their trade secret can ruin their brand reputation and loss of intellectual property [38]. Whiles integrity and confidentiality violation can ruin a company, compromise on availability such as DOS on XR device can result in operational downtime [39] which can affect business processes.

Remote work and the rise of XR has made it easy and has reduced cost in several means for a lot of companies. Some organizations use XR and digital twin to create a digital copy of their cyber physical systems or business for remote services. They can become vulnerable to criminals who will replicate and use to scam clients in a virtual space. This can reduce companies to financial fraud when fake companies advertise their products as coming from real suppliers. They can become victims of DOS which can result in breach of availability. Man-in-the-middle (MitM) attacks can be launched by criminals between industrial machinery and the remote operators which will breach and integrity. Business products can be altered to affect brand or production [40].

Another disturbing attack that could be possible in XR is Deepfakes. An example is Nancy Pelosi video with Mark Zuckerberg boasting that Facebook "owns" its users. Such attacks could ruin a company instantly. If it is associated with a bank, there will be panic withdrawal which can collapse the bank in a day [41].

Table 3. Summary of specific attacks in XR.

Ref	Threat	Threat Category	Breach Type
[32]	Social engineering	Identity theft/impersonation	Confidentiality
[25]	Session failure	DOS	Availability
[33]	Deepfakes	Data-tampering, Identity theft/impersonation	Confidentiality, integrity
[25]	Elevation of privilege (EOP)	Unauthorized access	Integrity
[30]	Chaperon attack	Unauthorized access, data-tampering	Integrity, confidentiality
[25]	Stolen Credentials	Identity theft/impersonation	Confidentiality
[34]	Eavesdropping	Unauthorized access	Confidentiality
[25]	Packet sniffing	Unauthorized access	Confidentiality
[30]	Disorientation attack	Unauthorized access, data-tampering	Integrity, confidentiality
[19]	Shoulder surfing	Content unawareness	Confidentiality
[30]	Overlay attack	Unauthorized access	Availability
[30]	Camera exfiltration	Unauthorized access	Confidentiality
[23]	Face-mic attack	Unauthorized access	Confidentiality
[35]	Man-in-the-room attack	Unauthorized access	Confidentiality
[36]	Spoofing	Impersonation	Authenticity

4.3 User Identity Risk (Identity Theft)

In the natural life, humans are known by the things around them by which they could be identified. Whereas in the digital world, identity is the collection of data that is stored electronically about a person, business, or electronic device [42]. These identities are subject to fraudulent activities. There is a perception that the immersive experience in XR will offer a more advanced scam than in the normal social sites – body language, behavior, tone, and diverse level of data points will all make these scams much difficult to spot than the traditional ones [40].

Ranging from local city servers to huge metropolitan server farms, users will be identified in their XR communities by the likeness and popularity of their avatar. XR users interact at an unprecedented intimacy level that occurs in a real time and leaves users no chance to authenticate the avatars they communicate with in XR environment. This gives fraudsters free movement in XR to fraud people. Fraud situations could be avatars whose identities are stolen and exploited to scam other VR users will exist. One of the most prevalent issues raised by the use of avatars, particularly customized avatars, is identity theft [14]. Identity theft occurs when one utilizes another person's identity without their permission to gain some form of advantage. Identity theft is already a significant issue in social media activity today, and VR is likely to make it worse [32]. Identity in XR covers all the information about a user including the biometric data that identifies a user in virtual world. The sensitivity of the user profile in XR makes it unique than existing social platforms [27].

4.4 Common Attack Vectors of Identity Theft in XR

There are several ways users can be exploited in the XR environment. One of the ways is social engineering (SE). SE is a deception based attack that involves interactions with victim that produce a sense of urgency, anxiety, or other emotions, resulting in the individual revealing (accidentally or not) something of value [32]. In XR, it is easy for identity theft to occur through shoulder surfing [43]. Phishing attacks in XR is the most known scam which may occur in a virtual private room [35] either through messages where the attacker can attach malicious file or link to the user to take vital information from the user. Phishing is a type of SE that happens through an emails. The emails could purport to be from reliable sources, such as XR developers or other users.

Digital footprint of a user in an XR environment can be tailed by an attacker to lunch social engineering attack against the user.

4.5 Risks Associated with Identity Theft

A compromised XR Identity allows an attacker to pretend as a genuine user and influence others to expose other sensitive data or to behave in ways they would usually not [44]. Users could give account information to the deceiver. Account details connected to user's credit card could lead to financial fraud. Users will be frustrated and be bankrupt [40]. Fake news resulting from deepfakes can ruin a user's reputation. Deepfake is a machine learning algorithm that is used to manipulate a video or voice to look like the original. In 2020, a marketing campaign starring cybersecurity specialist Chris Sistrunk was spotted on Meta whilst he has no idea [33].

Impersonation associated with traditional social media platforms may be different from that in XR. This is because the unique identity in XR could make it hard for the user to justify himself from a crime should it be involved with biometric identity. When users Identity is stolen in XR, the cybercriminal can take over the users virtual spaceans will deny access to the owner. Users can lose their digital assets [40]. Users whose identity is stolen can be victims of cyber bullying if the cybercriminal use the user's avatar to commit immoral act in the virtual space [32]. The immersive experience will be lost to users if the virtual space becomes full of fake avatars. Sexual harassment and all kinds of natural crime can be replicated when identity theft happens in the XR environment [14, 32]. Stealing someone's identity can cause psychological problem especially when the attacker impersonates the user for fraud activities.

In this section, we defined threat categories and breach. We classified threats according to confidentiality, integrity and availability. Threats connected with Confidentiality normally exploited privacy in XR whilst availability and integrity threat related exploits either privacy or security vulnerabilities. These security breaches can affect organization and individual. Risk like identity theft and deepfakes can ruin the reputation of their victims. Either of them can be exploits social engineering as the attack vector. On the other hand, phishing can also be use.

4.6 Existing Mitigation Suggestions for Privacy and Security

The challenges are great and go beyond the conventional scope of cybersecurity and security professionals' normal work. So how can we continue with the use of XR to experience all the immersiveness, delivering our sensitive information without compromising on security and privacy? We present a summary of the mitigation plans suggested by existing research.

In the case of remote XR interactions, end-to-end security with high-bandwidth IPsec and TLS secure connections can provide adequate protection for data at rest and data in transit [45]. The privacy threat of bystanders should be taken serious and awareness programs and consent should be strongly encouraged in AR usage [46, 47]. The author of [11] proposed blockchain technology to handle user authentication and further suggests policy and consent compliance. Piumsomboon. T proposed visual or auditory cues be incorporated within the virtual environment to remind users of their physical surroundings can help maintain awareness and prevent content unawareness. Exploration of privacy-enhancing technologies that can selectively facilitate awareness and consent based on the AR activity type and relationship to bystanders [48].

4.7 Mitigation Consideration Proposals

Based on our study, we propose the following security and privacy mitigation plans to be considered. Developers of android phones and XR should make secure boot default. Secure boot checks integrity of operating system before it boots. Secure boot should be coupled with other security solutions like state separation and isolation used in HoloLens 2 [49] to provide a multi-layered security approach [45]. We propose image authentication [50] be adopted to authenticate user's avatar each time they enter the VE to mitigate avatar takeover. A unique copy of user image should be tied to user's avatar and used to verify and avatar authenticity. XR is used in many applications. The design parameters may change depending on the specific application. It is important to maintain a design standard for cybersecurity inclusive irrespective of the application. There is the possibility for XR user to encounter obstacles or go beyond boundary in the face of a chaperon attack [14], environmental monitoring systems that can monitor the environment to provide alert or warning when users approach boundaries or encounter obstacles to enhance safety. Again, for bystanders, we propose VR headset should have ambient light sensors that should change the brightness of a VE when bystanders are captured or approaches. AR developers should adopt the PATRON model to split user storage data between server and client to enhance privacy [51].

4.8 Ethical Policies for XR and Their Impacts on the Adoption and Use of XR Systems

Ethical Policies for XR

Big tech companies and big organizations are getting cyber insurance, very soon individuals will be required to have cyber insurance. In the event of metaverse where you shall own a digital copy of yourself and probably almost all the things you own in the VE. The very nature of XR makes it unique and hence cannot rely on the existing data protection policies like GPDR [52], internet laws, etc. One experience relies on a large number of personal data from users generated by a whole lot of technologies, each having their own issues of privacy and security [53]. Adopting a common ethical codes could alter the way VR ethics are practiced [27]. Ethical design policy could be transparent enough to ensure third parties who store or collect XR data request consent to collect data to reduce the level of risk [54]. There is concern about the ethical standards [55] of the firms that manufacture XR technology for their focus is not on user privacy protection but money [27].

A study performed by [56] found out that, out of 140 popular apps, only 38 applications did not offer any privacy policy at all. The EU law is looking to complement the requirement of GDPR for XR-based services. But this is not enough since one policy cannot enable compliant for all the diverse technologies involved in XR. The metaverse forum is an association of different standard companies, tech giants, different stakeholders and developers whose main activity is to develop standards for metaverse. This will enable XR to be covered and help provide a standard for developers to build XR applications. The forum is aiming to pervasive and transparent XR environment [57]. XRA is an association of stakeholders coming together to provide best practices for development and use of XR. The XRA mediates between the public and private stakeholder and make sure their released guidelines provide training and education to manufacturers and users [58]. This promotes transparency and creates user awareness of their privacy in XR and the protection measures to take.

XRSI developed the first XR privacy framework [59]. The framework provides guidelines to public-private companies, governments, and academic organizations in order to establish transparency, inclusiveness, and awareness to enhance accountability and trust in spatial computing and XR ecosystems. These Standards will help manufacturers and developers to incorporate privacy measures at the production stage of XR devices and applications. Depending on the uniqueness of XR application and on the services it performs, one framework cannot satisfy all XR services. In view of this, XRSI has different frameworks for different XR domains. Among the many are Medical XRSI, Child Safety Initiative [60]. A case study conducted showed users interest for the code of ethics design for the usage of XR [61]. Therefore, having policies for different categories of XR applications will build users trust, hence encouraging the adoption of it.

5 Discussions

New technologies bring new threats of which XR is not exempted. To be able to understand the current risk related with privacy and security in XR we explored and analyzed the already work done in this area and present some results and conclusions from our analysis. We discuss the contributions made from our study in this section. We were able to identify and present security and privacy threats associated with XR systems. We found out that, the uniqueness of the XR sensors and body detectors makes privacy in XR critical. Also, the cybersecurity attacks that are traditional are applicable to XR, meanwhile, virtual worlds have introduced a different set of unique attacks like chaperon attack, human joystick, disorientation attack, vision tracking attack [30], face-mic [23], man-in-the-room attack [35], and many to be discovered in the future.

To analyze the organizational risks and individual risks we introduced the concept of cybersecurity model, CIA Triad for proper classification of threats. The analysis of the classification shows that XR environment will experience privacy related threats more. The user privacy will be exploited most to breach confidentiality. At the same time, privacy of XR system and traditional security threats will be exploited to breach integrity and availability. We went a little further to explore Identity theft which we discovered it is associated with serious cyber-attacks. Both organizations and users are all victims of deepfakes and identity theft. The severity of such breach calls for attention to be given to privacy and security by researchers and developers to identify solutions to safely adopt this technology.

Existing studies have proposed mitigation solutions which we summarized in our study. We saw it appropriate to propose some mitigation considerations out of our study and we deemed these suggestions practical. Ethical policies are considered important to help with these challenges and to provide a smooth and safe adoption of XR. Though current GDPR cannot fully protect users of XR, it could be considered as the foundational standard for further standard implementation.

6 Conclusions

XR technologies have the potential to revolutionize many aspects of our lives, but they also present new cybersecurity and privacy risks and challenges such as data breaches, hacking and unauthorized access to sensitive information. By understanding these risks and developing effective mitigation strategies, we can ensure that XR technologies are safe and secure for all users. In our study, we made analysis of the current security and privacy issues in XR and present results of threats, breaches and associated risks. We identified and explored the area that is not much focused in previous surveys and proposed mitigations solutions for future research consideration. An exploration of present ethical policies was examined and argued that, a proper security and privacy measures put in place will encourage the adoption of XR without fear of data breach. We discovered in our study that current applications of XR is growing and hence, earlier attention given to the security challenges will encourage its adoption. Ultimately, the presented threats and their classification and the proposed mitigations will help academicians, developers and law makers to make proper judgements during a new system development and studies.

References

1. Serras, M., García-Sardiña, L., Simões, B., Álvarez, H., Arambarri, J.: Dialogue enhanced extended reality: interactive system for the operator 4.0. Appl. Sci. **10**(11), 3960 (2020). https://doi.org/10.3390/app10113960

2. Giaretta, A.: Security and privacy in virtual reality – a literature survey. arXiv, 20 May 2022. http://arxiv.org/abs/2205.00208. Accessed 03 May 2023
3. Morrow, M.M.M.J.: The IEEE Global Initiative on Ethics of Extended Reality (XR) Report–Extended Reality (XR) and the Erosion of Anonymity and Privacy. IEEE Xplore, p. 24 (2021)
4. MacPherson, R.: Wearable technology is helping us amplify the power of our workforce
5. HoloLens 2 powers faster fixes for Mercedes-Benz USA. https://iot-automotive.news/hololens-2-powers-faster-fixes-for-mercedes-benz-usa/. Accessed 03 May 2023
6. Microsoft Customer Story-L'Oréal is revolutionizing work with Dynamics 365 Remote Assist on HoloLens 2. https://customers.microsoft.com/en-us/story/853016-loreal-retailers-dynamics-365-hololens. Accessed 03 May 2023
7. Chukwunonso, A.G., Njoku, J.N., Lee, J.-M., Kim, D.-S.: Security in metaverse: a closer look
8. Yang, G., Xu, M.: Research on network architecture and communication protocol of network virtual reality based on image rendering. IOP Conf. Ser. Mater. Sci. Eng. **740**(1), 012119 (2020). https://doi.org/10.1088/1757-899X/740/1/012119
9. Virtual Reality Security and Privacy - XR Today. https://www.xrtoday.com/virtual-reality/virtual-reality-security-and-privacy/. Accessed 13 May 2023
10. The Dark Version of Metaverse can Strip you off Your Identity. https://www.analyticsinsight.net/the-dark-version-of-metaverse-can-strip-you-off-your-identity/. Accessed 13 May 2023
11. Qamar, S., Anwar, Z., Afzal, M.: A systematic threat analysis and defense strategies for the metaverse and extended reality systems. Comput. Secur. **128**, 103127 (2023). https://doi.org/10.1016/j.cose.2023.103127
12. Odeleye, B., Loukas, G., Heartfield, R., Sakellari, G., Panaousis, E., Spyridonis, F.: Virtually secure: a taxonomic assessment of cybersecurity challenges in virtual reality environments. Comput. Secur. **124**, 102951 (2023). https://doi.org/10.1016/j.cose.2022.102951
13. Bao, T., Ok, H.: Secure augmented reality (AR) for telehealth and emergency medical services (EMS): a survey, p. 7, July 2021
14. Lin, J., Latoschik, M.E.: Digital body, identity and privacy in social virtual reality: a systematic review. Front. Virtual Real. **3**, 974652 (2022). https://doi.org/10.3389/frvir.2022.974652
15. O'Hagan, J., et al.: Privacy-enhancing technology and everyday augmented reality: understanding bystanders' varying needs for awareness and consent
16. Lebeck, K.: Security and privacy for emerging augmented reality technologies (2019)
17. Steed, A., et al.: Evaluating immersive experiences during Covid-19 and beyond. Interactions **27**(4), 62–67 (2020). https://doi.org/10.1145/3406098
18. XR in Government and Public Sector | Vection Technologies. https://vection-technologies.com/solutions/industries/public-sector/. Accessed 11 July 2023
19. Ane, B.K., Roller, D.: Ubiquitous virtual reality: the state-of-the-art. IJCSMC **8**(7), 11 (2019)
20. O'Hagan, J., et al.: Privacy-enhancing technology and everyday augmented reality: understanding bystanders' varying needs for awareness and consent. In: Proceedings of the ACM Interactive, Mobile Wearable Ubiquitous Technologies, vol. 6, no. 4, Article no. 177, December 2022, 35 p. (2023). https://doi.org/10.1145/3569501. Accessed 1 July 2023
21. Zhang, X., Chen, Y., Hu, L., Wang, Y.: The metaverse in education: definition, framework, features, potential applications, challenges, and future research topics. Front. Psychol. **13**, 1016300 (2022). https://doi.org/10.3389/fpsyg.2022.1016300
22. New Infographic Highlights XR Technology Data Flows and Privacy Risks - Future of Privacy Forum. https://fpf.org/blog/new-infographic-highlights-xr-technology-data-flows-and-privacy-risks/. Accessed 08 May 2023
23. Shi, C., et al.: Face-mic: inferring live speech and speaker identity via subtle facial dynamics captured by AR/VR motion sensors. In: Proceedings of the 27th Annual International Conference on Mobile Computing and Networking, New Orleans Louisiana, pp. 478–490. ACM, October 2021. https://doi.org/10.1145/3447993.3483272

24. Rawson, A.: White Paper | Perceptual Computing: Inflection Point for Embedded Applications, p. 7
25. Gulhane, A., et al.: Security, privacy and safety risk assessment for virtual reality learning environment applications. In: 2019 16th IEEE Annual Consumer Communications & Networking Conference (CCNC), Las Vegas, NV, USA, pp. 1–9. IEEE, January 2019. https://doi.org/10.1109/CCNC.2019.8651847
26. Cybersecurity: Will AR & VR Open New Doors for Security and Privacy Challenges? https://www.bbntimes.com/technology/cybersecurity-will-ar-vr-open-new-doors-for-security-and-privacy-challenges. Accessed 12 May 2023
27. Viswanathan, K., Yazdinejad, A.: Security considerations for virtual reality systems. arXiv, 23 January 2022. http://arxiv.org/abs/2201.02563. Accessed 12 May 2023
28. Security and Privacy research lab, University of Washington: 2019 Industry-Academia Summit On Mixed Reality Security, Privacy, and Safety. Industry-Academia Summit (2019)
29. Dick, E.: Balancing User Privacy and Innovation in Augmented and Virtual Reality. Information Technology (2021)
30. Casey, P., Baggili, I., Yarramreddy, A.: Immersive virtual reality attacks and the human joystick. IEEE Trans. Dependable Secur Comput. 18(2), 550–562 (2021). https://doi.org/10.1109/TDSC.2019.2907942
31. Alspach, K.: Data integrity cyberattacks are an emerging security threat - Protocol, protocol, 22 August 2022. https://www.protocol.com/enterprise/data-integrity-security-cyberattacks-threat. Accessed 11 July 2023
32. Lake, J.: Hey, you stole my avatar!: virtual reality and its risks to identity protection. Emory Law J. 69
33. How Underground Groups Use Stolen Identities and Deepfakes. https://www.trendmicro.com/en_us/research/22/i/how-underground-groups-use-stolen-identities-and-deepfakes.html. Accessed 15 May 2023
34. Langfinger, M., Schneider, M., Stricker, D., Schotten, H.D.: Addressing security challenges in industrial augmented reality systems. In: 2017 IEEE 15th International Conference on Industrial Informatics (INDIN), Emden, pp. 299–304. IEEE, July 2017. https://doi.org/10.1109/INDIN.2017.8104789
35. Vondráček, M., Baggili, I., Casey, P., Mekni, M.: Rise of the metaverse's immersive virtual reality malware and the man-in-the-room attack & defenses. Comput. Secur. 127, 102923 (2023). https://doi.org/10.1016/j.cose.2022.102923
36. AR Security & VR Security. https://usa.kaspersky.com/resource-center/threats/security-and-privacy-risks-of-ar-and-vr. Accessed 12 May 2023
37. Mlinek, E.J., Pierce, J.: Confidentiality and privacy breaches in a university hospital emergency department. Acad. Emerg. Med. 4(12), 1142–1146 (1997). https://doi.org/10.1111/j.1553-2712.1997.tb03697.x
38. O'Brien, D.: Privacy, confidentiality, and security in information systems of state health agencies. Am. J. Prev. Med. 16(4), 351–358 (1999). https://doi.org/10.1016/S0749-3797(99)00024-0
39. 5 Damaging Consequences of a Data Breach | MetaCompliance. https://www.metacompliance.com/blog/data-breaches/5-damaging-consequences-of-a-data-breach. Accessed 13 May 2023
40. Metaverse or Metaworse? Cybersecurity Threats Against the Internet of Experiences
41. Deepfake Types, Examples, Prevention. https://www.spiceworks.com/it-security/cyber-risk-management/articles/what-is-deepfake/. Accessed 15 May 2023
42. What is digital identity? | Definition from TechTarget. https://www.techtarget.com/whatis/definition/digital-identity. Accessed 14 May 2023
43. What is identity theft? Definition from SearchSecurity. https://www.techtarget.com/searchsecurity/definition/identity-theft. Accessed 14 May 2023

44. Happa, J., Glencross, M., Steed, A.: Cyber Security threats and challenges in collaborative mixed-reality. Front. ICT **6**, 5 (2019). https://doi.org/10.3389/fict.2019.00005
45. Koon, J.: Design and Security Challenges for VR, Semiconductor Engineering, 10 August 2022. https://semiengineering.com/design-and-security-challenges-for-vr/. Accessed 08 May 2023
46. Roesner, F., Kohno, T.: Security and privacy for augmented reality: our 10-year retrospective. In: VR4Sec: 1st International Workshop on Security for XR and XR for Security. https://par. nsf.gov/biblio/10312790. Accessed 1 July 2023
47. Lebeck, K.: Security and privacy for emerging augmented reality technologies
48. Piumsomboon, T., Dey, A., Ens, B., Lee, G., Billinghurst, M.: The effects of sharing awareness cues in collaborative mixed reality. Front. Robot. AI **6**, 5 (2019). https://doi.org/10.3389/frobt. 2019.00005
49. State separation and isolation | Microsoft Learn. https://learn.microsoft.com/en-us/hololens/ security-state-separation-isolation. Accessed 15 May 2023
50. Gharsallaoui, R., Hamdi, M., Kim, T.-H.: A novel privacy technique for augmented reality cloud gaming based on image authentication. In: 2017 13th International Wireless Communications and Mobile Computing Conference (IWCMC), Valencia, Spain, pp. 252–257. IEEE, June 2017. https://doi.org/10.1109/IWCMC.2017.7986295
51. Sekhavat, Y.A.: Privacy preserving cloth try-on using mobile augmented reality. IEEE Trans. Multimedia **19**(5), 1041–1049 (2017). https://doi.org/10.1109/TMM.2016.2639380
52. Goddard, M.: The EU general data protection regulation (GDPR): European regulation that has a global impact. Int. J. Mark. Res. **59**(6), 703–705 (2017). https://doi.org/10.2501/IJMR-2017-050
53. Reality Check: How is the EU ensuring data protection in XR Technologies? — The Digital Constitutionalist. https://digi-con.org/reality-check-how-is-the-eu-ensuring-data-protection-in-xr-technologies/. Accessed 12 May 2023
54. Lee, J.J., Hu-Au, E.: E3XR: an analytical framework for ethical, educational and eudaimonic XR design. Front. Virtual Real. **2**, 697667 (2021). https://doi.org/10.3389/frvir.2021.697667
55. The ethical dilemmas of virtual reality application in entertainment. In: 2019 IEEE International Conference on Computational Science and Engineering (CSE) and IEEE International Conference on Embedded and Ubiquitous Computing (EUC), New York, NY, USA. IEEE (2019)
56. Trimananda, R., Le, H., Cui, H., Ho, J.T., Shuba, A., Markopoulou, A.: OVRseen: auditing network traffic and privacy policies in oculus VR. arXiv, 19 November 2021. http://arxiv.org/ abs/2106.05407. Accessed 12 May 2023
57. The Metaverse Standards Forum. https://metaverse-standards.org/. Accessed 13 May 2023
58. About - XR Association. https://xra.org/about/. Accessed 13 May 2023
59. The XRSI Definitions of Extended Reality (XR): XR Data Classification Framework Public Working Group, California, USA
60. XRSI – XR Safety Initiative | Helping Build Safe Immersive Environments. https://xrsi.org/. Accessed 13 May 2023
61. Adams, D., Bah, A., Barwulor, C., Musabay, N., Pitkin, K., Redmiles, E.M.: Ethics emerging: the story of privacy and security perceptions in virtual reality. In: Proceedings of the Fourteenth USENIX Conference on Usable Privacy and Security (SOUPS 2018), pp. 443–458. USENIX Association, USA (2018)

Semantic Explorable Representation of 3D Content Behavior

Jakub Flotyński(✉) ⓘ, Mikołaj Maik ⓘ, Paweł Sobociński ⓘ,
and Michał Śliwicki ⓘ

Poznań University of Economics and Business, Poznań, Poland
{flotynski,maik,sobocinski,sliwicki}@kti.ue.poznan.pl
http://www.kti.ue.poznan.pl/

Abstract. Extended reality (XR) environments are successfully used in various domains, such as medicine, education, training, and industry. The essential element of every XR environment, apart from the XR/3D content, is the domain knowledge encoded in the environment, which is expressed by the behavior of the content, including its autonomous actions and interactions with the XR users. Such knowledge covers the processes occurring in the environment, characteristics of its objects, and skills of the users. However, the available approaches to XR creation and usage focus on the sensory perception of XR, including its visual, haptic, and aural elements, and knowledge acquisition using human senses, but they do not enable knowledge acquisition based on automated reasoning and queries. It strongly limits the possibilities of knowledge discovery from XR, in particular on a massive scale in web based environments and repositories. In this paper, we propose a knowledge-based model to 3D content behavior representation. The model permits generic representation of temporal properties of XR environments with domain terminology, which can be subject to semantic exploration with queries and reasoning. Our solution may contribute to broader and more efficient dissemination of knowledge using XR.

Keywords: Extended reality · Knowledge · Exploration · Temporal

1 Introduction

Extended reality (XR) is increasingly used in many companies and institutions. They introduce XR systems to improve their basic operations, such as employee training, merchandising, product design, marketing, preserving cultural heritage, and education. XR environments are built using multiple 3D objects. While using an XR environment, its 3D objects change their properties—states, appearance, and geometry—in response to user interactions, mutual interactions with other objects as well as autonomous actions. Such interactions and actions constitute the XR behavior and express the knowledge in the domain for which the environment has been developed. However, currently, the acquisition of knowledge by users is possible mostly by immersing into the environment and directly interacting with its 3D content.

L. T. De Paolis et al. (Eds.): XR Salento 2023, LNCS 14218, pp. 121–138, 2023.
https://doi.org/10.1007/978-3-031-43401-3_8

Actions and interactions within XR environments could also be subject to exploration based on semantic queries and automated reasoning. Such exploration has the potential to enrich various application domains, especially in the context of the collaborative network- and web-based XR providing additional information about users' behavior, e.g., past, current, and possible future actions.

Furthermore, such exploration can be used as a method for analyzing and improving the user experience. By using the exploration of content behavior, we can increase the understanding of the relationship between objects in the scene, the user and their interactions. Exploration can provide an efficient tool for measuring the user experience, for example, which interactions in the scene were the most difficult and time-consuming, and the differences in interaction with different objects. Such information can be used for evaluating the system to improve the user experience. Additionally, semantic queries can be used to predict the activity in the virtual scene, so the system can be adjusted for the user to improve the quality of use.

For the possibility of this kind of exploration, XR environments need to use an appropriate representation for interactive 3D content behavior. That can be created using knowledge representation technologies such as the semantic web standards (the Resource Description Framework—RDF [19], the RDF Schema—RDFS [20], the Web Ontology Language—OWL [18] and the SPARQL query language [17]) and ontologies, which gain increasing attention in 3D modelling and multimedia description [14,15].

The main contribution of this paper is a knowledge-based model for 3D content behavior representation. The primary goal of the model is to enable the expression of behavior semantics in any domain, regardless of the specific XR environment's 3D graphics and animation technologies. The proposed model consists of two sub-models responsible for the representation of different types of behavior using different knowledge representation technologies: the ontology-based component and the rule-based component. The model uses Semantic Web standards - RDF, RDFS and OWL.

The proposed model has been used to represent the behavior of the virtual environment in the industrial XR training system developed for Amica S.A (Poland's main house appliances manufacturer) to train employees how to operate specialized industrial devices.

The remainder of the paper is structured as follows: Sect. 2 provides an overview of the current state of modelling 3D content behavior. Then, Sect. 3 explains the proposed semantic model of 3D content behavior. Section 4 provides an example and overview of the generated knowledge base for the XR training system. Finally, Sect. 5 concludes the paper and indicates possible future research.

2   Related Work

The area of semantic representation of 3D content behavior has gained little attention in the scientific literature and is not present in the available XR environments. So far, ontologies have been used mostly for the representation of the structure, geometry, appearance, and animation of 3D content, which has been summarized in [6].

A few approaches have been developed to model the behavior of 3D content using ontologies and semantic web standards. One such approach, proposed in [9,10,12], provides temporal operators and allows for the expression of both primitive and complex behavior. Based on this approach, a graphical tool has been implemented to model complex behavior using diagrams, with the ability to encode the specified behavior in X3D scenes [11]. In another approach, presented in [5], primitive actions such as move, turn and rotate are combined to represent complex behavior in a manner that is easily understandable to end users, without requiring knowledge of 3D graphics and animation

In [8], a tool that utilizes semantic concepts, services, and hybrid automata to describe the behavior of 3D content elements is presented. The client is based on a 3D content presentation tool, such as an XML3D browser, while the server is composed of various services that facilitate content selection and configuration of 3D content. Additionally, a separate module is responsible for managing intelligent avatars, including their perception of the scene.

In [1], XSD-based semantic metadata schemes were proposed for describing the interactivity of 3D objects using events, conditions, and actions. Ontologies presented in [3,4] provide a means of representing multi-user virtual environments and avatars. These ontologies define the geometry, space, animation, and behavior of 3D content, with concepts that are semantic equivalents to those used in commonly-used 3D content formats such as VRML and X3D. Environmental objects, the main entities of 3D content, are described using translation, rotation, and scale. Avatars, on the other hand, are described using names, statuses, and user interfaces (UIs), and their behavior is described using code bases.

In the academic literature, researchers have proposed several approaches for spatiotemporal reasoning on semantic descriptions of evolving human embryos and 3D molecular models. For instance, in [13], the authors proposed an approach that leverages RDF, OWL, and SPARQL, along with an ontology that describes stages, periods, and processes. In a similar vein, [16] proposed an approach that combines different input and output modalities to enable presentation and interaction tailored to specific types of content and tasks. While there has been more research on the semantic representation of animations than interactions, the existing approaches in both areas remain preliminary and face several challenges, particularly in terms of content exploration

There is also another recent work that focuses on humans and their interactions in virtual reality and on creating an ontology for experimentation of human-building interaction that uses virtual reality (VHBIEO) [2]. The proposed solution aims to create a standardized approach to virtual human-building interaction experimentation. To achieve this, an ontology has been developed that builds on existing ontologies and semantic models, such as EXPO, STED, DNAs, ifcOWL, SSN, SUR, and UO. The DOGMA methodology has been employed to establish the internal structure of the ontology. In a similar vein, another ontology has been introduced in [7]. This ontology focuses on human-centred analysis and design of virtual reality conferencing, with goals that include enhancing user experience, facilitating research on VR-conferencing (especially psychological and behavioral), and enabling the sharing of research findings. Although both ontologies are still in their early stages of development.

3   Semantic Behavior Model

The presented knowledge-based model is a formal representation of 3D objects' behavior, including their interactions (with users and other objects) and autonomous actions. Knowledge exploration is made possible through the use of complex domain terminology, which is tailored to a specific application domain. The model may be used for any domain ontology.

The model allows for the representation of the behavior of XR objects and environments. The behavior of an XR environment encompasses the actions of its users and objects. The model consists of two main components based on distinct knowledge representation technologies, which differ in expressiveness.

1. The ontology-based behavior representation component provides a foundation for representing the behaviors of explorable XR environments. This component encompasses classes and properties defined in ontologies based on Semantic Web standards that implement description logic. The component consists of three main elements:
   (a) Domain ontologies, which are formal specifications of the conceptualization of individual application domains for which explorable XR environments are created.
   (b) A fluent ontology, which defines domain-independent classes and properties of temporal entities and the relationships between them. The ontology also specifies entities for the visual representation of the behaviors of XR components and environments. Additionally, it enables visualization associated with knowledge exploration.
   (c) Visual semantic logs, which represent knowledge about the behavior of users and objects demonstrated during sessions of using explorable XR environments.
2. The rule-based component for behavior representation provides complex relationships between temporal entities defined in the fluent ontology component. In particular, this component enables transitions between events and states that are essential for describing the behavior of XR components and environments. Entities and relationships are specified in a fluent set of rules. The rule set is defined using logic programming, which allows for describing relationships between the properties of individual objects.

The model utilizes knowledge representation technologies to provide axioms that allow for the representation of behaviors, features of components, and XR environments. An XR component is a reusable module, which is a collection of classes with methods that can be combined with other XR components in an XR environment.

3.1   Ontology-Based Component for Behavior Representation

This component is part of the behavior model used for representing the features as well as past and current behaviors of XR environments in the form of behavior logs, which encompass the actions of users and objects described using temporal statements. This component is based on Semantic Web standards - RDF, RDFS, and OWL.

States and Events. The fundamental units representing the behavior of explorable XR environments are states. A state is a representation of a fragment of the XR environment, specifically a set of concepts describing users and objects. States are described using terms, while their occurrence can be evaluated using predicates. In the presented method, we assume that an *Instantaneous State* is a state that occurs at a specific point in time, while an *Interval State* is a state that occurs over a time interval.

States are initiated and terminated by events. Like states, events are denoted using terms, while their occurrence can be evaluated using predicates.

1. The *begins* predicate is used to indicate that an event initiates a state. This predicate is true for a given event and state if and only if the event starts the state. It is denoted as *begins(event, state)*, for example, *begins(startOfRun, run)*.
2. The *finishes* predicate is used to indicate that an event terminates a state. This predicate is true for a given event and state if and only if the event ends the state. It is denoted as *finishes(event, state)*, for example, *finishes(endOfRun, run)*.

Fluent Ontology. The fluent ontology defines fundamental temporal entities - classes and properties - that allow for the representation of users' and objects' behaviors. The fluent ontology extends domain ontologies with temporal terminology, which can be used in conjunction with domain-specific classes and properties. The fluent ontology is an invariant part of the approach, which is common to all explorable XR environments, regardless of individual application domains.

1. The predicate *start* is used to indicate that a temporal entity begins at a specific point in time. This predicate is true for a given temporal entity and time point if and only if the temporal entity starts at that time point. It is denoted as *start(temporalEntity, tp)*.
2. The predicate *end* is used to indicate that a temporal entity terminates at a specific point in time. This predicate is true for a given temporal entity and time point if and only if the temporal entity ends at that time point. It is denoted as *end(temporalEntity, tp)*.

The fluent ontology defines a variety of distinct entities, such as:

1. *State:* An OWL class encompassing all states.

2. *InstantState:* A subclass of *State* representing all instantaneous states.
3. *IntervalState:* A subclass of *State* representing all interval states, which is disjoint from *InstantState*.
4. *Event:* An OWL class that includes all events.
5. *TemporalEntity:* An RDFS class that covers all temporal entities.
6. *TimePoint:* A subclass of both RDFS *datatype* and *TemporalEntity*, representing all time points. The use of RDFS *datatype* allows for specifying time domains according to the requirements of individual applications.
7. *TimeInterval:* A subclass of *TemporalEntity*, among others, that constitutes all time intervals. TimeInterval is described by two properties, *start* and *end*, which indicate the time points at which the interval begins and ends, respectively.
8. *TimeSlice:* An OWL class representing all time slices, each of which possesses two obligatory properties determined by qualified cardinality restrictions in OWL.
9. *VisualDescriptor:* An OWL class encompassing all visual descriptors.

Domain ontologies and fluent ontologies are used to create visual semantic behavior logs consisting of temporal statements. The concept of temporal statements is illustrated in Fig. 1. In the figure, every pair of nodes connected by a predicate represent a single RDF statement.

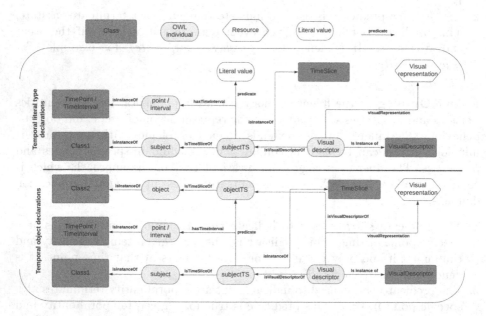

Fig. 1. Time statements (yellow) of the visual semantic behavior log. Entities that are related but not part of the time statements are highlighted in blue. (Color figure online)

Temporal Reasoning. We also define predicates for time points and intervals based on event calculus predicates and time ontology. Such predicates allow for temporal reasoning on time points and intervals.

- The predicate *in* is a predicate that is true for a given time point and time interval if and only if the time point is greater than or equal to the time point that starts the time interval and less than or equal to the time point that ends the time interval.

As examples of relationships between time intervals, we define three predicates from the Time Ontology proposed by Allen and Ferguson [18]: *before, after,* and *starts.*

- The predicate *before* is a predicate that is true for a given time interval ti1 and time interval ti2 if and only if ti1 ends before ti2 begins. *before(ti1, ti2)* is equivalent to *after(ti2, ti1).*
- The predicate *starts* is a predicate that is true for a given time interval ti1 and time interval ti2 if and only if ti1 and ti2 begin at the same time and ti1 ends before ti2 concludes.

3.2   Rule-Based Component for Behavior Representation

The rule-based component extends the formal representation of states and events provided by the ontology-based component and defines the relationships between them.

The compound term *begin* signifies an event that initiates a state. It is denoted as *begin(state),* for example, *begin(run) = startOfRun.* Additionally, *begin(begin(state), state).*

The compound term *finish* signifies an event that concludes a state. It is denoted as *finish(state),* for example, *finish(run) = endOfRun.* Moreover, *finishes(finish(state), state).*

Every state is initiated by an event and concluded by an event. Therefore, from the occurrence of states, we can infer the occurrence of the events associated with them.

An event initiating an interval state occurs at the time point that starts the time interval of that state. An event concluding an interval state occurs at the time point that ends the time interval of that state. The event that initiates an instantaneous state is equal to the event that concludes the state, and it occurs at the time point when the state appears.

1. An event initiating an interval state occurs at the time point that starts the time interval of that state.
2. An event concluding an interval state occurs at the time point that ends the time interval of that state.
3. The event that initiates an instantaneous state is equal to the event that ends the state, and it occurs at the time point when the state appears.

The *eventStartEnv* atom represents the event that initiates the XR environment. Therefore, it can be stated that no event can occur earlier than *eventStartEnv*.

The *eventStopEnv* atom represents the event that concludes the XR environment. Consequently, it can be said that no event can occur later than *eventStopEnv*.

Events signify the beginning and end of states, thereby determining their duration. The duration of a state is the difference between the time point of the event that concludes the state and the time point of the event that initiates the state. It is defined in the domain of time points and denoted by a compound term.

The duration can be utilized to calculate the length of time a particular state lasts in a selected time domain. Since each state is initiated and concluded by an event that determines the duration of the state.

In the case of an instantaneous state, the events that initiate and conclude the state are equal, which means the duration of an instantaneous state is zero. On the other hand, for an interval state, the events that initiate and conclude the state are different. As a result, the duration of an interval state is greater than zero.

Behavior. In practical applications, there is a need for direct relationships between states and the temporal entities in which these states occur. The concepts of event calculus can be used to achieve this goal.

The immediate evaluation predicate (IEP) is true for a given state or event and a timepoint if and only if the state or event occurs at that timepoint. In particular, IEP predicates include *holdsAt* and *time*. *holdsAt(state, tp)* assesses whether a state occurs at a timepoint tp. This predicate can be applied to both instantaneous and interval states, as each state can be evaluated at a timepoint.

To evaluate whether a state is initiated or terminated at a given timepoint, the IEP can be used. This evaluation can be performed using the time predicate along with the *begin* and *finish* terms, which represent events. The predicates *time(begin(state), tp)* and *time(finish(state), tp)* assess whether a state is initiated and terminated, respectively, at a timepoint tp.

Similarly, we define a predicate that evaluates the occurrence of states in time intervals (ETOI). It is true for a given interval state and a time interval if and only if the interval state occurs within the time interval. The ETOI predicate is *holds(state, ti)*.

The temporal evaluation predicate (TEP) is either IEP or ETOI and can be used to evaluate the occurrence of states in timepoints or time intervals.

State Transitions. States and events can trigger other states and events. For instance, the XR environment is active (state) from the moment it begins (event). In a factory, a stamping press initiates operation (state) when the start button is pressed (event) and proceeds to shape the product (state) as a result of contact with the metal material (event). Moreover, states can depend on other states, such as a house being fully illuminated if each room has been illuminated, regardless of the order in which lights were turned on in individual rooms. This allows for the creation of arbitrary cause-and-effect chains described by transitions that are consistent with the event-condition-action model. There are two types of transitions: event-based transitions and state-based transitions. An event-based transition is a Horn clause that consists of:

1. Body, which is a conjunction of a statement based on the IEP predicate that evaluates the occurrence of an event, and any number of statements based on predicates that are not fluent,
2. Head, which is a statement based on the TEP predicate.

The *assert* predicate is a predicate that is true for a given statement if and only if the statement exists in the rule set or it is possible to add the statement to the rule set. The predicate is denoted as *assert(statement)*. In examples, the predicate is often used to associate time points with time intervals in transitions. We assume that the *assert* predicate is satisfied unless stated otherwise.

4   Example

4.1   General Information

The introduced semantic behavior model was used to represent the virtual environment of the industrial worker training XR system, which allows trainees to learn how to act safely in an industrial setting.

The system has been developed in the Unity game engine and uses an Oculus Quest 2 VR headset. Users can interact with objects using their own hands, which was archived by using the Oculus Integration plug-in together with supplementary plug-ins to ensure a high level of immersion.

The training scenario implemented in the system focuses on safe work with the industrial press. It was developed using resources from Amica S.A., a major producer of household equipment in Poland. The prepared virtual scene in which the training takes place is shown in Fig. 2.

The scenario consists of several steps:

1. The worker pulls the metal sheet out of the container
2. The worker visually inspects the physical condition of the metal sheet to be processed looking for flaws
3. The worker places a metal sheet in the press
4. The worker lubricates/sprays the metal sheet parts with oil
5. The worker starts the press using the button
6. The worker takes the finished product from the press

Fig. 2. An industrial press in a factory hall

4.2   Knowledge Base Example

In the scene, there are three main objects which are used in the scenario: the metal sheet, the industrial press and the button for turning on the industrial press. The system generates a knowledge base that describes these objects. The example of such a knowledge base presents Listing 1.1. The objects are described in lines 1–15. Every object has its name, id and possible states; for example, Object2 (lines 6–9) - the industrial press has id: 2, and three possible states: empty press, press with inserted metal sheet and working press. The first two states are instant states, while the last state is an interval state. Additionally, object3 (a press button) is part of the industrial press, which is described in line 13 by object property isObjectOf. In lines 17–47, the rest possible states are described, also by their name and id.

Listing 1.1. A fragment of knowledge base describing objects in the scene and their possible states

```
1   fo:Object1 rdf:type owl:NamedIndividual , fo:Object ;
2               fo:hasState fo:SheetState1 , fo:SheetState11 , fo:
                    SheetState2 , fo:SheetState3 , fo:SheetState4 , fo:
                    SheetState5 ;
3               fo:id "1"^^xsd:int ;
4               fo:name "metal␣sheet"^^xsd:string .
5
6   fo:Object2 rdf:type owl:NamedIndividual , fo:Object ;
7               fo:hasState fo:PressState10 , fo:PressState6 , fo:
                    PressState7 ;
8               fo:id "2"^^xsd:int ;
9               fo:name "industrial␣press"^^xsd:string .
10
11  fo:Object3 rdf:type owl:NamedIndividual , fo:Object ;
12              fo:hasState fo:buttonState8 , fo:buttonState9 ;
```

```
13                    fo:isObjectOf fo:Object2 ;
14                    fo:id "3"^^xsd:int ;
15                    fo:name "press_button"^^xsd:string .
16
17   fo:PressState10 rdf:type owl:NamedIndividual , fo:IntervalState ;
18                    fo:id "10"^^xsd:int ;
19                    fo:name "working_press"^^xsd:string .
20
21   fo:PressState6 rdf:type owl:NamedIndividual , fo:InstantState ;
22                   fo:id "6"^^xsd:int ;
23                   fo:name "empty_press"^^xsd:string .
24
25   fo:PressState7 rdf:type owl:NamedIndividual , fo:InstantState ;
26                   fo:id "7"^^xsd:int ;
27                   fo:name "press_with_inserted_metal_sheet"^^xsd:string
                      .
28
29   fo:SheetState11 rdf:type owl:NamedIndividual , fo:InstantState ;
30                    fo:id "11"^^xsd:int ;
31                    fo:name "trimmed_sheet"^^xsd:string .
32
33   fo:SheetState3 rdf:type owl:NamedIndividual , fo:InstantState ;
34                   fo:id "3"^^xsd:int ;
35                   fo:name "Visualy_checked"^^xsd:string .
36
37   fo:SheetState4 rdf:type owl:NamedIndividual , fo:InstantState ;
38                   fo:id "4"^^xsd:int ;
39                   fo:name "metal_sheet_inside_press"^^xsd:string .
40
41   fo:buttonState8 rdf:type owl:NamedIndividual , fo:InstantState ;
42                    fo:id "8"^^xsd:int ;
43                    fo:name "unpressed"^^xsd:string .
44
45   fo:buttonState9 rdf:type owl:NamedIndividual , fo:InstantState ;
46                    fo:id "9"^^xsd:int ;
47                    fo:name "pressed"^^xsd:string .
```

Every action that happens in the scene is presented in the knowledge base as an event. Each described event has its own name and informs which states it begins and finishes. Moreover, each event has assigned a time slice, which informs when the event took place.

The Listing 1.2 presents the knowledge base generated by the system when the user inserts a metal sheet into an industrial press (Fig. 3). It generates an event (lines 1–7) that finishes two states: pressState6 (empty press) and Sheet-State3 (Visually checked), and begins two states pressState7 (press with inserted metal sheet) and SheetState4 (metal sheet inside press). The event has an object TimeSlice assigned (lines 9–12). Since the event happened over a period of time, additionally time interval was assigned (TimeInterval13). Time interval inform when the event started and ended (lines 14–17).

Listing 1.2. Example of knowledge base generated when user inserts metal sheet into press

```
1   fo:Event4 rdf:type owl:NamedIndividual ,
2                      fo:Event ;
3             fo:begins fo:PressState7 ,
4                       fo:SheetState4 ;
5             fo:finishes fo:PressState6 ,
6                         fo:SheetState3 ;
7             fo:name "inserting_metal_sheet_into_hydraulic_press"^^xsd:
                string .
8
```

```
 9   fo:TimeSlice4 rdf:type owl:NamedIndividual ,
10                        fo:TimeSlice ;
11                        fo:hasTimeInterval fo:TimeInterval3 ;
12                        fo:isTimeSliceOf fo:Event4 .
13
14   fo:TimeInterval3 rdf:type owl:NamedIndividual ,
15                        fo:TimeInterval ;
16                        fo:end "2023-04-26T09:07:52"^^xsd:dateTime ;
17                        fo:start "2023-04-26T09:06:34"^^xsd:dateTime .
```

Fig. 3. User inserts metal sheet into industrial press

Another fragment of the generated knowledge base is presented in the Listing 1.3. When the user pushes the button (Fig. 4) to activate the industrial press, the event is generated (lines 1–7). This event finishes two states: pressState7 (press with inserted metal sheet) and ButtonState8 (button unpressed), and begins two states pressState10 (working press) and ButtonState9 (button pressed). Event has assigned the time slice (lines 9–12), which by data property time point informs in what exact time the event happened (line 12). After that, another event (stopping the operation of the press) is generated, which describes when and what happens in the scene when the press stopped working (lines 14–24).

Listing 1.3. Example of knowledge base generated when user pushes the button of the industial press

```
1   fo:Event6 rdf:type owl:NamedIndividual ,
2                        fo:Event ;
```

```
3               fo:begins fo:PressState10 ,
4                         fo:ButtonState9 ;
5               fo:finishes fo:PressState7 ,
6                           fo:ButtonState8 ;
7               fo:name "pressing turn on button of the press"^^xsd:string
                .
8
9   fo:TimeSlice6 rdf:type owl:NamedIndividual ,
10                          fo:TimeSlice ;
11              fo:isTimeSliceOf fo:Event6 ;
12              fo:timePoint "2023-04-26T09:09:02"^^xsd:dateTime .
13
14  fo:Event7 rdf:type owl:NamedIndividual ,
15                      fo:Event ;
16              fo:begins fo:SheetState11 ;
17              fo:finishes fo:PressState10 ,
18                          fo:SheetState5 ;
19              fo:name "stopping the operation of the press"^^xsd:string .
20
21  fo:TimeSlice7 rdf:type owl:NamedIndividual ,
22                          fo:TimeSlice ;
23              fo:isTimeSliceOf fo:Event7 ;
24              fo:timePoint "2023-04-26T09:09:36"^^xsd:dateTime .
```

Fig. 4. User pushes the button to activate the press

4.3   Exploration Queries

After generating the knowledge base, it is possible to explore it using semantic queries. It gives the possibility to gain a broad range of information about the progress of training, for example, what events happened during the training process, when they happened, how the states of objects in the scene changed etc.

The exploration is possible due to the use of queries encoded using SPARQL, which is the main query language for RDF-based ontologies and knowledge bases. Below are presented examples of such queries and their results:

Query 1. Which events had happened before the press button was pushed?

```
    numberstyle
1   SELECT  ?eventName
2   WHERE { ?event rdf:type fo:Event   .
3                   ?timeSlice fo:isTimeSliceOf ?event .
4                   ?event fo:name ?eventName .
5                 { ?timeSlice fo:timePoint ?time . }
6                 UNION
7                 {
8                   ?timeSlice fo:hasTimeInterval ?timeInterval .
9                       ?timeInterval fo:start ?time .
10                }
11
12                ?PushButtonEvent fo:name "pressing␣turn␣on␣button␣of␣the␣
                      press"^^<http://www.w3.org/2001/XMLSchema#string> .
13                ?PushButtonTimeSlice fo:isTimeSliceOf ?PushButtonEvent .
14                ?PushButtonTimeSlice fo:timePoint ?pushButtonTime .
15
16                FILTER ( ?time < ?pushButtonTime)
17  }
18  ORDER BY ?time
```

eventName
"Starting the scenario"^^<http://www.w3.org/2001/XMLSchema#string>
"unpacking the metal sheet"^^<http://www.w3.org/2001/XMLSchema#string>
"visually controlling the metal sheet"^^<http://www.w3.org/2001/XMLSchema#string>
"inserting metal sheet into hydraulic press"^^<http://www.w3.org/2001/XMLSchema#string>
"putting oil on metal sheet"^^<http://www.w3.org/2001/XMLSchema#string>

Fig. 5. Results of query 1

The first query provides information about what happened in the scene before the trainee pushed the press button. The query searches for events and their assigned time slices that happened before the event with the name "pressing the turn on the button of the press". The result consists of event names ordered by time, which is shown in Fig. 5.

Query 2. How long the metal sheet was inspected?

```
    numberstyle
1   SELECT ?start ?end
2   WHERE { ?event fo:name "visually␣controlling␣the␣metal␣sheet"^^<http
          ://www.w3.org/2001/XMLSchema#string> .
3                   ?timeSlice fo:isTimeSliceOf ?event .
4                   ?timeSlice fo:hasTimeInterval ?timeInterval .
5                   ?timeInterval fo:start ?start .
6                   ?timeInterval fo:end ?end .
7           }
```

start	end
"2023-04-25T09:04:04"^^<http://www.w3.org/2001/XMLSchema#dateTime>	"2023-04-26T09:04:50"^^<http://www.w3.org/2001/XMLSchema#dateTime>

Fig. 6. Results of query 2

The second query gives information about the duration of the visual inspection of the metal sheet. The query searches for the time slice of the event named "visually controlling the metal sheet", then using the time interval object, access the information when the event started and ended. The result of the query is shown in Fig. 6.

Query 3. When and What states the sheet metal transitioned into?

```numberstyle
1   SELECT ?begins  ?stateName ?stateID
2   WHERE{ ?state rdf:type fo:InstantState .
3          ?object fo:hasState ?state .
4          ?object fo:name "metal␣sheet"^^xsd:string .
5          ?state fo:name ?stateName .
6          ?state fo:id ?stateID .
7          ?event fo:begins ?state .
8          ?timeSlice fo:isTimeSliceOf ?event .
9          ?event fo:name ?eventName .
10      { ?timeSlice fo:timePoint ?begins . }
11        UNION
12        {
13          ?timeSlice fo:hasTimeInterval ?timeInterval .
14          ?timeInterval fo:start ?begins .
15        }
16      }
17   ORDER BY ?begins
```

begins	stateName	stateID
"2023-04-26T09:00:00"^^<http://www.w3.org/2001/XMLSchema#dateTime>	"kept in a container"^^<http://www.w3.org/2001/XMLSchema#string>	"1"^^<http://www.w3.org/2001/XMLSchema#int>
"2023-04-26T09:01:22"^^<http://www.w3.org/2001/XMLSchema#dateTime>	"Unpacked"^^<http://www.w3.org/2001/XMLSchema#string>	"2"^^<http://www.w3.org/2001/XMLSchema#int>
"2023-04-26T09:04:04"^^<http://www.w3.org/2001/XMLSchema#dateTime>	"Visualy Checked"^^<http://www.w3.org/2001/XMLSchema#string>	"3"^^<http://www.w3.org/2001/XMLSchema#int>
"2023-04-26T09:06:34"^^<http://www.w3.org/2001/XMLSchema#dateTime>	"inserted into hydraulic press"^^<http://www.w3.org/2001/XMLSchema#string>	"4"^^<http://www.w3.org/2001/XMLSchema#int>
"2023-04-26T09:08:34"^^<http://www.w3.org/2001/XMLSchema#dateTime>	"inserted into hydraulic press and oiled"^^<http://www.w3.org/2001/XMLSchem	"5"^^<http://www.w3.org/2001/XMLSchema#int>
"2023-04-26T09:09:36"^^<http://www.w3.org/2001/XMLSchema#dateTime>	"trimmed sheet"^^<http://www.w3.org/2001/XMLSchema#string>	"11"^^<http://www.w3.org/2001/XMLSchema#int>

Fig. 7. Results of query 3

The last query provides information about what happened sequentially with the metal sheet. The query searches for events that changed the states of the scene object named "metal sheet". Then using proper time slices, the query determines the time by which the states are ordered. The results consist of the name and ID of the states and the time when they have begun. The query result is shown in Fig. 7.

Such queries can provide information about user experience with the training system. For example, how many mistakes the user made, how long the interaction with different objects took, and how complex and hard were the activities for the user. This information can be then used to evaluate the system and training scenario in order to increase the functionality and user-friendliness of the system and boost the efficiency of the virtual training.

5 Conclusions and Future Work

The use of knowledge-based representation for interactive 3D content, especially in the context of the collaborative network- and web-based VR/AR systems, has the potential to benefit various application domains by providing additional information about users' and objects' behavior. The paper presents a new approach to semantically representing the behavior of XR environments, including users' and objects' interactions and autonomous actions. The proposed model allows for the representation of temporal characteristics of XR environments with domain-specific terminology, which can be further explored through queries and reasoning. This approach could potentially lead to a more effective and widespread distribution of domain knowledge using XR. Furthermore, the information acquired by semantic queries can improve the user experience by measuring the performance of the users inside the virtual scene, which can lead to evaluating the system and training scenario in order to enhance the usability of the training system.

Additionally, an example and overview of the generated knowledge base for the VR training system have been presented, which is a real training scenario based on the requirements of the training process house appliances manufacturer. Additionally, on generated knowledge base the semantic queries were performed and results and overview were presented.

Possible future research directions can focus on the development of semantic repositories with domain knowledge collected using the proposed model as well as the development of machine learning methods for analyzing and classifying the collected data. It could be especially useful to discover patterns in users' behavior in training sessions, e.g., common problems and mistakes, to improve the overall training performance. In addition, we plan to develop graphical tools supporting the execution of queries against training ontologies and knowledge bases, which would facilitate the use of our approach by non-IT-specialists. Moreover, formal responses to semantic queries can be enriched by the accompanying visualization recorded during the training session.

Acknowledgements. The presented research was co-funded by the National Center for Research and Development under grant number LIDER/55/0287/L-12/20/NCBR/2021.

References

1. Chmielewski, J.: Describing interactivity of 3d content. In: Cellary, W., Walczak, K. (eds.) Interactive 3D Multimedia Content, pp. 195–221. Springer, London (2012). https://doi.org/10.1007/978-1-4471-2497-9_8
2. Chokwitthaya, C., Zhu, Y., Lu, W.: Ontology for experimentation of human-building interactions using virtual reality. Adv. Eng. Inform. **55**, 101903 (2023). https://doi.org/10.1016/j.aei.2023.101903, https://www.sciencedirect.com/science/article/pii/S1474034623000319

3. Chu, Y.L., Li, T.Y.: Realizing semantic virtual environments with ontology and pluggable procedures. In: Applications of Virtual Reality. IntechOpen, Rijeka (2012). https://doi.org/10.5772/36761
4. Chu, Y., Li, T.: Using pluggable procedures and ontology to realize semantic virtual environments 2.0. In: Proceedings of The 7th ACM SIGGRAPH International Conference on Virtual-Reality Continuum and Its Applications in Industry. VRCAI '08, pp. 27:1–27:6. ACM, New York, NY, USA (2008)
5. De Troyer, O., Kleinermann, F., Pellens, B., Bille, W.: Conceptual modeling for virtual reality. In: Grundy, J., Hartmann, S., Laender, A.H.F., Maciaszek, L., Roddick, J.F. (eds.) Tutorials, Posters, Panels and Industrial Contributions at the 26th International Conference on Conceptual Modeling - ER 2007. CRPIT, vol. 83, pp. 3–18. ACS, Auckland, New Zealand (2007)
6. Flotyński, J., Walczak, K.: Ontology-based representation and modelling of synthetic 3D content: a state-of-the-art review. Comput. Graph. Forum, 1–25 (2017). https://doi.org/10.1111/cgf.13083
7. Heitmayer, M., Russell, M.G., Lahlou, S., Pea, R.D.: An ontology for human-centered analysis and design of virtual reality conferencing. In: TMS Proceedings 2021, 3 November 2021. https://tmb.apaopen.org/pub/3rbumwgw
8. Kapahnke, P., Liedtke, P., Nesbigall, S., Warwas, S., Klusch, M.: ISReal: an open platform for semantic-based 3D simulations in the 3D internet. In: International Semantic Web Conference (2), pp. 161–176 (2010)
9. Pellens, B., De Troyer, O., Bille, W., Kleinermann, F.: Conceptual modeling of object behavior in a virtual environment. In: Proceedings of Virtual Concept 2005, pp. 93–94. Springer, Biarritz (2005). https://doi.org/10.1007/2-287-28773-6
10. Pellens, B., De Troyer, O., Bille, W., Kleinermann, F., Romero, R.: An ontology-driven approach for modeling behavior in virtual environments. In: Meersman, R., Tari, Z., Herrero, P. (eds.) OTM 2005. LNCS, vol. 3762, pp. 1215–1224. Springer, Heidelberg (2005). https://doi.org/10.1007/11575863_145
11. Pellens, B., De Troyer, O., Kleinermann, F.: Codepa: a conceptual design pattern approach to model behavior for x3D worlds. In: Proceedings of the 13th International Symposium on 3D Web Technology, pp. 91–99. Los Angeles, 09–10 August 2008
12. Pellens, B., Kleinermann, F., De Troyer, O.: A development environment using behavior patterns to facilitate building 3D/VR applications. In: Proceedings of the 6th Australasian Conference on International Entertainment. IE '09, pp. 8:1–8:8. ACM (2009)
13. Rabattu, P.Y., et al.: My corporis fabrica embryo: an ontology-based 3D spatio-temporal modeling of human embryo development. J. Biomed. Semant. 6(1), 36 (2015). https://doi.org/10.1186/s13326-015-0034-0
14. Sikos, L.F.: 3D model indexing in videos for content-based retrieval via X3D-based semantic enrichment and automated reasoning. In: Proceedings of the 22Nd International Conference on 3D Web Technology. Web3D '17, pp. 19:1–19:7. ACM, New York, NY, USA (2017). https://doi.org/10.1145/3055624.3075943, http://doi.acm.org/10.1145/3055624.3075943
15. Sikos, L.F.: Spatiotemporal reasoning for complex video event recognition in content-based video retrieval. In: Hassanien, A.E., Shaalan, K., Gaber, T., Tolba, M.F. (eds.) AISI 2017. AISC, vol. 639, pp. 704–713. Springer, Cham (2018). https://doi.org/10.1007/978-3-319-64861-3_66
16. Trellet, M., Ferey, N., Baaden, M., Bourdot, P.: Interactive visual analytics of molecular data in immersive environments via a semantic definition of the content

and the context. In: 2016 Workshop on Immersive Analytics (IA), pp. 48–53. IEEE (2016)
17. W3C: Sparql query language for RDF (2008). http://www.w3.org/TR/2008/REC-rdf-sparql-query-20080115/. Accessed 24 Mar 2015
18. W3C: Owl (2015). http://www.w3.org/2001/sw/wiki/OWL. Accessed 24 Mar 2015
19. W3C: Rdf (accessed March 24, 2015), http://www.w3.org/TR/2004/REC-rdf-concepts-20040210/
20. W3C: RDFs (2015). http://www.w3.org/TR/2000/CR-rdf-schema-20000327/. Accessed 24 Mar 2015

A Conceptual Framework for Maturity Evaluation of BIM-Based AR/VR Systems Based on ISO Standards

Ziad Monla[(✉)] [iD], Ahlem Assila [iD], Djaoued Beladjine, and Mourad Zghal [iD]

CESI LINEACT Laboratory UR 7527, Lille, France
{zmonla,aassila,dbeladjine,mzghal}@cesi.fr

Abstract. Maturity evaluation of BIM-based Augmented Reality (AR) and Virtual Reality (VR) systems is a challenging issue that requires ensuring their effectiveness and reliability. However, the lack of appropriate evaluation methods, tools, and standards for these systems makes this task even more complex. In this context, this paper proposes a conceptual framework for evaluating the maturity of BIM-based AR/VR systems, by using ISO standards. It represents a first and important step towards developing a standardized maturity model for such systems. The proposed framework enables the identification of fundamental concepts related to the evaluation of BIM-based AR and/or VR systems' maturity. This ranges from identifying the evaluation goals to interpreting the final findings to identify mechanisms to evaluate outcomes. This framework is based on ISO/IEC TS 33061 standard for determining maturity levels and ISO/IEC 15939 for identifying measurement concepts. Evaluation can be performed either globally or in a customized way. The global evaluation considers all aspects of the system, while customized evaluation allows users to select specific key elements according to their requirements. A feasibility study, conducted by academic experts in the field, has been carried out in order to validate the proposed framework.

Keywords: Maturity · Evaluation · BIM-based AR · BIM-based VR · ISO standards

1 Introduction

The Architecture, Engineering, and Construction (AEC) industry has been significantly impacted by technology, especially with the introduction of Building Information Modeling (BIM), which has been developed and adopted to help countries achieve accelerated growth [1, 2]. BIM has been recognized as a transformative force that can revolutionize project processes by offering a unique approach to asset design and construction. It induces increased productivity, reduced failure costs, and innovative collaboration methods [3]. However, the practical application of BIM presents challenges that can prevent projects from realizing their potential advantages [4]. For this reason, immersive technologies such as Augmented Reality (AR) and Virtual Reality (VR) have been integrated to address these challenges and improve the construction process. This has given rise to

© The Author(s), under exclusive license to Springer Nature Switzerland AG 2023
L. T. De Paolis et al. (Eds.): XR Salento 2023, LNCS 14218, pp. 139–156, 2023.
https://doi.org/10.1007/978-3-031-43401-3_9

BIM-based AR and BIM-based VR systems, which provide an engaging and immersive environment for creating and visualizing multi-dimensional simulations of construction projects [5–7]. These systems can also highlight diverse project aspects and provide invaluable assistance throughout all stages of the project [7]. However, to ensure the ongoing development and improvement of these innovative systems, it is essential to evaluate their maturity. Maturity evaluation is generally considered an essential process that helps companies make decisions when it comes to implementing these technologies and refining them to meet the needs of the construction industry [8].

In this context, maturity evaluation for BIM-based AR/VR systems can help companies make more informed decisions regarding investment in technology and develop more effective strategies for adopting augmented and virtual reality.

When reviewing the literature, only two research studies have currently been found on the maturity evaluation of these systems [8, 9], which suffer from several limitations. The first study [8] proposes a framework applied exclusively to BIM-based VR systems. The second study [9] proposed an approach for BIM-based AR/VR maturity evaluation without taking into account basic evaluation concepts such as measures and evaluation criteria. In this paper, we propose a more comprehensive maturity evaluation framework that can be applied to both BIM-based AR and VR systems, based on standards and measurement concepts. This framework serves as a first step towards creating a standardized maturity model.

To address this need, the objective of this study is to propose a conceptual framework for assessing the maturity of BIM-based AR/VR systems using ISO standards, specifically ISO/IEC TS 33061 [10] and ISO/IEC 15939 [11]. It enables the identification of key concepts related to the evaluation of BIM-based AR/VR systems' maturity, from defining the evaluation objective to interpreting the final results. Two modes of evaluation are used: a global evaluation that assesses all aspects of the system and identifies any issues, and a customized evaluation that allows users to select specific key elements according to their requirements. Further, our framework not only measures the maturity level of BIM-based AR/VR systems, but also provides analyses and interpretations of the results based on ISO/IEC 15939 standards, which can help identify mechanisms for transitioning from one maturity level to another.

The remaining part of this article is structured as follows: Sect. 2 introduces a synthesized background and the current state of the art on our subject. Section 3 describes the main concepts of the proposed maturity evaluation framework for BIM-based AR/VR systems based on ISO Standards. Section 4 presents a feasibility study of the proposed framework in order to demonstrate its validity in an academic context. It subsequently discusses the main findings and presents future perspectives of the proposed framework. Finally, Sect. 5 concludes the paper.

2   Background and Current State of the Art

Over the past decade, BIM-based AR/VR systems have undergone extensive research and development. In this section, we aim to provide a comprehensive background on these systems and review the existing related works on methods for evaluating their maturity.

2.1 BIM-Based AR/VR Systems

BIM-based AR/VR is a natural progression from the adoption of BIM in the AEC industry [12]. The lack of interoperability and difficulty in visualizing complex geometries in the BIM model made it challenging to incorporate AR/VR technologies [13]. However, experts in immersive technology worldwide are working diligently to develop pragmatic AR/VR solutions that align with BIM processes and meet clients' specific requirements and objectives [14]. Recently AR and VR technologies have demonstrated an excellent capability for improving current technologies and offering a better quality of life [15]. By overlaying virtual information into the real world or creating immersive virtual environments, these technologies provide new ways of visualizing and interacting with the built environment [16]. The use of AR and VR in the AEC industry shows capacity to enhance design, construction, and operation processes, as well as improve communication and collaboration among stakeholders. These technologies are bringing out unimaginable modification and advancement in various construction issues, as it enables users to interact with a building model in a more intuitive and immersive way [7]. The importance of BIM-based AR/VR systems has had an enormous impact on the construction industry, and many applications can benefit a construction project, from design and visualization to construction sequencing and safety analysis [7].

Most research has revealed that the BIM-based AR and/or VR system has the potential to enhance the construction industry by improving many of its current practices. As stated by Lopez et al. [17], the design phase is one of the primary areas in the construction industry that has implemented VR for BIM. This is done to facilitate collaborative visualization, enhance various aspects of the construction process, and design applications. Moreover, using VR to visualize and interact with a realistic representation of a BIM 3D model enables users to detect errors and identify risks. Additionally, this research shows that VR can potentially enhance the performance of professionals in the AEC industry by facilitating the creation of project timelines, cost estimation, and logistics planning. By using a BIM-based VR system, stakeholders can engage with the project by visualizing and selecting finishing elements within the construction project, such as color and texture of carpet, window types and styles, wood types, etc.

In another study [18], it was noted that BIM-based AR has multiple applications across the various phases of a construction project, including design, construction, and post-construction. During the design phase, it can aid in communication and marketing efforts before any physical construction work begins. However, during construction, AR can optimize tasks such as layout, excavation, positioning, inspection, coordination, supervision, commenting, and strategizing. Moreover, AR can be utilized in building lifecycle applications after the construction process is complete.

In a study by Li et al. [14], three different applications of AR and VR in construction safety were presented. The first application concerns hazard identification or risk recognition, which depends on the planning team's ability to detect and analyze potential dangers that may occur during the construction process. The second application concerns safety training and education, based on improving the cognitive learning experience of users during the construction phase. The third application of AR technology concerns safety inspection and instruction in construction. AR can be used to visualize construction drawings in a 3D representation, instead of physically carrying 2D drawings to the site. This enables quicker and more efficient decision-making during safety inspections and instruction. Furthermore, AR can be used as a tool to analyze disaster damage by comparing a previously saved base image to the actual image of the structure after an event such as an earthquake, facilitating faster decision-making and response times.

2.2 Related Works on the Maturity Evaluation of BIM-Based AR/VR Systems

As the adoption of BIM, AR, and VR technologies in the AEC industry continues to grow, various researchers have proposed maturity models to evaluate it and identify potential areas for improvement, and optimize the benefits of these technologies in accordance with the needs of construction companies [9]. This section discusses existing maturity models for BIM-based AR/VR systems as a starting point for establishing our framework.

A maturity model is a tool used to evaluate an organization's level of maturity based on predefined Key Performance Indicators (KPIs) (Assila et al. 2020). It typically consists of a maturity matrix that outlines the essential key elements of the project to be evaluated, including aspects, criteria, sub-criteria, and evaluation measures. This can include data interpretation methods and evaluation methods that are generally based on the classification of maturity levels, with higher levels indicating a greater degree of maturity [19, 20].

There have been only a few research papers published to evaluate the maturity of BIM-based AR/VR systems. Among these papers, we mention the study by Assila et al. [9]. The proposed maturity model in this study resulted from a mapping between the BIM maturity model proposed by Dakhil et al. [21] and the augmented reality and virtual reality maturity models suggested by Hammershmid et al. [22]. The matrix of the maturity model consists of three levels of maturity classification. The first level focuses on the visualization of BIM using AR and VR, the second level involves the interaction, configuration, and collaboration of BIM with AR and VR, while the third level emphasizes full BIM collaboration, immersion, problem detection, and solution suggestion through AR and VR. The model outlines seven aspects, including visualization, interaction, configuration, full immersion, full collaboration, problem detection, and finding solutions, to provide a comprehensive assessment of the implementation of BIM-based AR/VR technologies. The proposed maturity model aims to help companies determine their current level of maturity and identify opportunities for improvement. However, the model has two main limitations. Firstly, it is a conceptual approach that lacks a validation method. Secondly, the model does not define evaluation measures, which may affect its effectiveness in practice.

In another study, a new evaluation tool was proposed by Alarcon et al. [23] to assess the maturity of AR in the aerospace industry. This method primarily focuses on the technology components, including hardware elements such as sensors, chips, speakers, and display systems, as well as software features such as object recognition, tracking, interaction libraries, and remote assistance tools. The authors subjectively examined each component and estimated its related maturity. The framework was validated through multiple statistical tests, while also identifying opportunities for enhancement and areas that require further exploration. The study provides valuable perspectives to guide future advancements. However, the evaluation method utilized in the study is not well-defined, which presents a limitation.

More recently, [8] proposed a maturity model for evaluating BIM-based VR systems' maturity during the project's design phase. The proposed model was developed based on expert interviews and a review of research from other industries as similar research was lacking in the AEC industry. The model identifies three distinct stages of VR implementation: commissioning, usage, and post-usage, which are segmented into five main areas based on their focus: preparation, immersion, inspection, collaboration, and side effects. The team established criteria and measures for each area, resulting in a framework that can assist users in selecting BIM-based VR systems based on their preferences and requirements. Moreover, this model provides a consistent quantitative assessment method using well-defined and comprehensive measures and criteria. However, some inconsistencies in the scoring metrics still exist due to the varying characteristics of participants. It's worth noting that BIM-based VR evaluation services are limited to the design phase, and the final evaluation score was calculated using a five-point Likert scale.

To conclude this section, it is worth noting that several limitations have been identified in existing maturity models, including issues related to the stage of application, lack of validation methods, evaluation methods, and consistency. Therefore, this paper proposes a conceptual framework based on measurement concepts, standards, and best practices in evaluation. This framework serves as a first step towards developing a more standardized maturity model for the evaluation of BIM-based AR/VR systems.

3 The Proposed Conceptual Framework for BIM-Based AR/VR Systems Maturity Evaluation Based on ISO/IEC Standards

3.1 The Main Concepts of the Proposed Conceptual Framework

This section aims to present the overall structure of the proposed framework to ensure a clear understanding of its components and how it operates. Figure 1 illustrates the main concepts of the proposed conceptual framework for the evaluation of BIM-based AR and VR systems maturity.

The framework is composed of three parts, based on the most relevant guidelines and measurement standards to ensure its effectiveness and consistency.

The initial part defines the necessary key elements for maturity evaluation and offers concrete examples. These key elements were established from the Capability Maturity Model Integration (CMMI) and the Project Management Maturity Model (PMMM) [24, 25] that state the necessity of defining areas of interest to be evaluated. According to these models, areas of interest indicate the aspects of the studied project or system to be covered and evaluated. In our study, as shown in Fig. 1, the areas of interest represent the aspects of BIM-based AR/VR systems such as technology and collaboration. In addition, ISO/IEC 15939 standard emphasizes the importance of using specific criteria and measures for evaluation purposes and provides guidelines on how to develop and interpret them [11]. This standard [11] provides a comprehensive process for defining a suitable set of measures that address specific information needs. It allows for the determination of how the measures and analysis results are applied, as well as for determining the validity of the analysis results. In turn, the criteria specify the particular elements within the studied aspect that will be evaluated and provide a better understanding of the intended goal. Usually, breaking down criteria into sub-criteria provides additional details and clarity, leading to greater precision and understanding of the aspect being evaluated. These criteria and/or sub-criteria can be evaluated in a subjective or objective manner through measures. The measures serve as a way of achieving the intended objective by providing defined metrics that can be applied to reach a final decision on the maturity [11]. For example, in our study on BIM-based AR/VR systems, technology is an aspect that needs evaluation. It is segmented into software and hardware criteria. As illustrated in Fig. 1, navigation is a sub-criteria for the software criterion that can be measured via two measures: convenience and capability of navigation, in order to achieve the intended evaluation objective.

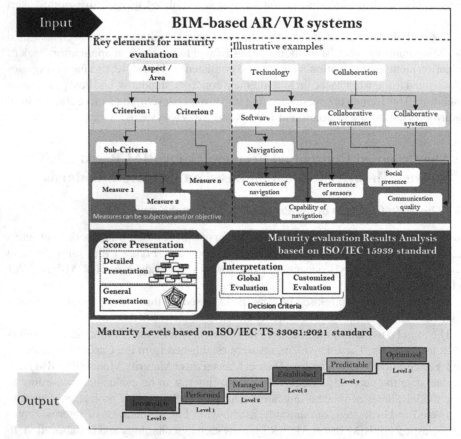

Fig. 1. The proposed conceptual framework for BIM-based AR/VR maturity evaluation based on ISO measurement standards and guidelines.

The second part of the framework focuses on the process of analyzing the measurement results obtained from the first part in accordance with the ISO/IEC 15939 standard

[11]. The analysis can be either detailed or more general and can be performed based on predefined decision criteria, which will be detailed in the following section.

Finally, the third part of the framework defines the maturity levels that have been selected to evaluate the studied key elements and generate a final decision as the output of the process. This step is based on the ISO/IEC TS 33061 standard [10], which provides guidelines for assessing the maturity of an organization's software engineering processes and identifies six maturity levels: (0) incomplete, (1) performed, (2) managed, (3) established, (4) predictable, and (5) optimized.

Further details regarding the proposed framework will be described in the next section.

3.2 Conceptual Framework Description for BIM-Based AR/VR Systems Maturity Evaluation

This section aims to provide a detailed description of the proposed framework, including an in-depth analysis of each of its components (parts) as presented above.

The Key Elements for BIM-Based AR/VR Systems Maturity Evaluation. The essential key elements for evaluating BIM-based AR/VR maturity include aspects, criteria, sub-criteria (if necessary), and measures. We identified these concepts as a first step in our framework by conducting an in-depth analysis of existing studies proposed by [8, 9, 23]. This analysis involved two main steps. The first step involved identifying and removing repetitive aspects, criteria, sub-criteria, and measures. The second step focused on determining elements that address the same subject, keeping only one, and placing it in the appropriate category. The key elements obtained concerning the main covered aspects, criteria, and sub-criteria, along with a list of examples of measures, are presented in Table 1.

As illustrated in Table 1, a maturity evaluation of a BIM-based AR/VR system consists of six essential evaluation aspects: technology, immersion, collaboration, side effects, BIM interaction/configuration with AR/VR, and detecting problems and suggesting solutions with AR/VR. Each aspect is further divided into corresponding criteria and sub-criteria, as necessary, with a list of examples of corresponding measures.

Starting with the technology aspect, it encompasses a set of criteria that ensure the efficiency and productivity of the experienced system in the AEC sector. This includes the information system, represented by software criterion, and the equipment, represented by hardware criterion [7, 35]. According to Alarcon et al. [23], Kim et al. [8] and Kozlenko et al. [26], software criterion includes two sub-criterion. The first is the BIM software, which is measured by its convenience [26]. The second sub-criterion includes the interaction system [8, 23], referring to the interaction libraries, AR/VR authoring tools, and remote assistance tools, which are evaluated based on their capability and convenience. On the other hand, hardware criterion refers to all physical components that make up BIM-based AR and/or VR systems, such as sensors, chips, optics, display systems, and speakers [23]. Typically, these elements are evaluated based on their efficiency [23]. The second aspect addressed is immersion. In the AEC industry, immersion refers to the degree of realism experienced when visualizing and interacting with the augmented or virtual environment of the BIM model [8]. Immersion evaluation depends

Table 1. The key elements for evaluating BIM-based AR/VR maturity, along with a list of examples of measures based on existing studies.

Aspects (Area)	Criteria	Sub-Criteria	Measures Examples
Technology [23]	Hardware [23]		System efficiency (sensors, chips, display, speakers) [23]
	Software [23]	Interaction system [8, 23]	Capability and convenience of the interaction system [8, 23]
		BIM software [26]	Convenience of BIM software [26]
Immersion [8]	Visual immersion [8]		Immersion consistency [27]
	Behavior [28]		Physical presence in a virtual environment [28]
	Interactivity [29]		Sense of agency [29]
Collaboration [9]	Collaborative environment [9]		Social presence or co-presence [30]
			Awareness [30]
			Interpersonal trust and spatial faithfulness [31]
	Collaborative system [9]	Real-time modification [8]	The ability of users to modify and visualize data in real-time [9]
		Communication quality [32]	Quality of text-based tools, avatars, visual sharing, and voice chat
		Multiple users platform [8]	Capability and convenience of Multiple users platform [8]
Side effect [8]	Dizziness [8]		Occurrence time [8]
			Severity [8]
	Fatigue [8]		Occurrence time [8]
			Severity [8]
BIM interaction and configuration with AR/VR [9]	Data visualization [9]		Ability of AR/VR devices to change the type of data [33]

(continued)

Table 1. (*continued*)

Aspects (Area)	Criteria	Sub-Criteria	Measures Examples
			Effectiveness of visualization in improving BIM data understanding [33]
	Tangible interaction [9]		Effectiveness of AR/VR in supporting tangible interactions with virtual models [34]
			Range and ease of use of options and tools available for modifying virtual elements [34]
	BIM file [8]		File format compatibility, Convenience, and complexity [8]
Detection problems and suggestion solutions with AR/VR [9]			Effectiveness of solutions in resolving problems [23]

on several criteria. Firstly, the visual immersion refers to the similarity between the virtual representation and the real world [8]. This can be measured by its consistency, accuracy, and level of detail [27]. The second criterion concerns the behavior of users in a virtual environment and whether it is realistic or not. This is evaluated based on the user's physical presence in the virtual world. Users are considered behaviorally immersed if their actions in the virtual environment are similar to those in reality [28]. The third criterion concerns the interactivity between users and the virtual environment, and it is measured by the level of naturalism in manipulating or controlling objects in the virtual environment. In other words, it is the "sense of agency" experienced by the user [29].

An essential aspect to consider when evaluating BIM-based AR/VR systems is the collaboration. Its importance lies in the success or failure of the work. Effective collaboration leads to a better understanding between users and successful task completion. Poor communication, on the other hand, may result in incomplete tasks and failure [8]. According to [9], the collaboration aspect depends on two criteria. The first criterion evaluates the collaborative environment, while the second criterion evaluates the collaborative system. The collaborative environment refers to the environment in which participants interact and is usually measured through three measures. The first measure is social presence or co-presence, which depends on verbal and nonverbal cues such as facial expressions, vocal cues, gestures, and physical appearance [30]. The second measure refers to awareness, such as mutual awareness related to the responsiveness of the participants to others' needs, and collaborative awareness that involves being aware of what others are doing in the project [30]. The third measure refers to interpersonal trust and spatial faithfulness between users, which is reflected in people's performances when they are doing a task [31].

The evaluation of collaborative system criteria depends on real-time modifications, which are measured through the ability of users to modify and visualize data in a virtual or augmented environment [9]. The quality of communication is also important, and this includes the quality of text-based tools, avatars, visual sharing, and voice chat [32]. In addition, the evaluation process should consider the capability and convenience of multiple user platforms [8].

The side effects aspect refers to the undesired effects and symptoms that occur after using BIM-based AR/VR systems. According to [8], the side effects aspect is divided into two criteria referred to dizziness and fatigue, and both are measured through their occurrence time and severity.

Assila et al. [9] presented an interesting perspective on the correlation between BIM and AR/VR. They suggested that there is another aspect to consider in the evaluation process, specifically the interaction and configuration between BIM and AR/VR, which involves three distinct criteria that are important to understand this relationship. The first criterion concerns data visualization, which is usually measured by evaluating the ability of AR and VR devices to change the type of data and the effectiveness of these devices in improving the user's understanding of BIM data [33]. While the second criterion concerns object manipulation in the virtual environment which is known as tangible interaction, and it is measured by evaluating how well and easily these VR and AR technologies support this type of interaction [34]. In addition, [8] added that the correlation between AR/VR and BIM software involves an important criterion for evaluation, which relates to the BIM files. These files have a significant impact on the communication between software tools and AR/VR technologies, and their importance can be determined based on factors such as the complexity of the BIM model, format compatibility, and convenience.

Lastly, the ability of a BIM-based AR/VR system to identify problems and suggest solutions was considered the last aspect to consider [9]. The effectiveness of the proposed solutions in addressing problems serves as the evaluation measure for this aspect [23].

Results Representation and Interpretation Based on ISO/IEC 15939 Standard for BIM-Based AR/VR Systems Maturity Evaluation. The interpretation of measurement results is a crucial step in developing a correct and efficient analysis. As illustrated in Fig. 2, our framework first ensures a global evaluation of the maturity of BIM-based AR/VR systems, taking into account all aspects to be evaluated. Second, it allows for a customized evaluation, providing evaluators with greater flexibility in choosing the elements to be evaluated. In this case, evaluators can select the relevant elements aligned with their needs and project requirements for a customized evaluation. Regardless of the type of evaluation chosen, this phase is based on the ISO/IEC 15939 standard, which defines an analysis process for presenting and interpreting the results of measures based on decision criteria.

According to this standard, decision criteria are defined as thresholds that describe the level of confidence in a given result [11]. The use of this concept allows the definition of rules to interpret the results of one or more measures at a time, and therefore identify, in our study, the level of maturity of the evaluated element (criterion/ sub-criterion/ aspect). Initially, we have defined three possible formats to represent a rule, where M is a measure used for evaluating a criterion or a sub-criterion; X and Y are the thresholds to be set by the evaluator; and SCL is Sub-Criteria Level; CL is Criteria Level; and AL is Aspect Level. As a reminder, we have six levels of maturity ranging from 0 to 5 based on the ISO/IEC TS 33061 standard [10]. In the following, we provide examples of rules in case a criterion or sub-criterion is evaluated by a single measure:

- (1) *if* (score M (> or <) X) *then* criteria/sub-criteria Level is SCL/CL
- (2) *if* (X < score M < Y) *then* criteria/sub-criteria Level is SCL/CL
- (3) *if* (criteria1 Level = CL1 and criteria 2 Level = CL2.... Criteria n = CLn) *then* Aspect Level is AL (in the case where an aspect is composed of n criteria, AL is calculated as the sum of level scores divided by the number of criteria)

The first two rules (1) and (2) allow determining the maturity level of a criterion or sub-criterion when it is evaluated by a single measure. Meanwhile, the third rule enables determining the maturity level of an aspect composed of one or more criteria.

The resulting maturity level is represented by a rounded integer. To provide more information on the calculated aspect score level and the maturity levels of each criterion, we propose presenting the result graphically as illustrated in Fig. 2 (see detailed presentation). This representation helps the evaluator identify the source of problems described by the lowest maturity level(s) and, consequently, determine the necessary recommendations to improve maturity and facilitate the transition from one maturity level to another. Moreover, we suggest a radar graph that highlights the final score level of each evaluated aspect to obtain a more general presentation (see Fig. 2 general presentation). These presentation options allow users to visualize the results clearly and communicate them effectively to designers.

In the following section, we present more details on the maturity levels.

Maturity Evaluation Levels for BIM-Based AR/VR Systems. As mentioned earlier, the maturity levels in our study are based on the ISO/IEC TS 33061:2021 [10] standard, which includes six levels ranging from 0 to 5. These levels are grouped into categories such as Incomplete, Performed, Managed, Established, Predictable, and Optimized. They range from basic process organization to continuous process improvement and refinement at the highest levels. In our proposed framework, we assess the criteria that can include sub-criteria and aspects elements rather than the overall system evaluation. Thus, as illustrated by Fig. 3, we have adapted the six maturity levels, defined by ISO/IEC TS 33061:2021 [10] standard, to address all key elements for maturity evaluation. This is based on satisfaction level, relevance, and appropriateness of measure's obtained results, as well as their suitability to meet our specific needs. Taking into account these six levels of maturity, five thresholds must be defined during the evaluation in order to identify the ranges of each level of maturity. For your information, the selection of these thresholds is crucial. However, it is very delicate to decide on the appropriate values for these thresholds. Therefore, the intervention of an expert at this stage is important [36]. The expert must take into account the contextual information of the system being evaluated,

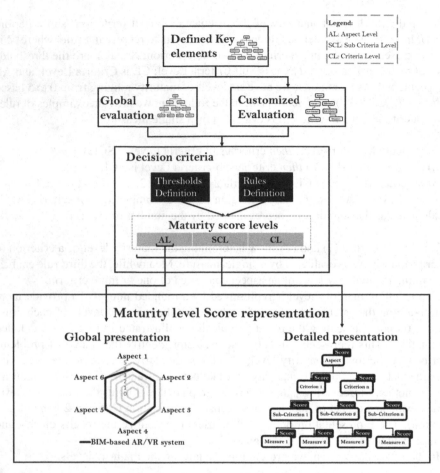

Fig. 2. The proposed maturity evaluation analysis process.

including the users involved in the evaluation, the software and hardware equipment, and the physical environment.

As illustrated in Fig. 3, the significance of each level is as follows:

- **Level 0 (Incomplete):** Represents the beginner level. It refers to a situation in which the score of the measured element is below the defined threshold X. In this case, the element being studied has not yet reached the minimum level of satisfaction required to meet the needs of users. Furthermore, the results obtained are inadequate and may result in a negative user experience.
- **Level 1 (Performed):** Represents the under development level. It describes a scenario where the score of the measure falls within the first two predetermined thresholds (X and Y). This indicates that there is progress toward increasing satisfaction levels, achieving desired outcomes, and comprehending user expectations. However, there are still areas that require enhancement.

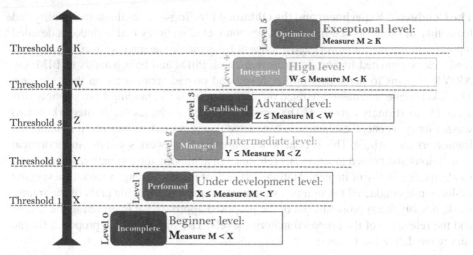

Fig. 3. ISO/IEC TS 33061:2021 maturity levels and their significance according to BIM-based AR/VR systems.

- **Level 2 (Managed):** Represents the intermediate level. It refers to a situation in which the score of the studied measure falls between the second and third defined thresholds (Y and Z). This indicates that the studied elements are delivering acceptable results, meeting user expectations, and yielding satisfactory levels of satisfaction. Nevertheless, there are still some minor improvements to be made.
- **Level 3 (Established):** Represents the advanced level. It corresponds to a scenario where the studied measure score falls between the third and the fourth predefined thresholds (Z and W), suggesting that the analyzed components are producing relevant results. The users are highly satisfied with their experience, and their expectations are mostly fulfilled, except for only a small number of areas requiring additional enhancements.
- **Level 4 (Predictable):** Represents the high level. It refers to a situation where the measured score falls between the fourth and fifth predefined thresholds (W and K). This indicates that the elements being studied are generating extremely relevant outcomes, exceeding the users' expectations, and resulting in an excellent level of satisfaction.
- **Level 5 (Optimized):** Represents the exceptional level. It refers to a situation in which the score of the studied element is higher than the fifth defined threshold K resulting in extremely relevant outcomes. In such cases, user satisfaction is exceptional, as their expectations are not just surpassed but also anticipated, leading to a delightful experience.

4   Feasibility Study and Discussion

In this section, we first present the conducted experimentation to study the feasibility of our framework, followed by a discussion reporting the limitations and new perspectives based on the analysis of the results obtained.

The Conducted Experiment and the Obtained Findings. To evaluate the validity and feasibility of our proposed framework, we conducted a survey that included a detailed report outlining the framework and a series of Likert scale statements aimed at gathering feedback. We invited five academic experts with PhDs and backgrounds in BIM and AR/VR systems to participate in the survey and provide comments on their choices. The Likert scale statements are rated on a seven-point scale, ranging from strongly disagree (1) to strongly agree (7). The proposed survey evaluates the framework in two ways. Firstly, a general evaluation is conducted that requires respondents to evaluate the framework as a whole. This is done to measure the framework's solidity in theoretical foundations and proven practices, its relevance in achieving the evaluation's objectives, its clarity, feasibility of implementation, and ease of understanding. Secondly, a specific evaluation is conducted through two statements to evaluate specific parts of the framework, notably the appropriateness of the proposed approach for interpreting the results and the relevance of the proposed maturity levels. The statements we proposed for the survey are defined as follows:

- *Statement 1:* The proposed framework is based on a sound theoretical basis or established best practices
- *Statement 2:* The proposed framework is relevant to evaluate the maturity of BIM-based AR/VR systems
- *Statement 3:* The proposed framework offers a clear and structured process for evaluating the maturity of BIM-based AR/VR systems.
- *Statement 4:* The proposed framework is practical and feasible to implement.
- *Statement 5:* The proposed framework is easy to understand.
- *Statement 6:* The results interpretation approach provides a clear way to interpret the results of the evaluation
- *Statement 7:*The proposed maturity levels for evaluating BIM-based AR/VR systems are coherent, clear, and understandable.

It is worth noting that statements 1 to 5 evaluate general aspects of the framework, while statements 6 and 7 evaluate specific parts within the framework. In addition, we provided an opportunity for academic experts to add any comments they wish.

The gathered scores on defined statements are illustrated in Fig. 4 below.

The histogram in Fig. 4 represents the feedback obtained from the experts who participated in the survey. The x-axis shows the seven statements, while the y-axis represents the frequency of responses, ranging from one to five. The bars for each statement indicate the different response options, which are color-coded to indicate the level of agreement or disagreement, ranging from strongly disagree to strongly agree.

According to the survey results, all participants provided overall highly positive feedback regarding the proposed framework. In fact, for statement 1, all participants strongly agreed with a score of "6" and "7", confirming that the proposed framework is based on solid theoretical foundations and established best practice standards. These ratings indicate that the framework is thoughtful, effective, and has the potential to provide a robust and credible approach to evaluating the maturity of BIM-based AR/VR systems.

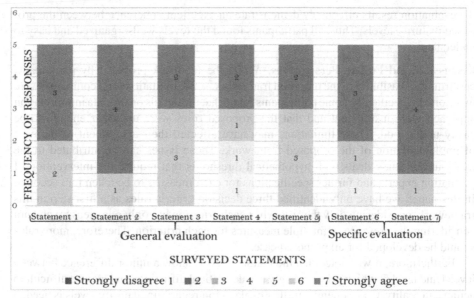

Fig. 4. Academic expert findings based on a seven-point Liker scale for the seven defined statements.

In addition, as shown in Fig. 4, the findings revealed that the proposed framework is well aligned with the intended objectives of evaluating the maturity of BIM-based AR/VR systems, as all participants strongly agreed as reflected in the score of "6" and "7" on statement 2. This indicates that the experts who participated in the survey perceived the proposed framework as relevant to the evaluation's objectives.

Regarding the clarity and structure of the proposed evaluation process, a total satisfaction of all participants was observed. This is supported by the results of Statement 3, which received 40% ratings of "7" and 60% ratings of "6".

The feedback on statements 4 and 5 further reinforces the positive perception of the proposed framework's usability and applicability. For Statement 4, the majority of participants expressed high levels of satisfaction regarding the feasibility of implementing and using the proposed framework. For Statement 5, all participants reported being fully satisfied with the framework's ease of understanding. These results confirm that the framework is not only feasible and easy to implement but also easily comprehensible. Note that the presence of a neutral response for Statement 4 implies that there may be some areas for improvement.

The survey results on statements 6 and 7 indicate a highly positive perception regarding the evaluation of specific areas. The proposed approach for interpreting results was found to be clear and useful by the participants, demonstrating the framework's success in providing a feasible approach to understanding, presenting, and interpreting the results of BIM-based AR/VR systems. Sixty percent of participants rated it with a score of "7," while the remaining 40% gave it a rating of "6" and "5," respectively. Moreover, the evaluation results effectively demonstrate an excellent coherence between the proposed maturity levels. Thus, all participants found the levels well-organized and easy to understand.

Discussion and Future Perspectives. While the feedback provided by participants confirms the feasibility of the proposed framework, some limitations and comments were mentioned. Specifically, some participants found that the details on the data interpretation approach were insufficient and that the proposed rules were not clear enough to be easily understood. These limitations may have affected their assessment of the ease of implementation of the proposed framework. These issues can be attributed to the fact that our study deals with hypothetical thresholds that require the intervention of evaluation experts and further specifications for each measure to be taken into account. In this paper, we have only identified three decision criteria rules as a first step in this framework, considering only the case when each criterion has only one measure and not considering the presence of multiple measures for each criterion. Therefore, more rules should be developed for all proposed cases.

Furthermore, it was noted that the maturity levels show a minor difference between level 4 and level 5, which is limited only to a theoretical difference and may be difficult to achieve in reality. Consequently, further explanation regarding maturity levels is needed to clarify their significance and practicality.

In addition to the limitations identified from the survey feedback, several other limitations of the study should be noted. The validation method used in the study only involved feedback from academic experts, which may not fully capture the perspectives of industrial experts who have more practical experience. Therefore, it is important to consider input from industrial experts in future studies to assess the applicability of the proposed framework. The identified key evaluation elements in this study are not exhaustive and are considered as examples from the literature. Thus, more research should be conducted to validate and identify more key elements through interviews with experts.

In conclusion, to enhance the usefulness and applicability of the proposed framework, future work should consider the transition between levels. This could be achieved by defining recommendations for each level to help companies and users improve their project's maturity and move from one stage to another.

5 Conclusion

This paper presents a conceptual framework for evaluating the maturity of BIM-based AR/VR systems in the AEC industry. The framework serves as an important step for establishing a more standardized maturity model with the same goal. It was developed by analyzing existing frameworks and based on known models and standards such as CMMI, PMMM, ISO/IEC 15939, and ISO/IEC TS 33061:2021. The evaluation process begins with identifying key elements and then defining aspects, criteria, and sub-criteria with appropriate evaluative measures. The proposed framework includes an analysis process for data interpretation and results representation. The framework defines six levels of maturity for assessing the maturity findings of the studied system. To validate the framework, a descriptive report containing evaluation statements was evaluated by five academic experts. Feedback revealed a positive response to the overall framework and specific evaluation aspects, although some comments were made regarding the maturity levels and the analysis process to understand the results.

References

1. Lu, W., Chen, K., Zetkulic, A., Liang, C.: Measuring building information modeling maturity: a Hong Kong case study. Int. J. Constr. Manag. **21**(3), 299–311 (2021)
2. Dadashi Haji, M., Taghaddos, H., Sebt, M.H., Chokan, F., Zavari, M.: The effects of bim maturity level on the 4d simulation performance: An empirical study. Int. J. Eng. **34**(3), 606–614 (2021)
3. Giel, B., Issa, R.R.: Synthesis of existing BIM maturity toolsets to evaluate building owners. Comput. Civil Eng. 451–458 (2013)
4. Siebelink, S., Voordijk, J.T., Adriaanse, A.: Developing and testing a tool to evaluate BIM maturity: sectoral analysis in the Dutch construction industry. J. Constr. Eng. Manag. **144**(8), 05018007 (2018)
5. Ahmed, S., Hossain, M.M., Hoque, M.I.: A brief discussion on augmented reality and virtual reality in construction industry. J. Syst. Manage. Sci. **7**(3), 1–33 (2017)
6. Wang, P., Wu, P., Wang, J., Chi, H.L., Wang, X.: A critical review of the use of virtual reality in construction engineering education and training. Int. J. Environ. Res. Public Health **15**(6), 1204 (2018)
7. Ververidis, D., Nikolopoulos, S., Kompatsiaris, I.: A review of collaborative virtual reality systems for the architecture and engineering (Virtual Tour), Int. J. Eng. Res. Technol. (IJERT) **11**(11) (2022)
8. Kim, J.I., Li, S., Chen, X., Keung, C., Suh, M., Kim, T.W.: Evaluation framework for BIM-based VR applications in design phase. J. Comput. Des. Eng. **8**(3), 910–922 (2021)
9. Assila, A., Beladjine, D., Messaadia, M.: Towards AR/VR maturity model adapted to the building information modeling. Product Lifecycle Management Enabling Smart X: 17th IFIP WG 5.1 International Conference, PLM 2020, Rapperswil, Switzerland, July 5–8 (2020)
10. ISO/IEC TS 33061:2021 Information technology—Process assessment—Process assessment model for software life cycle processes
11. ISO/IEC 15939. International Organization for Standardization/ International Electrotechnical Commission. Systems and software engineering—Measurement process (ISO/IEC 15939:2007 (E)).Geneva, Switzerland (2007).
12. Ververidis, D., Nikolopoulos, S., Kompatsiaris, I.: A review of collaborative virtual reality systems for the architecture, engineering, and construction industry. Architecture **2**(3), 476–496 (2022)
13. Sidani, A., et al.: Recent tools and techniques of BIM-Based Augmented Reality: a systematic review. J. Build. Eng. **42**, 102500 (2021)
14. Li, X., Yi, W., Chi, H.L., Wang, X., Chan, A.P.: A critical review of virtual and augmented reality (VR/AR) applications in construction safety. Autom. Constr. **86**, 150–162 (2018)
15. Ahmed, S.: A review on using opportunities of augmented reality and virtual reality in construction project management. Organ. Technol. Manage. Construct. Int. J. **10**(1), 1839–1852 (2018)
16. Alizadehsalehi, S., Hadavi, A., Huang, J.C.: From BIM to extended reality in AEC industry. Autom. Constr. **116**, 103254 (2020)
17. Lopez, J., Bhandari, S., Hallowell, M.R.: Virtual reality and construction industry: review of current state-of-practice and future applications. Construct. Res. Congress 174–184 (2022)

18. Meža, S., Turk, Ž, Dolenc, M.: Component based engineering of a mobile BIM-based augmented reality system. Autom. Constr. **42**, 1–12 (2014)
19. Wu, C., Xu, B., Mao, C., Li, X.: Overview of BIM maturity measurement tools. J. Inform. Technol. Construct. (ITcon) **22**(3), 34–62 (2017)
20. Yilmaz, G., Akcamete, A., Demirors, O.: A reference model for BIM capability assessments. Autom. Constr. **101**, 245–263 (2019)
21. Dakhil, A., Alshawi, M., Underwood, J.: BIM client maturity: literature review. In: 12th International Post-Graduate Research Conference (2015)
22. Hammerschmid, S.: Developing and testing of a virtual and augmented reality maturity model. Systems, Software and Services Process Improvement: 25th European Conference, pp. 279–288. EuroSPI 2018, Bilbao, Spain (2018)
23. Alarcon, R., et al.: Augmented Reality for the enhancement of space product assurance and safety. Acta Astronaut. **168**, 191–199 (2020)
24. Crawford, J.K.: Project Management Maturity Model. Auerbach Publications (2006)
25. Constantinescu, R., Iacob, I.M.: Capability maturity model integration. J. Appl. Quant. Methods **2**(1), 31–37 (2007)
26. Kozlenko, T.A., Pridvizhkin, S.V.: BIM and VR: development of a software module for the integration of building information modelling and virtual reality. Russian Autom. Highway Indust. J. **18**(4), 440–449 (2021)
27. Carroll, J., Hopper, L., Farrelly, A.M., Lombard-Vance, R., Bamidis, P.D., Konstantinidis, E.I.: A scoping review of augmented/virtual reality health and wellbeing interventions for older adults: redefining immersive virtual reality. Front. Virtual Real. **2**, 655338 (2021)
28. Lepecq, J.C., Bringoux, L., Pergandi, J.M., Coyle, T., Mestre, D.: Afforded actions as a behavioral assessment of physical presence in virtual environments. Virtual Real. **13**(3), 141–151 (2009)
29. Jeunet, C., Albert, L., Argelaguet, F., Lécuyer, A.: "Do you feel in control?": towards novel approaches to characterise, manipulate and measure the sense of agency in virtual environments. IEEE Trans. Visual Comput. Graph. **24**(4), 1486–1495 (2018)
30. Dey, A., Chen, H., Zhuang, C., Billinghurst, M., Lindeman, R.W.: Effects of sharing real-time multi-sensory heart rate feedback in different immersive collaborative virtual environments. In: IEEE International Symposium on Mixed and Augmented Reality (ISMAR), pp. 165–173 (2018)
31. Jacques, P.H., Garger, J., Brown, C.A., Deale, C.S.: Personality and virtual reality team candidates: the roles of personality traits, technology anxiety and trust as predictors of perceptions of virtual reality teams. J. Bus. Manage. **15**(2) (2009)
32. Li, J., et al.: Measuring and understanding photo sharing experiences in social virtual reality. In: Proceedings of the CHI Conference on Human Factors in Computing Systems (2019)
33. Xiong, J., Hsiang, E.L., He, Z., Zhan, T., Wu, S.T.: Augmented reality and virtual reality displays: emerging technologies and future perspectives. Light: Sci. Appl. **10**(1), 216 (2021)
34. Bekele, M.K., Champion, E.: A comparison of immersive realities and interaction methods: cultural learning in virtual heritage. Front. Robot. AI **6**, 91 (2019)
35. Succar, B.: Building information modelling maturity matrix. Handbook of Research on Building Information Modeling and Construction Informatics: Concepts and Technologies. IGI Global, pp. 65–103 (2010)
36. Assila, A., Marçal de Oliveira, K., Ezzedine, H.: Integration of subjective and objective usability evaluation based on IEC/IEC 15939: a case study for traffic supervision systems. Int. J. Hum. Comput. Interact. **32**(12), 931–955 (2016)

Design and Development of a Dynamic Fire Signage System for Building Evacuation: A VR Simulation Study

Orjola Braholli[1](✉), Mariana Ataide[1], Julius Emig[1], Ilaria Di Blasio[1],
Elias Niederwieser[1], Dietmar Siegele[1], and Dominik Matt[1,2]

[1] Fraunhofer Italia, Alessandro Volta 13a, Bolzano, Italy
orjola.braholli@fraunhofer.it
[2] Free University of Bozen-Bolzano, Piazza Università 5, 39100 Bolzano, Italy

Abstract. The paper presents a dynamic fire signage system for simulating emergency evacuation in the case of fire through dynamic pathfinding towards the nearest and safest exit in a virtual environment. Conventional fire signs and fire escape plans are becoming outdated and less effective due to their static nature and inability to adapt to different emergency scenarios. Experimental studies have shown that dynamic signs can be effective in guiding users of any age and can highly influence their direction choices during evacuation. A VR tool for simulating emergency evacuation through dynamic pathfinding towards the safest and nearest exit was designed using a BIM model as a basis to create a virtual environment for the simulation. Newly created fire signals, referred to as Fire Signal Cubes (FSCs) were used. They were specifically developed and implemented for this project as input for the node database and pathfinding algorithm to define navigable spaces. The FSCs have from one to four active sides, depending on their position in the floor plan and their relation to pathways and exit doors. Each side of the FSC that faces a path, or an exit door is active, and the FSC can show the correct signal according to the input of the pathfinding algorithm that instantly calculates the safest escape path. The paper provides a detailed description of the methodology and presents the results of implementing the dynamic pathfinder using a BIM model of an office environment.

Keywords: Virtual reality · dynamic fire signal · emergency evacuation · BIM · Unity

1 Introduction

Fire evacuation is a critical aspect of building safety that has been a subject of interest in the Architecture, Engineering, Construction, and Operations (AECO) industry for decades. Traditional methods of fire evacuation involve the use of fire alarms and signage to guide occupants towards the nearest exit. However, these methods are becoming

---

O. Braholli, M. Ataide, J. Emig, I. Di Blasio—All authors contributed equally to this work.

L. T. De Paolis et al. (Eds.): XR Salento 2023, LNCS 14218, pp. 157–171, 2023.
https://doi.org/10.1007/978-3-031-43401-3_10

outdated and do not take advantage of the new and advanced technologies emerging in the AECO industry. The use of Building Information Modelling (BIM) and Virtual Reality (VR) environments have shown great potential in creating strategies that enhance safety and reduce time in emergency situations [1, 2].

The current literature regarding the application of VR for fire safety has demonstrated potential in improving fire evacuation planning and training. Some studies have explored the use of VR environments to enhance emergency response times [3] and to create more efficient evacuation paths based on specific conditions [4]. However, most studies have primarily focused on using VR for training [5], BIM for building risk management [6] and evacuation plan efficiency [7].

Although the results of these studies are encouraging, there is still a gap in the investigation of the interoperability between BIM and VR for fire safety, as well as the implementation of innovative techniques for signaling fire escape routes. Traditional fire signage is becoming outdated with the new and advanced technologies emerging in the AECO industry. Thus, there is a need for a dynamic system that can adapt to different fire scenarios and provide real-time information about the best escape path, reducing the time it takes to leave the building and preventing people from being blocked between emergency doors and fire or smoke.

The purpose of this study is to develop a dynamic fire signal that offers real-time information on the safest escape route during a fire emergency based on the location of the fire or smoke source. The tool was developed using a pathfinder algorithm that utilizes BIM data to provide real-time updates. The study also aimed to assess the effectiveness of VR in fire evacuation simulations, explore the interoperability between BIM and VR, and evaluate the use of dynamic fire signals in identifying the correct fire escape routes. Using VR for this purpose has been shown to be a safer and more efficient use of resources and time.

The primary goal of our study is to enhance building safety and safeguard users by introducing a new method of guiding individuals during emergencies. Our system aligns with existing building management and operation technologies, leveraging data extracted from digital simulations. By utilizing a VR environment, we highlight the potential benefits of incorporating advanced technologies across all areas of the AECO industry. The expected outcomes include a reduced evacuation time and improved safety measures for building occupants. Additionally, our research will contribute to the growing body of literature on VR and BIM interoperability for fire evacuation simulations, thereby adding to the current knowledge on building safety.

As a result, we developed a three-dimensional cube that serves as an interactive tool for signaling fire escape routes. To determine the optimal evacuation path for building occupants during a fire emergency, we employed a pathfinder algorithm that considers the location of emergency exits and the source of the fire. This information is transmitted to the cube, which then provides guidance to users towards the safest path. To assess the effectiveness of the application, a virtual environment was created using Unity and tested by human users.

The paper has five sections. Section 2 presents the state of the art on the topics of fire safety, VR and BIM. Section 3 details the methodology used to create the smart system and the workflow between the integration of BIM and VR tools. Section 4 discusses the results and implementation of the system in a virtual environment. Finally, Sect. 5 presents a discussion on the paper and prospects for future research.

2 State of the Art

Fire safety is one of the primary concerns for Architecture, Engineering, Construction, and Operations (AECO) professionals as it ensures the safety of building users. Fire Safety Engineering (FSE) is a process that uses engineering principles to create or assess designs in the built environment to protect occupants [8]. Its main objective is to prevent fire emergencies and secure occupants, buildings, and other facilities. In general, the design of safe spaces considers possible fire hazards, such as materials and configurations that could lead to a fire outbreak. Additionally, FSE strategies are employed to mitigate the impact of fire and ensure occupant safety in the event of an emergency. Many building regulations incorporate these strategies to ensure the safety of building occupants. Although different countries have various regulations, similarities exist in terms of core aspects of fire safety [9, 10], highlighting the challenges involved in providing a safe environment for users.

The main objective during a fire emergency is the safe evacuation of building occupants. The escape routes are crucial as they represent the path that leads the building occupant to a safe space. Building regulations typically specify a maximum distance to safe exits [11], which can be increased when the escape route has aids such as sprinklers, light and sound alarms, and so on. The success of the route also depends heavily on how familiar the building users are with it [12, 13].

However, some building types, such as airports, shopping malls, and performance halls, have mostly transient occupants. In such cases, the guidance of occupants depends solely on the use of signs for directing safe exits, which are widely used in building designs to compensate for a lack of user awareness or possible behavior changes during a fire. Studies underscore the importance of designing effective signage for emergency exits to ensure that people can safely and quickly evacuate a building during an emergency [14, 15].

Regarding the building type, escape routes should always be flagged with clear signs to guide users when navigating the path. The goal is to lead the occupants in a quick evacuation of the building during an emergency, reducing the number of casualties. Training and drills are regular practices used in fire protection methodologies. Training helps occupants acquire knowledge of the spaces and escape routes, while drills simulate an emergency without putting the users at risk. These practices are essential in making occupants aware of their environment and training them for potential casualties [15].

Virtual Environments (VE) are used in different sectors for training purposes when there is a risk of harming the users in real-case situations. For example, VE simulations are used in flight training for pilots. One of the VE applications, the Virtual Reality (VR) provides users with a detailed, controlled, and safe experience that is not achievable in other scenarios. Therefore, the use of VR for safety purposes in the construction sector is highly promising. VR has been employed in workspace planning testing for a construction project in Italy, where the simulation helped identify potential safety hazards and improve the workspace configuration [16]. Additionally, VR has been used to study fire behavior and how to prevent and protect people and facilities [17, 18]. Numerous studies have focused on this subject, analyzing human responses to fire escapes using VR tools for testing and studying the potential applications of virtual reality environments to train construction workers regarding safety concerns [19]. Other studies create mathematical simulations for improving escape paths and use VR to test the final results [20].

The main advantage of using VR for safety training is the ability to simulate a real-case scenario without the risk of physical harm. However, a big disadvantage is that human behavior changes when the person knows there is no real threat in the simulation environment [1].

BIM (Building Information Models) is widely used in the AECO (Architecture, Engineering, Construction, and Operations) industry. BIM creates digital environments to simulate real-world scenarios [21], providing benefits to the industry, including the ability to study the behavior of fire and smoke. BIM data can be used across platforms to simulate scenarios according to the necessity of each study.

Several studies show that the use of BIM models can improve fire safety in built assets [2]. Integrating BIM models with algorithms and applications can create escape paths based on data gathered from the environment [3]. For instance, a study uses a pathfinding algorithm and BIM model to create paths for workers on a construction site to ensure their safety [4]. Another study presents a dynamic escape plan for buildings using fire simulation to create safe escape routes during a fire event [22]. Additionally, a BIM 3D visual model with a mobile guiding system assists firefighters in locating risk areas and planning optimal rescue routes [23].

However, studies linking BIM, VR, and fire safety mostly relate to building inspections or professional training [3, 24, 25]. While many studies focus on the automatic updating and increasing efficiency of escape routes [4, 23], no studies combine the automatic creation of those paths with VR drills. Moreover, a study by [3] found that guidance during escape in an emergency is crucial. The difference in moving routes for the two trial groups when escaping a facility was heavily supported by personal experience. For those without previous knowledge of the building, the moving route was timelier and more complicated. Thus, the necessity of good signage emerges to protect real users during emergencies.

Furthermore, past research correlating VR and means of escape mostly concentrates in China [3, 4, 17, 22, 24, 26], with limited studies conducted in Europe where building age and type may differ significantly. Although these studies showcase innovative technologies, they do not represent a significant technological advancement in advancing means of escape. The systems to manage data from a building in distress may have changed, but guidance for users inside buildings still relies on traditional analog formats. In a study by [27], they present the idea of dynamic signing for fire escape. However, there is still a gap in the literature on this topic, such as exploring the combination of a new type of signage that integrates live data and management, such as through BIM, or the use of virtual simulations such as VR.

In summary, BIM is a valuable technology for the AECO industry that can improve fire safety. Nevertheless, more adaptable systems are necessary for all building types. Moreover, while innovative technologies exist, further research is needed to advance means of escape and improve guidance for users inside buildings during emergencies.

3 Methodology

3.1 Conventional Fire Signage System and the Premise for a Dynamic System

Conventional fire signs and fire escape plans have been the primary means of providing information on evacuation routes and emergency procedures in buildings for many years. However, the conventional fire signage system is becoming outdated and less effective for several reasons.

Firstly, conventional fire signs provide static information that cannot adapt to different emergency scenarios. Many studies are showing that conventional signs may not be visible in certain areas of the building or may not be easily understandable by the occupants in moments of emergency. So, their effectiveness becomes questionable [27].

On the other hand, experimental studies have shown that dynamic signs can be effective in guiding users of any age and highly influencing their direction choices during evacuation. Networked digital escape routes could significantly improve the safety and efficiency of the process [18].

Secondly, a general and static fire escape plan may not provide clear and actionable instructions due to the complexity of the building and the lack of familiarity with it. This can lead to delays and confusion for the occupants and put their lives at risk [27].

The rapid developments of the AECO industry in the design and construction of the built environment demand the same regarding their safety. On these premises and with the technological means available, we built a dynamic fire signage system and simulated it in a VR environment. The concept of dynamic fire signs has been early introduced in various studies [27, 28], but its definition in the standards and regulations is still utterly inferior to the conventional one. In this study, the term dynamic fire sign refers to a fire sign that is able to change its display of indications in real time according to an instant input from a monitoring and signaling system, leading the occupants to the nearest safe exit. In this project the monitoring and signaling system is simulated in the VR environment, along with the fire scene.

3.2 Concept of the VR Tool

In this paper, we present the design and development of a VR tool for simulating emergency evacuation in case of fire, using dynamic path finding to determine the safest and nearest exit. We used a BIM model as the foundation to create the virtual environment for the simulation. A fire signal is placed at every crossing of the pathways in the floor plan. In this paper, we will refer to it as Fire signal cube (FSC). Depending on the number of pathways, each side of the FSC is equipped with signs for every available direction (left, right, forward) and the Stop sign. The FSCs serve as an input to create the database of nodes and the relationships between them for the path finding algorithm. Finally, we created a VR environment to simulate a lifelike evacuation scenario and implement the dynamic pathfinder.

3.3 BIM Model and Creation of the FSC

For this project, a BIM model of the Fraunhofer Italia office environment was used and adapted to simulate the escape scenarios added. The model is an identical representation of our current environment, with a total area of 922 m². It is composed of one floor, eleven rooms, multiple corridors, open areas, two staircases, and two exit doors for evacuation. Autodesk Revit environment was used to build and modify the model during this study.

For the scope of this study, we have made additions to the model by incorporating newly created fire signals that were specifically developed and implemented for this project. They were created as BIM objects containing geometric and non-geometric attributes [29] that serve as input for the node database's pathfinding algorithm to define the navigable spaces. Sixteen FSCs are placed in the model to cover the fire escape evacuation for the whole area (see Fig. 1). Each one of them is placed where two or more paths intersect and where an emergency exit door is present. An ID letter is assigned to each of the FSCs, ranging from A to P. Being positioned in front of each path at every crossing, the fire sign will be highly visible to the occupants and will provide a clear and sole indication of the direction that they must follow. This would lower the level of confusion and stress among the occupants, as they have fewer chances to make independent decisions in a moment of emergency evacuation.

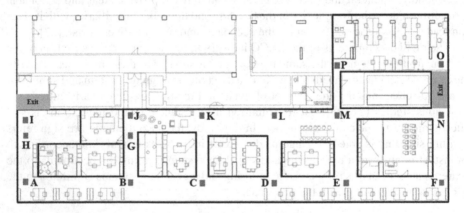

Fig. 1. Placement of the Fire signal cubes (FSC) in the floor plan of the office model.

The FSC has from 1 to 4 active sides, depending on its position in the floor plan, its relations to the pathways, and the exit doors. The sides that face a path or an exit door are active. The sides that face a dead end (ex. a wall) are inactive.

Every side of the cube has the possibility to display four fire signals (stop, forward, left, and right) (see Fig. 2) depending on the location where it is placed, and the emergency situation presented. The FSC is capable of displaying the correct signal according to the input of the path finding algorithm that instantly calculates the safest escape path.

The FSC is created as a BIM object using Autodesk Revit. Three identity parameters are added to it as Revit family parameters: the "ID" parameter, the "neighbor" parameter, and the "exit" parameter. Each of the FSCs has a unique ID, which is a letter from A to P that fills the ID parameter. The adjacent FSCs of each FSC are considered neighbors, and their IDs are inserted in the "neighbor" parameter of each of the FSCs. The "exit" parameter is active in the case that FSC leads directly to an emergency exit door and inactive in every other case. These three parameters are read by the pathfinding algorithm, and according to the correct path, each sign is analyzed and activated. After determining the shortest path, the FSCs activate the signs that direct towards the available neighboring FSC until the exit door is reached.

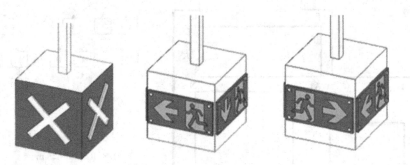

Fig. 2. Illustration of the Fire signal cube (FSC) displaying fire signals in three different evacuation scenarios.

3.4   Path Finding Algorithm

The basis for the dynamic adaptation of the fire signs that indicate the escape routes is the dynamic calculation of paths to the nearest exit. For a real case scenario, a path finder must provide results in real-time. For this reason, we discretized the problem and applied a rather simple search algorithm. The area of interest is discretized with nodes, where each FSC position represents one node. The relationships between the nodes — information about which nodes are neighbors and which nodes exist—is known from the digital building model and accessible to the path finder through a database. The database contains a list of nodes, in which each node has a unique identifier, a list of identifiers of the neighbors, a list of distances to the neighbors and a logical value indicating whether the node is an exit or not. Furthermore, that database is continuously updated in the sense that nodes that are within a certain distance of a fire event are excluded.

The implemented search algorithm takes a node database as input and returns the shortest path to an exit for each node in the form of a sequence of nodes that leads to the closest exit. A Breadth-First Search (BFS) approach [30] was conducted in this study. BFS discovers first all neighbor nodes before moving on to the next level (neighbors of the neighbor) until all nodes that are reachable from the root node are discovered. BFS has the advantage over other algorithms such as Depth-First Search (DFS), where first all nodes in one direction are discovered (all levels of the search tree), that it is guaranteed to find the optimal solution. Therefore, BFS generally takes longer to find a solution. For our specific case of the fire escape route, the implemented BFS algorithm returns all the possible paths to all the existing exits and then calculates the shortest path based on the total length of each path (see Fig. 3). It should be noted that we refer to the length as the physical distance measured in meters, whereas in typical search problems, the length is referred to as the number of steps from one node to another.

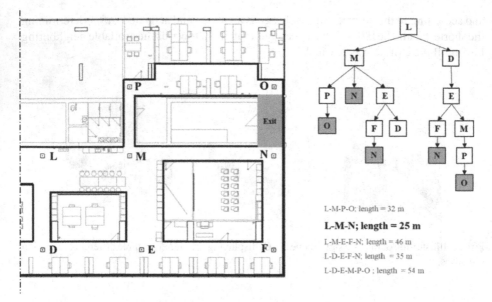

Fig. 3. Illustration of discretization of building floor plan (nodes denoted with capital letters) and example of exit path finding from node "L".

3.5 VR Escape Simulation

In order to create an immersive and lifelike emergency evacuation experience, a VR fire escape simulation has been defined. The VR experience should allow users to navigate through a virtual building and encounter realistic scenarios, such as burning objects, blocked exits, or smoke-filled hallways. To achieve this, the definition of the VR experience is based on a two-step approach, as shown in Fig. 4. Firstly, the realistic scenarios were created using Unity Reflect [31] and Unity (Unity Real-Time Development Platform) [32]. Unity Reflect can integrate seamlessly with multiple design tools, such as Autodesk Revit. This integration allows both the BIM model and associated data to be imported into Unity, which can then be used to create immersive VR simulations. Using this approach, the case-study's BIM model, including fire signage and related data, was imported into Unity. Afterwards, fire and smoke elements and path finding functionality were integrated into the model. The pathfinding algorithm was integrated by including C# scripts in the Unity project. During simulation the path finding algorithm is executed in every frame. This enables the identification of the safest evacuation paths based on the location of fire and smoke elements during run time. These elements were created using the *ParticleSystem* Unity component. It allows moving flames and smoke to be simulated, thus creating a lifelike fire scenario. In addition, the location of fire and smoke elements can be modified to simulate different fire scenarios.

Secondly the navigation system was defined using the Cyberith Virtualizer ELITE 2 [33] and the HP Reverb G2 VR-Glasses [34]. Cyberith Virtualizer ELITE 2 is a VR locomotion device that allows users to walk and run within a virtual environment. It has sensors that detect the user's movements and translate them into corresponding actions in the virtual environment, so that the user can react to a fire scenario in a more intuitive and realistic way. The locomotion device was integrated by including the *CVirtPlayerController Prefab* player object into the Unity project. The *CVirtPlayerController Prefab* consists of an abstract user representation and a set of functionalities for moving. Finally, the HP Reverb G2 VR-Glasses was set to work in conjunction with the locomotion device. This was done by integrating the *TrackedPoseDriver* component into the Unity project. In this way, users' movements, such as the position and orientation of the head, are tracked in real-time and translated into corresponding actions in the virtual environment. By immersing users in a realistic virtual environment, the VR-Glasses allow users to visualize the fire scenario while moving around using Cyberith Virtualizer ELITE 2.

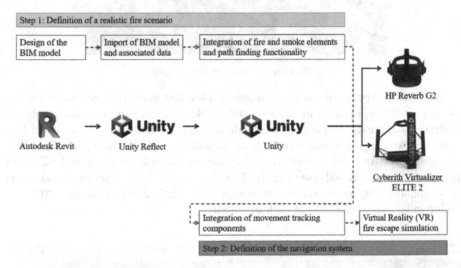

Fig. 4. The two-step approach for VR fire escape simulation definition.

4   Results and Analysis

We successfully developed a dynamic fire signage system that was implemented in a VR environment. The system is capable of changing its display of indications in real-time based on an instant input from a controlling central system, leading occupants to the nearest safe exit. In comparison to traditional signals, the dynamic fire signs were found to be easier to spot and follow, providing more certainty for the user that they are following the safe path to the exit. Overall, our study demonstrates the potential for dynamic fire signage systems to improve building safety and enhance the evacuation experience for occupants.

During this study, we created and virtually implemented a new dynamic fire sign and signage system. In this paper, we referred to the new fire sign as the FSC, which was created as a BIM object. It later served as input for the node database and pathfinding algorithm used to define the navigable spaces in the environment in which that we tested the escape scenarios. Sixteen FSCs were placed throughout the model, strategically positioned at each crossing where two or more paths intersected and where emergency exit doors were located. Each FSC was assigned an ID letter from A to P and was placed in front of each path at every crossing, providing a clear and visible indication of the direction that occupants must follow (see Fig. 5).

Fig. 5. Illustration of the FSC in Unity.

The FSCs had between one and four active sides, depending on their location in the floor plan and their proximity to pathways and exit doors. Each active side was capable of displaying four fire signals (stop, forward, left, and right), which were selected according to the input of the pathfinding algorithm to calculate the safest escape path. The FSCs were able to activate the correct signs that directed towards neighboring FSCs until the exit door was reached. (see Fig. 6) This approach reduced confusion and stress for occupants during an emergency evacuation, particularly as they may have difficulty making independent decisions in such situations.

Fig. 6. Illustration of the Fire signal cube (FSC) in Unity, displaying how the FSC changes the displayed signal during fire emergency.

The pathfinding algorithm developed in this study has the advantage of being easily applicable to any BIM model without requiring significant modifications or interventions. This is due to the fact that the algorithm is based solely on the locations of the fire signs, which serve as nodes for the pathfinding process. As a result, this approach can be used in an authoring environment with minimal effort, as long as the fire signs are placed according to the evacuation principles and the exit doors are defined. This makes the algorithm highly adaptable and potentially useful in a wide range of scenarios where emergency evacuation planning is required.

5 Discussion

5.1 Conclusions

The aim of this study was to develop and implement a dynamic fire signage system in a VR environment. In this section, we present the results of the implementation phase and discuss the effectiveness of the system in guiding occupants towards safe exits during fire emergencies. The concept of dynamic fire signs has been introduced in previous studies, but its definition in standards and regulations is still inferior to conventional signage. Our system utilizes real-time input from a controlling central system to provide occupants with clear and easy-to-follow signage leading them to the nearest safe exit. The purpose of this section is to present the outcomes of the implementation and evaluate the effectiveness of the dynamic fire signage system. Additionally, we discussed the level of certainty that the system provides for users following the safe path to the exit.

Multiple human users (see Fig. 7) actively engaged in trialing the system in the virtual environment created. Various fire scenarios were simulated for each case. It resulted that the users were effectively navigated to the secure exit in all instances through the guidance provided by the FCS system.

In this case, VR proved to be an effective and successful way to experiment with fire evacuation scenarios without the need for creating a real case scene, which can be both costly and risky. By using VR technology, we created a safe and controlled environment to simulate various emergency situations and assess the effectiveness of different evacuation strategies. This approach can lead to more efficient and accurate evacuation plans and ultimately improve the safety of occupants in the event of a fire.

Fig. 7. Human users trying the dynamic fire signage system evacuation routes in the VR environment.

5.2 Limitations

Regarding the implemented pathfinding algorithm, there are some limitations and potential optimizations. Even though the implemented BFS algorithm is guaranteed to find the shortest path, there are more time-efficient algorithms that could be investigated as alternatives. For example, A* or Alpha-Beta [35] could be more efficient in terms of computing time.

5.3 Future Prospects for Implementation

Although the dynamic fire signage system in a VR environment proved to be effective in guiding the human users towards a safe exit, it is important to note that this is just the first step in implementing the system in a real-world scenario. As such, it is necessary to test the system with the participation of multiple users simultaneously and evaluate its effectiveness in guiding crowds towards safe exits during an emergency situation. This would require the exploration of dynamic escape routes and the coordination of multiple individuals in a high-stress environment. The results of such testing will provide valuable insights into the feasibility of the system and its ability to improve the safety of building occupants in emergency situations.

In order to advance the study, additional assessments will be conducted to quantify and gather data for comparative analysis with respect to a conventional fire evacuation scenario. Participants would be positioned to experience both the dynamic signage system and the traditional signage system, allowing for the measurement and comparison of evacuation times.

Since operating within a VR environment, it is imperative to assess the user experience from a human and psychological perspective, aiming to gather their feedback for evaluating the quality of the simulated environment and identifying opportunities for design enhancement. Subsequent investigations will be carried out to evaluate the intensity of the users' experience, their emotional responses, and the extent of confusion encountered. This assessment will be accomplished through meticulous external observations of their experiences and the administration of questionnaires subsequent to the tests. The collected data will be further analysed with the scope of improving the user virtual environment.

In addition, the study can be taken further to integrate it with IOT sensors and test it in real case scenarios.

Author Contributions Statement. O.B worked on the BIM model and creation of FSC, M.A worked on the literature research, J.E worked on the pathfinding algorithm, I.D.B worked on the VR simulation, E.N reviewed the manuscript, D.S and D.M supervised the development.

References

1. Kinateder, M., et al.: Virtual Reality for Fire Evacuation Research. Presented at the 2014 Federated Conference on Computer Science and Information Systems, pp. 313–321 (2014). https://doi.org/10.15439/2014F94
2. Malagnino, A., Corallo, A., Lazoi, M., Zavarise, G.: The digital transformation in fire safety engineering over the past decade through building information modelling: a review. Fire Technol. **58**(6), 3317–3351 (2022). https://doi.org/10.1007/s10694-022-01313-3
3. Ma, G., Wu, Z.: BIM-based building fire emergency management: Combining building users' behavior decisions. Autom. Constr. **109**, 102975 (2020). https://doi.org/10.1016/j.autcon.2019.102975
4. Kim, K., Lee, Y.-C.: Automated generation of daily evacuation paths in 4D BIM. Appl. Sci. **9**(9), 1789 (2019). https://doi.org/10.3390/app9091789
5. Corelli, F., Battegazzorre, E., Strada, F., Bottino, A., Cimellaro, G.P.: Assessing the usability of different virtual reality systems for firefighter training. In: Proceedings of the 15th International Joint Conference on Computer Vision, Imaging and Computer Graphics Theory and Applications, pp. 146–153. SCITEPRESS - Science and Technology Publications, Valletta, Malta (2020). https://doi.org/10.5220/0008962401460153
6. Sun, Q., Turkan, Y.: A BIM-based simulation framework for fire safety management and investigation of the critical factors affecting human evacuation performance. Adv. Eng. Inform. **44**, 101093 (2020). https://doi.org/10.1016/j.aei.2020.101093
7. Zheng, H., Zhang, S., Zhu, J., Zhu, Z., Fang, X.: Evacuation in buildings based on BIM: taking a fire in a university library as an example. Int. J. Environ. Res. Public. Health **19**(23), 16254 (2022). https://doi.org/10.3390/ijerph192316254
8. Athanasopoulou, A., Sciarretta, F., Sousa, M.L., Dimova, S.: The Status and Needs for Implementation of Fire Safety Engineering Approach in Europe. Publications Office of the European Union, Luxembourg (2023)
9. Osácar, A., Trueba, J.B.E., Meacham, B.: Evaluation of the legal framework for building fire safety regulations in Spain. Buildings **11**(2), 51 (2021). https://doi.org/10.3390/buildings11020051

10. Sheridan, L., Visscher, H., Meijer, F.: Building regulations in Europe. Presented at the CIB-CTBUH International Conference on Tall Buildings, Malaysia (2003)
11. British Standards Institution, BS 9999: 2017 - Fire safety in the design, management and use of residential buildings – Code of Practice, BSI British Standards (2017). https://doi.org/10.3403/30314118
12. Kobes, M., Helsloot, I., de Vries, B., Post, J.G.: Building safety and human behaviour in fire: a literature review. Fire Saf. J. **45**(1), 1–11 (2010). https://doi.org/10.1016/j.firesaf.2009.08.005
13. Ding, N., Zhang, H., Chen, T.: Experimental study of egress selection behavior between stairs and elevators during high-rise building evacuation. Fire Technol. **55**(5), 1649–1670 (2019). https://doi.org/10.1007/s10694-019-00822-y
14. Olander, J., Ronchi, E., Lovreglio, R., Nilsson, D.: Dissuasive exit signage for building fire evacuation. Appl. Ergon. **59**, 84–93 (2017). https://doi.org/10.1016/j.apergo.2016.08.029
15. Jeon, G.-Y., Na, W.-J., Hong, W.-H., Lee, J.-K.: Influence of design and installation of emergency exit signs on evacuation speed. J. Asian Archit. Build. Eng. **18**(2), 104–111 (2019). https://doi.org/10.1080/13467581.2019.1599897
16. Getuli, V., Capone, P., Bruttini, A., Isaac, S.: BIM-based immersive Virtual Reality for construction workspace planning: a safety-oriented approach. Autom. Constr. **114**, 103160 (2020). https://doi.org/10.1016/j.autcon.2020.103160
17. Cha, M., Han, S., Lee, J., Choi, B.: A virtual reality-based fire training simulator integrated with fire dynamics data. Fire Saf. J. **50**, 12–24 (2012). https://doi.org/10.1016/j.firesaf.2012.01.004
18. Kwee-Meier, S.T., Mertens, A., Jeschke, S.: Recommendations for the design of digital escape route signage from an age-differentiated experimental study. Fire Saf. J. **110**, 102888 (2019). https://doi.org/10.1016/j.firesaf.2019.102888
19. Bhoir, S., Esmaeili, B.: State-of-the-Art review of virtual reality environment applications in construction safety. In: AEI 2015, pp. 457–468. American Society of Civil Engineers, Milwaukee, Wisconsin (2015). https://doi.org/10.1061/9780784479070.040
20. Lorusso, P., De Iuliis, M., Marasco, S., Domaneschi, M., Cimellaro, G.P., Villa, V.: Fire emergency evacuation from a school building using an evolutionary virtual reality platform. Buildings **12**(2), 223 (2022). https://doi.org/10.3390/buildings12020223
21. I. 19650 ISO. Organization and digitization of information about buildings and civil engineering works, including building information modelling (BIM). Information management using building information modelling. Part 1, Concepts and principles. London: British Standards Institution (2018)
22. Wang, J., Wei, G., Dong, X.: A dynamic fire escape path planning method with BIM. J. Ambient Intell. Humaniz. Comput. **12**(11), 10253–10265 (2021). https://doi.org/10.1007/s12652-020-02794-2
23. Cheng, M.-Y., Chiu, K.-C., Hsieh, Y.-M., Yang, I.-T., Chou, J.-S.: Development of BIM-Based Real-time Evacuation and Rescue System for Complex Buildings. Presented at the 33th International Symposium on Automation and Robotics in Construction, Auburn, AL, USA (2016). https://doi.org/10.22260/ISARC2016/0120
24. Yan, F., et al.: Interactive WebVR visualization for online fire evacuation training. Multimed. Tools Appl. **79**(41–42), 31541–31565 (2020). https://doi.org/10.1007/s11042-020-08863-0
25. Zhang, D., Zhang, J., Xiong, H., Cui, Z., Lu, D.: Taking advantage of collective intelligence and BIM-based virtual reality in fire safety inspection for commercial and public buildings. Appl. Sci. **9**(23), 5068 (2019). https://doi.org/10.3390/app9235068
26. Tang, Y., et al.: BIM-based safety design for emergency evacuation of metro stations. Autom. Constr. **123**, 103511 (2021). https://doi.org/10.1016/j.autcon.2020.103511
27. Wong, H.Y., Zhang, Y., Huang, X.: A Review of Dynamic Directional Exit Signage: Challenges & Perspectives (2022). https://doi.org/10.13140/RG.2.2.11437.97761

28. Olyazadeh, R.: Evaluating Dynamic Signage for Emergency Evacuation using an Immersive Video Environment (2013). https://doi.org/10.13140/RG.2.1.4464.7282
29. Barbini, A., Malacarne, G., Massari, G., Monizza, G.P., Matt, D.T.: BIM objects library for information exchange in public works: the use of proprietary and open formats. Presented at the BIM 2019, pp. 269–280. Seville, Spain (2019). https://doi.org/10.2495/BIM190231
30. Cormen, T.H., Leiserson, C.E., Rivest, R.L., Stein, C.: Introduction to Algorithms, 4th edn. The MIT Press, Cambridge, Massachusett (2022)
31. Unity Technologies, "Unity Reflect," Unity. https://unity.com/products/unity-reflect. Accessed 30 April 2023
32. Unity Technologies, "Unity Real-Time Development Platform," Unity. https://unity.com. Accessed 30 April 2023
33. Cyberith, "Virtualizer ELITE 2 I Cyberith Virtualizer." https://www.cyberith.com/virtualizer-elite. Accessed 30 April 2023
34. HP Development Company, "HP Reverb G2 VR Headset." https://www.hp.com/it-it/vr/rev erb-g2-vr-headset. Accessed 30 April 2023
35. Heineman, G.T., Selkow, S., Pollice, G.: Algorithms in a Nutshell. O'Reilly, Beijing, Sebastopol [Calif.] (2009)

Effortlessly Populating Immersive Training Simulations with Background Characters

Jean-Benoît Culié[1,3]($\boxtimes$), Stéphane Sanchez[2,3], and David Panzoli[1,3]

[1] INU Jean-François Champollion, 81000 Albi, France
[2] University of Toulouse Capitole, 31200 Toulouse, France
[3] IRIT UMR 5505, 31400 Toulouse, France
Jean-Benoit.Culie@irit.fr

Abstract. Immersive training simulations engage users in compelling environments with interactive and pedagogically meaningful activities. Integrating virtual characters in these simulations has proven highly beneficial, especially in technical contexts where social interactions are key in the training. Although most of the research on the topic endeavours to model tutoring agents endowed with natural interaction, cognitive, or even emotional abilities, there is a more modest yet widespread need for background characters with lower capabilities but higher ease of integration on the developer's behalf. In this paper, we demonstrate how informed environments, which already constitute an appropriate framework for designing interactive environments, can be leveraged for simulating the realistic behaviour of background characters, even allowing for scripted events and scenario control during the training session. The model presented in the paper, called CRITS (CRowds for Immersive Training Simulations), has been applied to a large-scale crisis management scenario and has produced satisfying results in terms of the behaviours obtained and ease of integration.

Keywords: Immersive training · Virtual agents · Informed environment · Smart objects

1 Introduction

Technical training in Virtual Reality (VR) environments, usually referred to as "Immersive Learning" gains in popularity within prestigious companies or institutions for which efficiently training employees to technical tasks is key. Although most of the core learning activities may focus on operating technical machinery or following protocols, social aspects, manifested by the presence of public, users or employees in the environment, represents an important part of the training, especially in socio-technical systems where risks often arise from the collective nature of the activity rather than individual mistakes. Collaborative Virtual Environments for Training (CVET) typically resort to animated characters to train learners in complex socio-technical contexts such as surgery, aeronautics or industry in general, sales and customer relationship management,

L. T. De Paolis et al. (Eds.): XR Salento 2023, LNCS 14218, pp. 172–183, 2023.
https://doi.org/10.1007/978-3-031-43401-3_11

etc. Non-playing characters may assume different roles, ranging from virtual collaborators [1] working "hand in hand" with the learners to personal assistants [2] endowed with conversational abilities or even the capacity, for pedagogical purposes, to demonstrate and explain their own actions and decisions [3]. To that end, a variety of existing, generic and reusable AI techniques [4,5] have been identified over the years. Nevertheless, designing the behaviours of these virtual autonomous agents remains a complex task which requires experienced designers and programmers. Besides, the models that are used for architecting what is known as the action selection process of a virtual character (meaning the algorithms whose role is to replicate with a variable level of realism the mental processes of a human being) are still cumbersome and intricate.

Yet, some use-cases do not necessitate the agents to team-up with the human players or have conversations. A crowd of virtual characters walking throughout the environment can fulfil the needs of the training, either for the sake of populating the area with lively animation or to help the human players comprehend the purpose of each location or piece of equipment inside the environment. This is particularly the case with cultural heritage VR applications for instance [6]. Such background characters would not be regarded for their ability to conduct complex tasks on their own, make decisions, have conversations or meaningful interactions with the human players. In the contrary, successful design criteria would include ease of integration, adaptivity to a highly dynamic environment (partially due to the presence of human players interacting) and plausibility with respect to the educational role of the environment.

The following sections describe a software architecture that enables an immersive training environment to be populated with background characters fitting to these criteria without any more engineering than what is already required to make the environment interactive for the human player(s).

2   Generic Virtual Crowds for Immersive Training Simulations (CRITS)

The objective of CRITS is to provide a generic virtual crowd for immersive training simulations. This crowd is composed of virtual humanoid agents which are expected to behave autonomously in the environment in order to populate the scene, bring some life to it and give a sense of the ongoing activity inside the area. The behaviours of the agents are described as "plausible", in the sense that human players would not be able to detect anomalies or discrepancies affecting their feeling of immersion in the environment, as opposed to "realistic", which would suppose to guarantee a certain conformity of the observed behaviour to reality (i.e. to real humans acting in similar situations). More prosaically, the agents provide a convincing background that adds to the immersion of the scene, even actively participating in it by taking part in the scenario, but the degree of fidelity of their reactions or their behaviour does not allow them to be given a more important role. For example, they are not able to simulate crowd effects in a panic situation or to assist the learner in a collaborative task. That said, the virtual agents adapt their behaviour dynamically to changes occurring in the environment, reflecting actions from the players and therefore playing a role in the scenario, albeit minor.

The model and the processes that are described are generic, which means they are designed to adapt to any type of situation. In the following sections, the features of CRITS will take as illustration a banking agency populated with agents with multiple roles : customers, employees (customer advisor, teller) and distinctive agents with scripted behaviours in order to unfold the scenario.

2.1   Overarching Principles

The basic principles of the agent control mechanism is inspired by the Sims, as originally designed by Will Wright in the late 1990s. Before being introduced into the scene, each agent is provided with a list of tasks to be performed as well as a set of needs, and finally attributes influencing the decision making. Table 1 exemplifies tasks, needs and attributes that were used in the banking agency scenario. Each item from the lists can be drawn randomly or predefined in a configuration file. Once introduced into the scene, an agent is programmed to fulfil its needs and to perform the tasks it is assigned to, when it gets a chance to, by interacting with the objects in its field of vision, or by actively exploring the environment. The random initialization of the list of tasks as well as the variability of the profiles (needs, attributes) is the reason that makes all the agents behave differently and follow each a different routine, in spite of sharing the same simple behaviour program.

Table 1. Agents in CRITS are provided with tasks and needs. Their decisions are mostly contextual, depending on tasks and needs to be fulfilled, yet influenced by personal attributes.

Tasks	Needs	Attributes
• withdraw money	• thirst	• sociability
• book an appointment	• hunger	• humor
• request a loan	• tiredness	• fear
		• courage

In CRITS, the interactions between objects and agents constitute the basis of character crowd activity. For this reason, the objects available in the environment are more than static or animated 3D models. They also embed semantic properties that define the actions they make possible in the environment (called "affordances"), and which are proposed to the agents, and the scripts that describe how these interactions take place once engaged. For example, the cash dispenser meets the need for withdrawing money. The illustration in Fig. 1 gives an overview of how objects expose (or broadcast) their affordances to every agent. From the interaction opportunities collected from the environment, and with respect to its affected tasks, needs and attributes, the agent is in a position to select which interaction to favour. This process, called action selection, is described in next Sect. 2.3. In addition, the interactions proposed by an object can take into account the character traits (attributes) of the agents. For example, the cash dispenser does cater for sociability, whereas the counter does require from the agent a higher level of sociability. Still, both share the same goal : to allow one agent to withdraw money. In the illustration in Fig. 1, the agent pictured is tasked to withdraw money : availability and personal preferences towards sociability will elicit the interaction with the ATM.

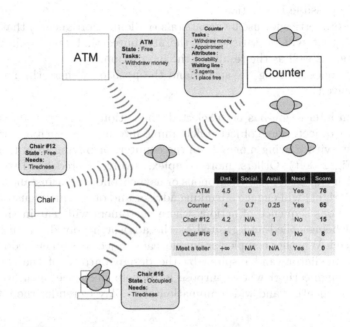

	Dist.	Social.	Avail.	Need	Score
ATM	4.5	0	1	Yes	76
Counter	4	0.7	0.25	Yes	65
Chair #12	4.2	N/A	1	No	15
Chair #16	5	N/A	0	No	8
Meet a teller	+∞	N/A	N/A	Yes	0

Fig. 1. The affordances collected from the surrounding smart objects are constantly re-sorted by relevant with respect to the agent's assigned tasks, needs and personal attributes. Selecting an interaction is then easy as picking the most relevant available one.

2.2 Smart Objects

The objects of the environment constitute the essence of the know-how developed in CRITS. Smart objects are widely used in games, simulations and by extension immersive learning applications. In addition to breaking the complexity of the code-base, they also help reducing the critically time-consuming design process by easily sharing the interactive objects from one project to another [7]. In CRITS's logic, the environment is built by the designer from a library of ready-to-use objects that are compatible with virtual agents.

Such objects that encapsulate a graphic representation along with interaction abilities are called "smart objects" as they encapsulate data, code for multiple related behaviours and embed intelligence in the environment. They are necessary since the complexity in the behaviours of the non-playable characters (NPC) has increased in the past years, making it difficult to maintain the script code-base. Smart objects allow to break the NPC's behaviours into smaller manageable pieces [8]. In practice, in game engines like Unity3D that are nowadays widely used for assembling immersive training tools, each smart object comes as a prefab which embeds everything that is necessary for its usage in the environment:

- Graphic representations of the object, including animations that visually depict the possible interactions.
- Semantic properties for use by agents (also called "affordances") that describe the needs that will be satisfied or the attributes that are required for the interaction, as well as the results of the interaction.
- Semantic zones defining the spaces and the positions where the interactions will be played.

When an interaction has been selected, the actions to trigger are controlled by the smart object. Some objects offer simple interactions, such as sitting on a chair to rest, withdrawing money from the counter, or buying from the vending machine (Fig. 2, left). Others, more complex, involve a predefined sequence of actions which can either be synchronous or asynchronous. For instance, the loan desk (Fig. 2, right) will engage a banking adviser and one or more customers into an asynchronous sequence of actions where customers will seat in the waiting space, until being called and greeted by the advisor, received for an interview and then freed. Whether complex or simple, each object has an embedded script, acting as a mediator (and inspired by the design pattern of the same name in software engineering) whose purpose is to help both the agent(s) and the object communicating and which animation(s) to play to render the interaction graphically.

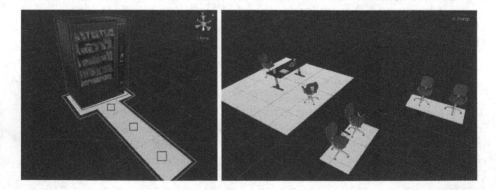

Fig. 2. (Left) A food dispenser with interaction slots and waiting line positions. (Right) A loan application desk with the associated spaces (chairs) for the reception of the adviser, the customer, and the seats for the customers waiting.

2.3   Action Selection

A few models are fit to implement decision making, that is to orchestrate the agent's routine consisting of seeking in the environment ways to fulfil its goals and needs. Finite State Machines (FSM) represent an easy way to handle the complexity of behaviours, although their main problem is scalability, unlike Behavior Trees (BT) which are a practical scalable solution [9] yet more complex. BTs can also be based on Q-Learning algorithms to determine the best action that can be achieved based on an expected reward value [10]. However, since we don't need the deep level of complexity allowed by BTs, we decided to implement an FSM combined with a set of decision rules for each state. The FSM implemented in CRITS, illustrated in Fig. 3, is composed of 5 states which are common to all agents, regardless of their job. Those are named *Idle*, *Tasks*, *Waiting*, *Execute-Task* and *ExecuteScenario*. They constitute the core of the agent's behaviour. For the purpose of the illustration in a banking agency, there will be an armed agent in the bank as a part of an unexpected event. This adds 2 more states to the agents, the state *Emergency* which is used by customers and employees once the threat is spotted, then the state *Aggressive* which is used by the armed agent in the bank.

The objective of an agent is to achieve the tasks assigned to him. To do this, as Fig. 4 illustrates, the agent, having knowledge of its environment, will look for an object which allows him to perform one of his tasks in order to interact with it, which is done by the state *Tasks*. If an item cannot be used immediately, the agent will check if it can stand in line to use it. If the waiting line is full, the agent will look for another task from its list while waiting for

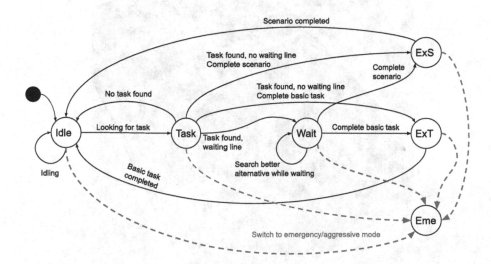

Fig. 3. The FSM used in CRITS features 6 states : Idle; Task, Waiting, Execute Task (ExT), Execute Scenario (ExS) and Emergency/Aggressive (Eme), a specific state reachable from any other state and triggering a specific behaviour depending on the agent's role in the simulation : causing a mayhem, or reacting to mayhem by escaping or fear.

a more favorable condition to undertake the action (freeing up a place in the waiting line, discovery of a new object allowing completion of the task). This part is done by the state *Waiting*. If none of the tasks are feasible, the agent will go for a walk, use his phone, or try to fulfill a need by looking for an object to interact with, such as sitting in a chair if they are tired, done by the state *Idle*. A task can either be a basic task (e.g. withdrawing money at the ATM) or a scenario task (e.g. Request a loan.). Since they are completely different, they are also executed in a different way, this is why there are 2 states, respectively *ExecuteTask* and *ExecuteScenario*, which are responsible of the correct execution of the selected task. When an agent has emptied the list of tasks assigned to him, it leaves the scene and is replaced by a new agent. To ensure the consistency of the tasks assigned to an agent, the tasks are grouped by profession. An agent is first assigned to a profession (customer, customer advisor, receptionist, armed robber, etc.) then receives a list of tasks corresponding to this profession.

The adaptability of behaviours is highlighted when an unexpected event is triggered. For instance, in case of the presence within the bank of one or more armed agents, fear will be propagated between agents, either customers or employees, and they will dynamically adopt new behaviours in response to the perception of the threat. Doing so, an agent who is not aware of the unexpected event will continue doing his task until it realises that something is going wrong. The reaction of each agent depends on its attributes (here: fear/courage) and the reactions observed are thus very varied: some try to flee the scene or to hide, while others will remain on the ground, paralyzed.

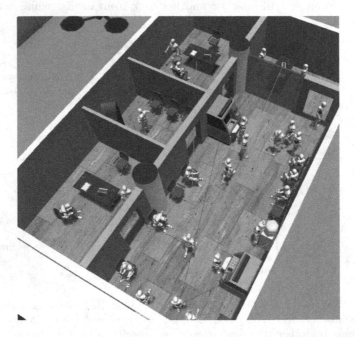

Fig. 4. Green lines represent the communication between an agent and an object. Purple lines show the object selected by the agent once the decision making process is achieved. (Color figure online)

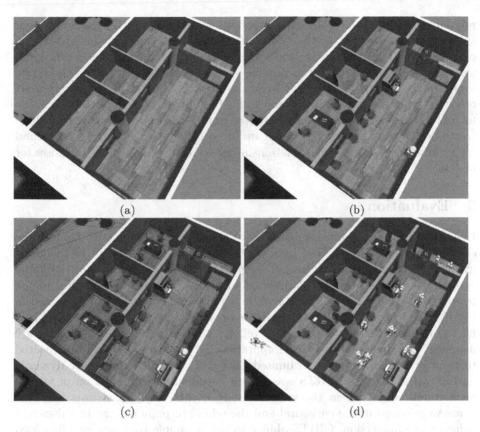

Fig. 5. The process of adding a crowd of characters to a training environment is facilitated by the use of smart objects, as described in the 4 following steps. (a) The modeler starts with an empty environment representing the location inside which the training is set to happen. (b) Smart objects are added from an existing library, and arranged in the building. (c) The navigation script is run to calculate the semantic zones within the building. Those will later restrain the coming and goings of the characters depending on their respective roles: blue zones are public, pink ones are restricted to bank staff (d) The environment is ready for welcoming at runtime a crowd of virtual characters, some designated to work in the branch, others to act as customers. (Color figure online)

2.4   Game Engine Integration

CRITS integrates very well in Unity3D engine and exploits several built-in features. Firstly, smart objects use the ability to bundle *prefab* (i.e. prefabricated objects) embedding multiple different components like graphical representations, animations or scripts. Secondly, Unity's integrated 3D scene editor lets designers compose the training environment by simply arranging objects in a graphical and simplified manner. Lastly, Unity's integrated *Navmesh* (AI navigation mesh) calculator script has been enhanced with the ability to compute navigation areas related to activities and jobs, so that agents would occupy the space in a consistent way with respect to their occupation and/or the context: for instance, a customer could not walk in an office uninvited, unless there is an emergency and some furniture in the office can provide shelter. Apart from running the script every time the environment has been modified, adding and arranging smart objects within the pre-designed model of a building or a location is all it takes for obtaining a lively crowd of characters populating the scene. Figure 5 illustrates how a bank branch can be set up in no time to serve as the background for training users to customer relationship or security management purposes for instance.

3   Evaluation

EGCERSIS [11] is a multi-user immersive environment designed to train learners to crisis management and improve their preparedness toward forthcoming hypothetical crisis. Multiple learners engage in a large-scale scenario combining several co-occurring threats at different locations (a fire in a cathedral in the town of Albi and a terrorist outbreak in a public school nearby, as depicted in Fig. 6). The scenario relies on a coordinated response from the authorities, played by the learners (firefighters, security officers, etc.). Background characters are necessary for the situations to be appraised by the learners who are expected to react and make decisions in limited time and cope with the highly dynamic nature of the training. CRITS was chosen to integrate a population of virtual background characters in the various environments. Civilian visitors and students were added in the cathedral and the school to populate the premises and enhance the immersion. CRITS ability to define simple routines was also used to script the specific behaviours of some teammate firefighters (protect artworks in the cathedral) and the terrorists themselves (wander aggressively following a pattern).

This experiment allowed us to evaluate different factors like ease-of-integration on the developer's end, and plausibility and coherence of the virtual characters as assessed by the players. Both environments were furnished

Fig. 6. (Left) Civilians being evacuated from the *Sainte-Cécile cathedral* in Albi (France) by firefighters. (Right) A terrorist attack where one or more armed terrorists are threatening people at the École Mines-Télécom of Albi-Carmaux (France).

with smart objects (artworks in the cathedral, common furniture in the school, etc.) so as to enable the CRITS background characters to move around purposefully while showing enough behavioural variability to convey a feeling of convincingness. The detection of a threat during the scenario (fire, terrorists) yielded coherent reactions such as escaping or freezing out of fear. Players interviewed after the experience unanimously declared the presence of the background characters was undoubtedly a benefit for immersion and for better understanding the situation. EGCERSIS developers confirmed that integrating CRITS was straightforward, as it merely implies adding to the scene scripted furniture that was provided to them, or adapting pre-existing objects to CRITS requirements.

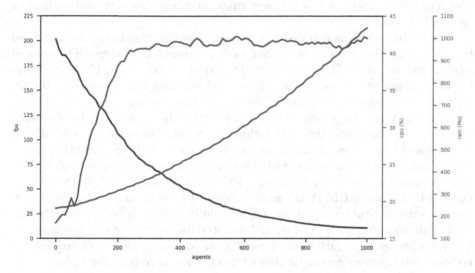

Fig. 7. CRITS performance under optimal conditions. Tests were performed on an Intel I7-11370H processor @3.30Ghz, with an NVidia RTX 3050-Ti GPU and 32 GB of RAM.

In terms of performance, CRITS is expected to have a minimal footprint on CPU usage, as most of the processing time has to be allocated to the training simulation and the user's interactions. Moreover, CRITS should be able to cope with a substantial number of characters. A performance benchmarking test was conducted to evaluate how CRITS would perform when scaling up to several hundred agents. The results are summarized as a graph in Fig. 7. CPU usage is low up to 200 characters and seems to plateau when increasing the number of agents (as reported by Windows 10 task manager). Number of frames per seconds (fps) degrades steadily and starts to be problematical passed 4 to 5 hundred agents, which is far beyond necessary in most cases. As expected, memory footprint grows with the number of agents. This could be improved by switching to a more modern system, as discussed in future work section.

4 Conclusion

In this paper, we have proposed a tool, named CRITS (CRowds for Immersive Training Simulations), which facilitates the implementation of a living background of animated humanoid characters in an immersive training environment. Running in Unity 3D, CRITS allows to easily setup a crowd of virtual autonomous agents capable of populating the environment or even to participate to pedagogical activities through the scripting of actions or behaviours of one or more entities. Scriptable agents can be useful when scenario events must be conveyed by means of people's actions, like making a mistake or creating a hazard at a specific moment. CRITS's agents are based on a Finite-state Machine (FSM) and a set of decision rules, allowing diversity and realism in agent's behaviours.

The evaluation demonstrated how informed environments can be leveraged for simulating the realistic behaviour of background characters. The ease of implementation of CRITS in a Unity 3D project allows to quickly setup a living background as well as creating simple and complex tasks, even allowing for scripted events and scenario control during the training session.

As future work, the priority is to upgrade CRITS by using Unity DOTS which is a multi-threaded Data-Oriented Technology Stack. Doing so, it would allow a better scalability by improving performance, although CRITS currently keeps a decent frame rate (above 60 fps) with 300+ active agents on the scene (cf. Fig. 7). Another priority would be to replace the FSM by a BT (cf. Sect. 2.3). Despite the fact the FSM used in CRITS allows the degree of freedom needed by the agents, there is some limitation to this model, especially with scripted agents where it is difficult to allow both freedom and scripted behaviours simultaneously. By using BT, scripted agents would benefit from the same degree of freedom as non-scripted agent as well as be allowed to execute more complex tasks.

Acknowledgment. This research has been funded by Toulouse Tech Transfer's technological development program. The authors also wish to thank Pr Frédérick Benaben and the folks at the CGI working on the EGCERSIS project for giving us the opportunity of a full-scale integration of CRITS.

References

1. Panzoli, D., Lelardeux, C.P., Galaup, M., Lagarrigue, P., Minville, V., Lubrano, V.: Interaction and communication in an immersive learning game: the challenges of modelling real-time collaboration in a virtual operating room. In: Ma, M., Oikonomou, A. (eds.) Serious Games and Edutainment Applications, pp. 147–186. Springer, Cham (2017). https://doi.org/10.1007/978-3-319-51645-5_7
2. Lopez, T., et al.: Collaborative virtual training with physical and communicative autonomous agents. Computer Animation Virtual Worlds 25(3–4), 485–493 (2014)
3. Harbers, M., van den Bosch, K., Meyer, J.-J.: A methodology for developing self-explaining agents for virtual training. In: Dastani, M., El Fallah Segrouchni, A., Leite, J., Torroni, P. (eds.) LADS 2009. LNCS (LNAI), vol. 6039, pp. 168–182. Springer, Heidelberg (2010). https://doi.org/10.1007/978-3-642-13338-1_10

4. Westera, W., et al.: Artificial intelligence moving serious gaming: presenting reusable game AI components. Educ. Inf. Technol. **25**(1), 351–380 (2020)
5. Sanselone, M., Sanchez, S., Sanza, C., Panzoli, D., Duthen, Y.: Constrained control of non-playing characters using monte Carlo tree search. In: 2014 IEEE Conference on Computational Intelligence and Games, pp. 1–8. IEEE (2014)
6. Panzoli, D., et al.: A level of interaction framework for exploratory learning with characters in virtual environments. Intell. Comput. Graph. **321**, 123–143 (2010)
7. Getuli, V., Capone, P., Bruttini, A., Sorbi, T.: A smart objects library for BIM-based construction site and emergency management to support mobile VR safety training experiences. Construct. Innov.(2021)
8. Černý, M., Plch, T., Marko, M., Gemrot, J., Ondráček, P., Brom, C.: Using behavior objects to manage complexity in virtual worlds. IEEE Trans. Comput. Intell. AI Games **9**(2), 166–180 (2016)
9. Sekhavat, Y.A.: Behavior trees for computer games. Int. J. Artif. Intell. Tools **26**(02), 1730001 (2017)
10. Zhu, X.: Behavior tree design of intelligent behavior of non-player character (NPC) based on unity3D. J. Intell. Fuzzy Syst. **37**(5), 6071–6079 (2019)
11. Congès, A., Evain, A., Chabiron, O., Graham, C., Benaben, F.: Virtual reality to train for crisis management. In: ISCRAM 2020–17th International Conference on Information Systems for Crisis Response and Management, pp. 1100–1112 (2020)

The Experience of A Self-Assessment Tool for Enhancing XR Technology Adoption in SMEs and HEIs across Europe

Ahmet Köse[✉] [iD], Aleksei Tepljakov[iD], Saleh Alsaleh[iD], and Eduard Petlenkov[iD]

Department of Computer Systems, Tallinn University of Technology, Akadeemia tee 15a, 12618 Tallinn, Estonia
ahmet.kose@taltech.ee

Abstract. Extended Reality (XR) technology has emerged as a cutting-edge innovation, facilitated by the availability of low-cost head-mounted display (HMD) devices and augmented features in affordable mobile devices. Despite its accessibility, XR technology has yet to realize its full potential in small and medium-sized businesses (SMEs) due to concerns surrounding its applicability in business-related activities. To address this gap, we presented a novel approach utilizing a self-assessment tool aimed at identifying specific challenges and difficulties inhibiting XR technology adoption for SMEs and higher education institutions (HEIs). This paper outlines the implementation and experience of the self-assessment tool, which serves multiple purposes. Firstly, it allows SME representatives to validate their XR technology experience, thereby providing a comprehensive understanding of their current XR capabilities. Additionally, the tool incorporates a specialized module for HEIs to refine their curricula, ensuring graduates possess the necessary skills to leverage XR technology for business needs effectively. The experience observed through the self-assessment tool is statistically analyzed to gauge the level of understanding and familiarity with XR technology among over two hundred participants across Europe. Preliminary findings indicate the efficacy of the self-assessment tool in assisting both SMEs and HEIs in recognizing the advantages of XR technology and identifying knowledge gaps. Moreover, the survey outcomes provide valuable statistical insights into the expectations and interests of SMEs across various sectors, offering XR developers and experts a deeper understanding of the specific requirements and preferences of SMEs. This statistical analysis aids in customizing XR solutions to meet the distinct needs of SMEs and promotes further adoption of XR technology. These insights may contribute to the advancement of XR technology and its utilization within the business landscape.

Keywords: Self Assessment Tool · Extented Reality · Skills Gap Detector · Training Gap Detector · SMEs · HEI

Supported by organization Erasmus+ Project entitled "VAM Realities"

L. T. De Paolis et al. (Eds.): XR Salento 2023, LNCS 14218, pp. 184–197, 2023.
https://doi.org/10.1007/978-3-031-43401-3_12

1   Introduction

Virtual Reality (VR) is a sophisticated interface between humans and computers, encompassing four fundamental components: a virtual world, immersion, sensory feedback, and interactivity [5]. VR enables unprecedented levels of interaction between humans and machines, as well as between humans themselves, by capitalizing on modern computing, visualization, and motion-tracking technologies. It effectively transports users into an artificial reality, engaging their visual and auditory senses. In contrast, Augmented Reality (AR) is closely related to VR but functions on a different principle. The terms VR and AR are often combined under the umbrella term Mixed Reality (MR). Additionally, in last years, the term *eXtended Reality* (XR) is commonly employed as a comprehensive term for both AR and VR.

The global XR market size reached 64 billion in 2022, rising to close to 300 billion U.S. dollars by 2024 [7]. While extended reality (XR) has great potential as a powerful medium, there are still several challenges that need to be addressed for it to reach its full potential. In other words, the accuracy of these predictions often applies to various usage scenarios, including both consumer and enterprise. Consequently, the current level of XR utilization within organizations, particularly small and medium-sized enterprises (SMEs), remains unclear and requires further investigation. Moreover, leading technology companies are actively engaged in developing XR solutions explicitly designed for enterprise implementation. SMEs have been slower in embracing digital transformation compared to their larger counterparts.

According to recent research on the adoption of XR in SMEs, it was found that although they generally recognize the existence and advantages of XR technologies, there are several significant barriers preventing their integration into relevant business models. Among these barriers, the technological aspect is considered to be one of the most significant factors. This is primarily due to the unique and interdisciplinary nature of XR, which demands addressing numerous implementation and adoption challenges [3].

As a result, research and development capacity has increased in research institutions, but not in SMEs, which cannot typically afford a dedicated R&D department focused on emerging technology adoption. However, even in the case of higher education institutions (HEIs) there are various limiting factors related to skills and knowledge gaps that prohibit the efficient adoption of XR technology [8]. One can conclude that a holistic approach towards identifying these gaps and proposing the best possible scenarios for bridging them with relevant information. What concerns XR technologies specifically, no relevant research regarding the design of a tool for automatic skills gap detection has been identified.

As the pace at which technology is adopted increases SMEs risk being left behind. This can have direct consequences for societies as SMEs constitute the majority of all businesses and employ the majority of people. It is therefore crucial to understand the overall organizational situation and the challenges that accompany XR in order to support companies in their adoption efforts. Due to a lack of resources and more focused competencies, which affect their innovation capability and readiness to digitalize their operations [2]. It is, therefore, crucial to understand the overall organizational situation and the challenges that accompany XR in order to support companies in their adoption efforts [4]. What complicates matters even more, is that XR is a technology that requires a wide range of skills from developers. Even if the SME business model is not centered on development *per se*, a set of micro-skills and knowledge are still required to engage and succeed with this novel technology. Accordingly, the serious game in immersive environments (SG) approach has been considered to enhance learning and training by a number of researchers. A common conclusion of conducted results in those researches indicates higher user satisfaction with the SG experience than with other learning methodologies. This may also refer to higher learning rates or skills improvement rather than traditional learning methods. However, although the users may enjoy the experience, they might not be able to benefit from the full potential for learning and training sufficiently. Thus, the design of SG should therefore include an extensive pre-training stage, let users familiar with the interfaces, and gain sufficient skills through their interaction with the XR-related applications. [1].

In our earlier work [6], we introduced a novel assessment tool aimed at assisting relevant stakeholders in understanding the gaps in their skills and knowledge related to XR technology. The tool serves as a skills gap detector for SMEs and a training gap detector for HEI representatives. Upon completing the survey, users receive a set of recommendations based on their survey responses, which are tailored to address their specific skills or knowledge gaps. This research paper presents our experience with the assessment tool, including data collected from over two hundred participants across Europe. The distribution map to illustrate the diversity is depicted in Fig. 1. The tool was developed and promoted under the same ERASMUS+ project entitled "VAM Realities"[1] in collaboration with dedicated partners.

Furthermore, we briefly outline our approach to developing the assessment tool and discuss improvements based on internal evaluations with an aim to provide a systematic approach for such online tools designed by researchers in the XR technology domain. The implemented tool has also been enhanced to collect and store necessary data for future years using the same access point. Additionally, we explore whether the level of XR technology adoption is consistent among SMEs and HEIs across Europe. One notable advantage of this framework is the storage of concrete outputs and the provision of realistic recommendations based on user input.

The main original contribution of the present paper is that we present the results and explore the user experience stemming from the use of the developed tool. We discuss the preferred methods used to derive novel findings and the outcomes of using the Skills/Training Gap Detector. Finally, we conclude by addressing the implications of XR technology for SMEs and HEIs through the application and outline potential ideas for future research. For completeness, we

---

[1] The official website for the project is located at https://vam-realities.eu/

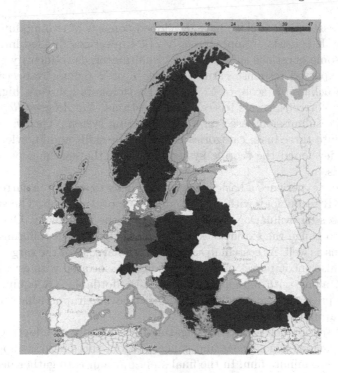

Fig. 1. Participants distribution across Europe

also briefly review the most important aspects of the assessment tool. We also describe the development process of the tool, including its components.

The structure of the paper is as follows. In Sect. 2, the model of the proposed solution is discussed. Our novel materials to bridge the gaps towards XR technology and technical description with evaluation rounds are also explained in this section. The experience and statistical results are presented in Sect. 3. Finally, the planned use cases and conclusions are drawn in Sect. 4.

In the paper, the authors present the results of research based on conducting a structured survey. The study confirms that technological knowledge was one of the key factors influencing the decision to use AR in the retail business. Lack of external support for technology adoption was also identified as a critical issue. In what follows, we describe the model for the XR skills gap detector for SMEs and training gap detector for HEIs, provide information about the implementation, and discuss the resulting solution.

2   Implementation of Self Assessment Tool

Our implementation aims to explore the required knowledge, skills, and competencies for personnel in SMEs to facilitate the adoption of VR/AR/MR adoption. Additionally, we address to investigate the necessary training features for educational activities offered by HEIs and provide assistance to SMEs in their adoption.

The self-assessment tool we have developed consists of two modules for each target group. It consists of approximately 21-24 questions divided into four sections, with some questions supported by visual materials to identify gaps. Each correct or expected response earns the user 1 or 2 points, respectively, with a maximum achievable score of 42 points. Participants can earn higher scores by providing correct answers to technical questions. *XR Advisor Report* is created after the submission based on a unique rating system. The system divides individuals into three main categories based on the skills and knowledge assessments. We developed the scoring system to assist the coaching program that targets SMEs.

First, users experience a basic background check to assess the current level of interest in XR technology within the company or organization. The subsequent section focuses on evaluating the accessibility of the technology. Questions are formulated to gauge the extent of knowledge and experience, offering multiple-choice options as well. As cost analysis plays a crucial role for the target audience, this section also encompasses projected expenses associated with establishing an XR project, along with anticipated prices for affordable XR equipment. The report later presents readers with an informative infographic that provides an initial comparative analysis.

The next section delves into investigating the feasibility of adopting XR technology. To enhance engagement and concentration, this phase is supplemented with a brief half-minute film. In the final step, our aim is to gather insights into people's experiences. Given that the primary objective of VAMR's coaching program is to support SMEs across all levels in their utilization of XR technology, it is essential to examine existing knowledge and ideas on the subject. Upon completion of the journey, participants are provided with an immediate PDF report, typically consisting of 4-5 pages. This report offers personalized advice based on the user's input. Additionally, relevant materials are made available to the user. If the tool identifies existing knowledge and experience gaps, the report recommends studying specific materials to enhance business-related activities. The workflow to illustrate the complete self-assessment tool is depicted in Fig. 2.

We have developed a set of materials as part of this project to bridge the gap between XR technology, SMEs, and HEIs. One of the goals of the developed tool is to help deliver those materials to the target groups. The set contains the State-of-the-Art (SotA) Report, Handbook, Experts Panel, Showcases, and Survey that are explained in our earlier work [6].

2.1 Development and Evaluation

We explored different approaches for building web-based applications and were in search of a flexible tool that could meet all the requirements of our project. The chosen tool needed to have built-in functionalities for essential communication tasks such as user authentication, form management, and content uploads (such as images and videos). As a result, we decided to utilize Django [11] as the core framework for developing our application.

1. Background check

2. XR Knowledge Inspection

3. Gap Identification

   a. Theoretical knowledge barrier

   1. General Overview
   2. Hardware
   3. Software
   4. Use cases
   5. Application areas

   b. Practical Challenges

   1. Feasibility
   2. Cost Analysis

   c. Specific issue to consult

4. XR Experience Validation

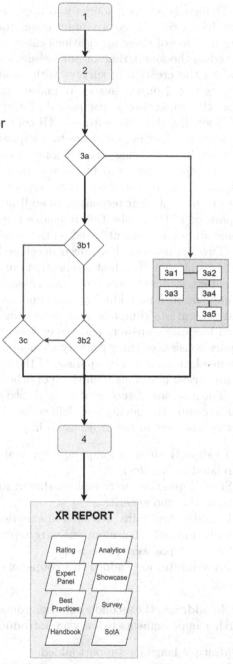

Fig. 2. Workflow of the Self-Assessment Tool

Django is an open-source web application framework based on Python. It is widely used and has a vibrant community that has created numerous applications. One of these applications called the "Django survey application" [10], served as the foundation for our website's development. This survey application enables the creation of surveys with various types of questions and generates reports based on the survey responses. By incorporating the matrix question type, the application encompassed all the question types required for our tool. Additionally, given the nature of XR content, it was essential to include the ability to attach images and videos to the questions. This interactive content proved valuable in showcasing VR/AR solutions before posing relevant questions.

The application also includes a significant functionality where the user's responses can be saved for future retrieval and utilized to generate statistical data to present their responses. In addition, the assessment tool necessitated an expansion of the application to enable the evaluation of answers, enabling us to make a final assessment based on the user's responses.

Two applications have been developed to cater to different aspects of the assessment tool. The first application enables the creation of surveys that can be categorized and scored in various assessment categories. It also allows for the storage of both individual answers and overall results in the database. The second generates a comprehensive report, incorporating recommendations derived from the user's answers and scores collected in the first application. The final report consists of three primary elements: an overall score, category-based recommendations, and a comparison of the user's responses to a predetermined set of numerical questions with those of other users.

The assessment tool went through two evaluation rounds; internal and external to ensure the quality and deliverable. The first evaluation round was carried out by partners in the project and improvements were as follows:

- To allow the user to compare, the actual price range was added to the question related to XR devices;
- Several questions were rephrased, and some were changed, especially the ones that were too generic;
- Periodic checks are presented in experience and activity-related questions;
- Some multiple-choice options were replaced to increase awareness;
- Several typos were corrected;
- Prerequisites were added to a couple of questions to give a better understanding;

In addition, the second evaluation round was handled by external parties and further improvements below were introduced:

- Multiple language support added;
- Country origin of the user is available to increase the precision;
- Rephrased a couple of questions and provided additional questions;

3   Main Result: The experience with the Self-Assessment Tool

SUBMISSIONS

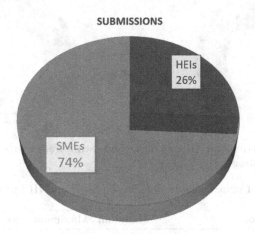

Fig. 3. The distribution of 229 submissions among HEIs and SMEs

Our aim has been to achieve participation from 50 individuals from HEIs and 200 individuals from SMEs across Europe. Surpassing the target, a total of 229 individuals engaged with the self-assessment tool, showing the attainment of the desired sample size. Consequently, the tool will remain accessible online and undergo maintenance for an extended period, thereby accomplishing the intended goal. The latest overview of submissions, as of May 2023, is illustrated in Fig. 3.

An analysis of the participants' experience with XR technology reveals that a majority of them possess limited exposure to such technologies. Approximately one-third of the participants reported having no prior experience, while over 30 percent acknowledged having less than two years of experience. In contrast, only approximately 10 percent of the participants indicated having over five years of experience in XR technology. These findings indicate that the current adoption rate of XR technology among SMEs and HEIs is relatively low. However, The latest participants' experiences demonstrate an increasing level of interest in XR technology, with nearly 60 percent of the participants finding it relevant. While around 20 percent of the participants remained neutral in their assessment, the overall sentiment suggests a positive inclination towards XR technology. Detailed information regarding the participants' XR experience and individual ratings can be observed in Fig. 4.

SMEs and HEIs went through the background check and fundamental XR knowledge and experience within the organization and region. The distributed responses to closed questions can be founded in Fig 6.

THE SUBSET OF XR EXPERIENCE

■AR ■MR ■VR ■NONE

THE LATEST XR EXPERIENCE RATE

■1 ■2 ■3 ■4 ■5 ■0

Fig. 4. Overall the individual XR experience and rating from 1 to 5 (bad to very good) and 0 refers to no rating

Table 1. List of numerical questions in the SME and HEI assessment tool.

Question	Minimum	Maximum	Average
Oculus Quest 2 Stand-alone VR Headset Price Estimate	4€	50k€	1.24k€
AR scenario similar to the one shown in the video (in euros) with available necessary 3D models	3€	500k	16.38k€
VR Project Cost Estimate with available 3D drawings	5€	250k	18.16k€

The second section of the report encompasses a statistical and visual analysis that compares the responses of the participants to questions requiring numeric

Preparing XR Course Cost Estimate

Your estimate was 4k€. Your estimated value is less than the average estimated value of 5.35k€ reported via this survey (N=16). Your estimated value is also greater than or equal to the minimum reported value. The lower boundary is set to the minimum value which is 0€. The upper boundary is set to the maximum reported value which is 20k€.

Fig. 5. An example of the statistical and visual comparison calculated based on the users' estimates to the numerical questions.

input and multiple-choice selection. These questions are formulated to aid users in comprehending how their expectations correspond to those of their peers by assigning a numerical value to the cost of XR hardware or solutions. The report provides the users with their estimations compared to the average, minimum, and maximum estimates provided by others. An instance of the statistical and visual comparison can be observed in Fig. 5, while a comprehensive listing of the numerical questions is available in Table 1.

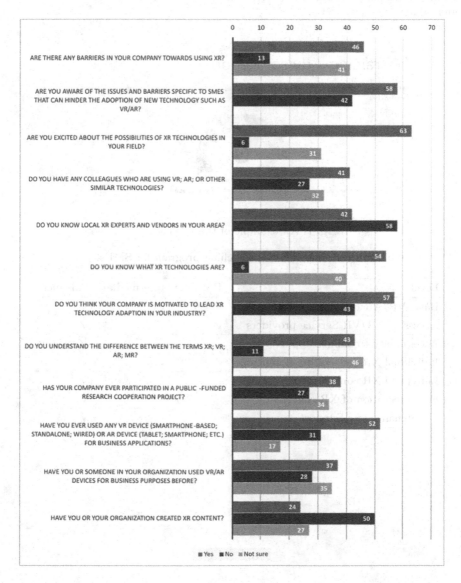

Fig. 6. List of closed questions with distributed responses in the SME and HEI assessment tool.

Next, the overall score is calculated based on the answers to all the questions within a given survey. The overall level is categorized into different categories. A scalable vector graphic-based gauge is used to indicate the total score. An example of the total score is shown in Fig. 7. Furthermore, a table is used to show the user's identified strengths and identified opportunities based on the calculated total score. The recommendations in the second section of the report are based on the user's results in several assessment categories; the written recommendations are embedded with videos and links to the relevant VAMRs deliverables.

Fig. 7. An example of the total score.

Table 2. VAMRS XR Coaching program for SMEs.

Level	Beginner	Intermediate	Advanced
Basic VR/AR training	✓	✓	✓
Access to AR/VR Service providers	✓	✓	✓
Accessibility to online support systems	✓	✓	✓
Individual XR concept development		✓	✓
Individual XR concept deployment		✓	✓
Full integration of XR concept			✓
Maintenance and Support			✓

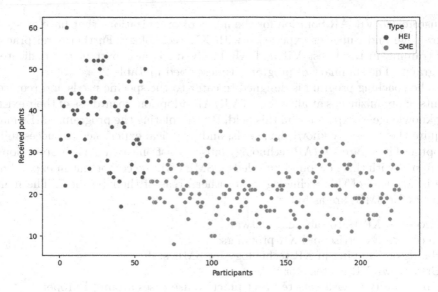

Fig. 8. The collected points by participants

4 Conclusion and future work

Initially, the comprehensive score is computed by aggregating the responses within the self-assessment tool. The overall level is then categorized into distinct classifications. A visually representative gauge, based on scalable vector graphics, is employed to indicate the cumulative score. Furthermore, a tabular format is utilized to present the identified strengths and opportunities of the user, derived from the calculated aggregate score and the example is depicted in Fig. 7. One of the major challenges in XR technology is enabling consumers to explore the potential for business-related activities across multiple domains. XR applications often offer interactivity, which can significantly influence SMEs in their decision to modify their operational processes, services, and product offerings [9]. After analyzing the collected data, the VAMRS project recommends that SMEs interested in embracing XR technology consider enrolling in the corresponding coaching program.

The coaching program is structured into three distinct levels, determined by accumulated points; Beginner XR Bootcamp program (0-14 points), Advanced XR SME Launchpad (14-28 points), and Pro XR Business (28-42 points), the programs that may take up to 9 months, 6 months, 3 months respectively. The first program is the first level of the coaching program and it serves as an introduction to VR/AR and teaches basic concepts, with a selection of use cases to help individuals to understand the technologies' potential for the industry. The second program is dedicated to guiding organizations in the adoption of both VR and AR in specific areas of business operation areas such as product design, collaboration, remote maintenance, enhancing work processes, sales, and marketing. The most advanced program means a collaboration to mutually develop a customized VR/AR Solution for the needs of organizations that have existing knowledge and sufficient experience with XR technology. Furthermore, practical training in the latest VR and AR hardware is also part of the dedicated programs. The summary of programs is described in Table 2.

The coaching program is designed to cater to the specific needs and requirements of organizations at all stages of VR/AR adoption, regardless of their existing knowledge or experience in this field. By completing the program, SMEs may acquire the necessary knowledge, skills, and practical experience to successfully adopt and integrate VR/AR technology into at least one area of their operations. Equipped with this newfound knowledge, SMEs will be competent in expanding the integration of this technology into other areas of their business. The main benefits for SMEs are as follows:

- Access to XR Hardware and Software;
- Access to Expertise and XR providers;
- Hands-on Training in XR technology for SME staff;
- Create own XR content for SME;
- Opportunity to visit selected best practice use-cases around Europe;
- No consulting fee, no purchase obligation for participation.

Additionally, Higher Education Institutions (HEIs) will acquire the essential knowledge to position themselves as proficient consultants in XR adoption for SMEs. They will also be equipped to develop relevant training programs and study courses tailored to the industry's needs, effectively addressing the increasing significance of VR/AR technology. This will enable them to establish an exemplary XR center of excellence, setting new benchmarks for other European HEIs to emulate. It is important to emphasize that HEIs might receive up to 60 points due to the dedicated content.

While it may appear that AR and VR, in particular, have numerous obstacles in terms of large-scale adoption by SMEs, this is due to the fact that the technology is still relatively new and changing rapidly. At the same time, current concerns present great opportunities for those who can address them. HEIs may also benefit from the situation by improving their curricula, allowing graduates to be better equipped for current business needs, and assisting them in adapting to this technology and cooperating with SMEs. The results of participants are depicted in Fig. 8.

Therefore, we developed a self-assessment tool aimed at bridging the gap between XR Technology, SMEs, and HEIs. We developed the tool as a web-based application to provide data-driven results and comparisons. Besides giving pertinent recommendations and ratings, the application allows participants to compare their financial perspectives with those of other people via an automated report. Since the current tool is intended to be used to adapt XR technology with coaching programs based on the assessment of given responses, additional development efforts should be exhibited to provide statistical conclusions in order to feed the output of collected information to the tool, as the estimated amount of participants from Europe is over 300 by the end of 2023. Furthermore, the approach given here may help other organizations that are having similar challenges adapting XR technology for corporate, educational, and training purposes. XR developers may also have a better understanding to support redirection strategies in XR-based applications in target groups. In the future, the assessment tool will have the calculation of ROI for industrial projects in order to stimulate interest.

References

1. Checa, D., Bustillo, A.: A review of immersive virtual reality serious games to enhance learning and training. Multimedia Tools Appl. **79**(9–10), 5501–5527 (2019). https://doi.org/10.1007/s11042-019-08348-9
2. Denicolai, S., Zucchella, A., Magnani, G.: Internationalization, digitalization, and sustainability: are SMEs ready? a survey on synergies and substituting effects among growth paths. Technol. Forecasting Soc. Change **166**, 120650 (2021). https://doi.org/10.1016/j.techfore.2021.120650
3. Jalo, H., Pirkkalainen, H., Torro, O., Pessot, E., Zangiacomi, A., Tepljakov, A.: Augmented and virtual reality in small and medium-sized European industrial companies: level of awareness, diffusion and enablers of adoption. Virtual Reality (2022), revised version submitted for review
4. Jalo, H., Pirkkalainen, H., Torro, O., Pessot, E., Zangiacomi, A., Tepljakov, A.: Extended reality technologies in small and medium-sized European industrial companies: level of awareness, diffusion and enablers of adoption. Virtual Reality **26**(4), 1745–1761 (2022). https://doi.org/10.1007/s10055-022-00662-2
5. Jerald, J.: The VR Book. Association for Computing Machinery (2015). https://doi.org/10.1145/2792790
6. Köse, A., Tepljakov, A., Alsaleh, S., Petlenkov, E.: Self assessment tool to bridge the gap between XR technology, SMEs, and HEIs. In: Extended Reality, pp. 296–311. Springer International Publishing (2022). https://doi.org/10.1007/978-3-031-15546-8_25
7. Lee, J.J., Hu-Au, E.: E3XR: an analytical framework for ethical, educational and eudaimonic XR design. Front. Virtual Reality 2 (2021). https://doi.org/10.3389/frvir.2021.697667, https://www.frontiersin.org/article/10.3389/frvir.2021.697667
8. Matsika, C., Zhou, M.: Factors affecting the adoption and use of AVR technology in higher and tertiary education. Technol. Soc. **67**, 101694 (2021). https://doi.org/10.1016/j.techsoc.2021.101694
9. Merino, L., Ghafari, M., Anslow, C., Nierstrasz, O.: CityVR: gameful software visualization. In: 2017 IEEE International Conference on Software Maintenance and Evolution (ICSME). IEEE (2017). https://doi.org/10.1109/icsme.2017.70
10. Pierre Sassoulas: Github repository of the Django survey app. https://github.com/Pierre-Sassoulas/django-survey, retrieved 18.04.2022
11. The Django Software Foundation: The official website of the Django project. https://www.djangoproject.com/, retrieved 18 Apr 2022

Game Engine Platforms Supporting Metaverse-Linking Process: A Proposed Case Study on Virtual 3D Printing

Elisabetta Lucia De Marco$^{(\boxtimes)}$ ⓘ, Antonella Longo ⓘ, and Marco Zappatore ⓘ

Department of Engineering for Innovation, University of Salento, 73100 Lecce, Italy
{elisabettalucia.demarco,antonella.longo,
marcosalvatore.zappatore}@unisalento.it

Abstract. In the era of digital learning, the Metaverse is expected to be the frontier of the educational research, resulting in the increased popularity of related technologies and applications in recent years and gradually becoming the focus of 3D learning environments. Since the Metaverse, as a link between the real world and its virtual counterpart, can provide learners with immersive experiences, many researchers and instructional designers begin to focus on the educational Metaverse or Edu-Metaverse. Therefore, this study is based on an "integrated-Metaverse" system, which combines a learning environment implemented in Unity3D Game Engine with a traditional Moodle-based Learning Management System.

Keywords: Metaverse · virtual lab · e-learning

1 Introduction

The Metaverse is emerging as one of the most promising technologies with educational potential to be explored, as it represents an appealing opportunity for pedagogy to challenge traditional theories and models.

We can address the Metaverse as a complex technology that requires the integration of multidisciplinary research perspectives [1], and therein lies its relevance as a multidimensional concept that refers to a combination of formal and informal learning experiences. The current perception of the Metaverse encompasses games, experiences, technologies, and social applications [2]. These are suitable components of the Metaverse that can be used effectively in education to enhance learning experiences.

This study aims to investigate the functional applicability of the integration between a traditional Learning Management System or LMS (based on Moodle) and an additional learning environment exploiting a cross-platform game engine (i.e., Unity3D), in order to determine the extent to which the learning experience of users changes. This work's purpose is to establish a relation between the user's learning experience and the adoption of "integrated-Metaverse" system, focusing on indicators of the skills acquired in a virtual 3D printer laboratory on Moodle.

© The Author(s), under exclusive license to Springer Nature Switzerland AG 2023
L. T. De Paolis et al. (Eds.): XR Salento 2023, LNCS 14218, pp. 198–209, 2023.
https://doi.org/10.1007/978-3-031-43401-3_13

1.1 From Metaverse to Edu-Metaverse

Metaverse is a combination of prefix "meta" (beyond), which implies transcending with the word "verse" (the root of "universe," cosmos; the whole world), which describes a new virtual universe created beyond the real world and linked to the physical. In 1992, Neal Stephenson, author of Snow Crash, coined the term Metaverse. Snow Crash is a science fiction novel about a future globalised society in which online life is often more important than real life. Stephenson imagines the 'Metaverse' as a successor to the Internet based on virtual reality (VR).

A main characteristic of the Metaverse is the constant interaction with the real world; the Metaverse is not a separate universe, a universe of fiction, but a universe in relation with the real world. The Metaverse as a digital mapping of reality that interacts and conditions reality. This is not a simple combination of the world and virtual reality, but an interaction. According to Tlili et al. [3] the Metaverse "does not simply combine the physical and virtual worlds; it is instead a continuity of the physical world in the virtual world to create an ecosystem that merges both worlds (physical and virtual)." The Metaverse does not simplify the reality to which it refers but increases its complexity. Reality is enriched with information and data that is not immediately available and usable.

Educational mediation is configured as an action of immersion in the learning experience and an action of management and monitoring of the data referable to the learning processes. It is what Wu and Gao [4] call the "Edu-Metaverse", which the authors define as the Metaverse applied to education.

1.2 Online learning and Metaverse

Ever since its conception, online education mainly relies on two main system types: asynchronous and synchronous e-learning. Both types depend on software or web applications in two-dimensional (2D) digital environments.

Standard asynchronous online learning tools include LMS (e.g., Moodle, Blackboard), and sometimes also collaborative web applications and social networks. Asynchronous tools serve the flexible, in other words, anytime, anywhere communication and interaction among educators, students and content [5].

However, online learning without interaction is not significantly different from traditional learning and has a negative effect on learners' motivation, participation and learning attitude. Indeed, in a distance-learning environment, the use of first-generation digital resources (e.g., textbooks, links, SCORM, webpages, videos, and quizzes) is not as effective for learning as the approaches based on and real, social experiences, since a low level of interaction and a lack of synchronous activities prevent meaningful interactions for learning.

Synchronous e-learning systems enable the online meeting of educators and students at the same time in a digital, virtual space and enhance motivation and participation. Synchronous online learning is typically implemented through web conferencing and web collaboration platforms (e.g., Zoom, WebEx, Microsoft Teams, Adobe Connect, Google Classroom).

Over the last decade, Massive Open Online Courses (MOOCs) have attracted a considerable attention, being attended by thousands of students worldwide, even if they have a typical completion rate not exceeding 10% [6].

Recently, a number of studies have reported the educational benefits of using a Metaverse platform to sustain students' interest and engagement in distance learning [7–9]. The high levels of engagement in the Metaverse platforms and the gamified elements seem to elicit the student's interest and motivation of learning and autonomy towards academic engagement. Education in the Metaverse can facilitate student experiences to ensure multimodal learning opportunities based on a real human interaction. Supporting meta-modal learning in the Metaverse plays a crucial role in implementing VR contents in a digital environment as it encourages students and teachers to experience multimodal learning contents based on a real human interaction.

Accordingly, to solve the problems of online learning, a method of delivering value based on gameful experiences in the Metaverse has been explored. The 'gameful experience,' considered by researchers to be the essence of gamification, plays a significant role in positively affecting behavior in learning organizations. In existing gamification literature, the gameful experience refers to a set of experiences elicited by games or gamification, and even [10]. Given the multiplicity of disciplinary perspectives that have contributed to its definition, gamification has evolved as an interdisciplinary subject. Gamification has been defined as the "use of game design elements in non-game contexts" [11]. Recently, Eppmann et al. [12] define that "gameful experience in a non-game context refers to the positive emotional and involving qualities of using a gamified application". There is an increased interest in "virtual world metaverse-supported gameful experience-based education". Educators have thus focused on exploiting knowledge/skills delivery approaches based on gameful experiences to induce learners' motivation, participation, interaction, and continuity [13]. Metaverse-supported gameful learning is a new way of learning that, empowered not only by the already mentioned VR, but also by AR (Augmented Reality), MR (Mixed Reality), and brain-computer interfaces, utilizes immersive games integrating with knowledge and entertainment for achieving learning enjoyment. Due to its immersive nature, gaming is expected to be a foundational use case for the Metaverse. In the emerging Metaverse space, gaming is a key component. A gameful experience as an experience similar to playing a game but in a non-game context that is interpreted differently from a game-like experience. A Metaverse based environment is becoming essential to design a quality experience of playing and learning. Gameful experience is related to gamification an integrated system of game elements such as points, badges, levels, and leaderboards in a non-game context, including a variety of study field (e.g. education, business, health care). Gamification in education induces the effects of learner motivation, learning participation, and attitude improvement through these game elements.

Currently, the Metaverse model is under intense development and it is expected to allow social, immersive VR platforms to be compatible with massive multiplayer online video games, open game worlds and AR collaborative spaces, thus overcoming the typical limitations now existing within a single platform. In the field of VR, the Metaverse was conceived as the 3D Internet or Web 3.0.Digital environment generated by AR, VR and MR have begun to find their way into a multitude of areas related to teaching and learning. From an instructional-educational perspective is of great interest to mention that such technologies have several differences in regard to the common LMS like Moodle, giving users the opportunity to experience combining digital and physical contents or materials.

VR and AR have the advantage of creating a sense of reality based on a high level of immersion in a virtual space with mixed environments. In VR, users can immerse themselves in a virtual environment and interact with virtual objects in it. VR provides gameful and visual education to make it easier to understand complex content while improving communication efficiency. VR can be subdivided into two types: non-immersive and immersive. Non-immersive VR involves the users partially inserting themselves into a virtual environment by means of a monitor, while immersive VR allows the users to fully insert themselves into the virtual environment using a head-mounted display (HMD) [14]. This study focuses primarily on non-immersive VR.

In terms of interactivity and presence, it remains important to select VR technologies that offers a learning experience through social communication with other learners, tutors, or teachers. Except for VR games that can allow synchronous 3D experiences with other users, the majority of educational VR content is nowadays meant to deliver semi-immersive experiences to a single user who is connected to his or her physical surroundings [15].

According to this rationale, it is imperative the need to be provided possible ways or approaches which enable instructors or teachers to create and assess successfully those AR technologies and LMS which can be the most appropriate for their teaching interventions.

2 "Integrated-Metaverse" System: Moodle and Unity

To address the above challenge, this work investigates whether the combination of the Unity3D game engine described above with specific design features and characteristics can support teachers in developing interactive LMS that can support students in acquiring awareness learning practices. Therefore, the development of a suitable virtual distance learning platform that combines game engines with traditional LMS has a good role to play in promoting student learning.

This work proposes an integration of the Learning Management System (Moodle) with a game engine platform (Unity) in order to make the user experience more immersive and to improve the didactic effectiveness of the virtual laboratory (3D Printer Lab). The purpose is to establish a relation between users' learning experience and adoption of "integrated-Metaverse" system, focusing on indicators of the skills acquired in a virtual 3d printer laboratory on Moodle.

This "integrated-Metaverse" system consists of three modules, whose operational flow is shown in Fig. 1.

After detecting the user's feedback, Unity3D can catch the data objects from Moodle LMS, as shown in Fig. 1. Developers can get a feedback from learners on LMS after observing the learner's behaviour in the 3D Printer Lab, as shown in Fig. 1. Thus, developers (e.g. teachers, tutors) can get a feedback from learners on LMS after observing the learner's behavior in the 3D Printer Lab.

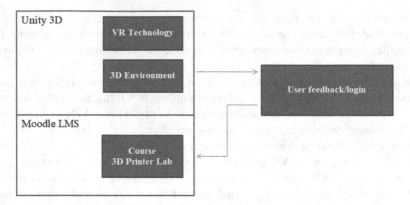

Fig. 1. "Integrated-Metaverse" system modules (arrows represent data objects flow).

2.1 Moodle

Learning Management Systems (LMS) are widespread around the world and Moodle (Modular Object-Oriented Dynamic Learning Environment) is a leading example. Moodle is an open-source product that collects a large type of data including all the interactions of registered participants (students, teachers, and editors, among others). These collection of data can offer insight into the online behavior of students, improving both learning and teaching. Moodle is an excellent platform for resources and communication tools but has all limitation of the 2D learning environment. The effectiveness of the e-learning system depends on the level of interaction provided among the students and tutors. The Moodle community supports its expansion which greatly facilitates new developments of the package and research.

Despite these typical limitations of the 2D environment, Moodle includes a learning analytics (LA) system, which offers educators analyses of students' learning and makes predictions about their success chances.

Learning analytics (LA) are "the measurement, collection, analysis, and reporting of data about learners and their contexts, for purposes of understanding and optimizing learning and the environments in which it occurs" [16]. Research in the area of learning analytics increased quickly in recent years [17] also with the emergence of MOOCs. With MOOCs, the amount of educational data useful for defining the effectiveness of teaching and learning strategies has increased.

There are two kinds of LA models in Moodle: static and machine learning (ML) based LA. Static LA uses simple rules to recognize specific situations, whereas ML-based LA predicts events, e.g., "students at risk of dropping out". The provided ML-based LA models are not pre-trained. Thus, users (institutions) should administer the ML-process, e.g., data collection, training, evaluation, and prediction locally [18]. The evolution of LMS has contributed greatly in transforming education and has enabled researchers to gather and process multivariate datatypes to provide engaged users with meaninful learning experiences.

2.2 Unity

In a similar manner, immersive technologies – such as VR– have demonstrated a strong potential to facilitate the formation of open, interconnected spaces with countless opportunities for interaction, collaboration, and knowledge sharing.

Unity is a worldwide renowned 3D-based, cross-platform game engine, whose potential for being applied in educational context is significant, thanks to its versatility, effective user interface, and extensive set of functionalities. One of its main advantages is the possibility for learning professionals (educators, teachers, tutors) to coordinate their work in a unified environment because it is an open and user-friendly tool. More specifically, the adaptability of Unity3D makes it not only an ideal choice for video game development but also a suitable option for educational settings.

The incorporation of Unity3D in STEM educational curricula can be performed by either introducing Unity-based learning environments (i.e., students and teachers use already designed and developed environments) or creating them directly as a curricular activity.

As for the latter option, Unity3D intuitive UI allows both educators and students to learn the basics of game development slightly rapidly, thus facilitating the creation of engaging learning experiences. Unity3D supports a wide array of platforms (e.g., desktop PCs, mobile devices, and VR), so that educators are supported to deliver content through diverse mediums and reach a broader audience. Furthermore, its scripting language, C#, is widely used in the software industry, affording involved students an opportunity to develop valuable programming skills.

When properly incorporated, Unity3D can promote active learning by enabling students to directly create contents and by allowing them to design and implement game mechanics through hands-on experiences, problem solving and critical thinking skills can be activated. Moreover, Unity3D facilitates interdisciplinary learning, allowing students to merge various subjects, such as art, mathematics, and physics, in the creation of immersive virtual environments.

However, several challenges have to be addressed as well. First, the learning curve required to proficiently master the engine's large set of functionalities is not smooth and educators from non-computer-science sectors would need time to become effectively helpful to students. In addition, hardware and software assets required to implement learning environments with Unity3D could be a hindrance in resource-limited educational settings.

3   Case Study: 3D Printer Lab

In the context of this work, we propose the combination of a LMS (verbal content representation) and a VR platform (visual content representation) for the design and development of a learning environment, which can support personalized and efficacy-based learning interventions.

The proposed work is a fictional 2D-3D online learning environment, where students can connect and interact with each other and with a set of 3D learning objects. In this work, Moodle is used as an e-learning analysis resource integrated with Unity for the rendering of the learning environment (login, course visualisation, 3D Printer lab). Indeed, online learning platforms allow to analyze student activity and performance in relation to course learning objectives. Moodle is a widely used LMS with a large number of additional tools for e-Learning Analytics (e-LA), Educational Data Mining (EDM), and visual analytics to help teachers arrive at relevant decisions for the teaching process.

3D Printer Lab is an open-source solution that integrates the multi-user virtual environment Unity with the Moodle LMS.

The 3D Printing Virtual LAB is an ultra-concurrent lab, and it is devoted to 3D printing process. Ultra-concurrent laboratories are based on a set of pre-recorded experiences carried out at a real lab. Then, the ultra-concurrent laboratory interface allows the user to have the same experience as in a real-time laboratory. The 3D Printing Virtual LAB introduces beginners to the process simulating the configuration setup and the printing of a plastic part. The 3D Printer Lab is available in the course Virtual labs@DEfI on the Moodle platform (https://elearning.unisalento.it/) and it is organised in 4 sections: 1. Introduction, 2. Part configuration, 3. Print configuration, 4. Observation (Fig. 2).

Fig. 2. Sections of 3D Printer Lab

The traditional Moodle course (3D Printer Lab) establishes communication and interaction between the objects in Unity and the learning contents and activities that are provided in Moodle. It is functionally configurable to adapt to any standard Moodle learning course or object. Therefore, this system is based on Moodle, which shares the Unity3D with the database.

As a first step, learners must identify themselves with a login/password. Validation with the Moodle login/password is integrated with Unity interface (Fig. 3).

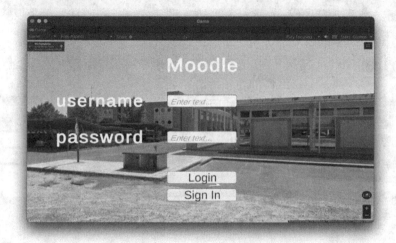

Fig. 3. Unity scene for login in Moodle

Then, learners access Moodle and view the list of available courses, including the 3D Printer lab. Users can see the Unity game scene based on Moodle courses, as shown in Fig. 4.

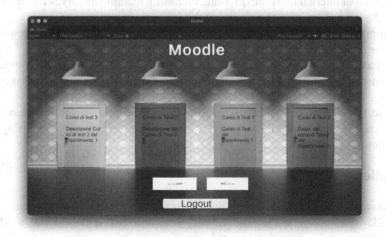

Fig. 4. Unity scene for course visualization in Moodle

Once the learner has connected to the Moodle server and selected a particular course, the course content is provided for visualization and study. In Fig. 5, we show an initial preview of the main screen when the course has been loaded.

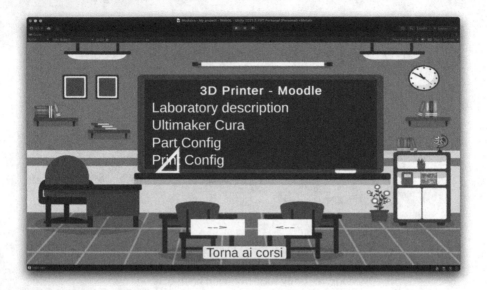

Fig. 5. Unity scene for course topics

By synthesizing the findings from this study, a set of recommendations building upon the experience gained from this proposed case study are the following:

1. Integration of internal tools into Moodle, including learning analitycs for teachers, to guide design and improve the quality of the learning experience.
2. Development of an immersive environment with Unity offering a user-friendly way to create Moodle learning context based on gaming.
3. Unity has to run in an environment, which equips learning content with objectives and competence profiles, therefore dealing with Moodle information based on data analysis
4. Moodle is the platform, where the courses take place, so course data have to be transferred from the Moodle to Unity; a mechanism for exporting/importing those data, has to be provided.

4 Challenges

The Metaverse is attracting attention as an alternative to overcome the limitations of existing 2D-based online and remote learning environments. It can provide a differentiated experience value from the current internet era due to the complex use of various technologies [19]. However, the Metaverse faces a number of challenges related to the underlying VR technologies. Therefore, new models of Metaverse-powered distance education can emerge to break the limitations of 2D platforms.

First, it is necessary to study students' activity patterns, level of immersion in the Metaverse, and its positive and negative effects on students' learning activities. Therefore, teachers/educators and, in general, learning professionals can become instructional designers who want to utilize the Metaverse for education. For this reason, it is necessary understand each type of Metaverse technical characteristics and design classes so that they can solve problems or perform projects collaboratively and creatively.

Second, developing an educational Metaverse platform to enhance the teaching processes based on learning data is required. Evaluation studies on data collection to support teaching and learning are also required.

Despite the availability of a variety of digital tools for online education, existing technologies have not been able to face the challenges on how to properly design fully the virtual learning approaches to accommodate courses' needs, meet learning objectives, and maintain students' high learning experience [20].

The "integrated metaverse" system brings a lot of unique advantages and immersive applications can better utilize spatial memory, create a strong sense of presence, provide an additional dimension for displaying information, and take advantage of natural ability to navigate 3D worlds, such as the virtual classroom.

Similarly, for distance education platform developers, the improvement of human-computer interaction interface and interaction quality can also significantly improve the teaching effect. Human-computer interaction in distance education is actually the interaction between learners and teaching resources. In order to improve the learning interest and quality of learners, teaching platforms should strengthen the interactive design of learning content.

Metaverse can offer an elevated version of VR and AR experiences combined with interactions between real and virtual space.. Educational implementations in the Metaverse are still at an early stage, when considering that a complex Metaverse system not yet been widely implemented and the use of Metaverse and real space interactions remains scarce.

Nonetheless, the potential is probably there with further developments and maturity of the Metaverse being expected to go together with the ongoing development of related technologies, leading to the wider use of the Metaverse for learning.

5 Limitation and Conclusion

In this paper, we briefly described the user experience on the Moodle platform integrated with Unity game engine platform for educational purposes. Furthermore, the study aims to investigate functional applicability of the integration between a traditional LMS (Moodle) and a cross-platform game engine (Unity). This study demonstrates that the adoption of "integrated-Metaverse" system, as presented above, can be functional to overcoming certain limits in learning arising from the use of 2D learning environments. Nevertheless, the "integrated-Metaverse" of 3D Printer Lab adds the Metaverse as a small part of the proposed system. Subsequently, the Metaverse should include all the parts of the proposed framework because virtual reality is a core part of the Metaverse. Future work will measure and evaluate the "integrated metaverse" system on Moodle and improve the model to simplify the Unity platform design process for educational purposes. Future studies should focus on strengthening the reliability of the integrated Metaverse system on Moodle through the analysis of learning experiences.

References

1. Dwivedi, Y.K., et al.: Metaverse beyond the hype: multidisciplinary perspectives on emerging challenges, opportunities, and agenda for research, practice and policy. Int. J. Inform. Manage. **66**, 102542 (2022). https://doi.org/10.1016/j.ijinfomgt.2022.102542
2. Yang, S.-H., et al.: Development of a game-based e-learning system with augmented reality for improving students' learning performance. Internat. J. Eng. Ed. **2**, 1–10 (2020). https://doi.org/10.14710/ijee.2.1.1-10
3. Tlili, A., et al.: Is Metaverse in education a blessing or a curse: a combined content and bibliometric analysis. Smart Learn. Environ. **9**, 24 (2022). https://doi.org/10.1186/s40561-022-00205-x
4. Wu, J., Gao, G.: Edu-Metaverse: Internet Education Form with Fusion of Virtual and Reality: Presented at the 2022 8th International Conference on Humanities and Social Science Research (ICHSSR 2022), Chongqing, China (2022). https://doi.org/10.2991/assehr.k.220504.197
5. Mystakidis, S.: Metaverse. Encyclopedia. **2**, 486–497 (2022). https://doi.org/10.3390/encyclopedia2010031
6. Jordan, K.: Initial trends in enrolment and completion of massive open online courses. IRRODL **15** (2014). https://doi.org/10.19173/irrodl.v15i1.1651
7. Mystakidis, S.: Distance education gamification in social virtual reality: a case study on student engagement. In: 2020 11th International Conference on Information, Intelligence, Systems and Applications (IISA), pp. 1–6. IEEE, Piraeus, Greece (2020). https://doi.org/10.1109/IISA50023.2020.9284417
8. Yu, E.: A study of a korean speaking class using online platforms during COVID-19. IJICC 1026–1035 (2021). https://doi.org/10.53333/IJICC2013/15272
9. Jeon, J.H.: A study on education utilizing metaverse for effective communication in a convergence subject. Int. J. Internet Broadcast. Commun. **13**, 129–134 (2021). https://doi.org/10.7236/IJIBC.2021.13.4.129
10. Thomas, N.J., Baral, R., Crocco, O.S., Mohanan, S.: A framework for gamification in the metaverse era: how designers envision gameful experience. Technol. Forecast. Soc. Chang. **193**, 122544 (2023). https://doi.org/10.1016/j.techfore.2023.122544
11. Deterding, S., Dixon, D., Khaled, R., Nacke, L.: From game design elements to gamefulness: defining "gamification."
12. Eppmann, R., Bekk, M., Klein, K.: Gameful experience in gamification: construction and validation of a gameful experience scale [GAMEX]. J. Interact. Mark. **43**, 98–115 (2018). https://doi.org/10.1016/j.intmar.2018.03.002
13. Chen, X., Zou, D., Xie, H., Wang, F.L.: Metaverse in education: contributors, cooperations, and research themes. IEEE Trans. Learning Technol. 1–18 (2023). https://doi.org/10.1109/TLT.2023.3277952
14. Kirner, C., Shneider, C., Goncalves, T.: Using augmented reality cognitive artifacts in education and virtual rehabilitation. In: Eichenberg, C. (ed.) Virtual Reality in Psychological, Medical and Pedagogical Applications. InTech (2012). https://doi.org/10.5772/46416
15. Lee, H., Hwang, Y.: Technology-enhanced education through VR-making and metaverse-linking to foster teacher readiness and sustainable learning. Sustainability **14**, 4786 (2022). https://doi.org/10.3390/su14084786
16. Long, P., Siemens, G.: Penetrating the Fog: Analytics in Learning and Education

17. Dawson, S., Joksimovic, S., Poquet, O., Siemens, G.: Increasing the impact of learning analytics. In: Proceedings of the 9th International Conference on Learning Analytics & Knowledge, pp. 446–455. ACM, Tempe AZ USA (2019). https://doi.org/10.1145/3303772.3303784
18. Tagharobi, H., Simbeck, K.: Introducing a framework for code based fairness audits of learning analytics systems on the example of moodle learning analytics: In: Proceedings of the 14th International Conference on Computer Supported Education, pp. 45–55. SCITEPRESS - Science and Technology Publications, Online Streaming, Select a Country (2022). https://doi.org/10.5220/0010998900003182
19. Kye, B., Han, N., Kim, E., Park, Y., Jo, S.: Educational applications of metaverse: possibilities and limitations. J. Educ. Eval. Health Prof. **18**, 32 (2021). https://doi.org/10.3352/jeehp.2021.18.32
20. Pappas, I.O., Giannakos, M.N.: Rethinking learning design in IT education during a pandemic. Front. Educ. **6**, 652856 (2021). https://doi.org/10.3389/feduc.2021.652856

Investigating Age Differences in Passive Haptic Feedback for Immersive Virtual Reality: A Pilot Study on Configuration Tasks

Markus Dresel[✉] [iD], Julia Plaumann, and Nicole Jochems[iD]

University of Lübeck, Lübeck, Germany
m.dresel@uni-luebeck.de, jochems@imis.uni-luebeck.de

Abstract. Since the aging process leads to a variety of cognitive and perceptual changes, this might also impact the use of immersive virtual reality (IVR) systems. This study investigated age-related differences in IVR configuration tasks by comparing passive haptics, mid-air, and controller interaction in an age-heterogenious sample (N=38). Although older participants took significantly longer for task-completion, this was not reflected in subjective usability ratings, which did not differ significantly between age groups (young, middle-aged, older adults). However, the sense of presence (IPQ) was significantly higher in the middle-aged group, independent of the interaction technique used. This highlights the importance of including middle-aged adults in age-differentiated IVR research (alongside young and older adults) to obtain a holistic picture of the ageing process. Unexpectedly, the three interaction techniques did not differ significantly in subjective usability, presence, and task completion times, suggesting that passive haptics, mid-air, and controller interaction in IVR might be equally well-suited for simple one-dimensional configuration tasks, regardless of users' age. Whether this also applies to multi-dimensional configuration, has to be explored in future studies. Additionally, follow-up studies should measure key perceptual and cognitive variables to define age groups beyond chronological age. This may especially shed light on how middle-aged adults differ from young and older adults in terms of user characteristics and how these relate crucial IVR aspects, i.e. presence and usability.

Keywords: virtual reality · presence · usability · passive haptics · age differences

1 Introduction

Immersive virtual reality (IVR) devices, like head-mounted displays (HMDs) have reached broad consumer-level availability in recent years [17,54]. Nevertheless, the design of IVR systems has mainly focused on young adults as the primary target group, neglecting the factor of age and the multitude of related variables that impact the interaction with technology [38]. In the field of Human-Computer Interaction (HCI), IVR research focuses not only on usability but

© The Author(s), under exclusive license to Springer Nature Switzerland AG 2023
L. T. De Paolis et al. (Eds.): XR Salento 2023, LNCS 14218, pp. 210–222, 2023.
https://doi.org/10.1007/978-3-031-43401-3_14

especially on the sense of presence as a quality measure [3,12,17,50]. Defined as the sense of "being there", [24] presence is considered one of the few results of a Virtual Environment (VE) that can be used to measure its effectiveness regardless of its application context [52]. However, very few studies aim to identify age-related differences in presence or usability. Current findings are based almost exclusively on the separate observation of either younger or older users, whereas studies considering older adults are often limited to very specific (mostly medical) contexts and studies including middle-aged adults are even more scarce (see Sect. 2). Nevertheless, IVR offers great potential to benefit users of all ages, e.g. by improving social participation [13], as a tool for cognitive and physical training [42,49], or for entertainment purposes [13,49]. With this technology, experiences can be made possible with lower demands on mobility and financial situation [5,30]. Growing technologization of our society and demographic change make it imperative to consider all user groups in an age-differentiated system-design in order to improve accessibility and universal access [55]. Thus users of all ages must be included in the systematic research on usability and presence in IVR in order to design VEs that are especially suited to their needs [21,33]. In particular, the influence of age-related changes on presence needs to be examined more closely. An age-differentiated analysis of the sense of presence is conducted in very few studies [14,21,27,37,43].

Furthermore an important step towards reducing the age-specific digital gap, is system-design that focuses on age-related needs, preferences, and abilities, making technology more useful and usable [31], and achieving positive effects on medium and long-term use [39]. Previous research suggests that age-specific barriers of Virtual Reality adoption and use are for instance cybersickness, system workload, frustration, fatigue, and discomfort [19], but the variety of age-related changes in perception and cognition suggests that there are many more to be discovered. Thus, age differences in usability of VEs must also be identified systematically.

Configurability of VEs represents a promising approach to (1) identifying and (2) compensating for age differences, enabling users to adapt the virtual environment to their individual needs, preferences, and abilities. This would enable the adaptation of a VE's properties, which interact with sensory perception (visual, auditory, haptic, etc.) and cognitive load, to the user's individual ability profiles. However, the configuration task itself must not become an additional barrier for IVR usability and presence. Therefore, a suitable interaction technique must be found. Classical IVR interaction techniques, such as mid-air interaction or controllers, may lack the necessary sensory richness or biomechanical symmetry to known real-world tasks, respectively. Utilizing passive haptics in IVR by mapping virtual objects with physical proxy objects, has the potential to match visual and haptic Stimuli during IVR Interaction and to improve conformity to expectations and learnability [26]. In addition, haptic perception is less affected by the aging process than other perceptual senses [37,38]. Consequently this pilot study is to compare passive haptics to traditional VR-Interaction for configuration tasks in an age-differentiated manner.

2   Age Differences Relevant for IVR Use

Literature has not clearly defined the group of older users due to its heterogeneity and interindividual ability profiles. However, individuals with a chronological age of 60+ years are often referred to as "older adults" [18]. This differentiation is based on the analysis of age-related changes in performance and can vary according to the focus of abilities considered (perceptual or cognitive). In research on the age-differentiated design of human-technology interfaces, the consideration of specific user characteristics (ability profiles) has become established as an important predictor in addition to the chronological age of the users [46]. The interindividual variability of sensory, cognitive, and sensorimotor systems places high demands on the flexibility and adaptability of usable human-technology interfaces. Age-related changes that are of particular importance for the design of VEs have been identified by McGlynn and Rogers [37,38], focusing particularly on the sense of presence. The visual system, attention and memory performance (esp. working memory) have been pointed out as the most important influencing factors in this context, being mainly responsible for the perception of (virtual) stimuli. Visual perception is strongly influenced by the aging process. The amount of light that passes through the lens, the ability of the lens to adapt and focus at different distances and the ability to adapt to changing lighting situations are examples of aspects that are affected by the aging process [22]. Besides, older adults are more susceptible to glare, which especially impairs the recognition of contrasts [18]. The contrast sensitivity decreases continuously from the age of 20 [23]. Also, the eye's accommodation ability, which enables depth perception, decreases with age, so well-known negative effects of 3D-Displays (e.g., the vergence-accommodation conflict [28]) may be even more severe in older adults. Attention, particularly selective and distributed attention, are affected by the aging process as well [16,34]. In the case of distributed attention, age-related changes in performance intensify depending on the attentional demands [23]. Also, older adults need more time to shift from one point of attention to the next and are more likely to be affected by salient events such as blinking, high-intensity lights or other alarming stimuli [23]. They also have a reduced signal-to-noise ratio compared to younger adults [16]. The age-related decline in memory capacity has been demonstrated by many studies, particularly concerning working memory [11]. Often this is the main limiting factor for the performance of older adults. In addition, older adults often have less technology experience compared to younger adults, so that mental models of technology use are less sophisticated [39]. In contrast to the deterioration in almost all other perceptual senses, the haptic system remains relatively stable in the aging process [37,38]. Therefore, it could be the preferred feedback for older adults and provide a way to compensate for usability and presence differences between age groups when using IVR systems.

It must be noted that the focus of age-differentiated IVR research lies primarily on older adults [37,38]) and differences to young adults (e.g., [14,19,27]). The full adult lifespan is almost exclusively considered in age correlation approaches (e.g., [48]), but rarely in age group comparisons. Middle-aged users[1] are underrepresented especially in studies of cognitive aging and health [29]. For instance, changes in cognitive abilities are far less well researched in midlife than in old age (60+) [25]. Therefore, it seems promising to consider not only the specific characteristics of users in early and late adulthood, but also those in the transitional period which lies in between (midlife), to gain a more nuanced understanding of age-related changes in IVR interaction.

3 Related Work

Typically age-differentiated IVR studies on passive haptic have focused on the comparison of IVR with a corresponding real-world task, being mostly limited to medical context like rehabilitation [4, 20]. Although these works do not consider the sense of presence, they demonstrate that age differences in performance can persist after transferring tasks to IVR. Previous IVR studies comparing presence in subjects of different ages led to contradictory results. Both a positive [19, 43, 48] and a negative correlation [6] between age and presence were identified. Other studies, however, did not find any significant differences in presence between older and younger subjects [14, 21, 27, 37]. Thus, there is no consistent empirical evidence, so that the relation between age and the sense of presence in IVR remains unclear.

Considering the relationship between user characteristics and the sense of presence in IVR, numerous age-related changes are assumed to have an impact (e.g., visual perception, attention, working memory; see Sect. 2). However, no empirically verified findings are available in this regard [37, 38]. Previous studies did either not include older subjects (e.g., considering visual [56] and spatial imagination [7, 15]) or investigated user characteristics that are not directly related to age (e.g., control beliefs [40], extraversion [2]). Moreover, the few existing empirically grounded design recommendations on increasing presence specifically for older adults [1] do not allow for conclusions on age differences between users of different ages.

Although presence is considered a key aspect of HCI research in IVR, its relationship to the various aspects of usability has yet to be clarified [7, 41]. Studies that investigated this issue led to contradictory results. Brade et al. [7] found a significant correlation between presence and subjective usability ratings in an IVE. No such correlation was found in a corresponding real environment, indicating that presence only plays a vital role for IVR-usability. However, other study results [9] led to the conclusion that presence is equally important in both contexts. A frequently measured objective usability indicator is task performance, quantified by error rates (effectiveness) and completion times (efficiency). Previous IVR-studies found both negative [35] and positive correlations [53] or even no correlation [36] between presence and task performance. The conflicting results suggest that the relationship between presence and usability (especially performance [41]) depends strongly on the specific task and its requirements, e.g., gait

---

[1] typically defined as being between 35 and 55 to 60 years old [18, 32].

performance seems to be less dependent on presence in older than in younger adults [27]. Bystrom et al. [10] suggest that presence does not facilitate or hinder performance per se, but that "having some sense of presence in an environment is a necessary condition for performance to occur." Furthermore it has been shown that the extensiveness of sensory stimuli in IVR can enhance presence. The more senses are involved in the virtual experience, the higher is the potential sense of presence (e.g., by adding auditory/tactile feedback [45]). This also seems promising in terms of usability, especially for older adults. Incorporating more senses allows for enhanced information transfer and may even improve IVR interaction, by enabling older adults to compensate for one impaired sense with a different one. However, it is important to ensure the coherence of (virtual) stimuli (e.g., sound and haptics, matching visual impressions) to maintain predictability and plausibility in the VE, which are affecting usability and particularly presence [51,57].

Fig. 1. The experimental setup in the three conditions Mid-Air (left), Haptic (middle), and Controller (right).

4   Experiment

4.1   Method

To investigate age differences in haptic/non-haptic IVR interaction, we chose a mixed study design with age as the between-subject and interaction technique as the within-subject factor. The IVR application was developed using the Unity 3D game engine[2] with the Oculus Integration Toolkit[3] and displayed using an Meta Quest[4] head-mounted display.

At the beginning of the experiment participants filled out an informed consent and a demographic questionnaire. Next, they experienced all three conditions, namely mid-air, haptic, and controller interaction (see Fig. 1), in a randomized

---

[2] https://unity.com/.

[3] https://assetstore.unity.com/packages/tools/integration/oculus-integration-82022.

[4] Formerly known as Oculus Quest 1.

and counterbalanced order. The VE was the same in all conditions. It depicted a furnished room with the participant sitting at a table with a tablet on it. In the mid-air condition the built-in hand-tracking of the Meta Quest was used to interact with the VE without providing haptic feedback. The haptic condition additionally used a real Surface Pro Tablet to act as a haptic proxy for the virtual tablet. The controller condition used the standard Meta Quest controllers to implement a pointer interaction on the virtual tablet. In this experiment we chose a simple configuration task in combination with a perception task. Participants were tasked to configure the illumination intensity of the scene 1) to the maximum value, 2) to the minimum value, 3) to the degree were they can barely read what is written on the wall in front of them, and to read it out loud. The virtual tablet subsequently displayed two different configuration UIs and the configuration was executed twice, once in discrete steps using radio buttons and then in a continuous way using a horizontal slider. After every condition participants removed the HMD and filled out the presence and usability questionnaires specified below.

Measures. Presence was assesed using the IGroup Presence Questionnaire (IPQ) by Schubert et al. [44, 47]. The 14-item questionnaire consists of the three subscales "Spatial Presence", "Involvement" and "Experienced Realism" as well as the additional "General Presence" item. For the assessment of subjective usability the System Usability Scale (SUS) by Brooke [8] was used. In addition task completion times (TCT) were recorded during IVR exposure to provide a supplementary objective indicator for usability.

Participants. An age-heterogenious group of 38 participants was recruited for this pilot study. Participants were between 18 and 83 years old (M = 42.5, SD = 20.95). 19 participants were young adults (18–35), 8 were middle-aged (35–60) and 11 were older adults (>60). Prior IVR experience (assessed on a 4-Point Likert-Scale ranging from 1 - "never used" to 4 - "regularly used") was highest for young adults (M=2.21, SD=0.85) followed by middle-aged (M=1.63, SD=0.52) and older adults (M=1.27, SD=0.65).

4.2   Results

A mixed ANOVA was calculated for each of the resulting questionnaire scores (SUS, IPQ) as well as TCT. Age group (young, middle-aged, older) was entered age as between-participant factor and interaction technique (mid-air interaction, passive haptics, controller) was entered as a within-participant factor. Mixed ANOVA is preferred over multiple regression/correlation for this study because it allows for direct examination of within-subjects effects and is less vulnerable to problems such as multicollinearity and violation of assumptions of independence of residuals. Data was tested for outliers, normal distribution and homogeneity of variance/covariance. Greenhouse-Geisser sphericity correction was applied where necessary.

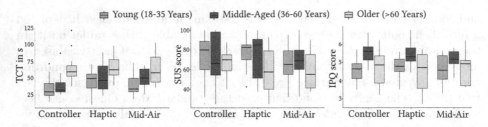

Fig. 2. Boxplots of the task completion time (left), the SUS scores (middle), and the IPQ scores (right).

With regard to the SUS scores no significant main effects of age group ($F = 1.735, p = 0.191$) or interaction technique ($F = 1.364, p = 0.262$) were found and there was no interaction effect ($F = 0.772, p = 0.547$).

For the IPQ scores, homogeneity of variance assumption was slightly violated only in the passive haptics condition ($p = 0.0491$). Here, we found a significant main effect of age group ($F = 3.832, p = 0.031$) but not for interaction technique ($F = 0.332, p = 0.719$) and no interaction effect ($F = 1.395, p = 0.245$). Multiple pairwise paired t-tests for the age group variable, ignoring interaction technique (p-values adjusted via Bonferroni correction), revealed significant differences between the middle-age group and both the young ($p < 0.001$) and older ($p = 0.00106$) groups, but no difference between the older and the young group ($p = 0.856$).

For the task completion times, assumption of normal distribution was violated in the controller condition only for the middle-aged ($p = 0.008$) and young ($p = 0.024$) groups. A strongly significant main effect of age group ($F = 19.389, p < 0.001$) was found but none for interaction technique ($F = 1.375, p = 0.26$) nor an interaction effect ($F = 0.298, p = 0.878$). Multiple pairwise paired t-tests for the age group variable, ignoring interaction technique (p-values adjusted via Bonferroni correction), revealed significant differences between the older group and both the young ($p < 0.001$) and middle-aged ($p = 0.003$) groups, but no difference between the middle-aged and the young group ($p = 0.319$). Descriptive statistics for all experimental conditions and age groups are shown in Fig. 2.

5   Discussion and Future Work

In this pilot study we conducted an age-differentiated investigation of the effects different interaction techniques, namely passive haptics, controller, and mid-air interaction may have on presence as well as objective and subjective indicators of usability in an IVR configuration task.

Several age-related effects could be identified. As seen in previous IVR-studies, performance (i.e., TCT) deteriorated substantially with higher age, with older participants taking significantly longer for task completion than young and middle-aged ones. This is consistent with the literature and thus could be explained by the age-related decline in memory capacity and sensorimotor precision limiting older adults' performance [11, 22]. However, this tendency was not reflected in either subjective usability ratings or reported presence within the IVE. Concerning presence, the results of this experimenet initially suggest a non-linear relationship between age and presence. IPQ scores were significantly higher for middle-aged participants than they were for the older and young age groups, regardless of interaction technique. We suspected that this might be related to differences in IVR experience between age groups, so we performed pairwise T-tests for reported IVR experience. There was no significant difference between middle-aged and older (p=0.2), but there was significant difference between young and older (p<0.01) and between young and middle-aged (p<0.05). Therefore, it is possible that a novelty effect might have affected the presence scores, especially in the middle-aged group, where none of the participants reported to have used an IVR device more than once. However, since the mean IVR experience of the older group was still lower, this relation needs to be investigated more closely in further studies. Moreover, these results suggest that paying closer attention to middle-aged users as a separate age group (alongside young and older users) will be important in future IVR studies. Analogous to the other age groups, middle-aged adults are in a unique phase of life with different physical, cognitive and psychosocial characteristics. As mentioned, middle adulthood is a transitional period where individuals may experience changes in their social roles, lifestyle, and health status. All this may affect their use and experience of IVR in different ways compared to young and older adults. Including a middle-aged group in the study design allows for a more sensitive analysis of the age effects on the dependent variables. This could reveal age-related differences that may not be apparent when comparing only young and older groups, as it was predominantly done in previous research (see Sect. 2).

Considering usability, mean SUS scores fell roughly within the 'acceptable' range of the SUS questionnaire for all combinations of age group and interaction technique (ranging from 59.6 to 78.2). Older Adults had the lowest overall SUS score ($M = 62.2$), followed by the middle aged ($M = 70, 4$) and the young adults ($M = 73.2$), however these differences were not significant. Thus, although it took older subjects significantly longer to complete the task with either interaction technique, this did not reduce their perceived usability.

Surprisingly, no differences were found between interaction techniques in any of the independent variables. We had expected that in direct comparison to passive haptics, at least the mid-air interaction would perform significantly poorer, due to the lack of sensory feedback. It seems that not only young and middle-aged adults have been able to compensate for non-existent haptic feedback. Since the impact of the aging process on haptic perception is comparatively small [37, 38], older adults might also have been able to cope better, than they would with other discrepancies in perceptual stimuli (e.g. visual or auditory). Thus, results suggest that passive haptics, mid-air, and controller interaction in IVR can be equally well suited for simple one dimensional configuration tasks regardless of users' age. However it remains unclear whether this also applies to multidimensional configuration tasks. In this experiment we focused exclusively on the configuration of illumination intensity, as a relevant aspect for viusal perception, which is subject to age-related changes. However, as we plan to incorporate more perceptual and cognitive variables and their combinations in further studies, configuration tasks will become far more complex and more extensive. This may enable certain interaction techniques to unfold their full potential of compensating for age-related differences in user characteristics.

Another question that needs to be investigated in future studies is whether more sophisticated age differentiation could have better identified age differences between interaction techniques. This study exclusively used chronological age in years as an age indicator. As previously mentioned the additional consideration of age-specific ability profiles is an upcoming approach in research on the age-differentiated design of human-technology interfaces [46]. Thus, follow-up studies should apply neuropsychological tests to precisely measure perceptual and cognitive key variables to enable a refined definition of age groups compared to classifications merely based on chronological age in years. In particular, this could shed light on how the group of middle-aged adults (as a transitional stage) is defined in terms of user characteristics and how these relate to the use and experience of IVR systems (i.e. usability and presence). This offers the opportunity to further clarify potentially non-linear relationships, such as the one between age and presence found in this experiment. As a starting point for this differentiation we plan to focus on the individual performance of the visual system (e.g., visual acuity, spatial vision, accommodation ability, color and contrast vision), the visual short-term memory capacity (block span), and spatial imagination. This may allow us to systematically determine how age-specific ability profiles are interrelated with presence and usability in addition to mere age correlations.

6   Limitations

Our pilot study has several limitations to the generalizability of its results that should be adressed. First, the different (and in part very small, e.g., middle-aged: n=8) sample size of the three age groups limits the comparability of their data. Second, experiments were conducted in three different locations, a laboratory, a community house, and a private space. Future studies should use a single controlled laboratory environment. Third, the haptic proxy was only placed in a predetermined fixed position to overlap with the virtual tablet. This could have resulted in an impairment of the previously mentioned coherence of the stimuli (see Sect. 3). Utilizing positional tracking could enable more dynamic interaction and achieve better haptic fidelity. Finally, future studies should include usability testing and/or inspection methods (e.g., usability heuristics, cognitive walkthrough) for a more sophisticated and complete usability measurement.

Acknowledgements. We thank the LandFrauen Berkenthin und Umgebung e.V. for their active support and for making their venues available for our studies.

References

1. Abeele, V.V., Schraepen, B., Huygelier, H., Gillebert, C., Gerling, K., Van Ee, R.: Immersive virtual reality for older adults: empirically grounded design guidelines. ACM Trans. Accessible Comput. (TACCESS) **14**(3), 1–30 (2021). https://doi.org/10.1145/3470743
2. Alsina-Jurnet, I., Gutiérrez-Maldonado, J.: Influence of personality and individual abilities on the sense of presence experienced in anxiety triggering virtual environments. Int. J. Human-Comput. Stud. **68**(10), 788–801 (2010). https://doi.org/10.1016/j.ijhcs.2010.07.001
3. Ankomah, P., Vangorp, P.: Virtual reality: a literature review and metrics based classification. Comput. Graph. Vis. Comput. (CGVC) **2018**, 173–181 (2018). https://doi.org/10.2312/cgvc.20181222
4. Arlati, S., Keijsers, N., Paolini, G., Ferrigno, G., Sacco, M.: Age-related differences in the kinematics of aimed movements in immersive virtual reality: a preliminary study. In: 2022 IEEE International Symposium on Medical Measurements and Applications (MeMeA), pp. 1–6. IEEE (2022). https://doi.org/10.1109/MeMeA54994.2022.9856412
5. Baker, S., Waycott, J., Carrasco, R., Hoang, T., Vetere, F.: Exploring the design of social VR experiences with older adults. In: Proceedings of the 2019 on Designing Interactive Systems Conference, pp. 303–315 (2019). https://doi.org/10.1145/3322276.3322361
6. Bangay, S., Preston, L.: An investigation into factors influencing immersion in interactive virtual reality environments. In: Virtual Environments in Clinical Psychology and Neuroscience, pp. 43–51. IOS Press (1998)
7. Brade, J., Lorenz, M., Busch, M., Hammer, N., Tscheligi, M., Klimant, P.: Being there again-presence in real and virtual environments and its relation to usability and user experience using a mobile navigation task. Int. J. Hum.-Comput. Stud. **101**, 76–87 (2017). https://doi.org/10.1016/j.ijhcs.2017.01.004
8. Brooke, J.: Sus-a quick and dirty usability scale. Usability Eval. Ind. **189**(194), 4–7 (1996)
9. Busch, M., Lorenz, M., Tscheligi, M., Hochleitner, C., Schulz, T.: Being there for real: presence in real and virtual environments and its relation to usability. In: Proceedings of the 8th Nordic Conference on Human-Computer Interaction: fun, fast, foundational, pp. 117–126 (2014). https://doi.org/10.1145/2639189.2639224
10. Bystrom, K.E., Barfield, W., Hendrix, C.: A conceptual model of the sense of presence in virtual environments. Presence: Teleoperators Virtual Environ. **8**(2), 241–244 (1999). https://doi.org/10.1162/105474699566107
11. Charness, N., Best, R., Souders, D.: Memory function and supportive technology. Gerontechnology: Int. J. Fundamental Aspects Technol. Serve the Ageing Society **11**(1) (2012). https://doi.org/10.4017/gt.2012.11.01.006.00
12. Coelho, C., Tichon, J., Hine, T.J., Wallis, G., Riva, G.: Media presence and inner presence: the sense of presence in virtual reality technologies. From communication to presence: cognition, emotions and culture towards the ultimate communicative experience **11**, 25–45 (2006)
13. Coldham, G., Cook, D.M.: VR usability from elderly cohorts: preparatory challenges in overcoming technology rejection. In: 2017 National Information Technology Conference (NITC), pp. 131–135. IEEE (2017). https://doi.org/10.1109/NITC.2017.8285645

14. Corriveau Lecavalier, N., Ouellet, É., Boller, B., Belleville, S.: Use of immersive virtual reality to assess episodic memory: a validation study in older adults. Neuropsychol. Rehabil. **30**(3), 462–480 (2020). https://doi.org/10.1080/09602011.2018.1477684

15. Coxon, M., Kelly, N., Page, S.: Individual differences in virtual reality: are spatial presence and spatial ability linked? Virtual Reality **20**(4), 203–212 (2016). https://doi.org/10.1007/s10055-016-0292-x

16. Craik, F.I.M., Byrd, M.: Aging and cognitive deficits. In: Aging and cognitive processes, pp. 191–211. Springer (1982). https://doi.org/10.1007/978-1-4684-4178-9_11

17. Cummings, J.J., Bailenson, J.N.: How immersive is enough? a meta-analysis of the effect of immersive technology on user presence. Media Psychol. **19**(2), 272–309 (2016). https://doi.org/10.1080/15213269.2015.1015740

18. Czaja, S.J., Boot, W.R., Charness, N., Rogers, W.A.: Designing for older adults: principles and creative human factors approaches. CRC Press (2019)

19. Dilanchian, A.T., Andringa, R., Boot, W.R.: A pilot study exploring age differences in presence, workload, and cybersickness in the experience of immersive virtual reality environments. Front. Virtual Reality **2**(October), 1–11 (2021). https://doi.org/10.3389/frvir.2021.736793

20. Dong, Y., et al.: A haptic-feedback virtual reality system to improve the box and block test (BBT) for upper extremity motor function assessment. Virtual Reality, pp. 1–21 (2022). https://doi.org/10.1007/s10055-022-00727-2

21. Felnhofer, A., Kothgassner, O.D., Hauk, N., Beutl, L., Hlavacs, H., Kryspin-Exner, I.: Physical and social presence in collaborative virtual environments: exploring age and gender differences with respect to empathy. Comput. Hum. Behav. **31**, 272–279 (2014). https://doi.org/10.1016/j.chb.2013.10.045

22. Goldstein, E.: Sensation and Perception. Cengage learning, 2013 (2016)

23. Hawthorn, D.: Possible implications of aging for interface designers. Interact. Comput. **12**(5), 507–528 (2000). https://doi.org/10.1016/S0953-5438(99)00021-1

24. Heeter, C.: Being there: the subjective experience of presence. Presence: Teleoperators Virtual Environ. **1**(2), 262–271 (1992)

25. Hughes, M.L., Agrigoroaei, S., Jeon, M., Bruzzese, M., Lachman, M.E.: Change in cognitive performance from midlife into old age: findings from the midlife in the united states (MIDUS) study. J. Int. Neuropsychol. Soc. **24**(8), 805–820 (2018). https://doi.org/10.1017/S1355617718000425

26. Insko, B.E.: Passive haptics significantly enhances virtual environments. The University of North Carolina at Chapel Hill (2001)

27. Janeh, O., Bruder, G., Steinicke, F., Gulberti, A., Poetter-Nerger, M.: Analyses of gait parameters of younger and older adults during (non-) isometric virtual walking. IEEE Trans. Vis. Comput. Graph. **24**(10), 2663–2674 (2017). https://doi.org/10.1109/TVCG.2017.2771520

28. Kramida, G.: Resolving the vergence-accommodation conflict in head-mounted displays. IEEE Trans. Vis. Comput. Graph. **22**(7), 1912–1931 (2015). https://doi.org/10.1109/TVCG.2015.2473855

29. Lachman, M.E.: Development in midlife. Annu. Rev. Psychol. **55**, 305–331 (2004). https://doi.org/10.1146/annurev.psych.55.090902.141521

30. Lai, X., Lei, X., Chen, X., Rau, P.-L.P.: Can virtual reality satisfy entertainment needs of the elderly? The application of a VR headset in elderly care. In: Rau, P.-L.P. (ed.) HCII 2019. LNCS, vol. 11577, pp. 159–172. Springer, Cham (2019). https://doi.org/10.1007/978-3-030-22580-3_13

31. Lee, C.C., Czaja, S.J., Moxley, J.H., Sharit, J., Boot, W.R., Charness, N., Rogers, W.A.: Attitudes toward computers across adulthood from 1994 to 2013. Gerontologist **59**(1), 22–33 (2019). https://doi.org/10.1093/geront/gny081

32. Liu, L., Watson, B., Miyazaki, M.: VR for the elderly: quantitative and qualitative differences in performance with a driving simulator. Cyberpsychol. Behav. **2**(6), 567–576 (1999). https://doi.org/10.1089/cpb.1999.2.567

33. Lombard, M., et al.: Measuring presence: a literature-based approach to the development of a standardized paper-and-pencil instrument. In: Third International Workshop on Presence, Delft, The Netherlands, vol. 240, pp. 2–4 (2000)

34. Madden, D.J., Langley, L.K.: Age-related changes in selective attention and perceptual load during visual search. Psychol. Aging **18**(1), 54 (2003). https://doi.org/10.1037/0882-7974.18.1.54

35. Makransky, G., Wismer, P., Mayer, R.E.: A gender matching effect in learning with pedagogical agents in an immersive virtual reality science simulation. J. Comput. Assist. Learn. **35**(3), 349–358 (2019). https://doi.org/10.1111/jcal.12335

36. Mania, K., Chalmers, A.: The effects of levels of immersion on memory and presence in virtual environments: a reality centered approach. Cyberpsychol. Behav. **4**(2), 247–264 (2001). https://doi.org/10.1089/109493101300117938

37. McGlynn, S.A.: Investigating age-related differences in spatial presence formation and maintenance in virtual reality. Ph.D. thesis, Georgia Institute of Technology (2019)

38. McGlynn, S.A., Rogers, W.A.: Design recommendations to enhance virtual reality presence for older adults. In: Proceedings of the Human Factors and Ergonomics Society Annual Meeting, vol. 61, pp. 2077–2081. SAGE Publications Sage CA: Los Angeles, CA (2017). https://doi.org/10.1177/1541931213602002

39. Mitzner, T.L., et al.: Technology adoption by older adults: findings from the prism trial. Gerontologist **59**(1), 34–44 (2019). https://doi.org/10.1093/geront/gny113

40. Murray, C.D., Fox, J., Pettifer, S.: Absorption, dissociation, locus of control and presence in virtual reality. Comput. Hum. Behav. **23**(3), 1347–1354 (2007). https://doi.org/10.1016/j.chb.2004.12.010

41. Nash, E.B., Edwards, G.W., Thompson, J.A., Barfield, W.: A review of presence and performance in virtual environments. Int. J. Hum.-Comput. Interact. **12**(1), 1–41 (2000). https://doi.org/10.1207/S15327590IJHC1201_1

42. Optale, G., et al.: Controlling memory impairment in elderly adults using virtual reality memory training: a randomized controlled pilot study. Neurorehabil. Neural Repair **24**(4), 348–357 (2010). https://doi.org/10.1177/1545968309353328

43. Rand, D., et al.: Comparison of two VR platforms for rehabilitation: video capture versus HMD. Presence: Teleoperators Virtual Environ. **14**(2), 147–160 (2005). https://doi.org/10.1162/1054746053967012

44. Regenbrecht, H., Schubert, T.: Real and illusory interactions enhance presence in virtual environments. Presence: Teleoperators Virtual Environ. **11**(4), 425–434 (2002). https://doi.org/10.1162/105474602760004318

45. Reinhardt, J., Wolf, K.: Go-through: disabling collision to access obstructed paths and open occluded views in social VR. In: Proceedings of the Augmented Humans International Conference, pp. 1–10 (2020). https://doi.org/10.1145/3384657.3384784

46. Schlick, C.M., Frieling, E., Wegge, J.: Age-differentiated work systems. Springer (2013). https://doi.org/10.1007/978-3-642-35057-3

47. Schubert, T., Friedmann, F., Regenbrecht, H.: The experience of presence: factor analytic insights. Presence: Teleoperators Virtual Environ. **10**(3), 266–281 (2001). https://doi.org/10.1162/105474601300343603

48. Schuemie, M.J., Abel, B., Van Der Mast, C.A., Krijn, M., Emmelkamp, P.M.: The effect of locomotion technique on presence, fear and usability in a virtual environment. In: Euromedia, vol. 2005, p. 11th. Citeseer (2005)
49. Silva, R.S., Mol, A.M., Ishitani, L.: Virtual reality for older users: a systematic literature review. Int. J. Virtual Reality 19(1), 11–25 (2019). https://doi.org/10.20870/IJVR.2019.19.1.2908
50. Skarbez, R., Brooks, F.P., Jr., Whitton, M.C.: A survey of presence and related concepts. ACM Comput. Surv. (CSUR) 50(6), 1–39 (2017). https://doi.org/10.1145/3134301
51. Skarbez, R.T.: Plausibility illusion in virtual environments. Ph.D. thesis, The University of North Carolina at Chapel Hill (2016)
52. Slater, M.: How colorful was your day? why questionnaires cannot assess presence in virtual environments. Presence 13(4), 484–493 (2004). https://doi.org/10.1162/1054746041944849
53. Snow, M.P.: Charting presence in virtual environments and its effects on performance. Ph.D. thesis, Virginia Polytechnic Institute and State University (1996)
54. Steed, A., Takala, T.M., Archer, D., Lages, W., Lindeman, R.W.: Directions for 3D user interface research from consumer VR games. arXiv preprint arXiv:2106.12633 (2021)
55. Stephanidis, C., et al.: Seven HCI grand challenges. Int. J. Hum.-Comput. Interact. 35(14), 1229–1269 (2019). https://doi.org/10.1080/10447318.2019.1619259
56. Wallach, H.S., Safir, M.P., Samana, R.: Personality variables and presence. Virtual Reality 14(1), 3–13 (2010). https://doi.org/10.1007/s10055-009-0124-3
57. Witmer, B.G., Singer, M.J.: Measuring presence in virtual environments: a presence questionnaire. Presence 7(3), 225–240 (1998). https://doi.org/10.1162/105474698565686

The Social and hUman CeNtered XR: SUN XR Project

Luca Greci[✉], Ferdinando Bosco, and Vincenzo Croce

Engineering Ingegneria Informatica Spa, Rome, Italy
luca.greci@eng.it

Abstract. In the recent years, Extended Reality (XR) technology has emerged as a powerful tool, revolutionizing various industries, offering immersive experiences and making experiences available to individuals who may face physical barriers. XR technology, combined with hyper-realistic avatars and innovative interfaces, holds great promise for revolutionizing rehabilitation practices and improving the quality of life for individuals with serious mobility and verbal communication diseases. In this context the SUN project aims to explore and develop XR solutions that merge the physical and virtual realms, focusing on human and social aspects. The project addresses challenges such as hyper-realistic human interaction interfaces, resource limitations of end-user devices, and wearable haptics for enhanced physical interactions. The project also investigates gaze-based and gesture-based interaction and leverages artificial intelligence to optimize resource allocation and improve the XR experience.

This paper presents two use cases that will be developed as demonstrators of the SUN project: XR for Rehabilitation and XR for people with serious mobility and verbal communication diseases.

Keywords: Extended reality · limb rehabilitation · mobility diseases · verbal communication diseases · NFT and Metaverse

1 Introduction

Extended Reality (XR) technology has emerged as a powerful tool, revolutionizing various industries and offering immersive experiences.

XR technologies have the potential to greatly enhance accessibility, making experiences available to individuals who may face physical or geographical barriers. For example, individuals with disabilities or limited mobility can benefit from virtual experiences that provide them with opportunities to explore new environments, participate in educational activities, or engage in social interactions [1–3].

XR can level the playing field and ensure that everyone, regardless of physical limitations, can access and engage with various forms of content and experiences. Moreover, XR technologies offer opportunities for individuals to connect, collaborate, and engage in shared experiences regardless of their physical location [4]. Virtual reality platforms enable people from different parts of the world to come together in shared virtual spaces, fostering social inclusion and breaking down geographical barriers.

L. T. De Paolis et al. (Eds.): XR Salento 2023, LNCS 14218, pp. 223–231, 2023.
https://doi.org/10.1007/978-3-031-43401-3_15

XR can provide individuals who may feel isolated or marginalized in their physical environments with a sense of belonging and community. XR technologies have shown promise in the healthcare sector, particularly in the realms of mental health, rehabilitation, and assistive therapy [5]. Virtual reality-based interventions can provide accessible and controlled environments for individuals with anxiety disorders [6, 7, 8], phobias [9], facilitating exposure therapy and reducing barriers to mental healthcare.

This paper presents the real-life scenarios that will be used to evaluate the technologies developed by the SUN project in the field of upper and lower body rehabilitation and supporting people with verbal communication diseases: XR for rehabilitation and XR for people with serious mobility and verbal communication diseases.

2 Upper and Lower Limb Rehabilitation

Upper and lower limb rehabilitation is a vital component of medical care for individuals with impairments or injuries affecting their arms, hands, legs, or feet.

This type of rehabilitation aims to restore mobility, functionality, and independence in performing activities of daily living. Traditional rehabilitation approaches often involve repetitive exercises, manual therapy, and assistive devices to facilitate recovery [10]. While these methods have proven effective to some extent, they often lack engagement, personalization, and real-life context, leading to reduced motivation and adherence to therapy.

Traditional rehabilitation approaches face several limitations that can be addressed by incorporating XR technologies. Firstly, traditional methods often lack engaging and immersive experiences, which can result in boredom and reduced motivation for patients. XR technologies, such as virtual reality (VR) and augmented reality (AR), provide a more captivating and interactive environment, offering patients a sense of presence and enjoyment during their rehabilitation sessions [11–14].

Secondly, traditional approaches may lack personalization and customization. Each patient has unique needs and abilities, and traditional therapies often follow a one-size-fits-all approach. In contrast, XR technologies enable the creation of hyper-realistic avatars (HRA) that can mimic the patient's specific body movements and characteristics. This personalization aspect enhances the relevance and effectiveness of rehabilitation exercises, as patients can see themselves represented in the virtual environment, increasing their sense of ownership and engagement [15].

Lastly, traditional rehabilitation methods often lack real-life context, making it challenging for patients to transfer their skills and progress into their daily activities. XR technologies can simulate real-world scenarios and environments, providing patients with the opportunity to practice functional movements and tasks in a safe and controlled virtual setting. By bridging the gap between therapy and real-life situations, XR-based rehabilitation can improve the transfer of skills and boost patients' confidence in performing daily activities independently [16, 17].

3 Mobility and Verbal Communication Diseases

For individuals with limited mobility, XR offers virtual environments that can be accessed from the comfort of their homes. XR headsets provide a means of escape and exploration, enabling users to visit distant locations engage in physical activities, or even attend events they would otherwise be unable to access.

Through AR, users can experience simulations that mimic real-world scenarios, allowing them to practice and improve their mobility skills in a safe and controlled environment [19]. XR technology is empowering individuals with mobility challenges by granting them newfound freedom, independence, and a sense of inclusion.

People with verbal communication diseases often face significant challenges in expressing themselves and interacting with others. XR technology can bridge this communication gap by offering innovative solutions. With XR, individuals can leverage gesture recognition, eye tracking, and voice commands to communicate their needs, emotions, and thoughts more effectively [20].

AR overlays can display real-time subtitles, translating spoken language into written text, enabling smooth conversations with others. VR environments facilitate non-verbal forms of expression, such as body language and hand gestures, allowing individuals to connect with their surroundings and express themselves more fully. XR technology empowers people with verbal communication diseases to engage in meaningful social interactions and facilitates improved communication with their caregivers, family, and friends [21].

4 Hyper-Realistic Avatar and XR

4.1 For Rehabilitation

In SUN photorealistic avatars are used and represent new cutting-edge technology compared with low quality 2d avatars and cartonized version. They offer a realistic representation of yourself in the virtual world and facial expressions that make your avatar more human.

HRAs, in the context of rehabilitation, are digital representations that closely mimic the appearance and movements of individuals undergoing therapy. The hyper-realist factor represents a strong user engagement factor, in fact the experience shows that the engagement obtained by avatar that accurately resembles the user is significantly higher than the static and cartoon-like ones.

HRAs are designed using advanced 3D photogrammetry body scanning techniques and motion capture technologies to replicate the patient's unique physical characteristics, including body shape, limb movements, joint angles, and even facial expressions. HRAs are then integrated into VR or AR environments, where patients can interact with and control their virtual counterparts.

The role of HRA in rehabilitation extends beyond mere visual representation. They play a crucial role in enhancing patient engagement and motivation. By embodying the patient in a virtual environment, avatars provide a strong sense of presence and immersion, making the rehabilitation experience more interactive and compelling. Patients can see themselves performing movements and tasks through the avatar's perspective, which creates a powerful visual feedback loop [22]. This visual feedback can boost motivation by providing a clear understanding of progress and improvements, as well as highlighting areas that need further attention [23].

Furthermore, customization and personalization of avatars are essential features in individualized rehabilitation. HRA can be tailored to match the patient's specific needs, abilities, and preferences. This customization includes adjusting the avatar's physical attributes, such as limb lengths or joint ranges, to accurately represent the patient's impairments. Personalization extends to the virtual environment as well, allowing patients to choose different scenarios, difficulty levels, or even incorporating gamification elements to make the rehabilitation experience more enjoyable and engaging. By providing individualized avatars, rehabilitation programs can address the specific challenges and goals of each patient, enhancing their sense of ownership and promoting a higher level of commitment to the therapy process [24].

4.2 To Enhance Communication

HRA, Real-time 3D Human Pose-Motion Reconstruction and XR technologies have ushered in a new era of accessibility and inclusivity for individuals facing serious mobility and verbal communication diseases. By harnessing the power of virtual environments and lifelike avatars, these innovative solutions offer transformative opportunities for individuals to overcome their challenges and engage with the world on their terms.

Hyper-realistic HRA serve as digital representations of individuals, enabling them to express themselves, communicate, and interact with others in virtual spaces. For people with verbal communication diseases, these avatars become powerful tools for overcoming limitations [24]. Through the integration of XR, users can control their avatars' movements, gestures, and expressions, facilitating non-verbal communication. This empowers individuals to express their thoughts, emotions, and needs in a way that transcends verbal language barriers, leading to improved social interaction and a greater sense of connection with others [24].

5   The SUN XR Project

The main objective of The Social and hUman ceNtered XR (SUN) project is to explore and create XR solutions that effectively merge the physical and virtual realms, with a specific focus on human and social aspects. By utilizing the virtual world, this initiative seeks to enhance the physical environment by introducing new possibilities for socializing and engaging with others. The solution will be offered as SUN XR Platform, including digital twins, wearable sensors and haptic interfaces, artificial intelligence-based solutions to address limitations of wearable devices, hyper-realistic avatars of real people, blockchain-based solutions for the digital asset management. In relation to the latest a tokenized platform, leveraging on NFTs, will be embedded for the fair, transparent and secure management of the XR digital assets.

The SUN project aims to tackle certain challenges in XR by addressing the lack of hyper-realistic and immersive human interaction interfaces, as well as resource limitations of end-user devices. To overcome these limitations, the project will focus on developing innovative wearable sensors and haptic interfaces that enable natural and convincing interaction with the virtual environment.

The introduction of wearable haptics will enhance physical interactions, allowing users to engage with virtual menus and receive contextually-relevant information through tactile feedback. Furthermore, the project will explore solutions for providing body contextual information, such as skin stretch-vibration on different body parts and vibrotactile and thermal cues under fingertips. These enhancements will guide users in various tasks, including remote training, home physical exercises, and interacting with others in XR.

In addition, the project will investigate and develop advanced solutions for user interaction, specifically gaze-based and gesture-based interaction. These approaches will enable users to interact with the XR environment using their gaze or gestures, enhancing the immersion and usability of the experience.

To address the current limitations of wearable devices in terms of computing power, memory, and network connectivity, the project will leverage artificial intelligence-based solutions. These intelligent systems will optimize resource allocation, improve data processing capabilities, and overcome network constraints, ensuring a smoother and more efficient XR experience on wearable devices.

The solutions will be demonstrated in real-life scenarios, focusing on social interaction and collaboration.

5.1   XR for Rehabilitation

The objective of this scenario is to enhance adherence to the physiotherapy protocol, boost patient involvement, monitor physiological conditions, and offer immediate feedback to patients by real-time classification of exercises as correctly or incorrectly executed, based on the criteria set by physiotherapists.

It is widely recognized that combining visual and physical interaction yields better task performance compared to relying solely on visual interaction. Wearable haptics, such as EMG, can be employed to enhance the monitoring of physical interaction by providing contextual information about the body. Visual AI algorithms can aid in understanding body alignment, capturing outlines, and delivering personalized real-time feedback to enhance the quality of movement.

Ensuring adherence and fidelity to rehabilitation is particularly challenging, especially when it comes to motor learning with personalized feedback. Physiotherapy plays a crucial role in the complete rehabilitation of conditions like orthopedic surgery, "frozen shoulder," or severe hand arthritis, but it often becomes repetitive, monotonous, and time-consuming. In fact, achieving motor recovery often requires an extensive course of physiotherapy treatment, sometimes exceeding 50 sessions.

Therefore, it is essential to bridge the gap between evidence and practice and effectively implement digital innovations while improving their accuracy and portability in home environments. By starting with a visual representation of an exercise, conveyed through an avatar of the therapist performing it correctly, the patient will be asked to repeat the exercise or synchronize their movements with the avatar.

Wearable devices and wireless sensors will be utilized to measure and provide contextual information, including multiple IMUs (Inertial Measurement Unit) for dynamic motion, body and limb orientation kinetics and kinematics, and the maximum joint angle achieved. SEMG will assess neuromuscular potentials like activation and fatigue, while a smartwatch will monitor heart rate, oxygen saturation, and arterial blood pressure.

In specific cases, a flex sensor could replace a gyroscope to measure limb angles during bending, and a force-sensitive sensor can gauge limb pressure, potentially enabling classification of various rehabilitation exercises across a sensor network.

Real-time data from a camera and the sensors will be collected and sent to a GPU server, which could be cloud-based or edge-based, leveraging cloud-based AI infrastructure or edge AI technology, respectively. An AI algorithm will process the sensory input, adjusting the exercise difficulty-intensity based on muscle activation levels and providing personalized feedback on movement quality.

Clinicians can also contribute their feedback at any point during the automated feedback process to enhance accuracy, ensure safety, and further improve the algorithm. Prior to the application of these complex innovative digital tools, usability testing is necessary.

Additionally, the goal of this scenario is to increase user engagement among diverse populations. This can be achieved by incorporating personalization for diverse populations with varying rehabilitation needs and abilities.

An iterative-convergent-mixed-methods design will be employed to assess and address any significant usability issues, optimizing the user experience and facilitating adoption. This design approach will provide transparency and guidance throughout the development and implementation of the tool within clinical pathways.

5.2 XR for People with Serious Mobility and Verbal Communication Diseases

Individuals with motor disabilities or those recovering from strokes often face significant challenges in communication and meeting their essential needs.

The project aims to address this issue by establishing a dedicated communication pathway specifically designed for such individuals. This pathway will enable them to interact with specific social cues, transforming them into clear communication or actions. By leveraging residual abilities and assigning them meaning in terms of communication, the project will incorporate avatars in a virtual environment as needed. The objective is to develop low-cost, non-invasive tools that utilize existing biofeedback, facial expressions, and other input methods.

The main challenge lies in creating a solution that allows for person-specific XR interactions in various settings such as home, workplace, or school. The project also aims to develop innovative multi-user virtual communication and collaboration solutions that deliver cohesive multisensory experiences while effectively conveying relevant social cues.

Successful implementation of the pilot scenario will enable individuals with communication and motor disabilities to interact with friends and family, realistically meeting in an extended environment that combines the physical and virtual realms.

The person with disabilities will be represented by an avatar, interacting with others present in an augmented physical environment. Simultaneously, the individual with disabilities will experience the illusion of being present in the same physical environment as others, interacting with the new interfaces provided by the SUN project.

To achieve this, SUN will develop a new generation of non-invasive bidirectional body-machine interfaces (BBMIs). These interfaces will enable smooth and highly effective interaction between individuals with different types of sensory-motor disabilities and virtual reality environments with avatars. The BBMI will utilize printed electrode arrays to record muscle activities and inertial sensors, with the sensor positions tailored to the specific motor abilities of the individuals. For example, shoulder and elbow movements may be used, and muscle activities from auricular muscles could also be recorded.

These sensors will capture information during various upper limb and hand movements, and a tailored decoding algorithm will be implemented to identify the most useful signals for different tasks. This approach has already proven successful in controlling flying drones and is expected to yield promising results in this context as well.

Machine learning techniques will be utilized to decode the different tasks, relying on human-machine interfaces and extracting information from electrophysiological and biomechanical signals.

Furthermore, SUN aims to provide sensory feedback to the user regarding movement and interaction with the avatar in the virtual environment. This will be achieved through techniques such as transcutaneous electrical stimulation or small actuators for vibration.

6 Conclusion and Future Work

The paper describes the general objectives of the SUN focusing on the two scenarios aimed at improving rehabilitation and communication for individuals with physical disabilities.

The first scenario focuses on enhancing adherence to physiotherapy protocols and increasing patient engagement through real-time classification of exercises. The use of wearable haptics and visual AI algorithms allows for better monitoring of physical interactions and personalized feedback. The goal is to bridge the gap between evidence and practice by implementing digital innovations accurately and effectively in home environments. Various wearable devices and wireless sensors are employed to measure physiological conditions and provide contextual information. Real-time data from cameras and sensors are processed by an AI algorithm to adjust exercise difficulty and provide personalized feedback on movement quality. Clinician feedback is also incorporated to enhance accuracy and safety.

The second scenario addresses communication and essential needs for individuals with motor disabilities or those recovering from strokes. The project aims to establish a dedicated communication pathway using XR technologies. Hyper-realistic avatars in virtual environments will enable individuals to interact with social cues and convert them into clear communication or actions. The goal is to develop low-cost, non-invasive tools that utilize biofeedback, facial expressions, and other input methods. The project also aims to create multi-user virtual communication and collaboration solutions that effectively convey social cues. Non-invasive bidirectional body-machine interfaces (BBMIs) will be developed to enable smooth interaction between individuals with sensory-motor disabilities and virtual reality environments. Machine learning techniques will be used to decode different tasks based on electrophysiological and biomechanical signals. Finally, sensory feedback through electrical stimulation or vibration will enhance the user's experience and interaction with the avatar in the virtual environment.

The future phase of this project will involve implementing and assessing the pilots in terms of usability and performance. The results obtained from the pilots will be evaluated through focus groups, which will conduct interaction analysis and assess factors such as the sense of immersion, experience sharing, and engagement.

The assessment of the pilots will also involve the evaluation by professional users. For instance, in the rehabilitation scenario, a total of 10 subjects will be enrolled, and the outcomes will be evaluated using the QuichDASH scale. The QuichDASH scale is a shortened version of the DASH (Disability of the Arm, Shoulder, and Hand) scale, which can be found at https://dash.iwh.on.ca/about-quickdash.

References

1. Aasen, J., Galaaen, K., Nilsson, F., Sørensen, T., Lien, L., Leonhardt, M.: Promoting social participation and recovery using virtual reality-based interventions among people with mental health and substance use disorders: qualitative study. JMIR Form Res. **27**(7), e46136 (2023). https://doi.org/10.2196/46136.PMID:37104000;PMCID:PMC10176145
2. Kourtesis, P., et al.: Virtual reality training of social skills in adults with autism spectrum disorder: an examination of acceptability, usability, user experience, social skills, and executive functions. Behav. Sci. **13**(4), 336 (2023). https://doi.org/10.3390/bs13040336
3. Liu, L.: Virtual reality for social skills training of children and adolescents with ASD: a systematic review. J. Educ. Hum. Soc. Sci. **8**, 2061–2067 (2023). https://doi.org/10.54097/ehss.v8i.4645
4. Arlati, S., et al.: A social virtual reality-based application for the physical and cognitive training of the elderly at home. Sensors **19**(2), 261 (2019)
5. Weiss, P.L., Kizony, R., Feintuch, U.: Virtual reality in neurorehabilitation. Textbook of Neural Repair and Rehabilitation, pp. 1253–1265(2008)
6. Carl, E., et al.: Virtual reality exposure therapy for anxiety and related disorders: a meta-analysis of randomized controlled trials. J Anxiety Disord. **61**, 27–36 (2019). https://doi.org/10.1016/j.janxdis.2018.08.003. Epub 2018 Aug 10. PMID: 30287083
7. Malbos, E., Rapee, R. M., Kavakli, M., Kagan, C.: Virtual reality applications for the treatment of social anxiety disorder: an overview. J. Clin. Psychol. **75**(12), 2463–2479 (2019)
8. García-Palacios, A., Botella, C., Hoffman, H., Fabregat, S.: Comparing acceptance and refusal rates of virtual reality exposure vs. in vivo exposure by patients with specific phobias. CyberPsychol Behav. **10**(5), 722–724 (2007)
9. Veerbeek, J.M., et al.: What is the evidence for physical therapy poststroke? A systematic review and meta-analysis. PLoS ONE **9**(2), e87987 (2014)
10. Holden, M.: Virtual environments for motor rehabilitation: review. Cyberpsychol. Behav. Soc. Netw. **8**(3), 187–211 (2005)
11. Ou, Y., Wang, Y., Chang, H., Yen, S., Zheng, Y., Lee, B.: Development of virtual reality rehabilitation games for children with attention-deficit hyperactivity disorder. J. Ambient. Intell. Humaniz. Comput. **11**(11), 5713–5720 (2020)
12. Köktürk, E., Molteni, F., Bordegoni, M., Covarrubias, M.: Utilization of limb orientations for a home-based immersive virtual reality rehabilitation system to treat phantom limb pain. In: Miesenberger, K., Kouroupetroglou, G. (eds.) Computers Helping People with Special Needs, pp. 484–488. Springer International Publishing, Cham (2018). https://doi.org/10.1007/978-3-319-94274-2_71
13. Malaka, R.: How computer games can improve your health and fitness. Games for Training, Education, Health and Sports, pp. 1–7 (2014)

14. Montoya, M.F., Muñoz, J.E., Henao, O.A.: Enhancing virtual rehabilitation in upper limbs with biocybernetic adaptation: the effects of virtual reality on perceived muscle fatigue, game performance and user experience. IEEE Trans. Neural Syst. Rehabil. Eng. **28**(3), 740–747 (2020). https://doi.org/10.1109/TNSRE.2020.2968869
15. Kim, A., Schweighofer, N., Finley, J.M.: Locomotor skill acquisition in virtual reality shows sustained transfer to the real world. J. NeuroEng. Rehabil. **16**, 113 (2019). https://doi.org/10.1186/s12984-019-0584-y
16. Rose, F.D., Attree, E.A., Brooks, B.M., Parslow, D.M., Penn, P.R., Ambihaipahan, N.: Training in virtual environments: transfer to real world tasks and equivalence to real task training. Ergonomics **43**(4), 494–511 (2000). https://doi.org/10.1080/001401300184378. PMID: 10801083
17. Oncioiu, I., Priescu, I.: The use of virtual reality in tourism destinations as a tool to develop tourist behavior perspective. Sustainability **14**(7), 4191 (2022). https://doi.org/10.3390/su14074191
18. Demeco, A., et al.: Immersive virtual reality in post-stroke rehabilitation: a systematic review. Sensors **23**(3), 1712 (2023). https://doi.org/10.3390/s23031712
19. Dechsling, A., et al.: Virtual and augmented reality in social skills interventions for individuals with autism spectrum disorder: a scoping review. J. Autism. Dev. Disord. **52**(11), 4692–4707 (2022). https://doi.org/10.1007/s10803-021-05338-5. Epub 2021 Nov 16. PMID: 34783991; PMCID: PMC9556391
20. Rizzo, A.A., Kim, G.J.: A SWOT analysis of the field of virtual reality rehabilitation and therapy. Presence: Teleoper. Virtual Environ. **14**(2), 119–146 (2005). https://doi.org/10.1162/1054746053967094
21. Liu, L.Y., Sangani, S., Patterson, K.K., Fung, J., Lamontagne, A.: Real-time avatar-based feedback to enhance the symmetry of spatiotemporal parameters after stroke: instantaneous effects of different avatar views. IEEE Trans. Neural Syst. Rehabil. Eng. **28**(4), 878–887 (2020). https://doi.org/10.1109/TNSRE.2020.2979830
22. Masmoudi, M., Benrachou, D.E., Djekoune, O., Al, E.: Avatar-facilitated therapy and virtual reality: next-generation of functional rehabilitation methods. In: 2020 1st International Conference on Communications, Control Systems and Signal Processing (CCSSP), p. 298–304. IEEE (2020)
23. Rehm, I.C., Foenander, E., Wallace, K., Abbott, J.M., Kyrios, M., Thomas, N.: What role can avatars play in e-mental health interventions? Exploring new models of client-therapist interaction. Front Psychiatry **18**(7), 186 (2016). https://doi.org/10.3389/fpsyt.2016.00186. PMID:27917128;PMCID:PMC5114267
24. Hart, J.D., Piumsomboon, T., Lee, G.A., Smith, R.T., Billinghurst, M.: Manipulating avatars for enhanced communication in extended reality. In: 2021 IEEE International Conference on Intelligent Reality (ICIR), pp. 9–16. Piscataway, NJ, USA (2021). https://doi.org/10.1109/ICIR51845.2021.00011

Narrative Perspectives and Embodiment in Cinematic Virtual Reality

Tobías Palma Stade[1]([☒]) [iD], Guy Schofield[2] [iD], and Grace Moore[2] [iD]

[1] University of Arts London, London, UK
t.palmastade@lcc.arts.ac.uk
[2] University of York, York, UK
{guy.schofield,grace.moore}@york.ac.uk

Abstract. Along with the technological advancements of virtual reality over the years, has come the emergence of Cinematic Virtual Reality (CVR), where immersive 360-degree video approaches the high-quality found in feature film. Extensive research has been done on embodiment and presence in relation to Virtual Reality (VR), however, there is a lack of existing literature on the narrative effects of embodiment and perspective in narrative VR films. Exploring the concept of viewer embodiment and its connection to the cinematic concept of narrative perspective, we conduct a review of literature in relation to CVR and flat screen cinema, selecting five CVR films to conduct an analysis of how cinematic techniques for establishing perspective and embodiment can be translated from flat screen cinema. Considering embodiment and perspective in CVR, we propose a spectrum of embodiment between extreme distancing from and extreme identification with characters in the narrative. Areas for future exploration are considered in light of the lack of research in this area.

Keywords: Virtual Reality · Cinematic Virtual Reality · Filmmaking · VR · XR · Immersive Storytelling

1 Introduction

Embodiment and viewer perspective has long been a matter of interest in Virtual Reality (VR) research. Murray [19, 20], Lanier [14] and De La Peña [4] have commented on the importance of the viewer's role in VR stories, whether told using 3D Computer Graphic Imagery or 360-degree video. Chris Milk, a key proponent of the persuasive properties of VR, claims that the viewer's apparent presence within the scene is key to its power [17]. Much recent literature around VR storytelling emphasizes aspects of presence and immersion, arguably the key qualities that distinguish VR from forms of media presented on flat screens. Although considerations of embodiment in VR are not new, much research takes a purely functional approach, focusing on basic properties such as the effect of the viewer's apparent height [7, 16, 24] and ways to overcome 'sim-sickness' [28]. There is little existing literature on the narrative effect of embodiment and perspective in VR and - as VR storytelling is still relatively novel [5] - VR storytellers are not yet able to draw on an established narrative language of viewer embodiment.

© The Author(s), under exclusive license to Springer Nature Switzerland AG 2023
L. T. De Paolis et al. (Eds.): XR Salento 2023, LNCS 14218, pp. 232–252, 2023.
https://doi.org/10.1007/978-3-031-43401-3_16

In conventional filmmaking, by contrast, directors and cinematographers can draw on over 100 years of well-developed conventions and techniques regarding not only what the viewer sees in a scene but how they are apparently seeing it [35] and what this means for the story. Film audiences are able to make sophisticated distinctions between a disembodied view (e.g., from a camera looking over an actor's shoulder) to an embodied one (e.g., through the eyes of a character reading a letter).

2   Methodology

To explore perspective and embodiment in CVR, we first conducted a review of literature on embodiment and perspective in relation to CVR and to flat cinema. For flat screen cinema this is relatively straightforward due to the film and television industry's use of standardised directorial grammars and common terminology. Educators, practitioners and researchers are able to draw on texts such as Katz [12], Murch [18], etc. to describe filmmaking approaches. Until recently, this was not the case in CVR [16]. However, as VR gains popularity and dedicated VR production companies spring up, practical accounts of and guides to directing CVR are beginning to emerge. This has arguably led to a shift in emphasis in recent literature from theoretical speculation on how CVR might work to practice-based accounts from filmmakers [35].

Next, we selected a number of CVR films and conducted a shot-by-shot analysis of camera movement, placement and action in each. We explored how their creators use perspective and embodiment, considering these with reference to established techniques from flat screen cinema. Selecting CVR films for analysis was challenging as, due to the novelty of the medium, a universally agreed 'canon' of key works is yet to emerge. While certain films are better known than others, the exhaustive critical attention devoted to cinema means that the films analysed in the case study section of this paper were, therefore, selected both to represent a range of directorial approaches and commercial contexts and because they had received substantial critical attention or were high-profile pieces released by well-known directors or studios.

In attempting to compare approaches to embodiment in CVR and conventional cinema, several important factors should be considered. Firstly, the sophistication of devices used in flat screen cinema is due at least in part to the cultural dominance and longevity of the medium [12]. Viewers' ability to glean subtle narrative information from directing, cinematography and sound is often based on a life-time's exposure to film and television. CVR is a relatively new medium, and it may take time for viewers to become sufficiently familiar with the medium to engage with CVR films in the way they do with flat screen films. The comparative length of feature films compared to most VR films may also be a confounding factor. To date there have been very few feature-length VR films, possibly due to the novelty of the medium but also partly due to concerns about the health implications of lengthy exposure to VR.

Most importantly, the commercial and industrial contexts in which most VR films have been produced so far are arguably different from cinema. Film directors - especially directors of genre films - are able to target specific audiences with well-established expectations in terms of narrative, production value and style. CVR, by contrast, as an emerging medium, has yet to develop the production and distribution infrastructures that directors and producers of conventional cinema are able to access [16]. Several well-established film directors (most notably Doug Liman [40], Robert Rodriguez [41] and Justin Lin [42] have experimented with the medium and a number of individuals, such as Chris Milk, Nonny De La Peña and Felix and Paul, have risen to prominence as CVR filmmakers but there is yet to emerge a conventional framework for financing, producing and distributing high-quality VR films. Many of the most technically complex and widely watched VR projects have instead been produced as ancillary material to conventional cinema productions, especially Hollywood properties such as the Jurassic World and Marvel franchises. This has an effect not only on production context but also narrative intent: VR films are not necessarily attempting to tell the same sorts of stories in the same ways.

3 Definitions of Embodiment

Embodiment supposes one of the biggest challenges for storytelling in VR. While the use of first-person perspective in flat screen cinema is not rare and has been approached in different ways - the camera embodying a character/protagonist (*Lady in the Lake* [64], *Rope* [70]), a monster or creature (*E.T.,* [57], *Jaws* [61]), an object (*Cloverfield* [55], *Pulp Fiction* [67]), or a participative presenter in documentary-style narratives. CVR's narrative perspective is based on the trinomial user-camera-subject/object, an integrated unit we identify as a defining feature of the medium: In CVR, the user embodies the camera, which is in itself materialized in the immersive environment as a channel for the user. As it will be seen later, the user can be present in the virtual world through different levels of embodiment, depending on the specific conditions of each narrative, defining the third aspect of this trinomial: what is the user-camera embodying in the virtual world.

While embodiment can be associated with the notion of *having* a body, it also comprises cultural definitions regarding *experiencing* a body. From an anthropological perspective, embodiment is "how culture 'gets under the skin,' or the relationship of how sociocultural dynamics become translated into biological realities in the body." [1] An ontological vision suggests that "the idea that embodiment is key for the construction of our inner self representation by demonstrating that the sense of embodiment is also closely related to the sense of self." [15] And a phenomenological view sees it as "an existential condition in which the body is the subjective source or inter-subjective ground of experience" and "can be understood from the standpoint of bodily being-in-the-world." [3] These notions of embodiment allow a more critical yet creative approach to VR and HCI research, where "[b]oth presence and embodiment have a phenomenological sense, which can refer to the things we consciously notice about the role of our bodies in shaping our self-perception and identities through conscious introspection and deliberate reflection on our experience." [31].

There are several experiments conducted on how virtual reality affects the perception of our own body versus the one of a virtual body - famously, extensions of the 'rubber hand illusion' into virtual reality [10] - however, the creative characteristics of the embodiment trinomial seem to respond to a further extent to the relation with the rest of the virtual environment, more specifically through interactions organized in terms of creation, manipulation and communication of meaning. Dourish states that "the technologies of embodied action participate in the world they represent" [6] while Slater, Spanlang and Corominas argue that "there is evidence to suggest that a virtual body in the context of a head-mounted display based virtual reality is a critical contributor to the sense of being in the virtual location" [29] pushing further the conception of the HMD as an access to virtual worlds, facilitating the embodying trinomial user-camera-subject/object. However, we acknowledge that embodiment in virtual worlds is problematic, as it has repeatedly been argued by Murray [20, 21] and by Slater in numerous studies on the neurological effects of virtual reality. Both authors - and their collaborators - argue that, despite the instinctive reactions users have to virtual environments - as in 'rubber hand illusions' - they never really lose awareness of the real world, positioning users in a sort of divided consciousness of both environments.

This awareness is productive for narrative purposes, since it allows users to trigger an enhanced suspension-of-disbelief that allows them to voluntarily navigate virtual environments. While embodiment can be associated with having a body, awareness of a virtual body supposes a Sense of Embodiment (SoE), an "ensemble of sensations that arise in conjunction with being inside, having, and controlling a body especially in relation to virtual reality applications." [13] The SoE would consist of three subcomponents: sense of self-location, sense of agency, and sense of body ownership, and understands the virtual body as a "container, which can be any object in the context of virtual reality." [13].

The definition of SoE summarises the functions of embodiment for narrative purposes: The user ceases to be a passive, leaned-back spectator because of their own awareness. Moreover, the three components of the SoE, in addition to the participatory, co-creative and interactive nature of VR, grants the user with the ownership of a point of view. The challenge, then, is to converge the qualities of the trinomial with the conventions of narrative perspectives that have been the standard for filmmakers and narrators in almost every storytelling discipline. Like other immersive and participatory media, VR supposes a challenge to these conventions, inviting practitioners to innovate and subvert the traditional role of both creator and spectator.

4   Embodiment in Cinema

While viewers of CVR are surrounded by the action (at least in audio-visual terms) this is not to say that viewers of 2D cinema are not immersed in the films they watch. Depending on the genre, the type of action and the way it is presented through camera position, angle, framing and composition and editing, the viewer can be made to feel more or less involved. This sense of embodiment is contingent on empathy and the suspension of disbelief and can produce remarkably powerful effects [30]. Film viewers jump when the monster pounces, wince when the protagonist experiences pain, laugh along with comedic characters. Emotions, such as fear, anger, sadness, and joy can all be stimulated, as well as psychophysiological responses to situations, such as dizziness in high places, disgust at horrifying events. Gunning argues that in spectacular cinema, the viewer's involvement in the world of the film oscillates between unselfconscious immersion in the events of the story and detached appreciation of the craft skill involved in the making of the film [8]. Embodiment in cinema is inextricably entangled with the cinematic concept of perspective. Perspective "determines who the viewer identifies with" [12] and can be modulated through a number of different devices and techniques. Crucially, perspective establishes the viewer's relationship to the narrative and how this should be manifested, including whether and how they should be embodied in the world of the film.

Katz categorizes perspective into three broad types: First-person, where we see the world through the eyes of the character – from a subjective perspective; Third-person Restricted, where the action is observed by the viewer as an ideal witness; and Omniscient, where the viewer has a holistic comprehension of the dramatic actions. Other theorists and filmmakers including Proferes [26] and Vera-Meiggs [32, 33] have refined these categories, to describe more nuanced relationships between viewer and film.

- **Omniscient:** As defined by Katz, most common in epic sagas, such as *Lawrence of Arabia* [65], *The Lord of the Rings* trilogy [66], or *Schindler's List* [72]. An omniscient perspective may allow the viewer access to multiple characters' perspectives but also may include perspectives available to none of the characters, for example, the aerial shots of battles in *The Lord of the Rings*, the shots of the insides of racing car engines in *The Fast and The Furious* [58];
- **Third-person Distanced:** A privileged viewer, at the same level as the characters, that witnesses the action from a dispassionate perspective, more involved with the actions than with the emotional development of the characters, most common in detective stories, adventure films, or whodunnits, like *Knives Out* [63], or heists like *Ocean's Eleven* [68].
- **Third-person Participative:** Also a privileged, character-levelled viewer, who has a closer emotional engagement with the main characters, most common in coming-of-age stories, dramas, melodramas, or noir films, like in *The Shawshank Redemption* [73], *Sound of Metal* [74], or *Stand by me* [75].
- **First-person Indirect:** The viewer witnesses the dramatic action sharing the character's subjectivity, seeing the world coloured by their gaze, but not directly from their eyes. This is common in films – or sequences – where events are not presented as objective or factual, but rather as subjective interpretations of such events, like in Fellini's *8 ½* [52], *All that Jazz* [53], *Fear and Loathing in Las Vegas* [59], or *Rashomon* [69].
- **First-person Direct:** The viewer sees the world from the character's eyes, being possible or not to share their subjectivity. For Vera-Meiggs, this is more a technical category, that is rarely but purposely used in films. This can be seen in the opening sequence of *8 ½*, *The Blair Witch Project* [54], or *Russian Ark* [71].

As it will be observed, this typology is susceptible to be adapted into CVR, although the process is not without problems. On the other hand, we believe that merging narrative perspectives with different styles of embodiment can result in storytelling conventions for cinematic virtual reality.

4.1 Perspective Devices

In cinema, besides determining what the viewer sees, directors also establish perspective through the way we see, through well-established cinematographic and directorial grammars. Framing and Composition are key elements here and are deployed in combination with particular types of action, especially in relation to characters. The clearest example of this, the Point-of-View shot, mimics the character's view of the world by apparently placing the camera at their physical position and focusing it on their centre of attention [12]. The characteristics of other shot types also reinforce particular relationships to the action. The aerial shot - presented from a viewpoint not usually accessible to human beings - is usually read as a distancing device, presenting a dispassionate 'god's eye view' of the action [2].

Perspectival devices are deployed to determine both the viewer and the characters' relationships to the story and to each other. However, perspective is also used to expose power relationships within the narrative. By giving more or less screen time to characters (by including them in more or less, longer or shorter shots) the viewer can establish their importance to the story [12]. The power of characters in relation to each other can be manifested through higher or lower camera angles or through tighter or looser framing. Similarly, the viewers' visceral involvement in the action can be increased or decreased by measures such as faster or slower editing, lower or higher camera angles (especially in the case of action sequences such as fight scenes and car chases) and closer or wider framing [12].

It should be noted that films which are presented from a single uninterrupted perspective are relatively rare. Even 'one take' films such as *1917* [51] use a moving camera to provide shifts in perspective and viewer involvement throughout the film. Very few film (exceptions include *Lady in the Lake* [64], *Enter the Void* [56] and *Hardcore Henry* [60]) maintain a single consistent perspective on the action but many more films vary perspective from scene to scene and in some cases from shot to shot. For example, The *Blair Witch Project* [54] uses a consistent first-person direct perspective but from multiple characters' perspectives. *Jaws* [61] combines various 3rd person participative and first-person indirect perspectives on the actions of the human characters while presenting the killer shark's view of the world through a first-person direct perspective. *Cloverfield* [55] uses the 'found footage' format to present the action from a first-person perspective via a handheld camcorder, apparently used by the characters. However, this is disrupted at several points when the camcorder is left unattended presenting a 3rd person view of the action.

5 Embodiment in Cinematic Virtual Reality

Many of the devices described above rely on the use of the frame, constraining the viewer's gaze to characters and parts of the scene important to the story. The lack of a conventional frame in VR presents novel challenges to storytellers, not limited to cinematography, but extending to concerns such as blocking (the placement and movement of characters in a film scene), acting, and editing. At the centre of many of these challenges is the effect of physical viewpoint on the narrative. For audiences from societies dominated by conventional approaches to flat screen films, filmmakers must choose between adapting well-known and widely understood conventions for establishing embodiment and perspective from cinema or develop entirely new techniques that leverage the properties of VR.

Although CVR filmmaking is relatively new, theorists and practitioners have identified a number of key concepts in order to describe the properties of this medium for filmmakers. Williams, Love and Love [34] introduce the concept of 'gravity', conceptualising the camera as being at the centre of a cinematic universe around which the story revolves, both figuratively and literally. They suggest a useful distinction between 'Newtonian' approaches, where the action is predominantly arranged in front of the viewer, requiring little or no movement of the viewer's head or body, and 'Copernican' approaches, where the action requires the viewer to turn to view the action, which might be taking place behind them.

Importantly, William, Love & Love also specifically discuss a key problem of embodiment in CVR stories: the persona gap. This is characterised as narrative uncertainty in situations where a viewer knows they are seeing a story from a characters' physical point of view but have little or no information about the character. This is directly related to how the trinomial user-camera-subject/object is drawn within the narrative, and how it is embodied in the virtual world, whether its presence is material or not. To approach this, they have adapted traditional narrative points of view into CVR guidelines, identifying four possible observers. [34].

God: "neutral, all seeing, that the characters don't see," [34] with many similarities to the omniscient perspective that is invisible to the characters in the virtual world - hence, although not explicitly mentioned by the authors, a disembodied observer.

Griffin: "is an actual character who occupies space in the scene" and is acknowledged by other characters. However, it doesn't have a virtual body that the user can see or use. They also identify two types of Griffin: "a first person POV where the entire story revolves around the audience's perspective" [34] that is at the centre of the action; and a second person perspective that watches the action from the side.

Bod: "also a character - this time with a body" the user can recognize. This user gets to embody someone else (a character with their own body, clothing, race, sex, etc.) rather than being present as themselves. As with the Griffin, the Bod also can be identified as a first or a second person, although the authors make further distinctions: A passive Bod where the body doesn't do anything, and an active Bod, where the body moves but at its own accord, without responding to the user's agency.

Dog: a non-human perspective, where the user-camera is placed or embodied in an animal, object, monster, or any other non-human element.

Similarly, Nicolae [23] proposes three spectator perspectives in VR films, calling these spectatorship modes; 'the witness' (a viewer onto the action), 'the hero' (viewer is at the centre of the story, but retains their identity), and 'the impersonator' (viewer becomes an embodied character in the story).

These categories can be very useful to approach narrative perspectives in VR, but they are not exempt from complications, particularly regarding embodiment and how this can influence feelings of presence, engagement, and perspective-taking. The use of these POVs would depend on the narrative objectives of each film and would need to be observed case by case in order to assess potential problems or successes. These POVs provide a guide to identify different types of narrators in VR films and observe the characteristics that define the relation between such narrators and the embodied user. In other words, we are observing the narrative configuration between narrator and embodiment in CVR, to try to define potential narrative conventions.

6   Case Studies: Embodiment in Practice

6.1 *Jurassic World: Blue*: Spectacular Cinema in the Round

Jurassic World: Blue [43] was produced and directed by Félix Lajeunesse and Paul Raphaël as VR studio Felix and Paul in conjunction with Oculus Studios to coincide with the release of *Jurassic World: Fallen Kingdom* [62]. The VR experience was distributed exclusively through the Oculus store. The 7 min film combines live action footage and CGI elements created by Industrial Light and Magic and features as its protagonist, Blue the velociraptor; a well-known character from the film franchise.

The film consists of two separate sequences, each apparently consisting of a single take, separated by a transition to black. The camera moves smoothly forward in an extended dolly shot over the course of each sequence and all the key events in the story take place in front of the viewer. As the camera's position changes little during the film, changes of narrative perspective are achieved largely through character action and a number of directorial techniques from traditional cinema are used. As there is no dialogue and the scenes are almost static, the simple plot (a dinosaur hunts and encounters predators in the island environment in which the films are set) plays out entirely through character action. The viewer has no visible presence in the scene and there are no devices used to explain how and why they are there: the camera generally provides a third-person distanced perspective on the story. However, several devices are used to move from a view of the scene that prioritises understanding of narrative through characters' actions, to a more visceral, first-person experience of 'being in the scene'.

Much of the film is presented from a camera position which combines characteristics of a conventional Over-The-Shoulder shot and a Point of View shot, following the dinosaur from the left and slightly to the rear, leaving the centre of the field of view open (see Fig. 1). In 2D cinema, these two shots are used for slightly different purposes. While OTS shots provide a view of the character and what they are seeing, reinforcing their physical and narrative connection with the scene [12], POV shots are generally used to prioritise what they are experiencing, by placing the viewer directly in the space they inhabit [12]. In Jurassic World: Blue, the combination seems designed to enable the viewer to experience a perilous environment in as visceral a way possible while also receiving narrative cues from the dinosaur's reactions as to how to read events in the scene. However, the perspective in Blue is not a 'true' POV shot, instead conforming more closely to the Griffin perspective described by Williams, Love and Love[34].

Character eyelines are used to alert the viewer to events taking place at the edge of the field of view. For example: Blue moves close to the viewer and cranes her neck upwards, to foreshadow the eruption of a volcano and looks directly across the viewer's

Fig. 1. Two different views from the same viewpoint in *Jurassic World: Blue*

field of view to the left when another dinosaur appears in the scene from that direction (see Fig. 2). Changing power relations between characters as Blue encounters larger and larger predatory dinosaurs are reinforced by the scale of each character in the scene in relation to the height of the viewer's point of view: the viewer has to look up to see these dinosaurs, providing a close equivalent to a low-angle shot in conventional cinema. The simple narrative and short form of the film requires only that the viewer understands the context of the character's actions, principally the relationships between the predatory protagonist, her prey and the larger dinosaurs who might prey upon her. The final sequence of the film, in which helicopters fly overhead, is not explained and is seen from the perspective of the dinosaurs as a frightening, mysterious event.

Fig. 2. Clear direction of gaze in *Jurassic World:Blue*

6.2 *HELP*: Camera Positioning and Perspective

HELP [42] was produced and directed by Justin Lin, established director of Star Trek Beyond and various Fast & Furious films, in conjunction with Google Spotlight Stories in 2016. Much like *Jurassic World: Blue*, *HELP* also combines live action footage and CGI aspects in CVR but uses movement to progress the sequential narrative through a constantly evolving scene. Justin Lin claims *HELP* is, "the first cinema quality narrative in the VR space" [9], using fast action sequences and a range of audio and visual cues within the story to direct the viewer's attention towards the action.

The five-minute film consists of a young woman scrambling to escape from an alien creature that chases her across downtown Los Angeles. At a climax point, the young lady realises the alien is only asking for help, and after receiving aid it peacefully ascends back into space. The film appears to consist of a single take, with a tracking dolly shot that follows the action and fast paced movement of the narrative. Throughout the story the camera position is constantly changing, at the beginning it is in a 'god's eye view' looking down on the scene from above, and then progresses into more of a traditional eye-level view of the scene that closely follows the main characters. The steady camera movement stops at various points in the film to allow the viewer to reorient themselves in the scene, and to accentuate emotional narrative moments. At the climax, the camera pauses at a low angle which makes the humans and objects in the scene appear rather imposing. The camera is positioned specifically at level with the alien at this point to create a more empathic link between the viewer and the creature through the perspective of the narrative (see Fig. 3).

Fig. 3. Low camera angle in *HELP*.

The events of the narrative take place across the entire 360-degree space, causing the viewer to actively look around for relevant story elements. In turn, this increases the reviewability of the film, as the viewer is moved quickly through the evolving scene whilst multiple story elements are taking place around them. The director tries to tackle this by placing the two main characters throughout the chase, the young lady and the alien, directly in front and behind of the viewer (see Fig. 4). Character eyelines and audio cues, such as loud crashes, are used to alert the viewer to specific story elements taking place within the 360-degree field of view. This relates to the Copernican approach as interpreted by William, Love and Love.

Fig. 4. Viewpoints of the action taking place directly behind and in front of the viewer in HELP

The viewer has no visible presence in the scene, moreover the camera provides more of a third-person perspective of the narrative. This corresponds to the 'witness' spectatorship mode in VR film, where the viewer observes the scene as it unfolds in front of them, and there is no active engagement with the viewer from the characters in the story [23], evolving from the 'third-person restricted' perspective in cinema [12].

At the end of the film the camera follows the movement of the alien's ascension towards the stars. It is not explained as to why the viewer is following the alien here, potentially this is seen as an empathic device that isn't possible in cinema but is using the novelty of VR to engage the viewer through the perspective of the narrative.

6.3 *Clouds Over Sidra*: Empathetic Perspectives in Documentary CVR

VR's capability to embody another person started being explored by fundraisers around 2015, after Chris Milk famously called VR the "ultimate empathy machine." [17] This premise is based on the principle that embodying another person living in a different context could enhance feelings of empathy through perspective-taking tasks, placing "users in novel environments, showing them what it would be like to experience a specific situation from someone else's perspective." [11] Since then, numerous international non-profits and humanitarian organisations started using VR to promote engagement and participation in humanitarian causes, triggering a trend of VR documentaries made for such purpose. The most recognized is *Clouds over Sidra* [37], commissioned by the United Nations, and setting a certain narrative standard for this type of documentary.

The film shows a refugee camp in Jordan and starts with the user being in a room with a girl, while listening to the voice-over of the same girl, who introduces herself as Sidra. The film then shows various slices of the life within the camp, narrated by Sidra's voice over, although she can be seen as part of the scene - going to school, in the playground, back at her house, etc. - or not at all - bakery, men's gym, general view of the camp, etc. The formal characteristics of the film are simple. The camera is positioned at an adult's eye-line and is treated as a passive witness of life in the refugee camp. While Sidra appears and reappears as the main character, she doesn't play the role of a guide, addressing the camera directly only at the beginning of the film (see Fig. 5). This first - and only - acknowledgement of the user seems to be granting them presence in the camp - despite the user/camera not having a body, restricted to looking around itself - a user with Copernican gravity. From then on, it is a witness on a human level and at a human distance of the events around them; it is never again addressed directly - although it could be argued that it is towards the end, when a group of children form a circle around the camera, or in the next scene, back to Sidra's room, where she is there but doesn't talk or look directly at the camera anymore.

Fig. 5. On the left, at minute 0:33, when still introducing the film, Sidra acknowledges the embodiment of the user-camera in the refugee camp. This sets the tone for the overall narration, even for scenes where Sidra can't be seen (in the middle, in a men's gym at 3:48). On the right, at 6:43, the user-camera returns to Sidra's room; although she is not looking at the camera, the intimacy of the moment reinforces the emotional engagement to the character.

Following categorizations of narrative perspectives in cinema, *Clouds over Sidra* mostly relies on a third-person participative perspective, where the second person Griffin (character without a body) is invited to emotionally engage with the world and the characters they see. This is enhanced by Sidra's extra-diegetic voice-over, that narrates each scene from a subjective point of view, sharing intimate details and her own opinions, rather than an intellectualised vision of life in the camp. As a dramatic device, the voice-over is used in other VR short films as a subjective voice, to signify that the user-camera is embodying a character - i.e. *The Party* [45]. However, in *Clouds over Sidra*, the intimate relationship established from the beginning is then extended throughout the film through the non-diegetic voice-over that complements the image with a subjective narrator that participates emotionally in the scene and the portrayed world.

The conventions set in *Clouds over Sidra* have been replicated in similar documentaries thereafter: *Evelyn's Story* [38], *I am Rohingya* [39], *Layla Comes Home* [44], *The Source* [46], *Ready to Learn, Ready to Live* [47], to name a few. These all rely on similar third-person participatory perspectives that operate as witnesses despite not having a body and are guided by an extra-diegetic voice-over of a character that operates as a subjective narrator, while also appearing in the film themselves. This third-person participative is such because it participates in the narration on an emotional level, despite not actively taking part of the action - for instance, in being addressed directly by the characters, considering the constraints of cinematic VR. This type of narrative strategy is consistent with the intentions behind the organisations that commission this type of film: fundraisers appealing to the empathetic feelings of potential donors and volunteers. Certainly, this doesn't set a unique standard for this type of documentary. For instance, *A Journey to the Arctic* [36], commissioned by Greenpeace, relies on a similar witnessing use of camera but uses a neutral, objective, distanced, non-diegetic narrator as a voice-over that doesn't belong to any character, facilitating a more intellectual observation. There are other similar, more intellectual approaches to documentary narratives in VR. Nevertheless, this pool of films is starting to set certain conventions in cinematic VR that aims to generate emotional empathy towards characters and the worlds they inhabit.

6.4 Distanced Witnesses in *Rebuilding Notre Dame*

A different approach to documentary narratives in VR can be found in the work by Targo Stories, a virtual reality media company that has gained recognition in recent years. Their film *Rebuilding Notre Dame* [48] collects testimonies of relevant personalities around the reconstruction of the cathedral after the fire of 2019. The documentary opens with a collage of television news screens reporting the disaster in different languages, to then transition into an aerial shot flying above the cathedral. This shot immediately sets a difference with the third-person participative that is dominant in *Clouds over Sidra*, placing the user-camera in a non-human, god-like perspective. This omniscient view is not constant in the film but sets the more analytical relation between the camera and the topic, in comparison to the emotionality of the third-person participative.

The camera in *Rebuilding Notre Dame* is mostly placed on a human level - except for the aerial shots - and is presented as a Griffin (see Fig. 6), but the POV feels closer to the third-person distanced perspective for two reasons. First, the relationship established with the narrator. While in *Clouds over Sidra* the narrative is built on the emotional relation with the main character through their subjective view of the world, *Rebuilding Notre Dame* doesn't have a main character. It still relies on voice-overs: The first voice that is heard is anonymous, while the camera is still observing the cathedral from different angles (human and non-human), is then revealed to belong to Patrick Chauvet, rector-archpriest of Notre Dame, sitting in a studio looking directly at the camera, addressing the viewer. While the exercise is similar to *Clouds over Sidra*, this is not constant. A similar strategy is used throughout the film many times to reveal different characters, who share their testimonies presented in a rather formal fashion, similar to interviews, and without establishing an emotional link with the viewer. The film doesn't count with a main narrator, resulting in a collage of voices subordinated to the impressive images of the cathedral before and after the fire.

The second reason is related to the editing. In *Clouds over Sidra* the editing is subverted to the narration of the main character, which complements the images with her subjective view. The camera and the narration complement each other to give spatial consistency to the refugee camp, and even when some might feel sudden, the next shot still responds to the idea of the space that is being narrated. *Rebuilding Notre Dame*'s erratic relation to the space makes the gravitational pull less evident; there is an intermittency between general shots that invite the user to wander the gaze around the cathedral in a rather Copernican way, and abrupt cuts that redirect the sight towards an interviewee that directly addresses the camera, shifting into a Newton gravity. *Rebuilding*

Fig. 6. The alternating placements of the camera in Rebuilding Notre Dame, and the editing techniques used to jump from one perspective to another, facilitate a more distant observation of the events, the cathedral, and the testimonies. On the top left, the image shows an aerial omniscient perspective of the cathedral, which contrasts with the first-person point of view being addressed by a character in the top right image. The images in the middle illustrate the drastic cuts from one part of the cathedral to another, while the bottom images illustrate a jump cut, an editing technique commonly used for disruptions in the narrative.

Notre Dame uses more evident cuts, jumping between different areas inside the cathedral that are not always visually connected to the previous shot - different wings, different floors, inside the belltower, next to the stained-glass windows, etc. - and outside - from the street, external corridors, the roof, etc. - which causes a notorious disruption in the user-camera's spatial localization. Moreover, the use of jump-cuts within the church makes the artificiality of the editing more evident. Like in cinema, this technique generates a distance between the spectator and the object/subject of the film, facilitating a more analytical perspective on either this or on the film itself.

Rebuilding Notre Dame is an interesting case because it seems to set certain conventions towards the Targo's following documentaries. The series *When We Stayed Home* [49] and the film *Surviving 9/11* [50] seem to correct the intermittent narrator and rely on one voice that serves as the thread that unifies each film. Similarly, the style of editing is softer and avoids abrupt jumps from one space to another completely different. However, it is still open to interpretation how intimate and emotional the narrative is from a cinematic view. The narrator is still presented under the formalities of an observational documentary [22], which places the user-camera to a certain distance and in an artificial studio environment. Likewise, the editing in these films encourages the viewer not to look around him, locating all relevant objects in the same place in relation to the camera/viewer. These two characteristics give the documentaries a more televisual quality, making the narration generally more analytical than emotional.

6.5 Specific Embodiment in *The Party*

The Party [45] is a CVR production commissioned by The Guardian and directed by Annick Bregman and Shehani Fernando. The piece attempts to convey as directly as possible the experiences of a young autistic girl at a family party, illustrating the challenges she faces. The piece is presented entirely from the girl's point of view, via a single fixed camera position. This is reinforced using voiceover to convey her thoughts and to introduce the story. Postproduction effects such as blurring of faces and sound distortion are used to illustrate the effect of her condition on her experience of events (see Fig. 7). These include an artificial Depth of Field effect in which the viewer's attention is forced to a single point and the rest of the scene becomes blurred. This has the effect of making the viewer conscious of varying agency in the scene: at some points they can look around freely while at others, they are unable to focus on anything but a single point, again illustrating the protagonist's condition.

Fig. 7. Blurred faces used to simulate an autistic girl's experience of a party in The Party

Other characters move around the scene, talking directly to the viewer and she converses with them, with spatial sound used to distinguish between internal monologue and interpersonal dialogue. Unlike the other works described in this paper, *The Party* uses a 'Bod' approach [34]: the viewer has an implied body. Looking down, the viewer can see a coloured blur, occupying the space the girl's body would inhabit in the scene.

Although most events in *The Party* take place within the 180-degree area in front of the viewer, the action of characters is complex, with multiple conversations and character actions taking place at the same time. The action moves around the scene, requiring the viewer to turn to pay close attention. At several points, as in *Help*, the viewer's attention is split between several actions taking place within the same 'frame'. In the story, this is accompanied with a voiceover from the protagonist explaining that this confusion reflects her own state of mind.

7 Discussion

The films analysed above demonstrate a range of approaches to perspective and embodiment in CVR, correlating in each case to the specifics of each narrative. A well-known challenge to conventional filmmakers approaching CVR is the lack of a frame in which to compose conventional shots which would traditionally be used to construct meaning over a series of cuts. However, as seen in *Jurassic World: Blue*, and *HELP*, the immersive space of CVR is instead able to support multiple choices of 'shot' (e.g., OTS and POV) within a single take, with the viewer able to move smoothly from one to another through movements of the head, in a process roughly analogous to cutting. Furthermore, in *HELP* the viewer can select which part of the story they would like to engage with through this head movement, as the fast-paced narrative takes places across the entire 360-degree space. This gives the viewer a range of freedom that is specific to the medium itself.

Crucially, in *Jurassic World: Blue*, these choices are available within the viewer's immediate field of view: a situation different both to the sequential presentation of a film edit, or the selection of different narrative branches in an interactive film. In certain cases (such as moments when the viewpoint is directly alongside the protagonist dinosaur), the resulting effect is a combining of perspectives: both an OTS shot containing third-person narrative information about the dinosaur's reactions to the scene and a first-person POV shot, placing the viewer so close to the dinosaur's physical position that their points of view are almost coterminous.

The narrative proximity generated in *Jurassic World: Blue* is not strange to cinematic techniques that generate identification with characters - human and non-human - through the use of the camera, among other techniques. In *Clouds over Sidra* and other documentaries of its kind, this emotional proximity is generated through a combination of techniques, primarily the introduction of the main character as someone approachable and on the same level as the user, enhancing the sense of presence in the refugee camp. Thereafter, while Sidra herself is not present in every shot, the use of a subjective voice-over and an editing style that provides continuity to the user's presence in the camp, while connecting each location to the narration, enables a constant closeness to the character, who in this case also plays the role of the narrator.

In *The Party*, this identification with a single character is taken to extremes. A high-level of specific embodiment is achieved through the use of a fixed viewpoint, voiceover as internal monologue and the inclusion of an implied body, similar to the 'bod' observer. Rather than drawing the viewer's attention to a clear area of interest as in conventional cinema, confusing configurations of character action are used to reinforce the film's key narrative message: that the protagonist finds social situations difficult to make sense of.

In *Rebuilding Notre-Dame*, on the other hand, the formal cinematic techniques maintain the camera-user in a considerably more artificial position, compared to the organic nature of the embodiment in *Clouds over Sidra*. Here, the use of disjunctive editing, jump-cuts, non-sequential spaces, and aerial shots are a constant reminder of the artificiality of the observer. This is also reinforced by the inconstant narrators, or the absence of a sort of host - like Sidra or Blue - that provide the story with conducting thread, also keeping the user from establishing an emotional relation with any character and, instead, facilitating a more intellectual approach.

In considering embodiment and perspective in VR, it is possible to conceive of a spectrum of embodiment, between extreme distancing from and extreme identification with and embodiment of characters. In terms of narrative meaning, we argue that the distanced end of this spectrum is roughly equivalent to techniques in cinema. An aerial shot giving a 3rd person view of a scene in which action is taking place, has roughly the same affordances in VR as in flat screen cinema. However, at the end of extreme embodiment, CVR techniques have the capacity to more closely identify the viewer's perspective with that of a character (through a sense of presence in the scene, demonstrated through the inclusion of a body, viewer's agency in terms of directions of gaze etc.) than techniques from flat-screen cinema. Figure 8 shows this in graphical form, with the case studies discussed included at various points.

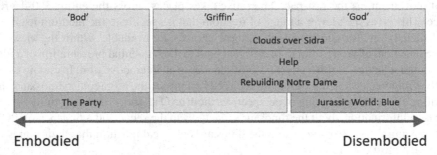

Fig. 8. Types of Embodiment in the Case Studies Discussed Above.

In CVR, power relations would involve a more direct consideration of the user, placing within the space where power tensions take place, becoming part of the mise-en-scéne with more or less prevalence depending on creative objectives. [25] The ability of VR to facilitate feelings of presence in a virtual environment can also be seen as a break of the fourth wall that separates the narrative from the spectator, generating the conditions for an emancipation [27] in which the user comes to integrate the creative experience.

8   Conclusions

While the POVs proposed by Nicolae and Williams, Love & Love are helpful in terms of how to treat the camera, these are still not problematized enough to address the extension of embodiment as a narrative experience rather than just as having a body. Moreover, we believe that exploring embodiment as a narrative category can expand on the understanding of VR's own and unique storytelling conventions.

We believe the spectrum of embodiment proposed is also tied to the notion of the trinomial user-camera-subject/object: If embodiment is a defining and unavoidable feature of CVR and it directly affects the way stories are narrated, then generating and/or identifying conventions for the different ways the user is embodied in the virtual world can potentially contribute to improving blocking and narrative techniques that are unique for CVR. Through CVR, certain modes of address change meaning, and effects can become exaggerated. For example, the direct to camera becomes very confrontational or didactic, depending on the type of relation that is meant to be generated with the character and/or environment. Meanwhile, the lack of a frame in which to compose conventional shots can allow for combined perspectives, such as the OTS and POV shot in Blue.

Narratively speaking, different techniques affect the sense of presence and, thus, the narrative perspective through which the user integrates into the story. In Blue, HELP, The Party and Clouds over Sidra, a more continuous editing enhances the sense of narrative presence, while in Rebuilding Notre Dame, the discontinuous editing facilitates a more intellectual or distanced approach. We are referring to a sense of narrative presence that considers qualities that are specific to the narrative objectives of a certain piece, and/or how the user is integrated to the story: subjectively, like in The Party; emotionally, like in Help, Blue or Clouds over Sidra; or intellectually, like in Rebuilding Notre Dame.

Further exploration of these potential grammars should facilitate the identification and design of narrative conventions for VR that consider the problem of embodiment through creative solutions. We have been able to observe how editing, camera, and sound techniques affect the sense of embodiment and the sense of presence from a narrative point of view. Future work should be able to assess these effects in a larger audience, to observe how different cinematic techniques can affect the storytelling possibilities of VR.

References

1. Anderson-Fye, E.P.: Anthropological perspectives on physical appearance and body image. In: Cash, T.E. (ed.) Encyclopedia of Body Image and Human Appearance, vol. 1, pp. 15–22. Academic, London, UK (2012)
2. Campbell, R.: Drone film theory: the immanentisation of kinocentrism. Media Theory 2(2), 52–78 (2018)
3. Csordas, T.J.: Embodiment and cultural phenomenology. In: Wiess, G., Haber, H.F. (eds.) Perspectives on Embodiment: The Intersections of Nature and Culture, pp. 143–164. Routledge, New York, NY, USA (1999)
4. de la Peña, N., Weil, P., Llobera, J., Spanlang, B., Friedman, D., Sanchez-Vives, M.V., Slater, M.: Immersive journalism: immersive virtual reality for the first-person experience of news. Presence: Teleoper. Virtual Environ. 19(4), 291–301 (2010). https://doi.org/10.1162/PRES_a_00005
5. Dooley, K.: Cinematic Virtual Reality: A Critical Study of 21st Century Approaches and Practices. Springer, Cham (2021). https://doi.org/10.1007/978-3-030-72147-3
6. Dourish, P.: Where the Action Is: The Foundations of Embodied Interactions. MIT Press, Cambridge, MA, USA (2001)
7. Michael, G., Frank, G., Dirk, S., Andreas, B.: Cinematic narration in VR – rethinking film conventions for 360 degrees. In: Chen, J.Y.C., Fragomeni, G. (eds.) Virtual, Augmented and Mixed Reality: Applications in Health, Cultural Heritage, and Industry: 10th International Conference, VAMR 2018, Held as Part of HCI International 2018, Las Vegas, NV, USA, July 15-20, 2018, Proceedings, Part II, pp. 184–201. Springer International Publishing, Cham (2018). https://doi.org/10.1007/978-3-319-91584-5_15

8. Gunning, T.: An aesthetic of astonishment: early film and the (in) credulous spectator. Film Theory Crit. Concepts Media Cult. Stud. **3**(2004), 76–95 (2004)

9. Google Spotlight Stories. 2016. Google Spotlight Stories: The Making of Help. Online video resource. https://www.youtube.com/watch?v=we6gK-rqCso. Accessed 9 Feb 2023

10. Jsselsteijn, W.A.I., de Kort, Y.A.W., Haansl, A.: Is this *my* hand i see before me? The rubber hand illusion in reality, virtual reality, and mixed reality. Presence: Teleoper. Virtual Environ. 2006 **15**(4), 455–464 (2006). https://doi.org/10.1162/pres.15.4.455

11. Herrera, F., Bailenson, J., Weisz, E., Ogle, E., Zaki, J.: Building long-term empathy: a large-scale comparison of traditional and virtual reality perspective-taking. PLoS ONE **13**(10), e0204494 (2018). https://doi.org/10.1371/journal.pone.0204494

12. Katz, S.D.: Film Directing Shot by Shot: Visualizing from Concept to Screen. Michael Wiese Productions. Massachusetts, USA (1991)

13. Kilteni, K., Groten, R., Mel, S.: The sense of embodiment in virtual reality. Presence: Teleoper. Virtual Environ. **21**(4), 373–387 (2012). https://doi.org/10.1162/PRES_a_00124

14. Lanier, J.: Dawn of the New Everything: A Journey Through Virtual Reality. Vintage Press, London (2017)

15. Matamala-Gomez, M., Donegan, T., Bottiroli, S., Sandrini, G., Sanchez-Vives, M.V., Tassorelli, C.: Immersive virtual reality and virtual embodiment for pain relief. Front. Hum. Neurosci. **13**,(2019). https://doi.org/10.3389/fnhum.2019.00279

16. Mateer, J.: Directing for cinematic virtual reality: how the traditional film director's craft applies to immersive environments and notions of presence. J. Media Pract. **18**(1), 14–25 (2017). https://doi.org/10.1080/14682753.2017.1305838

17. Milk, C.: How virtual reality can create the ultimate empathy machine. TED2015 (2015). https://www.ted.com/talks/chris_milk_how_virtual_reality_can_create_the_ultimate_empathy_machine. Accessed 10 Jan 2023

18. Murch, W.: In the Blink of an Eye, vol. 995. Silman-James Press, Los Angeles (2001)

19. Murray, J.: Hamlet on The Holodeck: The Future of Narrative in Cyberspace. MIT Press, Cambridge (1998)

20. Murray, J.: Did it make you cry? Creating dramatic agency in immersive environments. In: Subsol, G. (ed.) Virtual Storytelling. Using Virtual Reality Technologies for Storytelling, pp. 83–94. Springer Berlin Heidelberg, Berlin, Heidelberg (2005). https://doi.org/10.1007/11590361_10

21. Murray, J.: Virtual/reality: how to tell the difference. J. Vis. Cult. **19**(1), 11–27 (2020). https://doi.org/10.1177/1470412920906253

22. Nichols, B.: Representing Reality: Issues and Concepts in Documentary. Indiana University Press, Bloomington and Indianapolis (1991)

23. Nicolae, D.F.: Spectator perspectives in virtual reality cinematography: the witness, the hero and the impersonator. Ekphrasis. Images, Cinema, Theory, Media **2**, 168–180 (2018). DOI: https://doi.org/10.24193/ekphrasis.20.10

24. Passmore, P., Glancy, M., Philpot, A., Fields, B.: 360 Cinematic Literacy: a case study. TVX 2017 - 2017 ACM International Conference on Interactive Experiences for TV and Online Video. Netherlands Institute for Sound and Vision, Hilversum, The Netherlands (2017)

25. Pope, V.C., Dawes, R., Schweiger, F., Sheikh, A.: The geometry of storytelling: theatrical use of space for 360-degree videos and virtual reality. In: CHI 2017: Proceedings of the 2017 CHI Conference on Human Factors in Computing Systems. May 2017, pp. 4468–4478 (2017). https://doi.org/10.1145/3025453.3025581

26. Proferes, N.T.: Film Directing Fundamentals: See your film before shooting. Focal Press, Routledge, New York (2018)

27. Rancière, J.: The Emancipated Spectator. Verso, Brooklyn, London (2008)

28. Sharples, S., Cobb, S., Moody, A., Wilson, J.R.: Virtual reality induced symptoms and effects (VRISE): comparison of head mounted display (HMD), desktop and projection display systems. Displays **29**(2), 58–69 (2008). https://doi.org/10.1016/j.displa.2007.09.005

29. Slater, M., Spanlang, B., Corominas, D.: Simulating virtual environments within virtual environments as the basis for a psychophysics of presence. ACM Trans. Graph. **29**(4), 1–9 (2010). https://doi.org/10.1145/1778765.1778829

30. Stadler, J.: Empathy in film. In: The Routledge Handbook of Philosophy of Empathy, pp. 317–326. Routledge (2017)

31. Tham, J., Duin, A.H., Gee, L., Ernst, N., Abdelqader, B., McGrath, M.: Understanding virtual reality: presence, embodiment, and professional practice. IEEE Trans. Profession. Commun. **61**(2), 178–195 (2018). https://doi.org/10.1109/TPC.2018.2804238

32. Vera-Meiggs, D.: La Caverna Audiovisual o las razones del cine. Editorial Universitaria, Santiago, Chile (2011)

33. Vera-Meiggs, D.: La Verdad Imaginaria. Editorial Universitaria, Santiago, Chile (2013)

34. Williams, E., Love, M., Love, C.: Virtual Reality Cinema: Narrative Tips & Techniques. Focal Press, Routledge, Oxon, England (2021)

35. Zhang, Y., Weber, I.: Adapting, modifying and applying cinematography and editing concepts and techniques to cinematic virtual reality film production. Media Int. Australia **186**(1), 115–135 (2021). https://doi.org/10.1177/1329878X211018476

VR Filmography

36. A journey to the Arctic. MediaMonks, Greenpeace. Online resource (2016). https://vimeo.com/178321028. Accessed 7 Feb 2023

37. Clouds over Sidra. Chris Milk, and Gabo Arora. VRSE.works, UN SDG Campaign, UNICEF Jordan (2015). https://www.youtube.com/watch?v=mUosdCQsMkM&t=6s&ab_channel=Within. Accessed 7 Feb 2023

38. Evelyn's Story. Dave Denneen. Filmgraphics, Alt.vfx, We Love Jam Studios, Oxfam Australia (2017). https://www.youtube.com/watch?v=jZUnUCWqwFw. Accessed 7 Feb 2023

39. I am Rohingya. Zahra Rasool. 2017. Contrast VR, AJ+, Amnesty International. https://www.youtube.com/watch?v=_SL3aab8LAs. Accessed 7 Feb 2023

40. Invisible. Doug Liman. 30 Ninjas, Conde Nast Entertainment. Jaunt VR. [series] (2016). https://www.youtube.com/watch?v=WS0iXc9jMZo&t=38s. Accessed 9 Feb 2023

41. The Limit. Robert Rodriguez. STX Surreal (2018)

42. HELP. Justin Lin. 360 Google Spotlight Stories, The Mill (2016). https://www.youtube.com/watch?v=G-XZhKqQAHU&ab_channel=GoogleSpotlightStories. Accessed 7 Feb 2023

43. Jurassic World: Blue. Felix Lajeunesse and Raphael Paul. 2018. Felix & Paul Studios, Sailor Productions

44. Layla comes home. Andy Taylor Smith. We Are Caravan, Oxfam. Online resource (2018). https://www.youtube.com/watch?v=XA1esOet8Kk. Accessed 7 Feb 2023

45. The Party: A virtual experience of autism. Anrick Bregman and Shehani Fernando. The Guardian (2017). \https://www.youtube.com/watch?v=OtwOz1GVkDg&t=183s&ab_channel=TheGuardian. Accessed 7 Feb 2023

46. The Source. Imraan Ismail. Charity Water, Vrse.works (2016). https://www.youtube.com/watch?v=nlVIsVfWwS4&ab_channel=charitywater. Accessed 7 Feb 2023

47. Ready to Learn, Ready to Live. Thomas Nybo. 2018. Hatchet Story Lab, UNICEF Afghanistan. Online resource (2018). https://vimeo.com/252732591. Accessed 7 Feb 2023

48. Rebuilding Notre Dame. Chloé Rochereuil. Targo (2020)

49. When we stayed home. Chloé Rochereuil. Targo, Facebook's Oculus. [series] (2020)

50. Surviving 9/11 – 27 hours under the rubble. Chloé Rochereuil. Targo (2022)

Filmography

51. Mendes, S.: Dreamworks Pictures, Reliance Entertainment. New Republic Pictures, UK, USA, India, Spain (2019)
52. ½. Federico Fellini. Cineriz, Francinex. Italy, France (1963)
53. All that Jazz. Bob Fosse. Columbia Pictures, 20th Century Fox. USA (1979)
54. The Blair Witch Project. Daniel Myrick and Eduardo Sánchez. Haxan Films. USA (1999)
55. Cloverfield. Matt Reeves. Paramount Pictures, Bad Robot, Cloverfield Productions. USA (2008)
56. Enter the Void. Gaspar Noé. Fidélité Films, Wild Bunch, BUF. France, Germany, Italy, Canada, Japan (2009)
57. E.T. Steven Spielberg. Universal Pictures, Amblin Entertainment. USA (1982)
58. The Fast and the Furious. Rob Cohen. Universal Pictures, Original Film, Mediastream Film GmbH & Co, Productions KG. USA, Germany (2001)
59. Fear and Loathing in Las Vegas. Terry Gilliam. Fear and Loathing LLC, Rhino Films, Shark Productions. USA (1998)
60. Hardcore Henry. Ilya Naishuller. Bazelevs Production, Versus Pictures, Huayi Brothers Media. Russia, USA, China (2015)
61. Jaws. Steven Spielberg. Zanuck/Brown Productions, Universal Pictures. USA (1975)
62. Jurassic World: Fallen Kingdom. J.A. Bayona. Universal Pictures, Amblin Entertainment, Legendary Entertainment (2018)
63. Knives Out. Rian Johnson. Lionsgate, Media Rights Capital (MRC), T-Street. USA (2019)
64. Lady in the Lake. Robert Montgomery. Metro-Goldwyn-Mayer. USA (1947)
65. Lawrence of Arabia. David Lean. Horizon Pictures. UK (1962)
66. The Lord of the Rings trilogy. Peter Jackson. 2001, 2002, 2003. New Line Cinema, WingNut Films, The Saul Zaentz Company. New Zealand, USA
67. Pulp Fiction. Quentin Tarantino. Miramax, A Band Apart, Jersey Films. USA (1994)
68. Ocean's Eleven. Steven Soderbergh. Warner Bros., Village Roadshow Pictures, NPV Entertainment. USA (2001)
69. Rashomon. Akira Kurosawa. Daiei. Japan (1951)
70. Rope. Alfred Hitchcock. Warner Bros., Transatlantic Pictures. USA (1948)
71. The Russian Ark (*Russkiy Kovcheg*). Aleksandr Sokurov. The State Hermitage Museum, The Hermitage Bridge Studio, Egoli Tossell Pictures. Russia, Germany, Japan, Canada, Finland, Denmark (2002)
72. Schindler's List. Steven Spielberg. Universal Pictures, Amblin Entertainment. USA (1993)
73. The Shawshank Redemption. Frank Darabont. Castle Rock Entertainment. USA (1994)
74. Sound of Metal. Darius Marder. Caviar, Flat 7 Productions, Ward Four. USA (2019)
75. Stand by me. Rob Reiner. Columbia Pictures, Act III, Act III Communications. USA (1986)

Digital Twin

Towards a Digital Twin Implementation of Eastern Crete: An Educational Approach

Ilias Logothetis[1] ⓘ, Ioanna Mari[2], and Nikolas Vidakis[1](✉) ⓘ

[1] Department of Electrical and Computer Engineering, Hellenic Mediterranean University, 71004 Heraklion, Crete, Greece
{iliaslog,nv}@hmu.gr
[2] Water Directorate -D.A. of Crete, Crete, Greece

Abstract. In the age of digitalization, modern technologies have multiplied, changing how businesses work across a wide range of industries and organizations. Technologies under the extended reality (XR) umbrella can provide immersive user experiences, connectivity, and data collecting from devices and sensors via the Internet of Things (IoT), and digital twins (DT) allowing consumers to test their products and services in a safe virtual environment. This work describes an early use of digital twin technology to model and simulate regions, cultural buildings, fauna, and water-related circumstances within Sitia's Geopark. This paper presents 3D maps in AR while allowing users to interact with virtual items using various techniques. Additionally, digital reconstruction of cultural buildings and mechanisms are included in this study, which enables users to experience how they were and operated when in use. The result of this study is an application that aims to familiarize students with the topography, surface, and underground of a Plateau that simulates real-life conditions of a Plateau in the Sitia Geopark area.

Keywords: Augmented Reality · Extended Reality · Serious Games · Digital Twins · Human-Computer Interaction · Education · Tourism

1 Introduction

The age of digitization has brought with it a wealth of cutting-edge technologies that are changing how organizations function across a variety of industries. These include immersive and personalized experiences for users in augmented reality (AR), virtual reality (VR), mixed reality (MR), and extended reality (XR). Due to their interactive experience, they provide in both the real and virtual worlds, they have a wide variety of appliances [1]. Industries can now connect to and gather data from a broad network of devices and sensors thanks to the Internet of Things (IoT), which enables them to optimize their processes and boost productivity. Contrarily, digital twins (DT) allow businesses to test and improve their goods and services in a virtual setting by using data and simulation models to build a virtual counterpart of a physical asset and offer real-time monitoring and analysis of physical systems, which can help in the diagnosis of errors before they become serious problems.

L. T. De Paolis et al. (Eds.): XR Salento 2023, LNCS 14218, pp. 255–268, 2023.
https://doi.org/10.1007/978-3-031-43401-3_17

In recent years, the application of these technologies in education has also made tremendous progress. With the help of these technologies, students can engage in immersive and interactive learning experiences that make difficult concepts and ideas easier to understand and retain. Metaverse is built upon such technologies and has present great potential in education [2]. Digital twins can also be used to replicate and test procedures and experiments, giving students a risk-free and affordable way to explore and learn. By connecting students and teachers to a huge array of resources and data, the Internet of Things (IoT) has the potential to completely transform education by providing personalized and adaptable learning experiences. Education systems can equip students with the knowledge and abilities required for the digital age while also enhancing engagement and learning outcomes by embracing these cutting-edge tools [3].

An industry of interest in this paper is the tourism industry, where XR and digital twin technologies have great potential. They can provide digital representations of cultural buildings, artwork, and other attractions that travelers can explore and interact with. Studies to examine [4] how these technologies are used and adopted in tourism education have shown that students are positively influenced by technology.

1.1 Motivation

The INTERREG 2014–2020 Project "Waterways", concerns the improvement and enhancement of the attractiveness of areas of natural and cultural interest through the protection and highlighting of important "water features" on the E4 European path in Crete and Cyprus. E4 path runs through areas and monuments of special natural beauty that are part of European and international protection networks such as Natura 2000 and the UNESCO Geoparks network to which the Sitia (Crete) & Troodos (Cyprus) Geoparks belong. Their recognition, as a comparative advantage, provides unique development opportunities and possibilities for the sustainable development of local communities and their emergence as geotourism destinations of excellence. The project highlights the value & special characteristics of geological & cultural heritage, contributes to the protection and preservation of the natural & cultural environment, and raises awareness among citizens about climate change & sustainability.

Following the project's concerns, the purpose of this study is to expand the knowledge of the users in respect to the unique characteristics of Sitia's Geopark, to recognize geographical terms that relate to the surface and subsurface relief and the path of water in it but also to promote their critical thinking regarding the effects that may bring about human interventions both in the natural landscape and in our life itself. Usually, student textbooks, or common websites present general geographical depictions of places such as large flowing rivers, green lands, active volcanoes, and smooth land levels without focusing on the particularities of certain geographical divisions.

However, in most cases, such depictions do not concern the Greek landscape, and especially they do not belong to Crete and especially to the Eastern side, where the intense relief, the type of rocks, and the dry-thermal conditions have shaped one definite landscape entirely different from that of Northern Europe. A very characteristic example of this particularity is watercourses (rivers and torrents) which water does not flow throughout the year, and this is the reason they characterize them as "intermittent watercourses" which means that the water occurs in these only during the rainy season, while during the rest of the period in the summer, it is dry. At the other end of the "dry" season is the winter season, which in cases of rainstorms can lead to flooding phenomena.

Human activities have also adapted to this landscape. The people who live in these areas have built their settlements in the foothills of the mountains and not in the plain, to protect their houses from any floods while using groundwater to meet their needs either in water supply (for drinking, washing, and more) or irrigation (for crops). So, from ancient times until today, they have built wells through which they pump the underground water and use it during the summer season.

1.2 Objectives

For the reasons described above, this paper provides an early adoption of digital twin technology to model and simulate areas, cultural buildings, fauna, and conditions caused by water within Sitia's Geopark. This paper provides an alternative presentation of 3D maps in AR, while allowing users to interact with virtual objects with various techniques. Such techniques include haptic interaction, roaming in the environment (walking) and gaze interaction. This visualization technique allows many users to view the content collaboratively from a mobile phone or tablet providing a higher degree of freedom than a conventional application. Additionally, an early adaptation of DTs in tourism and cultural heritage promotion in offering remote tour experiences is explored. Finally, this study discusses how DTs might be used in the tourism sector to offer interactive tours that can be accessed remotely as well as educational initiatives to improve spatial awareness.

The aim of this study includes:

a) to familiarize students with topography and the surface and underground of a Plateau that simulates real-life conditions of a Plateau in the Sitia Geopark area through direct contact.
b) To be used as a base development platform for educational scenarios.
c) Explore how DT can be combined with AR to provide educational content based on spatial information.

The rest of the article is organized as follows: Sect. 2 outlines a brief background and review of the state-of-the-art approaches in similar work. Section 3 describes the methodology and implementation, while Sect. 4 presents and discusses the results of the current study. Finally, Sect. 5 concludes the article with final thoughts and insights for future directions.

2 Background

Several recent studies [5–7] show that the use of digital twins is spreading across a wide range of industries, including urban planning and design. Digital twins can be utilized in the industrial business, for example, to track equipment performance and predict when maintenance or repairs are required [8]. Digital twins can be used in the healthcare business to replicate the human body and assess the efficacy of therapies [9]. Another advantage of digital twins is their ability to improve physical system performance. Digital twins are an effective tool for optimizing the performance of physical systems and processes. They enable real-time monitoring, analysis, optimization, and augmentation, which increases productivity, reduces costs, and produces better results. AR and game technologies have also been investigated as techniques for increasing citizen participation in urban planning procedures [10]–[12]. Furthermore, digital twin technology has been demonstrated to be an excellent method for evaluating sustainability in the context of railway station buildings [13].

The use of digital twins in water infrastructure management is becoming increasingly popular, particularly with the growing threat of flooding. Pesantez et al. [14] utilize a digital twin to investigate the effects of the COVID-19 pandemic on water infrastructure, whereas Tarpanelli et al. [15] employ a digital twin to investigate the flooding of the Enza River in December 2017. Pedersen et al. [16] concentrate on the development of digital twins for urban water systems, emphasizing the possibility of creating multi-purpose value through the use of models and sensors. Furthermore, Wei et al. [17] provide a combined anomaly detection framework for digital twins of water treatment plants, emphasizing digital twins' potential to improve the efficiency and safety of water infrastructure.

Recent technological breakthroughs have increased interest in digital twins and augmented reality for the tourism business. According to Fischer-Stabel et al. [18], digital twins and explorer maps are becoming more appealing for outdoor tourism, particularly in rural areas. According to Yuce [19], digital twins can help with sustainable development in the tourist and hospitality industries. Furthermore, Ssin et al. [20] offer a business model for science tours based on digital twins. As Luther et al. [21] point out, digital twins and enabling technologies are also being used in museums and cultural heritage. Augmented reality has also been investigated as a helpful tool in tourism, with Cranmer et al. [22] concluding that it has significant promise. In addition, Noh et al. [23] and Wojciechowski et al. [24] examine the application of augmented reality in virtual and augmented reality museum exhibitions. Haugstvedt and Krogstie [25] found encouraging results in a technological acceptance study on mobile augmented reality for cultural assets.

Applications with digital twins of a tourist attraction, such as a historical site or museum, can be built to provide travellers with an immersive experience. Furthermore, digital twins allow visitors to examine the attraction in great detail, including its history, architecture, and artwork [26]. Digital twins can also be used by tourism operators to model and simulate tourist flows, allowing them to maximize visitor experiences and control congestion. For example, a theme park can use a digital twin to mimic visitor behaviour and flow, allowing operators to adjust staffing and ride capacity to optimize wait times and reduce crowding [27]. Additionally, customized recommendations are available to travellers based on their interests and inclinations through digital twins. A digital twin can recommend activities, venues, and experiences suited to a tourist's interests by analysing data from the tourist's previous behaviour and preferences [28]. Overall, digital twins are being used to improve tourist experiences, optimize operations, and deliver personalized recommendations in the tourism industry.

3   Methodology

The objective of the application is to promote cultural heritage inside the Sitia Geopark, advise users about locations to visit, and provide a preview of vistas. The area's water resources have received significant attention, particularly how the water and the problems caused by its misuse flow in the Ziros plateau. Augmented Reality was chosen for this project over VR or a standard 3D game because, according to the literature [29] and studies conducted by the authors, AR is a better technology for displaying spatial information and users can better receive and understand that information. The game's goal is to provide a 3D map of Lasithi Prefecture (eastern Crete) and mark notable locations on that map in the same way that a standard 2D digital map would. When annotated places are clicked, a 3D map of the area is displayed, and the user can execute actions relevant to the location within that map. The game is intended for elementary and high school children and is built for mobile devices as most of the people nowadays have one always with them, and most of the modern devices can run AR applications.

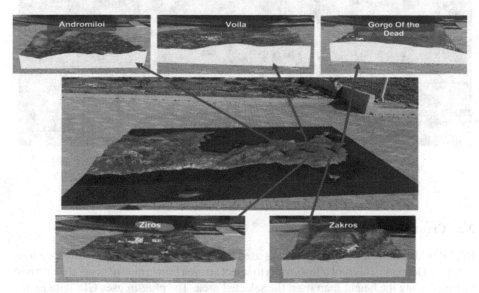

Fig. 1. Lasithi prefecture with the modeled areas

3.1   The Game

The Unity 3D game engine was used to create the game since it provides good support for the building of AR applications utilizing the AR Foundation framework. Furthermore, the Real-World Terrain asset was made available on Unity through the Unity Asset Store, allowing the creation of Digital terrain from GIS data. The game shows a map of eastern Crete (Lasithi Prefecture), which is the border of the Geopark of Sitia. Five selected communities and historical settlements are also given 3D digital analogs on this map. These are Andromuloi, Voila, Ziros, Zakros, and the Gorge of the Dead (see Fig. 1). The application incorporates game-based learning by offering engaging puzzle and matching mini-games to captivate users. To ensure an immersive experience without losing interest, the game carefully applies the principles of flow theory, striking a balance between providing tasks that are enjoyable yet challenging enough. Moreover, cognitive theory guides the presentation of content, ensuring it is delivered in a manner that optimizes learning. Furthermore, all activities feature a quest-like approach, serving as a gamification element that assigns a sense of purpose and achievement.

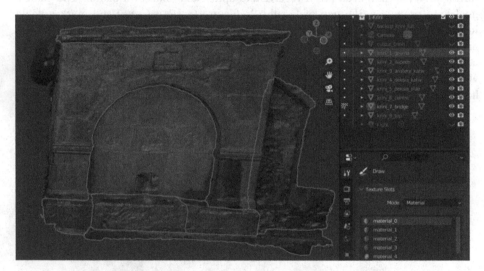

Fig. 2. Small fountain in Voila

3.2 Creating the Models

Real World Terrain, a Unity plug-in, was used to build the 3D models depicting locations in Sitia's Geopark. This tool allows users to select an area from a map to generate a Terrain in Unity using the height map from the selected area. The plug-in uses GIS data in this process. After the creation of the Terrain, configurations were made to fine-tune the Terrain's dimensions and texture quality. The final steps for the Terrain creation before the addition of objects are to create a "base" for the map that represents the underground layers of the areas and to carve the watercourse of rivers on the surface. Blender was used to carry out these tasks. Rivers configured as simple meshes, with a shader to imitate water flow were added later. Lastly, buildings and structures were placed on the generated maps to fit the real-world field. Watermill models were produced in Blender using real data from Zakros' Watermills. The textures are also produced using the exact materials and colors that the real objects used. Other models, such as the fountain in Voila, were 3D scanned using drones using photogrammetry.

3.3 Game Activities

Complete Puzzles
One of the activities offered through the game is the puzzle completion of cultural monuments like the fountain in Fig. 2. In this type of activity, the player has to gather the pieces placed around an empty outline of the fountain and place them in the corresponding position to successfully complete the puzzle and view the actual model. Puzzle games in AR have been found fun to play by children [29] but also might drop their confidence towards the game [30]. For that reason, the included puzzles are very simple to solve with a small number of pieces.

(a) Ziros plateau signs

(b) Andromiloi Agioi Apostoloi church

Fig. 3. Label Placing activity examples.

Matching Labels in the Correct Spots
This activity can be found on the Ziros plateau map in Fig. 3. The purpose of this activity is to inform the user about the basic terms and the topography of the plateau. The process of this activity is similar to the puzzle activity, with the difference that the "cards" containing the terms are in a fixed position in the UI of the application and the signs around the map. The player has to select a "card" with a term and walk towards the sign that is placed in a position that describes the place or object of the picked term (Fig. 4).

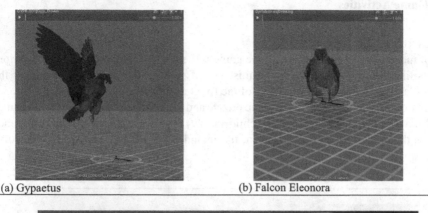

(a) Gypaetus   (b) Falcon Eleonora

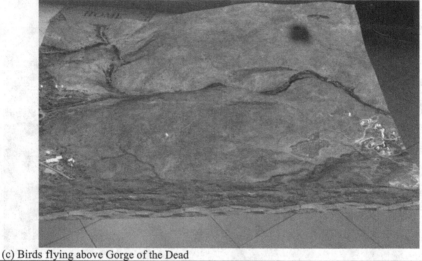

(c) Birds flying above Gorge of the Dead

Fig. 4. Modeled Birds from Geopark's fauna

Interact with the Fauna

When the player navigates in the Gorge of the Dead map, the opportunity to watch two of the most known and rare birds is located in Sitia's Geopark Fig. 6. The player can interact with them by tapping on their mobile screens and watching the birds perform actions like diving down to the ground to eat or drink water, changing flight directions, and more Fig. 6(c) presents the birds flying above the Gorge of the Dead (Fig. 5).

Navigate (& Interact) in Cultural Buildings

Zakros is another village within Sitia's geopark, in which the game offers the activities of navigating and interacting with cultural buildings. This activity requires a large area in order to be displayed correctly. This is because the projection of the buildings is in real size so that the user can enter inside and navigate around the place. Additionally, when looking at "points of interest" the ability to click on them and request more information

(a) watermill

(b)"Rasotrivio" – Local clothing washing mechanism

Fig. 5. Zakros cultural buldings

about those points is supported. Through this activity, the player can learn how cultural buildings were and how the mechanisms inside them were operating. The first building is that of a watermill house Fig. 7 (a) and Fig. 7 (b).

Moreover, a service has been developed that gathers weather forecasts for each location, and when a user navigates to that location the weather conditions are displayed on the map Fig. 6. This service is developed specifically for Ziros map as an activity on this map is for the user to play some scenarios where the user is called to solve problems related to water management. The service will allow each scenario to get triggered when the corresponding weather condition is applied. For example, if there is heavy rain and the ground can't absorb all the water, then the plateau will flood, and users will have to find solutions to prevent or fix this condition.

Fig. 6. Clouds Over Ziros plateau

4   Results and Discussion

Presenting a piece of land in AR offers a fascinating experience to the users while unlocking functionalities that otherwise would be impossible to produce. As the continent is presented, in the real world, through a mobile device, the users can actively engage with the content moving around and observe it from different angles. In the case of 3D maps, this offers an advantage over a typical desktop application as the engagement is more intense, while a VR application could imitate the same functionality it requires extra hardware that is still not commonly available to everyone. The same applies to the navigation and interaction inside the watermill cultural building and the puzzle completion activities. A drawback in AR can be considered the matching game, in which the users have to move their phones really near the map to be able to spot some hard objects to match such as wells. A limitation of the application is that it requires a large open area to be presented correctly due to the nature of the content, and the real-size buildings included in it, so the users would not be able to fully experience the application in a small place, as the digital models will attempt to shrink to fit in the provided space. Trying to place the watermill, for example, in a small area will result in poor user experience as the results will not be as intended.

4.1   Digital Versus Physical Model

The physical models are built to synergize with digital serious educational games, to provide an additional perspective to the basic learning process and knowledge. The Ziros plateau model Fig. 7 (a) activities are related to water such as the path of water as rain, its runoff through the rivers, its penetration into the underground aquifer, its use, and more,

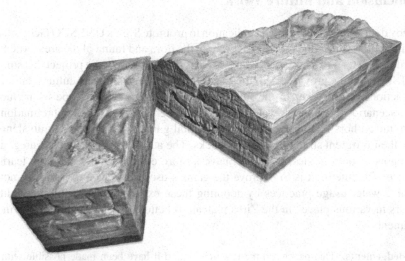

(a) Physical Model of Ziros Plateau

(b) 3D printed model of a watermill   *(c) Lego model of a watermill*

Fig. 7. Physical models

using real data from the Sitia Geopark area. The watermill in Fig. 7 (b) is a 3D printed version of the watermill mechanism, which one can break down and assemble again to learn the parts of the mechanism and how it operated. Figure 7 (c) presents a watermill created with Lego and is programmed to simulate the movement of the actual watermill. Through this second model of the watermill, the users can learn how to assemble a watermill with Lego and have an entry-level experience in programming. Future studies will explore the potential synergy between these physical models and Augmented Reality (AR), aiming to enhance the models by incorporating AR technology to enrich them with additional information and interactive features.

5   Conclusion and Future Work

This study demonstrates a gamified application to promote Sitia's UNESCO Geopark as a tourist attraction while educating its users about the flora and fauna of the area. Attention is towards the water and its uses as "Waterways" is the acronym of the project this study is a part of. Through the provided activities, users can examine and view cultural buildings and attractions in real size. In the future, to broaden the game's scope by including playable scenarios that address water abuse issues such as overuse or contamination. In addition, the authors intend to compare this digital game to its physical equivalents to evaluate their different strengths and drawbacks. The authors believe that by integrating the strengths of both modes, users will have a more effective and enjoyable learning experience. The intention is to improve the game's usefulness as a tool for promoting sustainable water usage practices by adopting these expansions. Finally, the addition of sensors in various places in the Ziros plateau to better capture the conditions in the environment.

Acknowledgements. This paper and the research behind it have been made possible with the support of the following project Water ways.

PROJECT TITLE: Waterways and Histories in E4 and Eastern Mediterranean Geoparks, PROJECT MIS CODE: 5048529, PROJECT ACRONYMS: WaterWays, PRIORITY AXES 2&3, FRAMEWORK OF THE INTERREG V-A COOPERATION PROGRAM GREECE – CYPRUS 2014–2020, PRIORITY AXIS 3 - Preservation and protection of the environment and risk prevention, ERDF Fund.
CONSORTIUM

1. Beneficiary (Complete Name)	2. Role	3. Country	4. NUTS II / NUTS III
5.	6.	7.	8.
9. Hellenic Mediterranean University (HMU)	10. Main Partner	11. Greece	12. EL431
13. Foundation for Research and Technology (ITE)	14. Partner	15. Greece	16. EL431
17. Eforia of Antiquities Lassithiou (St Nicholas)	18. Partner	19. Greece	20. EL432
21. Municipality of Sitia	22. Partner	23. Greece	24. EL432
25. Troodos Development Company Ltd	26. Partner	27. Cyprus	28. CY000
29. Frederick Research Center	30. Partner	31. Cyprus	32. CY000

References

1. Minaee, S., Liang, X., Yan, S.: Modern augmented reality: applications, trends, and future directions (2022)
2. Jagatheesaperumal, S.K., Ahmad, K., Al-Fuqaha, A., Qadir, J.: Advancing Education Through Extended Reality and Internet of Everything Enabled Metaverses: Applications, Challenges, and Open Issues (2022)

3. Crittenden, W.F., Biel, I.K., Lovely, W.A.: Embracing digitalization: student learning and new technologies. J. Mark. Educ. **41**, 5–14 (2019). https://doi.org/10.1177/0273475318820895/ ASSET/IMAGES/LARGE/10.1177_0273475318820895-FIG4.JPEG

4. Shen, S., Xu, K., Sotiriadis, M., Wang, Y.: Exploring the factors influencing the adoption and usage of augmented reality and virtual reality applications in tourism education within the context of COVID-19 pandemic. J. Hosp. Leis. Sport. Tour. Educ. **30**, 100373 (2022). https://doi.org/10.1016/J.JHLSTE.2022.100373

5. Dembski, F., Wössner, U., Letzgus, M., Ruddat, M., Yamu, C.: Urban Digital Twins for smart cities and citizens: the case study of Herrenberg, Germany. Sustainability **12**, 2307 (2020). https://doi.org/10.3390/SU12062307

6. Saßmannshausen, S.M., Radtke, J., Bohn, N., Hussein, H., Randall, D., Pipek, V.: Citizen-centered design in urban planning: how augmented reality can be used in citizen participation processes. In: DIS 2021 - Proceedings of the 2021 ACM Designing Interactive Systems Conference: Nowhere and Everywhere, pp. 250–265 (2021). https://doi.org/10.1145/3461778. 3462130

7. Wolf, M., Söbke, H., Wehking, F.: Mixed reality media-enabled public participation in urban planning, 125–138 (2020). https://doi.org/10.1007/978-3-030-37869-1_11

8. Tao, F., Cheng, J., Qi, Q., Zhang, M., Zhang, H., Sui, F.: Digital twin-driven product design, manufacturing and service with big data. Int. J. Adv. Manufact. Technol. **94**, 3563–3576 (2018). https://doi.org/10.1007/s00170-017-0233-1

9. Croatti, A., Gabellini, M., Montagna, S., Ricci, A.: On the integration of agents and digital twins in healthcare. J. Med. Syst. **44**, 1–8 (2020). https://doi.org/10.1007/S10916-020-01623-5/FIGURES/2

10. Fegert, J., Pfeiffer, J., Peukert, C., Weinhardt, C.: Enriching E-participation through augmented reality: first results of a qualitative study. In: WI2020 Zentrale Tracks, pp. 560–567 (2020). https://doi.org/10.30844/WI_2020_E5-FEGERT

11. Raghothama, J., Meijer, S.: Gaming, urban planning and transportation design process. Lecture Notes Geoinform. Cartography **213**, 297–312 (2015). https://doi.org/10.1007/978-3-319-18368-8_16/COVER

12. Kavouras, I., Sardis, E., Protopapadakis, E., Rallis, I., Doulamis, A., Doulamis, N.: A low-cost gamified urban planning methodology enhanced with co-creation and participatory approaches. Sustainability **15**, 2297 (2023). https://doi.org/10.3390/SU15032297

13. Kaewunruen, S., Xu, N.: Digital twin for sustainability evaluation of railway station buildings. Front Built Environ **4**, 77 (2018). https://doi.org/10.3389/FBUIL.2018.00077/BIBTEX

14. Pesantez, J.E., Alghamdi, F., Sabu, S., Mahinthakumar, G., Berglund, E.Z.: Using a digital twin to explore water infrastructure impacts during the COVID-19 pandemic. Sustain Cities Soc **77**, 103520 (2022). https://doi.org/10.1016/J.SCS.2021.103520

15. Tarpanelli, A., Bonaccorsi, B., Sinagra, M., Domeneghetti, A., Brocca, L., Barbetta, S.: Flooding in the digital twin earth: the case study of the enza river levee breach in December 2017. Water **15**, 1644 (2023). https://doi.org/10.3390/W15091644

16. Pedersen, A.N., Borup, M., Brink-Kjær, A., Christiansen, L.E., Mikkelsen, P.S.: Living and prototyping digital twins for urban water systems: towards multi-purpose value creation using models and sensors. Water **13**, 592 (2021). https://doi.org/10.3390/W13050592

17. Wei, Y., Law, A.W.K., Yang, C., Tang, D.: Combined anomaly detection framework for digital twins of water treatment facilities. Water **14**, 1001 (2022). https://doi.org/10.3390/W14071001

18. Fischer-Stabel, P., Mai, F., Schindler, S., Schneider, M.: Digital twins, augmented reality and explorer maps rising attractiveness of rural regions for outdoor tourism. In: Kamilaris, A., Wohlgemuth, V., Karatzas, K., Athanasiadis, I.N. (eds) Advances and New Trends in Environmental Informatics. Progress in IS. Springer, Cham, pp. 243–253 (2021). https://doi.org/10.1007/978-3-030-61969-5_17

19. Yuce, A.: Digital Twins and Sustainable Developments in the Tourism and Hospitality Industry. https://services.igi-global.com/resolvedoi/resolve.aspx?doi=https://doi.org/10.4018/978-1-6684-6821-0.ch027 1AD, 461–472. https://doi.org/10.4018/978-1-6684-6821-0.CH027

20. Ssin, S., Suh, M., Lee, J., Jung, T., Woo, W.: Science tour and business model using digital twin-based augmented reality. In: Tom Dieck, M.C., Jung, T.H., Loureiro, S.M.C. (eds.) Augmented Reality and Virtual Reality. Progress in IS, pp. 267–276. Springer, Cham. https://doi.org/10.1007/978-3-030-68086-2_20

21. Luther, W., Baloian, N., Biella, D., Sacher, D.: Digital twins and enabling technologies in museums and cultural heritage: an overview. Sensors **23**(3), 1583 (2023). https://doi.org/10.3390/s23031583

22. Cranmer, E.E., Tom Dieck, M.C., Fountoulaki, P.: Exploring the value of augmented reality for tourism. Tour. Manag. Perspect. **35**, (2020). https://doi.org/10.1016/j.tmp.2020.100672

23. Noh, Z., Sunar, M.S., Pan, Z.: A Review on Augmented Reality for Virtual Heritage System. Lecture Notes in Computer Science (including subseries Lecture Notes in Artificial Intelligence and Lecture Notes in Bioinformatics), vol. 5670 LNCS, pp. 50–61 (2009). https://doi.org/10.1007/978-3-642-03364-3_7/COVER

24. Wojciechowski, R., Walczak, K., White, M., Cellary, W.: Building virtual and augmented reality museum exhibitions. In: Web3D Symposium Proceedings, pp. 135–144 (2004). https://doi.org/10.1145/985040.985060

25. Haugstvedt, A.C., Krogstie, J.: Mobile augmented reality for cultural heritage: a technology acceptance study. In: ISMAR 2012 - 11th IEEE International Symposium on Mixed and Augmented Reality 2012, Science and Technology Papers, pp. 247–255 (2012). https://doi.org/10.1109/IS-MAR.2012.6402563

26. Buhalis, D., Leung, D., Lin, M.: Metaverse as a disruptive technology revolutionising tourism management and marketing. Tour Manag. **97**, 104724 (2023). https://doi.org/10.1016/J.TOUR-MAN.2023.104724

27. Digital Twins: A Model of Efficiency for Travel. https://www.linkedin.com/pulse/digital-twins-model-efficiency-travel-kumar-parama-sivam?trk=articles_directory. Accessed 26 April 2023

28. Zhao, J., Guo, L., Li, Y.: Application of Digital twin combined with artificial intelligence and 5G technology in the art design of digital museums. Wirel. Commun. Mob. Comput. (2022). https://doi.org/10.1155/2022/8214514

29. Hapsari, G.I., Mutiara, G.A., Chaidir, R.: Dental health education game based-on IRVO model in augmented reality technology. J. Infotel. **14**, 108=115–108=115 (2022). https://doi.org/10.20895/INFOTEL.V14I2.760

30. Lu, S.J., Liu, Y.C., Chen, P.J., Hsieh, M.R.: Evaluation of AR embedded physical puzzle game on students' learning achievement and motivation on elementary natural science. Interact. Learn. Environ. **28**, 451–463 (2018).https://doi.org/10.1080/10494820.2018.1541908

Digital Twin and Extended Reality in Industrial Contexts: A Bibliometric Review

Vito Del Vecchio(✉) [iD], Mariangela Lazoi [iD], and Marianna Lezzi [iD]

University of Salento, Lecce, Italy
vito.delvecchio@unisalento.it

Abstract. Digital twin and extended reality technologies, including augmented reality, virtual reality and mixed reality, are among the key digital technologies of Industry 4.0. While digital twin enables the representation of the virtual counterpart of a physical system, the extended reality attempts to improve the user experience by augmenting the perception of the reality through digital information. The combined use of such technologies contributes to leverage the creativity of experts in collaboration with intelligent industrial systems. Although their benefits for industries are widely discussed in the literature, few studies are available on the implications of their combined use. Therefore, based on a systematic literature review and a bibliometric analysis, the paper aims to investigate the intersection of digital twin and extended reality technologies in industry, in order to discover the implications and reveal future research directions. Six main clusters resulted from the analysis: advanced digital services, extended robotized twin, virtualization, scalable analysis, multi-layered digitalization, digital lymph. Both academics and practitioners can benefit from such results in order to evaluate potential applications and to address their current research and activities.

Keywords: Digital Twin · Extended Reality · Smart Manufacturing · Bibliometric Analysis · Research Directions

1 Introduction

Industry 4.0, through the use of a range of advanced technologies (including digital twin and extended reality), enables the fusion of the physical and digital worlds, the creation of new knowledge in real time, valuable decision-making and product and process innovation [1]. This allows flexible manufacturing, adapting to quick changes in demand, while increasing the quality of products/services offered and productivity, as well as the efficiency of the processes executed according to customer needs [2].

In this industrial context, while digital twin (DT) technology is based on the principle of making physical objects interact with their digital counterparts, extended reality (XR) technology rather focuses on improving the user experience in terms of digital content visualization, interaction and remote or collaborative operation [3]. In other words, a manufacturing DT gives the opportunity to simulate, monitor and optimize the machine; whereas, the XR enhances human-machine interaction (HMI) in the industrial domain

L. T. De Paolis et al. (Eds.): XR Salento 2023, LNCS 14218, pp. 269–283, 2023.
https://doi.org/10.1007/978-3-031-43401-3_18

[4]. According to [5], DTs utilize XR capabilities to digitally model physical objects, enabling users to interact with digital contents.

The combined use of digital twin and extended reality technologies contributes to the Industry 5.0 goal of leveraging the creativity of human experts in collaboration with intelligent machines. In particular, DT and XR could enable humans to access critical knowledge and control different machines, systems and processes [6].

Although the benefits of using DT and XR technologies within industrial contexts have been widely discussed in the literature [4, 7], research is lacking in identifying the implications of their combined use, as well as in defining supporting guidelines for their successful integration.

Based on a systematic literature review and a bibliometric analysis, this study aims to explore the most important emerging research directions related to the application of DT and XT technologies in the modern industrial contexts, in order to highlight their main implications. Due to the nature of the bibliometric analysis, this study proposed a set of emerging topics surrounding the research on DT and XR, to be intended as future research actions. Thus, it explores a new field of the literature which seems to be still immature. In particular, the paper intends to provide an answer to the following research question: What are the implications of applying digital twins and extended reality technologies in industry? To answer this research question, a network analysis and a graphical investigation of the bibliographic textual data, exported from Scopus, were conducted with the aim of creating a co-occurrence map through the use of VOSviewer, as a bibliometric analysis software.

The results of the analysis show the identification of six clusters (i.e., advanced digital services, extended robotized twin, virtualization, scalable analysis, multi-layered digitalization and digital lymph) as potential research actions for understanding the implications of DT and XR technologies in current industrial contexts.

Therefore, this study provides both theoretical and practical implications, extending the boundaries of knowledge through the formulation of potential future research directions in industry, and supporting managers and experts in understanding useful strategies to strengthen the sustainability of their business through the adoption of DT and XR technologies.

The paper is structured as follows: the next section provides an overview of the literature on DT and XR applications in industry; Sect. 3 describes the methodology adopted by the researchers; and Sect. 4 presents the results of the exploratory study. Finally, Sect. 5 closes the paper, by discussing the main findings and limitations of the research.

2 Background

2.1 Digital Twin Applications in Industry

Digital twin is recognized as one of the key technological pillars of the Industry 4.0 [8]. It is characterized by a seamless integration within industrial internet of things environments. This technology attracted an increasing attention over the years, from both academics and practitioners, due to its wide declinations and applications [9].

According to [10], a DT can be defined as "a digital representation of a real-world entity or system; the implementation of a digital twin is an encapsulated software object or model that mirrors a unique physical object, process, organization, person or other abstraction". It has the potential to achieve smart configurations of industries [11] and the ability to digitalize business processes. The term "digital twin" appeared for the first time in 2006, when Michael Grieves presented the Information Mirroring Model, as its ancestor, having common features such as the real space, the virtual space and their connection through bidirectional data flows [12]. By leveraging different digital technologies (e.g., Internet of Things, Cyber Physical Systems, Artificial Intelligence, Big Data, Advanced Analytics, Cloud, Simulation) [9], the DT creates a link between the physical and virtual worlds by providing a mean for simulation, monitoring and analysis in multiple sectors, for a huge set of purposes and creating various benefits [13].

An interesting study within the smart manufacturing contexts was provided by [14], who presented an extensive systematic review of the literature that allows for understanding the key building blocks of a DT in industry. A multi-layered conceptual framework was introduced consisting of six layers: i) physical layer, which encompasses the sources of data belonging to the physical world (e.g., objects, people, processes); ii) network layer, that is responsible for sensing, communicating and transmitting data to the virtual world; iii) model layer, including sub-modules for the virtual abstraction as the physical counterpart; iv) data integration layer, that focuses on integrating the available streaming data flows with the datasets stored in corporate repositories or managed in enterprise applications; v) knowledge layer, that leverages enabling technologies and techniques to highlights insights from data; vi) application layer, that allows users to access DT services according to specific objectives (e.g., predictive maintenance, process monitoring, quality predictions, production planning). Then, such framework was also experimented within a manufacturing aerospace scenario as the process-counterpart of the material handling process for supporting the monitoring of critical part numbers [15].

Relevant DT applications were reported for product design and manufacturing as well as production processes [16], enabling organizations to make more accurate predictions, rational decisions, and informed plans. For instance, [17] considered data feedback of DT to support and better implement design-oriented DTs. It is also an enabler of iterative optimization, data integrity, virtual evaluation and verification [18]. Also, [19] proposed a model to manage 3D products and to strengthen the collaboration between designers and producers, by envisioning its use in different development phases such as planning, conceptualization and detailed design. According to [20], DTs represent the next generation of simulation. The authors proposed a study for assisting and optimizing the production process, by developing an advanced cyber-physical system that synchronize the physical and virtual spaces. The concept of shop-floor DT was presented in [21], which comprises a specific service system for exploiting the value of production data. In manufacturing, DTs enable real-time monitoring, production control, workpiece performance prediction, asset management and production planning [18]. An interesting application of the DT is also related to the human-robot collaboration and interaction, as discussed by [22]. In this case, benefits arise in terms of task allocation, workstation layout optimization, human ergonomic analysis and robot program test. Also, DTs can support the service phase of product development in terms of predictive maintenance, fault detection and diagnosis, status monitoring, performance prediction, virtual test [18]. It supports manufacturers and suppliers to have control of systems, gain access to real time data and realize a closed-loop stream [23].

2.2 Extended Reality Applications in Industry

Extended reality technologies, including virtual reality (VR), augmented reality (AR) and mixed reality (MR), embody a paradigm that enhances and underpins Industry 4.0 in different contexts [4]. Indeed, these technologies enable faster and easier implementation of new practices of virtual representation of complex scenarios that, in turn, can lead to greater value creation [3]. In particular, virtual reality allows the user to immerse himself, through the computer screen, in a virtual world based on three dimensions (3D); whereas, augmented reality augments the user's field of view with information necessary to perform the current task. Finally, mixed reality, being a mix of real and virtual, causes the virtual to augment the real and the real to augment the virtual [24]. In the manufacturing context, VR is most commonly used in product development and marketing, but can also be used for training, ergonomics and visualization of digital factories [25]. On the other hand, AR is mainly employed for the remote guidance and visualization of instructions for complex assemblies, and disruptive or training activities [26], and MR is used to visualize new products and particular procedures (such as picking) [24].

XR technologies consist of hardware systems that create a feeling of immersion for users. Moreover, these technologies employ tools and methods to design and implement software systems in the underlying environment, create user-centered designs for XR experiences (prioritizing human behavior, capabilities and needs), and prepare three-dimensional content to be displayed in XR scenes by creating and assigning properties (e.g., geometry, materials, textures, animations, collisors and physical relationships to relevant data) [27]. Therefore, the adoption of XR technologies in industrial contexts involves considerable technological complexity, high hardware costs and the need for users with appropriate experience and knowledge.

According to [6], XR is recognized as a pivotal role in the realization of various HMI applications. Indeed, XR technologies refer to the combined environment of all real and virtual resources in which humans interact with machines, thus transforming the concept of manufacturing. The merging of the digital/cyber/virtual and physical worlds through XR can result in significant time savings at almost every stage of production (from design and prototyping to marketing, logistics and maintenance) [24]. Furthermore, such technology can be useful in increasing so-called time-room flexibility (i.e., the need of not being in the same place at the same time when working on a project and needing to adopt a faster and more powerful decision-making process) [28].

The application fields of XR technologies are varied, such as [3]: automotive, construction, energy, manufacturing, recreational, maritime, aerospace, health and safety, petrochemical, education and research, business, and many others. The literature review work conducted by [3] on XR applications in industry provides multiple examples of applications in the industries mentioned here.

2.3 Combined Use of Digital Twin and Extended Reality

The possibility to enhance the value and effectiveness of DT solutions is represented by the use of immersive technologies, such as virtual reality, augmented reality and mixed reality. Overall, immersive technologies significantly enhance the user experience and applicability of DT across industries, leading to improved decision-making, cost savings, and increased efficiency. In parallel, different challenges occur, such as VR interaction design, networking optimization, and optimized hardware controls [29].

Immersive technologies can provide a more realistic and immersive visualization experience through a VR experience. Users can explore and interact with the DT in a simulated environment, enhancing their understanding of physical systems [30]. For example, engineers can virtually walk through a digital representation of a factory to analyze operations, identify bottlenecks, and plan improvements. Also, VR enable training and simulations in safe virtual environments, so that operators can practice operating and maintaining complex systems using the digital twin, reducing the risk of real-world mistakes or accidents [31].

Another interesting value coming from the use of DT and immersive technologies is to facilitate remote collaboration and communication [32]. Indeed, users can access and interact with the DT simultaneously from remote locations, improving coordination and knowledge sharing. In addition, such technologies can support iterative design processes by enabling designers to virtually test and simulate their ideas, by creating and manipulating DTs of real systems, visualizing how changes or modifications affect their performance [33]. This also helps in reducing physical prototypes and associated costs, accelerating the overall design process.

Finally, immersive technologies combined with DT can enhance maintenance and support activities [34]. Technicians can use immersive reality to overlay DT information into the physical system, providing real-time instructions for repairs or maintenance. Remote experts can guide onsite technicians via augmented information, reducing downtime and improving efficiency.

3 Methodology

The research methodology was designed to achieve the understanding of the use of DT and XR technologies in modern industry. These fields were combined in order to discover their implications and the potential future research directions, in the attempt to extend their knowledge boundaries [35]. The paper aims to provide an answer to the following research question: What are the implications of applying digital twins and extended reality technologies in industry?

A systematic literature review (SLR) has been carried out as the reference methodology for collecting the sample of data. It is a transparent, scientific and replicable process that allows for the identification, highlighting and evaluation of several sources of information in order to catalogue and compare the results in a structured way [36]. In addition, a bibliometric analysis has been carried out to analyze the obtained sample and to provide an exploratory understanding of the reference fields of interest. The bibliometric analysis is recognized as a fundamental methodology for exploring research of any disciplines and areas and highlighting their nature [37]. It is particularly useful when approaching to a still immature research field [38].

As also suggested by [39], three main phases comprised the reference methodology of this study: i) definition of search schema and data sample; ii) preliminary analysis of the sample; iii) data analysis. Figure 1 details steps and sub-steps of the methodology.

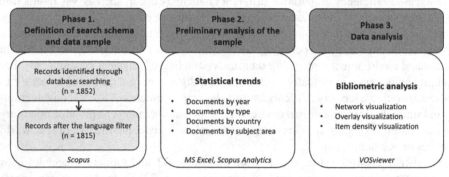

Fig. 1. Research methodology

3.1 Definition of Search Schema and Data Sample

In line with the objective of this study and considering the SLR procedure [36], the following keywords were selected for the investigation of the fields of interest: "Digital Twin"; "Extended Reality", "Mixed Reality", "Virtual Reality", "Augmented Reality", "Immersive Technolog*", "AR", "VR", "MR", "XR"; "Industry 4.0", "Industry 5.0", "Industrial Internet of Things", "IIoT", "Smart Manufacturing", "Smart Factory", "Industrial Internet", "Industr*", "CPS", "Cyber Physical System*", "ICS", "Industrial Control System*". The selection of such keywords comes from the consideration of similar concepts, synonyms and acronyms observed in the theoretical background. Specifically, their combination has been implemented by accurately using mathematical logical connectives (Boolean operators). Also, to build a homogeneous data sample useful for the following bibliometric analysis, the language filter has been used to considered only contributions written in English. Below, the designed query:

(TITLE-ABS-KEY ("digital twin") AND TITLE-ABS-KEY ("extended reality" OR "mixed reality" OR "virtual reality" OR "augmented reality" OR "immersive technolog*" OR "AR" OR "VR" OR "MR" OR "XR") AND TITLE-ABS-KEY ("Industry 4.0" OR "Industry 5.0" OR "industrial internet of things" OR "iiot" OR "smart manufacturing" OR "smart factory" OR "industrial internet" OR "industr*" OR "cps" OR "cyber physical system*" OR "ics" OR "industrial control system*")) AND (LIMIT-TO (LANGUAGE, "English")).

Papers containing such terms in their title, abstract and keywords, were searched (in April 2023) into Scopus (www.scopus.com), an important electronic scientific database, recommended as a robust source of data. The initial sample of 621 papers was refined up to 597, due to the language filter. The results have been exported in csv and txt files, storing all the information necessary to provide next analysis (e.g., title, authors, affiliation, abstract, keywords).

3.2 Preliminary Analysis of the Sample

The second step of the methodology focused on analyzing the statistical trends of the literature contributions, through the use of MS Excel and Scopus Analytics.

Figure 2 shows the trend in quantity of papers published over the years. It is possible to note that the consideration of DT and XR technologies in industry is relatively recent. Indeed, starting from 2016, some scientific studies start to appear. A positive growth of publication can be observed over the years, with exception of 2020, with an approximated tax of production grown of 183% from 2021 to 2022.

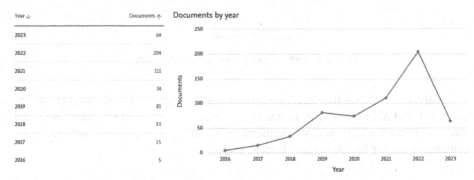

Fig. 2. Publishing trend of papers over the years

In addition, according to the Scopus classification, out of 597 documents, 52.5% represents conference papers, 35.6% are journal articles, 8.2% are review and 2.2% are book chapters (Fig. 3).

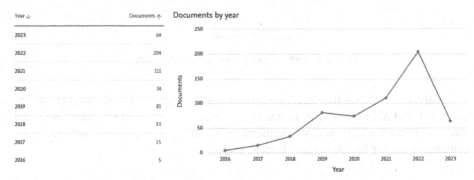

Fig. 3. Document types distribution

The interest towards these research fields and their relationships comes from all over the world (Fig. 4). In fact, the top five countries that provided such studies are:

Germany (77 papers), China (63), United States (57), Italy (35), United Kingdom (31). A predominant trend is observed in European countries.

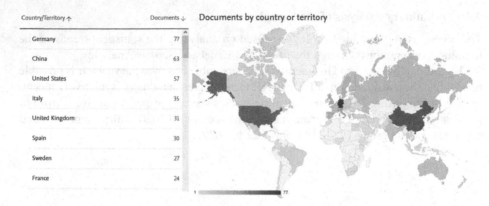

Fig. 4. Distribution of papers around the globe

Finally, Fig. 5 shows that there are several research areas that addressed the attention on DT and XR technologies in industry. Particularly, the most important areas are represented by technical sources: "engineering" (33.5%), "computer science" (27.9%), "mathematics" (7.9%), "decision sciences" (3.8%).

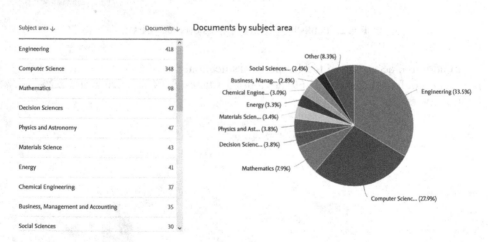

Fig. 5. Distribution of papers in subject areas

3.3 Data Analysis

Finally, the third phase of the methodology focused on analyzing the total amount of 597 documents by carrying out a bibliometric analysis. Such type of analysis was useful for a macro assessment of the most relevant topics coming out from the data sample.

Therefore, in this study, it helps to define implications and future research directions related to the use of DT and XR technologies in industry. The bibliometric analysis has been applied to: i) understand the most recurrent topics that surround the fields of analysis; ii) identify their relationships; iii) underline emerging topics and trends over the time. A network analysis and graphical investigation on text data have been carried out in order to create a co-occurrence map by using VOSviewer software. Such tool focuses on the graphical representation of bibliometric terms, functionally useful for displaying large maps in an easy-to-interpret way [40, 41]. As suggested by [37] and [42], the analysis has been based on counting the recurring terms in "title" and "abstract" with a minimal frequency of 10. Out of 4339 terms, 102 meet the threshold. The following section shows a qualitative analysis.

4 Digital Twin and Extended Reality in Industry: Implications as Future Research Directions

The bibliometric analysis revealed as a useful tool for a general understanding of the main topics related to the use of DT and XR technologies in industry. Particularly, the bibliometric analysis allowed for a network analysis based on term co-occurrence.

Figure 6 shows the co-occurrence map, which encompasses six main clusters. Each recurring term identifies a node of the network that can be in relationship not only with other nodes of the same cluster, but also with those of other clusters. The node size is the mirror of the occurrence of the term, so, the larger the nodes, the more frequent the terms in the pool of analysis. Moreover, the centrality of the nodes is representative of the relevance for the cluster and for the overall network as well. The link between two nodes means that those terms are included in the same paper, and the thickness is proportional to the number of times they are used.

The co-occurrence analysis highlighted six clusters, which are identified by different colors:

- Cluster 1 (red) is composed of 21 terms (e.g., big data, data analytics, digital storage, extended reality, real time systems, digital technologies, digital transformation, architectural design, accident prevention, maintenance) referred to the "advanced digital services" topic, in which digital twin and extended reality technologies are considered as key enablers for the creation of valuable digital services within industrial contexts.
- Cluster 2 (green) is composed of 18 terms (e.g., computer software, human robot interaction, human robot collaboration, industrial robots, intelligent robots, collaborative robot, robot programming, machine design, remote control, user interface) referred to the "extended robotized twin" topic, that emphasizes the use of robotics technology for building autonomous or semi-autonomous counterparts of systems.
- Cluster 3 (blue) is composed of 18 terms (e.g., virtual reality, virtual models, virtual representations, cyber physical system, embedded systems, flow control, optimization, real-time) referred to the "virtualization" topic, as the need to digitalize industrial systems in order to gain the benefits coming from the exploitation of available data flows.
- Cluster 4 (yellow) is composed of 17 terms (e.g., industry 4.0, digital twin, automation, machine tools, machinery, 3d printers, manufacturing process, process control,

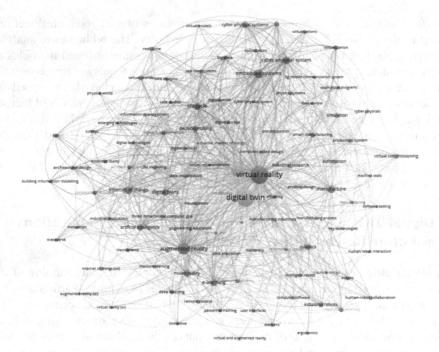

Fig. 6. Network visualization. (Color figure online)

product design, simulation, software testing, virtual and augmented reality, virtual commissioning) related to the "scalable analysis" topic, in which the use of both digital twin and extended reality technologies for analyzing hardware, as well as software components and processes is considered.

- Cluster 5 (purple) is composed of 17 terms (e.g., augmented reality, virtual reality, mixed reality, artificial intelligence, machine learning, deep learning, digital twins, internet of things, immersive, metaverse) referred to the "multi-layered digitalization" topic, as the possibility to use multiple digital technologies, at different levels, for the realization of an integrated digital working environment.
- Cluster 6 (light blue) is composed of 11 terms (e.g., data acquisition, data visualization, digital devices, cyber physicals, industrial internet of things, information management, production systems) referred to the "digital lymph" topic, in which data is considered the essence of digital industrial architectures, from its collection to its visualization, able to generate relevant business insights.

Furthermore, Fig. 7 shows the overlay visualization map. It is similar to the co-occurrence map, but it adds the temporal dimension. Through the use of different colors, it distinguishes recent and older terms. While older terms are in blue, recent terms are in yellow, and terms in the middle are in green. To observe a significant difference with colors, the temporal range of reference spans from 2020 to 2022. Indeed, before and after such years, no relevant differences could be observed. It is interesting to note that, most recently, the following main terms appear: virtualizations, real-time, architectural

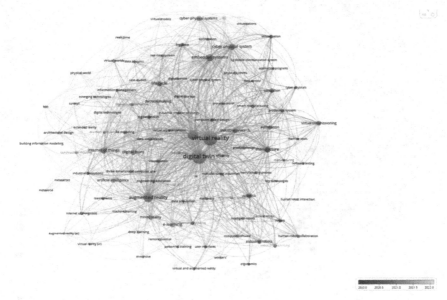

Fig. 7. Overlay visualization

design, building information modelling, deep learning, e-learning, remote control, artificial intelligence, metaverse, collaborative robots, human robot interaction. This suggests how the integrated use of DTs and XR technologies is promising in industries at different levels and purposes, such as from the analysis of business assets and remote control of operations to people training and engagement. On the contrary, older terms include: data acquisition, big data, information management, flow control, digital devices, virtual representations, industrial internet of things. These terms highlight common elements that are now well-metabolized in the digital culture of industry. Finally, in the middle, it is possible to find these terms: embedded systems, cyber physical system, life cycle, data visualization, automation, industrial robots, maintenance.

Figure 8 shows the item density visualization map. Items are represented by their label and the area around them has a color and intensity that indicate the density of items at that point. The larger the number of items in the neighborhood of a point and the higher the weights of the neighboring items, the closer the color of the point is to red. On the contrary, the smaller the number of items in the neighborhood of a point and the lower the weights of the neighboring items, the closer the color of the point is to yellow.

The most relevant terms that concentrate the most representative items density are: digital twin, virtual reality, augmented reality. It is as expected, since the research was set on DT and XR technologies as keywords of interest. However, other important terms are: internet of things, industrial robots, life cycle, cyber physical systems.

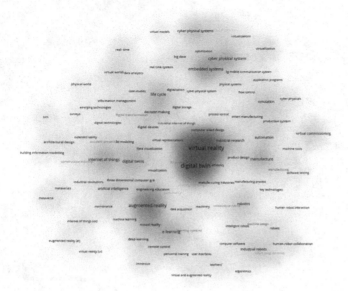

Fig. 8. Item density visualization

5 Conclusions

The bibliometric analysis made it possible to identify, through the application of a transparent and objective procedure, the distributional structure of the literature on the combined use of digital twin and extended reality technologies in modern industrial contexts. In particular, six key topics (i.e., advanced digital services, extended robotized twin, virtualization, scalable analysis, multi-layered digitalization and digital lymph) were identified, as potential research directions useful for understanding the implications of the use of such technologies. These topics demonstrate a positive relationship between the application of DT and XR technologies and machine, system and process performance within the industrial 4.0 scenario. In addition, in contrast of common concepts related to their use (e.g., information management, flows control), emerging concepts appear such as metaverse and collaborative human-robot interaction, as a signal of a potential yet to be exploited.

Therefore, the study, which aims to guide studies in the literature in the integrated application of DT and XR technologies in industry, provides promising indications for future research. However, it has some limitations that allow it to point academics to new insights for future investigations. In particular, the bibliometric analysis, relying only on the Scopus database, allows for a preliminary investigation; in the future, further studies could consider scientific articles from other sources (such as Web of Science and PubMed). In addition, considering the nature of the bibliometric analysis, the paper just limits to provide a set of directions for addressing future investigations on DT and XR; deeper content analysis should be focused on their potential combined applications, benefits and limitations. Furthermore, as the interpretation of the resulting clusters could be distorted by the subjectivity and background of the researchers, in the future, content analysis could be implemented with the aim of improving the quality of the research and highlighting further insights.

References

1. Slavkovic, N., Zivanovic, S., Milutinovic, D.: An indirect method of industrial robot programming for machining tasks based on STEP-NC. Int. J. Comput. Integrat. Manufact. **32**(1), 43–57 (2019). https://doi.org/10.1080/0951192X.2018.1543952
2. Frank, A.G., Dalenogare, L.S., Ayala, N.F.: Industry 4.0 technologies: implementation patterns in manufacturing companies. Int. J. Product. Econ. **210**, 15–26 (2019). https://doi.org/10.1016/j.ijpe.2019.01.004
3. Adriana Cárdenas-Robledo, L., Hernández-Uribe, O., Reta, C., Antonio Cantoral-Ceballos, J.: Extended reality applications in industry 4.0. – a systematic literature review. Telematics Inform. **73**, 101863 (2022). https://doi.org/10.1016/j.tele.2022.101863
4. Yang, C., et al.: Extended reality application framework for a digital-twin-based smart crane. Appl. Sci. **12**(12), 6030 (2022). https://doi.org/10.3390/app12126030
5. Attaran, M., Celik, B.G.: Digital twin: benefits, use cases, challenges, and opportunities. Decision Analy. J. **6**, 100165 (2023). https://doi.org/10.1016/j.da-jour.2023.100165
6. Maddikunta, P.K.R., et al.: Industry 5.0: a survey on enabling technologies and potential applications. J. Ind. Inf. Integr. **26**, 100257 (2022). https://doi.org/10.1016/j.jii.2021.100257
7. Stacchio, L., Angeli, A., Marfia, G.: Empowering digital twins with extended reality collaborations. Virtual Real. Intell. Hardware **4**(6), 487–505 (2022). https://doi.org/10.1016/j.vrih.2022.06.004
8. Singh, M., Fuenmayor, E., Hinchy, E., Qiao, Y., Murray, N., Devine, D.: Digital twin: origin to future. ASI **4**(2), 36 (2021). https://doi.org/10.3390/asi4020036
9. Pires, F., Cachada, A., Barbosa, J., Moreira, A.P., Leitao, P.: Digital twin in industry 4.0: technologies, applications and challenges. In: 2019 IEEE 17th International Conference on Industrial Informatics (INDIN), Helsinki, Finland, pp. 721–726. IEEE (2019). https://doi.org/10.1109/INDIN41052.2019.8972134
10. Gartner, Digital Twin. Gartner Inc (2023). https://www.gart-ner.com/en/information-technology/glossary/digital-twin
11. Shao, G., Helu, M.: Framework for a digital twin in manufacturing: scope and requirements. Manufact. Lett. **24**, 105–107 (2020). https://doi.org/10.1016/j.mfglet.2020.04.004
12. Shafto, M., et al.: DRAFT Modeling, Simulation, Information Technology & Processing Roadmap (2010). https://www.nasa.gov/pdf/501321main_TA11-MSITP-DRAFT-Nov2010-A1.pdf
13. Schroeder, G., et al.: Visualising the digital twin using web services and augmented reality. In: 2016 IEEE 14th International Conference on Industrial Informatics (INDIN), Poitiers, France, pp. 522–527. IEEE (2016). https://doi.org/10.1109/INDIN.2016.7819217
14. Corallo, A., Del Vecchio, V.D., Lezzi, M., Morciano, P.: Shop floor digital twin in smart manufacturing: a systematic literature review. Sustainability **13**(23), 12987 (2021). https://doi.org/10.3390/su132312987
15. Corallo, A., et al.: Internet of things and shop-floor digital twin: an aerospace case study. In: 2022 7th International Conference on Smart and Sustainable Technologies (SpliTech), Split/Bol, Croatia: IEEE, pp. 1–6 (2022). https://doi.org/10.23919/SpliTech55088.2022.9854314
16. Tao, F., et al.: Digital twin and its potential application exploration. Comput. Integrat. Manufact. Syst. **24**(1) (2018)

17. Canedo, A.: Industrial IoT lifecycle via digital twins. In: Presented at the International Conference on Hardware/Software Codesign and System Synthesis, Pittsburgh, PA, USA (2016)
18. Liu, M., Fang, S., Dong, H., Xu, C.: Review of digital twin about concepts, technologies, and industrial applications. J. Manuf. Syst. **58**, 346–361 (2021). https://doi.org/10.1016/j.jmsy.2020.06.017
19. Yu, Y., Fan, S., Peng, G., Dai, S., Zhao, G.: Study on application of digital twin model in product configuration#br# management. Aeronaut. Manufact. Technol. **60**(7), 41–45 (2017)
20. Weyer, S., Meyer, T., Ohmer, M., Gorecky, D., Zühlke, D.: Future modeling and simulation of CPS-based factories: an example from the automotive industry. IFAC-PapersOnLine **49**(31), 97–102 (2016). https://doi.org/10.1016/j.ifacol.2016.12.168
21. Tao, F., Zhang, M.: Digital twin shop-floor: a new shop-floor paradigm towards smart manufacturing. IEEE Access **5**, 20418–20427 (2017). https://doi.org/10.1109/ACCESS.2017.2756069
22. Li, L., Li, H., Gu, F., Ding, N., Gu, X., Luo, G.: Multidisciplinary collaborative design modeling technologies for complex mechnical products based on digital twin. Comput. Integr. Manuf. Syst. **25**(6), 1307–1319 (2019)
23. Anderl, R., Haag, S., Schützer, K., Zancul, E.: Digital twin technology – an approach for Industrie 4.0 vertical and horizontal lifecycle integration. it – Inf. Technol. **60**(3), 125–132 (2018). https://doi.org/10.1515/itit-2017-0038
24. Fast-Berglund, Å., Gong, L., Li, D.: Testing and validating extended reality (xr) technologies in manufacturing. Procedia Manuf. **25**, 31–38 (2018). https://doi.org/10.1016/j.promfg.2018.06.054
25. Lawson, G., Salanitri, D., Waterfield, B.: Future directions for the development of virtual reality within an automotive manufacturer. Appl. Ergon. **53**, 323–330 (2016). https://doi.org/10.1016/j.apergo.2015.06.024
26. Regenbrecht, H., Baratoff, G., Wilke, W.: Augmented reality projects in the automotive and aerospace industries. IEEE Comput. Grap. Appl. **25**(6), 48–56 (2005). https://doi.org/10.1109/MCG.2005.124
27. Krodel, T., Schott, V., Ovtcharova, J.: XR technology deployment in value creation. Appl. Sci. **13**(8), 5048 (2023). https://doi.org/10.3390/app13085048
28. Seth, A., Vance, J.M., Oliver, J.H.: Virtual reality for assembly methods prototyping: a review. Virtual Reality **15**(1), 5–20 (2011). https://doi.org/10.1007/s10055-009-0153-y
29. Pirker, J., Loria, E., Safikhani, S., Kunz, A., Rosmann, S.: Immersive virtual reality for virtual and digital twins: a literature review to identify state of the art and perspectives. In: 2022 IEEE Conference on Virtual Reality and 3D User Interfaces Abstracts and Workshops (VRW), Christchurch, New Zealand, pp. 114–115. IEEE (2022). https://doi.org/10.1109/VRW55335.2022.00035
30. Oyekan, J.O., et al.: The effectiveness of virtual environments in developing collaborative strategies between industrial robots and humans. Robot. Comput.-Integrat. Manufact. **55**, 41–54 (2019). https://doi.org/10.1016/j.rcim.2018.07.006
31. Kaarlela, T., Pieska, S., Pitkaaho, T.: Digital twin and virtual reality for safety training. In: 2020 11th IEEE International Conference on Cognitive Infocommunications (CogInfoCom), Mariehamn, Finland, pp. 000115–000120. IEEE (2020). https://doi.org/10.1109/CogInfoCom50765.2020.9237812
32. Wang, X., Liang, C.J., Menassa, C., Kamat, V.: Real-time process-level digital twin for collaborative human-robot construction work. In: Presented at the 37th International Symposium on Automation and Robotics in Construction, Kitakyushu, Japan (2020). https://doi.org/10.22260/ISARC2020/0212

33. Eyre, J.M., Dodd, T.J., Freeman, C., Lanyon-Hogg, R., Lockwood, A.J., Scott, R.W.: Demonstration of an industrial framework for an implementation of a process digital twin. In: Volume 2: Advanced Manufacturing, Pittsburgh, Pennsylvania, USA: American Society of Mechanical Engineers, p. V002T02A070 (2018). https://doi.org/10.1115/IMECE2018-87361

34. Coupry, C., Noblecourt, S., Richard, P., Baudry, D., Bigaud, D.: BIM-based digital twin and XR devices to improve maintenance procedures in smart buildings: a literature review. Appl. Sci. **11**(15), 6810 (2021). https://doi.org/10.3390/app11156810

35. Tranfield, D., Denyer, D., Smart, P.: Towards a methodology for developing evidence-informed management knowledge by means of systematic review. Br. J. Manag. **14**(3), 207–222 (2003). https://doi.org/10.1111/1467-8551.00375

36. Corallo, A., Crespino, A.M., Vecchio, V.D., Lazoi, M., Marra, M.: Understanding and defining dark data for the manufacturing industry. IEEE Trans. Eng. Manage. **70**(2), 700–712 (2023). https://doi.org/10.1109/TEM.2021.3051981

37. Donthu, N., Kumar, S., Pattnaik, D., Lim, W.M.: A bibliometric retrospection of marketing from the lens of psychology: insights from psychology & marketing. Psychol. Mark. **38**(5), 834–865 (2021). https://doi.org/10.1002/mar.21472

38. Shao, Y., Shi, X.: Bibliometric analysis and visualization of research progress in the diabetic nephropathy field from 2001 to 2021. Oxidative Med. Cell. Longevity **2023**, 1–16 (2023). https://doi.org/10.1155/2023/4555609

39. Corallo, A., Latino, M.E., Menegoli, M., De Devitiis, B., Viscecchia, R.: Human factor in food label design to support consumer healthcare and safety: a systematic literature review. Sustainability **11**(15), 4019 (2019). https://doi.org/10.3390/su11154019

40. Hu, K., et al.: Global research trends in food safety in agriculture and industry from 1991 to 2018: a data-driven analysis. Trends Food Sci. Technol. **85**, 262–276 (2019). https://doi.org/10.1016/j.tifs.2019.01.011

41. Van Oorschot, J.A.W.H., Hofman, E., Halman, J.I.M.: A bibliometric review of the innovation adoption literature. Technol. Forecast. Soc. Chang. **134**, 1–21 (2018). https://doi.org/10.1016/j.techfore.2018.04.032

42. Fahimnia, B., Sarkis, J., Davarzani, H.: Green supply chain management: a review and bibliometric analysis. Int. J. Prod. Econ. **162**, 101–114 (2015). https://doi.org/10.1016/j.ijpe.2015.01.003

Towards the Development of a Digital Twin for Micro Learning Factory: A Proof of Concept

Mame Cheikh Sow[1]([✉]) [ID], Ahlem Assila[2] [ID], David Garcia[3] [ID], Sinuhé Martinez[2] [ID], Mourad Zghal[1] [ID], and David Baudry[4] [ID]

[1] CESI LINEACT Laboratory UR 7527, Strasbourg, France
{mcsow,mzghal}@cesi.fr
[2] CESI LINEACT Laboratory UR 7527, Reims, France
{aassila,smartinez}@cesi.fr
[3] CESI LINEACT Laboratory UR 7527, Lyon, France
dgarcia@cesi.fr
[4] CESI LINEACT Laboratory UR 7527, Rouen, France
dbaudry@cesi.fr

Abstract. The Learning Factory concept has gained importance in recent years to improve manufacturing education and prepare students for the workforce. Digital Twin (DT) technology is considered as a crucial tool to enhance the Learning Factory experience. Due to the novelty of this topic, there is limited research on developing DTs specifically for this purpose. Currently, a Micro Learning Factory (MLF), described as a smaller-scale version of the Learning Factory, has been developed mainly for educational purposes to offer a flexible, personalized, and effective learning solution. This platform incorporates a large number of equipment to reproduce industrial production lines with a good level of representativeness, including a 6-axis robotic arm, conveyor belts, grippers, cameras and computer vision tools. However, to fully realize its potential, the development of a DT for the MLF is crucial. This technology can simulate the learning environment, provide data analytics, and offer real-time feedback to students. Despite its potential, a digital twin for the MLF has not yet been developed. In this article, we propose a proof of concept for the development of a digital twin of one of the main components of the MLF, which is the 6-axis robotic arm. Firstly, we present the proposed architecture for the DT of the 6-axis robotic arm that we designed. Then, we present in detail two scenarios for its manipulation, one focused on the pick and place operations, and the other on conformity control. Finally, we discuss future perspectives, with a focus on the development of a MLF DT interfaced in Extended Reality.

Keywords: Digital Twin · Micro Learning Factory · Robotic · Automation · Learning tool

1 Introduction

The most widely discussed topic in the world of production in recent years is the factory of the future, also known as Industry 4.0. The Learning Factory is a broader concept that is particularly relevant in this context which is characterized by the use of advanced

L. T. De Paolis et al. (Eds.): XR Salento 2023, LNCS 14218, pp. 284–298, 2023.
https://doi.org/10.1007/978-3-031-43401-3_19

technologies such as artificial intelligence (AI), Digital Twin (DT), and robotics [1]. The Learning Factory is a collaborative learning environment that can be applied to various fields, such as engineering education [2], economics education [3], construction [4], and logistics [5]. It is known as a corporate training concept that aims to provide hands-on training and practical experience to students or employees [6]. Consequently, it helps them to develop their problem-solving abilities, teamwork skills, and practical skills that are relevant to the industry [7, 8]. By allowing experimentation with various manufacturing processes, technologies, and strategies, the Learning Factory provides a safe and controlled environment for learning without disrupting production in a real-world factory [8].

In recent years, the development of digital twin technology in learning factories has the potential to revolutionize manufacturing education and training. Digital twin is defined as the virtual replica of a physical object [9]. The digital twin is much more than a simple 3D representation used to run simulations. It can communicate with its real-life replica as it is fed with data sent by the latter. It also allows for a global representation of an entire system or process to test its feasibility and reliability. This can help avoid time and economic losses [10].

In a learning factory, digital twins can be used to create virtual models of manufacturing processes and production systems, allowing students and trainees to practice and experiment with different scenarios without the risk of damaging equipment or causing accidents [11]. One of the key benefits of digital twin technology in learning factories is that it allows for more personalized and adaptive learning experiences. By analyzing data from the virtual models, instructors can identify areas where students may need additional support or feedback, and adjust the learning experience accordingly. The digital twin concept for learning factory is a recently developed concept. Upon reviewing the literature, only a modest number of researchers have been published on this topic. One of the main obstacles for developing DT is the related cost. In general, the digital twin for learning factories are proprietary based solutions, which are often black boxes with limited possibilities to modify the architecture. This implies limited software possibilities and more or less expensive solutions. A method to develop open source solutions for DT is proposed in [12]. In addition to the open source solution, a changeable architecture is possible for exploring different configurations. The learning factory has proved its interest in education and it is an important learning material for the introduction of 4.0 ideas of the future industry [13]. Yasushi et al. [14] are emphasizing the importance of developing a digital twin for the learning factory to fully demonstrate the effectiveness of their 'Digital Triplet' concept. The developed DT offers enhanced effectiveness of engineering activities in the manufacturing industry and provides support to manufacturing system engineers. In fact, the digital twin functionality of the factory includes an operational log database and a 3D simulation system in the cyber world, and an Engineering Process Description subsystem in the intelligent activity world. Moreover, the authors discuss three critical points for constructing the digital twin of the learning factory, which are mapping the physical and cyber worlds, limitations in the modeling ability of the digital twin, and problems in supporting the execution of engineering cycles. As future work of this study, the authors envision developing the intelligent activity world further, expanding functions that support the execution of engineering cycles, and ultimately verifying the effectiveness of Digital Triplet in solving manufacturing system engineering problems. In another work, Park et al. [15] propose a production control method based on a digital twin (DT) and reinforcement learning (RL). To achieve efficient personalized production at an affordable cost, the authors developed a Micro Smart Factory (MSF), which uses cyber-physical production systems (CPPS) to enhance the system's resilience. The developed DT provides virtual event logs including states, actions, and rewards to support learning, and in coordination with the RL policy network, it helps decide what-next/where-next in the production cycle. The development of a digital twin for MSFs is also discussed, as it enables effective control of engineering activities in the manufacturing industry and provides support for manufacturing system engineers. This method can be applied in various manufacturing domains due to the frequent application of the priority rule concept.

More recently, Rasovska et al. [16] developed a digital twin of a learning factory called FleXtory, designed to provide opportunities for industrial projects and processes to acquire the necessary skills in the context of Industry 4.0. In their study, the authors proposed an architecture model for FleXtory that emphasizes the return on experience/information loop within the digital transformation of the learning factory. The paper focuses on the pedagogical specifications of the proposed learning models and their future perspectives. Furthermore, they suggested that the transformation to Industry 4.0 requires the development of professionals' abilities to work within a digital environment, and the pedagogical modules developed within FleXtory address the evolution of professional competencies and skills.

Despite the limited number of research studies in this subject, there is a diversification of proposed approaches. As we have noted, several perspectives have been proposed. We can observe that this subject is still evolving. In this context and as part of a project led by CESI LINEACT research laboratory, a Micro Learning Factory (MLF) has been developed. As its name suggests, it is a scaled-down version of the traditional learning factory, mainly dedicated to education and research. This platform is composed of 6-axis robotic arms, conveyors, and a wide range of grippers to adapt to the shapes of the parts. One of the main objectives of this project is to develop a digital twin for the MLF, which will allow learners to simulate the learning environment by manipulating different scenarios without the risk of damaging the physical equipment.

As the first step of this project, we began by developing a digital twin of the 6-axis robotic arm, which can interact with the other components of the platform. Therefore, in this article, we present a proof of concept for the designed digital twin. This includes creating a virtual model of the 6–axis robotic arm and simulating various scenarios to test its effectiveness in providing learners with a safe and immersive learning environment that closely replicates real-world scenarios.

The remainder of this article is structured as follows: Sect. 2 outlines the proposed proof of concept, presenting the Micro Learning Factory components and the architecture of the developed digital twin for the 6–axis robotic arm. Section 3 presents a use case study with two study scenarios for DT manipulation, followed by a discussion of the main findings and future project perspectives. Lastly, Sect. 4 concludes the paper.

2 The Development of a Digital Twin for the Micro Learning Factory 6-Axis Robotic Arm Equipment

2.1 The Micro Learning Factory (MLF): Goals and Components

In this study, we used the MLF platform, one of the tools available at CESI LINEACT research laboratory, as shown in Fig. 1, to develop or improve applications for the industry of the future. It is mainly used for education and research purposes in order to reproduce operations of an industrial production assembly line with a good level of representativeness: pick-and-place operations, product conveying, product conformity control, and so on.

Fig. 1. The Micro Learning Factory platform designed by CESI LINEACT research Laboratory

As depicted in Fig. 1, the MLF is based on two main pieces of equipment: 6-axis robotic arms and conveyor belts. These are capable of replicating manufacturing scenarios that align with the Industry 4.0 paradigm. As shown in Fig. 2, 6-axis robotic arms and conveyor belts are respectively complemented by a set of equipment (sensors, cameras, vacuum grabber systems…) to perform advanced automation functions such as pick and place assembling operations based on computer vision.

The main equipment used in MLF are developed by the NIRYO company (www. niryo.com): NED1 version of 6-axis robotic arm and conveyor equipment have been integrated today to MLF. Several programming tools based on ROS (Robotic Operating System) are provided to configure, control and program the 6-axis Robotic Arm.

MLF is an ambitious CESI Enegineering School project dedicated to teaching and research activities in the fields of robotics and automation of manufacturing processes. Today 6 of the 25 CESI campuses are in the process of integrating MLF. Undoubtedly, not all campuses will be able to physically host an MLF, the project roadmap has integrated from its beginning the need to develop a digital twin to operate this facility remotely and synchronously by several CESI campuses.

Fig. 2. Illustration of components dedicated to advanced automation functions. (Photo on the left) 6-axis robotic arm with integrated camera, (Photo on the right) Conveyor belts with integrated infrared sensors for product detection.

In the following, we present the architecture of the developed digital twin for the MLF, with an emphasis on all the design steps.

2.2 Digital Twin Architecture for MLF 6-Axis Robotic Arm

As shown in Fig. 2, we have proposed an architecture for developing the digital twin of our 6-axis robotic arm. The architecture consists of three main parts with specific tools used for each part. On the left side, we have the physical model of our robot, where we used Niryo Studio for simple task programming and Python in the VS Code development environment for more complex programming. Python allowed us to create OPC UA[1] servers and clients to facilitate data exchange. On the right side, we have the virtual model of our robot developed using Webots software, which serves as the digital twin of our physical model. We programmed the virtual model using Python to ensure communication between the client and server. In the middle, we have the communication layer dedicated to facilitating communication between the physical robot and its digital twin. This communication is enabled by the OPC UA protocol, which allows us to retrieve targeted data and send them to the other system in real-time. At the bottom, we added UAExpert, which is an OPC UA client used to easily identify the identifiers of each variable for reuse when programming the digital twin on Webots or another development environment.

---

[1] OPC UA (Open Platform Communications Unified Architecture) is a machine-to-machine communication protocol for industrial automation [17].

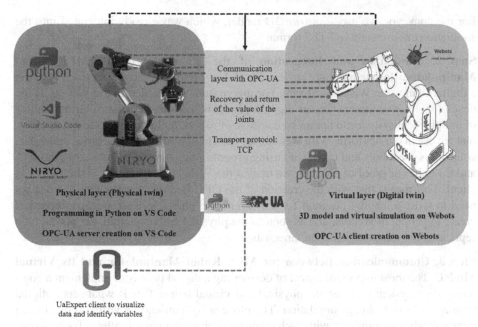

UaExpert client to visualize
data and identify variables

Fig. 3. The Proposed Digital Twin Architecture for MLF 6–axis robotic arm

In the following, we will detail the different steps to follow to develop a digital twin. These main steps are the 3D modeling of our physical system, the integration and simulation of this 3D model in a simulator and the communication between the physical system and its virtual replica.

Step 1. 3D Modeling of the MLF Robot Manipulator. Based on our review of the literature, we have identified several 3D modeling software packages that are commonly used for creating digital twins, including SolidWorks[2], Blender[3], Fusion 360[4] or NX[5] from Siemens. However, since our laboratory already possessed 3D models of the platform, we focused on using software to open and possibly convert those models for import into other software as needed. The robotic arm (Ned from Niryo) was already integrated into the simulation software we used, so we did not need to use our own 3D model of the robot. Instead, we focused on developing controllers for the robot and the conveyor.

---

[2] SolidWorks is a 3D computer-aided design (CAD) software used to create and design mechanical parts, assemblies, and drawings [18].

[3] Blender is a free and open-source 3D computer graphics software used for creating animated films, visual effects, video games, and 3D printed models [19].

[4] Fusion 360 is a cloud-based 3D CAD/CAM (computer-aided design/computer-aided manufacturing) software developed by Autodesk [20].

[5] NX is a computer-aided design (CAD), manufacturing (CAM), and engineering (CAE) software developed by Siemens Digital Industries Software [21].

For the conveyor, we used our own 3D model, which was already integrated into the simulation environment in STL[6] format.

Step 2. Simulation and Integration of the 3D model of the MLF Robot Manipulator. In our literature review, we did not find any references to developing a digital twin using Webots software. For this reason, we decided to use Webots as the development environment for our digital twin. This software provides a virtual replica of our physical system and has a vast database of robots, including the Ned manipulator that we use in our platform. With Webots, we can simulate different scenarios and create controllers for robots and conveyors using programming languages such as Python, C, and C++. In our proof of concept, we treated the Webots environment as the OPC UA client. This means that with the creation of the OPC UA server and client, we did not need to write a lengthy program for the simulation phase. Instead, we just needed to create the client in Webots, and as soon as the physical system started, the digital twin replicated the same actions simultaneously.

Step 3. Communication Between the MLF Robot Manipulator and its Virtual Model. The most important aspect of developing a digital twin is to implement a communication system between the physical and virtual twins. This is what sets a digital twin apart from a simple simulation. The physical system and its virtual replica must continuously communicate with each other by exchanging data. It allows for real-time monitoring of the physical system from its virtual replica, predictive maintenance operations, and remote control of the system. Updates can also be launched and new equipment can be tested in the virtual environment to assess their performance, adaptability, and feasibility of integration into the system.

In our study, we built the communication system using the OPC UA protocol, which is standardized and open source for cross-platform data transmission. The predecessor to OPC UA was OPC, which had the weakness of not being an independent protocol and only allowed data exchange through COM/DCOM, limiting compatibility to Windows operating systems. The OPC Foundation addressed this issue by developing OPC UA, a unified architecture that is independent and can communicate with a wider range of devices.

The old protocol, OPC, had several problems that the new OPC UA protocol overcame, such as configuration issues, poor security, and limited control over DCOM. OPC UA is now considered one of the most important industry standards for the future, as it plays a critical role in exchanging data between machines and other connected devices. Its independence, since the introduction of its unified architecture (UA), has made it widely used in developing applications for the industry of the future and for machine-to-machine communication.

The communication approach proposed in our study is based on the OPC UA communication protocol. As shown in Fig. 2, data is retrieved through the OPC UA server/client created to feed the other system. In the figure, only the robot is considered since our goal is to develop a PoC of our digital twin. Therefore, we developed the digital twin of the robot using Webots, an open-source software for robotic simulation. On Webots, we

---

[6] STL (STereoLithography) is a file format commonly used in 3D printing and computer-aided manufacturing (CAM) [22].

can develop controllers for robots, conveyors, and create OPC UA servers or clients. In our PoC, the OPC UA client was developed on Webots and the server on VS Code, both programmed in Python. UA Expert was used as another OPC UA client, which helped in finding the identifiers of the variables for retrieving their data in real-time. The data that is exchanged in our digital twin are the joint variables of our robot. Once the robot is launched, the values of each joint of the arm are retrieved and sent to the virtual system, which creates synchronization of the arm movements with its digital twin.

In order to demonstrate the feasibility of our proof of concept of the digital twin for the MLF Robot manipulator, we present in the next section the manipulation scenarios and use cases developed.

3   Case Study and Findings Discussion

This section aims to demonstrate the feasibility of the designed Digital Twin (DT) for the MLF 6-axis robotic arm. Figure 3 shows the digital twin of the Niryo Ned arm, which reacts immediately after the physical arm is activated. Both the physical arm and the DT react to the actions of the other.

Fig. 4. Communication between the physical robot and its digital twin

In Fig. 4, the variables exchanged by the physical robot and its digital twin are shown. Since the arm is a 6-axis robotic arm, we exchange the joint positions of each axis, which correspond to the variables motor1, motor2, motor3, motor4, motor5, and motor6. This data visualization during communication was done using UAExpert software. It should be noted that the synchronization between the DT and the robot is functioning properly.

In the following, we detailed two proposed scenarios for manipulating the designed DT, followed by a discussion on the main findings, limitations, and future perspectives of this project.

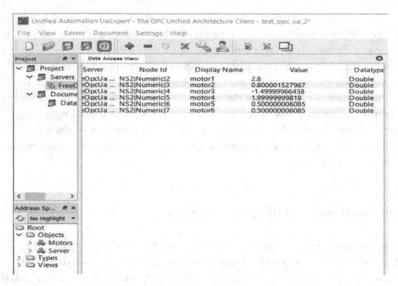

Fig. 5. Visualization of the exchanged data between the robot and its digital twin through UAExpert

3.1 Proposed Scenarios

The idea is to develop several types of learning applications using the MLF platform, aiming to provide learners with a wide variety of tasks to perform from the digital twin. As a first step, two scenarios have been developed. The first focused on the pick and place operations, and the second on conformity control.

Scenario 1: Pick-and-Place Operations. This first scenario involves two Ned robots sharing a conveyor, as depicted in Fig. 5, which shows a graphical representation of this scenario. As depicted in Fig. 5, the first robot picks up the part located next to it and places it on the conveyor. Once the part is deposited, the conveyor starts to move it. When the arrival of the part is detected, the conveyor stops and the second robot picks up the part to place it on the tray next to it. Then, the second robot picks up the part that is on its tray and places it on the conveyor. The same operation is repeated, but this time the sign of the velocity vector is changed so that the part can be moved in the opposite direction.

The simulation of this scenario was developed using Webots, as shown in Fig. 6.

Studying this scenario enabled us to validate the feasibility of developing its digital twin, taking into account all the machines involved, such as the two 6-axis robotic arms and the conveyor, as well as the data to be exchanged, such as positions detected by sensors, arm articulations, conveyor states, etc.

Scenario 2: Conformity Control. The second scenario is more complex than the first. In this scenario, we have developed a program that sorts parts based on their color and shape. As shown in Fig. 7, the robot picks up a part from the ramp where the parts are stored.

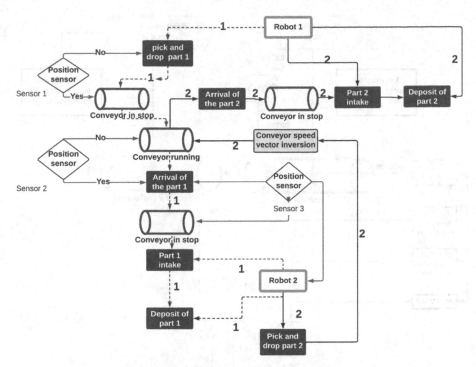

Fig. 6. Scenario 1: Pick and Place Operations using two robots and a conveyor

Fig. 7. Developing Scenario 1 using Webots

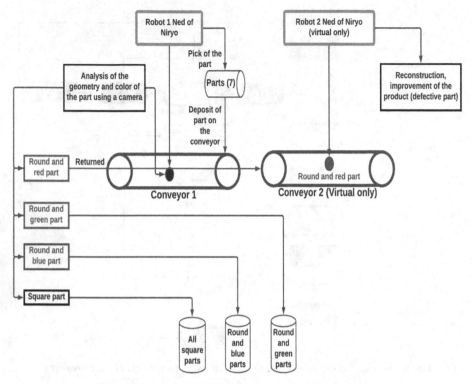

Fig. 8. Scenario 2: Conformity control by robotic vision

As illustrated in Fig. 7, it always picks up the first part at the bottom and places it on the conveyor. It then positions itself above the processing area and waits for the part to arrive. The processing area is defined by the four black and white rings. Once the part arrives in this area, the robot analyzes its color with its camera and retrieves the part to place it in the corresponding location based on its color and/or shape. In this scenario, we programmed the robot to reject any red and round part by controlling the conveyor and moving it to the other end, in the small box. The purpose here is to allow learners to understand that cameras are increasingly being used by robots for conformity control in the industry. They should also understand that defective parts are often present in real production lines and need to be sent back for rework. This is why the red and round parts are rejected as being defective.

The validation of this scenario has been tested and confirmed after developing it with the physical equipment of our platform, as shown in Fig. 8.

After implementing this scenario, we noticed that developing this digital twin will be much more complex compared to our first scenario. The complexity arises from the need to integrate visual recognition data from the camera. However, developing this digital twin is well feasible.

In the next section, we will discuss the handling of these scenarios, as well as the various findings and potential limitations and future perspectives.

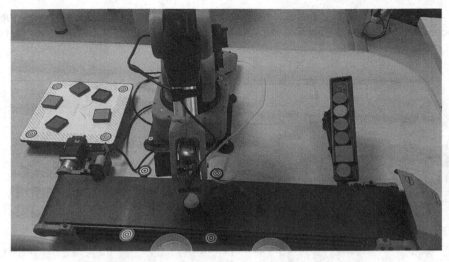

Fig. 9. Developing Scenario 2 using the physical equipment

3.2 Scenarios Validation, Findings and Discussion

By simulating and conducting real tests on the two proposed scenarios, we were able to explore the feasibility of developing a digital twin for each scenario. This allowed us to conduct a feasibility study and identify the most relevant variables to exchange during the digital twin's development. To assist in creating variables and retrieving data, we proposed using position sensors that detect the arrival of an object for the other robot to pick up. This will improve the synchronization and coherence between the movements of the two systems by sending position data from the virtual system to the physical system.

Moreover, this study enabled us to offer students various purely industrial tasks that can be practiced in both real and virtual settings through the digital twin. For example, the conformity control of parts scenario was significant, as robots are increasingly involved in this task in modern industries using robotic vision recognition tools on production lines.

However, while carrying out these scenarios, we discovered an issue regarding our robot's camera performance under varying lighting conditions. In fact, we noticed that when the light is strong enough, there are noises that prevent our camera from clearly identifying the object's color and shape. This discovery urges us to be cautious when setting up the digital twin of this scenario to avoid issues during exchanges between the physical system and its digital twin. To address this issue, we could either adjust the environment by reducing the brightness, enhance the camera's performance, or use objects that absorb light instead of diffusing it.

The next steps will be devoted to developing the digital twin of our platform by integrating other variables, such as the speed and direction of movement of the conveyor, as well as the variables related to visual recognition and the grippers.

In addition, we will be implementing a more advanced architecture to showcase the upcoming steps. Figure 9 presents this architecture, which consists of two main parts (Fig. 10).

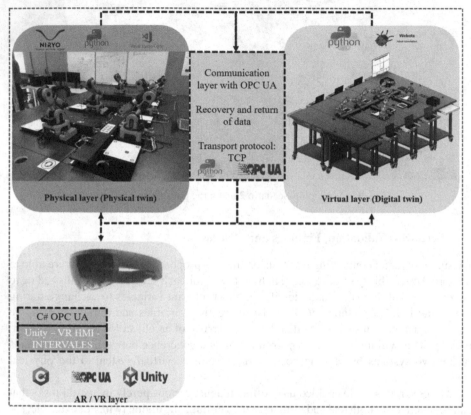

Fig. 10. Proposed architecture for the development of the MLF's digital twin and its interaction in AR/VR environment

The first task involves developing the digital twin of the entire platform, while the second task focuses on creating an interactive interface for our digital twin using augmented reality or virtual reality, as indicated in the proposed architecture (see Fig. 9).

The complete development of our digital twin will encompass all the physical and software tools utilized in our proof of concept, along with additional physical components such as additional robots to complete the platform, the integration of conveyors, the utilization of various grippers, sensors, and so on. Due to the growing volume of data to be collected, this stage of digital twin development becomes increasingly complex.

The second part of our project will focus on creating an interactive visualization interface using extended reality (XR). We plan to establish communication with OPC UA and develop our XR environment using Unity, as proposed by Havard et al. [23]. The integration between the digital twin and XR environments will be based on INTERVALES, a framework for XR industrial environments and scenarios introduced by Richard et al.

[24, 25]. By developing an interactive interface using HoloLens headsets, students will benefit from a fully immersive experience with the digital twin, facilitating their understanding. Furthermore, with XR technology, they will have the opportunity to interact with the platform and access key information necessary for comprehending the various equipment and developing scenarios.

4 Conclusion

In this paper, we propose a proof of concept for the development of the digital twin of our MLF platform. The digital-twin-proposed architecture is based on the Webots simulation software and the OPC UA protocol for communication between the physical system and its digital twin. Results were based on the development of the digital twin of one robot, and show excellent communication between the physical and virtual twins. This allows us to validate the first successful step towards the development of the entire MLF platform digital twin. Our communication approach enables us to control the digital twin by exchanging the 6 joint values of the physical robot. The movement synchronization was perfect, and we can now develop the digital twin of the two proposed scenarios for students. The design of an interactive visualization interface using extended reality (XR) is actually under development. This work will provide an interesting tool for the academic environment to remotely manipulate physical robotic systems.

References

1. Borangiu, T., Răileanu, S., Anton, F., Iacob, I., Anton, S.: A systems engineering-oriented learning factory for industry 4.0. In: Service Oriented, Holonic and Multi-Agent Manufacturing Systems for Industry of the Future. Proceedings of SOHOMA 2022, pp. 233–253. Cham, Springer International Publishing (2023). https://doi.org/10.1007/978-3-031-24291-5_19
2. Putnik, G.D., Alves, C., Varela, L., Pinheiro, P.: A contribution to the learning factory architecture implementations for engineering education. In: Managing and Implementing the Digital Transformation: Proceedings of the 1st International Symposium on Industrial Engineering and Automation ISIEA 2022, pp. 350–361. Cham: Springer International Publishing (2022). https://doi.org/10.1007/978-3-031-14317-5_30
3. Savchenko, I., Novotny, P., Fleck, H., Ropin, H.: Learning Factory Concept for Technical and Economic Education: An I4. 0 Solution with the Micro Factory. Festo Mps404. Available at SSRN 4073910 (2022)
4. Teizer, J., Chronopoulos, C.: Learning factory for construction to provide future engineering skills beyond technical education and training. In: Construction Research Congress 2022, pp. 224–233 (2022)
5. Behrendt, F., Lehner, O., Rettmann, A., Schmidtke, N., Wollert, T.: Process analysis of a teaching and learning factory environment to demonstrate Industry 4.0 solutions by using the smart logistics zone approach. In: 2022 IEEE 6th International Conference on Logistics Operations Management (GOL), pp. 1–10. IEEE (2022)
6. Veerasamy, N., Mkhwanazi, T., Dawood, Z.: Towards the usefulness of learning factories in the cybersecurity domain. In: International Conference on Cyber Warfare and Security, vol. 18, no. 1, pp. 412–419 (2023)
7. Reining, N., Kauffeld, S.: Empirical findings on learning success and competence development at learning factories: a scoping review. Educ. Sci. **12**(11), 769 (2022)

8. Bellucci, M., Chiurco, A., Cimino, A., Ferro, D., Longo, F., Padovano, A.: Learning Factories: a review of state of the art and development of a morphological model for an industrial engineering education 4.0. In: 2022 IEEE 21st Mediterranean Electrotechnical Conference (MELECON), pp. 260–265. IEEE (2022)

9. Loaiza, J.H., Cloutier, R.J., Lippert, K.: Proposing a small-scale digital twin implementation framework for manufacturing from a systems perspective. Systems 11(1), 41 (2023)

10. Tao, F., Xiao, B., Qi, Q., Cheng, J., Ji, P.: Digital twin modeling. J. Manuf. Syst. 64, 372–389 (2022)

11. Chau Khac Bao, C., Tran, T.T.: Development of a Digital Learning Factory Toward Multi Objectives for Engineering Education: An Educational Concept Adopts the Application of Digital Twin. Available at SSRN: https://ssrn.com/abstract=4378748 or http://dx.doi.org/ https://doi.org/10.2139/ssrn.4378748 (2023)

12. Al-Geddawy, T.: A digital twin creation method for an opensource low-cost changeable learning factory. Procedia Manufact. 51(2020), 1799–1805 (2020)

13. Elbestawi, M., Centea, D., Singh, I., Wanyama, T.: SEPT learning factory for industry 4.0 education and applied research. Procedia Manufact. 23, 249–254 (2018)

14. Umeda, Y., et al.: Developing a digital twin learning factory of automated assembly based on 'digital triplet' concept. In: Proceedings of the Conference on Learning Factories (CLF) (2021)

15. Park, K.T., Son, Y.H., Ko, S.W., Noh, S.D.: Digital twin and reinforcement learning-based resilient production control for micro smart factory. Appl. Sci. 11(7), 2977 (2021)

16. Rasovska, I., Deniaud, I., Marmier, F., Michalak, J.L.: Learning factory flextory: interactive loops between real and virtual factory through digital twin. IFAC-PapersOnLine 55(10), 1938–1943 (2022)

17. Muniraj, S.P., Xu, X.: An implementation of OPC UA for machine-to-machine communications in a smart factory. Procedia Manufact. 53, 52–58 (2021)

18. Łukaszewicz, A., Skorulski, G., Szczebiot, R.: The main aspects of training in the field of computer-aided techniques (CAx) in mechanical engineering. In: Proceedings of 17th International Scientific Conference on Engineering for Rural Development, pp. 865–870 (2018)

19. Blain, J.M.: The Complete Guide to Blender Graphics and Blender 2D Animation Two Volume Set, AK Peters/CRC Press (2021)

20. Bi, Z., Wang, X.: Computer Aided Design and Manufacturing. John Wiley & Sons (2020)

21. Duboeuf, F., et al.: Integration of AM process in design cycle of metallic parts: application to space components. In: ESAFORM 2021 24th International Conference on Material Forming (2021)

22. Iancu, C., Iancu, D., Stăncioiu, A.: From CAD model to 3D print via STL file format. Fiability Durability/Fiabilitate si Durabilitate, (1) (2010)

23. Havard, V., Courallet, A., Baudry, D., Delanin, H.,: Digital twin, virtual reality and opcua-based architecture for pedagogical scenarios in manufacturing and computer sciences curriculum. In: CLF 2023 13th Conference on Learning Factories (2023)

24. Richard, K., Havard, V., Baudry, D.: Authoring-by-doing: an event-based interaction module for virtual reality scenario authoring framework. In: De Paolis, L.T., Arpaia, P., Bourdot, P. (eds.) AVR 2021. LNCS, vol. 12980, pp. 519–527. Springer, Cham (2021). https://doi.org/ 10.1007/978-3-030-87595-4_38

25. Richard, K., Havard, V., His, J., Baudry, D.: Intervales : interactive virtual and augmented framework for industrial environment and scenariosAdv. Eng. Inform. 50, 101425 (2021)

State of the Art of Urban Digital Twin Platforms

Angelo Martella[✉] ⓘ, Amro Issam Hamed Attia Ramadan ⓘ,
Cristian Martella ⓘ, Mauro Patano ⓘ, and Antonella Longo ⓘ

DataLab, Department of Engineering for Innovation, University of Salento,
via per Monteroni, 73100 Lecce, Italy
https://www.unisalento.it

Abstract. Urban Digital Twin platforms are rapidly emerging as a powerful tool for urban planning and development, enabling city planners, architects, and other stakeholders to create virtual versions of real-world cities with extensive data on everything from traffic patterns to energy consumption. This work explores the present and future of Urban Digital Twin platforms, highlighting their potential to support a wide range of users in making informed decisions related to urban development challenges, by simulating the behaviour of cities and their residents using real-world data and advanced modeling approaches. The survey presented in this article examines a selection of state-of-the-art Urban Digital Twin platforms and discusses some of their key features, highlighting the differences in relation with their use cases. Furthermore, this work addresses some of the emerging trends and technologies in the field of Urban Digital Twins. Additionally, it considers how these developments might shape the future of urban planning and development by enabling more accurate predictions about how cities will evolve over time.

Keywords: digital twin · urban digital twin platform · smart city

1 Introduction

Digital twins are actually used in a variety of industries, including manufacturing, healthcare, and transportation, and consist of virtual replicas of physical objects or systems meant to simulate their behaviour in real-world conditions. Digital Twin models are at the basis of AR visualization, 3D Immersive Worlds, and integration with AR/VR Platforms. AR Visualization involves overlaying virtual information onto the physical environment, allowing users to interact with virtual objects and data in a more natural and intuitive way. 3D Immersive Worlds involve simulating urban environments in 3D, providing a highly interactive and engaging way to explore and experience urban spaces. Integration with AR/VR Platforms allows developers to create interactive and realistic simulations that enable users to explore and interact with urban spaces.

A Urban Digital Twin (UDT) represents a specialized digital twin which focuses on modeling and simulating urban environments. UDT platforms are a

L. T. De Paolis et al. (Eds.): XR Salento 2023, LNCS 14218, pp. 299–317, 2023.
https://doi.org/10.1007/978-3-031-43401-3_20

cornerstone in the development of smart cities, as they provide essential tools to allow planners to model and simulate different scenarios before implementing them in the real-world, fostering sustainable, resilient, and livable developments. Given the current scenario, a multitude of DT tools and platforms have been deployed and are tailored to the specific goals and tasks related to real-world use cases they are meant to address. Yet, such platforms exhibit various levels of industrial and technological maturity and may not be designed to address the recent needs for interoperability. Thus, this work focuses on the data acquisition layer of UDT platforms, since this is the core aspect to foster the creation of real Digital Twins of urban elements, at different layers and scopes. The requirements for successful creation of an integration layer made from a combination of all the platforms are investigated. Therefore, in this work some UDT platforms will be analyzed and compared based on their common features and aims. Finally, it is worth noting that at the moment there not exist full-fledged UDT platforms, but only limited approaches that are being maintained and are integrating new features over time. After Sect. 1 that introduces this work, the background is described in Sect. 2. Next, the surveyed platforms are presented in Sect. 3, whilst Sect. 4 discusses the survey criteria, how the platforms are located in the resulting framework and the results of the survey. Finally, in Sect. 5 the conclusions are summarized.

2   Background

Before providing a set of DT definitions, it is necessary to introduce and distinguish the DT concept from other similar ones like digital shadow, and digital model. The terms digital twin, digital shadow, and digital model are closely related, although they present precise and specific characteristics.

2.1   Digital Model

A digital model is a 3D streamlined representation of a physical object or system used for analysis, simulation, and optimization. Although it may not include all of the physical system's components or details, it can still represent a useful tool for different purposes, like testing and improving performance. It is important to highlight that a digital model consists of a mere real-world object representation, without any automatic data stream mechanisms between the real and digital models (as shown in Fig. 1 [19]). Therefore, whether necessary, this synchronization mechanism must be performed manually, regardless the level of accuracy of the model. The digital models have been discussed in several research works [23, 32, 40].

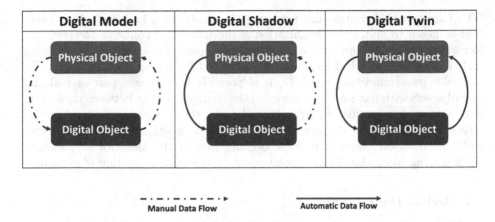

Fig. 1. Digital model, shadow and twin.

2.2 Digital Shadow

A Digital Shadow (DS) can be considered as a digital model that in addition provides an automated and uni-directional data flow from the physical model to the corresponding digital object (refer to Fig. 1). In this way, the state of the digital model always reflects its physical counterpart's. Vice versa, data synchronization between the digital model and the corresponding physical model is not realized.

2.3 Digital Twin

A virtual replica of a physical object, process, or system is referred to as a digital twin. Unlike the digital shadow, a DT provides a data synchronization mechanism with the corresponding physical one as well (as depicted in Fig. 1). A DT can be considered as a real-time view of its physical counterpart. For this reason, it can also be used to simulate, test, and optimize the physical system's performance.

After introducing these concepts of digital twin, digital shadow, and digital model, a DT definition can be provided. DT is yet to be a mature technology and considering that it is continuously evolving, many definitions exist in literature [11,20,21,34].

According to a recent definition provided in [11], a DT consists of a live digital coupling between the state of a physical asset or process and its virtual representation with a functional output. This definition is the most relevant for the purposes of this paper with respect to the characteristics and functions that a DT management platform must provide.

Similarly to what happens in real life, any asset of the real-world takes part to a specific environment with which the same asset mutually interacts. This prerogative of the real-world can be replicated to the corresponding scenario of DTs, where each DT corresponds to its physical counterpart. As a result, any

DT of this parallel context can be seen as located into a hierarchical structure that is meant to match the organization of the real-world context. The resulting hierarchical organization will be obtained by properly implementing and adding each DT of any physical asset of interest, at different scopes and levels. By mutually interconnecting two DTs, it is possible to realize a pair of real and digital assets with the aim of propagating the changes of state between them. DTs that belong to a specific hierarchical level can interact with upper level virtual assets, forming a complex network that fosters bidirectional interactions, with real-time data exchange. A possible organization of this network may include the following hierarchical levels: component, asset, system, system of systems.

2.4　Urban Digital Twin

In [19], an interesting review of the enabling technologies, challenges and ongoing research for Digital Twins is proposed. The review provides a discussion that is organized into three research areas related to manufacturing, healthcare, and especially smart cities. In this last area, the DTs that make up the basic technological infrastructure take the name of Urban Digital Twins (UDT). These kinds of DTs are sophisticated data models allowing for collaborative processes. Various studies regarding UDTs exist in literature [13, 18, 33]. A further review of the DT terminology for cities are borrowed from the corresponding similarities and relationships typical of the more well-known context of the 3D city models [24]. This review also includes details about how to implement DTs for cities, along with the application areas and potential challenges for their future development.

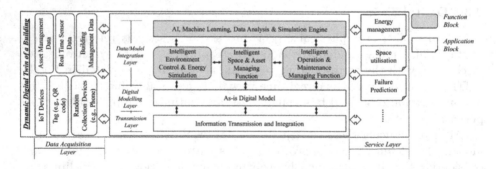

Fig. 2. Architecture of a Digital Twin.

An innovative vision of DT provides to express it as its informative structure, eventually obtained by also integrating the corresponding sub-DTs hierarchy. Indeed, the idea to consider a urban DT as a hierarchical structure of sub-DTs was already introduced in [27], where an architecture of UDTs is proposed at various levels. Considering a city as an asset that integrates different sub-assets (buildings, infrastructure, and people), the corresponding city DT can be obtain by combining and integrating the sub-UDTs related to each sub-asset. In this

way, it is possible to organize a hierarchical architecture of UDTs, by replicating
the structure of each sub-UDT. Such an architecture can be considered for presenting the logical composition of a generic DT. Specifically, the extract relating
to the UDT of a building can be considered for the following discussion and is
reported in Fig. 2 [27]. At the moment, the implementation of such an architecture is yet to be fully technologically supported, due to its high complexity.
For this reason, it can be considered as a challenging frontier for future research
efforts. The proposed architecture encompasses five layers: (1) data acquisition
layer, (2) transmission layer, (3) digital modeling layer, (4) data/model integration layer, and (5) service layer. For the needs of this paper, the attention must
be focused on the data acquisition layer. A detailed discussion about this layer
is proposed in the following.

Data Acquisition Layer. Considering the heterogeneity and large volume of data
a DT must deal with, the data acquisition represents the most complex and challenging layer of a DT architecture. Indeed, this layer must provide the necessary
support to a wide range of types, formats, sources, and content of data. Considering the hierarchical architecture of DTs, each sub-DT refers to its necessary
data/information/models when following up a query from the parent DT. Data
collection techniques must include contact-less data collection (radio-frequency
identification (RFID), and image-based techniques), distributed sensor systems,
wireless communication, and mobile access (e.g., WiFi environment). Observing
the image of the DT architecture, the data acquisition layer must implement
specific interactions with (1) IoT devices, (2) Asset Management Data, (3) Tag,
(4) Real-Time Sensor Data, (5) Random Collection Devices, and (6) Building
Management Data. Moreover, the data acquisition layer must support real-time
data collection, effective data management, and integration [22,28].

Urban Digital Twin Platforms. Urban Digital Twin platforms are software
tools that enable the creation and management of virtual replicas of urban environments. These platforms typically include a range of features designed to support urban planning and development, including tools for visualizing and analyzing data, as well as simulation capabilities that allow users to test different
scenarios and interventions. Referring to the definition of DT provided in [11], it
is possible to identify the key features to consider for its design and implementation. These features include the following: (1) Take care of receiving, formatting
and processing operational status data, (2) Provide a digital model representing
the salient properties, behaviour and functioning of the physical twin during its
twinned life cycle, and (3) Provide an interface that allows humans or systems
to output and interact with the DTs. In addition to the previous key features,
some optional ones should be considered, such as the following: (1) Provide data
storage and/or retrieval, (2) Include a toolkit that allows the analysis, simulation and visualization of the physical twin at appropriate levels of fidelity and
temporal granularity, and (3) Provide tools to enable data about the physical
entity and its environment to be curated.

In literature, various examples of DT platforms exist [10,12,17,25,30,31,40, 42] within the most various contexts.

3 Urban Digital Twin Platforms Survey

Given the above challenges (from the above section) and the critical nature of the procedure of creating DT models, many tools have been developed with the objective of creating Digital Twins by both the business world and the academic community to meet the needs of specific applications.

3.1 Survey Settings

Before giving a deep insight of the survey proposed in this paper, it is fundamental to highlight its main goal and characteristics, along with some information about how it was been organized. After a preliminary scouting of the most relevant DT platforms available on the market, the target solutions to consider for the survey have been selected. It is important to underline that the scouting is not meant to be considered as exhaustive, being the offer of DT platforms very large and in continuous ferment. The resulting list of DT platforms was then filtered by considering only the solutions are completely open-source or that at least provide a free trial period. At the best of our knowledge, the filtered list includes the most relevant DT platforms.

The goal of the proposed survey is to perform a comparative analysis of these platforms, by evaluating the main characteristics and features their data acquisition layer offers. The result obtained from the present survey aims at supporting various stakeholders in selecting the most flexible and suitable UDT platform, according to specific purposes and needs. Again, only solutions that are open-source or that offer a free trial period participate in the starting list of the UDT platforms. A more detailed discussion about both the reference criteria and the accomplished comparative analysis for the proposed survey is reported in the following.

Platform Features. The features that are crucial for selecting the UDT platforms to consider for the present survey must include the following.

Urban Simulation Support. It enables the modeling and analysis of urban environments, as well as the effects produced by various urban policies and interventions.

Digital Twin Modeling. Each platform can generate digital twin models of urban environments. These virtual representations of the physical world can be used for a variety of purposes such as urban planning, asset management, and emergency management.

3D Visualization. 3D visualizations of urban environments are fundamental for a UDT platform. Users can view and interact with urban spaces in a more intuitive and immersive manner, thanks to the visualizations this feature makes available.

Geospatial Analysis. A UDT platform makes available its models using geospatial data and analysis. Data on the physical environment, such as building footprints and street layouts, can be eventually integrated. Additional data can be related to population density and land use, which can be used to highlight social and economic factors.

Open-Source and Freely Accessible Platforms. The prerogative of a DT platform to be open-source or to provide a free trial period makes it possible to directly install, configure and evaluate it. This allows developers and users to tailor the platforms to their specific needs and use cases. In this way, it is possible to experience the platform's main features and investigate its capabilities and constraints.

3.2   Platforms Scouting

Before proceeding with the UDT platform evaluation, a scouting in literature has been performed to identify the majority solutions the market offers. Concerning commercial platforms, a valid contribution in this regard can be found in [35]. Regarding non commercial solutions, a more specific scouting in literature has been carried out, identifying these additional UDT platforms: TU Delft project [26], UrbanSIM [43], Digital Twin Cities Center (DTCC) [24], and ArcGIS City Engine [41]. A brief description of each DT platforms resulted from the scouting in literature is provided in the following paragraphs. The appearance order in which the DT platforms are introduced is strictly alphabetical.

Akselos. [8] is a commercial platform for engineering simulation based on finite-element analysis with a reduced basis. The platform can be used to create digital twins of energy infrastructures in order to enhance their design, maintenance, dependability, and lifetime.

Altair. [3] provides a commercial digital twin platform that connects various development disciplines. It optimizes performance by using CAE, IoT, machine learning, and data intelligence.

ArcGIS City Engine. [9] is the only solution that provides a free trial period among the DT platforms resulting from scouting. It is a powerful 3D modeling software for cities that enables users to quickly and easily create 3D models of cities and buildings.

Blockbax. [1] is a commercially available platform that generates a digital twin of any asset in order to generate real-time insights and reduce problems. It is the most efficient and user-friendly method for contextualizing IoT data and creating a dynamic virtual replica of any asset.

Open Cities Planner. [4] is a commercial urban planning and visualization solution that enables users to design and visualize digital cities, nonetheless, it enables the 3D visualization of CAD, BIM, and GIS data.

Digital Twin Builder. [2] is a commercial ScaleOut software that aims at enabling developers to create digital twin models of data sources and deploy them to ScaleOut. It is mainly a toolkit that enables developers to define object-oriented state information and analytics code for tracking telemetry. Its APIs allow developers to create digital twin models that incorporate application-specific algorithms and state data describing either physical or virtual objects.

Digital Twin Cities Center. [15] is an open-source solution that provides a city planning and management software platform that enables the creation of DT model for city's infrastructures and services. The platform can simulate different scenarios and can forecast the effects of changes on the corresponding city's environment.

Predix. [5] is a commercial tool provided by General Electric for creating and managing digital twins and their associated analytic models, making it easier for businesses to leverage the benefits of digital twins.

IoT Production Monitoring. [14] is a commercial IoT Digital Twin Implementation provided by Oracle that permits a data analyst to create a model based on external observation of a machine and to develop multiple models based on the user's requirements. Oracle IoT Digital Twin Simulator enables users to create simulated devices for their environment without the need to connect or configure hardware.

Seebo [6] is commercial platform delivered as Software-as-a-Service (SaaS) for Industry 4.0 that provides prepackaged solutions for Condition Monitoring, Predictive Maintenance, Digital Twin, and Smart Manufacturing. The Seebo Platform incorporates Digital Twin technology, which has been in use for some time to simulate conditions and predict outcomes. The Digital Twin methodology entails the creation of a virtual copy of a physical product or process, which can be used to monitor and optimize performance.

TU Delft Project. [7] is an open-source platform developed by The Delft University of Technology in the Netherlands that provides detailed 3D models of buildings and infrastructures in a country level scope, based on real-world data. The platform can be used to generate detailed simulations and visualizations of urban areas, providing a free and easy-to-use tool to aid in urban planning and decision-making tasks.

UrbanSIM. [39] is an open-source and AI-powered platform for sustainable urban planning and development that reduces the time, effort, and cost of planning urban development and infrastructure projects while increasing confidence that desired outcomes will be achieved. It is mainly used in the real-estate sector.

The resulting list of DT platforms obtained from the scouting was then filtered in order to meet the survey criteria previously introduced. These criteria are related to (1) the prerogative of a platform to be open (not commercial), and (2) the prerogative of a platform to foster the development of a city
DT. By considering these requirements, the following considerations for identifying the survey target platforms can be done: (1) Akselos, Altair, Blockbax,
Digital Twin Builder, IoT Production Monitoring, Open cities planner, Predix,
and Seebo must be excluded being commercial solutions. (2) UrbanSIM is not
accounted for in the present survey based on the second prerogative. Therefore,
the remaining UDT platforms to consider for the subsequent evaluation are:
ArcGIS CityEngine, DTCC and TU Delft Project.

3.3   Platforms Discussion

For each of the UDT platforms resulting from the scouting, a more detailed
discussion and a comparative analysis are provided in the following, with a particular focus on the corresponding data acquisition layer.

ArcGIS City Engine. ArcGIS City Engine is a powerful 3D modeling software
for cities that enables users to quickly and easily create 3D models of cities and
buildings. The platform proposes features that can be addressed to users with
different technical skills, including architects, urban planners, and GIS professionals.

ArcGIS City Engine supports the import of various data formats from a
variety of sources, such as GIS data, CAD files, and aerial imagery. Furthermore,
the platform includes a library of pre-built 3D models and textures in order to
make available a quick and simple city creation.

The platform provides specific functionalities for designing urban features,
such as streets, and sidewalks, along with powerful visualization and analysis
tools. ArcGIS City Engine enables simulations for various scenarios and can
highlight and analyse the impact of supposed changes within urban context.
Moreover, the platform can be fully integrated to other ArcGIS products, such
as ArcGIS Online.

The platform is capable of producing 3D models related to entire cities, but
also to smaller areas such as neighborhoods or individual buildings, by using
a simple procedure. In addition, this procedure offers the possibility to easily
change the look and feel of their models by using different textures, lighting,
and other visual effects.

The software supports terrain creation and editing tools, such as hills and
valleys, and can export the resulting model into a variety of formats, including
3D PDF, OBJ, Collada (DEA), DXF as well as VOB for Vue.

The platform allows to refer to a scripting language in order to implement
specific custom tasks. This is one of the most interesting features for automating
repetitive tasks and creating custom workflows that can enable collaboration and
sharing operations between users.

ArcGIS City Engine is a proprietary, closed-source, non-free system marketed by ESRI, however, the platform offers a free trial that gives users the chance to test the platform and understand its characteristics. It is strongly integrated with other software products, mainly of the GIS type, from ESRI to create interactive and immersive 3D environments to be used in other platforms such as ArcGIS Urban Suite. It uses Autodesk FBX to interact with game engines and VFX tools. It exports to Alembic or even Pixar's Renderman. 3D object layers are exported as scene layer package (SLPK) files. To the extent of our knowledge, it is a solid modeler oriented toward urban architecture. For this reason, it offers integration modules towards the main commercial 3D modeling software: Puma is a plug-in for Rhino and Grasshopper, Palladio is a plug-in for SideFX Houdini, Serlio is a plug-in for Autodesk Maya, Vitruvius is a plug-in for Unreal Engine.

Digital Twin Cities Center. The Digital Twin Cities Center (DTCC) engine is a city planning and management software platform that makes possible to create the DT model of a city's infrastructure and services. The platform can simulate different scenarios and can forecast the effects of changes on the corresponding city's environment.

The engine behind the DTCC platform can assist decision-makers in making data-driven decisions aimed to improve the city's sustainability, resilience, and livability. Indeed, the DTCC platform can support the gathering of real-time data from a variety of sources, including sensors, IoT devices, and social media. These data are then used to track the city's performance and identify areas for improvement.

The engine of the DTCC can contribute to emergency response and disaster management by providing to the decision-makers a centralized dashboard for monitoring the city's operations and performance.

The platform is highly customizable and can be tailored to support each city's specific needs and is compatible with a wide range of existing city management systems.

Using the DTCC platform, citizens and stakeholders can be involved in the planning and management process. Specifically, citizens can provide feedback and suggestions for city improvements by referring to the platform's user-friendly interface.

The DTCC platform allows to improve the communication and collaboration between decision-makers, stakeholders, and citizens. At the same time, the DTCC platform can support the design and development of urban projects. Proceeding in this way, decision-makers can use the platform to visualize and test various design scenarios before applying changes to the real-world, saving time and money. In [29], the authors propose the virtual copies creation of physical systems, specifically digital twins in cities. They highlight on using digital twins for a variety of purposes, including multi-physics simulations, what-if scenarios, and life-cycle analysis. The authors address the problem of creating 3D models of any urban environment at Level of Detail 1 (LoD1) in the form of both surface and volume meshes. The mesh is generated using publicly available datasets from

Sweden's Mapping, Cadastral, and Land Registration. In general, the authors hope to provide a solution for creating 3D models of urban environments that can be used for a variety of purposes, such as simulations and analysis. The DTCC platform can be particularly suitable in creating LoD1 models from publicly available datasets.

A final aspect to highlight corresponds to the creation of 3D models of historical cities, as well as to simulate the effects of historical events on urban environments.

The basis for building a digital twin of a city is the generation of a 3D city model, often represented as a mesh. The system developed by DTCC is based on an algorithm and its implementation for automatic, efficient and robust mesh generation for large-scale city modeling and simulation. The mesh generation algorithm uses a limited number of parameters initially loaded from a JSON format file and two geographic data files, in particular 2D cadastral maps (building footprints) and 3D point clouds obtained from LIDAR-type aerial surveying. The algorithm generates LoD1.2 city models in the form of triangular surface meshes, suitable for visualization, and high-quality tetrahedral volume meshes, suitable for simulation. In particular, DTCC Builder is capable of generating large-scale conformal tetrahedral volume meshes of cities suitable for finite element simulation (FEM). The long-term goal is to build a system capable of generating a three-dimensional meshed digital twin of city volume in (near) real-time in LoD2.x.

The DTCC system is completely open-source and is developed in a modular way using both Python and C++ in a Unix environment.

TU Delft Project. The Delft University of Technology in the Netherlands developed a platform that provides detailed 3D models of buildings and infrastructures in a country level scope, based on real-world data. Target end users are urban planners, architects, and other city development professionals.

The platform includes buildings information such as function, type of infrastructure (i.e. road, bridge, building, and so forth), location, geometry, and height. The primary source of such information is the Dutch national address and building database, which is constantly kept up to date with new data.

The project encompasses a number of packages that are tailored to address specific use cases [7,36], spanning from 3D representation of cities in country-wide scenarios, with 3D BAG [37], to solar irradiance simulations with Solar3Dcity [38].

The platform can be accessed via a web interface or an API and it is available with an open license. Thus, it has been used in a variety of applications, including flood risk assessment and building energy performance assessments.

Regular updates enrich the platform with new features and capabilities, allowing it to be an important tool for urban planning and development in the Netherlands, with the potential to be used and applied in other countries as well. The Dutch Kadaster and the 3D Geoinformation research group at TU Delft are actively collaborating [16] to create and disseminate 3D city models of the entire Netherlands. The workflow includes automated reconstruction from existing countrywide data, maintenance of 3D data in a unified database, quality control, and making the data available in an open 3D standard. The 3D model is made up of three data products: 3D Basisbestand Volledig, 3D Basisbestand Gebouwen, and building height statistics 3D Hoogtestatistieken Gebouwen.

The model is regularly updated based on new versions of BAG and BGT data, as well as up-to-date height data obtained from aerial images. The data is aligned on a grid for accuracy and stored with mm precision. The 3D data is reconstructed using another open-source model, City3D, and the 3D BAG service, which generates several reference heights per building. The data is disseminated using CityJSON, CityGML, GeoPackage, Wavefront OBJ, PostgreSQL, WMS, WFS exchange formats. The platform also tackles the challenges related to the reconstruction of underground parts of buildings, as well as the workflow from reconstruction to 3D data dissemination.

The ultimate goal is to provide applications with standardized, future-proof 3D topographic data. The Kadaster is working on a workflow to generate and distribute a 3D topographic dataset covering the entire Netherlands. The workflow is scheduled to be re-run every year with new input data. Based on feedback, the Kadaster intends to improve the workflow and research new applications that require 3D data. They also intend to investigate how to make the best use of updated point clouds, as well as integrate and align 3D city models from other governments. Future work will concentrate on generating a single aggregated quality value per building, as well as developing a 3D viewer and a download service.

3D BAG is built by combining two open datasets:

- The Building and Address Register is the most detailed and openly available data set on buildings and addresses in the Netherlands. It contains information about each address in a building, such as its current use, date of construction, or registration status. The data set is regularly updated as new buildings are registered, constructed or demolished.
- The National Height Model of the Netherlands is the openly available elevation dataset of the Netherlands. It is captured by aerial laser scanning (LIDAR), with an average dot density of 8 dots per square meter for the current version.

Three levels of detail are available: LoD1.2, LoD1.3 and LoD2.2. In addition to the 3D models, 2D projections of the roof surfaces are provided with the relative height references.

4   Survey Discussion

In this section, an overview of the criteria used to evaluate Urban Digital Twin platforms is provided, along with a description of how the surveyed platforms are located in the resulting framework, portraying the results of the survey.

4.1 Survey Criteria

Evaluation Criteria. The UDT platforms featured in this work are described according to a set of characteristics related to their input, output, and the simulations they perform. Further information is provided about the level of detail of represented objects and the supported data formats. An additional important feature to consider for evaluating a UDT platform regards the integration with AR/VR platforms. Considering that this paper aims to be a first analysis, this aspect can be faced and discussed within its already planned future evolution. Before discussing the survey results, it is fundamental to anticipate that none of the UDT platforms included in the survey is capable of supporting data streams from sensors and of implementing a bi-directional data flow between a physical asset and the corresponding digital replica. Thus, these are not to be intended as full-fledged DTs, but rather as tools to enable and foster the future development of DT platforms. Each of the features considered for the survey is discussed in the following paragraphs.

Users. UDT platforms are generally tailored to help users in performing their activities. Considering that the user base of a UDT platform can be wide and varied, the prerogative of a platform to be supportive of more or fewer user categories is a decisive and important factor for its evaluation. The categories of users that have been considered in this context are: policymakers, researchers, developers, city planners, architects, and infrastructure planners.

Input. The most common input data a UDT platform must support are aerial photography, LIDAR point clouds, and cadastral data. In this way, it is possible to reconstruct accurate 3D models of buildings, infrastructures, and other city assets of interest.

Output. For evaluating each UDT platform, the output we have considered includes 3D City Model, Solar irradiance, Solar shadow, Citizen interaction, Future city development, Digital infrastructure for IoT services, and Energy demand. These outputs are the reference results obtained within the common use cases that have been developed in most research efforts.

Object Representation. Concerning the object representation, several aspects were taken into account, starting with the level of detail (LoD) [26] of the model, the representation of natural elements like trees, the representation of building elements such as openings, roofs, doors, and windows, and finally, the representation of infrastructure elements like road networks.

Simulations. The platforms must enable the users to perform various simulations, leveraging high-performance computing and AI predictive tools to deploy realistic and accurate what-if analyses. For the purposes of this work, the aspects that are considered relevant are supporting models for geotechnical and future development, solar irradiance and shadowing, rain and sea level rise, wind, air quality, and noise models.

Supported Data Formats. As discussed in Sect. 2.4, interoperability between DT platforms can be achieved through open and standard data formats. Being compliant with these requirements, JSON, CityGML, IFC and shape files have been considered for performing the platform evaluation.

4.2 Platforms Comparison

As reported in Table 1, all platforms are suitable for a wide range of users, including policymakers, researchers, developers, city planners, architects, and infrastructure planners. Regarding the inputs, ArcGIS CityEngine and TU Delft Project do not support aerial photography.

In this context, all the platforms considered can ingest LIDAR-generated point clouds. Additionally, DTCC and ArcGIS CityEngine also support cadastral data as input.

Shifting the attention to the output side, the focus is on the type of models and simulations that the platforms can create. In this scenario, it was found that all provide a 3D city model.

DTCC and TU Delft Project support the simulation of solar irradiance and solar shadow, whereas ArcGIS CityEngine does not explicitly mention it. Moreover, DTCC supports digital infrastructure for IoT services and encourages citizen interaction with the platform. These characteristics have not been found in the other platforms. Furthermore, DTCC provides tools to assess and model the energy demand of cities and perform geotechnical and future development of cities, while ArcGIS CityEngine can perform rain and sea rise-related simulations.
To the extent of our knowledge air quality and noise, simulations could be done by Tu Delft with the help of additional tools and platforms.
Regarding the detail level of entities represented in each platform's virtual environment, it was found that DTCC represents objects at LoD 1, whereas ArcGIS CityEngine is designed to provide more advanced LoD 3 objects. Additionally, TU Delft Project can manage LoD 1 and LoD 2 entities for different objects.

Trees and other natural elements are well targeted by DTCC and TU Delft Project, which mention tree representation using terrain mesh and LIDAR, whereas ArcGIS CityEngine does not mention explicitly any kind of representation in this regard.
Doors and windows are represented only by TU Delft Project as a 3D polyline. Road network is represented by two platforms, DTCC and TU Delft Project as a terrain mesh.

As for the formats supported by the platforms, the goal is to assess the most common types that can be leveraged to achieve interoperability between different platforms and systems, such as JSON, CityGML, IFC, and Shapefile.

In particular, it was found that Shapefile and CityGML are supported by all considered platforms. TU Delft Project supports all of the file formats, making it a strong option to be considered when it comes to creating 3D models of cities.

Table 1. Comparison between the platforms considered in this work.

FEATURES		UDT PLATFORMS		
		DTCC	ArcGIS CityEngine	TU DELFT Project
Users	Policy makers	✓	✓	✓
	Researchers	✓	✓	✓
	Developers	✓	✓	✓
	City Planners	✓	✓	✓
	Architects	✓	✓	✓
	Infrastructure planners	✓	✓	
Input	Aerial Photography	✓		
	Point clouds (Lidar)	✓	✓	✓
	Cadastral data	✓	✓	
Output	3D City Model	✓	✓	✓
	Solar irradiance	✓		✓
	Solar shadow	✓		✓
	Citizen interaction	✓		
	Future city development			
	Digital infrastructure for IoT services	✓		
	Energy demand	✓		
Object representation	LoD level	LoD 1	LoD 3	LoD 1-2
	Trees	Terrain mesh		3d with Lidar
	Doors/Windows			polyline 3d
	Road network	Terrain mesh		Terrain mesh
Simulations	Wind			
	Air quality			
	Geotechnical/future development	✓		
	Solar shading/irradiance	✓		✓
	Noise			
	Rain/sea level rise		✓	
Supported data formats	JSON			✓
	CityGML	✓	✓	✓
	IFC			✓
	Shapefile	✓	✓	✓

4.3 Final Considerations

Various approaches can be taken into consideration to achieve compatibility and interoperability between the platforms analyzed in this survey. For instance, APIs can be used to enable data sharing and exchange between platforms. Data can also be transformed or converted into a common format that is supported by all platforms.

This survey highlighted the state-of-the-art features provided by the considered UDT platforms. It was found that currently, DTCC is the most mature platform, addressing the largest number user and stakeholder categories and supporting the largest set of input and output types. Yet, it does not provide advanced object representation support as other platforms, e.g. ArcGIS CityEngine and TU Delft Project, do.

Concerning the supported data formats, TU Delft Project is the strongest option, given its support to all the file formats accounted. Nevertheless, it is worth mentioning that the capabilities of all the platforms can be further expanded with additional plugins or through their regular updates.

5   Conclusion and Future Work

Urban Digital Twin platforms have the potential to break through urban planning and management by providing a comprehensive and integrated view of cities. In this paper, after introducing an architecture for UDTs and providing a survey of some UDT development solutions, a comparative analysis restricted to the open-source or free trial UDT platforms is performed. This analysis aims at evaluating for each platform the corresponding features, benefits, and potential applications by focusing on its data acquisition layer.

UDT platforms can support a wide range of users, including policymakers, researchers, developers, city planners, architects, and infrastructure planners, enabling them to perform simulations and make informed decisions in order to address urban development challenges, such as sustainability, resilience, and livability.

Future developments in UDT platforms will play a critical role in addressing the above challenges. Being not sufficiently mature, current UDT platforms are expected to evolve in two distinct directions in the future. The first is towards more advanced modeling methodologies, such as agent-based modeling and machine learning, which can deliver more accurate and realistic simulations of cities and their residents. The second direction is towards improved integration with other technologies, such as Internet of Things devices and cloud computing, which can enhance the capabilities of UDT platforms and distribute the computational requirements across the entire edge-cloud continuum spectrum.

Acknowledgements. This work is partially supported by ICSC-Italian Center on Supercomputing and Italian Research Center on High Performance Computing, Big Data and Quantum Computing, funded by European Union - NextGenerationEU, by CETMA DIHSME and Brindisi Smart City Port.

References

1. Digital Twin – blockbax.com. https://blockbax.com/digital-twin/. Accessed 18 May 2023
2. Digital Twin Builder – scaleoutsoftware.com. https://www.scaleoutsoftware.com/products/digital-twin-builder/. Accessed 18 May 2023
3. One Total Twin - Digital Twin Technology|Altair – altair.com. https://altair.com/one-total-twin. Accessed 18 May 2023
4. OpenCities Planner: Digital Twin Software | Bentley Systems – bentley.com. https://www.bentley.com/software/opencities-planner/#:~:text=What%20is%20Opencities%20Planner%3F%201%20Easily%20Share%20Information,Get%20Started%20Quickly%20with%20this%20Easy-to-use%20Application%20. Accessed 18 May 2023

5. What is Predix Platform?|Predix Edge 2.8.1 Documentation|GE Digital – ge.com. https://www.ge.com/digital/documentation/edge-software/c_what_is_ predix_platform.html. Accessed 18 May 2023
6. Seebo industry 4.0 solutions (2022). https://www.solidworks.com/media/seebo-industry-40-solutions. Accessed 18 May 2023
7. 3d geoinformation at tu delft. https://3d.bk.tudelft.nl/. Accessed 18 May 2023
8. Akselos - The Fastest Engineering Simulation Technology – akselos.com. https:// akselos.com/. Accessed 18 May 2023
9. arcgis.com. https://desktop.arcgis.com/es/cityengine/. Accessed 18 May 2023
10. Browning, J., et al.: Foundations for a fission battery digital twin. Nuclear Technol. **208**, 1089–1101 (2022). https://doi.org/10.1080/00295450.2021.2011574
11. Catapult, H.: Untangling the requirements of a digital twin. Univ. Sheff. Adv. Manuf. Res. Cent. (AMRC), p. p7 (2021), cited by: 1
12. Clemen, T., et al.: Multi-agent systems and digital twins for smarter cities. In: Proceedings of the 2021 ACM SIGSIM Conference on Principles of Advanced Discrete Simulation, pp. 45–55 (2021)
13. Dembski, F., Wössner, U., Letzgus, M., Ruddat, M., Yamu, C.: Urban digital twins for smart cities and citizens: the case study of Herrenberg, Germany. Sustainability **12**(6), 2307 (2020)
14. Developing Applications with Oracle Internet of Things Cloud Service – docs.oracle.com. https://docs.oracle.com/en/cloud/paas/iot-cloud/iotgs/oracle-iot-digital-twin-implementation.html. Accessed 18 May 2023
15. Dtcc. https://github.com/dtcc-platform/dtcc-core. Accessed 18 May 2023
16. Dukai, B., et al.: Generating, storing, updating and disseminating a countrywide 3D model. The International Archives of the Photogrammetry, Remote Sensing and Spatial Information Sciences XLIV-4/W1-2020, 27–32, September 2020. https:// doi.org/10.5194/isprs-archives-xliv-4-w1-2020-27-2020
17. Fan, C., Zhang, C., Yahja, A., Mostafavi, A.: Disaster city digital twin: a vision for integrating artificial and human intelligence for disaster management. Int. J. Inf. Manage. **56**, 102049 (2021). https://doi.org/10.1016/j.ijinfomgt.2019.102049
18. Ferré-Bigorra, J., Casals, M., Gangolells, M.: The adoption of urban digital twins. Cities **131**, 103905 (2022)
19. Fuller, A., Fan, Z., Day, C., Barlow, C.: Digital twin: enabling technologies, challenges and open research. IEEE Access **8**, 108952–108971 (2020). https://doi.org/ 10.1109/access.2020.2998358
20. Gelernter, D.: Mirror worlds: Or the day software puts the universe in a shoebox... How it will happen and what it will mean. Oxford University Press (1993)
21. Grieves, M., Vickers, J.: Digital twin: mitigating unpredictable, undesirable emergent behavior in complex systems. Transdisciplinary perspectives on complex systems: New findings and approaches, pp. 85–113 (2017)
22. Hu, Z.Z., Tian, P.L., Li, S.W., Zhang, J.P.: Bim-based integrated delivery technologies for intelligent mep management in the operation and maintenance phase. Adv. Eng. Softw. **115**, 1–16 (1 2018). https://doi.org/10.1016/j.advengsoft.2017. 08.007
23. Huang, X., Huang, P., Huang, T.: Multi-objective optimization of digital management for renewable energies in smart cities. Journal Européen des Systèmes Automatisés **53**(6), 893–902 (2020). https://doi.org/10.18280/jesa.530615
24. Ketzler, B., Naserentin, V., Latino, F., Zangelidis, C., Thuvander, L., Logg, A.: Digital twins for cities: a state of the art review. Built Environ. **46**(4), 547–573 (2020). https://doi.org/10.2148/benv.46.4.547

25. Kunzer, B., Berges, M., Dubrawski, A.: The digital twin landscape at the crossroads of predictive maintenance, machine learning and physics based modeling (6 2022)
26. Lehner, H., Dorffner, L.: Digital geotwin vienna: Towards a digital twin city as geodata hub (2020)
27. Lu, Q., et al.: Developing a dynamic digital twin at building and city levels: a case study of the west Cambridge campus. J. Manage. Eng. **36**, October 2019. https://doi.org/10.1061/(ASCE)ME.1943-5479.0000763
28. Mohammad, S., Fattah, M., Sung, N.M., Ahn, I.Y., Ryu, M., Yun, J.: Building IoT services for aging in place using standard-based IoT platforms and heterogeneous IoT products (2017). https://doi.org/10.3390/s17102311. https://www.mdpi.com/journal/sensors
29. Naserentin, V., Somanath, S., Eleftheriou, O., Logg, A.: Combining open source and commercial tools in digital twin for cities generation. IFAC-PapersOnLine **55**(11), 185–189 (2022). https://doi.org/10.1016/j.ifacol.2022.08.070
30. Pang, J., Huang, Y., Xie, Z., Li, J., Cai, Z.: Collaborative city digital twin for the covid-19 pandemic: a federated learning solution. Tsinghua Sci. Technol. **26**(5), 759–771 (2021). https://doi.org/10.26599/tst.2021.9010026
31. Riaz, K., McAfee, M., Gharbia, S.S.: Management of climate resilience: exploring the potential of digital twin technology, 3d city modelling, and early warning systems. Sensors **23**(5), 2659 (2023). https://doi.org/10.3390/s23052659
32. Ruiz-Zafra, A., Pigueiras, J., Millan-Alcaide, A., Larios, V.M., Maciel, R.: A digital object-based infrastructure for smart governance of heterogeneous internet of things systems. In: 2020 IEEE International Smart Cities Conference (ISC2). IEEE, September 2020. https://doi.org/10.1109/isc251055.2020.9239077
33. Schrotter, G., Hürzeler, C.: The digital twin of the city of Zurich for urban planning. PFG-J. Photogrammetry Remote Sens. Geoinform. Sci. **88**(1), 99–112 (2020)
34. Shafto, M., Conroy, M., Doyle, R., Glaessgen, E., Kemp, C., LeMoigne, J., Wang, L.: Modeling, simulation, information technology & processing roadmap. National Aeronautics Space Adm. **32**(2012), 1–38 (2012)
35. Teng, S.Y., Touš, M., Leong, W.D., How, B.S., Lam, H.L., Mávsa, V.: Recent advances on industrial data-driven energy savings: digital twins and infrastructures. Renewable Sustainable Energy Rev. **135**, 110208 (2021). https://doi.org/10.1016/J.RSER.2020.110208
36. Tudelft3d project repository. https://github.com/tudelft3d. Accessed 18 May 2023
37. Tudelft3d/bag3d: Software for generating a 3d version of the bag dataset and more. https://github.com/tudelft3d/bag3d. Accessed 18 May 2023
38. Tudelft3d/solar3dcity: An experimental utility to estimate the yearly solar irradiation of roof surfaces in citygml. https://github.com/tudelft3d/Solar3Dcity. Accessed 18 May 2023
39. urbansim.com. https://www.urbansim.com/about. Accessed 08 May 2023
40. White, G., Zink, A., Codecá, L., Clarke, S.: A digital twin smart city for citizen feedback. Cities **110**, 103064 (2021). https://doi.org/10.1016/j.cities.2020.103064
41. Xiong, H., Wang, Z., Wu, G., Pan, Y.: Design and implementation of digital twin-assisted simulation method for autonomous vehicle in car-following scenario. J. Sens. **2022** (2022)

42. Xue, F., Lu, W., Chen, Z., Webster, C.J.: From LiDAR point cloud towards digital twin city: clustering city objects based on gestalt principles. ISPRS J. Photogrammetry Remote Sens. **167**, 418–431 (2020). https://doi.org/10.1016/j.isprsjprs.2020.07.020
43. Ye, X., Du, J., Han, Y., Newman, G., Retchless, D., Zou, L., Ham, Y., Cai, Z.: Developing human-centered urban digital twins for community infrastructure resilience: a research agenda. J. Plan. Lit. **38**(2), 187–199 (2023)

 9783031434006

Artificial Intelligence

The Application of the Preoperative Image-Guided 3D Visualization Supported by Machine Learning to the Prediction of Organs Reconstruction During Pancreaticoduodenectomy via a Head-Mounted Displays

Klaudia Proniewska[1,2], Radek Kolecki[3,4], Anna Grochowska[4,5], Tadeusz Popiela[4,5], Tomasz Rogula[4], Krzysztof Malinowski[1,2], Damian Dołęga-Dołęgowski[6], Jakub Kenig[4,5,6], Piotr Richter[4,5,7,8], Julianna Dąbrowa[4], MHD Jafar Mortada[1,9], Peter van Dam[1,10], and Agnieszka Pregowska[11(✉)]

[1] Center for Digital Medicine and Robotics, Jagiellonian University Medical College, 7E Street, 31-034 Krakow, Poland
[2] Department of Bioinformatics and Telemedicine, Jagiellonian University Medical College, Medyczna 7 Street, 30-688 Krakow, Poland
[3] Department of Orthopedic Surgery, University Hospital in Krakow, Jakubowskiego 2 Street, 30-688 Krakow, Poland
[4] Jagiellonian University Medical College, Anny 12 Street, 31-008 Krakow, Poland
[5] University Hospital in Krakow, Jakubowskiego 2 Street, 30-688 Krakow, Poland
[6] Project LIDER XI NCBiR-HoloMed, Jagiellonian University Medical College, Anny 12 Street, 31-008 Krakow, Poland
[7] Department of General, Oncologic and Geriatric Surgery, Jagiellonian University Medical College, Anny 12 Street, 31-008 Krakow, Poland
[8] Chair and First Department of General Surgery, Jagiellonian University Medical College, Anny 12 Street, 31-008 Krakow, Poland
[9] Department of Information Engineering, Università Politecnica delle Marche, 60121 Ancona, Italy
[10] Department of Cardiology, University Medical Center Utrecht, Lundlaan 4, 3584 EA, Utrecht, The Netherlands
[11] Institute of Fundamental Technological Research, Polish Academy of Sciences, Pawinskiego 5B, 02-106, Warsaw, Poland
aprego@ippt.pan.pl

Abstract. Early pancreatic cancer diagnosis and therapy drastically increase the chances of survival. Tumor visualization using CT scan images is an important part of these processes. In this paper, we apply Mixed Reality (MR) and Artificial Intelligence, in particular, Machine Learning (ML) to prepare image-guided 3D models of pancreatic cancer in a population of oncology patients. Object detection was based on the convolution neural network, i.e. the You Only Look Once (YOLO) version 7 algorithm, while the semantic segmentation has been done with the 3D-UNET algorithm. Next, the 3D holographic visualization of this model as an interactive, MR object was performed using the Microsoft HoloLens2. The results indicated that the proposed MR and ML-based approach can precisely segment the pancreas along with suspected lesions, thus providing a reliable tool for diagnostics and surgical planning, especially when considering organ reconstruction during pancreaticoduodenectomy.

Keywords: Extended Reality · Mixed Reality · Augmented Reality · Head-Mounted Displays · Artificial Intelligence · Image-guided surgery

1   Introduction

Pancreatic cancer is most often diagnosed in a locally advanced stage, where local vessel involvement is more probable (Kenner et al. 2021), (Rawla et al. 2019). Since the early symptoms of the disease are mostly non-specific, an efficient diagnosis in the initial stages of the disorder is crucial in improving survival rates (Gheorghe et al. 2020). Experienced oncological surgical centers are capable of performing radical local resection with vessel reconstruction; however, this is often an intraoperative decision. Advances in 3D visualization of CT imagery provide a crucial preoperative decision-making tool to identify possible regions of vascular involvement, the feasibility of resection, and the extent of potential vessel reconstruction. This is particularly useful given that vascular invasion necessitating reconstruction is itself a negative prognosticator for long-term outcomes. Preoperative planning that shows the extent of invasion may avoid an operation, instead opting for alternatives such as neoadjuvant chemotherapy. Moreover, image-guided navigation fits in with the assumptions of an alternative to traditional solutions, minimally invasive surgeries (MIS) (Kochanski et al. 2019). Thus, early pancreatic diagnosis is of high importance.

Recently the development of head-mounted displays (HMDs) has opened many possibilities for the use of immersive technologies like Augmented Reality (AR), and Mixed Reality (MR) in various fields, particularly medicine with a special emphasis on the medical education sector (Klinker et al. 2020), (Garlinska et al. 2023), (Pregowska et al. 2022) and surgery (Wang et al. 2023). Since HMDs are the portable alternative to the standard computer monitors, they have the potential to revolutionize surgery by enabling augmenting the operating field through digital data visualization (Quero et al. 2019), (Acidi et al. 2023), (Brockmeyer et al. 2023). Overlaying an image, such as radiography (X-ray), magnetic resonance imaging (MRI), or computed tomography (CT) on anatomical landmarks allows the operator to visualize organs, vessels, and irregularities such as tumors (England et al. 2023) compared the perception of images by radiologists using HDMs or traditional monitor, finding that HDMs provided a higher quality and thus more actionable image. The application of HDMs in surgery may help to improve efficiency by providing the doctor with a more accurate preoperative image. (Patric & Baowei 2023) described the interface of the AR-based system for visualization of prostate biopsy with the color and transparency of each element of the 3D model being adjustable in real-time. (Pan et al. 2020) described AR-based navigation in deep anterior lamellar keratoplasty, finding that AR enables accurate detection and tracking of the corneal contour complex in real-time. Another interesting application of HMDs is a medical ultrasound-guided 3D visualization (Ruger et al. 2020) (Nguyen et al. 2022). (von Haxthausen et al. 2023) presented an MR-based real-time volumetric in situ ultrasound for guiding vascular punctures. The holographic remote mode was used to send the rendered images to the HMDs. One of the main issues in the wide application of AR/MR in surgery is providing a sense of depth perception for the operator. The main limitation of the proposed approach is the difficulty in distinguishing relevant structures from noise and occlusion.

Machine Learning (ML) and particularly deep neural networks (DNNs) have revolutionized image segmentation (Chen et al. 2018), (Polyviou & Zamani 2023), (Hasan et al. 2023), (Chen et al 2023). Precise segmentation of lesions may contribute to efficient diagnostics and more effective, targeted therapy. For example, (Hosny et al. 2019) presented an algorithm for the segmentation of pigmented skin lesions, which enables diagnoses at an earlier stage without invasive medical procedures. Given its flexibility and scalability, ML can be an efficient tool for cancer diagnosis, in particular, the early disease stages (Young et al. 2020), (Granata et al. 2023). (Hayward et al. 2010) assessed multi-layer perceptron neural networks, Bayesian nets, and locally weighted naive Bayesian nets for clinical performance in a pancreatic cancer database. They found that ML algorithms provide a substantial improvement in predicting clinical outcomes. The most commonly used ML-based algorithms in image semantic segmentation, in particular in segmentation of different tumors, are Convolutional Neural Networks (CNNs) (Badrinarayanan et al. 2017), particularly the U-Net (Li et al. 2020), and its variation U-Net++ (Zhou et al. 2018), R2UNet (Alom et al. 2019). (Ren et al. 2023) examined the application of Attention U-Net to the prediction of solid pancreatic tumors. The proposed approach was based on feature fusion to assess the extent and boundaries of solid tumors. This approach was particularly helpful in generating early-stage images of tumors, thereby augmenting the training and testing sets. In (Janssen et al. 2021)U-nets with a DenseNet161 encoder were applied to the segmentation of residual tumors in pancreatic cancer histopathology samples. The results obtained show that AI-based algorithms can help the assessment of residual tumor burden. Another application of ML was shown by (Lee et al. 2021), i.e. the evaluation of the survival prediction of pancreas cancer based on Random Forest and the Cox proportional-hazards model.

In this paper, we also propose a so-the virtual shared experience paradigm, in which the primary HMD is worn by physicians with a secondary HMD worn by patients. Mixed Reality and Artificial Intelligence were applied to prepare 3D visualizations of preoperative surgical oncology patients' imaging.

2 Research Methodology

The study "Holographic MedAssistant" was conducted following the Declaration of Helsinki, and approved by the Medical Ethical Committee of the Jagiellonian University Medical College (JUMC) in Krakow, Poland No: 1072.6120.27.2020 and 1072.6120.92.2022.

2.1 Image Segmentation Based on Opened Database Source

Pancreatic segmentation from abdominal computer tomography (CT) images is a challenge because the morphology of the pancreas, i.e., its shape and position, has significant variability and may result in blurred boundaries (Dai et al. 2023). Also, the pancreas makes up a small amount of an entire abdominal CT scan. Moreover, the often the border between the pancreas and background is very subtle making it especially challenging to precisely define its boundaries. Segmentation was usually done manually by an expert moving a pointer. This was highly inefficient and often subject to error depending on the experience of the expert, especially when considering such challenging organs as the pancreas. Thus, accurate and automated segmentation will be important in the future of surgical planning. However, automated pancreas segmentation will also face the challenges described in segmenting a pancreas manually (Bagheri et al. 2020). In this paper, the data were obtained and delivered as de-identified DICOM files from open datasets. We have selected from a large collection (-100 3D CT images -) of healthy patients, namely 1) 281 patients with pancreatic tumors, (Simpson et al. 2019) and 2) 80healthy patients (Roth et al. 2015), and the relevant anatomical structures were labeled using a series of Machine Learning-based segmentation algorithms by You Only Look Once (YOLO) version 7, which is open-source software to use under GNU General Public License v3.0 license (see, Fig. 1).

In this study, CT dicom files were processed in an open-source medical image analysis software, 3D Slicer (version 5.2.2, functiongrow from seeds function) to segment key structures. Anatomical landmarks including the pancreas, superior mesenteric vein (SMV), splenic vein (SV), portal vein (PV), abdominal aorta, and celiac trunk along with its branches were isolated and converted into a 3D mask using a combination of region-based segmentation to define organs and blood vessels as a volume rendering. An output surface matrix, or model, was obtained that identifies an object or instance to which each pixel belongs using input tags, or seeds. Object detection, i.e. localizing and identifying structures in a digital image or video was done first (Amit et al. 2020), followed by the bounding box, and ultimately object classification. Figure 2 shows an object detection example in a CT scan to show the liver and spine, i.e. it shows the bounding boxes around the detected regions. This is a different procedure than semantic segmentation, as in semantic segmentation the algorithm will classify each pixel (or voxel in 3D images) in a class (Thoma 2016). The semantic segmentation on a CT slice was visualized in Fig. 3 as a example.

The detection of pancreatic lesions consists of three stages. First, the region of interest (ROI) containing the pancreas, then the detection of a lesion in a pre-selected area of interest, and clinical validation consisting in comparing the results of the pancreatic lesion detection, including algorithms alone and combining the results of the algorithms with radiological verification to the standard approach, i.e. manual radiological assessment. The automated algorithm relies on a pipeline with two major steps, first is to detect the ROI i.e. the area around the pancreas, and then feed this detected ROI to another step that would perform the final segmentation. From a computer science point of view, the first step is called object detection and it relies on the YOLOv7 algorithm, while the second step is called semantic segmentation and relies on the 3D-UNET algorithm.

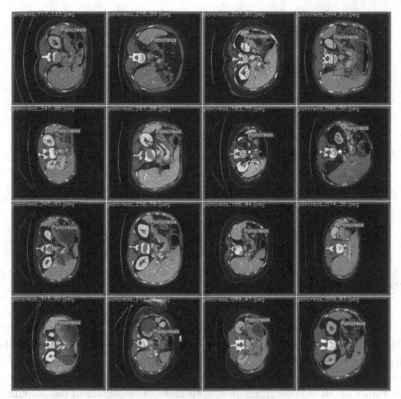

Fig. 1. Automatically generated region of interest by the YOLO training script

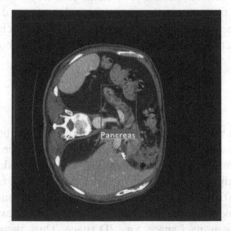

Fig. 2. Object detection in CT scan image. Red box around the pancreatic region. (Color figure online)

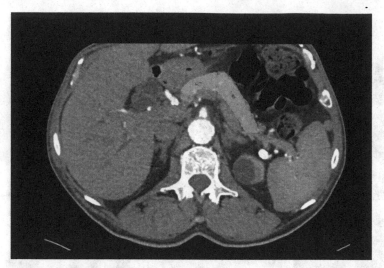

Fig. 3. Semantic segmentation in CT scan image. Note that the pancreas was marked by yellow color. (Color figure online)

The YOLO algorithm depends on deep learning for object detection (Redmon et al. 2016). It depends on the idea of the images passing only once through the neural network, hence the name, this is done by dividing the input image into a grid and predicting for each grid cell the bounding box and the probability of that class. The algorithm predicts different values about the object, i.e. the coordinates of the center of the bounding box around the object, the height and width of the bounding box, the class of the object, and the probability, or the confidence of the prediction. This way of working may cause the algorithm to detect the object multiple times, to avoid duplicate detections of the same object the algorithm uses non-maximum suppression (NMS), which works by calculating a metric called Intersection over Union or (IOU) between the boxes according to the following formula.

$$IOU = \frac{Area\ of\ overlap}{Area\ of\ Union}. \tag{1}$$

If the IOU between two boxes is larger than a threshold, the box with a higher confidence score is chosen and the other is ignored. There have been many improvements to the YOLO algorithm (Redmon & Farhadi 2017), (Bochkovskiy et al. 2020), (Zhu et al. 2021). In this study, YOLO version 7 (YOLOv7), which was released in 2022, is applied (Wang et al. 2022). It has several structural modifications that provide higher accuracy, faster performance, improved scalability, and greater flexibility for customization. YOLOv7 operates in pixel space, i.e., 2D space. Thus, there is a need to extract the three-dimensional ROI for the pancreas from different anatomical planes (Axial, Coronal, Sagittal) and combine this information to get the 3D ROI. Figure 4 shows the general idea of the YOLOv7 algorithm. The first row shows the pancreas detection in the three planes, combining this information would produce the coordinates in the voxel space.

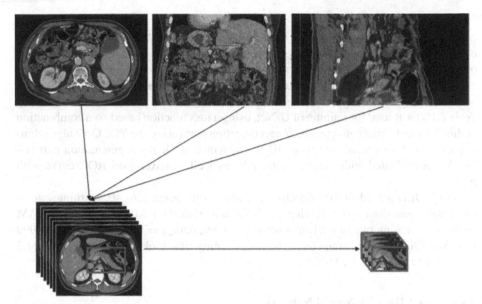

Fig. 4. The general functional structure of the YOLOv7 algorithm to detect the pancreas 3D ROI.

The next step, i.e., training the 3D UNET usually requires a substantial amount of computational power. However, since the image size will be significantly reduced, as shown in Fig. 4, the computational power will likewise be reduced allowing more freedom to optimize network parameters.

UNET is a convolutional neural network architecture, which was introduced by Ronneberger et. al (2015) (Ronneberger et al. 2015), it was built upon a well-established architecture called a fully connected network (FCN) (Shelhamer et al. 2014), to perform semantic segmentation on biomedical images, in the original paper, which was cited more than 62,000 times by the time this article was written, described the architecture as having two paths contracting path (also known as encoder) and an expansive path (also known as a decoder). The contracting path consists of 3×3 convolutional layers followed by 2×2 max-pooling layers with strides equal to two, after each max-pooling the number of features channels is doubled, while the expansive path is like a mirror for the contracting path with upsampling layers instead of max pooling, and a final 1×1 convolutional layer that should have a number of channels equal to the required number of classes, UNET also have skip connections between the two paths, which copies the images from steps of the contracting path to the mirrored stages of the expansive path.

The architecture showed promising results when applied to biomedical images especially when applying data augmentation with elastic deformation and trained with a weighted loss function with reasonable training time.

Although the original work considered 2D images only, the 3D UNET appeared later in 2016 to perform volumetric segmentation, using $3 \times 3 \times 3$ window convolutional layers followed by $2 \times 2 \times 2$ max-pooling layers with strides equal to two, This had many uses in segmenting CT images (Wu et al. 2020) and MRI images (Tomassini et al. 2023).

3D UNET would require more parameters which would apply limitations on the complexity of the model, also 3D data needs more memory space to handle, which might affect the size of the batches, we tend to deal with this problem by performing object detection step first to significantly reduce the size of the input data.

These steps were implemented using Python in the Google Colab Pro cloud service environment. NVIDIA T4 GPU was used for training of YOLO v7 algorithm whereas Tesla A100 was used for training of U-Net, using a loss function based on a combination of dice loss and Cross entropy. The object detection part (using the YOLO v7 algorithm) was evaluated for precision and recall. The semantic while the segmentation part (U-New) was evaluated with the dice sore, IOU as well as voxel-level ROC curve with AUC.

For YOLO a total of 100 epochs were used, with batch size 40, learning rate = 0.01, and momentum = 0.937, whereas U-Net was trained for 50 epochs, using ADAM optimizer, learning rate of 0.01, momentum = 0.99, beta_1 = 0.9 and beta_2 = 0.999 with 544,970 trainable parameters. The total training time took approximately 4 h (1.5 h for YOLO and 2.5 h for U-Net).

2.1.1 Input Data for Neural Network

The input data should be standardized to be inserted into a neural network using YOLOv7. The proper format of data is to have pairs of images and text files, where the text files contain information about the objects in the image, in it the class of the object should be specified, as well as the coordinates of the center of the bounding box with the high and width of that box, Fig. 4 shows the proper encoding of the data. Coordination and dimensional information should be normalized to have values between zero and one, this can be done by assuming that the top left corner of the image has the coordination of (0, 0) and the bottom right corner has the coordination of (1, 1), see Fig. 5.

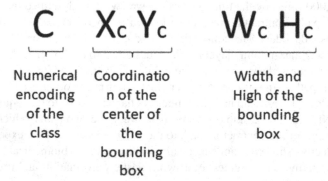

Fig. 5. Data encoding inside text files so that they can be used as input to the YOLOv7 algorithm.

Thus, even though the masks provided by experts have only the semantic segmentation information i.e., the class of each voxel, it is relatively easy to generate information about the bounding box, since the algorithm needs only to get the largest bounding box in each plane to build a good 3D box. We chose only to train on the 2D images that have bounding boxes with sizes greater than 95.00% of the largest bounding box in that image. In practice, the steps to generate the data for YOLOv7 are following repeat step two for the other planes.

- Step 1: Load the image.
- Step 2: Iterate through the slices in one plane.
- Step 3: Check if the image has a pancreas.
- Step 4: if not skip this slice.
- if yes:

  - Detect the bounding box.
  - Register its coordinates and its size,
  - Register the number of the slice.

- Step 5: When done from all slices, calculate the max bounding box size.
- Step 6: iterate through the registered sizes.
- Step 7: if the size of the bounding box is greater or equal to the max size:

  - Adjust the window/level of the image to the abdominal preset.
  - Export the image as a jpeg file.
  - Normalize the coordinates.
  - Add numerical encode for the plane (0 for Axial, 1 for Coronal, and 2 for Sagittal)
  - Export this information as a text file that has the same name as the image.

After generating all training data, it should be divided into three sets, i.e., training 60.00%, validation 10.00%, and testing 30.00%. The training set is the largest portion of the dataset and is used to train the model. It is used to optimize the model's parameters and learn patterns from the data. The model is exposed to both input data and corresponding output labels during training. The validation set is used to fine-tune the model and select the best hyperparameters. It is typically used for model selection, hyperparameter tuning, and performance monitoring. The validation set helps to evaluate the model's performance on unseen data and can be used to make adjustments to improve the model's generalization. The test set is a completely independent dataset that is used to evaluate the final performance of the model. It is used to simulate the model's performance on new, unseen data. The test set should be representative of the real-world data the model is expected to encounter. The model should not be exposed to the test set during the training or validation phases to prevent any potential bias or overfitting.

Training time took approximately 4 h (1.5 h for YOLO v7 algorithm and 2.5 h for U-Net). The YOLO v7 algorithm model performance expressed as a relation between the precision and recall is visualized on the precision-recall (PR) plot in Fig. 6.

The U-Net model performance expressed as a dice score in the test set (independent from model development) was 0.73 (95.00%CI: 0.68–0.77) for healthy subjects and 0.72 (95.00%CI: 0.7–0.74) for patients with cancer. The IOU was 0.58 (95%CI: 0.53–0.63) and 0.57 (95.00%CI: 0.54–0.6), respectively. Voxel-level AUCs were 0.9865 (95.00%CI: 0.98646–0.98658) and 0.9898 (95.00%CI: 0.98976–0.98989), respectively. High values

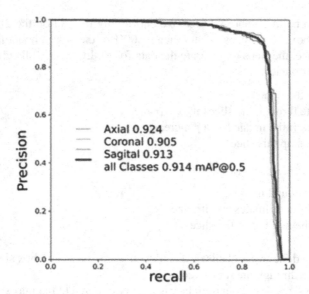

Fig. 6. Precision-Recall graph for YOLO algorithm.

of AUCs compared to the values of dice/IOU resulted in the good identification of background voxels, which are not taken into account in the dice/IOU metrics. The AUCs are voxel-level hence the number of observations is very large resulting in very narrow confidence intervals Fig. 7 and Fig. 8.

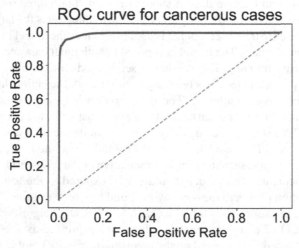

Fig. 7. ROC curve for cancerous cases.

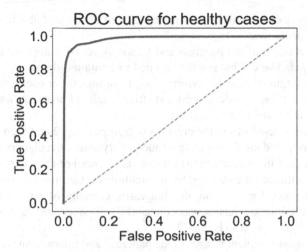

Fig. 8. ROC curve for healthy cases.

2.2 Future Manual Segmentation Approach to Machine Learning Concept

The next stage of this project is to gather data from local university hospitals and anonymized them, then data can be uploaded to the open-source medical imaging software, 3D Slicer (version 5.2.2). The resulting structures transfer into color-coded segments visible on CT scans and convert into a merged 3D file in STL format. Bearing in mind patient experience, additional structures also visualize to provide a more robust image that while largely not surgically relevant, helped them see and understand the relationship between local and overall anatomy, the extent of their surgery, and precisely what findings on a CT warranted them being scheduled for surgery to begin with. A standardized approach is to adopted to always visualize the same structures namely, bone, arterial, venous (portal and systemic), liver, gall bladder, stomach, spleen, kidneys, and pancreas, together with masses described by radiology along with separately marked areas of resection and potential anastomosis. According to this approach, several stages of manual segmentation have been provide:

- Step 1: independent radiologists make the characteristic points and the pancreas on each cross-section of each image according to a developed and strictly defined protocol, which served as partly a training set and partly as a bounding box.
- Step 2: detection models for each point and pancreas are constructed. The diagnostic capabilities of the constructed models, calculated based on the test set, are used to calculate the sample size required for validation, which will be performed on an independent, new dataset obtained from other centers. The new data set is evaluated by a panel of three independent experts, which enabled the selection of the so-called Ground Truth, based on which the diagnostic ability to detect characteristic points and the pancreas will be assessed. For each point, a binary decision will be determined, as well as the probabilities of the given class. Parameters like sensitivity, and specificity, the area under the ROC curve, and parameters related to the classical (JA) FROC methodology for MRMC-type problems are used as diagnostic endpoints. For each

point, a binary decision will be determined as well as the probability of cancer, i.e. semantic segmentation.

- Step 3: segmentation of the pancreas and tumor. A set of pancreatic cancer patient data is obtained. The CT images are cropped to contain only an area that included the pancreas. Segmentation is performed by radiologists on each cross-section of each image according to a developed and strictly defined protocol, which is treated as partly a training and partly a test set.
- Step 4: validation results from the previous two steps (Step 2 and Step 3) are used to calculate the required number of cases to adequately assess the diagnostic capacity of the created models in comparison to radiologists. A panel of three experts segmented the pancreas, with cancer confirmed by histopathology, forming the so-called Ground Truth – a reference for assessing the diagnostic capacity of both radiologists and algorithms. A validation dataset was collected from pancreatic cancer patients and non-pancreatic patients who had a CT.
- Step 5: radiologists segment images of the pancreas and tumors. An algorithm-based segmentation was performed independently (first detect the area of interest, then segment the pancreas and tumor).
- Step 6: The cases segmented by the algorithm are reviewed by radiologists. This allowed the radiologists' diagnostic capacity to be compared to the algorithm and radiologists assisted by the algorithm. The time to diagnose, cognitive load, and fatigue of the radiologist is also measured. Sensitivity, specificity, the area under the ROC curve, and parameters related to the classical (JA)FROC methodology for MRMC-type problems were diagnostic endpoints. The ability to segment was assessed using the Dice coefficient. Moreover, the number of observations in the validation set is sufficient to perform analogous analyses with subgroups defined by confounding factors.

2.3 Mixed Reality Application with the Possibility of Artificial Intelligence Enhancement as a Future Approach

Development of a mixed reality application that has the potential for enhancement through the integration of Artificial Intelligence (AI) technology. The mention of AI enhancement implies that the application could utilize AI algorithms, techniques, or functionalities to enhance its capabilities. AI can bring various benefits to mixed reality applications, such as improved object recognition, intelligent interaction, natural language processing, or personalized experiences. The specific AI enhancements would depend on the goals and requirements of the application, but the overarching idea is to leverage AI to augment and optimize the mixed reality experience for users. Based on our knowledge of manual individual case studies preprocedural planning, as described below, we can easily transfer this application to an AI approach based on dedicated algorithms like YOLO.

The creation of the Mixed Reality-based application, which will be tailored to run on HMDs, e.g., Microsoft HoloLens 2, to display Dicom data as 3D models can be described in the two steps. The first is to create the model, using data in the Dicom format. The second is the creation of the application to visualize the model. Before proceeding to step one, it is necessary to understand what kind of data will be processed in step one.

When performing an MRI or CT scan the human body is split into slices of varying millimeter thickness. Each slice is saved next as a grey-scale Dicom file similar to the picture. The quality of a model resulting from this data depends on the size of the pixel used to save the slice as a picture and the thickness between each slice. Typical thickness can be between 0.5–6 mm, depending on the purpose and quality needed. Thinner slices minimize the signal-to-noise ratio and produce optimal 3D segmentation models. The first step in segmentation utilizes the open-source software 3DSlicer. Model creation (step 1) is as follows:

- Load Dicom files into 3DSlicer. Data is displayed as grayscale pictures where the user can manipulate the slider to move between slices.
- Using the module "Segment Editor" the user creates layers on visible image slices signifying the anatomical structure to be segmented.
- The 3Dslicer function "Threshold", allows users to set a range of greyscale that will automatically label structures fitting within that range across all available slices. This involves specifying the minimum and maximum intensities based on the histogram of a region of interest in the slice view, i.e., where a high-intensity, white region such as bone is selected while omitting soft tissues. This allows users to preview what will be included. After confirming that the selected range captures the desired structures, the resulting mesh can be previewed in 3D.
- This mesh is referred to as a mask and provides the limits of structures that will be segmented.
- Additional algorithms applied to this mesh include seeding and filling slices. Seeding involves tagging two or more specific regions of interest in sagittal, coronal, and axial views of a CT scan. For example, an object and background, where the object corresponds to the desired organ and the background corresponds to all undesired regions. After tagging these respective seeds, a customized GrowCut algorithm is applied to grow the region of seeded interest while excluding the region of undesired structures. This expands the binary "object" and "background" tags voxel by voxel along with a statistical weight as to the probability a given voxel still corresponds to the object. Filling slices is similar except it seeds only an "object" in one view, i.e., axial predominantly for vertical structures such as the inferior vena cava. Upon manually tagging the object in multiple levels of the CT scan, the Fill between Slices algorithm, based on ND morphological contour interpolation, is applied to form a 3D mask corresponding to the object. These algorithms are automated, however, the resulting models require varying degrees of manual correction which is done before accepting the finalized 3D mask they generate.
- Exporting the finalized model will be done via the function "Export segment to file" with OBJ format. This will then be accepted by Unreal Engine.

Creating the MR-based application (step 2) with the Unreal Engine is as follows

- Install the Visual Studio package.
- Start Unreal Engine and create a simple new blank mobile application.
- Add the plugin "Microsoft OpenXR" which adds tools useful for Extended Reality devices.
- Create a new object which will use the HoloLens 2 positional data to create a virtual space.

This allows the application to understand the position and perspective from which a user wearing the HoloLens 2 will be watching the 3D model (see Figure 9).

- Create an AR session to allow applications to link with Augmented Reality devices.
- AR session configuration.
- A final plugin to the project, "Mixed Reality UX Tools" will control interactions between the user, environment, and the displayed model.
- Import the created 3D model and interact with it in a virtual space
- Finally, this bundle is packaged as a file that can be directly imported to any HoloLens 2 device (see Fig. 10).

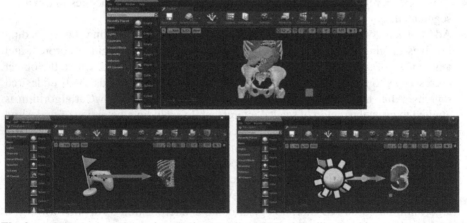

Fig. 9. A final plugin to the project, "Mixed Reality UX Tools" will control interactions between the user, environment, and the displayed model.

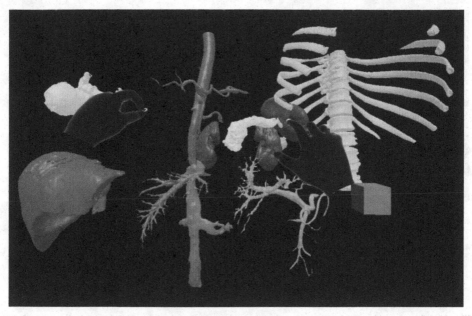

Fig. 10. Manual individual case studies preprocedural planning as a future approach for AI algorithms. 3D visualization of the pancreas and related organs as a digital file that can be directly imported to any HoloLens 2 device.

3   Case Study Description to Present the Concept of Automatization for Preprocedural Planning with 3D Visualization

The presented case study refers to a 74-year-old male with cancer involving the head of the pancreas who was scheduled for a pancreaticoduodenectomy. Upon review of the organ segmentation model, a region at the SMV/PV junction measuring approximately 2.5 cm was identified as likely requiring intraoperative reconstruction to avert changing the procedure into a prophylactic bypass anastomosis, see Fig. 11 and Fig. 12.

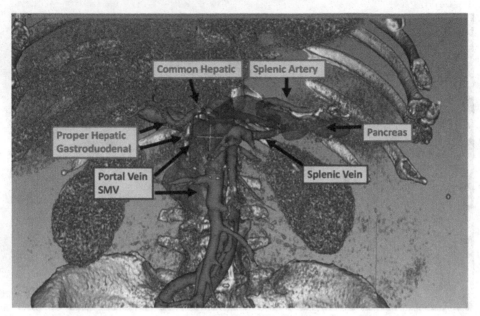

Fig. 11. Segmentation and volume rendering of key anatomical landmarks including arteries, veins, and pancreas. The arteries are red, the veins are purple, and the pancreas was marked by translucent blue color. The yellow crosshair indicates the region overall between the SMV/PV and pancreas, i.e., the area potentially requiring vessel reconstruction.

Based on the source data, is it possible to visualize images in the form of 3D images in the pre-procedural process (see Fig. 13) as well as interprocedural (see Fig. 14).

The results can beconfirmed intraoperatively where a patch was successfully applied following vessel dissection and pancreatic head resection (see Fig. 15).

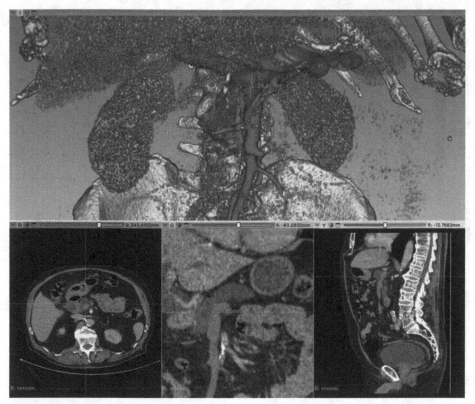

Fig. 12. Segmentation and volume rendering including CT scan image views of the approximately 2.5 cm region of potential vessel reconstruction. The arteries were marked by red color, veins are marked by purple color, while the pancreas was marked by translucent blue color. The yellow crosshair indicates the region overall between the SMV/PV and pancreas, i.e., the area potentially requiring vessel reconstruction (lower image: views from left to right – horizontal, coronal, sagittal). (Color figure online)

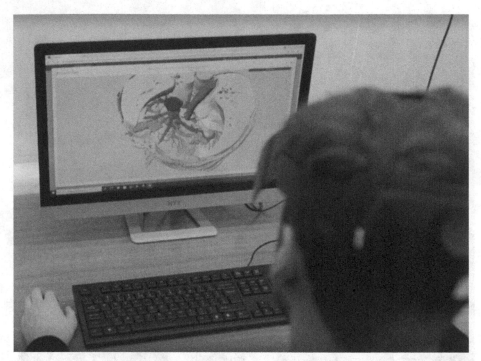

Fig. 13. Distal pancreatectomy sample. Superior view angled caudal to rostral showing a model rendering that is to be uploaded onto the HoloLens 2. Arteries are in red, systemic veins in blue, portal veins in purple, and lungs in pink, with a yellow lesion proximal to the pancreatic tail section in orange. (Color figure online)

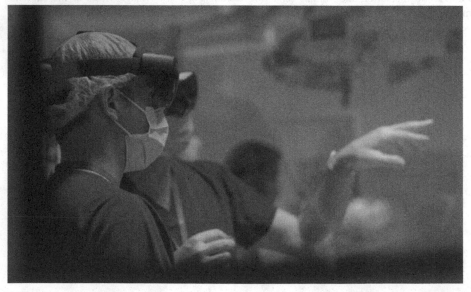

Fig. 14. Intraoperative use of the HoloLens2 depicting surgeons discussing a case in a shared experience virtual space.

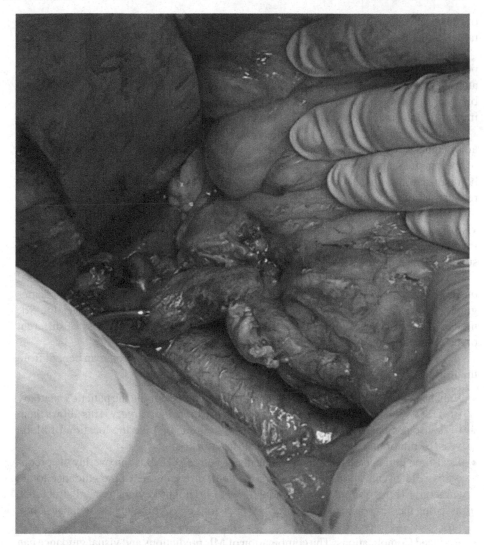

Fig. 15. Completed blood patch at the region predicted by 3D visualization.

4   Conclusion

The availability of an automated and non-invasive tool for visualization of the pancreas and its abnormalities can greatly improve the pre and intraoperative process along with providing previously impossible benefits to patient experience. Organ and vessel segmentation with subsequent 3D visualization with Artificial Intelligence and Mixed Reality enhancement can substantially improve planning, reduce the incidence of unforeseen intraoperative decision-making, and improve clinical outcomes. Thus, the proposed approach can be considered as both an accurate and efficient image segmentation tool of the pancreas and its abnormalities, which is crucial for diagnostics and delivery of targeted therapy.

In the future, the application of preoperative image-guided 3D visualization supported by Machine Learning to the prediction of organ reconstruction during pancreaticoduodenectomy via Head-Mounted Displays holds tremendous potential. This combination of technologies can revolutionize surgical planning and execution, leading to improved outcomes and enhanced patient care.

With advances in medical imaging techniques, including computed tomography and magnetic resonance imaging, surgeons have access to detailed 3D representations of the patient's anatomy. By utilizing ML algorithms, these preoperative images can be analyzed and processed to provide accurate predictions and simulations of organ reconstruction outcomes.

Head-Mounted Displays, such as augmented reality glasses, enable surgeons to visualize the patient's anatomy in a more immersive and intuitive manner. By wearing HMDs, surgeons can overlay the 3D visualizations onto the patient's body during surgery, enhancing their spatial awareness and precision.

Machine Learning algorithms play a crucial role in this process. They can be trained on large datasets of preoperative images, incorporating factors such as patient demographics, disease characteristics, and surgical outcomes. This training enables the ML models to learn patterns and make accurate predictions about the success of different organ reconstruction approaches.

By leveraging ML-supported 3D visualization and HMDs, surgeons can benefit from the following future perspectives:

- Enhanced Surgical Planning: Surgeons can thoroughly examine the patient's anatomy in 3D and visualize potential complications before the actual surgery. This allows them to devise personalized surgical plans, considering factors like the location of blood vessels, tumor margins, and other critical structures.
- Real-time Intraoperative Guidance: During the surgery, HMDs can overlay the preoperative 3D visualizations onto the surgical field, providing real-time guidance to the surgeon. ML algorithms can help identify and highlight key anatomical structures, assisting the surgeon in making informed decisions and optimizing the reconstruction process.
- Reduced Complications: The combination of ML predictions and visual guidance can help minimize the risk of complications during pancreaticoduodenectomy. Surgeons can anticipate potential issues, such as vascular involvement or inadequate margins, and adjust their approach accordingly, thereby reducing postoperative complications and improving patient outcomes.
- Training and Education: ML-supported 3D visualization via HMDs can be a valuable tool for training new surgeons. Trainees can benefit from interactive virtual simulations, allowing them to practice complex procedures and refine their skills in a controlled environment before performing surgeries on actual patients.
- Remote Collaboration and Expertise: The integration of ML and HMDs also enables remote collaboration and consultation with experts. Surgeons can share live surgical views and 3D visualizations with off-site specialists, allowing for real-time guidance

and support during complex cases. This can be particularly beneficial in regions with limited access to specialized surgical expertise.

While these future perspectives hold great promise, their realization requires further advancements in medical imaging, ML algorithms, and HMD technologies. Additionally, comprehensive validation through clinical trials and regulatory approvals will be essential to ensure the safety and efficacy of these applications.

In summary, the application of preoperative image-guided 3D visualization supported by Machine Learning to the prediction of organ reconstruction during pancreaticoduodenectomy via Head-Mounted Displays has the potential to transform surgical practices. By leveraging ML algorithms and immersive visualization, surgeons can enhance surgical planning, and intraoperative guidance, and ultimately improve patient outcomes in this complex surgical procedure.

Acknowledgments. This study was supported by the National Centre for Research and Development (Grant Lider No. LIDER/17/0064/L-11/19/NCBR/ 2020).

Data Availability The data that support the findings of this study are available from the corresponding author upon reasonable request.

References

Acidi, B., Ghallab, M., Cotin, S., Vibert, E., Golse, N.: Augmented reality in liver surgery. J. Visc. Surg. **160**(2), 118–126 (2023). https://doi.org/10.1016/j.jviscsurg.2023.01.008

Alom, M.Z., Yakopcic, C., Hasan, M., Taha, T.M., Asari, V.K.: Recurrent residual U-Net for medical image segmentation. J. Med. Imaging (Bellingham) **6**(1), 014006 (2019). https://doi.org/10.1117/1.Jmi.6.1.014006

Amit, Y., Felzenszwalb, P., Girshick, R.: Object detection. In Computer Vision: A Reference Guide, pp. 1–9. Springer International Publishing (2020). https://doi.org/10.1007/978-3-030-03243-2_660-1

Badrinarayanan, V., Kendall, A., Cipolla, R.: SegNet: a deep convolutional encoder-decoder architecture for image segmentation. IEEE Trans. Pattern Anal. Mach. Intell. **39**(12), 2481–2495 (2017). https://doi.org/10.1109/tpami.2016.2644615

Bagheri, M.H., et al.: Technical and Clinical factors affecting success rate of a deep learning method for pancreas segmentation on CT. Acad. Radiol. **27**(5), 689–695 (2020). https://doi.org/10.1016/j.acra.2019.08.014

Bochkovskiy, A., Wang, C.Y., Liao, H.-Y.M.: YOLOv4: Optimal Speed and Accuracy of Object Detection. ArXiv, abs/2004.10934 (2020)

Brockmeyer, P., Wiechens, B., Schliephake, H.: The role of augmented reality in the advancement of minimally invasive surgery procedures: a scoping review. Bioengineering (Basel), **10**(4), 501 (2023). https://doi.org/10.3390/bioengineering10040501

Chen, L.C., Papandreou, G., Kokkinos, I., Murphy, K., Yuille, A.L.: DeepLab: semantic image segmentation with deep convolutional nets, atrous convolution, and fully connected CRFs. IEEE Trans. Pattern Anal. Mach. Intell. **40**(4), 834–848 (2018). https://doi.org/10.1109/TPAMI. 2017.2699184

Chen, P.T., et al.: Pancreatic cancer detection on CT scans with deep learning: a nationwide population-based study. Radiology **306**(1), 172–182 (2023). https://doi.org/10.1148/radiol. 220152

Dai, S., Zhu, Y., Jiang, X., Yu, F., Lin, J., Yang, D.: TD-Net: trans-deformer network for automatic pancreas segmentation. Neurocomputing **517**, 279–293 (2023). https://doi.org/10.1016/j.neu com.2022.10.060

England, A., et al.: A comparison of perceived image quality between computer display monitors and augmented reality smart glasses. Radiography **29**(3), 641–646 (2023). https://doi.org/10. 1016/j.radi.2023.04.010

Garlinska, M., Osial, M., Proniewska, K., Pregowska, A.: The influence of emerging technologies on distance education. Electronics **12**(7), 1550 (2023). https://www.mdpi.com/2079-9292/12/ 7/1550

Gheorghe, G., et al.: Early Diagnosis of pancreatic cancer: the key for survival. Diagnostics (Basel), **10**(11), 869 (2020). https://doi.org/10.3390/diagnostics10110869

Granata, V., et al.: Risk assessment and pancreatic cancer: diagnostic management and artificial intelligence. Cancers (Basel), **15**(2), 351 (2023). https://doi.org/10.3390/cancers15020351

Hasan, M.M., Islam, M.U., Sadeq, M.J., Fung, W K., Uddin, J.: Review on the evaluation and development of artificial intelligence for COVID-19 containment. Sensors (Basel), **23**(1), 527 (2023). https://doi.org/10.3390/s23010527

Hayward, J., Alvarez, S.A., Ruiz, C., Sullivan, M., Tseng, J., Whalen, G.: Machine learning of clinical performance in a pancreatic cancer database. Artif. Intell. Med. **49**(3), 187–195 (2010). https://doi.org/10.1016/j.artmed.2010.04.009

Hosny, K.M., Kassem, M.A., Foaud, M.M.: Classification of skin lesions using transfer learning and augmentation with Alex-net. PLoS ONE **14**(5), e0217293 (2019). https://doi.org/10.1371/ journal.pone.0217293

Janssen, B.V., et al.: Artificial intelligence-based segmentation of residual tumor in histopathology of pancreatic cancer after neoadjuvant treatment. Cancers (Basel), **13**(20), 5089 (2021). https:// doi.org/10.3390/cancers13205089

Kenner, B., et al.: Artificial intelligence and early detection of pancreatic cancer: 2020 summative review. Pancreas **50**(3), 251–279 (2021). https://doi.org/10.1097/MPA.0000000000001762

Klinker, K., Wiesche, M., Krcmar, H.: Digital transformation in health care: augmented reality for hands-free service innovation. Inf. Syst. Front. **22**(6), 1419–1431 (2020). https://doi.org/ 10.1007/s10796-019-09937-7

Kochanski, R.B., Lombardi, J.M., Laratta, J.L., Lehman, R.A., O'Toole, J.E.: Image-guided navigation and robotics in spine surgery. Neurosurgery **84**(6), 1179–1189 (2019). https://doi.org/ 10.1093/neuros/nyy630

Lee, K.-S., et al.: Usefulness of artificial intelligence for predicting recurrence following surgery for pancreatic cancer: retrospective cohort study. Int. J. Surg. **93**, 106050 (2021). https://doi. org/10.1016/j.ijsu.2021.106050

Li, X., et al.: Multi-task refined boundary-supervision U-Net (MRBSU-Net) for gastrointestinal stromal tumor segmentation in endoscopic ultrasound (EUS) images. IEEE Access **8**, 5805–5816 (2020). https://doi.org/10.1109/ACCESS.2019.2963472

Nguyen, T., Plishker, W., Matisoff, A., Sharma, K., Shekhar, R.: HoloUS: augmented reality visualization of live ultrasound images using hololens for ultrasound-guided procedures. Int. J. Comput. Assist. Radiol. Surg. **17**(2), 385–391 (2022). https://doi.org/10.1007/s11548-021-02526-7

Pan, J., et al.: Real-time segmentation and tracking of excised corneal contour by deep neural networks for DALK surgical navigation. Comput. Meth. Progr. Biomed **197**, 105679 (2020). https://doi.org/10.1016/j.cmpb.2020.105679

Patric, B., Baowei, F.: An Advanced System with Advanced User Interfaces for Image-Guided Intervention Applications. SPIE, Proc (2023)

Polyviou, A., Zamani, E.D.: Are we nearly there yet? a desires & realities framework for Europe's AI strategy. Inf. Syst. Front. **25**(1), 143–159 (2023). https://doi.org/10.1007/s10796-022-102 85-2

Pregowska, A., Osial, M., Dolega-Dolegowski, D., Kolecki, R., Proniewska, K.: Information and communication technologies combined with mixed reality as supporting tools in medical education. Electronics, **11**(22), 3778 (2022). https://www.mdpi.com/2079-9292/11/22/3778

Quero, G., et al.: Virtual and augmented reality in oncologic liver surgery. Surg. Oncol. Clin. N. Am. **28**(1), 31–44 (2019). https://doi.org/10.1016/j.soc.2018.08.002

Rawla, P., Sunkara, T., Gaduputi, V.: Epidemiology of pancreatic cancer: global trends, etiology and risk factors. World J. Oncol. **10**(1), 10–27 (2019). https://doi.org/10.14740/wjon1166

Redmon, J., Divvala, S., Girshick, R., Farhadi, A.: You only look once: unified, real-time object detection. In: 2016 IEEE Conference on Computer Vision and Pattern Recognition (CVPR), pp. 779-788 (2016, 27–30 June 2016)

Redmon, J., Farhadi, A.: YOLO9000: Better, faster, stronger. In: 2017 IEEE Conference on Computer Vision and Pattern Recognition (CVPR), pp. 7263-7271 (2017, 21–26 July 2017)

Ren, Y., Zou, D., Xu, W., Zhao, X., Lu, W., He, X.: Bimodal segmentation and classification of endoscopic ultrasonography images for solid pancreatic tumor. Biomed. Sign. Process. Control **83**, 104591 (2023). https://doi.org/10.1016/j.bspc.2023.104591

Ronneberger, O., Fischer, P., Brox, T.: U-Net: Convolutional Networks for Biomedical Image Segmentation. ArXiv, abs/1505.04597 (2015)

Neher, P.F., Götz, M., Norajitra, T., Weber, C., Maier-Hein, K.H.: A machine learning based approach to fiber tractography using classifier voting. In: Navab, N., Hornegger, J., Wells, W.M., Frangi, A.F. (eds.) MICCAI 2015. LNCS, vol. 9349, pp. 45–52. Springer, Cham (2015). https://doi.org/10.1007/978-3-319-24553-9_6

Ruger, C., Feufel, M.A., Moosburner, S., Ozbek, C., Pratschke, J., Sauer, I.M.: Ultrasound in augmented reality: a mixed-methods evaluation of head-mounted displays in image-guided interventions. Int. J. Comput. Assist. Radiol. Surg. **15**(11), 1895–1905 (2020). https://doi.org/10.1007/s11548-020-02236-6

Shelhamer, E., Long, J., Darrell, T.: Fully convolutional networks for semantic segmentation. In: IEEE Conference on Computer Vision and Pattern Recognition (CVPR), pp. 3431–3440 (2014)

Simpson, A.L., et al.: A large annotated medical image dataset for the development and evaluation of segmentation algorithms (2019). arXiv:1902.09063. https://ui.adsabs.harvard.edu/abs/201 9arXiv190209063S. Accessed 01 Feb 2019

Thoma, M.: A Survey of Semantic Segmentation. ArXiv, abs/1602.06541 (2016)

Tomassini, S., Anbar, H., Sbrollini, A., Mortada, M.J., Burattini, L., Morettini, M.: A double-stage 3D U-net for on-cloud brain extraction and multi-structure segmentation from 7T MR volumes. Information, **14**(5), 282 (2023). https://www.mdpi.com/2078-2489/14/5/282

von Haxthausen, F., Rüger, C., Sieren, M.M., Kloeckner, R., Ernst, F.: Augmenting image-guided procedures through in situ visualization of 3d ultrasound via a head-mounted display. Sensors **23**(4), 2168 (2023). https://www.mdpi.com/1424-8220/23/4/2168

Wang, C.-Y., Bochkovskiy, A., Liao, H.-Y.M.: YOLOv7: Trainable bag-of-freebies sets new state-of-the-art for real-time object detectors. ArXiv, abs/2207.02696 (2022)

Wang, K., et al.: Fluorescence image-guided tumour surgery. Nature Rev. Bioeng. **1**(3), 161–179 (2023). https://doi.org/10.1038/s44222-022-00017-1

Wu, W., Gao, L., Duan, H., Huang, G., Ye, X., Nie, S.: Segmentation of pulmonary nodules in CT images based on 3D-UNET combined with three-dimensional conditional random field optimization. Med. Phys. **47**(9), 4054–4063 (2020). https://doi.org/10.1002/mp.14248

Young, M.R., Abrams, N., Ghosh, S., Rinaudo, J.A.S., Marquez, G., Srivastava, S.: Prediagnostic image data, artificial intelligence, and pancreatic cancer: a tell-tale sign to early detection. Pancreas **49**(7), 882–886 (2020). https://doi.org/10.1097/MPA.0000000000001603

Zhou, Z., Rahman Siddiquee, M.M., Tajbakhsh, N., Liang, J.: UNet++: a nested u-net architecture for medical image segmentation. In: Stoyanov, D., et al. (eds.) Deep Learning in Medical Image Analysis and Multimodal Learning for Clinical Decision Support Cham, pp. 3–11 (2018). https://doi.org/10.1007/978-3-030-00889-5_1

Zhu, X., Lyu, S., Wang, X., Zhao, Q.: TPH-YOLOv5: improved YOLOv5 based on transformer prediction head for object detection on drone-captured scenarios. In: IEEE/CVF International Conference on Computer Vision Workshops (ICCVW), pp. 2778–2788 (2021)

eXtended Reality & Artificial Intelligence-Based Surgical Training: A Review of Reviews

Giulia Pellegrino[1]([✉]), Maria Cristina Barba[1], Giovanni D'Errico[2], Muhammed Yusuf Küçükkara[3], and Lucio Tommaso De Paolis[1]

[1] Department of Engineering for Innovation, University of Salento, Lecce, Italy
giulia.pellegrino1@unisalento.it
[2] Department of Applied Science and Technology, Polytechnic University of Turin, Turin, Italy
[3] Computer Engineering Department, Sakarya University of Applied Sciences, Sakarya, Türkiye

Abstract. Recent technological innovations have profoundly transformed the approach to surgical training, necessitating a substantial paradigm shift by combining traditional approaches with new tools and methods. The use of simulated and interactive environments through eXtended Reality (XR) technologies, in combination with Artificial Intelligence (AI) techniques, is increasingly becoming a standard in this field.

In this paper, a review of reviews exploring the combined use of XR technologies and AI techniques for surgical training has been conducted. The specific objective is to analyze the attention that the scientific community has devoted to this topic, focusing on both specific surgical specialties and general applications.

The analysis suggests the need for a systematic and comprehensive update of the literature that examines studies across all surgical domains, includes a discussion of technological and methodological aspects, as well as clinical considerations, and contemplates the use of standardized metrics for study evaluation.

Keywords: extended reality · virtual reality · artificial intelligence · surgical training · review

1 Introduction

Surgical training represents a pivotal component within the realm of medicine. Its roots can be traced back to ancient times, with traditional surgical education primarily focusing on the training of aspiring surgeons through cadaver dissections and internships [7].

The 19th and 20th centuries witnessed notable advancements in medical and surgical technologies, consequently leading to substantial enhancements in the standards and methodologies of surgical training [25].

L. T. De Paolis et al. (Eds.): XR Salento 2023, LNCS 14218, pp. 345–355, 2023.
https://doi.org/10.1007/978-3-031-43401-3_22

Surgeons must acquire sufficient skills and experience to perform successful and safe operations on patients. Traditionally, these skills are developed through intensive practice and observation during internship and residency periods. However, the rapid development of technology and innovations in the digital age have significantly changed approaches to surgical training [5]. In this context, the COVID-19 pandemic has spurred a heightened focus on and advancement of remote education [22]. Therefore, medical education has also had to keep pace with innovations in the digital age. Combined methodologies in surgical education refers to the integration of traditional methods and technology-based approaches. It aims to provide more effective and safer surgical training with developing medical technology and training methods. Simulation in technology refers to the creation of digital replicas of real systems that provide a safe and controlled environment for analysing complex phenomena, testing hypotheses and predicting outcomes [28]. Interaction capabilities allow users to actively intervene in these digital models and change variables and inputs, not only enhancing experiential learning but also promoting creativity, problem solving and innovation [12]. Simulation-based training is the main combined methodology used to increase surgical skills and reduce error rates [6]. It is possible to achieve a simulated and interactive environment by making use of eXtended Reality (XR) technologies combined with Artificial Intelligence (AI) techniques. These technologies enable the creation of realistic, immersive, and interactive environments that closely resemble actual operating conditions [3]. Trainees can practice surgical procedures repeatedly, receiving instant AI-generated feedback without any risk to actual patients. Furthermore, integrating AI with XR provides the potential for telementoring [34]. Experienced surgeons can guide trainees remotely in real-time, demonstrating techniques, observing performance, and providing feedback, thereby overcoming geographical barriers and enriching the learning experience. This technologically-enhanced approach to surgical training has the potential to significantly improve surgical skill acquisition, reduce error rates, and ultimately lead to safer and more effective patient care [27]. XR is an umbrella term encompassing technologies such as Virtual Reality (VR), Augmented Reality (AR), and Mixed Reality (MR) [35]. These technologies enable users to interact with both the real and virtual worlds, finding applications in diverse fields such as military, education, industry, and entertainment [36]. XR technologies provide realistic and customised surgical training experiences, enabling students to receive training appropriate to their skills and knowledge levels [33]. AI is a branch of computer science focused on developing computer systems with learning and decision-making capabilities [26]. Nowadays, it is used in education, robotics, military, industry and many other fields [30]. AI-based XR technologies in surgical training provide students and young surgeons the chance to practice in a safe, controlled environment before performing complex procedures. These technologies can expedite the acquisition and application of surgical skills, bolster the confidence of inexperienced surgeons, and reduce medical errors [8]. In addition, AI-based XR technologies also significantly improve the surgical learning curve [23]. Such simulations accelerate students and young surgeons to gain experience so that they can deal with more complex procedures faster and more effectively [13]. By giving reproducible feedback of each procedure and immediate feedback of errors, these technologies make the learning process more efficient [9,10]. This can significantly reduce the learning curve, especially in surgical disciplines where practical experience is critical. The combined use of these technologies represents a recent and emerging paradigm in the scientific literature [24]. There is a growing need to organise the existing body of knowledge to address contemporary guidelines and trends. Currently, a systematic review of the literature regarding XR- and AI-based surgical training is underway, aiming to offer a comprehensive overview of the role played by these technologies in surgical training and establish a foundation for further improvements in this field. In this preliminary study, our objective is to assess and review the current landscape of systematic reviews conducted thus far, aiming to gain insights into the focal points of the scientific community regarding this topic. In Sect. 2, the Methods section is presented, detailing how the research was conducted (including the databases used, the search query, and the eligibility criteria for the review work). The results of the research are provided in Sect. 3, accompanied by a critical discussion of the current attention of the scientific community to the chosen research topic. Finally, Sect. 4 reports the conclusions of the study.

2 Methods

The review was conducted covering the period between March 2003 to February 2023 and the main databases in the engineering-medical area were queried (Scopus, PubMed and IEEEXplore). The following query was used, by taking into account titles, abstracts and keywords: ("extended reality" OR "virtual reality" OR "augmented reality" OR "mixed reality") AND ("artificial intelligence" OR "machine learning") AND "surgery" AND "training" AND (LIMIT-TO (DOC-TYPE, "review")). A total of 31 results were obtained, removing scientific articles obtained from more than one database. Analyzing the titles, abstracts and structure of the articles found, only half were consistent with the conducted research. In particular, 6 articles were excluded because they were not written in English, 4 because they did not concern surgical training, 4 because they were not reviews, 2 because they did not contemplate XR technologies, and 1 because it did not deal with AI and ML techniques.

3 Results and Discussion

3.1 Classification of the Selected Reviews

The 16 reviews that met the aforementioned exclusion criteria were categorized into two main groups. The first cluster encompasses the review papers focused on studies across various surgical specialties, while the second cluster comprises reviews focused on a single surgical specialty or a specific type of surgery. For the purpose of this study, we will refer to the first group as "general" and the second group as "specific" (see Fig. 1).

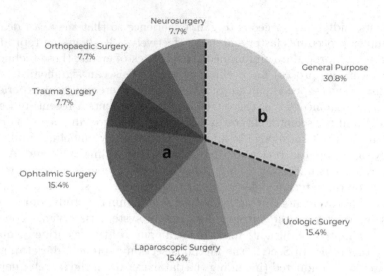

Fig. 1. Pie chart illustrating the percentage distributions of the two clusters in which the collected reviews were classified: a) specific and b) general. The chart includes the percentage distribution of specialties within cluster a).

3.2   Analysis of General Purpose Papers

The reviews that fall into the general purpose cluster are 4 [1, 16, 31, 32]. Among these, a systematic analysis is only evident in [32], although the specific search criteria used are unknown. However, the sample analysed with respect to the total, the database from which the results were extracted, and a table focusing on specific parameters are disclosed. Within this analysis, only 8 of the 32 results found are relevant to the topic of ML and AI applied to virtual reality-based surgical training. Furthermore, the analysis period covers only the years between 2015 and 2020, excluding the past two and a half years (2021–2023), which have witnessed a rich influx of studies in this field. The surgical specialties mentioned in this review paper encompass Thoracic Surgery, Neurosurgery, General Surgery. The review concludes that evidence in the literature is still scarce with regard to AI applied to VR simulators, and existing contributions focus mainly on its potential to stratify surgical performance and provide synthetic feedback in this regard. The review presented in [1] is provided as a narrative review of applications for surgical training and intra-operative guidance, focusing on the topics of autonomous surgery, robotic surgery and surgical navigation combined with AI and AR. Within this review, seven articles extracted from Scopus, PubMed and MEDLINE, published between January 2015 and January 2019, are analysed. The authors conclude that the use of AI in robotic surgery for both surgical training and intra-operative procedures increases the quality of the care [1]. In contrast, the overview [31] focuses on the use of autonomous and self-adaptive systems and data-driven training within VR-based training environments. The consulted databases are Medline, IEEE Xplore, ASME Digital Collection, ACM Digital Library, Google Scholar, and IET/IEEE Electronic Library (IEL). Adaptation was applied to the five major technologies in VR training: adaptive technology, haptic devices, head-mounted displays, evaluation, and autonomous agents. In medical VR training, adaptation is used in Bayesian network systems that have proven effective for automated adaptive virtual training. Frameworks, models, libraries and software tools are needed to enable adaptive systems for games. In VR training for rehabilitation, exercise difficulties can adapt, using a Bayesian framework, to the individual patient's abilities and functional status, thus avoiding maladaptation. Input data can be collected from a level of abstraction using wireless or audiovisual tracking devices to adapt to the patient's improvement over time. There is still no common infrastructure that makes automated technologies more combined and portable. A key step forward would be to produce a portable framework for VR automation that combines adaptation with each core technology in VR training. This would increase the benefits of automation and make adaptation more accessible. The [16] reflects how AR, AI, and ML can be combined together to form a surgical training system. It's a small and not systematic review.

3.3 Analysis of Non-general Purpose Papers

There are 10 specific reviews and they are listed in Table 1 together with a summary of their main characteristics. Among the surgical specialties there are 3 reviews concerning ophthalmology, 2 laparoscopy, 1 urology, 1 open trauma, 1 neurosurgery and 1 spinal surgery (see Fig. 1).

The reviews [2,14,19], are focused on ophthalmic surgery. While the first two are limited to surgical training, the third extends to techniques and applications related to surgical planning and intraoperative guidance. The latter deals with a wider range of techniques that are not limited to AI, but also include ML and Deep Learning (DL). None of them are systematic: the databases and the keywords are not stated, nor is the sample of works analyzed explicitly stated. Therefore, the three reviews have slightly different focuses. In [14] there are included distance educational training techniques that make use of both AI and VR/AR technologies. In [2], the applications of AI and VR are exclusively explored in relation to future trends in ophthalmic surgical education, while [19] highlights the intersection between computer vision, machine learning and ophthalmic microsurgery. The reviews agree in considering the rapid development and profitable use of these technologies in ophthalmic surgery to be relevant. However, the authors point out that training in the use of new teaching methodologies for academic staff [14], but also rigorous standardization and validation before implementation [2] are necessary for their acceptance. Ophthalmology is set back from other surgical specialties both because one goal is to fight blindness in the world [2], and because it operates in a small surgical field, and because patients in ophthalmology are often awake during surgery [14].

The reviews identified for laparoscopic surgery (minimally invasive surgery) applied to various surgical specialties both focus on training systems [15,21]. The first review analyzes the usefulness of AI techniques in such systems, while the second exclusively discusses ML techniques. Humm et al. aims to provide a critical analysis of the identified training systems [15], while in [21] it's conducted a systematic search and analysis of literature on the topic. Competence evaluation metrics were analyzed, which are necessary to provide evidence of the reliability and validity of the system as a tool for evaluating surgical performance. Surgical tasks were studied, and the classification of these tasks depends on the environment in which they are performed and can vary if built for a trainer box or virtual simulator. Surgical tasks were classified according to the laparoscopic skill taxonomy presented by Lamata [20]. A total of 32 studies were selected that intersected the basic tasks and valid metrics, both in trainer boxes and virtual reality simulators. The different VR simulators used by the systems found were analyzed based on modules, scenarios, environments, force feedback, construct validity, concurrent validity, and predictive validity. Human motion tracking systems in devices were classified based on the technology used, range of application, recorded metrics, portability, construct validity, and concurrent validity. Automatic analysis techniques for evaluating skills were studied based on methodology, scenario, tasks, sample size, and success rate [21]. Both articles conclude by emphasizing the importance of objective evaluation of the psychomotor skills of laparoscopic surgeons to improve surgical competence training and evaluation and ensure patient safety. Digital technologies can play an important role in supporting this process. The choice of laparoscopic surgery as the area of study is because it is a surgical specialty that requires particularly sophisticated and precise manual and psychomotor skills. Additionally, laparoscopic surgery has become increasingly widespread in recent years due to its numerous advantages over traditional open surgery, such as greater precision, less postoperative pain, and faster patient recovery times [15,21].

The two articles aimed at urological surgery [4,17] describe applications for both surgical training and surgery planning, but also for assistance during surgery by exploiting Ai, machine learning and deep learning. In [4] it's considered only one type of surgery: the removal of large, complex kidney stones through percutaneous nephrolithotomy (PCNL). Both propose a non-systematic review of the literature, but in [4] it's nevertheless explicitly listed the databases that produced 20 results. While Ma et al. [17] propose to analyse and describe the recent discoveries and applications of machine learning in robotic-assisted urological surgery, Checcucci et al. [4] propose the analysis through the following characteristics: type of study, type of virtual image-guided surgery, setting (surgical planning or simulation/planning/intraoperative guidance), number of cases, outcomes evaluated, main findings. Both articles conclude that these technological aids have positive effects both in the planning phase of the operation and during the operation itself, increasing its precision and effectiveness.

The only specific systematic review concerns open trauma surgeries. The applications sought are for training using Machine Learning techniques. The databases yielded 422 results. Searches included terms related to VR, AR, MR and haptic reality as well as specific procedures. No date limits were applied to the searches. Results were limited to the English language. Studies describing AR, VR MR and haptic tests for trauma-specific open surgical procedures, emergency open surgical procedures or vascular procedures relevant to trauma management, such as acute thoracic, abdominal, pelvic and extremity procedures, were included in the systematic review. Surgical procedures performed on patients, cadavers, physical model simulators or partial trainers were included. Studies that were only concerned with technical development, testing of physical models of trauma procedures without VR, AR, MR or haptics, evaluation of team and non-individual performance, non-technical skills and elective surgery were excluded. All studies examining minimally invasive laparoscopic or endovascular surgical procedures were also excluded from the systematic review, as these require different skills and assessment tools than open surgery. Therefore, the total sample analysed is 14 scientific articles. Covidence software was used for screening and data extraction. The analysis of the results considered was based on VR, AR, MR tools, study design, use of controls, Kirkpatrick's Level evidence, intended trainees, technology cost, procedures tested number of trainees, basis, evaluation metrics used, Machine Learning to Asses Surgical Expertise (MLASE) score, strengths, limitations, outcomes and way forward [18].

Neurosurgical simulations are presented as an overview in [29]. In order to outline the status of simulated surgical environments, extensive research was conducted on MEDLINE, the Internet and other databases between 1960 and 2002. An overview of the state of surgical simulation in terms of its adaptability to current surgical training regimes in 2003 was outlined. As expected, the widest application of simulations in the field of endoscopic (and laparoscopic) procedures is demonstrated, most likely as a result of the reduced engineering burden compared to the incorporation of a haptic interface. The realisation of ergonomically acceptable haptic interfaces remains difficult. Improvements in graphical rendering and the incorporation of artificial intelligence functions signal the certain emergence of surgical simulators as a valuable adjunct to surgical training [29].

The only review, which has spine surgery as its speciality, is defined as narrative and covers AI, ML and DL techniques in applications aimed at both training, surgical planning and intra-operative phase [11]. Google scholar and PubMed databases were queried. An output of 250 scientific articles was obtained from which 89 were selected by reading only the abstracts and finally 67 were analysed in their entirety. The articles were divided into four categories: articles on technologies, applications in surgery, applications in spine education and training, and general applications in orthopaedics. For each of the categories, an attempt was made to provide the most up-to-date state of the art. The results of the study show that head-mounted devices, which are the preferred hardware of surgeons, cause headaches, dizziness and discomfort, that the learning curves of AR and VR systems are high, that current VR systems cannot effectively simulate physical touch, which is of great importance to surgeons. Skin marker tracking systems are affected by the relative displacement and/or deformation of soft tissue relative to bone. It is worth noting that AR and VR in healthcare are ways to provide information to the physician and/or surgeon, students and trainers or the patient and have the ability to work as a link between the surgeon and an operating module such as robots. Therefore, AR and VR integrate naturally with different technologies in healthcare. Gaming is the leading technology for AR and VR that can be used in healthcare for patient and student education and to distract patients from pain. Spinal surgery, as a leading field of orthopaedics, should be ready and willing to adopt these new technologies.

Table 1. Table of Reviews included in the Study. Each entry comprises the bibliographic reference of the analyzed article (Cit.); the surgical specialty (Surgical spec.); the purpose of the described technologies (T = Training, P = Planning, I = Intraoperative guidance); review type; the query used to extract the results described in each article; the databases (DB) consulted in each article; the sample of articles extracted through the query.

Cit.	Surgical spec.	Aim	Type	Query	DB	Sample
[14]	Ophthalmology	T	Review	NA	NA	NA
[18]	Open trauma	T	SLR	cf. Appendix 1	PubMed, Embase, CENTRAL	14
[2]	Ophthalmology	T	Review	NA	NA	NA
[19]	Ophthalmology	T/P/I	Review	NA	NA	NA
[15]	Laparoscopy	T	Critical	NA	NA	NA
[17]	Urology	T/P/I	Review	NA	NA	NA
[32]	Generic	T	Review	NA	MEDLINE	8
[1]	Generic	T/I	Narrative	Artificial intelligence, autonomous surgery, machine learning, robotic surgery, surgical navigation	MEDLINE, Pubmed and Scopus	7
[31]	Generic	T	Overview	NA	MEDLINE, IEEE Xplore, ASME Digital Collection, ACM Digital Library, Google Scholar, IET/IEL, EPO	NA
[21]	Laparoscopy	T	Systematic research	Laparoscopy, minimally invasive surgery, surgical assessment, psychomotor skills, objective evaluation, validation, virtual reality, motion analysis.	PubMed, Google Scholar	NA
[29]	Neurosurgery	T	Overview	NA	MEDLINE, Internet	NA
[11]	Orthopaedics	T/P/I	Narrative review	Augmented reality, virtual reality, spine surgery, orthopaedic	Google scholar, PubMed	67
[4]	Urology	T/P/ I	Short overview	Percutaneous nephrolithotomy; PCNL; Endoscopic combined intrarenal surgery; ECIRS and kidney stones; Renal stones and 3D models; Three-dimensional; 3Dprinting; 3D virtual models.	Medline, PubMed, Cochrane DB, Embase	20
[14]	Presentation	T	Short review (overview)	NA	NA	10

The systematic review conducted, reveals a comprehensive picture of the literature present in this area of research, highlighting potential and gaps to be filled. Reviews in all areas of surgery are clearly in the minority and the most recent was published in 2020. Therefore, there is no article that reports a comprehensive overview. Only one general article [32] focuses exactly on the topic, but at the same time it does not analyze it systematically and therefore considers a small sample of articles. The analysis is not conducted by going into the specifics of technical features, but from a medical point of view.

4 Conclusions

This paper examines the literature corpus of reviews that explore the combined use of XR technologies and artificial intelligence techniques for surgical training. The aim of this review was to analyze the attention that the scientific community has devoted to this topic thus far, both focusing on specific surgical specialties and in terms of general-purpose applications. The analysis reveals that generalist reviews are significantly outnumbered by reviews with a specific focus. The only paper with a broader focus, published in a medical journal, lacks critical discussion on the technical aspects and does not appear to provide a systematic analysis, considering a limited sample of reviewed papers. Furthermore, there is a noticeable lack of literature coverage in the past three years, suggesting the need for a systematic and comprehensive update of the literature that: i) examines studies across all surgical domains in a general sense, ii) includes a discussion on technological and methodological aspects, in addition to clinical aspects, and iii) considers the use of standardized metrics for study assessment.

References

1. Andras, I., et al.: Artificial intelligence and robotics: a combination that is changing the operating room. World J. Urol. **38**, 2359–2366 (2020)
2. Bakshi, S.K., Lin, S.R., Ting, D.S.W., Chiang, M.F., Chodosh, J.: The era of artificial intelligence and virtual reality: transforming surgical education in ophthalmology. Br. J. Ophthalmol. **105**(10), 1325–1328 (2021)
3. Bowyer, M.W., Streete, K.A., Muniz, G.M., Liu, A.V.: Immersive virtual environments for medical training. In: Seminars in Colon and Rectal Surgery, vol. 19, pp. 90–97. Elsevier (2008)
4. Checcucci, E., et al.: Percutaneous puncture during pcnl: new perspective for the future with virtual imaging guidance. World J. Urol. **40**, March 2022. https://doi.org/10.1007/s00345-021-03820-4
5. Co, M., et al.: Distance education for anatomy and surgical training-a systematic review. The Surgeon **20**(5), e195–e205 (2022)
6. Cook, D.A., et al.: Comparative effectiveness of instructional design features in simulation-based education: Systematic review and meta-analysis. Med. Teacher **35**(1), e867–e898 (2013). https://doi.org/10.3109/0142159X.2012.714886. https://doi.org/10.3109/0142159X.2012.714886, pMID: 22938677

7. Cuschieri, A.: Whither minimal access surgery: tribulations and expectations. Am. J. Surg. **169**(1), 9–19 (1995)
8. De Luca, V., Meo, A., Mongelli, A., Vecchio, P., De Paolis, L.T.: Development of a virtual simulator for microanastomosis: new opportunities and challenges. In: De Paolis, L.T., Mongelli, A. (eds.) AVR 2016. LNCS, vol. 9769, pp. 65–81. Springer, Cham (2016). https://doi.org/10.1007/978-3-319-40651-0_6
9. De Paolis, L.T., De Luca, V.: The impact of the input interface in a virtual environment: the vive controller and the myo armband. Virtual Reality **24**(3), 483–502 (2020)
10. De Paolis, L.T., De Luca, V.: The effects of touchless interaction on usability and sense of presence in a virtual environment. Virtual Reality **26**(4), 1551–1571 (2022)
11. Ghaednia, H., et al.: Augmented and virtual reality in spine surgery, current applications and future potentials. Spine J. **21**(10), 1617–1625 (2021)
12. Gonzalez, F., Gosselin, F., Bachta, W.: Analysis of hand contact areas and interaction capabilities during manipulation and exploration. IEEE Trans. Haptics **7**(4), 415–429 (2014)
13. Howard, V.M., Englert, N., Kameg, K., Perozzi, K.: Integration of simulation across the undergraduate curriculum: student and faculty perspectives. Clin. Simul. Nurs. **7**(1), e1–e10 (2011)
14. Hu, K.S., Pettey, J., SooHoo, J.R.: The role of technology in ophthalmic surgical education during covid-19. Current Surgery Reports, pp. 1–7 (2022)
15. Humm, G., Harries, R., Stoyanov, D., Lovat, L.: Supporting laparoscopic general surgery training with digital technology: The united kingdom and ireland paradigm. BMC Surgery **21**, March 2021. https://doi.org/10.1186/s12893-021-01123-4
16. Khandelwal, P., Srinivasan, K., Roy, S.S.: Surgical education using artificial intelligence, augmented reality and machine learning: a review. In: 2019 IEEE International Conference on Consumer Electronics-Taiwan (ICCE-TW), pp. 1–2. IEEE (2019)
17. Ma, R., Vanstrum, E., Lee, R., Chen, J., Hung, A.: Machine learning in the optimization of robotics in the operative field. Current Opinion Urology **30**, September 2020. https://doi.org/10.1097/MOU.0000000000000816
18. Mackenzie, C.F., Harris, C.T.E., Shipper, A.G., et al.: Virtual reality and haptic interfaces for civilian and military open trauma surgery training: a systematic review. Injury (2022)
19. Mishra, K., Leng, T.: Artificial intelligence and ophthalmic surgery. Curr. Opin. Ophthalmol. **32**(5), 425–430 (2021)
20. Oropesa, I., et al.: Relevance of motion-related assessment metrics in laparoscopic surgery. Surgical Innov. **20**(3), 299–312 (2013). https://doi.org/10.1177/1553350612459808. https://doi.org/10.1177/1553350612459808, pMID: 22983805
21. Oropesa, I., et al.: Methods and tools for objective assessment of psychomotor skills in laparoscopic surgery. J. Surgical Res. **171**(1), e81–e95 (2011). https://doi.org/10.1016/j.jss.2011.06.034. https://www.sciencedirect.com/science/article/pii/S0022480411005841
22. Özacar, K., Ortakcı, Y., Küçükkara, M.Y.: Vrarcheducation: Redesigning building survey process in architectural education using collaborative virtual reality. Computers & Graphics (2023)
23. Park, J., Tiefenbach, J., Demetriades, A.: The role of artificial intelligence in surgical simulation. Frontiers in Medical Technology 4 (2022)

24. Reiners, D., Davahli, M.R., Karwowski, W., Cruz-Neira, C.: The combination of artificial intelligence and extended reality: a systematic review. Front. Virtual Real. **2**, 721933 (2021)
25. Rutkow, I.M.: Surgery: An Illustrated History. Mosby-Year Book (1993)
26. Sardar, P., Abbott, J.D., Kundu, A., Aronow, H.D., Granada, J.F., Giri, J.: Impact of artificial intelligence on interventional cardiology: from decision-making aid to advanced interventional procedure assistance. Cardiovascular Interventions **12**(14), 1293–1303 (2019)
27. Schiza, E.C., et al.: Co-creation of virtual reality re-usable learning objectives of 360 video scenarios for a clinical skills course. In: 2020 IEEE 20th Mediterranean Electrotechnical Conference (MELECON), pp. 364–367. IEEE (2020)
28. Shafto, M., Conroy, M., Doyle, R., Glaessgen, E., Kemp, C., LeMoigne, J., Wang, L.: Modeling, simulation, information technology & processing roadmap. National Aeronaut. Space Adm. **32**(2012), 1–38 (2012)
29. Spicer, M.A., Apuzzo, M.L.: Virtual reality surgery: neurosurgery and the contemporary landscape. Neurosurgery **52**(3), 489–498 (2003)
30. Svenmarck, P., Luotsinen, L., Nilsson, M., Schubert, J.: Possibilities and challenges for artificial intelligence in military applications. In: Proceedings of the NATO Big Data and Artificial Intelligence for Military Decision Making Specialists' Meeting, pp. 1–16 (2018)
31. Vaughan, N., Gabrys, B., Dubey, V.N.: An overview of self-adaptive technologies within virtual reality training. Comput. Sci. Rev. **22**, 65–87 (2016)
32. Veneziano, D., Cacciamani, G., Rivas, J.G., Marino, N., Somani, B.K.: Vr and machine learning: novel pathways in surgical hands-on training. Curr. Opin. Urol. **30**(6), 817–822 (2020)
33. Woon, A.P.N., et al.: Effectiveness of virtual reality training in improving knowledge among nursing students: a systematic review, meta-analysis and meta-regression. Nurse Educ. Today **98**, 104655 (2021). https://doi.org/10.1016/j.nedt.2020.104655. https://www.sciencedirect.com/science/article/pii/S0260691720315057
34. Yoon, H.: Opportunities and challenges of smartglass-assisted interactive telementoring. Appl. Syst. Innov. **4**(3), 56 (2021)
35. Zagury-Orly, I., et al.: What is the current state of extended reality use in otolaryngology training? a scoping review. Laryngoscope **133**(2), 227–234 (2023)
36. Ziker, C., Truman, B., Dodds, H.: Cross reality (xr): challenges and opportunities across the spectrum. Innovative learning environments in STEM higher education: Opportunities, challenges, and looking forward, pp. 55–77 (2021)

Smart Meters and Customer Consumption Behavior: An Exploratory Analysis Approach

Ahmed Ala Eddine Benali[1] , Massimo Cafaro[1,2] , Italo Epicoco[1,2(✉)] ,
Marco Pulimeno[1] , Enrico Junior Schioppa[3] , Jacopo Bonan[2,4] ,
and Massimo Tavoni[2,4]

[1] University of Salento, 73100 Lecce, Italy
{benali.ahmedala,massimo.cafaro,italo.epicoco,
marco.pulimeno}@unisalento.it
[2] Euro Mediterranean Center on Climate Change Foundation, 73100 Lecce, Italy
{massimo.cafaro,italo.epicoco,jacopo.bonan,massimo.tavoni}@cmcc.it
[3] Inmatica S.p.A., 73010 Monteroni, LE, Italy
eschioppa@inmatica.com
[4] Politecnico di Milano, Milan, Italy
{jacopo.bonan,massimo.tavoni}@polimi.it
http://www.unisalento.it, http://www.cmcc.it, https://www.inmatica.com/,
https://www.polimi.it/

Abstract. As the economy and technology continue to advance, the
need of energy for humans' activities is growing, placing significant pressure on power distribution to reach this demand instantly. Household
energy behaviors can be tracked by using Smart Meters (SM), whose
data undoubtedly contains valuable insights into household electricity
consumption. However, it is challenging to effectively perceive customers'
behavior from the massive SM data. Moreover, this information needs
to be captured by a data model; the workflow to understand customer
behavior needs to be clearly defined. Our research main goal is three-
fold: we aim to exploit SMs data to train unsupervised Machine Learning
(ML) models to forecast the energy load for a specific customer; we want
to cluster customers into appropriate equivalence classes characterized
by a distinct consumption pattern; and, last but not least, we pursue
the profiling of customers according to their habits, with the goal of discriminating the appliances actually in use and/or the charging of electric
vehicles. Since this is currently work-in-progress, in this manuscript we
briefly describe our research and report the current preliminary achievements.

Keywords: Smart Meters · energy consumption · customer behavior

1 Introduction

Nowadays analyzing the energy consumption plays a crucial role in energy sectors and companies (e.g., [5,9]). This analysis provides the stakeholders and

decision-makers with the behavior of consumers and the ability to forecast the energy load [9]. The consumers' behaviour can be mined from the Smart Meters (SM) data, which are essentially a stream and can be used to develop analytical models, identify repeated patterns over time and across households, forecast future consumption, and estimate the impact of external interventions and other potentially disruptive events. [17].

Customer behavior analysis has the potential to drive the business, and has been pioneered in various domains like telecommunications, retail, and banking [1]. In the energy sector, knowledge of the customer behavior is an essential element to grow a successful business, since it can provide the information required by retailers and aggregators to propose a custom contract and related services to customers. Moreover, the information can also be used to define contracts thought for a specific class of users. However, designing and implementing a solution to customer behavior is a non-trivial task and is very challenging, as it requires significant work to analyze different factors impacting the customer's journey whilst simultaneously taking into account risky situations and/or opportunities. Figure 1 presents a conceptual model of impact factors that can be seen as an aggregation to understand and analyze the customer's behavior [6].

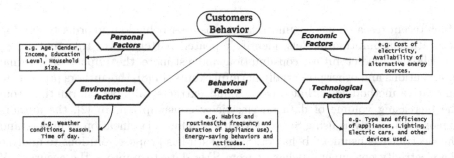

Fig. 1. Summary of impact factors on energy consumption.

For instance, the low energy consumption during a given period of a specific customer can be analyzed and interpreted by the consumer profile (e.g., married or single, gender, income), the presence at home (e.g., physical work, remote work), technology in use at home (e.g., the efficiency of appliances, presence of electric cars), the behavioral habits (e.g., routines, frequency, and duration of appliance use, energy-saving behaviors, and attitudes).

To efficiently handle the power consumption demand, decision-makers and managers of companies often need to explore and understand customers behaviors. For example, how do most customers use energy during a specific period of time? When does the peak of electricity consumption occur, and why? The detailed scenarios of how customers consume electricity need to be analyzed to answer these questions. The challenge here arise considering the huge amount of data, the time required to execute suitable data mining algorithms in order to represent and model the customer behavior, the design of what-if scenarios to predict the customer response to changing factors such as the energy price, the availability of novel sustainable technologies to produce energy and the awareness campaigns.

Our research main goal is three-fold: we aim to exploit SMs data to train unsupervised Machine Learning (ML) models to forecast the energy load for a specific customer; we want to cluster customers into appropriate equivalence classes characterized by a distinct consumption pattern; and, last but not least, we pursue the profiling of customers according to their habits, with the goal of discriminating the appliances actually in use and/or the charging of electric vehicles. Since this is currently work-in-progress, in this manuscript we briefly describe our research and report the current preliminary achievements.

The manuscript is structured as follows. Section 2 summarizes the related work. In Sect. 3, we present the proposed conceptual overview of the approach and develop the workflow to analyze the customers' behavior. Section 4 presents our preliminary results. We draw our conclusions in Sect. 5 and highlight future work.

2   Related Work

Much recent research has begun to study consumer behaviour in order to develop accurate consumption models, identify repeated patterns over time and across households, predict future consumption and estimate the impact of external interventions and other potentially harmful events. In [8], the authors propose an innovative methodology that organizes and extracts valuable information from the increasing volume of data on electricity consumption. In [2], the authors explored the analysis using Support Vector Machine classification to understand the electricity consumers' behavior. Several studies propose solutions to analyze the electricity consumers' behavior from SMs data to improve the accuracy of short term load forecasting (nowcasting) [10,12,14]. Additionally, several studies propose a predictive modeling approach based on Artificial Neural Network (ANN) models to learn the individual customer's behavior in response to electricity price changes [3,7,13]. Similar efforts have been conducted using profile clustering analysis to explore customer behavior during energy consumption [16]. In [15], the authors use a clustering-based probability distribution model for monthly residential electricity consumption analysis.

3   Methodology

For our analysis we shall use a dataset spanning 28 months from December 2019 to March 2022. The data were collected hourly and each instance includes a timestamp, a customer identification number and the energy consumed in the last hour. The dataset is related to 321, 561 customers and contains 20, 400 observations for each customer.

We pre-processed the available data, filtering out misleading data such as the customers exhibiting unusually low electricity consumption, since the corresponding contracts are clearly related to unused households; moreover, we also filtered out those contracts characterized by a hourly consumption greater than 12 kWh, since the corresponding contracts were deemed business contracts. This may be thought of as a standard approach to data cleaning, in which we remove the outliers in order to deal only with inliers. Next, we perform an exploratory data analysis to understand the statistical properties of the data being examined. In particular, we build histograms, draw a heatmap and perform Fast Fourier Transform (FFT) analysis to highlight recurring patterns. In order to model the customers' behaviour, we perform sequence mining to determine the most frequent sequences arising from the data. We then cluster the customers according to their measured electricity consumption, by using a density based approach (e.g. DBSCAN [4]). This can be done in several ways, aggregating the available data with regard to the time of consumption (e.g., night, morning, afternoon and evening) grouping by weekday or weekend. Finally, we use the data to train an unsupervised Machine Learning model to be used to forecast the electricity load.

Here we report our initial findings, related to the analysis of one month of data. The data is available in parquet file format, and one month of data includes 744 observations for each customer (there are $321,561$ customers). We use Python for data analysis and, in particular, the well-known libraries numpy, pandas, and matplotlib.

4   Preliminary Results

Figure 2 depicts the histogram for the dataset. The x-axis of the histogram represents the consumption values, while the y-axis represents the occurrences.

Next, we built a heatmap to visualize the energy usage patterns.

The resulting heatmap, shown as Fig. 3, depicts on the x axis the hourly bins and on the y axis the electricity consumption bins. The occurrences are represented by using the provided color map, using a log scale.

The heatmap allows identifying patterns visually, and gaining insight into the energy usage. The picture shows that, during the weekends and the holidays the majority of the consumers has a reduced or regular consumption; the peak consumption happens during the weekdays.

We perform Fast Fourier Transform analysis, as depicted in Fig. 4, with the aim of identifying patterns in time series data determining the dominant frequencies in the dataset, which were found to be respectively 0.042, 0.083, 0.125, 0.167 and 0.208 cycles/hour. The time periods for each of these frequencies were also computed: 24, 12, 8, 6 and 5 h.

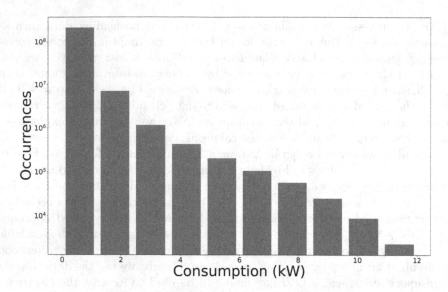

Fig. 2. Number of occurrences of energy consumption binned into 10 uniform intervals of 1.5 kWh.

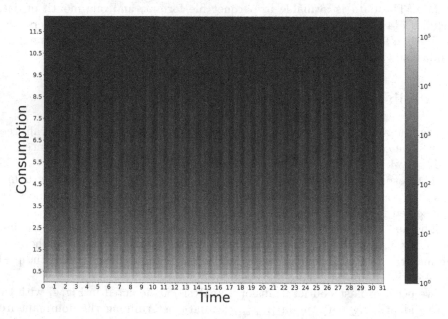

Fig. 3. Heatmap of one month.

Next, we report our preliminary results obtained by performing sequence mining in order to determine households' electricity consumption patterns identifying the most frequent sequence in the data. The obtained results may be used to cluster households according to their energy consumption behavior. For

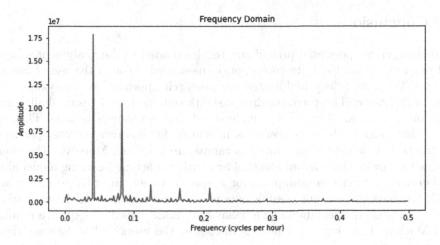

Fig. 4. Dominant frequencies.

this analysis, we focus on standard 3 kWh contracts only, since these are the most common ones. We process the data by finding frequent sequential pattern; each sequence is a list of transactions ordered by transaction-time, and each transaction is a power consumption. The analysis amis to discover all sequential patterns with a user-specified minimum support; to this end we used the Generalized Sequential Pattern (GSP) algorithm [11]. In particular, we partition the 24 h in a day into three 8 h time intervals. Therefore, a sequence will be represented by three itemsets, corresponding to the maximum values in each interval. Since small consumption values are more frequent than large ones, we use a non uniform binning approach in which we define the following bins representing the consumption expressed in kWh: [0, 0.1, 0.2, 0.3, 0.5, 1, 3]. The GSP algorithm's output is the following (we only report here the 3 most frequent sequences):

Table 1. Results of sequence mining.

Sequence	Support
[1, 3, 3]	81, 879
[0.5, 3, 3]	75, 762
[1, 1, 1]	73, 776

As shown in Table 1, the most frequent sequence is [1, 3, 3], which means that the consumption in the first interval (spanning from midnight to 8.00 AM) is at most 1 kWh, whilst the consumption in the next two intervals (spanning respectively from 8:00 AM to 4:00 PM and from 4:00 PM to midnight) is at most 3 kWh.

5   Conclusions

In this paper, we presented preliminary results related to the analysis of a large dataset related to electricity consumption measured through the use of Smart Meters. We have briefly highlighted our research approach for analyzing customers' behavior. The corresponding insights obtained as a result shall allow decision makers to visualize and understand how customers behave. This, in turn, shall lead to different scenarios in which, for instance, custom per-user contracts may be defined or awareness campaigns initiated. Moreover, the main goal is to provide the relevant stakeholders with a machine Learning model able to forecast electricity consumption for a specified user, in order to anticipate peak demands and prevent possible outages. Future work include characterizing different classes of users, building a behavioral model based on sequence mining and Machine Learning based models to cluster the users and to forecast their consumption.

References

1. Abbasimehr, H., Shabani, M.: A new methodology for customer behavior analysis using time series clustering: a case study on a bank's customers. Kybernetes **50**(2), 221–242 (2021)
2. AbuBaker, M.: Data mining applications in understanding electricity consumers' behavior: a case study of Tulkarm district, palestine. Energies **12**(22), 4287 (2019)
3. Balachander, K., Paulraj, D.: Retracted article: ann and fuzzy based household energy consumption prediction with high accuracy. J. Ambient. Intell. Humaniz. Comput. **12**(7), 7543–7557 (2021)
4. Deng, D.: Dbscan clustering algorithm based on density. In: 2020 7th International Forum on Electrical Engineering and Automation (IFEEA), pp. 949–953. IEEE (2020)
5. Iqbal, N., Kim, D.H., et al.: IoT task management mechanism based on predictive optimization for efficient energy consumption in smart residential buildings. Energy Build. **257**, 111762 (2022)
6. Liu, J., et al.: Analysis of customers' electricity consumption behavior based on massive data. In: 2016 12th International Conference on Natural Computation, Fuzzy Systems and Knowledge Discovery (ICNC-FSKD), pp. 1433–1438. IEEE (2016)
7. Nakabi, T.A., Toivanen, P.: An ANN-based model for learning individual customer behavior in response to electricity prices. Sustain. Energy Grids Networks **18**, 100212 (2019)
8. Oprea, S.V., Bâra, A., Tudorică, B.G., Călinoiu, M.I., Botezatu, M.A.: Insights into demand-side management with big data analytics in electricity consumers' behaviour. Comput. Electr. Eng. **89**, 106902 (2021)
9. Prakash, K.P., et al.: A comprehensive analytical exploration and customer behaviour analysis of smart home energy consumption data with a practical case study. Energy Rep. **8**, 9081–9093 (2022)
10. Quilumba, F.L., Lee, W.J., Huang, H., Wang, D.Y., Szabados, R.L.: Using smart meter data to improve the accuracy of intraday load forecasting considering customer behavior similarities. IEEE Trans. Smart Grid **6**(2), 911–918 (2014)

11. Srikant, R., Agrawal, R.: Mining sequential patterns: generalizations and performance improvements. In: Apers, P., Bouzeghoub, M., Gardarin, G. (eds.) EDBT 1996. LNCS, vol. 1057, pp. 1–17. Springer, Heidelberg (1996). https://doi.org/10.1007/BFb0014140

12. Viegas, J.L., Vieira, S.M., Melício, R., Mendes, V., Sousa, J.M.: Classification of new electricity customers based on surveys and smart metering data. Energy **107**, 804–817 (2016)

13. Wang, H., Mahato, N.K., He, H., An, X., Chen, Z., Gong, G.: Research on electricity consumption behavior of users based on deep learning. In: 2020 IEEE/IAS Industrial and Commercial Power System Asia (I&CPS Asia), pp. 1491–1497. IEEE (2020)

14. Wang, Y., Chen, Q., Gan, D., Yang, J., Kirschen, D.S., Kang, C.: Deep learning-based socio-demographic information identification from smart meter data. IEEE Trans. Smart Grid **10**(3), 2593–2602 (2018)

15. Xu, J., Kang, X., Chen, Z., Yan, D., Guo, S., Jin, Y., Hao, T., Jia, R.: Clustering-based probability distribution model for monthly residential building electricity consumption analysis. Building Simulation **14**(1), 149–164 (2020). https://doi.org/10.1007/s12273-020-0710-6

16. Yang, J., Zhao, J., Wen, F., Dong, Z.: A model of customizing electricity retail prices based on load profile clustering analysis. IEEE Trans. Smart Grid **10**(3), 3374–3386 (2018)

17. Yildiz, B., Bilbao, J.I., Dore, J., Sproul, A.B.: Recent advances in the analysis of residential electricity consumption and applications of smart meter data. Appl. Energy **208**, 402–427 (2017)

User Experience in eXtended Reality

Are Virtual Reality Serious Games Safe for Children? Design Keys to Avoid Motion Sickness and Visual Fatigue

Kim Martinez[1]([✉]) [iD] and David Checa[2] [iD]

[1] Department of History, Geography and Communication, Universidad de Burgos, Burgos, Spain
kmartinez@ubu.es
[2] Department of Computer Engineering, Universidad de Burgos, Burgos, Spain

Abstract. Designing serious games in virtual reality (VR) may raise a health and safety concern as to whether children should use this technology. This paper attempts to clarify this issue by studying VR impact on children's physical, cognitive and psychosocial development. With a supervised and controlled use over time, it is found that VR could cause physical problems as motion sickness and visual fatigue. To avoid these issues, a series of VR design guidelines are collected so researchers can follow them to develop serious games for children. To avoid motion sickness, developers have to: 1) regulate free movement in the virtual environment and add visual effects or references, 2) help to maintain a stable body posture during the game, 3) bring interactive objects closer and allow their manipulation in non-gravity condition, 4) adjust the difficulty of the tasks and make them as interactive as possible, and 5) implement quality visual and sound content. Regarding the reduction of visual fatigue, developers need to: 1) regulate and supervise the game time, 2) choose an HMD that offers good graphic definition, and 3) design the user interface to be easily understandable and legible.

Keywords: Virtual reality · Children · Motion sickness · Visual fatigue

1 Introduction

Serious games are tools that have proven to be very useful for education in different fields. One of the target audiences that can benefit the most from the advantages of video games are children [1]. Playful learning increases their engagement to develop skills in various areas, such as problem solving, decision making, creativity and collaboration. In addition, serious games offer immediate feedback and the option to adapt to the individual needs of each child. This is fundamental when adjusting the difficulty of challenges for accessibility [2].

Developing serious games in virtual reality (VR) enhances their educational capacity by adding new functions [3]. Scenarios and situations can be simulated to learn physical or psychosocial skills that would be more complicated in real life. There is also greater immersion in the virtual environment, along with increased interactivity, which enhances user engagement and information retention.

However, in the development of virtual reality serious games for children, researchers may face a health and safety issue. The vast majority of VR head-mounted displays (HMD) manufacturers, such as Oculus and HTC, include the following indication in their manuals: "not recommended for use by children under 13 years of age". This statement raises the question of whether it is appropriate to develop VR applications for children as it could be harmful to their health and development.

This paper aims to determine what these problems may be and to provide design keys for researchers to develop serious games that are safe for children. The current research that studies the possible harms of virtual reality in children will be reviewed. We will analyze which of these issues are possible in the controlled use of serious games and how they can be avoided. For this purpose, a compilation of design guidelines will be made according to the latest studies in the development of VR applications. Therefore, researchers can use them as references for their future work.

2 Possible Physical, Cognitive and Psychosocial Damage from the Use of Virtual Reality in Children

VR HMD manufacturers recommend to avoid its use in children under 13 years of age due to the lack of evidence on the VR effects on their development. This may give rise to health issues regarding the development of VR serious games for children. However, several scientific studies are showing the requirements to ensure their safe and controlled use. Kaimara et al. [4] reviewed the most significant studies of the last 10 years that group the main problems that can be associated with the use of virtual reality in children. They recognized 3 types of development that virtual reality can affect: physical, cognitive, and psychosocial. Each of these areas may present individualized problems, which are defined below along with studies that have tested children for developmental impact.

2.1 Possible Damage to Physical Development

The possible short- and long-term physical damages that are more determinant to discourage the use of virtual reality in children are [4]:

- Motion sickness: oculomotor problems, nausea and disorientation can occur during and after the experience. Oculomotor symptoms may cause headache, eyestrain and tiredness. Nausea is known as malaise, stomach awareness and even vomiting. Disorientation refers to difficulty concentrating, dizziness and lightheadedness [5].
- Visual impairment: the impact on the immature oculomotor system could lead to adverse effects on accommodation, vergence and stereoscopic vision, as well as visuomotor coordination [6].

However, its controlled and short-term use has been proved to be safe. The study by Tychsen and Foeller [6] tested 50 children aged 4 to 10 years who used virtual reality for visual impairment and cybersickness in 2 sessions of 30 min each. They confirmed that the results regarding heterophoria and near point accommodation were not significant. In addition, no evidence of accommodative myopia or degradation in stereo acuity measurements was revealed. Moreover, the symptoms of visual fatigue or dizziness that these children experienced were lower than that of adults exposed to the same virtual reality tests.

Other studies have confirmed that playing for controlled periods of time does not lead to visual impairment. Rechichi et al. [7] conducted a cross-sectional study of potential vision impairment. Their conclusion was that only using video games for 30 min or more per day can affect and compromise the visual development of children up to 10 years of age. In addition, most of the children did not suffer from headaches while playing. Also, Hirota [8] studied objective and subjective visual fatigue, which was alike between the use of virtual reality goggles and a two-dimensional display. Likewise, the incidence of motion sickness between a large screen and virtual reality goggles is quite similar [5].

In fact, not only have these virtual reality tests been found not to cause harm, but they may even be beneficial. The work of Bennett et al. [9] provides a robust assessment of cognitive spatial processing skills in people with visual impairment. It also tested the safety and usability of this technology in more susceptible children with Autism Spectrum Disorder (ASD). The 35 study participants showed no visual or cybersickness problems and 74% preferred virtual reality to traditional screens [10].

Other potential physical damages that may result from virtual reality use [4] include the following:

- Cardio-metabolic deficiencies: disorientation and non-active video game habits can lead to a sedentary lifestyle and obesity [11]. This may result in long-term cardio-metabolic deficiencies and, physical and psychological problems, like low self-esteem [12].
- Radiation: children's eyes and brains absorb significantly higher doses of local radiation by wireless adults than adults. For the time being, it is still under study which could be the long-term health risks because more research data is needed [13].
- Sleep disorders: have been shown to be directly related to low secretion of melatonin [13]. It starts to be produced about 2 h before the natural bedtime. Virtual reality goggles emit blue light that reduces melatonin production, especially in children. Consequently, it can affect sleep and the circadian system [14].

These damages correspond to long-term habits of the participants' daily life. Therefore, they are not applicable to the use of serious games in virtual reality. These experiences are usually performed at a short time and during daytime [1], so they will not affect the melatonin production and sleep of the children.

2.2 Possible Damage to Cognitive Development

Cognitive development regards children's mental abilities as attention, learning, perception, thinking, and language. There is extensive research on the benefits of serious games [15]. They promote learning with very positive cognitive, behavioral, and affective outcomes [16]. These experiences use rules, goals and objectives, feedback, challenges, interaction, and story that attract, engage, and motivate children. The main positive effects found are increased attention, motivation in the face of failure, mood management and prosocial behaviors [17].

Different authors have tested the additional benefits of serious games on virtual reality devices:

- Dalgarno and Lee [18] determined improved spatial awareness, greater opportunities for experiential learning, increased motivation and engagement, better contextualization of learning.
- Parong and Mayer [19] investigated the effects of playing through immersive virtual reality on specific components of cognition: perceptual attention, mental rotation, working memory, field of view (FoV) and visual processing speed. They argued that immersion could increase a learner's sense of presence, motivation, and attention in a virtual world. Likewise, its use could improve cognitive and daily skills, besides academic results.
- Nolin et al. [20] recommended virtual reality as an assessment tool because of the selective and sustained attention it creates in children.
- Passig et al. [21] indicate that teaching in a virtual reality environment contributes to children's cognitive modifiability.

In fact, for these reasons virtual reality has been used in minors with ASD, as they foster emotional and social skills [22]. In the work of Newbutt et al. [23] children determined that the goggles were physically and visually comfortable and easy to use. They also felt at ease within the immersive environment and better identified learning opportunities. On the other hand, it has been proven effective with children with ADHD [24]. Training in virtual reality environments allows them to acquire self-regulation skills and transfer them to everyday situations.

Finally, a concern found in the cognitive perspective was the confusion between the virtual world and the real world [4]. This is a stage of child development, which is directly related to metacognitive limitations [25]. This relationship between fiction and reality can affect all digital media, not just virtual reality. However, as this technology is mainly based on realism, immersion and presence, it is important for the learner to help them differentiate the situation.

2.3 Possible Damage to Psychosocial Development

Psychosocial development regards children's personality, emotions and interpersonal relationships. Problems that have been raised by the use of virtual reality are anxiety, negative emotional and social behaviors, and isolation [4].

Pallavicini and Pepe [26] highlighted the ability of virtual reality video games as effective tools to elicit positive emotions and decrease negative emotions and anxiety state in individuals. This technology has been used in treatments to overcome feelings of confusion and anxiety in unfamiliar or crowded environments (agoraphobia), through stress management training. Another study of 29 participants with ASD [27] also highlighted that for these more susceptible individuals it did not create anxiety or sensory problems.

Lobel et al. [28] studied the effect of video games on children's psychosocial well-being and concluded that only competitive games, played for more than 8 h per week, may be a risk factor for decreasing prosocial behavior. Similarly, isolation relates to the belief that playing too much time disconnects children from social and family activities, in addition to physical activities.

However, it was shown that children and adolescents who play less than one hour a day have better prosocial behavior and life satisfaction. At the same time, they have lower negative effects like sleep disorders, peer problems, hyperactivity, and emotional difficulties [17]. Specifically, virtual reality has been applied to the training of children and adolescents with ASD to improve emotional and/or social skills, including emotion recognition, collaboration, and social interaction tasks [28].

Most virtual reality interventions with minors have focused on these psychosocial aspects. These experiences seek the improvement of social and emotional skills with situations that train flexibility development, identity formation, construction of social norms, emotional recognition, and improvement of social interaction and collaboration [29]. These successful trials again demonstrate the safety of virtual reality in short periods of immersion [30].

3   Design Keys to Avoid Motion Sickness and Visual Fatigue

Section 2 displays many evidence supporting that the use of virtual reality does not cause cognitive and psychosocial damage to children. In fact, the studies cited above show how serious games help them in the development of their emotions and skills. As for physical damage, in experiences such as serious games that are controlled and limited in time, the main concerns are motion sickness and visual fatigue. This section will provide a series of design guidelines, collected in Fig. 1, that researchers can adopt to avoid them.

3.1   How to Avoid Motion Sickness

First, it is necessary to identify how motion sickness is generated. The main cause is the conflict between sensory signals, especially between visual information and information coming from the vestibular system [31]. The visual system indicates that the user is moving, but the vestibular information tells that they are standing still. The design keys in this section are going to focus on reducing these conflicts to avoid motion sickness.

Movement in VR serious games can be mainly classified into 3 types of navigation: 1) free teleportation in which the user can move to any destination, 2) teleportation nodes between predefined points, and 3) flying/walking with freedom in direction. When choosing a type of movement for the game researchers have to think about several aspects [32]: a) characteristics and dimensions of the scenario; b) main tasks of the game; c) type of user and possible special needs; d) adjustment of different parameters and options of the game design.

Using teleportation can be useful in many games to reduce motion sickness since the user is not aware of the movement and there are no conflicts of information [33]. However, this reduces immersion and presence, so there would be no point in using VR technology. It is always preferable that the player can move freely through the scenario by walking or driving, although this movement increases the mental demand and the chances of motion sickness [34]. To avoid motion sickness, different researchers use the following techniques:

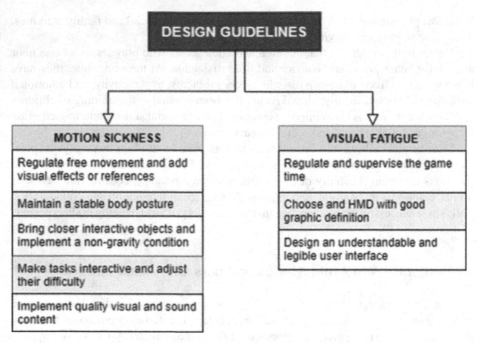

Fig. 1. Diagram of the VR design guidelines collected.

- Dynamically constrain the FoV as the player moves [35]. For example, a tunnel effect or a Gaussian blur can be applied to reduce the view to a circle in the direction of movement. However, the restriction of the FoV should be limited to certain parts of the scene, leaving at least the ground plane and the horizon line visible [36]. In this way the user does not lose excessive visual information and therefore, the feeling of immersion.
- Include a stable visual reference that relates to the Earth on which the player is physically sitting or standing [37]. This reference should be visually close to the environment in which the task is performed or where the texts or objects of interest are located. Other different concepts such as "a virtual nose" or a "rest frame" have also been proposed.
- Smoothing virtual movements while moving on a terrain with rough trajectory [38]. That is, the surface on which the player moves is smooth even if visually it looks different.
- Regulate the speed motion factor during gameplay [39]. Speed affects motion sickness quite a lot, but it is also observed that players that get used to the virtual environment prefer to move fast. Therefore, it is optimal to allow the user to choose the speed or have it inherent in the controls (e.g., the pressure level of the joysticks).

In addition to these design adjustments, there are other aspects of player movement that must be taken into account. The user's body posture while interacting in the virtual environment is vital. If it causes musculoskeletal loads and discomfort, as well as instability, the user is more likely to suffer from muscle fatigue and motion sickness [40]. To avoid these symptoms there are several options [33]. The first is to sit the user down to play, although this decreases the sense of realism and freedom of interaction. The second is to "force" the user to adopt a wider and upright posture (legs parallel and apart). It can be implemented through a game mechanic to make it unobtrusive or totally invisible to them.

The gestures with which the objects in the virtual environment are manipulated are also relevant. Depending on the game mechanics, children may have to pick up, move or rotate objects to accomplish objectives. This can be a problem because it forces them to move around the object or to turn their body or head to look at them. To avoid this, it is ideal to manipulate objects in a non-gravity condition to allow the free use of the hands and 360-degree manipulation that avoids unnecessary body movement [41]. Similarly, the virtual environment should be designed so that these objects are in the FoV close to them. This prevents the user from having to turn their head excessively and helps them to focus their gaze on a stable visual referent [39].

The game design should contemplate the tasks it requires to fulfill the objectives. On the one hand, if the duration is excessive and children spend too much time in the virtual environment, motion sickness symptoms increase. Hot environment conditions also influence because the user's discomfort increases [42]. The same happens if children are assigned several complicated tasks that they have to solve in a row [43]. To avoid this situation, it is necessary to mix simple tasks with the difficult ones and plan some breaks to stop playing. On the other hand, VR HMD that offer passive experiences in 3 degrees of freedom (DoF) and decrease the user's control and sense of presence have been found to cause more motion sickness [44]. Therefore, it is better to use 6 DoF HMD that involve children in the task and at the same time increase their immersion.

Finally, the last aspect to take into account to avoid motion sickness is the quality of the audiovisual content. Latency is one of the most determinant factors since the asynchronization between the frame rate of the VR content and the refresh rate of the HMD generates motion sickness [45]. The best solution is to use quality equipment that offers good latency. Another option is to replace dynamic scenes with more static scenes, so that image complexity is reduced and users do not have to process a lot of visual information [31]. Similarly, implementing pleasant sounds in the virtual environment reduces motion sickness because they help users to relax [46]. However, the volume of these sounds should be adjusted to the position and movements of the child to give a realistic feeling.

3.2 How to Avoid Visual Fatigue

The main aspect of serious game design that needs to be taken into account to avoid visual fatigue is play times. As with any digital device with a screen, prolonged use of VR HMD causes eyestrain and tiredness. Therefore, the American Academy of Ophthalmology suggests to apply the 20–20-20 time rule [47]. That is, games should be designed to play for 20 min, stop for another 20 min to rest, and play again for another 20 min.

The choice of VR HMD is also fundamental [31]. As well as to avoid motion sickness, visual fatigue will be less using the latest HMDs on the market such as HTC Vive Focus 3 or the upcoming Meta Quest 3. This technology is in constant development and its technical characteristics are increasing its quality. In particular, latency should be as low as possible to avoid constant flickering and low frame rates that cause eye discomfort [48]. Also, a frame rate of 60 frames per second (FPS) is recommended for images and videos, and 90 FPS for interactive content. This frame rate, together with a high resolution, will display quality content on the screens that does not cause visual fatigue.

Finally, the user interface should be designed to avoid visual fatigue. On the one hand, it is essential to have a usable design that clearly shows what the interactive elements are and how to manipulate them. The easier these texts or icons are, the less time it will take children to understand them so they will not get tired looking for a solution [31]. In addition, text design is especially relevant regarding contrast sensitivity, sentence length and font size [49]. Some basic rules are: 1) contrast between background and text should be from 50% to 75%; 2) sentence length ratio should be 33.3% to 50%; 3) font size should be 96 pixels or more. As for the color of the text, it shall be given luminosity on a dark background because this mix makes the font appear slightly larger and makes it easier to read [50].

4 Conclusions

This paper reviews the latest relevant studies on the effect of VR on children's development. These focus on the possible physical, cognitive and psychosocial damages that can be suffered. Evidence is found that, not only is VR not dangerous for children, but that VR serious games can help them in their development. The only possible health issues that can affect the controlled and supervised use of a VR serious game are motion sickness and visual fatigue.

To help researchers to develop VR serious games safely for children, this paper investigates the latest trends in VR development and compiles guidelines. In order to avoid motion sickness, developers have to: 1) regulate free movement in the virtual environment and add visual effects or references, 2) help to maintain a stable body posture during the game, 3) bring interactive objects closer and allow their manipulation in non-gravity condition, 4) adjust the difficulty of the tasks and make them as interactive as possible, and 5) implement quality visual and sound content. Regarding the reduction of visual fatigue, developers need to: 1) regulate and supervise the game time, 2) choose an HMD that offers good graphic definition, and 3) design the user interface to be easily understandable and legible.

The next step of this research should be to adopt customized solutions to avoid motion sickness and visual fatigue. It is known that children and young people are less likely to suffer from these symptoms while using VR, but it is still an effect that is highly dependent on the individual. Therefore, some of these design guidelines may annoy users who do not need them. The solution should be to implement artificial intelligence in the serious game so it can detect if the child is starting to show symptoms. In that case, the game will automatically implement these design keys to avoid any further discomfort.

References

1. Martinez, K.K., Menéndez, M.I.M., Bustillo, A.: Awareness, prevention, detection, and therapy applications for depression and anxiety in serious games for children and adolescents: systematic review. JMIR Serious Games 9(4), e30482 (2021). https://doi.org/10.2196/30482

2. Martinez, K.K., Menéndez, M.I.M., Bustillo, A.: A new measure for serious games evaluation: gaming educational balanced (GEB) model. Appl. Sci. **12**(22), 11757 (2022). https://doi.org/10.3390/app122211757

3. Checa, D., Bustillo, A.: A review of immersive virtual reality serious games to enhance learning and training. Multimedia Tools Appl. **79**(9–10), 5501–5527 (2020). https://doi.org/10.1007/s11042-019-08348-9

4. Kaimara, P., Oikonomou, A., Deliyannis, I.: Could virtual reality applications pose real risks to children and adolescents? Virtual Reality. Published, A systematic review of ethical issues and concerns (2021). https://doi.org/10.1007/s10055-021-00563-w

5. Rebenitsch, L., Owen, C.: Review on cybersickness in applications and visual displays. Virtual Real **20**, 101–125 (2016). https://doi.org/10.1007/s10055-016-0285-9

6. Tychsen, L., Foeller, P.: Effects of immersive virtual reality headset viewing on young children: visuomotor function, postural stability, and motion sickness. Am. J. Ophthalmol. **209**, 151–159 (2020). https://doi.org/10.1016/j.ajo.2019.07.020

7. Rechichi, C., De Moja, G., Aragona, P.: Video game vision syndrome: a new clinical picture in children? J. Pediatr. Ophthalmol. Strabismus. **54**, 346–355 (2017). https://doi.org/10.3928/01913913-20170510-01

8. Hirota, M., et al.: Comparison of visual fatigue caused by head-mounted display for virtual reality and two-dimensional display using objective and subjective evaluation. Ergonomics **62**, 759–766 (2019). https://doi.org/10.1080/00140139.2019.1582805

9. Bennett, C.R., Bailin, E.S., Gottlieb, T.K., Bauer, C.M., Bex, P.J., Merabet, L.B.: Assessing visual search performance in ocular compared to cerebral visual impairment using a virtual reality simulation of human dynamic movement. In: Proceedings of the Technology, Mind, and Society (TechMindSociety 2018). ACM Press, New York, pp 1–6 (2018)

10. Malihi, M., Nguyen, J., Cardy, R.E., Eldon, S., Petta, C., Kushki, A.: Short report: evaluating the safety and usability of headmounted virtual reality compared to monitor-displayed video for children with autism spectrum disorder. Autism **24**, 1924–1929 (2020). https://doi.org/10.1177/1362361320934214

11. Gheller, B.J.F., et al.: Effect of video game playing and a glucose preload on subjective appetite, subjective emotions, and food intake in overweight and obese boys. Appl. Physiol. Nutr. Metab. **44**, 248–254 (2019). https://doi.org/10.1139/apnm-2018-0281

12. Cappuccio, F.P., Miller, M.A.: Sleep and cardio-metabolic disease. Curr. Cardiol. Rep. **19**, 110 (2017). https://doi.org/10.1007/s11886-017-0916-0

13. Gottschalk, F.: Impacts of technology use on children: exploring literature on the brain, cognition and well-being. OECD Educ. Work Pap. **195**, 45 (2019). https://doi.org/10.1787/8296464e-en

14. Tosini, G., Ferguson, I., Tsubota, K.: Effects of blue light on the circadian system and eye physiology. Molvis **22**, 61–72 (2016)

15. Fokides, E.: Digital educational games in primary education. In: Daniela, L. (ed.) Epistemological Approaches to Digital Learning in Educational Contexts, pp. 54–68. Routledge (2020)

16. Boyle, E.A., et al.: An update to the systematic literature review of empirical evidence of the impacts and outcomes of computer games and serious games. Comput. Educ. **94**, 178–192 (2016). https://doi.org/10.1016/j.compedu.2015.11.003

17. Granic, I., Lobel, A., Engels, R.C.M.E.: The benefits of playing video games. Am. Psychol. **69**, 66–78 (2014). https://doi.org/10.1037/a0034857

18. Dalgarno, B., Lee, M.J.W.: What are the learning affordances of 3-D virtual environments? Br. J. Educ. Technol. **41**, 10–32 (2010). https://doi.org/10.1111/j.1467-8535.2009.01038.x

19. Parong, J., Mayer, R.E.: Cognitive consequences of playing braintraining games in immersive virtual reality. Appl. Cogn. Psychol. **34**, 29–38 (2020). https://doi.org/10.1002/acp.3582

20. Nolin, P., et al.: Clinica VR: classroom-CPT: a virtual reality tool for assessing attention and inhibition in children and adolescents. Comput. Human Behav. **59**, 327–333 (2016). https://doi.org/10.1016/j.chb.2016.02.023

21. Passig, D., Tzuriel, D., Eshel-Kedmi, G.: Improving children's cognitive modifiability by dynamic assessment in 3D immersive virtual reality environments. Comput. Educ. **95**, 296–308 (2016). https://doi.org/10.1016/j.compedu.2016.01.009

22. Mesa-Gresa, P., Gil-Gomez, H., Lozano-Quilis, J-A., Gil-Gomez, J-A.: Effectiveness of virtual reality for children and adolescents with autism spectrum disorder: an evidence-based systematic review. Sensors **18**, 2486 (2018). https://doi.org/10.3390/s18082486

23. Newbutt, N., Sung, C., Kuo, J., Leahy, M.J.: The acceptance, challenges, and future applications of wearable technology and virtual reality to support people with autism spectrum disorders. In: Brooks, A., Brahnam, S., Kapralos, B., Jain, L. (eds.) Recent Advances in Technologies for Inclusive Well-being, Intelligent Systems Reference Library, vol. 119, pp. 221–241. Springer, Cham (2017)

24. Blume, F., et al.: NIRS-based neurofeedback training in a virtual reality classroom for children with attention-deficit/hyperactivity disorder: study protocol for a randomized controlled trial. Trials **18**, 41 (2017). https://doi.org/10.1186/s13063-016-1769-3

25. Woolley, J.D., Ghossainy, M.E.: Revisiting the fantasy-reality distinction: children as Naive skeptics. Child Dev. **84**, 1496–1510 (2013). https://doi.org/10.1186/s13063-016-1769-3

26. Pallavicini, F., Pepe, A.: Virtual reality games and the role of body involvement in enhancing positive emotions and decreasing anxiety: within-subjects pilot study. JMIR Serious Games **8**(2), e15635 (2019). https://doi.org/10.2196/15635

27. Newbutt, N., Bradley, R., Conley, I.: Using virtual reality headmounted displays in schools with autistic children: views, experiences, and future directions. Cyberpsychol. Behav. Soc. Netw. **23**, 23–33 (2020). https://doi.org/10.1089/cyber.2019.0206

28. Lobel, A., Engels, R.C.M.E., Stone, L.L., Burk, W.J., Granic, I.: Video gaming and children's psychosocial wellbeing: a longitudinal study. J. Youth Adolesc. **46**, 884–897 (2017). https://doi.org/10.1007/s10964-017-0646-z

29. Adjorlu, A., Serafin, S.: Head-mounted display-based virtual reality as a tool to reduce disruptive behavior in a student diagnosed with autism spectrum disorder. In: Brooks, A., Brooks, E.I. (eds.) Interactivity, Game Creation, Design, Learning, and Innovation: 8th EAI International Conference, ArtsIT 2019, and 4th EAI International Conference, DLI 2019, proceedings, pp. 739–748. Springer, Cham (2020)

30. Madary, M., Metzinger, T.K.: Recommendations for good scientific practice and the consumers of VR-Technology. Front. Robot. AI **3**, 1–23 (2016). https://doi.org/10.3389/frobt.2016.00003

31. Chen, Y., Wu, Z.: A review on ergonomics evaluations of virtual reality. Work J. Prevent. Assess. Rehabil. **74**(3), 831–841 (2022). https://doi.org/10.3233/wor-205232

32. Kamal, A., Andujar, C.: Designing, testing and adapting navigation techniques for the immersive web. Comput. Graph. **106**, 66–76 (2022). https://doi.org/10.1016/j.cag.2022.05.015

33. Bailey, G.S., Arruda, D.G., Stoffregen, T.: Using quantitative data on postural activity to develop methods to predict and prevent cybersickness. Front. Virtual Real. **3**,(2022). https://doi.org/10.3389/frvir.2022.1001080

34. Rhiu, I., Kim, Y.J., Kim, W., Yun, M.H.: The evaluation of user experience of a human walking and a driving simulation in the virtual reality. Int. J. Ind. Ergon. **79**, 103002 (2020). https://doi.org/10.1016/j.ergon.2020.103002

35. Groth, C., Tauscher, J., Heesen, N., Alldieck, T., Castillo, S., Magnor, M.: Mitigation of cybersickness in immersive 360°videos. In: 2021 IEEE Conference on Virtual Reality and 3D User Interfaces Abstracts and Workshops (VRW), pp. 169–177 (2021). https://doi.org/10.1109/vrw52623.2021.00039

36. Wu, F., Bailey, G.S., Stoffregen, T.A.: Rosenberg, E. S.: Don't block the ground: reducing discomfort in virtual reality with an asymmetric field-of-view restrictor. In: Symposium on Spatial User Interaction, pp. 1–10 (2021).https://doi.org/10.1145/3485279.3485284
37. Cao, Z., Jerald, J., Kopper, R.: Visually-induced motion sickness reduction via static and dynamic rest frames. In:IEEE Virtual Reality Conference(2018). https://doi.org/10.1109/vr. 2018.8446210
38. Dorado, J., Figueroa, P.: Ramps are better than stairs to reduce cybersickness in applications based on a HMD and a Gamepad. In: Symposium on 3D User Interfaces, pp. 47–50 (2014). https://doi.org/10.1109/3dui.2014.6798841
39. Lohman, J., Turchet, L.: Evaluating cybersickness of walking on an omnidirectional treadmill in virtual reality. IEEE Trans. Hum. Mach. Syst. **52**(4), 613–623 (2022). https://doi.org/10. 1109/thms.2022.3175407
40. Chardonnet, J., Mirzaei, M.A., Merienne, F.: Visually induced motion sickness estimation and prediction in virtual reality using frequency components analysis of postural sway signal. In HAL (Le Centre pour la Communication Scientifique Directe). Le Centre pour la Communication Scientifique Directe (2015)
41. Baykal, G.E., Leylekoğlu, A., Arslan, S., Ozer, D.: Studying children's object interaction in virtual reality: a manipulative gesture taxonomy for vr hand tracking. In: Extended Abstracts of the 2023 CHI Conference on Human Factors in Computing Systems, pp. 1–7 (2023). https://doi.org/10.1145/3544549.3585865
42. Bogerd, C.P., et al.: A review on ergonomics of headgear: thermal effects. Int. J. Ind. Ergon. **45**, 1–12 (2015). https://doi.org/10.1016/j.ergon.2014.10.004
43. Venkatakrishnan, R., Venkatakrishnan, R., Anaraky, R.G., Volonte, M., Knijnenburg, B.P., Babu, S.V.: A structural equation modeling approach to understand the relationship between control, cybersickness and presence in virtual reality. In: IEEE Virtual Reality Conference (2020). https://doi.org/10.1109/vr46266.2020.1581195115265
44. Sepich, N.C., Jasper, A., Fieffer, S., Gilbert, S.B., Dorneich, M.C., Kelly, J.W.: The impact of task workload on cybersickness. Front. Virt. Real. **3**,(2022). https://doi.org/10.3389/frvir. 2022.943409
45. Watanabe, K., Takahashi, M.: Head-synced drone control for reducing virtual reality sickness. J. Intell. Rob. Syst. **97**(3–4), 733–744 (2020). https://doi.org/10.1007/s10846-019-01054-6
46. Keshavarz, B., Hecht, H.: Pleasant music as a countermeasure against visually induced motion sickness. Appl. Ergon. **45**(3), 521–527 (2014). https://doi.org/10.1016/j.apergo.2013.07.009
47. Boyd, K.: Computers, digital devices, and eye strain. American Academy of Ophthalmology (4 March 2020). https://www.aao.org/eye-health/tips-prevention/computer-usage
48. Standard Activities Board. IEEE Standard for Head-Mounted Display (HMD)-Based Virtual Reality (VR) Sickness Reduction Technology (2020)
49. Lee, S., Kim, J.H., Son, H., Kwon, S., Lee, S.H.: A study of human factor for virtual reality text information implementation on head mounted-display. Asia-pacific J. Multimedia Serv. Convergent Art Hum. Sociol. **7**(1), 229–238 (2017). https://doi.org/10.14257/ajmahs.2017. 01.19
50. Erickson, A., Kim, K., Bruder, G., Welch, G.C.: Effects of dark mode graphics on visual acuity and fatigue with virtual reality head-mounted displays. In: 2020 IEEE Conference on Virtual Reality and 3D User Interfaces (VR), pp. 434–442 (2020). https://doi.org/10.1109/ vr46266.2020.00064

The Impact of Usability and Learnability on Presence Factors in a VR Human Body Navigator

Valerio De Luca$^{(\boxtimes)}$ iD, Giulia Pellegrino, and Lucio Tommaso De Paolis iD

Department of Engineering for Innovation, University of Salento, Lecce, Italy
{valerio.deluca,giulia.pellegrino1,lucio.depaolis}@unisalento.it

Abstract. Alongside the traditional concept of usability, dealing with the ease of use of a product, over the years the concept of learnability has been introduced, which refers to the possibility of learning to use a system easily and quickly. In contexts characterised by a significant level of user involvement, the traditional concept of usability has evolved into the more complex concept of user experience, which also includes emotional, cognitive or physical responses. In the specific case of virtual environments, an important factor of user experience is the sense of presence, defined as the subjective experience of being in a place.

This work aims at experimentally assessing which components of presence are significantly influenced by usability and learnability in a Virtual Reality environment for the navigation in the human body developed for the HTC Vive. The presence factors analysed in this work were *Realism, Ability to act, Interface quality, Ability to examine* and *Self-assessment of performance*. The results showed a significant impact of usability mainly on the perception of realism and a limited impact of learnability on the ability to act in the virtual environment.

Keywords: Usability · Learnability · User Experience · Presence · Realism

1 Introduction

User experience [1] has developed over the years as an extension of the traditional concept of usability by including emotional and aesthetic factors [2]. ISO 9241-210 [3] defines it as a combination of "perceptions and responses that result from the use or anticipated use of a product, system or service".

Furthermore, some works [4,5] have separated the concept of usability from that of learnability, which refers to the ease of learning to use a system.

A fundamental factor characterising the user experience in a Virtual Reality (VR) environment is the sense of presence, which refers to the subjective experience of being in one place or environment, independently of where a subject is actually located [6,7].

L. T. De Paolis et al. (Eds.): XR Salento 2023, LNCS 14218, pp. 378–396, 2023.
https://doi.org/10.1007/978-3-031-43401-3_25

Realism has been defined as the extent of experiential authenticity and perceived illusion of non-mediation and correlates with an increase in attention to the stimuli and entertainment space. It depends on a combination of perceptual and conceptual cues [8]. A distinction is made between evaluative realism and felt realism: the former arises from reflective processes such as the evaluation of the similarity of the representation to subjective experiences or expectations; the latter deals with perceptual persuasiveness, emotional involvement and the feeling of presence [8].

Immersion is the ability to stimulate the user through several external (sensory) and internal perceptual channels [9]. It increases the perception of realism and makes the experience more interesting and involving. The sense of presence is regarded as the psychological product of immersion. The user is partially or totally unaware of the mediating role played by technology [10].

In interacting with the world, the human brain continuously makes predictions about what is going to happen [11] and generates an "embodied simulation": the multiperceptive representation of the body and the surrounding space defines the so-called body matrix [12]. Virtual Reality is also based on a model of the body, the environment and the interaction between them and aims to produce multisensory stimuli consistent with the predictions of this model. It produces an alteration of the body matrix and previous perceptions by generating a feeling of presence in a virtual body and in the environment around it [13].

The features of presence and immersion make VR particularly suitable for enhancing the practice of Mindfulness meditation, as it is able to isolate from external distractions by helping the user to establish multisensory connections [14, 15].

This work aims to assess the influence of usability and learnability, defined as the ability to learn to use a system quickly, on various aspects that contribute to creating a sense of presence in a virtual environment. Adopting one of the proposed decompositions for the Presence Questionnaire, employed for the post-experience analysis conducted in this study, the following factors are analysed: *Realism, Ability to act, Interface quality, Ability to examine* and *Self-assessment of performance*.

The rest of the paper is structured as follows: Sect. 2 reports on the state of the art on presence and realism in Virtual Reality; Sect. 3 introduces the VR application considered for the experimental scenario; Sect. 4 describes the methodology employed for user experience evaluation; Sect. 5 presents and discusses the results; Sect. 6 concludes the paper.

2   Related Work

Numerous studies in the literature have explored the concepts of presence, usability, and ergonomics within virtual environments. In works that employed the Presence Questionnaire [6, 16–20], the sense of presence was often evaluated in terms of *Involvement, Interface quality, Adaptation/immersion* and *Visual fidelity*. Other works considered other presence factors: for instance, a virtual environment simulating the International Space Station [21] was evaluated in terms of *sensory, distraction, realism* and *involvement.* Another scale for the interpretation of presence scores in virtual environments was proposed in [22] starting from the Igroup Presence Questionnaire (IPQ), which encompasses *spatial presence, involvement* and *experienced realism.*

Various models have been developed to represent the relationships between the various components of the user experience. An extended Technology Acceptance Model [23] was specifically developed for Virtual Reality considering an aeronautical assembly task: according to such model, perceived ease of use does not influence the intention to use, which is positively influenced by perceived usefulness and negatively influenced by cybersickness. The analysis presented in [24] identified expectance, realism and prevention of disbelief as the main factors enabling a deep sense of presence. The study in [25] proved that physical coherence in terms of force, occlusion, lighting and material has a significant influence on presence: in particular, the predominant contribution of force suggests that the influence of interactivity on presence is higher than the influence of visual fidelity. A systematic review of presence-based strategies [26] highlighted that better hardware/software allocation and more accuracy in objects and characters enhance immersion and the spatial dimension of presence, also known as place illusion. Moreover, realism and external stimuli are enabling factors for the coherence dimension, known as plausibility illusion. An experimental study [27], focusing on an underwater seascape, revealed that the interaction with the virtual environment enhances immersion, leading to significant impacts on satisfaction and loyalty, but social interactions limit the influence of immersion on satisfaction, likely due to interferences with perceived immersion.

Other works have experimentally compared the user experience offered by various visualisation modes. The study in [28] evaluated depth perception, presence and comfort in medical endoscopic teleoperation, highlighting a significant improvement in user experience when stereoscopic 3D visualization was employed. The effects of CAVE and head-mounted displays in the edutainment field were compared in [29]. The findings suggested that CAVE offered a superior user experience in terms of presence, engagement, flow, skill, judgment, and experience consequence. However, no substantial differences were found regarding immersion, usability, emotion, and technology adoption. The study in [30] evaluated presence, workload, usability, and flow by comparing a video display terminal and a head-mounted display in walking and driving scenarios. The video display terminal demonstrated superior workload, while the head-mounted display provided a higher sense of presence and flow during direct interaction. However, in mediated interaction, such as driving a vehicle, the head-mounted display exhibited lower usability.

Another crucial aspect studied for usability and ergonomics in virtual environments is locomotion [31], which affects accuracy and timing of execution, particularly due to the need for covering long distances and precise movement control. In [32] several interaction and locomotion modes employed in immersive environments were compared in terms of presence, cybersickness and usability: teleportation achieved high scores in cybersickness and presence, but it exhibited limitations in the ability to interact with objects. For abstract data exploration [33], a comparison of teleportation and natural walking with a traditional 2D tablet interface revealed a tradeoff between efficiency and user interest, with no discernible difference in model understandability.

Several works have compared the ways of interaction in a virtual environment offered by various devices by analysing the effects on usability and user experience. An empirical study [34] compared hand-held, bare-hand and hand-worn devices in terms of learnability, effectiveness and estensibility: according to the collected feedback, users think hand-worn and bare-hand devices can be employed to provide a more intuitive and immersive experience, even though they are more familiar with hand-held devices. The impact of touchless interaction devices based on hand gestures, which are associated with commands within the virtual environment, was also widely discussed. Oculus Touch yielded better performance than the Leap Motion gesture controller in selection tasks and was perceived as more usable [35]. Also the Vive handheld controller, bundled with the HTC Vive headset, offered superior performance than Leap Motion in terms of task execution time and accuracy [36]. On the contrary, users encountered difficulties with the Leap Motion device, likely due to the absence of tactile feedback and tracking interruptions when hands moved out of the sensor's field of view [37].

Two previous works [17,18] compared, in the same virtual navigator considered in this paper, the interaction based on Vive controller with a touchless interaction based on the Myo armband. In the first work, the correlations between presence factors (*involvement, interface quality, adaptation/immersion* and *visual fidelity*) were evaluated. The second investigated the possible causes of the differences in these factors related to the peculiarities of the two devices.

In [38], gaze tracking and forearm contractions detected through electromyography were combined to control cursor movements and selections in a virtual environment, achieving better performance than HTC Vive controller, Xbox gamepad, dwelling time and eye-gaze dwelling time.

3   Case Study: A VR Navigator of the Human Body

The application, developed with the Unity game engine [39] and the SteamVR API [40] for the HTC Vive headset [41], provides three scenarios showing virtual models reconstructed from CT images:

- cardio explorer, which focuses on a case of study for mitral valve surgery;
- neuro explorer, which focuses on a case of cerebral aneurysm in a non-haemorrhagic state;
- body explorer, which represents most of the remaining organs of the human body.

After the selection of a virtual scenario, the user can interact by means of the Vive controller (Fig. 1). When he/she gets closer to the organs, he/she has also the possibility to enter them and navigate inside their internal structure, as illustrated in the right-hand column of Fig. 2. The 3D models are intersected by a plane, called TAC slicer, representing the CT images used to reconstruct the visualized virtual organs.

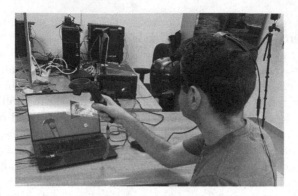

Fig. 1. User interaction through the Vive controller

The commands for model zoom and rotation are associated with the central button of the Vive controller (Fig. 3): pressing the lower or the upper side of the

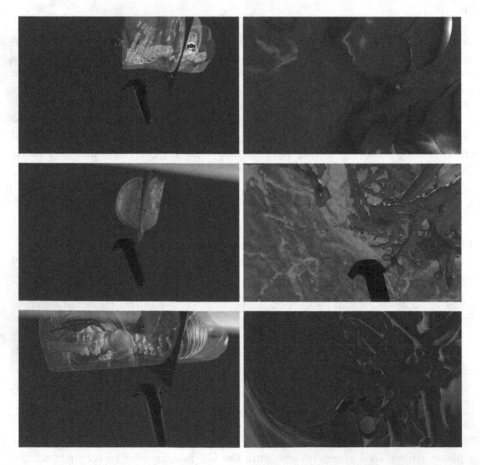

Fig. 2. Scenarios for virtual navigation of the human body: cardio explorer (at the top), neuro explorer (in the middle) and body explorer (at the bottom)

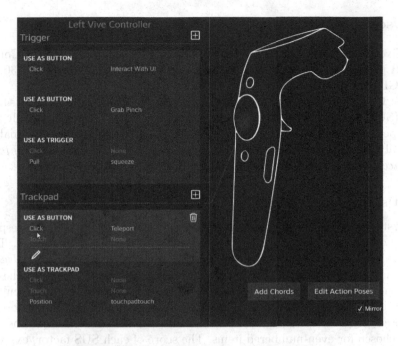

Fig. 3. The trackpad on the Vive controller

button allows increasing (zoom-in) or decreasing (zoom-out) the model dimensions, while pressing the left or the right side enables a left or right rotation.

The plane containing CT slices can be moved by keeping the grab pinch button (Fig. 4) pressed and moving the controller on the left and on the right.

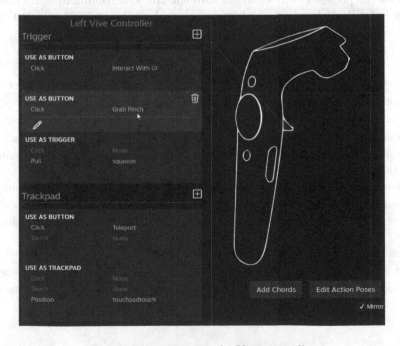

Fig. 4. The trigger on the Vive controller

4 User Experience Evaluation

The Vive headset was connected to a VR ready PC equipped with a Core i9-12900H processor, 32 GB of DDR5 RAM and a NVIDIA GeForce RTX 3070 Ti 8 GB GDDR6 graphic card.

The tests involved 69 users who were asked to fill in the System Usability Scale (SUS) [42] and the Presence Questionnaire (PQ) [16] immediately after the experience with the virtual environment: the former provides learnability and usability scores, while the latter provides scores for *Realism*, *Ability to act*, *Interface quality*, *Ability to examine* and *Self-assessment of performance*.

4.1 Usability Evaluation

The System Usability Scale (SUS) [42] is a 10-item questionnaire with response options on a scale from 1 ("Strongly disagree") to 5 ("Strongly agree"). These items can be grouped into two factors [4], namely *Learnability* and *Usability* in the narrow sense, which are weakly correlated [5]. Table 1 reports the SUS items and shows how they are grouped into the two factors. In the calculation of average *Usability* and *Learnability* scores, the scale values chosen for odd-numbered items are subtracted from 5, while 1 is subtracted from the scale values chosen for even-numbered items. The score of each SUS factor, expressed as a value from 0 to 4, is calculated as the average of the scores of its component items.

4.2 Presence Evaluation

The sense of presence was assessed through the Questionnaire sur l'État de Présence (QÉP) of the UQO Cyberpsychology Lab [16], a 2004 revision of the

Table 1. Items and factors of the System Usability Scale

SUS item	Factor
1. I think that I would like to use this system frequently	Usability
2. I found the system unnecessarily complex	Usability
3. I thought the system was easy to use	Usability
4. I think that I would need the support of a technical person to be able to use this system	Learnability
5. I found the various functions in this system were well integrated	Usability
6. I thought there was too much inconsistency in this system	Usability
7. I would imagine that most people would learn to use this system very quickly	Usability
8. I found the system very cumbersome to use	Usability
9. I felt very confident using the system	Usability
10. I needed to learn a lot of things before I could get going with this system	Learnability

Presence Questionnaire (PQ) introduced by Witmer and Singer in 1998 [6]. From this version, which includes 24 items with 7 response options, items concerning audio and haptic interaction were discarded, as the current version of the virtual navigator does not include these features. Following the indications of the UQO Cyberpsychology Lab [16], the 19 items considered were grouped into 5 factors,

Table 2. Items and factors of the Presence Questionnaire

PQ item	Factor
1. How much were you able to control events?	Ability to act
2. How responsive was the environment to actions that you initiated (or performed)?	Ability to act
3. How natural did your interactions with the environment seem?	Realism
4. How much did the visual aspects of the environment involve you?	Realism
5. How natural was the mechanism which controlled movement through the environment?	Realism
6. How compelling was your sense of objects moving through space?	Realism
7. How much did your experiences in the virtual environment seem consistent with your real world experiences?	Realism
8. Were you able to anticipate what would happen next in response to the actions that you performed?	Ability to act
9. How completely were you able to actively survey or search the environment using vision?	Ability to act
10. How compelling was your sense of moving around inside the virtual environment?	Realism
11. How closely were you able to examine objects?	Ability to examine
12. How well could you examine objects from multiple viewpoints?	Ability to examine
13. How involved were you in the virtual environment experience?	Realism
14. How much delay did you experience between your actions and expected outcomes?	Interface quality
15. How quickly did you adjust to the virtual environment experience?	Self-assessment of performance
16. How proficient in moving and interacting with the virtual environment did you feel at the end of the experience?	Self-assessment of performance
17. How much did the visual display quality interfere or distract you from performing assigned tasks or required activities?	Interface quality
18. How much did the control devices interfere with the performance of assigned tasks or with other activities?	Interface quality
19. How well could you concentrate on the assigned tasks or required activities rather than on the mechanisms used to perform those tasks or activities?	Ability to examine

namely *Realism, Interface quality, Ability to examine, Ability to act* and *Self-assessment of performance*, as shown in Table 2. The scores of items 14, 17 and 18 were computed by subtracting from 7 the value chosen by the user (since for such items higher values denote worse opinions expressed by the users). The scores of all the remaining items are computed by subtracting 1 from the value chosen by the user. The score of each PQ factor, expressed as a value from 0 to 6, is calculated as the average of the scores of its component items.

5   Results and Discussion

The density plot in Fig. 5 shows the distributions of *Usability* and *Learnability* scores, while the density plot in Fig. 6 shows the distributions of *Realism, Interface quality, Ability to examine, Ability to act* and *Self-assessment of performance* scores.

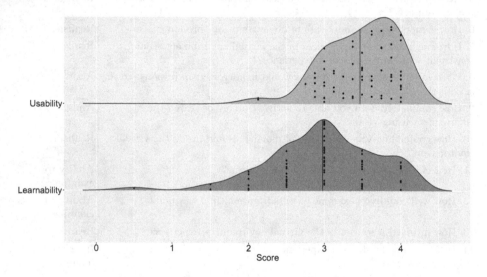

Fig. 5. Distribution of *Usability* and *Learnability* scores calculated for the 69 users involved in the tests

The waveforms suggest that most users rated *Usability* higher than *Learnability*. *Interface quality, Ability to examine* and *Ability to act* exhibit a fairly wide variability, while the more pronounced promontories of the waveforms representing *Realism* and *Self-assessment of performance* suggest a lower level of disagreement among users, who gave the highest scores to these two factors.

A hierarchical cluster analysis, depicted in Fig. 7, was performed on SUS and PQ factors using the ICLUST *R* package [43], which aims at maximizing internal consistency and homogeneity, represented by Cronbach's *alpha* [44] and Revelle's

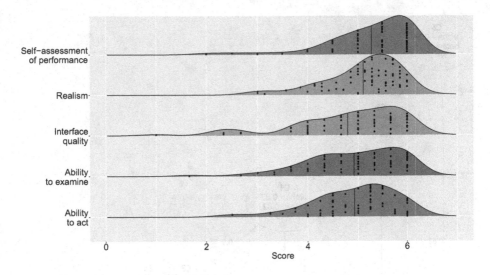

Fig. 6. Distribution of presence factor scores calculated for the 69 users involved in the tests

beta [45] respectively: the former is defined as the mean of all the possible split-half reliabilities of a scale, while the latter is defined as the minimum value among all the possible split-half reliabilities, to assess the scale homogeneity.

In addition to the intuitive link between *Ability to act* and *Ability to examine*, which in turn significantly influence *Self-assessment of performance*, the diagram shows a strong correlation between *Usability* and *Realism*. *Interface quality* is correlated to the macro-cluster formed by these 5 factors, but the significant difference between *alpha* and *beta* in cluster *C5* suggests a low reliability for this prediction. Similarly, the correlation between *Learnability* and cluster *C5* appears unreliable due to the clear difference between *alpha* and *beta* in cluster *C6*.

The learnability scores were divided by means of the k-means algorithm into three clusters, relating to users who expressed low, medium and high learnability scores.

Since not all samples follow a normal distribution, only non-parametric methods can be applied to detect whether there are statistically significant differences between the groups. Fligner-Killeen test and Levene's non-parametric test (Tables 3, 4, 5 and 6) suggest that homogeneity of group variances can be assumed (as p-value is always greater than 0.05 for at least one of the two tests), so the Kruskal-Wallis method can be applied to check whether significant differences exist between the different levels of learnability and usability considered.

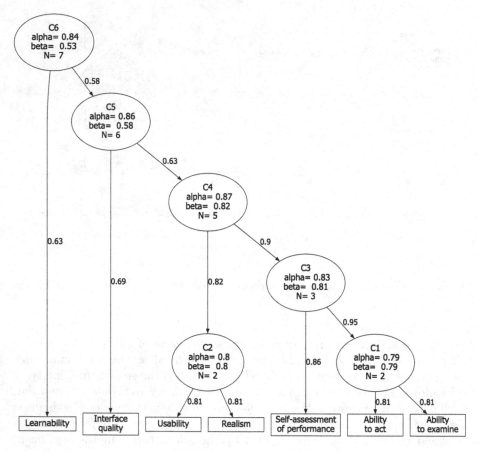

Fig. 7. Hierarchical cluster between learnability, usability and presence factors (Cluster fit = 0.85, Pattern fit = 0.99, RMSR = 0.07)

Table 3. Fligner-Killeen test and non-parametric Levene test when comparing low learnability and medium learnability scores

Factor	Fligner-Killeen test		Non-parametric Levene test	
	χ^2	p-value	Test statistic	p-value
Usability	2.7707	0.09601	3.0665	0.07992
Realism	0.017197	0.8957	0.79391	0.3729
Ability to act	1.8004	0.1797	2.4207	0.1197
Interface quality	0.099738	0.7521	0.31506	0.5746
Ability to examine	2.9032	0.0884	2.8416	0.09186
Self-assessment of performance	0.90913	0.3403	0.97653	0.3231

The Kruskal-Wallis rank sum test shows significant differences in terms of *Usability*, *Ability to act* and *Self-assessment of performance* when moving from a low to a medium level of learnability (Table 7).

Table 4. Fligner-Killeen test and non-parametric Levene test when comparing medium learnability and high learnability scores

Factor	Fligner-Killeen test		Non-parametric Levene test	
	χ^2	p-value	Test statistic	p-value
Usability	0.06363	0.8008	0.0098293	0.921
Realism	2.1169	0.1457	2.0785	0.1494
Ability to act	1.534	0.2155	3.7203	0.05376
Interface quality	0.11707	0.7322	0.020517	0.8861
Ability to examine	2.2276	0.1356	4.8217	0.0281
Self-assessment of performance	0.01526	0.9017	1.233	0.2668

Table 5. Fligner-Killeen test and non-parametric Levene test when comparing low usability and medium usability scores

Factor	Fligner-Killeen test		Non-parametric Levene test	
	χ^2	p-value	Test statistic	p-value
Learnability	0.84291	0.3586	0.00064785	0.9797
Realism	0.54522	0.4603	0.040714	0.8401
Ability to act	2.7318	0.09837	2.229	0.1354
Interface quality	0.27199	0.602	2.2967	0.1296
Ability to examine	0.91772	0.3381	0.4996	0.4797
Self-assessment of performance	4.0773	0.04346	2.0493	0.1523

Table 6. Fligner-Killeen test and non-parametric Levene test when comparing medium usability and high usability scores

Factor	Fligner-Killeen test		Non-parametric Levene test	
	χ^2	p-value	Test statistic	p-value
Usability	0.19802	0.6563	0.18226	0.6694
Realism	1.9693	0.1605	4.9137	0.02664
Ability to act	1.3387	0.2473	1.5663	0.2107
Interface quality	0.067982	0.7943	0.25479	0.6137
Ability to examine	0.11842	0.7308	0.18136	0.6702
Self-assessment of performance	0.10505	0.7459	0.0004185	0.9837

On the other hand, no factors show substantial differences when comparing the group with medium learnability and the group with high learnability (Table 8): in this case, users do not even notice an increase in their performance.

Table 7. Kruskal-Wallis rank sum test comparing factors between low learnability and medium learnability (p-values less than 0.05, which reveal significant differences, are highlighted in bold)

Factor	χ^2	p-value
Usability	5.1908	**0.02271**
Realism	1.1919	0.275
Ability to act	7.3561	**0.006684**
Interface quality	0.048971	0.8249
Ability to examine	2.8416	0.09186
Self-assessment of performance	5.9858	**0.01442**

Table 8. Kruskal-Wallis rank sum test comparing factors between medium learnability and high learnability

Factor	χ^2	p-value
Usability	0.05967	0.807
Realism	0.11684	0.7325
Ability to act	1.8427	0.1746
Interface quality	1.1568	0.2821
Ability to examine	0.41768	0.5181
Self-assessment of performance	0.0012433	0.9719

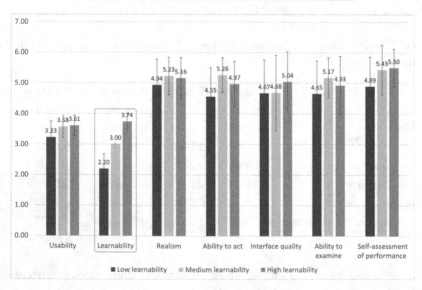

Fig. 8. Average scores of presence factors for 3 different levels of learnability (usability and learnability scores are expressed on a scale of 0 to 4, whereas PQ factor scores are expressed on a scale of 0 to 6)

For each of the three clusters (corresponding to low, medium and high learnability), the mean values and standard deviations of the corresponding usability and presence scores were calculated and represented in the multi-column histogram in Fig. 8.

Probably the *Ability to examine* was not significantly influenced by learnability as is the *Ability to act* because users preferred to examine the virtual organs by exploring them from the inside, which was more fascinating than, for example, the rotation performed by the controllers. *Interface quality* also does not show any significant differences, as confirmed by the histogram in Fig. 8: the average values are almost identical, although the very high standard deviation, evidenced by rather long error bars, reveals a high variability.

The standard deviations of the other factors tend to be quite large for the cluster with low learnability but then in the cluster with medium learnability always tend to decrease for all factors except *Interface quality*. On the other hand, there does not seem to be any further significant decreases in standard deviations in the cluster with high learnability, where *Ability to examine* actually shows a slight increase in standard deviation.

The users were then divided into three clusters according to usability scores. When comparing low and medium usability, the Kruskal-Wallis rank sum test shows significant differences in terms of *Learnability*, *Realism*, *Ability to act* and *Self-assessment of performance* (Table 9).

Table 9. Kruskal-Wallis rank sum test comparing factors between low usability and medium usability (p-values less than 0.05, which reveal significant differences, are highlighted in bold)

Factor	χ^2	p-value
Learnability	5.4891	**0.01914**
Realism	7.0382	**0.007979**
Ability to act	10.342	**0.0013**
Interface quality	0.20857	0.6479
Ability to examine	1.1086	0.2924
Self-assessment of performance	11.575	**0.0006686**

On the other hand, when comparing medium and high usability, the Kruskal-Wallis rank sum test shows significant differences in terms of *Realism* and *Ability to examine* (Table 10).

For each of the three clusters (corresponding to low, medium and high usability), the mean values and standard deviations of the corresponding learnability and presence scores were calculated and represented in the multi-column histogram in Fig. 9.

Table 10. Kruskal-Wallis rank sum test comparing factors between medium usability and high usability (p-values less than 0.05, which reveal significant differences, are highlighted in bold)

Factor	χ^2	p-value
Learnability	0.057904	0.8098
Realism	8.091	**0.004448**
Ability to act	0.53617	0.464
Interface quality	2.3233	0.1274
Ability to examine	8.4119	**0.003728**
Self-assessment of performance	0.4043	0.5249

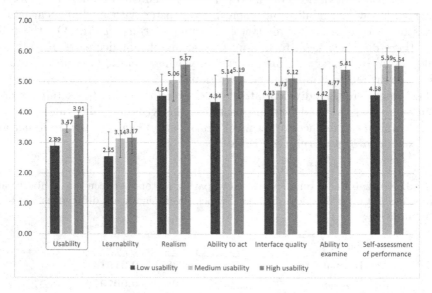

Fig. 9. Average scores of presence factors for 3 different levels of usability (usability and learnability scores are expressed on a scale of 0 to 4, whereas PQ factor scores are expressed on a scale of 0 to 6)

Ability to examine is not affected by the level of usability when it does not go beyond the intermediate level, probably because users preferred to examine the virtual organs by simply exploring them from the inside, without performing any special actions requiring the use of controllers. This dual possibility offered by the system thus makes it possible to examine without necessarily having to act and ensures that *Ability to act* and *Ability to examine* are not directly related as in other experimental scenarios. However, while learnability does not influence *Ability to examine* in any case, a high level of usability leads to a significant increase in *Ability to examine*, as the histogram in Fig. 9 also shows. This suggests that only users who are very skilled in the use of controllers can benefit further when exploring virtual models: only in this case the use of controllers proves to be an extra gear that enriches the possibilities provided by the exploration of organs from the inside.

In the medium usability cluster, a decrease in the standard deviations of all factors can be observed, which this time, contrary to the clusters based on learnability, also affects *Interface quality*. In the low usability cluster, the standard deviation is rather high not only for *Interface quality*, but also for *Self-assessment of performance*. The high variability of opinions on these aspects, resulting from the high standard deviation, indicates that not all users think that the difficulty in using the system significantly affects their ability to adapt and interact in the virtual environment. On the contrary, opinions tend to converge in the perception of *Realism*, characterised by a low standard deviation even in the case of low usability. The impact of usability on the perception of *Realism* appears very clear: the improvement is significant both in the transition to the medium usability cluster and in the transition to the high usability cluster.

6 Conclusions and Future Work

This paper reported a post-hoc analysis conducted for a virtual navigator of the human body to evaluate the effects of learnability and usability on the sense of presence. The results revealed only a limited influence of learnability on the ability to act in the virtual environment and a much stronger influence of usability especially on the perception of realism.

Future work will evaluate the influence of factors such as users' age, new modes of interaction such as voice commands, and study new factor decompositions for the questionnaires used. The impact of forms of interaction, such as teleportation associated with controller commands, that allow the user to move himself in a virtual environment, will also be assessed.

References

1. Tullis, T., Albert, B.: Measuring the User Experience: Collecting, Analyzing, and Presenting Usability Metrics: Second Edition (2013)
2. Bachmann, D., Weichert, F., Rinkenauer, G.: Review of three-dimensional human-computer interaction with focus on the leap motion controller (2018)
3. ISO: Human-centred design for interactive systems. Ergonomics of human system interaction Part 210 (ISO 9241–210). ISO 9241210 (2010). https://doi.org/10.1039/c0dt90114h
4. Lewis, J.R., Sauro, J.: The factor structure of the system usability scale. In: Kurosu, M. (ed.) HCD 2009. LNCS, vol. 5619, pp. 94–103. Springer, Heidelberg (2009). https://doi.org/10.1007/978-3-642-02806-9_12
5. Borsci, S., Federici, S., Lauriola, M.: On the dimensionality of the system usability scale: a test of alternative measurement models. Cogn. Process. **10**(3), 193–197 (2009). https://doi.org/10.1007/s10339-009-0268-9
6. Witmer, B.G., Singer, M.J.: Measuring presence in virtual environments: a presence questionnaire. Presence: Teleoperators Virtual Environ. **7**(3), 225–240 (1998)

7. Sanchez-Vives, M.V., Slater, M.: From presence to consciousness through virtual reality. Nat. Rev. Neurosci. **6**(4), 332–339 (2005). https://doi.org/10.1038/nrn1651

8. Christophers, L., Lee, C.T., Rooney, B.: Exploring subjective realism: do evaluative realism and felt realism respond differently to different cues? Int. J. Hum. Comput. Stud. **175**, 103027 (2023). https://doi.org/10.1016/j.ijhcs.2023.103027

9. Bohil, C.J., Alicea, B., Biocca, F.A.: Virtual reality in neuroscience research and therapy. Nat. Rev. Neurosci. **12**(12), 752–762 (2011). https://doi.org/10.1038/nrn3122

10. Gorini, A., Capideville, C.S., De Leo, G., Mantovani, F., Riva, G.: The role of immersion and narrative in mediated presence: the virtual hospital experience. Cyberpsychology Behavior Soc. Netw. **14**(3), 99–105 (2011). https://doi.org/10.1089/cyber.2010.0100

11. Clark, A.: Whatever next? Predictive brains, situated agents, and the future of cognitive science. Beh. Brain Sciences **36**(3), 181–204 (2013). https://doi.org/10.1017/S0140525X12000477

12. Moseley, G.L., Gallace, A., Spence, C.: Bodily illusions in health and disease: physiological and clinical perspectives and the concept of a cortical body matrix. Neurosci. Biobehav. Rev. **36**(1), 34–46 (2012). https://doi.org/10.1016/j.neubiorev.2011.03.013

13. Riva, G., Wiederhold, B.K., Mantovani, F.: Neuroscience of virtual reality: from virtual exposure to embodied medicine. Cyberpsychol. Behav. Soc. Netw. **22**(1), 82–96 (2019). https://doi.org/10.1089/cyber.2017.29099.gri

14. De Paolis, L.T., Arpaia, P., D'Errico, G., Gatto, C., Moccaldi, N., Nuccetelli, F.: Immersive VR as a promising technology for computer-supported mindfulness. In: De Paolis, L.T., Arpaia, P., Bourdot, P. (eds.) AVR 2021. LNCS, vol. 12980, pp. 156–166. Springer, Cham (2021). https://doi.org/10.1007/978-3-030-87595-4_12

15. Arpaia, P., D'Errico, G., De Paolis, L.T., Moccaldi, N., Nuccetelli, F.: A narrative review of mindfulness-based interventions using virtual reality. Mindfulness **13**(3), 556–571 (2022). https://doi.org/10.1007/s12671-021-01783-6

16. UQO Cyberpsychology Lab: Presence Questionnaire (2004). https://marketinginvolvement.files.wordpress.com/2013/12/pq-presence-questionnaire.pdf. Accessed 11 Jul 2023

17. De Paolis, L.T., De Luca, V.: The impact of the input interface in a virtual environment: the Vive controller and the Myo armband. Virtual Reality **24**(3), 483–502 (2020). https://doi.org/10.1007/s10055-019-00409-6

18. De Paolis, L.T., De Luca, V.: The effects of touchless interaction on usability and sense of presence in a virtual environment. Virtual Reality **26**(4), 1551–1571 (2022). https://doi.org/10.1007/s10055-022-00647-1

19. De Paolis, L.T., Chiarello, S., Gatto, C., Liaci, S., De Luca, V.: Virtual reality for the enhancement of cultural tangible and intangible heritage: the case study of the Castle of Corsano. Dig. Appl. Archaeol. Cult. Heritage **27**, e00238 (2022). https://doi.org/10.1016/j.daach.2022.e00238

20. De Paolis, L.T., Faggiano, F., Gatto, C., Barba, M., De Luca, V.: Immersive virtual reality for the fruition of ancient contexts: the case of the archaeological and Naturalistic Park of Santa Maria d'Agnano in Ostuni. Digital Appl. Archaeol. Cult. Heritage **27**, e00243 (2022). https://doi.org/10.1016/j.daach.2022.e00243

21. Seedhouse, E.: Presence within the virtual reality environment of the international space station. Virtual Reality **26**(3), 1145–1153 (2022). https://doi.org/10.1007/s10055-021-00615-1

22. Melo, M., Goncalves, G., Vasconcelos-Raposo, J., Bessa, M.: How much presence is enough? qualitative scales for interpreting the Igroup presence questionnaire score. IEEE Access **11**, 24675–24685 (2023). https://doi.org/10.1109/ACCESS.2023.3254892

23. Sagnier, C., Loup-Escande, E., Lourdeaux, D., Thouvenin, I., Valléry, G.: User acceptance of virtual reality: an extended technology acceptance model. Int. J. Hum. Comput. Interact. **36**(11), 993–1007 (2020). https://doi.org/10.1080/10447318.2019.1708612

24. Kelly, N.J.: Using interpretative phenomenological analysis to gain a qualitative understanding of presence in virtual reality. Virtual Reality **27**(2), 1173–1185 (2023). https://doi.org/10.1007/s10055-022-00719-2

25. Lim, C., Ji, Y.G.: The effects of physical coherence factors on presence in extended reality (XR). Int. J. Hum. Comput. Stud. **172**, 102994 (2023). https://doi.org/10.1016/j.ijhcs.2022.102994

26. Caldas, O.I., Sanchez, N., Mauledoux, M., Avilés, O.F., Rodriguez-Guerrero, C.: Leading presence-based strategies to manipulate user experience in virtual reality environments. Virtual Reality **26**(4), 1507–1518 (2022). https://doi.org/10.1007/s10055-022-00645-3

27. Hudson, S., Matson-Barkat, S., Pallamin, N., Jegou, G.: With or without you? Interaction and immersion in a virtual reality experience. J. Bus. Res. **100**, 459–468 (2019)

28. Livatino, S., et al.: Stereoscopic visualization and 3-D technologies in medical endoscopic teleoperation. IEEE Trans. Ind. Electron. **62**(1), 525–535 (2015)

29. Tcha-Tokey, K., Loup-Escande, E., Christmann, O., Richir, S.: Effects on user experience in an edutainment virtual environment: Comparison between CAVE and HMD. vol. Part F131193, pp. 1–8. Association for Computing Machinery (2017). https://doi.org/10.1145/3121283.3121284

30. Rhiu, I., Kim, Y.M., Kim, W., Yun, M.H.: The evaluation of user experience of a human walking and a driving simulation in the virtual reality. Int. J. Ind. Ergonomics **79**, 103002 (2020). https://doi.org/10.1016/j.ergon.2020.103002

31. Corelli, F., Battegazzorre, E., Strada, F., Bottino, A., Cimellaro, G.P.: Assessing the usability of different virtual reality systems for firefighter training. In: VISIGRAPP 2020 - Proceedings of the 15th International Joint Conference on Computer Vision, Imaging and Computer Graphics Theory and Applications, pp. 146–153. INSTICC, SciTePress (2020). https://doi.org/10.5220/0008962401460153

32. Mayor, J., Raya, L., Sanchez, A.: A comparative study of virtual reality methods of interaction and locomotion based on presence, cybersickness, and usability. IEEE Trans. Emerg. Top. Comput. **9**(3), 1542–1553 (2021). https://doi.org/10.1109/TETC.2019.2915287

33. Zenner, A., Makhsadov, A., Klingner, S., Liebemann, D., Krüger, A.: Immersive process model exploration in virtual reality. IEEE Trans. Vis. Comput. Graph. **26**(5), 2104–2114 (2020). https://doi.org/10.1109/TVCG.2020.2973476

34. Lee, J.T., Rajapakse, R.J., Miyata, K.: An Empirical Study on Intuitive Gesture Manipulation in Virtual Reality. vol. 2022-May, pp. 216–224. Institute of Electrical and Electronics Engineers Inc. (2022). https://doi.org/10.1109/ICVR55215.2022.9848105

35. Santos-Torres, A., Zarraonandia, T., Díaz, P., Aedo, I.: Exploring interaction mechanisms for map interfaces in virtual reality environments. In: Proceedings of the XIX International Conference on Human Computer Interaction, pp. 7:1–7:7. Interacción 2018, ACM, New York, USA (2018)

36. Gusai, E., Bassano, C., Solari, F., Chessa, M.: Interaction in an immersive collaborative virtual reality environment: a comparison between leap motion and HTC controllers. In: Battiato, S., Farinella, G.M., Leo, M., Gallo, G. (eds.) ICIAP 2017. LNCS, vol. 10590, pp. 290–300. Springer, Cham (2017). https://doi.org/10.1007/978-3-319-70742-6_27

37. Caggianese, G., Gallo, L., Neroni, P.: The Vive controllers vs. leap motion for interactions in virtual environments: a comparative evaluation. In: De Pietro, G., Gallo, L., Howlett, R.J., Jain, L.C., Vlacic, L. (eds.) KES-IIMSS-18 2018. SIST, vol. 98, pp. 24–33. Springer, Cham (2019). https://doi.org/10.1007/978-3-319-92231-7_3

38. Pai, Y., Dingler, T., Kunze, K.: Assessing hands-free interactions for VR using eye gaze and electromyography. Virtual Reality **23**(2), 119–131 (2019). https://doi.org/10.1007/s10055-018-0371-2

39. Unity Technologies: Unity (July 2023). retrieved from https://unity.com

40. Steam: SteamVR (July 2023). retrieved from https://steamcommunity.com/steamvr

41. HTC: HTC Vive (July 2023). retrieved from https://www.vive.com/

42. Brooke, J.: SUS - A quick and dirty usability scale (1996)

43. Revelle, W.: ICLUST: a cluster analytic approach to exploratory and confirmatory scale construction. Behav. Res. Methods Instrum. **10**(5), 739–742 (1978). https://doi.org/10.3758/bf03205389

44. Cronbach, L.: Coefficient alpha and the internal structure of tests. Psychometrika **16**(3), 297–334 (1951). https://doi.org/10.1007/BF02310555

45. Revelle, W.: Hierarchical cluster analysis and the internal structure of tests. Multivar. Behav. Res. **14**(1), 57–74 (1979). https://doi.org/10.1207/s15327906mbr1401_4

Seamless Virtual Object Transitions: Enhancing User Experience in Cross-Device Augmented Reality Environments

Robin Fischer[1]([✉])(ID), Wei-Xiang Lian[1], Shiann-Jang Wang[2], Wei-En Hsu[2], and Li-Chen Fu[1](ID)

[1] National Taiwan University, Taipei, Taiwan (ROC)
{d08922027,b06611038,lichen}@ntu.edu.tw
[2] JorJin Technologies Inc., New Taipei, Taiwan (ROC)
{lerdah.wang,vincent.hsu}@jorjin.com

Abstract. The integration of augmented reality (AR) headsets and projector displays has the potential to enhance shared experiences in various fields. However, the seamless transition of virtual objects between these devices remains a challenge. In this paper, we present a combined cross-device system that evaluates user experience based on different virtual object transition methods during both passive and active interactions. We hypothesize that certain transition techniques may result in confusion, discomfort, or disorientation, while others can improve immersion and ease of use. Our study comprises a virtual zoo scenario, where participants observe and interact with virtual alpacas, providing insights into their experiences with the different transition methods. The results reveal the impact of the content type and size on transitions between devices. We explain how to minimize confusion and discomfort while maximizing immersion and ease of use. Based on our findings, we propose future research directions to further refine cross-device interaction techniques, with the goal of creating more immersive, accessible, and user-friendly experiences in diverse applications, such as education, entertainment, and professional settings.

Keywords: Mixed/augmented reality · Cross-Device · Cross-Reality · Visualisation · SLAM

1 Introduction

Shared experiences in AR environments have not yet reached their full potential, primarily due to the high cost of AR headsets. This financial barrier has limited the widespread adoption of AR technology and its application in various fields, such as education, entertainment, and professional settings.

Low-cost AR headsets offer a more accessible alternative but often come with a limited field of view (FOV), which can hinder user experience. One potential solution to this limitation is the integration of an additional projector, which can expand the available display area and improve the overall experience.

L. T. De Paolis et al. (Eds.): XR Salento 2023, LNCS 14218, pp. 397–409, 2023.
https://doi.org/10.1007/978-3-031-43401-3_26

However, seamlessly combining a projector with a virtual object transition in an AR environment presents a unique challenge. The design and implementation of a cross-device system must account for the complexities of transitioning between different display devices while maintaining user immersion and minimizing disorientation.

In this research, we propose a combined cross-device system that addresses these challenges through the evaluation of user experience based on various virtual object transition methods. Our user study focuses on both passive and active interactions, enabling us to explore the impact of different transition techniques on the user experience. We implemented an example with two transitioning objects through hand interactions. By developing a better understanding of user preferences and needs in cross-device AR experiences, we aim to contribute to the ongoing development of more immersive, accessible, and user-friendly AR systems.

2   Related Works

The motivation to connect the real and virtual worlds has existed for many decades, and numerous aspects of sharing and collaborating with virtual content have been studied. In this section, we review some of the relevant works in the field of cross-device interactions and the integration of various XR modalities.

An early example by Billinghurst et al. demonstrates a marker-based collaboration space, emphasizing the potential for shared virtual experiences [5]. Gugenheimer et al. aimed to visualize VR for non-VR users by incorporating both projectors and smaller tablet screens to interact with the VR space [10]. These studies laid the groundwork for further exploration into cross-device virtual environments.

Cools et al. conducted more recent research on improving transitions between AR and VR and vice versa, showing enhanced workflows through the integration of different reality modalities [6]. In another study, they investigated how to incorporate desktop PC workflows into the AR space, with a focus on mirroring different input modalities in AR and desktop environments [7]. Batmaz et al. explored a specific spatial setup in which a user faced a wall with various virtual objects placed on it, but the interaction was limited to a VR headset [4]. This research offered insights into how physical spaces can be integrated with virtual environments. Another challenge in our research is the alignment of perception between the screen space and HMD space. As has been explored by Ghinea et al. [8] there is an objective discrepancy between the two modalities due to various factors. Combe et al. confirmed this theory.

The motivation for low-cost AR positioning and integration for long-range positioning and distant virtual objects has been investigated by Zhang et al. [18]. Hobson et al. proposed a system in which multiple devices could work on a shared topic, focusing on the technical limitations of web-based AR and websites in one system [11].

Martin-Gomez et al. aligned virtual content with real objects, emphasizing the algorithmic processing of mirror orientation for virtual object alignment [12].

These works highlight the importance of accurate positioning and alignment in creating immersive cross-device experiences.

The most related research to our work so far is by Schwajda et al. [15], which supports our hypothesis regarding the relevance of transitions. Their study includes different animations and object links but focuses more on data analysis than on user experience. Our research builds on these findings and emphasizes the evaluation of user experience in cross-device virtual object interactions.

3   Methodology

This chapter outlines the methodology for integrating a projector screen with multiple AR headsets. It covers the hardware, software components, communication protocol, and the SLAM localization system used in the Android-based AR headsets. The interconnection between each device during object transitions is shown in Fig. 1.

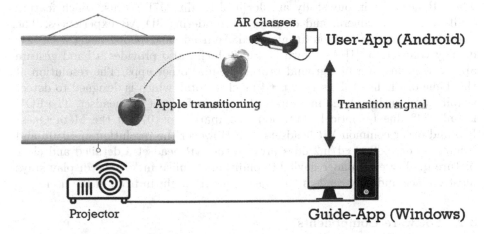

Fig. 1. Jorjin J-Reality J7EF Plus (left), ToF based hand gesture app (right)

3.1   Hardware Components

A. Projector Screen Connected to Windows PC

The static setup consists of various projector screens, and a Windows PC. The PC generates visual content and receives user interactions from the AR headsets. During development the PC can be connected to a single flat screen monitor for testing. However for the user study we attached 3 individual projector screens, which are each facing a different wall creating a large U-shaped screen space. This setup has the advantage that the user can look left and right while still being immersed in the virtual environment. The background also provides better visual features so the tracking of the AR headset becomes more stable.

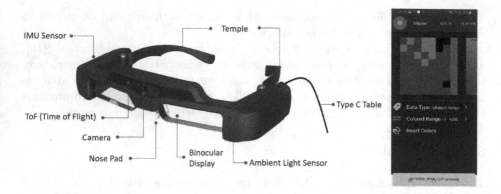

Fig. 2. Jorjin J-Reality J7EF Plus (left), ToF based hand gesture app (right)

B. Android-Based AR Headsets

The AR headsets in our study are Jorjin J-Reality J7EF Plus, which feature built-in sensors, camera, and displays for rendering 3D AR experiences. The applications have to run on an attached Android smartphone using a USB-C display connection. [1] As shown in Fig. 2 Jorjin also provides a hand gesture app which runs in a background process behind other apps. The resolution of the Time of Flight (ToF) sensor is 64 pixel in total, which is designed to detect swiping and pushing hand motions within 1m in front of the headset. The FOV is only 34° due to optical limitations, compared to 107° in the Meta Quest Pro and other common VR headsets. [13] However the resolution of 1080p and brightness of 1000 cd cd/m2 does provide the AR headset a detailed and clear picture quality even under daylight conditions. Unlike in VR the display stays mostly black and only renders an object once it's right in front of the user.

3.2   Software Components

A. Windows PC Based Guide-App

The PC software manages content generation, user interactions, and communication with the AR headsets. It includes various scene backgrounds, and intractable objects. When a user is joining the scene, it also processes the user interaction input, and communication with the user. The guide can control the pace of the experience, and trigger the next interaction part for the users based on keyboard commands. To evaluate the application in a standardized way, we focus on a simple repeatable experience, where an alpaca appears in front of the user, and then transitions out of the projected screen into the AR-headset. Secondly the guide can enable an apple tree to appear, which the user can interact with to feed the alpacas. We implemented a simple pathfinding system so the closest alpaca would go to eat the apple.

B. Android-Based AR User-App

The AR headset is rendering single virtual objects based on the users' actions or triggered by the guide. Both devices run a Unity [2] application using the same 3D assets, to maintain consistency throughout different object transitions. The app also includes a network client managing the communication with the guide app. For the sensor interface to the AR headset, we rely on the SDK provided by Jorjin. To track the user's position and orientation we implemented a custom SLAM localization system which is described separately in the following chapter.

Fig. 3. Android app screenshot, including blue dots, which represent feature points detected by our SLAM system. Only the alpaca is rendered in the app. (Color figure online)

SLAM Localization Implementation

For our customized SLAM system, we utilize the built-in sensors and cameras of the AR headset to create a map of the environment and determine the user's location. This information allows for accurate content overlay on the user's field of view. Since the headsets are running on Android we incorporated the Android version of ORB-SLAM2 from Mur-Artal et al. [14]. The original implementation was not build on Uinty, but we were able to use a suitable GitHub project as template for our Unity plugin. [17] ORB-SLAM2 establishes a coordinate system based on its initial estimated poses, but we needed to adapt the SLAM coordinate system to align with the smart space for a more robust application design. To accomplish this, we integrated the map saving and loading functionality from another GitHub repository [3] into our SLAM system. To transform the coordinate system to our desired frame in Unity, we extracted and visualized the point cloud data from the map file. By analyzing the point cloud, we determined the transformation matrix required to align the points with the projected smart space's wall. In our application, we loaded the map and applied the calculated transformation matrix to each estimated camera pose.

In a preliminary study we discovered several problems with the limited visual targets on the 2D screen for the SLAM system. If the scene was changed, or the virtual camera moved, the tracking would get lost. Even if plants in the scene were moving slightly in the wind, the localization inside the AR-display would constantly shift around. External localization systems would be needed to better stabilize the AR-headset localization. For this system we decided to limit the virtual environment to be mostly static, and only move one virtual object at a time, see Fig. 3.

3.3 Communication Protocol

The Windows PC and the Android-based AR headsets are using the Protobuf standard [9] for encoding wireless communication messages. The socket-based server runs on the Windows PC, ensuring low-latency and reliable data transfer. We did not measure the exact network latency, since we consider it negligible in our setup with a single router and two connected devices. The Windows PC hosting the guide app can initiate the scene for the AR user, and enable/disable what the user can interact with. These triggers are also send to the AR-user, who would see the corresponding virtual objects in the AR-display. Using hand gestures the user can send back commands to the guide app, which are synchronized to the virtual environment, to maintain seamless transitions between the devices.

4   User Study

As identified in related works, there is a lack of evaluation in cross-device virtual object interactions. This paper aims to assess the impact of these cross-device interactions on user experience, with a special emphasis on simultaneous multi screen visualizations. We propose the following hypotheses:

- H1: Users are sensitive to changing object size after transition. So the original size has to be maintained for better immersion.
- H2: Very rapid transitions can be distracting and uncomfortable for users.
- H3: Transitions that happen in the center of a users attention are inherently more immersive then hidden transitions. (e.g., hidden by other objects or at the screen's edge)

4.1 Study Scenario

We designed a virtual zoo experience for this study, in which participants explore and interact with a herd of alpacas with the help of a guide controlling the scenario. The study consists of two parts: passive observation and active engagement with the user. The guide has to supervise the participants, and also initiates the scenario, and enables or disables interactions.

Passive Observation

During passive observation, participants observe the transition of a virtual alpaca from the flat projection to the AR display. Users evaluate different animations for the alpaca's transition. This phase aims to assess user preferences for transition

Fig. 4. Alpaca transitioning from projector to AR glasses with a blue portal animation in the background (Color figure online)

animations and their effects on immersion and stability. The guide has to trigger the transition, which causes one alpaca to walk out of the screen, and reappear on the participants AR glasses as seen in Fig. 4. After the user had a moment to observe the alpaca more closely, the guide can trigger the alpaca to move back out of the glasses into the projection, and enable the active interaction with the alpacas.

Active Interactions
In the active engagement phase, participants pick virtual apples from a tree and throw them to the alpacas to feed them. This part of the experience features various methods of integrating and executing the transition between the AR-display and the projector screen. The guide can enable an apple tree to appear in front of the participant. Using the ToF sensor the AR glasses can detect a pull hand gesture, which triggers to pick the apple currently in focus of the AR-glasses. The apple will then be held in the center of the AR display, until the participant performs the push hand gesture, to throw the apple back into the projected environment. The closest alpaca will then move to the apple to eat it. Participants' opinions on these transitions are collected through a user opinion questionnaire (Fig. 5).

4.2 Participants and Procedure

17 participants (14 male/3 female) between 20 and 38 years old (M=26.59, SD=5.01) were recruited for the study both from academia and employees of an IT company, ensuring a more diverse sample. The experiment was conducted in a controlled environment, with each participant going through both passive

(a) pull hand to pick apple   (b) push hand to throw apple

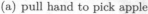

Fig. 5. Hand motions for apple interactions. Small phone screen is showing the what the user sees in AR

observation and active engagement phases. After completing the experience, participants filled out a questionnaire to provide feedback on the different transition methods and animations. In total 8 questions had to be answered, 4 about the passive observations, 3 for the active interactions, and 1 overall evaluation of the app.

5   Discussion of Results

The study results highlight the importance of optimizing transitions in cross-device interactions. We observed a potential for confusion and discomfort during transitions if they are not well-designed. In summary the virtual zoo experience was well received, as can be seen in the overall ranking of the complete system. We asked the participants to evaluate their general impression after observing the alpaca transition and apple interaction. Especially the immersion received high scores shown in Table 1. This results indicate our system's advantage over non-immersive applications using only 2D screens. Further feedback from the participants provided additional insights on different factors, which can maximize immersion in our application.

Table 1. Evaluation of general ranking of animations and general score.

Overall score	mean score	standard deviation
Entertainment	3.73	0.79
Immersion	3.91	0.83

5.1   Evaluation of Passive Observations

Impact of Object Size on Immersion

Since we hypothesized in H1 that the virtual object size would influence the user's impression of the transition, we designed 3 different alpaca sizes which

Fig. 6. Through lens photo of differently sized alpacas after transition.

were moving through the same transition, as shown in Fig. 6. The portal behind the alpaca stayed the same size.

User feedback indicated that the smallest alpaca seemed further away, and not consistent to be the moving out of the projected screen. The bigger sizes received higher scores, as shown in Fig. 7 b), however the biggest size was clipping out of the AR-headsets' FOV, which also distracted the participants. Therefore the middle size showing the upper body of the alpaca received the highest scores, which also maintained the size of the alpaca before the transition, confirming Hypothesis H1.

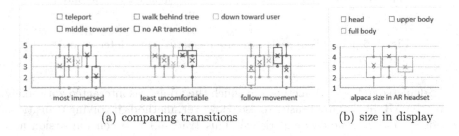

(a) comparing transitions   (b) size in display

Fig. 7. 5-point Likert scale response for passive alpaca observations.

Impact of Different Transition Methods

As shown in Fig. 7 a), methods that employed seamless visual transitions received higher scores in terms of immersion and the ability to follow the alpaca's movement. The "walk through middle" animation emerged as the more most immersive and easy-to-follow methods. This supports Hypothesis H3, suggesting that transitions through a virtual portal in the middle of the screen are inherently more immersive than indirect transitions where the alpaca moves out of view before reappearing. It would be valuable to further examine the specific factors that contribute to this increased sense of immersion, such as the visual continuity or spatial consistency provided by the portal.

On the other hand, the "walk behind three" and "down toward user" methods scored lower in terms of immersion and ease of following the alpaca's movement. This may indicate that the need to move one's head to observe the transitions can be disorienting for users, supporting Hypothesis H2. Especially the discomfort score further underlines the problem of excessive movements during the transition. Future research could explore ways to minimize this confusion and enhance the user experience in situations where transitions take place over larger areas with multiple objects, creating a more challenging environment for the user. The "no AR transition" and "teleport" options were designed as options with minimal discomfort, due to lack of movement of the alpaca. But apparently confused the participants, which caused more negative scores.

5.2   Evaluation of Active Interactions

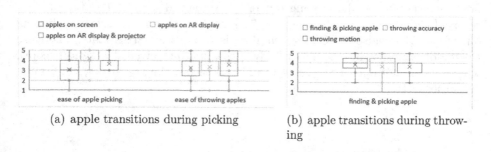

(a) apple transitions during picking

(b) apple transitions during throwing

Fig. 8. 5-point Likert scale response for active apple interaction.

As depicted in Fig. 8 a), methods in which the apple was interacted with solely within the AR display were easier to use. However, methods involving transitions provided a more immersive experience. This trade-off between immersion and ease of use highlights the importance of finding a balance when designing cross-device interactions. It may be beneficial to explore adaptive techniques that adjust the level of immersion or the complexity of the interaction method based on user skill level or familiarity with the technology.

Additionally, the results suggest that users prefer methods where the interaction occurs primarily within a single device. This could be due to the reduced cognitive load or the lower risk of disorientation associated with single-device interactions. Especially for the throwing action user's might feel disoriented by the apple. Fig. 8 b) Further investigation of the factors that contribute to this preference, such as the role of visual attention or the impact of device switching on task performance, could help inform the design of more effective and user-friendly cross-device experiences.

5.3   Limitations

The current study has revealed promising a system to create immersive AR experiences on low cost devices. However throughout the course of this work, we noticed the following limitations:

- The scenario is limited to a single scene and interaction, which may not fully represent the range of possible cross-device interactions.
- Limited movement was allowed due to the weak SLAM performance of the AR headsets, potentially impacting the user experience.
- Improved alignment through external tracking solutions or IMUs could enhance the overall experience, but were not utilized in this study.
- A larger scale user study, which also compares different types of devices for immersive AR applications could provide further insights on the impact of the device setup.

Many of these shortcomings can be addressed by integrating additional external hardware and additional data processing techniques. In the future, advancements in AR headset sensing capabilities and high-fidelity hand tracking may enable more nuanced user actions and interactions with virtual objects. The work by Tang et al. Presents a promising outlook for realistic hand interactions with virtual objects which would be suitable for low cost AR-headsets [16].

6   Conclusion and Future Work

In this study, we investigated the impact of different transition animations and interaction methods on user experience in a cross-device virtual zoo scenario. The results highlighted the importance of carefully designing and optimizing transitions to minimize confusion, discomfort, and disorientation while maximizing immersion and ease of use.

Our findings suggest that seamless visual transitions, which the user can perceive through the middle of the screen, can enhance user immersion and the ability to follow virtual objects during cross-device interactions. Conversely, methods without AR transitions were found to be less immersive and more disorienting for users. Additionally, the trade-off between immersion and hardware limitations, underscores the need for finding a balance that optimizes user preferences in context with the given hardware.

We propose that future work should focus on the following aspects:

1. Investigating a broader range of scenarios, interactions, and user groups to gain a more comprehensive understanding of user preferences and needs in cross-device experiences.
2. Exploring adaptive techniques that adjust the level of immersion or complexity of interaction methods based on user familiarity or skill, to provide a more personalized and user-centered experience.

3. Examining the long-term effects of using different transition animations and interaction methods, including the impact of familiarity and the learning curve associated with these techniques.
4. Assessing the cognitive load associated with different transition animations and interaction methods, and exploring the relationship between cognitive load and user experience.
5. Investigating the role of audio and haptic feedback in cross-device experiences, examining their impact on user engagement, immersion, and satisfaction.

Through continued research and development, we can refine and enhance cross-device interaction techniques to create more immersive, accessible, and user-friendly experiences for a wide range of applications, from entertainment and education to professional and industrial settings.

Acknowledgements. We'd like to acknowledge that various open source images from https://www.pngegg.com were used in this study. This work was supported in part by a grant from Jorjin Technologies Inc. and the Ministry of Science and Technology of Taiwan, and NTU Center for Artificial Intelligence Advanced Robotics, under the grant numbers MOST 110-2634-F-002-049, MOST 110-2221-E-002-166-MY3, MOST 111-2622-E-002-032.

References

1. Jorjin j7ef plus ar smartglasses. https://www.jorjin.com/products/ar-smart-glasses/j-reality/j7ef-plus/. Accessed 02 Jun 2023
2. Unity. https://unity.com/. Accessed 02 Jun 2023
3. Alejandro, S.: Github repository for slam saving and loading. https://github.com/AlejandroSilvestri/osmap. Accessed 02 Jun 2023
4. Batmaz, A.U., Mutasim, A.K., Malekmakan, M., Sadr, E., Stuerzlinger, W.: Touch the wall: comparison of virtual and augmented reality with conventional 2D screen eye-hand coordination training systems. In: 2020 IEEE Conference on Virtual Reality and 3D User Interfaces (VR), pp. 184–193 (2020). https://doi.org/10.1109/VR46266.2020.00037
5. Billinghurst, M., Poupyrev, I., Kato, H., May, R.: Mixing realities in shared space: an augmented reality interface for collaborative computing. In: 2000 IEEE International Conference on Multimedia and Expo. ICME2000. Proceedings. Latest Advances in the Fast Changing World of Multimedia (Cat. No.00TH8532). vol. 3, pp. 1641–1644 vol 3 (2000). https://doi.org/10.1109/ICME.2000.871085
6. Cools, R., Esteves, A., Simeone, A.L.: Blending spaces: cross-reality interaction techniques for object transitions between distinct virtual and augmented realities. In: 2022 IEEE International Symposium on Mixed and Augmented Reality (ISMAR), pp. 528–537 (2022). https://doi.org/10.1109/ISMAR55827.2022.00069
7. Cools, R., Gottsacker, M., Simeone, A., Bruder, G., Welch, G., Feiner, S.: Towards a desktop-AR prototyping framework: Prototyping cross-reality between desktops and augmented reality. In: 2022 IEEE International Symposium on Mixed and Augmented Reality Adjunct (ISMAR-Adjunct), pp. 175–182 (2022). https://doi.org/10.1109/ISMAR-Adjunct57072.2022.00040

8. Ghinea, M., Frunză, D., Chardonnet, J.-R., Merienne, F., Kemeny, A.: Perception of absolute distances within different visualization systems: HMD and CAVE. In: De Paolis, L.T., Bourdot, P. (eds.) AVR 2018. LNCS, vol. 10850, pp. 148–161. Springer, Cham (2018). https://doi.org/10.1007/978-3-319-95270-3_10

9. Google: Protocol buffers. https://protobuf.dev/. Accessed 02 Jun 2023

10. Gugenheimer, J., Stemasov, E., Frommel, J., Rukzio, E.: ShareVR: enabling co-located experiences for virtual reality between HMD and non-HMD users. In: Proceedings of the 2017 CHI Conference on Human Factors in Computing Systems, pp. 4021–4033. CHI 2017, Association for Computing Machinery, New York, USA (2017). https://doi.org/10.1145/3025453.3025683

11. Hobson, T., Duncan, J., Raji, M., Lu, A., Huang, J.: Alpaca: AR graphics extensions for web applications. In: 2020 IEEE Conference on Virtual Reality and 3D User Interfaces (VR), pp. 174–183 (2020). https://doi.org/10.1109/VR46266.2020.00036

12. Martin-Gomez, A., Winkler, A., Yu, K., Roth, D., Eck, U., Navab, N.: Augmented mirrors. In: 2020 IEEE International Symposium on Mixed and Augmented Reality (ISMAR), pp. 217–226 (2020). https://doi.org/10.1109/ISMAR50242.2020.00045

13. Meta Platforms Inc,: Quest hardware specifications (2023). https://en.wikipedia.org/wiki/Meta_Quest_Pro

14. Mur-Artal, R., Tardós, J.D.: ORB-SLAM2: an open-source slam system for monocular, stereo, and RGB-D cameras. IEEE Trans. Robot. **33**(5), 1255–1262 (2017). https://doi.org/10.1109/TRO.2017.2705103

15. Schwajda, D., Friedl, J., Pointecker, F., Jetter, H.C., Anthes, C.: Transforming graph data visualisations from 2D displays into augmented reality 3D space: a quantitative study. Front. Virtual Reality **4**, 28 (2023)

16. Tang, X., Hu, X., Fu, C.W., Cohen-Or, D.: GrabAR: occlusion-aware grabbing virtual objects in AR. In: Proceedings of the 33rd Annual ACM Symposium on User Interface Software and Technology, pp. 697–708. UIST 2020, Association for Computing Machinery, New York, USA (2020). https://doi.org/10.1145/3379337.3415835

17. Ying: Github repository for unity slam integration. https://github.com/ygx2011/AR_course. Accessed 02 Jun 2023

18. Zhang, Y., Tang, L.: Collaborative mixed reality annotations system for science and history education based on UWB positioning and low-cost AR glasses. In: De Paolis, L.T., Arpaia, P., Sacco, M. (eds.) Extended Reality. XR Salento 2022. Lecture Notes in Computer Science. vol. 13446. Springer, Cham (2022). https://doi.org/10.1007/978-3-031-15553-6_12

Usability Evaluation of Mixed Reality Applications in VET Training

Nadia Catenazzi[✉] ⓘ, Lorenzo Sommaruga ⓘ, and Chiara Locatelli

University of Applied Sciences and Arts of Southern Switzerland, Manno, Switzerland
nadia.catenazzi@supsi.ch

Abstract. This paper presents a usability study of wearable and handheld Mixed Reality and hypervideo technologies to support procedural learning in the vocational education and training context. As a case study an application based on the Tangram game was developed for HoloLens 2, Android smartphones and hypervideo. The app is structured as a procedural learning activity with incremental levels of scaffolding. The usability of these applications was evaluated in a user testing involving 90 students. No remarkable difference has emerged among the three applications in terms of completion rate during the learning process, but in the retention and transfer tasks HoloLens 2 users performed worse than users of the other devices. Considering the time on task metric, HoloLens 2 users time was aligned with hypervideo, while smartphone users generally took more time, probably because smartphones are not hand-free devices. An expert review was also conducted, providing a number of suggestions for improvements, mainly concerning the interaction design, and the positioning of holograms in the physical space. In the comparison among the devices, none was clearly preferred over the other: HoloLens 2 presented higher attractiveness, motivation of use, sense of immersion, but also greater cognitive load; handheld devices resulted easy to use but required considerable physical effort in activities where they needed to be hold for a long time. Hypervideo was easy to access, with an intuitive interaction, but less attractive.

Keywords: Usability · User experience · Interaction · wearable MR · handheld MR · hypervideo

1 Introduction

Vocational education and training (VET) plays a pivotal role in the Swiss educational landscape [1]. The Swiss VET system is described as dual since it is at the intersection of the educational and production tracks. Since VET strongly sustains procedural knowledge development, an interesting area of research concerns technologies that support this kind of knowledge. In particular, interactive technologies such as hypervideo and augmented/mixed reality are the object of this study, since they stimulate active learners' engagement.

L. T. De Paolis et al. (Eds.): XR Salento 2023, LNCS 14218, pp. 410–423, 2023.
https://doi.org/10.1007/978-3-031-43401-3_27

Hypervideo (HV) is a form of interactive video that allows users to interact with the content and other users through features such as navigation control, annotations, hyperlinks, quizzes, etc. [2]. It has been used for teaching and learning in various VET contexts, providing support for learners' motivation, declarative and procedural knowledge acquisition and transfer, reflection, error analysis, and feedback processes [3].

Concerning Augmented Reality (AR) and Mixed Reality (MR), there is not a common unique definition of the terms [4]. As firstly introduced by Milgram in 1994 [5], MR could be considered to cover a continuum ranging between the real and the virtual environment. More recently, according to Rokhsaritalemi et al. [6], MR is well characterized by three features: immersion, interaction, information. Immersion refers to the real-time processing and interpretation of the user's environment; interaction of the user with MR space is performed without any controller, using natural communication modes such as gestures, voice, and gaze; information refers to virtual objects being registered in time and space in the user environment. While immersion and information are present also in Augmented Reality, interaction is a distinctive feature of MR. Nowadays, the concept of mixed reality includes interesting new features, experimented also on handheld devices, as highlighted in [7], including: environmental understanding (spatial mapping and anchors); human understanding (hand-tracking, eye-tracking, and speech input); spatial sound; locations and positioning in both physical and virtual spaces; collaboration on 3D assets in mixed reality spaces. In our work, MR can be considered a space that combines real and virtual objects, reciprocally aligned, and enables user interaction in real time. From the state of the art about the use of augmented/mixed reality in VET, on the basis of systematic literature reviews of more than 80 empirical studies published between 2000 and 2021 [8, 9], it emerges that AR has a significant potential to improve learning, motivation and skills of students, by creating immersive and engaging experiences, but that further studies are needed to explore the mediating factors, the pedagogical implications and the technical and organizational challenges of MR.

In conclusion, both HV and MR have demonstrated to be promising technologies to support VET. A distinctive feature of MR compared to HV is its physical dimension. In MR users have the possibility of physical manipulation and natural interaction, especially when tangible objects are exploited [10]. While HV is a consolidated technology the use of MR in VET is relatively new and deserves additional investigation.

This paper presents a usability study of MR and HV technologies to support procedural learning with emphasis on MR as an emerging solution. In particular, it compares three different technological approaches: wearable MR with HoloLens 2, handheld MR with smartphones, and hypervideo on desktop computers. As a case study for this comparison a specific application based on the Tangram game was developed. The app is structured as a procedural learning activity with different levels of scaffolding. A user testing was conducted with the purpose to compare the three approaches mainly in terms of usability, but also in terms of motivation, cognitive load, presence, etc. As an additional usability study method, an expert review was also carried out with the objective to identify usability issues, collect suggestions for improvements, and compare the different approaches.

This work has been carried out within the MARHVEL research project (project number 1315002129, 2021–2025) funded by the Swiss State Secretariat for Education, Research and Innovation, about the assessment of use of hypervideo and Mixed Reality, both wearable and handheld, for skills development in VET. One of the main project objectives was to investigate the usability of MR compared to hypervideo, in terms of efficiency, effectiveness and satisfaction. Considering the potential of MR and HV technologies, the MARHVEL project investigates the design and development of different scenarios of use of HV and handheld and wearable MR for skill development. The Tangram study described in this paper, was carried out after a first project phase, where a MR technological review and a feasibility study were conducted. The development of different demonstrators allowed us to identify potentials and issues of HoloLens 2. The most representative was the *computer assembly* prototype, developed both as a handheld and wearable app, which aims to teach how to assemble a computer, by positioning different components on a computer motherboard [11]. The major challenges emerged during the development concerned object detection, tracking and registration. The main issues were connected to the size of the objects to be manipulated, the environment lighting and the distance between the manipulated objects and the viewer's eye. During the demonstration events, participants recognized some strengths of the prototype: they appreciated the engaging experience, the immersion feeling and the learning by doing approach. The *computer assembly* prototype, together with other demonstrators about the HoloLens 2 interaction modalities, has posed the basis for the Tangram application described in this study.

This paper firstly describes the Tangram applications, then reports the user testing experience with particular focus on the MR approaches, by presenting the testing methodology and emerged findings. Finally, it summarizes the expert review results.

2 The Tangram Applications

A specific application to teach the learner how to solve the tangram puzzle was developed according to the multimedia learning principles [12] in three versions: for HoloLens 2, for Android smartphones and for desktop computer as a hypervideo.

The learning process foresees different steps, with incremental levels of scaffolding:

- in the first step (or first attempt) the user is asked to assemble the tangram without any help;
- in the second attempt some instructions are given about which tiles to place first, in particular the suggestion is to start from the biggest tiles;
- in the third attempt, visual clues about where to place the two biggest tiles are provided with holograms appearing over the board;
- in the fourth attempt, the step is decomposed into some sub-steps, and visual clues and animations are provided about the position of four tiles.

At the end of this process, the learner is asked to try again to compose the tangram without any help (*retention* task). Finally, he/she is asked to make a different shape using the same tiles (*transfer* task). It is worth noting that if the user performs one of the first three steps correctly, then he/she skips the following ones and goes directly to the retention activity.

In order to help users to acquire familiarity with the devices and their interaction modalities, a short Tutorial was also developed in a similar way for the three devices.

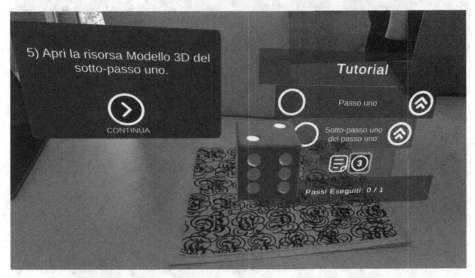

Fig. 1. A step of the Tutorial as it appears on a handheld device.

The Tutorial is structured in a sequence of different steps and sub-steps including some additional resources in the form of text, images, and 3d object holograms. The user is asked to follow some instructions in order to complete simple activities, such as expanding a step, showing/hiding a panel with extra textual information, solving a quiz, etc. For example, considering the handheld version, Fig. 1 shows the red dice 3d hologram resource, displayed by means of the highlighted button ("3"), of the Sub-step one ("Sotto-passo uno") of Step One ("Passo uno"). These actions require a number of basic interactions with the app interface that permit the user to get acquainted with both the device and its interaction modalities. Allowing a more homogenous level of knowledge among the end users on the three different devices.

The next sections provide additional details of the Tangram app for the three devices.

2.1 Wearable MR Tangram

The wearable version of the MR Tangram was developed as an app for the HoloLens 2 device by means of the Mixed Reality Toolkit (MRTK). The prototype was also implemented using the Unity development environment and Vuforia Engine. In addition to the panels showing the steps, sub-steps and resources of the tangram activity, some holographic geometric objects (red contour) are overlayed to the real board in order to give specific signals to the user, as presented in Fig. 2. In particular, a holographic fuchsia tile is animated for representing the correct insertion of this piece. It is worth noting that the appearance of the holograms occurs in-time, in-space and in-context only when the end user needs some helping hints for progressing, following a scaffolding approach.

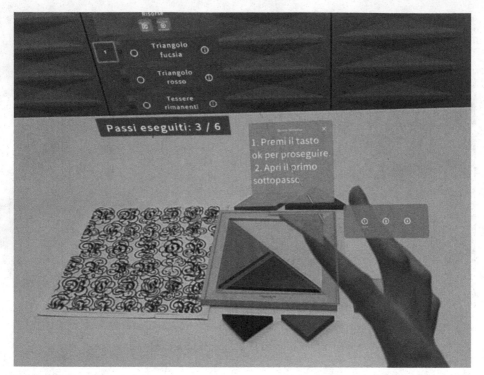

Fig. 2. The fourth step of the MR Tangram presented on the HoloLens 2 with the animation of a suggested fuchsia tile insertion.

2.2 Handheld MR Tangram

The handheld version of the MR Tangram was developed as an app for an Android smartphone device, basing the implementation on the Unity development environment and AR Foundation framework. In addition to the panel showing the steps, sub-steps and resources of the tangram activity, some holographic geometric objects (red contour) are also here overlayed to the real board in order to give specific signals to the user, as presented in Fig. 3.

2.3 Hypervideo Tangram

The Hypervideo version of the Tangram was developed as an interactive video on the iVideo platform (http://ivideo.education), previously developed by SUFFP together with SUPSI. One of the main features of an iVideo, exploited here, is that a video presentation can be played on a laptop or other devices as a traditional video with, in addition, some active points. These introduce more interactive functionalities, such as jumping and stopping, that allow the instructional Tangram procedure to be presented in the form of an hypervideo. The main interface of the Tangram iVideo is presented in Fig. 4, showing the fourth step of the MR Tangram procedure.

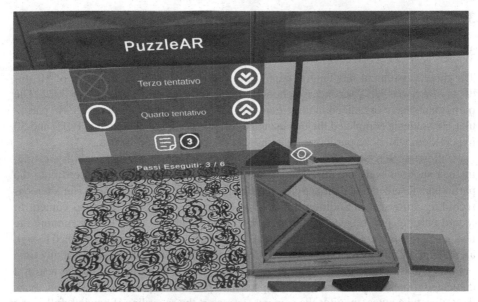

Fig. 3. The fourth step of the MR Tangram presented on a handheld device.

Fig. 4. The fourth MR Tangram step presented as an hypervideo on laptop.

3 User Testing of the Tangram Applications

3.1 Methodology

The three versions of the Tangram application were evaluated by a sample of 90 students of a Swiss VET secondary school in the period November-December 2022. The participants were organized in three randomized groups, one for each device. In particular, 28 students completed the test using HoloLens 2 (HL), 31 HandHeld (HH) and 30 hypervideo, while one participant withdrew at the beginning of the test.

Following Bennan's recommendations [13] about mobile AR app usability testing, the test sessions were organized in such a way that it was possible to record both the participants' screen and their activity in the testing room. The applications run a screen-recording software. In addition, the room was equipped with an external camera to record participants' fingers as they were interacting with the apps. Before running the test, participants were informed about what to expect during the study and asked to sign an Informed Consent form. They were allowed to withdraw from the study at any time before or during test. One student at a time was invited to participate in the test in a dedicated room, where a facilitator was present to provide help during the session, mark the times, take notes, monitor the cameras, or restart the recording if needed, following a precise protocol.

The methods used to collect data include *direct observation*, useful to record the participant's activity, the time taken to perform a specific task, whether the user was able to complete it, any feedback and unexpected behavior; *automatic logs* of the user activity recorded in logfiles; *questionnaires* submitted at the end of crucial phases of the test to collect additional information about cognitive load, motivation, sense of presence, etc.

The next sections mainly present the results collected through direct observation, in particular concerning task completion and time on task, and provides additional findings got through logfile processing. *Task completion* and *time on task* are the two main metrics used for usability testing in this study. The elaboration of the questionnaires results is currently in progress, taking into consideration also non-parametric tests.

3.2 Task Completion and Time on Task Results

Data concerning task completion and time on task, manually collected by the observer during the testing sessions, are reported in the following tables. The assigned task is composing the puzzle, and can be completed in any of the four steps of the procedure.

Table 1 reports the number of students completing the different attempts, the retention and the transfer task, respectively out of 28 for HL, 31 for HH and 30 for HV. It also highlights in gray the completion rate in all the attempts, retention and transfer tasks for each device.

A first observation emerged from the table is that the number of students able to solve the puzzle in the first three attempts is lower with HL (1) compared to HH (6) and HV (4). In other words, most of the HL users required the maximum support to be able to complete the puzzle. Nevertheless, concerning the percentage of students able to compose the puzzle in the four attempts, i.e., during the learning process, we can notice that there is not a significant difference among the three devices in the task completion

Table 1. Number of successful students and completion rate comparison among the three devices.

	MR-HL	MR-HH	HV
Attempt_1	0	1	0
Attempt_2	1	1	2
Attempt_3	0	4	2
Attempt_4	13	11	11
Total #	14	17	15
Total %	50.00%	54.84%	50.00%
Retention #	16	24	28
Retention %	57.14%	77.42%	93.33%
Transfer #	13	21	19
Transfer %	46.43%	67.74%	63.33%

(50% with HL, 54.84% with HH, 50% with HV); the only remark is that smartphone users performed slightly better. However, there is a remarkable difference in the *retention* task, where students reached 93.33% of completion rate using HV, 77.42% using HH and 57.14% using HL. In the transfer task, the best performances were reached using HH, followed by HV, and HL. A possible reason explaining the retention performance can be that MR devices, especially HoloLens 2, induce more distraction because they require focusing the attention on the device usage rather than on the task being performed. The lower familiarity with MR applications and devices could be the reason of this result.

Table 2 summarizes for each device the average time on task, expressed in seconds, for each attempt and for all the attempts together (Average Time on all attempts). This value is calculated as an average of the time required to complete the puzzle in all the attempts by all students using a specific device, independently from the step where the task is completed. Empty cells in the table represent attempts where no students were able to complete the task by the maximum time.

The results indicate that the "Average time on all attempts" about HH is higher than the average time of the other 2 devices, which are very similar. This can be justified by the fact that HH devices have to be placed on the table in order to have hands free to operate on the Tangram tiles.

Concerning the retention task, the differences are less remarkable, slower with the HH and quicker with HV. In the transfer task, the average time for HV and HH is significantly higher compared to HL. As shown in Table 1, few students were able to compose a different puzzle (transfer task) with HL compared to HH and HV, but they did it quicker. It is worth noting that the retention and transfer task are independent from the device, since participants do not receive any help beyond the initial instructions.

Other findings came out from direct observation of the participants' behavior:

Table 2. Average Time on task comparison in seconds among the three devices.

	MR-HL	MR-HH	HV
Attempt_1 Average Time		32.85	
Attempt_2 Average Time	39.00	56.65	49.58
Attempt_3 Average Time		37.09	23.87
Attempt_4 Average Time	31.30	40.66	30.25
Average Time on all attempts	31.85	39.19	31.76
Average Retention Time	26.01	29.77	23.06
Average Transfer Time	69.02	81.95	83.25

- a large majority users had little or no familiarity with HL interaction and found difficulties with some gestures such as the double pinch, and in some cases even pressing a holographic button because it was difficult to understand how far the active area is;
- after an initial difficulty with HH devices in locating the marker and finding the holograms in the physical space, participants proceeded quickly. Another observation is that, since the smartphone is not a hand-free device, the execution of some tasks required users to temporarily place the device on the table or accomplish the task with one hand;
- *hypervideo* was found quite simple and intuitive for its similarity with traditional videos, although sometimes participants expected to interact with linear videos. In some cases, it was not clear where to click on the screen to activate a particular object. A specific behavior in interacting with hypervideo is that participants placed the cursor in the next right position while they were still listening to the audio instructions.
- A general observation concerning all the devices is that participants were not willing to listen to the entire message and were impatient to proceed.

3.3 Additional Findings from Logfile Analysis

During this experiment, logfiles of the user activity were automatically recorded. Their analysis was useful, on one hand, to confirm the manually collected data and, on the other hand, to bring additional findings about the user interaction with the application.

HoloLens 2 Logfile of the Tangram App Usage. In the log files different data were stored such as an event start and end-time. The analysis of logfile data of the HoloLens 2 device allowed conclusions to be drawn about the same usability metrics collected by hand during the user testing: *task completion* and *time on task*. At the end of each step the participant was asked to check a confirmation button whether he/she had accomplished the required task; this information was used to state that the completion condition was fulfilled and to record the time taken. For each step a maximum time was given. If the student was not able to accomplish the task by this time, the completion condition was automatically set to false.

Concerning *task completion*, by analysing the logfiles of the 28 students who used the *Tangram* application for HoloLens 2, it emerges, as shown in Table 3, that:

- no student managed to compose the tangram at the first attempt;
- 1 student at the second attempt;
- 13 students at the fourth attempt;
- 16 students were able to accomplish the retention task;
- 13 students were able to make a different puzzle (transfer task).

Table 3. Numbers of students completing the task in HoloLens 2.

	MR-HL
Attempt_1	0
Attempt_2	1
Attempt_3	0
Attempt_4	13
Retention #	16
Transfer #	13

The results indicate that most of the students needed all the training steps before being able to make the puzzle alone, reaching a completion rate of almost 60% in the retention activity. These data are aligned with what emerged in the manual recording accomplished by the observer during the user testing, confirming the manually collected data.

Considering the *time on task* metric, a discrepancy was observed between the log data and the time manually recorded. Since the completion of a specific task is self-declared by the users, it happened that they tapped before having completed task or forgot to check the completion button, since they can move to the next step without checking it.

This experiment provided interesting clues on how to create logfiles to record user interactions with HoloLens 2, and opened the way towards interesting developments for the future, for instance, the integration of hand or eye-tracking recording. Logfiles are a powerful tool to track user interaction, and to avoid the time-consuming activity of manual data recording, but they have to be properly designed considering the final usage.

Handheld and Hypervideo Logfiles of the Tutorial Usage. Logfiles were also used to get additional insights on the user interaction during the familiarization phase (tutorial). In particular, handheld and hypervideo logfiles about the tutorial usage were analysed, considering a sample of overall 43 users, 21 for HH and 22 for HV. HL logfile data for the tutorial were not correctly recorded because of a technical issue and are not considered here.

Data about the tutorial duration, the quiz duration and number of textual and 3D resources activations were collected. It was noted that the selection of resources was a difficult task for most participants, leading to further investigation.

The tutorial duration was calculated for each student starting from step 1 activation till the quiz completion. Table 4 reports the average tutorial and quiz duration time on each device. The results about the tutorial duration (119 s vs. 168 s) indicate that students were quicker in accomplishing the tutorial activities with HH devices compared to HV; this can depend on the fact that participants are more familiar smartphones than with hyper-videos. Concerning the average quiz duration, the results indicate that students on average took more time on HH devices than on HV (24 s vs. 19 s). A possible reason is connected to the way quizzes are presented in HH; the users have to open them and then to find the way to select the "check" button (only the small icon at the left is active and not the entire "controlla" text under the answers).

Concerning resource activation, a problem emerged with the HH devices in opening textual and 3D resources. In the tutorial the user is asked to open the resource once; the logfile results show that the most part of students opened it more than once; only 38% of them perform the task correctly. The same occurs for 3D resources, although the percentage of correct activations is higher (67%). This is probably due to the fact the user did not see the results of his/her action and tried to tap the button several times (since no other feedback was provided); a better result was got with the 3D resource where most students demonstrated to have learned. The same problem of resource activation occurred sometimes with HV but less frequently.

Table 4. Comparison between HH and HV tutorial usage.

	HH	HV
Average tutorial duration (s)	119	168
Average quiz duration (s)	24	19
Textual resource correct activation %	38	86
3D resource correct activation %	67	77

4   Expert Review Results

As an additional usability study method, an expert review was carried out by 7 experts with the objective to identify usability issues, collect suggestions for improvements, and compare the different approaches. The results, fully described by Sommaruga [14], are briefly summarized in this section.

Expert review was organized in two main phases: a *testing session*, where each expert worked individually on the three applications, while an observer took notes and answered occurring questions, and a *final discussion* where the three devices were compared on the basis of a number of user experience (UX) factors.

The main emerged issues from the first phase were related to the interaction design, and size and positioning of virtual objects in the physical space in MR applications. Concerning the interaction design, the main problems include: too long instructions, quite heavy interaction (repetitive confirmation requests) with potential decrease of attention, accessibility issues mainly concerning color choice, bad design of some buttons, not intuitive gestures in HoloLens 2. With respect to holograms' positioning, in some cases experts experienced a sense of disorientation because holograms were not visible. They highlighted that it was hard to find them in the physical space and sometimes it was not possible to activate buttons or other active areas, because holograms overlapped them. They also underlined that large movements of the head or arm were required, due to the limited field of view.

Experts' recommendations were mainly oriented towards solving these issues. An interesting comment was the need to take into greater consideration the peculiar affordances of the device, especially for HoloLens 2.

In the final discussion experts evaluated the usability of the devices; all the them were accepted and none was clearly preferred over the other. HoloLens 2 presented higher attractiveness, motivation of use, sense of immersion, but also implied a higher cognitive load compared to the other devices, and required an initial training. Handheld devices were well-known and easy to use but required a considerable physical effort in activities where they need to be hold for a long time. Hypervideo was easy to access, with an intuitive interaction, but less attractive.

Both *effectiveness* and *efficiency* were judged medium-high or high for the three devices, while the greatest *satisfaction* was obtained with HoloLens 2, probably for the "novelty" effect. *Learnability* was better for handheld compared to the other devices, probably because of the high familiarity with the device.

5 Conclusions

This paper has presented the results of a usability evaluation of a didactic application, aimed to teach how to solve the Tangram puzzle, developed in three versions: as a wearable MR app for HoloLens 2, as a handheld MR app for Android smartphones, as a hypervideo app for desktop computers. The app consists of different learning steps (attempts) with incremental levels of scaffolding. At end of the learning process, a retention and transfer task are foreseen to verify if the users have learned and are able to apply the acquired knowledge in a similar situation.

The applications were evaluated through a *user testing* involving 90 participants, with the purpose to compare the three approaches mainly in terms of usability, and through an *expert review*, in order to identify usability issues, collect suggestions for improvements, and compare the different approaches.

Two main metrics were considered during the user testing: *task completion* and *time on task*; data were manually collected by the observers during the testing sessions but also confirmed for HL by logfiles. No remarkable difference emerged among the three devices in terms of *completion rate* during the learning process, but in the retention and transfer tasks HoloLens users performed worse than users using the other devices. A possible reason is that HoloLens is a new device and users have no familiarity with its interaction modalities and gestures. Considering the *time on task* metric, HoloLens users time was aligned with hypervideo, while smartphone users generally took more time in task execution. This probably depends on the fact that smartphone are not hand-free devices and for some activities additional time is required.

An additional analysis of the data collected during the user testing, including the questionnaires data, is currently in progress using non-parametric tests such as Chi-square.

The expert review confirmed most of the findings emerged in the user testing, and provided a number of suggestions for improvements, mainly concerning the interaction design of the different apps, and the positioning of holograms in the physical space specifically in the MR apps. The most interesting remark was the need to take into greater consideration the affordances of each device, in particular the in-time and in-space distinctive feature of Mixed Reality. In the comparison among the devices, none was clearly preferred over the other: HL presented higher attractiveness, motivation of use, sense of immersion, but also greater cognitive load; HH devices resulted easy to use but heavy to be hold for a long time; HV was intuitive, but not less attractive.

After the usability evaluation, some changes were taken into account for the MR applications on the basis of the user testing results and the evaluators' recommendations. These concerned for instance the design of new solutions to show and position the holograms in the physical space, producing a "light" version of the procedure where only the current step is visible.

The lesson learned from this experience will be useful in the next phases of the project to design more user-friendly applications and to better exploit logfiles to extract valuable information such as eye and hand tracking.

Acknowledgments. The work described in this paper has been partially funded by the State Secretariat for Education, Research and Innovation (SERI) of Swiss Confederation within the research project "Augmented reality and hypervideo combined: Interactive technologies to support procedural learning in initial vocational education and training" (MARHVEL). We thank Alberto Cattaneo and Vito Candido from the Swiss Federal University for Vocational Education and Training SFUVET, Lugano, for their precious collaboration in this project activity.

References

1. Dillenbourg, P., Cattaneo, A., Gurtner, J.L., Davis, R.L.: Educational Technologies for Vocational Training, SFUVET-EPFL (2022). https://www.sfuvet.swiss/sites/default/files/2022-10/01-dualt%20book_Educational%20Technologies%20for%20Vocational%20Training.pdf. ISBN 9798354160044
2. Sauli, F., Cattaneo, A., van der Meij, H.: Hypervideo for educational purposes: a literature review on a multifaceted technological tool. Technol. Pedagog. Educ. **27**(1), 115–134 (2018). https://doi.org/10.1080/1475939X.2017.1407357
3. Cattaneo, A., Nguyen, A.T., Aprea, C.: Teaching and learning with hypervideo in vocational education and training. J. Educ. Multimedia Hypermedia **25**(1), 5–35 (2016)
4. Parveau, M., Adda, M.: 3iVClass: a new classification method for virtual, augmented and mixed realities. Procedia Comput. Sci. **2018**(141), 263–270 (2018). https://doi.org/10.1016/j.procs.2018.10.180

5. Milgram, P., Takemura, H., Utsumi, A., Kishino, F.: Augmented reality: a class of displays on the reality-virtuality continuum. In: Proceedings of SPIE - The International Society for Optical Engineering. vol. 2351 (1994)
6. Rokhsaritalemi, S., Sadeghi-Niaraki, A., Choi, S.: A review on mixed reality: current trends. Challenges Prospects Appl. Sci. **10**(2), 636 (2020). https://doi.org/10.3390/app10020636
7. Microsoft: What is mixed reality. https://docs.microsoft.com/en-us/windows/mixed-reality/discover/mixed-reality. Accessed 30 Jun 2023 (2021)
8. Van Riesen, S.A., Weinberger, A., Breyer, F.J.: The impact of augmented reality on vocational education: a review of the literature. Interact. Learn. Environ. **27**(4), 554–568 (2019)
9. Chiang, F.K., Shang, X., Qiao, L.: Augmented reality in vocational training: a systematic review of research and applications. Comput. Hum. Behav. **129**, 107125 (2022)
10. Cuendet, S., Dehler-Zufferey, J., Ortoleva, G., Dillenbourg, P.: An integrated way of using a tangible user interface in a classroom. Int. J. Comput.-Support. Collab. Learn. **10**(2), 183–208 (2015)
11. Locatelli, C. Catenazzi, N., Sommaruga, L., Besenzoni, M.: A Case Study to Explore Issues and Potentials of HoloLens 2 for Training. In: INTED2022 Proceedings, pp. 7342–7348 (2022)
12. Mayer, R. E. (Ed.): The Cambridge handbook of multimedia learning (2nd ed.). New York: Cambridge University Press (2014)
13. Bennan, S.: Guidelines for Testing Mobile Augmented-Reality Apps. https://www.nngroup.com/articles/testing-AR-apps/. Accessed 30 Jun 2023 (2022)
14. Sommaruga, L., Catenazzi N., Locatelli C.: The tangram study for mixed reality affordance comparison, innovative educational technologies track. In: EDULEARN 2023 15th International Conference on Education and New Learning Technologies, July, Palma de Maiorca, Spain, IATED, ISBN: 978–84–09–52151–7 ISSN: 2340–1117 (2023)

Design Strategies to Enhance Awareness in MR Collaborative Systems

Agnese Augello[1], Giuseppe Caggianese[2](✉), Luigi Gallo[2], and Pietro Neroni[2]

[1] Institute for High Performance Computing and Networking, CNR, Palermo, Italy
`agnese.augello@icar.cnr.it`
[2] Institute for High Performance Computing and Networking, CNR, Naples, Italy
`{giuseppe.caggianese,luigi.gallo,pietro.neroni}@icar.cnr.it`

Abstract. An increasing number of innovative technologies are fostering augmented collaborative systems, thus setting the milestones of future collaboration paradigms. By merging real and virtual elements, mixed reality technologies lead to an augmented perception of the working environment and, consequently, an enriched experience of collaborative task execution. However, at the same time, such technologies can also impede proper communication and understanding among the entities working in concert to reach a common goal. Wearing head-mounted displays and simultaneously managing two different interactions - human-human and human-machine can lead to misunderstandings with co-workers. This also can hinder awareness, a fundamental requirement for the effective execution of collaborative tasks. As a consequence, cognitive load can increase with a negative impact on task performance. This paper analyses the main elements of a collaborative practice. Specifically, our aim is to identify crucial factors that must be considered for designing an effective interface for a collaborative mixed reality system. Then, we discuss some solutions to ensure that technology can act as an aid, rather than an impediment, to the accomplishment of collaborative tasks.

Keywords: AR-CSCW · Augmented Collaborative Practices · Mixed Reality · Awareness · Social Practices

1 Introduction

The need to digitise many aspects of our lives has emerged in recent years, leading us to create various computer-mediated environments. In parallel, the recent improvement of Augmented Reality (AR) and Virtual Reality (VR) technologies and their increasing affordability accelerated the ongoing digital transformation leading our lives to be increasingly immersed in virtual environments. As a result of these events, it becomes important to address how to explore and manipulate synthetic information [4,5] and especially how to share it in hybrid contexts, both real and virtual.

© The Author(s), under exclusive license to Springer Nature Switzerland AG 2023
L. T. De Paolis et al. (Eds.): XR Salento 2023, LNCS 14218, pp. 424–436, 2023.
https://doi.org/10.1007/978-3-031-43401-3_28

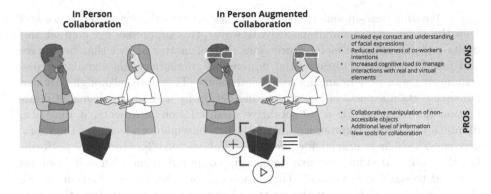

Fig. 1. Collaboration in Mixed Reality: Pros and Cons

Particular attention must be paid to collaboration when we move further towards the right side of the Real-Virtual Continuum introduced by Milgram et al. [13]. Different from AR, a Mixed Reality (MR) environment goes beyond simply overlaying virtual objects onto the physical environment, offering a more seamless blending and immersive experience. Virtual and real elements are more deeply integrated, allowing users to interact with virtual objects as if they were physical. Just as it happens with the usual digital tools that we all, especially after the COVID-19 pandemic, have learnt to use (i.e. video conferencing and realistic virtual meeting environments), MR technologies can bring out innovative ways of collaborating. The field of Computer-Supported Collaborative Work (CSCW) has been working for more than 30 years to determine how people utilise technology collaboratively to reach a shared goal, especially in the industrial field where multiple collaborators, even remotely, need to interact with each other. MR technologies and their forthcoming use in daily activities open up new scenarios to explore.

Collaboration can indeed represent an added value in MR environments, especially in situations where there is a need to enhance the users' sense of social presence, immersion, and engagement. Nevertheless, this requires an underlying efficient system and its relative interface, enabling multiple users to share the same virtual space and jointly observe and interact with the same virtual content, updating the results of manipulation activities in real-time. In particular, the concept of *awareness*, defined by Dourish et al. as the understanding of the activities of others, which provides a context for your own activity [9], is of central importance when it comes to social, cooperative contexts. There are several challenges to address, including enabling users to share their viewpoints on data, efficiently managing task control among different users, facilitating mutual use and manipulation of virtual content, balancing private and shared data, avoiding impediments to human-to-human communication and awareness, and preserving social protocols in collaborative contexts, as discussed in [21].

Some devices can impede proper communication among the individuals involved in the collaborative practice. Let us consider the scenario depicted in

Fig. 1. Wearing head-mounted displays enables users to share a mixed space and view the same content simultaneously. However, this suppresses eye contact and limits understanding of facial expressions. It is a matter of fact that both gaze and facial expressions are essential non-verbal communication signals for discriminating and understanding users' intentions. Therefore, although MR can enhance certain aspects of perception and action by adding new levels of information and allowing for a collaborative manipulation of objects, it may also diminish non-verbal communication and, as a consequence, decreases the users' awareness, which is crucial for effective collaboration [2]. Moreover, performing the task and simultaneously managing communication with collaborators can lead to cognitive overload. This can occur because the interaction among the co-workers and between the users and the system interface uses the same modalities (e.g. voice and gestures). The increased cognitive load required and the overlapping interactions (human-human and human-machine) can lead to misunderstandings with co-workers.

Current interaction modalities can be insufficient and need improvement to enable effective collaboration and awareness. To ensure that technology enhances opportunities and benefits its users, research in this field must address the urgent need for new solutions and interfaces that allow for optimal collaboration and easy awareness of participants' actions and the entire practice flow. This paper explores the key elements of social practices as a basis for the design of MR collaborative systems. Specifically, considering a synchronous co-located collaborative setting, the aim of this work is to discuss how a MR interface should be designed to effectively support and augment collaboration and awareness, highlighting difficulties and possible solutions.

2   Awareness in Collaborative Augmented Practices

2.1   Collaboration and Awareness in Mixed Reality

According to the literature, there is a growing trend towards developing collaborative systems in MR environments. In [22], a system enables remote collaborators to work in a shared virtual environment. The article highlights the importance of considering not only the objects in the shared workspace but also the empty spaces, referred to as "Negative Space", which can impact interaction and mutual understanding among remote collaborators. Miller et al. [14] propose a method for user localisation in multi-user AR sessions using inertial estimates and peer-to-peer ranging, allowing for determining relative distances between users. A microservice-based architecture for creating collaborative AR applications on different platforms is presented in [25]. The architecture enables real-time participant interactions on mobile devices, smart glasses, and projection screens. In [19], an asynchronous collaboration between immersive and non-immersive interfaces in data analysis is evaluated. The study demonstrates that combining both interfaces promotes effective communication and enhances interaction in asynchronous collaboration. The collaborative manipulation of shared objects in a virtual environment is faced in [17]. The authors explain the effectiveness of proposed strategies and potential applications in fields such as collaborative design. Erra et al. [10] present a collaborative system for evidence gathering in digital justice. The objective is to facilitate collaboration among professionals, allowing them to visualise, analyse, and discuss digital evidence efficiently. In [11], the authors address the topic of collaboration in the metaverse with agents proposing a framework for developing virtual agents that adhere to social conventions and enhance user interaction. The term "Collaborative AR" has been introduced as the intersection between Computer-Supported Collaborative Work (CSCW) and AR in [21]. The authors classified existing works according to six dimensions of interest: space, time, user roles symmetry, technology symmetry, input and output modalities. Regarding the space dimension, depending on the users' location, AR systems can be referred to as co-located collaborative or remote collaborative. Depending on whether or not the cooperation occurs in real-time, AR-CSCW can be either asynchronous or synchronous in terms of the temporal dimension. Synchronous collaboration is essential in scenarios where immediate feedback is needed. The authors in [24], extensively analyse the state of the art of AR tracking technologies and development tools to implement such experiences. The study also reviews collaboration in AR, splitting it into co-located AR and remote collaboration.

Almost all the proposed works strongly examine the importance of awareness since the immediate understanding of how others are interacting in the shared workspace contributes to the effectiveness of collaboration and ensures that team members have the necessary information to make informed decisions. In [1], the authors characterise the type of awareness for an application according to time, place and space. In more detail, they distinguish and evaluate six types of awareness (Collaboration, Location, Context, Social, Workspace, and Situation) based on the design elements of the application. The work proposed in [18] discusses the benefits and limitations of current systems for supporting awareness cues in MR remote collaboration by studying the effects of different combinations of awareness cues. Instead, the ambiguities originated by participants' opposing points of view are discussed in [22] by stressing the importance of workspace consistency and proposing a novel space for remote face-to-face collaboration. The system presented in [19] allows multiple users to explore data collaboratively using immersive and non-immersive interfaces. Next, the study proposed in [6] explores the effects of audio and visual notifications in remote AR collaboration, finding that a visual notifications channel is more suitable. Finally, in these papers [7,19], the evaluation of the effectiveness of collaborative systems, together with a measurement of awareness, is usually performed using questionnaires.

2.2   Augmented Collaborative Practices

The concept of awareness is central in every social activity, especially in those having a cooperative function. According to Schatzki, the social is a field of embodied, materially interwoven practices centrally organised around shared practical understandings [20]. We consider the concept of social practice and its formalisation provided in [3,8] as a guiding thread to understand which elements require attention in the design of a MR system supporting collaboration. We introduce the definition of "Augmented Collaborative Practice" (ACP) as shared and collaborative patterns of activities which occur in the real-virtual continuum and involve a set of interconnected elements, including bodily skills, norms, objects, ways of interaction which are used to achieve specific outcomes. Specifically, a practice is characterised by: a *Context*, i.e. the place and time in which a practice takes place, the actors involved and their roles, the elements that can be manipulated and the affordances they elicit; a *Meanings* i.e. purpose, promoted values of each action of the practice; *Expectations* and *Activities* [8].

In an ACP, the practice takes place in a mixed environment, in which both virtual and real actors/objects can be co or remotely located. Whether collaboration takes place in real-time or not, activities may be asynchronous or synchronous. Actors may have symmetrical or non-symmetrical roles. This means that users may or may not perform the same type of tasks. The difference in roles implies different permissions in using resources and enabled actions (skills or permission must be possessed to perform them). For instance, in classroom practice, the teacher has permission to walk along the benches, while the students need to be seated to avoid disturbing the lesson. Similarly, in surgical practice, the surgeon has permission to perform certain actions and use certain tools, while others have to observe or use a different set of tools. In addition, the type of social relationship between individuals affects the level of intimacy and sharing of private information. In a digital social perspective, such as in a video call, the sharing of resources is enabled by exposing only a few windows, and the same principle can be applied in a MR scenario.

Another important aspect to take into account regards expectations raised by the practice; if they conform to the practice's flow, awareness is better ensured. As an example, in an ACP turn-taking is crucial. Consider, for instance, the manipulation of a virtual object in a collaborative mode; it is essential to correctly manage the access request, grant permission, and use the resource within a certain time interval depending on the completion of a task or the need to release it. Control management is established by means of communicative actions, that may occur through voice, gaze and gestures. Other actions are those involving the interaction and manipulation of objects. The increase of physical space in the virtual real continuum has afforded new types of interaction [1]. The gestures used to interact in an environment that combines real and virtual elements may differ from those used in real environments, and virtual objects may elicit affordances different compared to real ones. Actions for interacting with MR elements typically consist of voice commands and gestures. In addition to being natural and intuitive, these actions must be easily understood and shared between the practice participants.

3 Addressing Challenges in Handling Co-located, Synchronous ACPs

3.1 Framing Scenario

In our context of analysis, we will focus on a co-located synchronous ACP, where individuals collaborate in real-time with a common purpose, by taking advantage from augmentation introduced by MR technologies. In this setting, two or more users are physically located in the same place and are able to interact with digital content using the same hardware technology. Specifically, we assume that users are wearing a head-mounted device. The choice of a device is not mandatory, as long as it is equipped with sensors and capabilities to support the intended MR experience. Specifically, it should allow placing virtual contents in the user's FOV according to the practice-oriented logic and task evolution. It should also allow users to interact with MR contents via voice commands and gestures to accomplish a designed task. As an example, considering the Microsoft Hololens 2, it is possible to exploit the Mixed Reality Toolkit project [16], to interact with virtual objects by means of raycasting [15] or direct touch [12], performing translation, rotation and scaling operations through unimanual and bimanual gestures. In the scenario, each user can interact with a hand menu, i.e., a private view containing information about the hologram and connected users. It is accessible at any time by the user by turning the palm of his open hand towards the viewer, and it can be explored via direct touch. Since simultaneous interaction of multiple users on shared holograms can generate manipulation conflicts, in our setting, a master-slave interaction protocol is adopted, where the control is allocated to the "master". When the users' roles are symmetric, at any time,

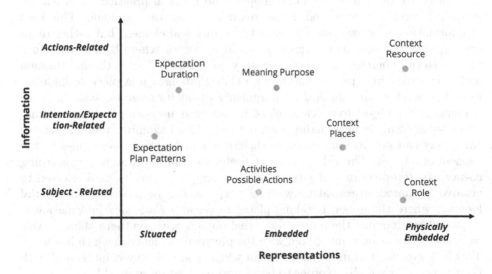

Fig. 2. ACP information conveyed by the envisioned collaborative MR system according to *Information* and *Representation* dimensions.

a user can acquire the master role. Otherwise, the master control over an object and the actions that can be performed on it can be limited to users according to their roles.

3.2 Dimensions of Interest

The information that can be conveyed by our envisioned collaborative MR system can be described according to the social practice's elements and by identifying two dimensions of interest. As a matter of fact, for a collaborative practice to happen, there must be at least two individuals actively collaborating, bringing their own knowledge and skills for fulfilling goals and a space in which the practice takes place and individuals and objects are located. Therefore, we can characterise the synthetic elements used to augment the scene with respect to an *Information*, and a spatial *Representation* dimensions, i.e. the type of information that is displayed and how it is placed in the shared space (see Fig. 2). The *Information* dimension represents a continuum from information regarding each subject's potential to contribute to the practice execution and information concerning what effectively happens in the practice flow. This dimension spans from *Subject-Related* information, typically static, such as information about a person's role, expertise, possible actions, to *Intention/Expectation-Related* information, regarding intentions and expectations for something that can happen, up to more dynamic and context-dependent information, namely *Actions-Related*, related to the dynamic actualisation of the practice such as information about a specific task or process actually performed, progress updates or task-specific instructions. The *Representation* dimension ranges from *Situated*, to *Embedded* and to *Physically Embedded* as described in [26]. *Situated* information can be introduced to foster awareness and support the users in practice execution, by providing context-specific knowledge, relevant to the task at hand. This kind of information is not specifically related to a physical element but rather to an ongoing process, such as the duration of an action or where it is located in a plan pattern. Therefore it is not necessary to spatially locate the information and it is shown in a part of the user's FOV. *Embedded* is a piece of information that overlays the physical environment so that its representation in space depends on the object to which it refers. In this case, users can find the information they need in the surrounding environment. As an example, possible actions that users can perform according to their role can be shown very close to the element of interest. This solution can be useful to improve awareness concerning co-workers' interactions and intentions; for example, a specific tool selected to act over a shared object, along with its purpose, can be placed in the spatial location where the action is taking place. *Physically Embedded* information is displayed by changing the properties of real objects with synthetic data. In this case, the information is integrated with the physical elements to which it relates. This happens, for instance, when certain widgets are displayed integrated with the tracked user's limbs in order to be viewed or used more quickly.

3.3   Designing ACPs Interfaces: Discussion and Possible Solutions

To explore potential solutions for designing a collaborative MR system interface, we will refer back to the framing scenario introduced in Sect. 3.1, using the scene depicted in Fig. 3 as a point of reference to guide our discussion. The figure shows a collaborative scene captured from the perspective of one of the participants. The scene involves three people, with two of them being framed from the third person's viewpoint. The black frame indicates the see-through device worn by the user, which enables the visualisation of the synthetic elements in the scene. These elements are spatially located in the scene following the continuum situated-embedded of the *Representation* dimension by showing informative contents to increase the awareness over the ACP flow.

Fig. 3. An illustrative scene in an ACP from the point of view of one of the participants. The black frame indicates the see-through device worn by the user, which enables the visualisation of the synthetic elements in the scene. Synthetic elements are represented in the situated-embedded continuum.

Access to Information About the ACP Context: Actors and Roles. In our scenario, the participants in the practice are not remotely connected and are well visible. However, their head-mounted displays may impede their identification, and the roles could change depending on the situation. One first consideration is, therefore, the importance of introducing information to make the users aware of the role of each participant. In our envisioned interface, an information layer can be physically embedded into the scene in the form of a disc-shaped element placed under the user's feet. This solution has the twofold advantage that it is anchored to the subject's position and can always be consulted without it constantly being displayed in the user's FOV, risking the occlusion of other information. In Fig. 3, the virtual disc-shaped element, reporting information about the subject on the right, is visible (since the user is looking under the feet of the man). To achieve the same information about the female collaborator, the user should change the direction of the point of view, turning it down to frame the woman's feet. Let's consider an example of a surgical practice that takes place in an augmented operating room, where a trainee who is not a regular member of the surgical team is present. The proposed solution allows the surgeon to obtain an immediate overview of the team and their roles by entering the room. This informative layer can increase the understanding of the users' intentions or provide directions about possible actions or ways of acting, regardless of whether they are symmetrical or asymmetrical. In an augmented educational practice, for example, to improve the trainee's understanding, the mentor can perform an action slower than usual.

Access to Information About the ACP Context: Resources and Their Affordances. For what concerns the resources, in the MR collaborative setting, they can be both real and computer-generated. In a situation where all participants are physically present, real resources present in the scene are intrinsically shared among the participants. Instead, virtual resources can be shared or can be kept private. Shared resources representing objects can be placed by integrating them into the physical space and, when possible, should be manipulated similarly as if they were real objects. This *physically embedded* visualisation allows defining an augmented working environment represented by a real part extended through virtual elements. It is a placement choice that simplifies their search, identification and comprehension and also the communication between collaborators who can use spatial references to refer to objects (e.g. "look at the object in front of me" or "the object near the desk"). Moreover, these shared resources associated with real objects should be manipulated when possible similarly as it could happen in the real environment. In fact, a manipulation similar as much as possible to what happens with real objects reduces the gap between intention and action [23], diminishing the user's cognitive load in learning and using the interface.

Virtual resources representing tools and widgets are often characterised by menus that can be called up when needed. In the analysed scenario, while interaction with a shared object by one of the participants can be easily understood by other participants, interaction with tools and widgets may not be as immediate. A participant may interact with something that is not visible, and even worse, as a result of this interaction, the presentation of shared information can appear altered without a shared understanding of the action that caused this change. To avoid this, the interactions with interface elements, namely information panels, menus, widgets and tools, must always be explicit for other participants. For instance, in Fig. 3, the rotation tool and the contextual menu recalled by the subject on the right become visible also to the other collaborators. However, due to the different point-of-views of the co-workers, it may be complex to show the specific user's interactions with the interface elements. In many cases, it is sufficient to make participants aware of the interaction type without sharing any details. On the other hand, in more specific use cases such as training, where the mentor's actions on the interface are relevant for the trainees, details on mentor actions can be projected directly into the trainees' FOV or on a shared virtual screen.

Despite the choice to use natural interaction methods, such as voice and gestures, it is necessary that the interface supports as much as possible the user in understanding the possible actions that can be made on a virtual object. When it is not possible to set in the MR environment an object manipulation similar to what happens in reality, the affordances of a virtual object may differ significantly from its real-life counterparts. For this reason, it is essential to provide clear visual cues on how the object can be manipulated. This can be achieved, for instance, by displaying widgets around the object (see the widgets around the cube in Fig. 1). A tailored display of affordances can be created based on the user's role and level of control in a specific ACP. For instance, in a classroom setting, the teacher may demonstrate possible ways to complete a task by interacting with an object. In this case, all possible actions are visualised, even if students are not allowed to perform them, in order to support their understanding of the process.

Access to Information About the ACP Context: Places. A user should have the possibility to keep some resources in a private space. However, physical space, shared virtual space, and private virtual space may overlap because the representations of the latter two require a location in the physical space. Ambiguities can therefore arise due to users' opposite points of view, as shown in Fig. 4 a). Indeed, when private space is aligned with a public resource, the gaze direction of a user engaged in observing his private space could be erroneously perceived as being directed toward that shared object.

One way to deal with this type of problem is to signal the users' private space when it is being used, using an appropriate graphical representation. In particular, the private space is made explicit by showing a panel whose contents cannot be known and manipulated by non-owner users, as shown in Fig. 4 b) and in Fig. 3 (behind the woman's back).

Access to Information About the ACP: Activities, Meaning and Expectations. In ACP, the main activities, possible plan patterns and the required competencies to perform them should be clear for the participants. This information, for example, is necessary to schedule an intervention based on the actions for which users are enabled. To increase awareness in the ACP, it can be useful to display information about intentions and actions purposes, for example, as discussed before, by graphically explicating the choice of a particular tool through icons placed near the user's hands (see Fig. 3). In this way, if a participant decides to modify a shared object by selecting, for instance, the "cutting" tool, the other participants will be able to understand the meaning of the gestures having a projection of the future state of the object upon completion of such actions. This is particularly important for those use cases where the

Fig. 4. Two users collaborating in an augmented shared environment. The icons next to the objects in the scene indicate who can view them. a) Ambiguity caused by overlapping of shared and private spaces. b) The ambiguity is resolved by displaying a panel that clearly indicates the private space.

actions should follow strict protocols (e.g. in surgery). In case the execution of a practice is characterised by a sequence of steps, the interface should be able to support collaboration by indicating the status of that action. Display this information and, if necessary, make explicit the expected duration or conditions that will lead the action to end, facilitate the planning of interventions, simplify the turnover on a shared resource, and allows verifying that the expectations elicited by the practice are met. The visualisations of such critical information must be available in the FOV of the user, as shown in Fig. 3, where a situated representation of a plan pattern is available to the users even when they are not framing the shared data.

4   Conclusion

This paper has addressed the critical issue of designing MR systems handling collaborative practices. It has been underlined that in this context, it is necessary to define new paradigms of communication among co-workers through proper interfaces. The discussion started by introducing a conceptualisation and formalisation of Augmented Collaborative Practices (ACPs), relying on Social Practice theory. Then, two meaningful dimensions to classify information about a current ACP have been identified. Each informative element of an ACP has been analysed, discussing both challenges and possible solutions to manage them in the MR environment and, at the same time, to increase awareness of practice participants with respect to that information and preserve human-human communication. This first analysis led to the definition of a collaborative interface in a co-located synchronous ACP, where all users wear the same mixed-reality headset. Our contribution aims to provide a foundation for the development of effective interfaces that enable successful ACPs in the future, which could facilitate the sharing of knowledge and information among co-workers and enable a continuous and almost instantaneous feedback loop of knowledge, adaptability, and group growth. Next works will focus on evaluating the interface in different case studies.

References

1. Antunes, P., Herskovic, V., Ochoa, S.F., Pino, J.A.: Reviewing the quality of awareness support in collaborative applications. J. Syst. Softw. **89**, 146–169 (2014)
2. Augello, A., Caggianese, G., Gallo, L.: Human augmentation: An enactive perspective. In: Extended Reality: First International Conference, XR Salento 2022, Lecce, Italy, 6–8 July 2022, Proceedings, Part I, pp. 219–228. Springer (2022). https://doi.org/10.1007/978-3-031-15546-8_19
3. Augello, A., Gentile, M., Weideveld, L., Dignum, F.: A model of a social chatbot. In: De Pietro, G., Gallo, L., Howlett, R.J., Jain, L.C. (eds.) Intelligent Interactive Multimedia Systems and Services 2016. SIST, vol. 55, pp. 637–647. Springer, Cham (2016). https://doi.org/10.1007/978-3-319-39345-2_57
4. Caggianese, G., Colonnese, V., Gallo, L.: Situated visualization in augmented reality: exploring information seeking strategies. In: 2019 15th International Conference on Signal-Image Technology & Internet-Based Systems (SITIS), pp. 390–395 (2019). https://doi.org/10.1109/SITIS.2019.00069
5. Caggianese, G., Gallo, L., Neroni, P.: An investigation of leap motion based 3D manipulation techniques for use in egocentric viewpoint. In: De Paolis, L.T., Mongelli, A. (eds.) AVR 2016. LNCS, vol. 9769, pp. 318–330. Springer, Cham (2016). https://doi.org/10.1007/978-3-319-40651-0_26
6. Cidota, M., Lukosch, S., Datcu, D., Lukosch, H.: Comparing the effect of audio and visual notifications on workspace awareness using head-mounted displays for remote collaboration in augmented reality. Augmented Hum. Res. **1**, 1–15 (2016)
7. Cooper, R.B., Haines, R.: The influence of workspace awareness on group intellective decision effectiveness. Eur. J. Inf. Syst. **17**, 631–648 (2008)
8. Dignum, F.: Social practices: a complete formalization (2022)
9. Dourish, P., Bellotti, V.: Awareness and coordination in shared workspaces. In: Proceedings of the 1992 ACM Conference on Computer-Supported Cooperative Work, pp. 107–114 (1992)
10. Erra, U., et al.: Collaborative visual environments for evidence taking in digital justice: A design concept. In: Proceedings of the 1st Workshop on Flexible Resource and Application Management on the Edge, FRAME 2021, pp. 33–37. Association for Computing Machinery, New York (2021). https://doi.org/10.1145/3452369.3463821, https://doi.org/10.1145/3452369.3463821
11. Gatto, L., Fulvio Gaglio, G., Augello, A., Caggianese, G., Gallo, L., La Cascia, M.: Met-iquette: enabling virtual agents to have a social compliant behavior in the metaverse. In: 2022 16th International Conference on Signal-Image Technology & Internet-Based Systems (SITIS), pp. 394–401 (2022). https://doi.org/10.1109/SITIS57111.2022.00066
12. Kang, H.J., Shin, J.h., Ponto, K.: A comparative analysis of 3d user interaction: how to move virtual objects in mixed reality. In: 2020 IEEE Conference on Virtual Reality and 3D User Interfaces (VR), pp. 275–284. IEEE (2020)
13. Milgram, P., Takemura, H., Utsumi, A., Kishino, F.: Augmented reality: a class of displays on the reality-virtuality continuum. In: Das, H. (ed.) Telemanipulator and Telepresence Technologies, vol. 2351, pp. 282–292. International Society for Optics and Photonics, SPIE (1995). https://doi.org/10.1117/12.197321

14. Miller, J., Soltanaghai, E., Duvall, R., Chen, J., Bhat, V., Pereira, N., Rowe, A.: Cappella: establishing multi-user augmented reality sessions using inertial estimates and peer-to-peer ranging. In: 2022 21st ACM/IEEE International Conference on Information Processing in Sensor Networks (IPSN), pp. 428–440. IEEE (2022)
15. Mine, M.R.: Virtual environment interaction techniques. UNC Chapel Hill CS Dept (1995)
16. Ong, S., Siddaraju, V.K., Ong, S., Siddaraju, V.K.: Introduction to the mixed reality toolkit. Beginning Windows Mixed Reality Programming: For HoloLens and Mixed Reality Headsets, pp. 85–110 (2021)
17. Pinho, M.S., Bowman, D.A., Freitas, C.M.D.S.: Cooperative object manipulation in collaborative virtual environments. J. Braz. Comput. Soc. **14**, 53–67 (2008)
18. Piumsomboon, T., Dey, A., Ens, B., Lee, G., Billinghurst, M.: The effects of sharing awareness cues in collaborative mixed reality. Front. Robotics AI **6**, 5 (2019)
19. Reski, N., Alissandrakis, A., Kerren, A.: An empirical evaluation of asymmetric synchronous collaboration combining immersive and non-immersive interfaces within the context of immersive analytics. Front. Virt. Reality, 148 (2022)
20. Schatzki, T.R.: Practice theory: An introduction. The practice turn in contemporary theory, pp. 1–14 (2001)
21. Sereno, M., Wang, X., Besancon, L., McGuffin, M.J., Isenberg, T.: Collaborative work in augmented reality: a survey. IEEE Trans. Visualiz. Comput. Graph. **28**, 2530–2549 (2022). https://doi.org/10.1109/TVCG.2020.3032761
22. Sousa, M., Mendes, D., Anjos, R.K.d., Lopes, D.S., Jorge, J.: Negative space: workspace awareness in 3d face-to-face remote collaboration. In: The 17th International Conference on Virtual-Reality Continuum and its Applications in Industry, pp. 1–2 (2019)
23. Starner, T.: Project glass: an extension of the self. IEEE Pervasive Comput. **12**(2), 14–16 (2013)
24. Syed, T., et al.: In-Depth review of augmented reality: tracking technologies, development tools, AR displays, collaborative AR, and security concerns. Sensors **23**(1) (2023). https://doi.org/10.3390/s23010146
25. Vaquero-Melchor, D., Bernardos, A.M., Bergesio, L.: Sara: A microservice-based architecture for cross-platform collaborative augmented reality. Appl. Sci. **10**(6), 2074 (2020)
26. Willett, W., Jansen, Y., Dragicevic, P.: Embedded data representations. IEEE Trans. Visual Comput. Graphics **23**(1), 461–470 (2016)

Comparison of User Intent for Mixed Reality and Augmented Reality in Hedonistic Shopping Experiences

Lingyao Jin(✉) ⓘ

Lancaster Institute for the Contemporary Arts, Lancaster University, Lancaster, UK
L.jin11@lancaster.ac.uk

Abstract. A mismatch between user-technology usage and a lack of user acceptance hinders the adoption and diffusion of technology. In this research paper, we focus on the differences in how mixed reality (MR) and augmented reality (AR) impact user adoption. We also examine the importance of user intentions in relation to MR and AR for purchase behaviour. A survey (n = 801) was conducted in the UK in May 2022 to investigate the relationship between AR and MR technologies and compare their compatibility for various intentions, including intent to use (9 factors), intent to experience (7 factors), and intent to purchase (7 factors). The results indicate that MR shows more promise than AR in the retail industry. MR significantly and positively affected five elements, such as shopping, while AR was primarily used for gaming. This study provides practical insights that can aid in technology adoption and evaluation. It also emphasises the importance and feasibility of incorporating product customisation functionality into MR retail purchase applications, which has inspired our subsequent development of the MR user interface.

Keywords: Augmented Reality · Mixed Reality · Shopping · User Intents · Consumer-machine Matching

1 Introduction

The rising research and adoption of augmented reality (AR) and mixed reality (MR) technologies have brought substantial benefits to the retail industry [1–5]. In the retail market, augmented reality is already being used in customer purchases to enable a better user experience, whilst a more comprehensive range of retailers is constantly observing or embarking on experimentation [6, 7]. The quality of matching users to emerging technologies can influence users' adoption of the technology or affect the efficiency of their implementation [8]. Consumer satisfaction with and adoption of technology are factors that drive the adoption of technology by retailers [9, 10]. Therefore, brands' decisions on technology selection need to consider the match between technology and consumer groups. Their needs and preferences for technology can also influence consumers' decision-making. Some retailers expressed concerns about the uncertainty of investing in technology [11]. Therefore, preliminary research on user groups, user environment

L. T. De Paolis et al. (Eds.): XR Salento 2023, LNCS 14218, pp. 437–455, 2023.
https://doi.org/10.1007/978-3-031-43401-3_29

preferences, and technology matching needs to establish to provide recommendations to stakeholders for matching and investing in technology.

This study proposed a comparison study of the intentions of augmented reality and mixed reality for shopping use. Both technologies' visual representations resemble as they rely on the real world for most of their existence, in contrast to virtual reality, which brings complete immersion and virtual environments [12]. Moreover, the vertigo-inducing effect of virtual reality technology on several users limits and diminishes the user experience [13]. Apart from this, multiple implementations of augmented reality shopping case studies validate its feasibility [14–16]. Research on mixed reality shopping relatively restrict [17] and is not yet broadly utilised in the marketplace as a selling medium. Accordingly, this paper seeks to compare the relationship between AR and MR for user adoption, providing usage directional guidance for situating and matching technologies for MR and AR developers, retailers, designers, and investors.

2 Related Work

As mentioned prior, AR in retail has been underpinned by a massive number of practical projects and research outputs, whereas MR has only been underpinned by restricted research and is barely available to the public for use in industry. In order to compare the research output of MR and AR in retail in academic research, we conducted a search in three large academic research databases in July 2023, by searching the keywords "mixed reality" and "retail", "augmented reality" and "retail" in all fields and years (see Table 1). Our findings indicate that there is less research on integrating MR with retail compared to AR. Apart from the financial incentives of technology investment and return, consumer technology acceptance and preference play an invaluable role in affecting the actual adoption of technology. Therefore, this paper focuses on comparing the two technologies primarily through consumer research. The mismatch between consumer expectations and the practical implementation of the technology should also be addressed. We will review various application cases that have been deployed and are being explored in brick-and-mortar retailing to identify their research gaps and limitations and contribute recommendations and inspirations for stakeholders.

Table 1. Key Words Search Results in Three Databases

Academic Research Database	"Mixed Reality" and "Retail"	"Augmented Reality" and "Retail"
Web of Science	36 Results	272 Results
Scopus	50 Results	284 Results
IEEE Xplore	14 Results	108 Results

AR has been familiarised and utilised by consumers in retail practices comparatively wider than MR. AR has been used in multiple retail segments, delivering it more conveniently and rapidly through access to smart devices (e.g., smartphones, computers).

Home furnishing category AR appeared, such as Dulux launched an app called Dulux Paint Expert: Decorator, which allows customers to see paint colours appear on their wall by tapping on the screen and generates portfolios to let shoppers compare different schemes. Apps from IKEA, Wayfair [18] and Target enable customers to see how furniture products can be placed in their homes from their smartphones (see Fig. 1).

Fig. 1. Wayfair AR Shopping App. Photography by Power, 2019

Skincare and beauty category AR Apps, for instance, Sephora's AR Makeup Match, which tries out make-up products through facial recognition technology. L'Oréal and Lancôme also offer AR lipstick products for facial colour trials. Fashion category apps like Nike and Gucci's AR Shoe fitting, where customers can see a digital product with a 360° coverage of their feet. Eyewear retailers Specsavers and Vision Express offer AR try-on frames. Tiffany & Co's jewellery try-on lets customers visualise how a ring will fit on their hands. AR try-on has increased online conversions and reduced returns for branded companies [19] and can also help retailers optimise the utilisation of warehouse space and navigation within warehouses [20]. During the pandemic in 2020, clothing sales fell by 21.5%, according to the UK Office for National Statistics (ONS), online sales rose to a historic peak of 33.9% of all retail expenditure [21]. Lockdown complicates retailers' routine operations, with clothing retailer ASOS developing See My Fit's app, digitally mapping each product onto the model, to help models keep social distance to avoid the necessity of entry to their studio to change clothes.

Compared to the established performance of AR, the application of MR in retail is a fairly young research phenomenon yet presents a rapidly growing interest. MR accomplishes the experience using optical see-through head-mounted displays. [3] Dou and Tanaka (2020) presented an MR Fashion Shop system that automatically layouts and decorates the interior through spatial recognition and responsive layouts and provides a virtual shop assistant for communication (see Fig. 2 left). [22] Fuchs et al. (2019) proposed a package recognition system for vending machines employing HoloLens. Retail packaged products tend to rely on barcode recognition, they evaluated the potential of multiple convolutional neural network (CNN) architectures in recognising product packages, providing an alternative to barcode recognition. Similarly, (see Fig. 2 right) regarding product identification and information provision, a system called MR Shopping Assistant for identifying information about groceries products and assisting in purchasing [23].

Fig. 2. MR Shop System. Dou and Tanaka, 2020 (Left); MR Shopping Assistant System. Jain et al., 2021 (Right).

However, these MR retail system studies mainly research and develop from the perspective of technological innovation, this study tries to innovate the user interface design and functionality from a designer's point of view. Leveraging this preliminary research draws a guideline for comparing user intentions against MR and AR.

3 Concepts and Research Questions

This study reports a preliminary partial quantitative dataset results intended to analyse and compare the match between MR and AR for consumers. It highlights the feasibility and necessity of product customisation functionality in MR retail purchase applications. It empirically demonstrated the applicability of MR technology to the user interface design of customised jewellery. In addition, it is propounded that the compatibility and development potential of MR in the retail sector is a superior match to its user preferences. As such, it is matching users and machines for ongoing mega projects, and validating the feasibility of future research orientations.

The theory for this study draws on theoretical research from several models [8, 24, 25]. The study addresses two main measurement domains. a) identifying consumer preferences for augmented reality and mixed reality technologies. b) describing user factors for both technologies in adoption and the complement environment. This research uses a mixed method to design a survey and raise three research questions.

RQ1. What are the associations between AR and MR on intent to use?
RQ2. What are the correlations between AR and MR on intent to experience, controlling for shopping?
RQ3. What are the correlations between AR and MR on intent to purchase, controlling for shopping?

4 Methodology

4.1 Research Framework and Methods

This study is an exaction of a pilot study on an ongoing large project. The entire project is based on empirical research, utilising mixed methods, including qualitative and quantitative research. In the early stages of the research, quantitative questionnaires were used to target our potential user groups and match applicable technologies. User testing is now underway to analyse user behaviour patterns and optimise user interface design and user experience. Subsequently, we will use qualitative in-depth interviews and iterative design to optimise the design proposals and software implementation. Ultimately, the study anticipates quantitative evaluation and feedback from users wearing HoloLens 2 and experiencing the mixed reality purchasing user interface we have developed. The final output of the study is expected to be an MR product customised user purchase interface app.

4.2 Questionnaire Design

This questionnaire was divided into introduction, user persona and user preference related questions. In the first section, the purpose of the questionnaire was briefly summarised and then the definitions and example pictures of the three technologies of extended reality (XR) were introduced. The participants began to complete the questionnaire with a fundamental cognition of the three different technologies of XR.

This complex questionnaire contains single-choice, scales, and multiple-choice interspersed with short text response arranged in the order of the questions. There are 17 questions with two logic jumps. There are four scale questions which designed on the five-point semantic scale of Likert (1932) [26]. The four scale questions' Cronbach α is 0.83, indicating that the questions data is of high-reliability quality. Nevertheless, we have only selected some multiple-choice questions to analyse in this paper.

4.3 Data Collection

A total of 878 data were collected which includes digital and paper. The questionnaires were culled to eliminate invalid questionnaires. Questionnaires with a response rate of less than 70% were removed and only retained those with a response rate of 70% or more. Removed those filled in indiscriminately, such as chose B for all of the options, or half for A and half for B. Removed the questionnaires were randomly filled in, meaning that respondents chose their answers randomly or gave incoherent or perfunctory answers to the previous and subsequent questions. After the screening, 807 samples remained in the complete data pooled. Data pooled collected in May 2022. We conducted in the UK, and distribution sites mainly focus on UK and China. Volunteers are recruited primarily through Qualtrics online questionnaire platform, offline distribution of questionnaires, snowballing and posters. Offline volunteers will be given a small packet of sweets as an incentive.

5   Results

5.1   Result 1: The Association Between AR and MR on Intent to Use

The original question for the above figure was the preference for technologies in extended reality. The reasons for comparing AR versus MR have already been articulated in existing research, so only the statistics for AR and MR are shown in the figure above. MR is distinctly preferable (see Fig. 3).

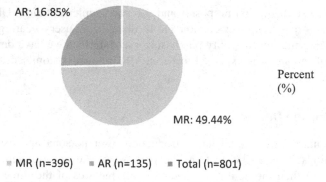

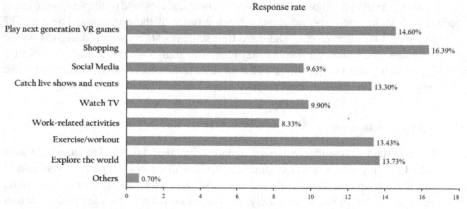

Fig. 3. Mixed Reality and Augmented Reality User Preferences

Fig. 4. Response Rate in Intent to Use

The response rate illustrates the percentage of each option. Shopping was the most popular, followed by playing VR games. Cross-tabulate it with AR and MR in the contingency table below (see Fig. 4).

MR is preferred for shopping, while AR is preferred for playing games (see Fig. 5).

Figure 6 boxed out factors imply a significant positive effect. MR evidently has a positive effect on multiple use intentions, whereas AR, apart from playing games, most factors have barely effect and negatively affect work-related activities.

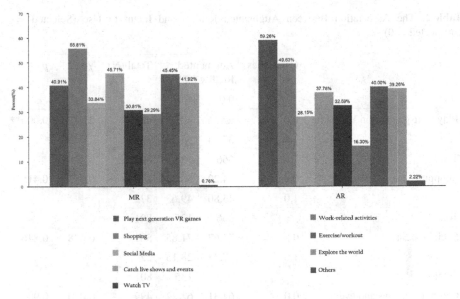

Fig. 5. MR Versus AR in Intent to Use

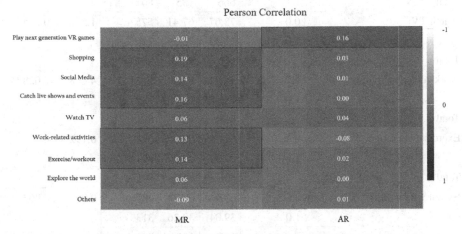

Fig. 6. Correlation in MR Versus AR in Intent to Use

The Chi-square analysed the relationship between augmented reality on the nine factors of intention to use. Users who preferred AR have a relatively positive acceptance of VR games which showed a significant association ($p < 0.05$). Instead, AR and work-related activities had a significant negative relationship (see Table 2).

Therefore, it is suggested that the user group playing VR games is highly likely to be a potential AR user group. Regarding response rates, AR is not applicable to the content of a pragmatic nature and is more beneficial for range of hedonistic activities.

Table 2. The Association Between Augmented Reality and Intent to Use (Selected = 1, Unselected = 0)

Items	Categories	Augmented Reality (%)		Total (N)	χ^2	p
		0.0	1.0			
Play next-generation VR game	0.0	62.16	40.74	469	21.224	0.000**
	1.0	37.84	59.26	332		
Total		666	135	801		
Shopping	0.0	54.20	50.37	429	0.663	0.415
	1.0	45.80	49.63	372		
Total		666	135	801		
Social media	0.0	72.67	71.85	581	0.038	0.846
	1.0	27.33	28.15	220		
Total		666	135	801		
Catch live shows and event	0.0	62.31	62.22	499	0.000	0.984
	1.0	37.69	37.78	302		
Total		666	135	801		
Watch TV	0.0	72.67	67.41	575	1.536	0.215
	1.0	27.33	32.59	226		
Total		666	135	801		
Work-related activities	0.0	74.92	83.70	612	4.798	0.028*
	1.0	25.08	16.30	189		
Total		666	135	801		
Exercise/workout	0.0	62.01	60.00	494	0.192	0.661
	1.0	37.99	40.00	307		
Total		666	135	801		
Explore the world	0.0	60.96	60.74	488	0.002	0.962
	1.0	39.04	39.26	313		
Total		666	135	801		
Others	0.0	98.05	97.78	785	0.042	0.838
	1.0	1.95	2.22	16		
Total		666	135	801		

* $p < 0.05$ ** $p < 0.01$

Table 3. The Association Between Mixed Reality and Intent to Use

Items	Categories	Mixed Reality (%)		Total (N)	χ^2	p
		0.0	1.0			
Play next-generation VR game	0.0	58.02	59.09	469	0.094	0.759
	1.0	41.98	40.91	332		
Total		405	396	801		
Shopping	0.0	62.72	44.19	429	27.622	0.000**
	1.0	37.28	55.81	372		
Total		405	396	801		
Social media	0.0	78.77	66.16	581	15.966	0.000**
	1.0	21.23	33.84	220		
Total		405	396	801		
Catch live shows and event	0.0	70.12	54.29	499	21.363	0.000**
	1.0	29.88	45.71	302		
Total		405	396	801		
Watch TV	0.0	74.32	69.19	575	2.601	0.107
	1.0	25.68	30.81	226		
Total		405	396	801		
Work-related activities	0.0	81.98	70.71	612	14.102	0.000**
	1.0	18.02	29.29	189		
Total		405	396	801		
Exercise/workout	0.0	68.64	54.55	494	16.832	0.000**
	1.0	31.36	45.45	307		
Total		405	396	801		
Explore the world	0.0	63.70	58.08	488	2.659	0.103
	1.0	36.30	41.92	313		
Total		405	396	801		
Others	0.0	96.79	99.24	785	6.151	0.013*
	1.0	3.21	0.76	16		
Total		405	396	801		

* $p < 0.05$ ** $p < 0.01$

Mixed reality showed statistically significant similarity with six factors of intention to use. MR significantly associated with shopping, social media, catching live shows and events, work-related activities, and exercise/workout ($p < 0.05$). As the option Others are text response, we do not consider it in statistical analysis. The remaining factors showed a consistency (p > 0.05). Of these five options, the rate of those who chose MR increased compared to those who did not select MR. This implies that this MR positively impacted these five usage intentions (see Table 3).

Hence, in contrast to Fig. 2, MR is explicitly more broadly adaptable than AR. Furthermore, our former findings suggest that prior experience with XR influenced users' preference for the technology that AR was not as high-intent to return to use as MR after being used [27]. Therefore, this study suggests that AR can be a good return for retail stakeholders with purely hedonic intentions at a relatively low cost. And for stakeholders with more financial commitment, MR can be used for both work and entertainment purposes, making it a promising technology investment. Notably, the main areas of implementation for MR nowadays, namely education, construction, healthcare and the military, also support the pragmatic nature of MR [28, 29].

5.2 Result 2: The Correlations Between AR and MR on Intent to Experience, Controlling for Shopping

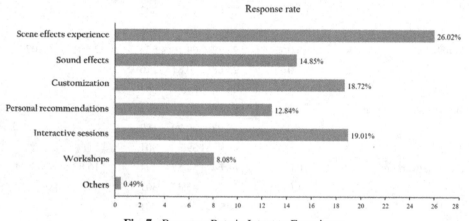

Fig. 7. Response Rate in Intent to Experience

Figure 7 and 8 demonstrates that scenarios, customisation and interaction are the three most anticipated experiential intentions in MR and AR. Figure 9 shows four factors positively influencing MR adoption, while these six are nearly neutral for AR.

Shopping had almost no correlation with AR ($R^2 = 0.001$, p > 0.05). F value increased after including the intent to purchase factors, which showed the model improved but did not show significance (F = 1.413, p = 0.196 > 0.05). Intent to experience has no statistically significant explanatory affected on AR shopping (see Table 4).

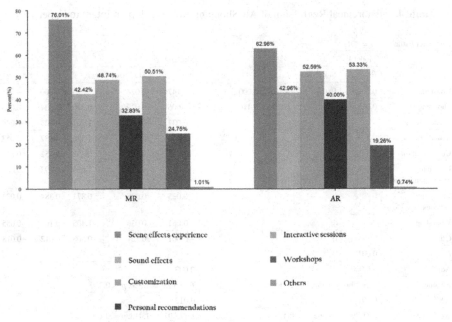

Fig. 8. MR Versus AR in Intent to Experience

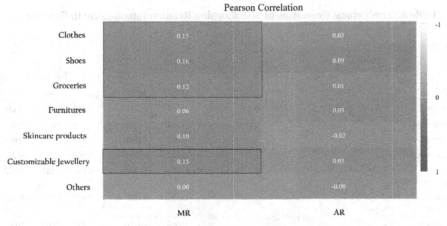

Fig. 9. Correlation in MR Versus AR in Intent to Experience

Table 4. Hierarchical Regression of AR Shopping Relationship on Intent to Experience

Parameter Estimates ($n = 801$)

	Model 1					Model 2				
	B	Std. Error	t	p	β	B	Std. Error	t	p	β
Constant	0.159**	0.018	8.763	0.000	–	0.147**	0.028	5.223	0.000	–
Shopping	0.022	0.027	0.814	0.416	0.029	0.006	0.029	0.210	0.834	0.008
Scene effects						−0.037	0.030	−1.207	0.228	−0.046
Sound effects						0.041	0.031	1.336	0.182	0.053
Customisation						0.022	0.029	0.752	0.452	0.029
Personal recommendations						0.052	0.031	1.686	0.092	0.064
Interactive sessions						0.025	0.028	0.871	0.384	0.033
Workshop						−0.051	0.036	−1.405	0.160	−0.055
Others						−0.061	0.121	−0.508	0.612	−0.018
R^2	0.001					0.013				
Adj R^2	−0.000					0.003				
F value	$F(1,799) = 0.662, p = 0.416$					$F(8,792) = 1.320, p = 0.230$				
ΔR^2	0.001					0.012				
ΔF Value	$F(1,799) = 0.662, p = 0.416$					$F(7,792) = 1.413, p = 0.196$				

Dependent Variable: Augmented Reality
$* p < 0.05 ** p < 0.01$

Table 5. Hierarchical Regression of MR Shopping Relationship on Intent to Experience

Parameter Estimates ($n = 801$)

	Model 1					Model 2				
	B	Std. Error	t	P	β	B	Std. Error	t	p	β
Constant	0.408**	0.024	17.177	0.000	–	0.318**	0.037	8.706	0.000	–
Shopping	0.186**	0.035	5.342	0.000	0.186	0.151**	0.037	4.068	0.000	0.151
Scene effects						0.172**	0.039	4.391	0.000	0.163
Sound effects						0.007	0.040	0.177	0.860	0.007
Customisation						−0.022	0.038	−0.594	0.552	−0.022
Personal recommendations						−0.023	0.040	−0.587	0.557	−0.022
Interactive sessions						−0.021	0.037	−0.570	0.569	−0.021
Workshop						0.086	0.047	1.831	0.067	0.069
Others						0.021	0.156	0.137	0.891	0.005
R^2	0.034					0.068				
Adj R^2	0.033					0.058				
F value	$F(1,799) = 28.537, p = 0.000$					$F(8,792) = 7.192, p = 0.000$				
ΔR^2	0.034					0.033				
ΔF Value	$F(1,799) = 28.537, p = 0.000$					$F(7,792) = 4.034, p = 0.000$				

Dependent Variable: Mixed Reality
$* p < 0.05 ** p < 0.01$

The F-test (F = 28.537, p < 0.05) indicates that shopping influences the relationship on MR, and the model equation is:

$$Mixed\ Reality = 0.408 + 0.186 * Shopping \qquad (1)$$

In model 1, shopping revealed a statistically significant relationship with MR (t = 5.342, p = 0.000 < 0.01), producing a significant positive correlation on MR. The model 2 changes in F-value showed statistical significance in intent to experience (p < 0.05). Scene effects showed a significant positive correlation on MR (t = 4.391, p = 0.000 < 0.01). The remaining factors did not show statistical significance, implying that they do not have correlations with MR (see Table 5).

Accordingly, result 2 shows that MR is a technology that is applicable to retail purchases, while AR does not show significant relevance. Among the experience factors, scene effects such as environment, user interface and spatial interaction contribute to the user's adaptation to MR. Therefore, visual presentation and environmental design represent a crucial dimension of MR adoption.

5.3 Result 3: The Correlations Between AR and MR on Intent to Purchase, Controlling for Shopping

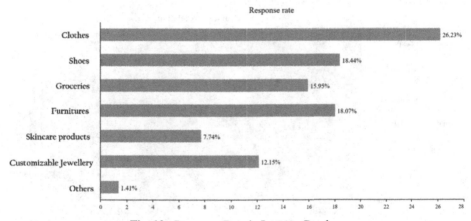

Fig. 10. Response Rate in Intent to Purchase

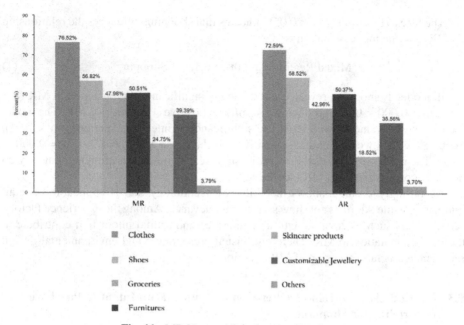

Fig. 11. MR Versus AR in Intent to Purchase

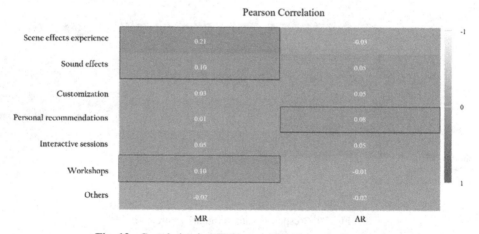

Fig. 12. Correlation in MR Versus AR in Intent to Purchase

MR and AR resemble in their purchase intentions (see Fig. 11). Scenes, sound effects and workshops positively influence the adoption of MR, whereas AR only has personalised recommendations (see Fig. 12).

In model 2, F value changes after including the intention to purchase factors did not show significance ($F = 1.148$, $p = 0.331 > 0.05$), implying that these seven factors had no statistically significant explanatory on AR shopping (see Table 6).

Table 6. Hierarchical Regression of AR Shopping Relationship on Intent to Purchase

Parameter Estimates ($n = 801$)										
	Model 1					Model 2				
	B	Std. Error	t	p	β	B	Std. Error	t	p	β
Constant	0.159**	0.018	8.763	0.000	–	0.142**	0.028	5.131	0.000	–
Shopping	0.022	0.027	0.814	0.416	0.029	0.011	0.030	0.347	0.729	0.014
Clothes						−0.014	0.035	−0.403	0.687	−0.017
Shoes						0.078*	0.033	2.382	0.017	0.105
Groceries						0.002	0.030	0.054	0.957	0.002
Furniture						0.004	0.029	0.131	0.896	0.005
Skincare Products						−0.056	0.037	−1.514	0.130	−0.061
Customisable Jewellery						0.008	0.032	0.239	0.811	0.009
Others						−0.002	0.071	−0.035	0.972	−0.001
R^2	0.001					0.011				
Adj R^2	−0.000					0.001				
F value	$F(1,799) = 0.662, p = 0.416$					$F(8,792) = 1.087, p = 0.370$				
ΔR^2	0.001					0.010				
ΔF Value	$F(1,799) = 0.662, p = 0.416$					$F(7,792) = 1.148, p = 0.331$				

Dependent Variable: Augmented Reality
* $p < 0.05$ ** $p < 0.01$

Table 7. Hierarchical Regression of MR Shopping Relationship on Intent to Purchase

Parameter Estimates ($n = 801$)										
	Model 1					Model 2				
	B	Std. Error	t	p	β	B	Std. Error	t	p	β
Constant	0.408**	0.024	17.177	0.000	–	0.318**	0.036	8.839	0.000	–
Shopping	0.186**	0.035	5.342	0.000	0.186	0.113**	0.039	2.860	0.004	0.112
Clothes						0.069	0.046	1.510	0.131	0.063
Shoes						0.054	0.043	1.262	0.207	0.054
Groceries						0.083*	0.039	2.133	0.033	0.082
Furniture						−0.043	0.038	−1.129	0.259	−0.043
Skincare Products						0.002	0.048	0.039	0.969	0.002
Customisable Jewellery						0.102*	0.041	2.475	0.014	0.096
Others						0.046	0.092	0.507	0.613	0.018

(continued)

Table 7. (*continued*)

Parameter Estimates ($n = 801$)										
	Model 1					Model 2				
	B	Std. Error	t	p	β	B	Std. Error	t	p	β
R^2	0.034					0.061				
Adj R^2	0.033	.				0.051				
F value	$F\,(1,799) = 28.537, p = 0.000$					$F\,(8,792) = 6.381, p = 0.000$				
ΔR^2	0.034					0.026				
ΔF Value	$F\,(1,799) = 28.537, p = 0.000$					$F\,(7,792) = 3.140, p = 0.003$				

Dependent Variable: Mixed Reality
* $p < 0.05$ ** $p < 0.01$

The F-test (F $= 28.537$, p < 0.05) indicates that shopping influences the relationship on MR, and the model equation is:

$$\text{Mixed Reality} = 0.408 + 0.186 * \text{Shopping} \qquad (2)$$

Shopping produced a significant positive correlation on MR (t $= 5.342$, p $= 0.000$ < 0.01). Clothes, shoes, furniture, and skin care products are almost unrelated to MR. Groceries show a significant positive correlation on MR (t $= 2.133$, p $= 0.033 < 0.05$). Customised jewellery presented a significant positive correlation on MR (t $= 2.475$, p $= 0.014 < 0.05$) (see Table 7).

Therefore, result 3 demonstrates a positive influence of MR on shopping and purchase intention, whereas AR is not significantly correlated with it. Bespoke jewellery and groceries positively influenced MR adoption, with bespoke jewellery having a more positive influence than groceries. This revealed that the hedonistic-premised use purpose was more favourable to the masses than the pragmatic-premised experience purpose in the user experience of MR retail purchases.

6 Conclusion

This study emphasises that MR holds more comprehensive promise compared to AR in the retail industry. In the retail market, utilising MR encompasses both hedonic and pragmatic intentions, whereas VR is more hedonic in nature. In particular, customised products like jewellery is a research gap that requires further investigation. As a pragmatic approach adapting MR into high-retention and high-value products. The Findings affirm the feasibility of the our future orientation of the research proposal. Therefore, a more in-depth exploration of customised jewellery function development in retail implementation will be undertaken (Fig. 13).

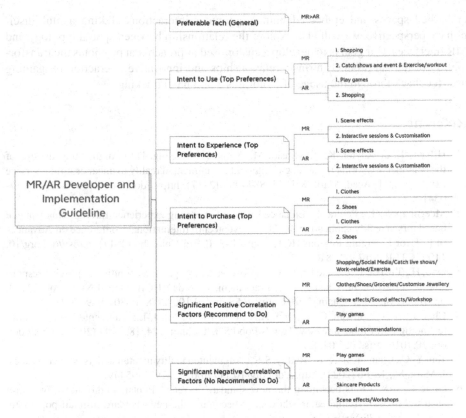

Fig. 13. MR/AR Developer and Implementation Guideline

7 Discussion and Future Work

In our study, we extracted a subset of data from a comprehensive survey and examined it from various perspectives. In this paper, we highlight the differences in the impact of mixed reality and augmented reality on user adoption and the relevance of user intent to MR and AR for purchase behaviour. Additionally, we revealed the strong relevance of MR in retail purchases. These findings have influenced our decision on which technology to utilise in ongoing large-scale projects. We also investigated the disparities in technology preferences and attitudes among consumers who have and have not experienced extended reality (XR) and modelled the influence of age and gender on technology acceptance [27]. The results helped to target user demographic.

This paper targeted the technology we intend to use, however, using questionnaires alone is insufficient to understand users' behaviour, psychology, and cognition. Therefore, further research will include in-depth interviews to analyse user behaviour towards psychological factors. Additionally, we will consider stakeholders' perspectives, such as retailers' attitudes towards accepting the technology and insights from user experience designers and experts. Furthermore, we also believe that the user interface and spatial environment directly impact user engagement and that the users should be afforded embodied spaces and embodied human-computer interactions. Taking a multidisciplinary perspective, we will also explore the relationship between spatial typology and MR interfaces. Our goal is to develop a customised approach that promotes the transformation of human-product intrinsic relationships and innovative interaction by gaining user feedback through the usage of HoloLens 2 and hand tracking.

References

1. Hilken, T., de Ruyter, K., Chylinski, M., Mahr, D., Keeling, D.I.: Augmenting the eye of the beholder: exploring the strategic potential of augmented reality to enhance online service experiences. J. Acad. Mark. Sci. **45**, 884–905 (2017). https://doi.org/10.1007/s11747-017-0541-x
2. Meegahapola, L., Perera, I.: Enhanced in-store shopping experience through smart phone based mixed reality application. In: 2017 Seventeenth International Conference on Advances in ICT for Emerging Regions (ICTer), pp. 1–8. IEEE, Colombo (2017). https://doi.org/10.1109/ICTER.2017.8257810
3. Dou, H., Tanaka, J.: A mixed-reality shop system using spatial recognition to provide responsive store layout. In: Chen, J.Y.C., Fragomeni, G. (eds.) HCII 2020. LNCS, vol. 12190, pp. 18–36. Springer, Cham (2020). https://doi.org/10.1007/978-3-030-49695-1_2
4. Chai, J.J.K., O'Sullivan, C., Gowen, A.A., Rooney, B., Xu, J.-L.: Augmented/mixed reality technologies for food: a review. Trends Food Sci. Technol. **124**, 182–194 (2022). https://doi.org/10.1016/j.tifs.2022.04.021
5. Tan, Y.-C., Chandukala, S.R., Reddy, S.K.: Augmented reality in retail and its impact on sales. J. Mark. **86**, 48–66 (2022). https://doi.org/10.1177/0022242921995449
6. Paige J.: How AR is becoming the new standard in retail: Poplar Studio. https://www.retail-insight-network.com/features/how-ar-is-becoming-the-new-standard-in-retail-poplar-studio/. Accessed 30 May 2023
7. GlobalData: Augmented Reality (AR) in Retail and Apparel - Thematic Research. https://www.globaldata.com/store/report/ar-in-retail-and-apparel-theme-analysis/. Accessed 30 May 2023
8. Scherer, M.J., Craddock, G.: Matching Person & Technology (MPT) assessment process. TAD. **14**, 125–131 (2002). https://doi.org/10.3233/TAD-2002-14308
9. Alnawas, I., Aburub, F.: The effect of benefits generated from interacting with branded mobile apps on consumer satisfaction and purchase intentions. J. Retail. Consum. Serv. **31**, 313–322 (2016). https://doi.org/10.1016/j.jretconser.2016.04.004
10. Foroudi, P., Gupta, S., Sivarajah, U., Broderick, A.: Investigating the effects of smart technology on customer dynamics and customer experience. Comput. Hum. Behav. **80**, 271–282 (2018). https://doi.org/10.1016/j.chb.2017.11.014
11. Williams, R.: 52% of retailers feel ill-prepared to support emerging mobile tech, study says. https://www.marketingdive.com/news/52-of-retailers-feel-ill-prepared-to-support-emerging-mobile-tech-study-s/560947/. Accessed 30 May 2023
12. Schubert, T.W.: A new conception of spatial presence: once again, with feeling. Commun. Theory **19**, 161–187 (2009). https://doi.org/10.1111/j.1468-2885.2009.01340.x
13. Viirre, E., Ellisman, M.: Vertigo in virtual reality with haptics: case report. Cycberpsychol. Behav. **6**, 429–431 (2003). https://doi.org/10.1089/109493103322278826
14. Zhu, W., Owen, C., Li, H., Lee, J.-H.: Personalized in-store E-Commerce with the PromoPad: an augmented reality shopping assistant, **1**(3) (2004)
15. Cruz, E., et al.: An augmented reality application for improving shopping experience in large retail stores. Virtual Reality **23**, 281–291 (2019). https://doi.org/10.1007/s10055-018-0338-3

16. Baytar, F., Chung, T., Shin, E.: Evaluating garments in augmented reality when shopping online. J. Fashion Market. Manag. Int. J. **24**, 667–683 (2020). https://doi.org/10.1108/JFMM-05-2018-0077
17. Jain, S., Werth, D.: Current state of mixed reality technology for digital retail: a literature review. In: Nah, F.F.-H., Siau, K. (eds.) HCII 2019. LNCS, vol. 11588, pp. 22–37. Springer, Cham (2019). https://doi.org/10.1007/978-3-030-22335-9_2
18. Power, D.: How Augmented Reality Is Driving the Evolution of Brands Like Wayfair. https://www.uschamber.com/co/good-company/launch-pad/augmented-reality-tra nsforming-wayfair. Accessed 11 July 2023
19. Dacko, S.G.: Enabling smart retail settings via mobile augmented reality shopping apps. Technol. Forecast. Soc. Chang. **124**, 243–256 (2017). https://doi.org/10.1016/j.techfore.2016.09.032
20. Program-Ace: Using Augmented Reality in Warehouse for Superior Logistics. https://pro gram-ace.com/blog/augmented-reality-warehouse/. Accessed 12 July 2023
21. Office for National Statistics: Impact of the coronavirus (COVID-19) pandemic on retail sales in 2020. https://www.ons.gov.uk/economy/grossdomesticproductgdp/articles/impactoft hecoronaviruscovid19pandemiconretailsalesin2020/2021-01-28. Accessed 12 July 2023
22. Fuchs, K., Grundmann, T., Fleisch, E.: Towards identification of packaged products via com-puter vision: convolutional neural networks for object detection and image classification in retail environments (2019). https://doi.org/10.1145/3365871.3365899
23. Jain, S., Schweiss, T., Bender, S., Werth, D.: Omnichannel retail customer experience with mixed-reality shopping assistant systems. In: Bebis, G., et al. (eds.) ISVC 2021. LNCS, vol. 13017, pp. 504–517. Springer, Cham (2021). https://doi.org/10.1007/978-3-030-90439-5_40
24. Davis, F.D.: Perceived usefulness, perceived ease of use, and user acceptance of information technology. MIS Q. **13**, 319 (1989). https://doi.org/10.2307/249008
25. Vijayasarathy, L.R.: Predicting consumer intentions to use on-line shopping: the case for an augmented technology acceptance model. Inf. Manag. **41**, 747–762 (2004). https://doi.org/10.1016/j.im.2003.08.011
26. Likert, R.: A technique for the measurement of attitudes. Arch. Psychol. **22**(140), 55 (1932)
27. Jin, L., Dalton, R., Fagan, D.: Extended reality (XR) survey: a consumer technology accep-tance preference study on retail. In: Nieto-Garcia, M., Acuti, D., Sit, J., Xavier, B. (eds.) Proceedings of the 8th Colloquium on European Research in Retailing 2023, pp. 207–218. University of Portsmouth, Portsmouth UK (2023).
28. Hughes, C.E., Stapleton, C.B., Hughes, D.E., Smith, E.M.: Mixed reality in education, enter-tainment, and training. IEEE Comput. Graph. Appl. **25**, 24–30 (2005). https://doi.org/10.1109/MCG.2005.139
29. Rokhsaritalemi, S., Sadeghi-Niaraki, A., Choi, S.-M.: A review on mixed reality: current trends, challenges and prospects. Appl. Sci. **10**, 636 (2020). https://doi.org/10.3390/app100 20636

Rapid Mixed Reality Prototyping for Novel Interaction Devices: Evaluating a Transparent Handheld Display

Markus Dresel[✉][iD], Bastian Schmeier, Nele Balke, Bjoern Emkes,
Wan Abdul Aliim Wanali, and Nicole Jochems[iD]

University of Lübeck, Lübeck, Germany
{dresel,schmeier,balke,emkes,jochems}@imis.uni-luebeck.de

Abstract. This paper proposes and evaluates a rapid mixed reality prototyping process for novel interaction devices. The process consists of five steps: ideation & visualization, CAD modeling, physical construction, MR augmentation, and comparative evaluation. It is exemplarily tested by developing a physical prototype of a transparent handheld display device and evaluating it against an opaque version ($N = 16$). Results show that rapid MR prototyping can detect certain UX differences without the need to actually realize the final device. The transparent version had significantly higher hedonic quality. However, no obvious advantage of transparency could be identified regarding task completion. It turned out that the tablet-based AR solution had limited ability to mediate the technological concept and led to ergonomic problems in the experimental setup. However, the proposed process is flexible enough to allow the use of high-quality MR augmentation solutions such as immersive head-mounted display AR, which could overcome the identified limitations.

Keywords: mixed reality · tangible augmented reality · prototyping process · physical proxy · transparent display · user study

1 Introduction

In the process of developing novel interaction devices, prototypes are a major success factor allowing designers to communicate, simulate, and evaluate ideas [7,18]. Given that *"advanced products demand advanced prototypes"* [18], they can be difficult to realize under economically feasible conditions [18]. In the past, however, these kinds of prototypes and their iterative user evaluations led to disruptive innovations such as touchscreens, RFID tags, or biometric sensors [11,21,24,33]. The use of digital tools such as computer-aided design (CAD) or, more recently, virtual prototyping [36] assists the prototyping process and has become an industry standard. This, however, presents a new challenge: the progressive virtualization of prototypes introduces the so-called *"intangibility problem"* [23], raising unmet expectations of tactile experiences

© The Author(s), under exclusive license to Springer Nature Switzerland AG 2023
L. T. De Paolis et al. (Eds.): XR Salento 2023, LNCS 14218, pp. 456–467, 2023.
https://doi.org/10.1007/978-3-031-43401-3_30

when users interact with high-quality 3D renderings of prototypes. To counter-act this, approaches which combine virtual and physical prototypes have emerged in recent years [4]. This enables the concurrent evaluation of ergonomic features and user experience (UX) through user studies [18]. Conducting user studies early in the development process enables the comparison between various initial ideas and early concepts, before actually beginning with the realization [9]. This requires early prototypes to be developed fast and cost-effectively.

Prior research has indicated the great potential of mixed reality (MR) tech-nology for the development of low-cost interactive prototypes [31] and has rec-ommended incorporating principles of rapid prototyping into the development process [5,6,34]. MR prototyping enables developers *"to evaluate the aesthetic, ergonomic, communicative and interactive features "* of a device prior to its tech-nical realization [5]. This paper defines and demonstrates a generalized time- and cost-efficient prototyping process for evaluating novel interactive devices. Trans-parent handheld displays are chosen as an example technology to showcase the rapid MR prototyping process in action by realizing an innovative, exemplary MR prototype from a mere concept idea. Starting as fictional concepts seen in movies and video games, transparent handheld displays are emerging as a viable technology in research [15,28]. However, as of writing, besides looking at the tech-nical feasibility there have been few attempts to validate this concept, especially concerning scientific user studies (i.e. UX evaluation of a stationary transpar-ent display by Moon and colleagues [26]). Transparent displays could provide numerous advantages, such as benefiting situation awareness during interaction and collaborative tasks. This paper investigates the suitability of MR proto-types for UX evaluations (RQ1) and further aims to identify advantages and possibilities of transparent displays compared to opaque displays (RQ2).

2 Terminology and Previous Approaches

The research area of utilizing MR technologies for device prototyping currently lacks consistent terminology and a uniform term for this field as a whole. How-ever, previous research named numerous specific approaches in this domain. The term *tangible augmented reality* (TAR) was coined as a combination of AR tech-nology, with the intuitiveness of tangible user interfaces [3,19]. It focuses on the seamlessness of display space and interaction space. In parallel, the term *interactive augmented prototyping* was defined as *"the combination of physical and virtual artifact models through augmented reality "* [35]. TAR, being a more widespread term, was used by other researchers, but slightly redefined as a low-cost prototyping approach for effective evaluations combining it with *virtual prototyping* (VP) [30–32,37]. Very similar prototyping approaches and evalua-tion processes, also using AR, were called *Mixed Prototyping* [8,12]. However, the same term was also used with an AR-based holographic prototype [27]. Other applications received more specific names. The projection of images on objects of rapid prototyping processes was described as *Workbench for Augmented Rapid Prototyping* [34]. Also, the term *configurable physical archetype* or *MR archetype* was introduced, focusing on movable physical interface elements (e.g. knobs) [2]. In this paper, the term *Mixed Reality Prototyping* is used, as it encompasses technology on all points of the reality-virtuality continuum [25] and is used in related research that also focuses on the development of novel interactive devices [5,10,20].

Over the years, different MR prototyping approaches used various physical construction methods for phyical proxies of objects. These include polystyrene foam models [23] or even more cost-effective origami-like paper prototypes [22,30,32]. Many approaches use CAD models leading up the physical contruction and aim to simulate or improve existing products. The modeled devices span a large range from mugs and robot vacuum cleaners [23], over to handheld game consoles and MP3 players [22,30,32], coffee machines [27], projectors [8,12], washing machines [1,2], and space heaters [10]. To model novel devices, creation tools for MR prototypes have been proposed [29]. Approaches differ in fidelity and often do not simulate the context of use in a plausible way (i.e. sense of presence) nor improve the prototypes iteratively. Adding circuit boards and microcontrollers can raise the fidelity of physical proxies, e.g. by enabling interactions like button presses [8,12].

3   Rapid Mixed Reality Prototyping Process

A generalized process is proposed to help approach MR prototyping systematically, adopting ideas from various previous research [2,22,30,34]. By extracting the key aspects of the analyzed models, a streamlined, flexible, and sequential five step process model was defined: *I) ideation & visualization, II) CAD modeling, III) physical construction, IV) MR augmentation*, and *V) comparative evaluation* (see Fig. 1). This approach is illustrated by reporting on the construction of a handheld interaction device using transparent display technology.

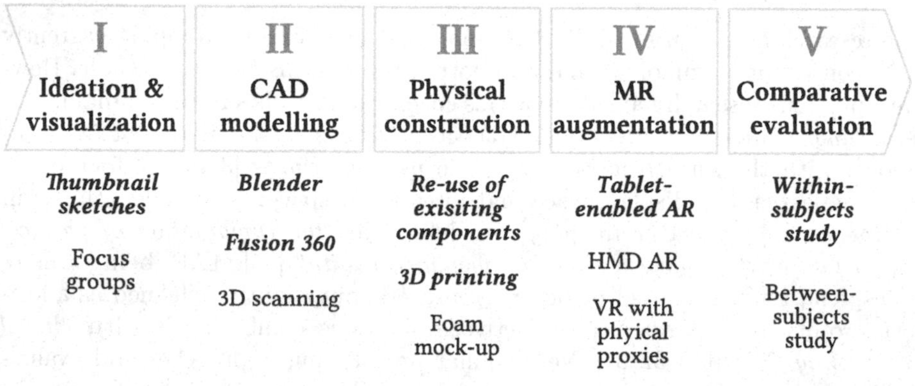

I Ideation & visualization	II CAD modelling	III Physical construction	IV MR augmentation	V Comparative evaluation
Thumbnail sketches	*Blender*	*Re-use of exisiting components*	*Tablet-enabled AR*	*Within-subjects study*
Focus groups	*Fusion 360*	*3D printing*	HMD AR	
	3D scanning		VR with phyical proxies	Between-subjects study
		Foam mock-up		

Fig. 1. The rapid MR prototyping process provides the flexibility to replace actions with context-adjusted alternatives on a step-by-step basis. Entries in italics indicate the actions adopted in this paper.

3.1 Conceptualization of the Handheld Interactive Prototype

Starting the prototyping process with the *I) ideation & visualization* step, the goal was to transform an abstract idea from a mere thought into a design concept. Several device ideas were visualized using thumbnail sketches, deliberately avoiding detailed modeling. The final sketch contained a Nintendo Joy-Con gaming controller[1] for interaction, making the later construction easier and faster. Alternatively, custom-built circuits could have been used.

3.2 CAD Model and Physical Construction

In the following *II) CAD modeling* step, a digital representation was made (see Fig. 2), using a design from Thingiverse[2]. The subsequent *III) physical construction* step used a 20 × 30 cm acrylic glass panel, 4 mm in thickness, as a mock display. Its bezels are taped down with black self-adhesive vinyl film. The grip handles were 3D printed using an Ultimaker 3 printer[3]. The right grip handle was designed to holster a wireless Joy-Con gaming controller for the desired button input. Cyanoacrylate adhesive ("Super Glue") was used to glue the handles onto the sides of the display panel. A magnetically detachable, lightweight cardboard on the display's back makes the display opaque to simulate both transparent and opaque displays. This allows the prototype to be converted swiftly between a transparent and an opaque display variant. The chosen MR augmentation solution (see Sect. 3.3) requires the attachment of an optical tracking marker. The physical construction costs less than 100 €, the most expensive part being the (reusable) Joy-Con controller.

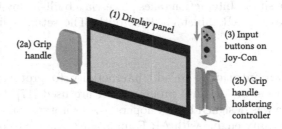

Fig. 2. The prototype model as the result of the CAD model phase, divided into three components

---

[1] https://www.nintendo.com/store/hardware/joy-con-and-controllers/.

[2] https://www.thingiverse.com/thing:2347696.

[3] https://www.ultimaker-3.de/.

3.3   MR Augmentation via Tablet-Enabled AR

Defining an Evaluation Task. Before deciding on how to implement an MR solution in the *IV) MR augmentation* step, an evaluation task needs to be defined to enable meaningful measurements and to address the research questions (see Sect. 1). A maze-solving task was developed to compare the display types. An additional screen – the *source display* (24–27 in. computer screen behind the prototype, 1 m away from the user) – is guiding users by showing the solution path to the current maze task. To solve the mazes efficiently, users need to look at both, the prototype as well as the source display (see Fig. 3, left). Holding the prototype with extended arms, users are able to see the displayed solution through the prototype's transparent display.

Multiple mazes were designed to counteract learning effects. Three difficulty levels ensured that the task will become challenging: easy (8×8 grid, approx. 20 turns), medium (13×13 grid, approx. 40 turns), and hard (18×16 grid, approx. 60 turns). To verify that all maze designs were suitable for comparison a preliminary analysis of task completion times (TCT) was conducted with ten participants.

AR Technology. A tablet-enabled AR solution was used to show the UI on the physical prototype, similar to the work of Choi [10] and Faust [12], who also highlight its simplicity, reliability, low cost, and less invasive nature. A tablet[4] mounted with a gooseneck tablet holder in the line of sight to the prototype displays runs the implemented software. In this video see-through solution users look through the AR tablet to see the maze task on the photorealistic augmented prototype. A 10×10 cm tracking marker allows the AR tablet to precisely track the prototype's position. Interaction takes place via a built-in Joy-Con controller, which connects to the AR tablet via Bluetooth. The setup is lightweight and portable.

Software Implementation. To add interactivity to prototypes, authoring tools based on visual or low-level programming are used [17]. Given that this paper's prototype was designed by developers, the prototype's mock display was simulated by the Unity engine with AR Foundation[5], similar to other MR studies [17]. The evaluation task was implemented corresponding to the evaluation procedure by sequencing the designed mazes (see Sect. 4.1). In terms of the implemented task, users can press the Joy-Con buttons like a directional pad to move through a maze in the corresponding cardinal direction step by step. The current position is marked by a large red dot, and the path traveled is indicated by green dots (see Fig. 3, top left). Acoustic feedback informs users after each step is taken and when they try to bump into a wall. The last step of the proposed process is the *V) comparative evaluation*. Here, study participants compared the different display variants against each other.

---

[4] Samsung Galaxy Tab S7, 12.4in display ($2,560 \times 600$px), 8 MP camera, Android 11.
[5] https://unity.com/   https://unity.com/unity/features/arfoundation.

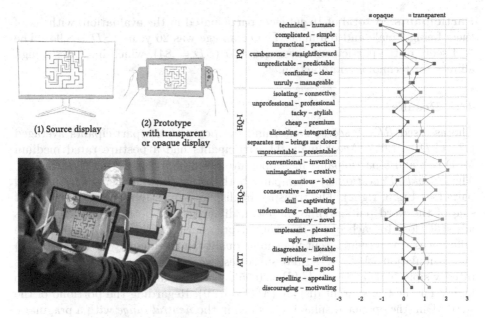

Fig. 3. Top left: content displayed on source display and prototype. Bottom left: experimental setup (staged photo). Right: word pair results of the AttrakDiff questionnaire results (scale ranging from -3 to 3, each $N = 16$) (right).

4   Comparative Evaluation

4.1   Study Design

Procedure and Measurements. The evaluation was conducted with a within-subjects design. Participants' affinity for technology interaction was assessed using the Affinity for Technology Interaction (ATI) scale [13]. The setup can be seen in Fig. 3 (bottom left). Subjects were counterbalanced assigned to begin with either the transparent or opaque display condition and with one of the two maze variants. The experiment started by explaining the goals of the study and the maze task. A trial run was performed for both display conditions to avoid learning effects. During the runs, the task completion times (TCT) for each maze were measured. Furthermore, the Rapid Entire Body Assessment (REBA) scale was used to assess musculoskeletal disorders (MSD), risks related to ergonomic design [16]. After finishing each display condition's mazes, the subjects filled out the AttrakDiff questionnaire [14] to compare the perceived hedonic and pragmatic quality. Finally, additional questions were asked investigating the participants' perception of as well as the interaction with the prototype and the underlying concept (see Table 1).

Participants. A total of 16 subjects participated in the evaluation, with six of them being female and ten male. The mean age was 26 years ($SD = 8.96$). The ATI score of the participants averaged 4.57 ($SD = .84$), which indicates a high affinity for technology interaction.

4.2   Results

The assessed *REBA scores* concerning the poses of the participants averaged 6.81 ($SD = 1.05$). Accordingly, 11 participants had a posture rated medium MSD risk and 5 participants had a posture rated high risk during the trial.

The *AttrakDiff questionnaire* compares both display variants using various word pairs (see Fig. 3, right). The transparent display is mostly assigned to the right side of the word pairs. While the mean differences of both display conditions are still close to each other in terms of pragmatic quality ($MD = 0.19$), the differences are more apparent in hedonic quality in the identity ($MD = -0.875$) and stimulation ($MD = -1.58$) subscales, were the transparent display was rated visibly higher overall ($MD = 0.55$). The measured attractiveness is also higher for the transparent display ($MD = 0.19$). Regarding the portfolio of the AttrakDiff, the opaque display is classified in the *neutral range* with a pragmatic quality of 0.28 and a hedonic quality of -0.11. The transparent display on the other hand is classified in the *self-oriented* category with a similar pragmatic quality of 0.06, but a significantly higher hedonic quality of 1.12. Paired t-tests for the different subscales of the AttrakDiff (at a Bonferroni corrected significance level of 0.125%) showed significant differences, between conditions within the identity ($t(15) = -5.374, p < .001$) and the stimulation ($t(15) = -5.477, p < .001$) subscales. The Shapiro-Wilk test was used to test the data for normal distribution. The p-values suggest a violation of the assumption of normality only for the scales of pragmatic quality and attractiveness. *Task Completion Times* increase noticeably with maze difficulty (easy $M = 14.675$ s, $SD = 4.57$; medium $M = 30.11$ s, $SD = 8.98$; hard $M = 55.34$ s, $SD = 21.96$). However, differences in TCT between display conditions were marginal within each difficulty setting (easy $MD = 1.71$ s; medium $MD = -2.18$ s; hard $MD = -0.814$ s). The participants were presented with several *additional questions* where they were asked indicate their level of agreement with different statement (see Table 1).

4.3   Limitations

Due to the COVID-19 pandemic, the study was not conducted in a controlled laboratory environment, but in several locations, differing in layout and furnishings, resulting in slightly varying sitting postures and lighting conditions. Most notably the size of the *source display*, varied between 24 and 27 in. It is not certain whether the differences found in the UX would also be found in a real (non-AR) study with a finished product, even though previous research indicates they might be [10]. To ensure normal distribution in resulting data and since participants were exclusively younger adults (students), replicating studies should also have larger and more diverse samples.

Table 1. Additional questions investigating the interaction with the prototype and the underlying concept (Likert scale ranging from 1–disapproval to 7–approval, $N = 16$).

Statement	Average approval
1. I found the input via the controller to be simple	6.25 ($SD = 1.06$)
2. The AR display worked well	4.56 ($SD = 1.59$)
3. The maze was easy to lay over the solution	3.63 ($SD = 2.03$)
4. I found it exhausting to hold up the prototype	6.69 ($SD = .79$)
5. I could not see any advantage in using the transparent display	3.75 ($SD = 2.05$)
6. The transparent display made the task easier for me	5.13 ($SD = 1.82$)
7. I can imagine using transparent displays in my everyday life	4.38 ($SD = 1.54$)
8. I would still prefer opaque displays in everyday life	4.63 ($SD = 1.36$)

5 Discussion

The *AttrakDiff* results show that the transparent display is marginally (not significantly) worse in pragmatic quality. This is possibly due to the experimental setup, which may have caused difficulties in overlaying the mazes. Here, the most noticable difference was the higher predictability of the opaque display, which the participants were clearly more familiar with. In contrast, the transparent display shows significantly higher hedonic quality, in both the identity and stimulation subscales. The highest differences in mean values were observed in the word pairs *"ordinary – novel"* ($MD = -2.69$), *"conservative – innovative"* ($MD = -2.13$), *"tacky – stylish"* ($MD = -1.88$), and *"conventional - inventive"* ($MD = -1.81$). These results may be related to the novelty of the transparent display prototype, possibly resulting in greater enthusiasm. Attractiveness was also rated noticeably higher in the transparent display condition, although not statistically significant. This could be explained by a conflict that arose from the transparent display triggering curiosity due to its novelty but leading to uncertainty due to unfamiliarity in using it. Many subjects (7) tended to (at least partially) agree that they would like to use transparent displays in everyday life. Only one subject disagreed with this question, six subject's where indifferent. However, only two subjects (at least partially) disagreed that they would still prefer opaque displays in their everyday lives. The rest either agreed (7) or were indifferent (7).

Participants reported numerous ideas for novel interaction possibilities using transparent displays. Predominantly, these were situations where it is necessary to maintain contextual awareness of collaborating users or non-users (social), and the environment (spatial). Examples include multiplayer gaming, collaborative drawing, photography, interior design planning, medical examinations, technical maintenance, navigation, and information retrieval (reading, looking at images).

Although TCT was similar between display conditions, participants tended to agree that the transparent display had made the task easier, likely due to the guidance provided by the solution on the source display. Since some subjects were able to line up the maze to the source display's solution, there is a medium level of agreement that the aligning of the mazes worked well and that there is an advantage to using the transparent display.

The prototyping process utilized tablet-enabled AR as the MR augmentation solution which presented issues. Regarding the experimental setup, the REBA scores indicate a medium to high MSD risk, which is consistent with the ratings on the statement that it was exhausting to hold the prototype, to which most subjects (14) fully agreed. Observed fatigue was occasionally commented on by some subjects during the experiment. Arguably, the tablet-enabled AR medium might have affected the UX of the tested prototype itself (in either condition), as the visual fidelity of the AR solution may have been too low and the physical inconvenience too great to convincingly convey the vision.

6   Conclusion

This paper investigated the potential of rapid MR prototyping for the evaluation of novel interaction devices. Based on the example of a transparent handheld display, an MR prototype was developed in a five-step process. The last step was a comparative evaluation between the opaque display and a transparent variant. The following answers to the research questions posed can be derived.

With respect to the suitability of MR Prototyping for UX evaluations (RQ1), the proposed process works to compare concept ideas. Certain UX differences (i.e., hedonic quality) can be measured without actually realizing the final device saving time and costs in further development phases and preventing wrong design decisions. However, in terms of pragmatic quality, attractiveness, or TCT, no differences were found between both prototype variants. Whether there were actually no such differences, or they were just not reflected sufficiently by the MR augmentation, cannot be said with certainty. More advanced MR augmentation alternatives like immersive AR technology might identify such differences.

Regarding advantages and possibilities of transparent displays compared to opaque ones (RQ2), results show that the trasparent variant performed significantly better in terms of hedonic quality for the identity and stimulation subscales of the AttrakDiff questionnaire. Referring directly to the evaluation task, the transparent display prototype did not seem to have noticeable advantages over the opaque variant. Differences in TCT and pragmatic quality were marginal and when asked directly most subjects were indifferent. This could differ in other tasks and contexts of use, like the many examples mentioned by the participants. Thus, further studies should focus especially on these contexts.

A follow-up study is being planned to repeat the proposed process using immersive head-mounted displays and more sophisticated object tracking in the MR augmentation step, adressing the limitations of tablet-based AR described above. By lowering the REBA scores and increasing visual fidelity, AR glasses in particular could increase the validity of comparing different prototype variants.

Acknowledgements. Our thanks to Malte Husung for his part in design and implementation, and to Rafael Wortmann and Pascal Stagge for 3D modelling/printing.

References

1. Barbieri, L., Angilica, A., Bruno, F., Muzzupappa, M.: An interactive tool for the participatory design of product interface. In: Proceedings of the ASME 2012 International Design Engineering Technical Conferences and Computers and Information in Engineering Conference, vol. 2, pp. 1437–1447. ASME, Chicago, Illinois, USA (Aug 2012). https://doi.org/10.1115/DETC2012-71097

2. Barbieri, L., Angilica, A., Bruno, F., Muzzupappa, M.: Mixed prototyping with configurable physical archetype for usability evaluation of product interfaces. Comput. Ind. **64**, 310–323 (2013). https://doi.org/10.1016/j.compind.2012.11.010

3. Billinghurst, M., Kato, H., Poupyrev, I.: Tangible augmented reality. In: ACM SIGGRAPH ASIA 2008 Courses on - SIGGRAPH Asia 2008, pp. 1–10. ACM Press, Singapore (2008). https://doi.org/10.1145/1508044.1508051

4. Bjoerkli, L.E.: A Review of Virtual Prototyping Approaches for User Testing of Design Solutions, p. 14 (2015)

5. Bordegoni, M., Polistina, S., Carulli, M.: Mixed reality prototyping for handheld products testing. In: Proceedings of IDMME - Virtual Concept 2010, Bordeaux, France, p. 6 (2010)

6. Bruno, F., Cosco, F., Angilica, A., Muzzupappa, M.: Mixed prototyping for products usability evaluation. In: 30th Computers and Information in Engineering Conference, Parts A and B, vol. 3, pp. 1381–1390. ASMEDC, Montreal, Quebec, Canada (Jan 2010). https://doi.org/10.1115/DETC2010-28841

7. Camburn, B., et al.: Design prototyping methods: State of the art in strategies, techniques, and guidelines. Design Sci. **3**, e13 (2017). https://doi.org/10.1017/dsj.2017.10

8. Catecati, T., et al.: Mixed prototyping in the evaluation of human-product interaction: issues and solutions. In: Proceedings of the 3rd International Conferenc on Integration of Design, Engineering & Management for Innovation, Porto, Portugal, pp. 269–276 (Oct 2013)

9. Choi, Y.M.: Utilizing end user input in early product development. Procedia Manuf. **3**, 2244–2250 (2015). https://doi.org/10.1016/j.promfg.2015.07.368

10. Choi, Y.M.: Applying tangible augmented reality for product usability assessment. J. Usability Stud. **14**(4), 14 (2019)

11. El-Abed, M., Charrier, C., Rosenberger, C.: Evaluation of biometric systems. In: Yang, J. (ed.) New Trends and Developments in Biometrics. InTech (Nov 2012). https://doi.org/10.5772/52084

12. Faust, F.G., et al.: Mixed prototypes for the evaluation of usability and user experience: simulating an interactive electronic device. Virtual Reality **23**(2), 197–211 (2019). https://doi.org/10.1007/s10055-018-0356-1

13. Franke, T., Attig, C., Wessel, D.: a personal resource for technology interaction: development and validation of the affinity for technology Interaction (ATI) scale. Int. J. Hum.-Comput. Interact. **35**(6), 456–467 (2019). https://doi.org/10.1080/10447318.2018.1456150

14. Hassenzahl, M., Burmester, M., Koller, F.: AttrakDiff: Ein Fragebogen zur Messung wahrgenommener hedonischer und pragmatischer Qualität. In: Szwillus, G., Ziegler, J. (eds.) Mensch & Computer 2003, vol. 57, pp. 187–196. Vieweg+Teubner Verlag, Wiesbaden (2003). https://doi.org/10.1007/978-3-322-80058-9_19

15. Hedili, M.K., Freeman, M.O., Urey, H.: Transmission characteristics of a bidirectional transparent screen based on reflective microlenses. Opt. Express **21**(21), 24636–24646 (2013). https://doi.org/10.1364/OE.21.024636

16. Hignett, S., McAtamney, L.: Rapid entire body assessment (REBA). Appl. Ergon. **31**(2), 201–205 (2000). https://doi.org/10.1016/S0003-6870(99)00039-3
17. Jain, K., Choi, Y.M.: Authoring interactions for tangible augmented reality. In: Stephanidis, C., Antona, M. (eds.) HCII 2020. CCIS, vol. 1225, pp. 43–50. Springer, Cham (2020). https://doi.org/10.1007/978-3-030-50729-9_6
18. Kanai, S., Verlinden, J.: Advanced prototyping for human-centered design for information appliances. Int. J. Inter. Design Manuf. (IJIDeM) **3**(3), 131–134 (2009)
19. Kato, H., Billinghurst, M., Poupyrev, I., Imamoto, K., Tachibana, K.: Virtual object manipulation on a table-top AR environment. In: Proceedings IEEE and ACM International Symposium on Augmented Reality (ISAR 2000), pp. 111–119. IEEE, Munich, Germany (2000). https://doi.org/10.1109/ISAR.2000.880934
20. Kent, L., Snider, C., Gopsill, J., Hicks, B.: Mixed reality in design prototyping: a systematic review. Des. Stud. **77**, 101046 (2021). https://doi.org/10.1016/j.destud.2021.101046
21. Lamel, L., Bennacef, S., Gauvain, J.L., Dartigues, H., Temem, J.N.: User evaluation of the MASK kiosk. Speech Commun. **38**(1), 131–139 (2002)
22. Lee, J.Y., Rhee, G.W., Park, H.: Ar/rp-based tangible interactions for collaborative design evaluation of digital products. Int. J. Adv. Manuf. Technol. **45**(7), 649–665 (2009)
23. Lee, W., Park, J.: Augmented foam: a tangible augmented reality for product design. In: Fourth IEEE and ACM International Symposium on Mixed and Augmented Reality (ISMAR 2005), pp. 106–109. IEEE, Vienna, Austria (2005). https://doi.org/10.1109/ISMAR.2005.16
24. Mäkelä, K., Belt, S., Greenblatt, D., Häkkilä, J.: Mobile interaction with visual and RFID tags: a field study on user perceptions. In: Proceedings of the SIGCHI Conference on Human Factors in Computing Systems, pp. 991–994. ACM, San Jose California USA (Apr 2007). https://doi.org/10.1145/1240624.1240774
25. Milgram, P., Takemura, H., Utsumi, A., Kishino, F.: Augmented reality: a class of displays on the reality-virtuality continuum. In: Das, H. (ed.) Proceedings, Telemanipulator and Telepresence Technologies, vol. 2351, pp. 282–292. SPIE, Boston, MA (Dec 1995). https://doi.org/10.1117/12.197321
26. Moon, B.S.: A study on the evaluation of ux elements for users' selective attention to the transparent public display. Arch. Design Res. **27**(2), 183–197 (2014). https://doi.org/10.15187/adr.2014.05.110.2.183
27. Morozova, A., Rheinstädter, V., Wallach, D.: MixedUX: a mixed prototyping framework for usability testing in augmented reality. In: Companion Publication of the 2019 on Designing Interactive Systems Conference 2019 Companion, DIS 2019 Companion, pp. 41–44. Association for Computing Machinery, New York (Jun 2019). https://doi.org/10.1145/3301019.3325146
28. Nakamura, T., et al.: 360-degree transparent holographic screen display. In: ACM SIGGRAPH 2019 Emerging Technologies, SIGGRAPH 2019, pp. 1–2. Association for Computing Machinery, New York (Jul 2019). https://doi.org/10.1145/3305367.3327974
29. Nam, T.J.: Sketch-based rapid prototyping platform for hardware-software integrated interactive products. In: CHI 2005 Extended Abstracts on Human Factors in Computing Systems, CHI EA 2005, pp. 1689–1692. Association for Computing Machinery, New York (Apr 2005). https://doi.org/10.1145/1056808.1056998
30. Park, H., Moon, H.C.: Design evaluation of information appliances using augmented reality-based tangible interaction. Comput. Ind. **64**(7), 854–868 (2013). https://doi.org/10.1016/j.compind.2013.05.006

31. Park, H., Moon, H.C., Lee, J.Y.: Tangible augmented prototyping of digital hand-held products. Comput. Ind. **60**(2), 114–125 (2009). https://doi.org/10.1016/j.compind.2008.09.001
32. Park, H., Park, S.J., Jung, H.K.: Note on tangible interaction using paper models for AR-based design evaluation. J. Adv. Mech. Design Syst. Manuf. **7**(5), 827–835 (2013). https://doi.org/10.1299/jamdsm.7.827
33. Repo, P., Kerttula, M., Salmela, M., Huomo, H.: Virtual product design case study: the Nokia RFID tag reader. IEEE Pervasive Comput. **4**(4), 95–99 (2005). https://doi.org/10.1109/MPRV.2005.92
34. Verlinden, J., de Smit, A., Peeters, A.W.J., van Gelderen, M.H.: Development of a flexible augmented prototyping system. WSCG **11**(1), 8 (2003)
35. Verlinden, J., Horváth, I.: Analyzing opportunities for using interactive augmented prototyping in design practice. Artif. Intell. Eng. Des. Anal. Manuf. **23**(3), 289–303 (2009). https://doi.org/10.1017/S0890060409000250
36. Wang, G.G.: Definition and review of virtual prototyping. J. Comput. Inf. Sci. Eng. **2**(3), 232–236 (2002). https://doi.org/10.1115/1.1526508
37. Zhang, X., Choi, Y.M.: Applying tangible augmented reality in usability evaluation. In: Shumaker, R., Lackey, S. (eds.) VAMR 2015. LNCS, vol. 9179, pp. 88–94. Springer, Cham (2015). https://doi.org/10.1007/978-3-319-21067-4_11

Virtual Reality for Neurofeedback, Biofeedback and Emotion Recognition

Emotion Tracking in Virtual Reality Fashion Shows

Marina Carulli⑩, Elena Spadoni(✉)⑩, Chiara Barone⑩, and Monica Bordegoni⑩

Politecnico di Milano, Milano, Italy
elena.spadoni@polimi.it

Abstract. Virtual Reality (VR) technologies are increasingly being adopted in fashion marketing to create innovative new channels for sales, advertising, brand communication, and strengthening relationships with consumers. In addition, virtual technologies can be useful for personalizing the offer, gathering insights, and user engagement. However, there seem to be few occurrences where the potential of virtual technologies on User eXperience (UX) and engagement is explored, evaluating the advantages compared to real-life experiences. Analyzing these aspects for virtual fashion experiences can be challenging. For measuring the UX, quantitative methods such as sensors capable of recording and examining the body's responses and automatic systems used to recognize emotions by tracking facial movements and expressions have been increasingly employed. In the context of fashion marketing, they can help analyze the implications that virtual experiences have, also considering content personalization and company promotion. This paper presents the design and development of a VR application that includes emotion-tracking technology that can be used to evaluate users' emotional reactions to virtual experiences and compare them with real ones. The final aim of the study is to increase the degree of user engagement and the quality of the virtual fashion show UX of the Italian clothing brand Bacon. Preliminary test sessions were organized to evaluate users' emotional reactions to the virtual experience and verify their effectiveness in relation to the objectives of the study.

Keywords: User eXperience · Emotion tracking · Virtual Fashion Show

1 Introduction

New and modern technologies, such as Virtual Reality (VR), are increasingly being used in the field of fashion marketing. Fashion brands, as well as others, are placed in a very competitive market environment. Therefore, it is necessary for corporate marketing to develop innovative business strategies focused on different objective, firstly, with the intention of increasing people's intent to purchase products, and then for more general purposes of communication, reputation, and brand name. In this sense, VR technologies may prove to be interesting tools at the service of marketing in the fashion sector, since they can be used as an innovative new channel for sales, advertising, communication and to strengthen the relationship with consumers.

However, there are not many fashion brands that measure themselves against all the potential offered by the innovative technology of VR in terms of improving the consumer's user experience or even personalizing and customizing this experience, as has happened in other sectors, such as engineering, entertainment, and video games. This is probably also due to the challenges these technologies pose. A pragmatic example is the measurement of the effectiveness of such systems in improving the user experience. User eXperience (UX) has many definitions in the literature today. We can say in a synthetic way that it leads back to different concepts related to the use of a product, including "usability, value and relevance, accessibility, ease of use, hedonic and pragmatic quality, visual/aesthetic attractiveness and human perception" [1] in terms of user's satisfaction.

There are still no defined metrics with which it is possible to have a certain result that suggests an effective increase in the quality of user experience when using VR technologies. However, given the high costs for the design and development of applications using these technologies, it is important for companies to understand if they lead to an improvement in UX and customer satisfaction and to benefits in terms of Return on Investment (ROI). It is, therefore, conceivable that the difficulty in measuring effectiveness could be a disincentive element for the marketing of some brands in the fashion sector, as it also happens in other sectors.

Both qualitative and quantitative criteria are used for analyzing UX. The former is usually used to investigate the depth of a phenomenon or psychological aspects or the impressions arising from the interaction between the user and the technological product. They are made up of an articulated set of methodologies widely analyzed in the literature [2]. They include, among others, questionnaires to analyze users' opinions, individual or group interviews, speaking aloud, and observations.

Progressively, for the analysis of performance, quantitative methods have been increasingly employed in an equal or greater way than qualitative ones [3]. In the case of UX, bio-feedbacks are frequently used as quantitative analysis methods, measured by sensors capable of recording and examining the body's responses to a given experience. An example of such technologies can be represented by eye tracking, capable of tracking the user's eye movement [4]. More in general, in several cases, sensors or emotion recognition systems have been used as methods for measuring the user experience and the level of engagement [5]. There are different systems and sensors used to map biological parameters (sensors that detect skin conductivity and heartbeat, breathing, etc.) and automatic systems that are used to recognize emotions using the recognition of facial movements and expressions.

These technological systems can detect and analyze the change in the expressions or other physical parameters of the users who are monitored at the exact moment in which they enjoy the virtual experience, thus providing interesting and useful inputs regarding the state of mind experienced by them. The use of emotion-sensing technologies has been tested in multiple domains so far. As far as marketing is concerned, to give an example, some studies have tried to demonstrate the effectiveness of the so-called "emotional targeting", which involves the possibility of sending personalized promotional messages to users on the basis of the state of mind recognized by them [6].

Research is actively continuing to test the validity of the inputs and data produced by using software, applications, and emotion recognition systems in general as UX measurement tools. They can also be useful as methods of verifying the opinions expressed by users during tests used to analyze the perceived quality of the user experience. In fact, it is known that the opinions expressed by users are frequently not very reliable as they are subject to distortions and biases of various types. Therefore, it seems useful to measure the responses that the body provides, both in terms of biofeedback and in terms of facial expressions. Emotion recognition systems can make it possible to understand whether these virtual experiences are perceived as of value by users and therefore to form an idea of their effectiveness in terms of involvement and responsiveness to market objectives. In the context of fashion marketing, they can help analyze the implications that these VR experiences have, also from the point of view of personalization and company promotion.

Several studies have investigated the opportunity to develop interactive VR applications to improve the user experience during fashion catwalks and evaluate their effectiveness. This paper presents the design and development of a VR application including emotions tracking that can be used to evaluate users' emotional reactions to virtual experiences. The final aim of the study is to increase the level of user engagement and the quality of the virtual experience of the fashion show of the Bacon clothing brand, an Italian company operating in the fashion sector.

The literature review in the relevant research areas and research objectives will be presented in the next section. Subsequently, the paper discusses a case study in which fashion catwalks were shot in VR and compared with the real ones. Preliminary test settings were organized to evaluate the users' emotional reactions to the VR environments and to verify their effectiveness in relation to the objectives defined.

2 Related Topics

The scientific literature presents numerous works focused on technologies and software aimed at the recognition and detection of human emotions [7] to collect data and get a global idea of the effectiveness of the User Experience in the most diverse fields. For example, in the field of gaming, it has been demonstrated that the detection of emotions is able to produce useful inputs to improve the user experience [8]. It can be used in the product development and design process to understand how to ensure a more rewarding and enjoyable gaming experience for players [9], and to increase the level of perceived empathetic engagement with the characters and the virtual narrative context [10]. The analysis of the adoption of human emotion recognition systems has also produced positive implications in other areas, including learning, where it has been proven that the integration of these systems correlates with higher levels of student motivation during the educational experience [11]. Through these technologies it is possible to develop personalized instruction programs for the individual student or even monitor the degree of difficulty felt by them while carrying out exercises or tasks [12]. This appears very interesting also regarding the possibility of improving the learning experience of children with disabilities, by acquiring information that allows for the development of teaching methodologies adapted to their needs [13]. Software capable of reading emotions and detecting the state of mind of users have also proved to be effective in developing personalized marketing messages. In this sense, a correlation has been found between the use of so-called emotional targeting and an increase in purchase intentions [14]. Finally, it also seems useful to mention the advantages of such systems to promote preferable behaviors in the social sphere. For example, they have been used to test different campaigns aimed at raising people's awareness of the issue of safe driving and understanding which of them were more impactful and effective [15]. As proved by various studies [5], these technologies have seen a progressive improvement over the last few years, to produce increasingly reliable results.

In the realm of Virtual Reality (VR) technology, existing literature highlights three distinct technological approaches linked to the notion of immersion: fully immersive VR, semi-immersive VR, and non-immersive VR solutions [16]. Fully immersive VR systems typically employ devices like Head Mounted Displays (HMD) to detach the user from their surroundings entirely. Semi-immersive systems, on the other hand, represent a hybrid approach, often utilizing environmental projections. Non-immersive VR systems refer to desktop-based VR, where content is displayed on a conventional computer screen, enabling virtual experiences. Building upon these distinctions, extensive research has demonstrated the advantages that VR solutions, offering varying degrees of immersion, can offer to marketing in the fashion industry. For example, studies have proved useful for the purpose of personalizing the offer, gathering insights and user engagement [17]. In the retail sector, they can be used to give users immersive and valuable experiences, as well as to increase purchase intention [18]. The use of VR technology in the field has also proved to be extremely advantageous also regarding the general theme of brand communication [19]. Various research works are moving in this direction, trying to understand how VR technologies can be introduced in the context of the customer journey [20] or questioning the impact that they could have on consumers [21].

Discussions relating to the potential of VR technologies are fueled today by the fervent debate regarding the metaverse, defined as "the post-reality universe, a perpetual and persistent multiuser environment merging physical reality with digital virtuality. It is based on the convergence of technologies that enable multisensory interactions with virtual environments, digital objects, and people such as Virtual Reality (VR) and Augmented Reality (AR)" [21].

In addition, following the conditions resulting from the Covid-19 pandemic, the urgency was felt in some areas to try and test the potential of these virtual tools, especially considering non-immersive virtual solutions. An example is the testing of theater performances in virtual environments using the metaverse, thus maintaining contact between art and the public, which has achieved exciting results [22].

Cases like this allow us to reflect on the fact that through the introduction and integration of the metaverse into the fashion world, it could also prove possible to create collaborative fashion shows, with the possibility for users to purchase virtual garments and accessories. This is also encouraged by the positive implications obtained from research on the effects of the metaverse and the use of VR technology in the retail sector [23].

Scholars also aimed at raising awareness and paying attention to the theme of acceptance of these technologies by consumers [24], which recall the importance of verifying the problems posed by the possible risks perceived by users, such as regarding the issue of privacy and psychological health. The user and their characteristics therefore appear to be essential elements to consider in the creation of the virtual environment [25]. In both cases, the studies cited are aimed at testing the effectiveness of the use of these technologies, to collect data that suggest how to increase the quality of the user experience and, consequently, their satisfaction.

3 Experimental Case Study

While Virtual Reality technologies have been utilized to communicate fashion content as well as create fashion shows and events, there appears to be a smaller number of occurrences where the impact of virtual technologies on user experience and engagement is explored. This may involve evaluating the potential benefits or advantages in comparison to real-life experiences. Analyzing the user experience and satisfaction levels for virtual fashion experiences can be challenging.

We identified the potential to create and implement an interactive non-immersive Virtual Reality application intended to assess the user experience and engagement of virtual fashion catwalks while also examining aspects related to fashion marketing. The case study utilizes clothing items designed by Bacon, an Italian fashion company (https://www.baconclothing.com) recognized for its signature lightweight puffer jackets, inspired by underground youth cultures and the grunge aesthetic of the 1990s.

The case study incorporates features for customizing the Bacon product line and gathering information on users' needs and preferences. The primary objective of the experimental case is to compare virtual and real fashion catwalks, evaluating users' experiences and emotional responses during these experiences. To investigate this aspect, the virtual application integrates an innovative tool named *EMOJ* (https://www.emojlab. com/), which enables mapping facial expressions and associating them with distinct emotions. The data collected, both qualitative and quantitative, are deemed valuable for informing future brand communication and customer experience decisions.

We took inspiration from interesting examples of VR technologies implemented in the fashion industry in the last few years to define the application concept. As an example, "The Fabric of Reality" is a fully immersive fashion show that was launched within the virtual Museum of Other Realities (MOR) in 2021. The show aimed to take audiences on a journey to explore the story and narrative behind the designers' collection [26].

Fashion events organized in the metaverse are also common. For example, "Unplanned Paths: A Metaverse Fashion Week Exhibition" was the first metaverse fashion week presented by The Chockablock in April 2022. The tension between the handmade and the digitally made was at the focus of this exhibition [27].

Another interesting example is the "Somnium Space Mixed Reality VR Fashion Show", which was organized in Prague in 2022 [28]. The event aimed to expand the way fashion is presented to the public by connecting people from all over the world simultaneously. During the event, different technologies such as Augmented Reality, Virtual Reality, Full Body Tracking, and Holograms were integrated.

3.1 Application Design Concept

The experimental case study consists of a Virtual Reality (VR) application showcasing a fashion catwalk in both digital and physical forms. The emotions of users are tracked using facial recognition technology to compare the two varieties of catwalks. Additionally, this feature enables the assessment of user engagement throughout the whole experience and helps uncover the preferred fashion options presented.

The design concept of the VR application is shown in Fig. 1 and explained in detail in the next section.

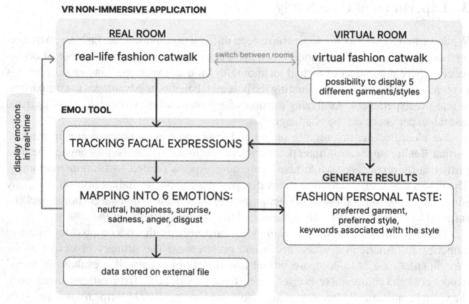

Fig. 1. The design concept of the experimental case study.

The fashion catwalk application provides users with access to both virtual and real catwalks through a non-immersive VR environment that can be accessed directly on personal computers. This decision was driven by the intention to utilize the EMOJ tool for mapping users' emotional responses. Consequently, technologies such as Head Mounted Displays (HMD) that hinder facial recognition were deliberately avoided in favor of PC-based access.

In the application, there are two distinct areas called the "real room" and the "virtual room" that showcase Bacon clothing on physical and virtual catwalks, respectively. These separate catwalks display the same garments, enabling users to make an accurate comparison between the two experiences.

At the start of the experience, the user has the option to choose between the two rooms through a Graphical User Interface (GUI) panel. This panel remains accessible throughout the experience, allowing the user to switch between the two rooms at any time. After selecting a room, the user will be automatically transported inside. Furthermore, the user can navigate freely within the virtual environment and engage with various virtual elements using the mouse and keyboard.

The "real room" contains a spacious area with a large screen situated in the center, as shown in Fig. 2. The screen showcases a video representing an actual catwalk. To enhance user engagement, the visual content presentation is accompanied by music. Users have the freedom to move around the space to find the best viewing angle. On the other hand, the "virtual room" comprises an open virtual environment with a screen displaying a video of the virtual catwalk on the wall at the far end of the room. Users can choose from five different videos that showcase various fashion styles and clothing items. This feature provides users with greater control over their experience and enables them to watch their favorite styles and clothes multiple times.

The application incorporates the *EMOJ* tool, which enables real-time recognition of users' emotions throughout their experience. Users' facial expressions are monitored both in the "real room" and the "virtual room," and the collected data is analyzed to determine the user's emotional state. This analysis encompasses six fundamental emotions: neutral, happiness, surprise, sadness, anger, and disgust. The data associated with these identified emotions are processed in real-time and stored in a cloud-based file for future reference and analysis. Specifically, these values are included in the file by establishing an automatic correlation with the timing of the fashion catwalk videos' playback. This value allows for linking the emotion to the displayed garment within a specific timeframe in the video, enabling the reconstruction of the user's emotional response. Subsequently, the recorded emotions are examined to calculate an average value for each garment.

Fig. 2. Screenshot showcasing the "real room" setting featuring the catwalk.

After concluding the "virtual room" experience, users have the opportunity to discern their preferred outfit based on the detected emotions. At this stage, the data stored in the cloud-based file is automatically analyzed to extract the users' positive emotions associated with the showcased garments. By selecting a GUI button, a dashboard is presented, outlining the clothing and style preferences derived from the extracted data. The dashboard features a preview of the preferred apparel and associated keywords (for example, casual, chic, cool, minimalist), providing insight into fashion tastes. This information can be advantageous in making educated shopping attitudes in the future. Moreover, the data gathered has the potential to be a valuable resource for Bacon fashion company to analyze customers' preferences and incorporate them into upcoming marketing strategies.

3.2 Application Development

Virtual Reality Environment

The Unity3D platform (https://unity.com) was utilized to create the virtual experience in this case study. All of the panels, texts, and buttons were designed and implemented directly in Unity, along with user interactions programmed with various scripts. Additionally, background music was included to enrich the experience by importing audio files into Unity. The virtual environment was developed by utilizing assets freely available on the Unity Assets Store (https://assetstore.unity.com/), which simplified the development process.

To emphasize the difference between physical and digital fashion shows, a metaphor was employed that equates the virtual catwalk with a futuristic, post-human realm, largely due to the incorporation of anthropomorphic avatars. This theme is conveyed by the ambiance created within the virtual setting.

The "real room" presents a luminous ambiance, where an industrial building hosts the experience, with the aim of recreating a realistic catwalk setting.

The "virtual room", on the other hand, features a futuristic atmosphere with a slightly dimmer tone and selected light strips illuminating only the crucial elements, as depicted in Fig. 3.

In addition, the GUI has been designed to reflect the post-human futuristic vision as well. In fact, the texts, panels, and graphical elements respect a common basic line for both rooms, but they present little differences in color and style to fit the atmosphere of the futuristic "virtual room" in terms of bright outlines and squared shapes.

Fig. 3. Captured images showcasing the "real room" and the "virtual room" settings.

Users' Facial Expressions Detection

To identify users' emotions, the *EMOJ* tool was integrated with Unity. This tool utilizes the RGB camera of the device for face detection, and recognizes facial expressions based on the individual's facial features and structure. The six emotions of happiness, sadness, anger, disgust, surprise, and neutral are mapped from these expressions. Additionally, *EMOJ* can measure the degree of involvement and emotional valence. The collected data is transmitted to Unity in real-time and stored as quantitative data in an external file. This file records the emotional value associated with the displayed garment, while ensuring that there is no reference to the individual being analyzed during the experience.

Of the analyzed data, those pertaining to the formation of user preferences for suggested garments and styles were particularly noteworthy. The findings were generated automatically by computing the average data for each garment and emotion experienced, followed by identifying the highest scores to determine user favorites. In Fig. 4, each garment is associated with a particular style and a set of keywords that reflect the user's fashion preferences based on the recorded emotional feedback.

Fig. 4. The generation of the user's favorite garments and styles, along with the corresponding keywords,

3.3 Preliminary Tests

An initial testing session was carried out on a specific cohort of 10 individuals, predominantly consisting of Politecnico di Milano's Master of Science students in Design. The test aimed to evaluate the feasibility and user-friendliness of the virtual application proposed and identify prospective areas for improvement. The test subjects were instructed to partake in the virtual experience and complete the System Usability Scale (SUS) questionnaire [29]. The SUS survey comprises 10 questions covering usability matters and is commonly utilized to comprehend the complete user experience and satisfaction. Each question offers five Likert scale choices, extending from "strongly agree" to "strongly disagree". The test yields a score between 1–100, with an average of 68 being considered to assess the overall experience [30].

To gather qualitative feedback on users' satisfaction and ideas for future enhancement, open-ended questions were utilized. The following questions were posed:

1. What do you like most about the application, and why?
2. What do you dislike about the application, and why?
3. In what areas do you believe the application falls short?
4. Which aspect of the application do you think requires the most improvement?
5. Are there any additional recommendations or feedback you have related to the application?

In this session, more accurate data was gathered by collecting the feedback of users. The gathered results indicated that the application was highly usable and left the users with a positive impression. Specifically, the SUS score obtained was 75.2, which is "excellent" as demonstrated in Fig. 5.

Additionally, the open-ended questions revealed some recommendations from users, particularly concerning the enhancement of the GUI icons to facilitate more effective communication of certain actions. According to user feedback, the Generate Results prompt, which is related to producing the users' preferred clothing items and styles, was not easily comprehensible.

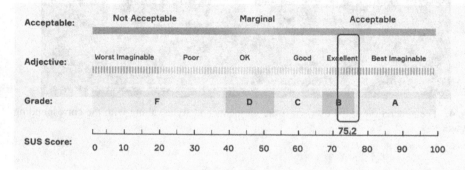

Fig. 5. Results obtained from the SUS questionnaire.

4   Improvement of the User Experience

Starting from the test results, we decided to conceptualize some improvements that can be applied to the experimental case study, mainly to enhance the virtual environment by incorporating new features that adapt to the users and their emotional reactions. In this revision phase, new interactive scenarios have been imagined, which can be effectively adopted depending on the type of collection presented and the feelings to evoke. As an example, Fig. 6 shows an alternative scenario in which the virtual environment has been modified, and new interactive features have been integrated to increase user engagement.

Specifically, some aspects that could be incorporated into the Virtual Reality application took inspiration from the research conducted on current fashion trends. For instance,

Fig. 6. Alternative scenario presenting new features, i.e., varying lighting hues and music choices.

we analyzed Prada's recent virtual catwalk show, which was crafted by Raf Simmons in collaboration with Koolhaas and AMO. As per Metalocus.com, Koolhaas and AMO created four rooms of varying shapes that were linked by doorways. These circular and polygonal areas were arranged in such a way as "to create the illusion of a never-ending route," said the architect Giulio Margheri [31]. This concept served as an inspiration to revise the 3D layout of the environment by connecting the two rooms and separating them by using doorways. In this way, the environment can be explored freely by the users instead of adopting the GUI icon to switch between the two rooms.

Moreover, the application can incorporate dynamic elements, such as varying lighting hues and music choices, depending on the user's emotions. Using the EMOJ tool, the application persistently identifies the user's emotions, and the room's lighting color scheme could be modified in real-time. For example, happiness can be represented by a yellow color, sadness by blue, surprise by pink, anger by red, disgust by violet, and neutrality by green. To enhance the changes in the lighting colors, the general atmosphere of the "virtual room" can be revised to present a brighter setting. In addition, users can be encouraged to interact with the show by taking screenshots of their preferred garments while watching the catwalks using a GUI button.

5   Conclusions

The objective of the research presented in the paper was to examine the perception of Virtual Reality fashion shows as interactive and valuable experiences for the participants, while also evaluating the effectiveness of virtual experiences using appropriate metrics.

To achieve this goal, an experimental scenario was set up consisting of a non-immersive Virtual Reality application displaying a fashion catwalk in both digital and physical form. Users' emotions were tracked using facial recognition technology to compare the two catwalk varieties. The experimental scenarios demonstrated the possibility of understanding the level of user involvement during the Virtual Reality experiences of the physical and virtual shows and proved to be a valid means to collect data relating to users' preferences with respect to the clothing items seen during fashion shows.

The conducted experiments aimed to investigate the potential of utilizing emotion recognition systems for providing feedback on the quality of User eXperience. Moreover, the experimental data present a potential solution for gaining insights into the clothing items that are highly valued by the general public. This information opens up intriguing possibilities for customization and promotional initiatives in corporate marketing.

Building upon this study, future endeavors will involve more comprehensive testing phases to assess the user's emotional response to both virtual and real solutions implemented in the fashion industry. The objective is to provide a valuable comparison of User Experience and satisfaction, offering meaningful insights.

The constant advancement of technologies has resulted in an ongoing reassessment of how individuals and businesses communicate and interact. It is crucial to recognize that younger generations are accustomed to and enthusiastic about the digital realm, making them more inclined to try novel virtual experiences. Further research in this field could yield valuable insights into the potential applications of emerging technologies for fashion brands and other industries.

Acknowledgments. The authors want to thank students Yuxia Ren, Ying Wang, Jessica Megan Jarvis, Annamaria Villa, Kertu Kivisik, Virtual and Physical Prototyping course, School of Design, Politecnico di Milano, Academic Year 2021/22, for their contribution in the project.

References

1. Abdul Ghani, M.S.A., Wan Shamsuddin, S.N.: Definitions and concepts of User Experience (UX): a literature review. Int. J. Creative Future Heritage (TENIAT) **8**(1), 130–143 (2020)
2. Kasinath, H.M.: Understanding and using qualitative methods in performance measurement. MIER J. Educ. Stud. Trends Practices **3**(1), 46–57 (2013)
3. Robinson, J., Candice, L., Weber, R.: The Past, Present, and Future of UX, Empirical Research, Communication Design Quarterly, 5(3), Association for Computing Machinery, New York, NY, USA (2018)
4. Soler-Dominguez, J.L., Camba, J.D., Contero, M., Alcañiz, M.: A Proposal for the Selection of Eye-Tracking Metrics for the Implementation of Adaptive Gameplay in Virtual Reality Based Games International Conference on Virtual, Augmented and Mixed Reality. Lecture Notes in Computer Science, vol. 10280, pp. 369–380 (2017)
5. Liu, X., Lee, K.: Optimized Facial Emotion Recognition Technique for Assessing User Experience, Games, Entertainment, Media Conference (GEM), pp. 1–9. IEEE (2018)
6. Garaus, M., Wagner, U., Rainer, R.C.: Emotional targeting using digital signage systems and facial recognition at the point-of-sale. J. Bus. Res. **131**, 747–762 (2021)
7. Mehta, D., Siddiqui, M.F.H., Javaid, A.Y.: Facial emotion recognition: A survey and real-world user experiences in mixed reality. Sensors 18.2 (2018)
8. Ilves, M., Gizatdinova, Y., Surakka, V., Vankka, E.: Head movement and facial expressions as game input. Entertainment Computing, **5**(3), pp. 147–156, Elsevier B.V, Amsterdam, Netherlands (2014)
9. Sekhavat, Y.A., Sisi, M.J., Roohi, S.: Affective interaction: Using emotions as a user interface in games. Multimedia Tools and Applications, vol. 80, pp. 5225–5253. Springer Nature (2021)
10. Turečková, Š.: Using player's facial emotional expressions as a game input: Effects on narrative engagement (2016)
11. Garcia-Garcia, J.M., Víctor M. R., Penichet, V.M.R., Lozano, M.D., Garrido J.E., Law, E.L.: Multimodal Affective Computing to Enhance the User Experience of Educational Software Applications, Hindawi, Mobile Information Systems, vol. 2018 (2018)
12. Behera, A., Matthew, P., Keidel, A., Vangorp, P., Fang, H., Canning, S.: Associating facial expressions and upper-body gestures with learning tasks for enhancing intelligent tutoring systems. Int. J. Artif. Intell. Educ. **30**, 236–270 (2020)

13. Ouherrou, N., Elhammoumi, O., Benmarrakchi, F., Kafi, J.E.: Comparative study on emotions analysis from facial expressions in children with and without learning disabilities in virtual learning environment. Educ. Inf. Technol. **24**, 1777–1792 (2019)
14. Garaus, M., Wagner, U., Rainer, R.C.: Emotional targeting using digital signage systems and facial recognition at the point-of-sale. J. Bus. Res. **131**, 747–762. Elsevier (2021)
15. Hamelin, N., Moujahid, O.E., Thaichon, P.: Emotion and advertising effectiveness: a novel facial expression analysis approach. J. Bus. Res. J. Retailing Consumer Serv. **36**, 103–11, Elsevier (2017)
16. Beck, J., Rainoldi, M., Egger, R.: Virtual reality in tourism: a state-of-the-art review. Tourism Rev. **74**(3), 586–612 (2019)
17. Jung, J., Yu, J., Seo, Y., Ko, E.: Consumer experiences of virtual reality: insights from VR luxury brand fashion shows. J. Bus. Res. **130**, 517–524 (2021). Elsevier B.V, Amsterdam, Netherlands
18. Xue, L., Parker, C.J., Hart, C.: How to design fashion retail's virtual reality platforms. Int. J. Retail Distrib. Manage. **48**(10), 1057–1076 (2020). Emerald Publishing Limited, Bingley, United Kingdom
19. Donatiello, L., Morotti, E., Marfia, G., Di Vaio, S.: Exploiting immersive virtual reality for fashion gamification. In: Annual International Symposium on Personal, Indoor and Mobile Radio Communications (PIMRC). IEEE, Bologna, Italy (2018)
20. Farah, M.F., Ramadan, Z.B., Harb, D.H.: The examination of virtual reality at the intersection of consumer experience, shopping journey and physical retailing. J. Retailing Consumer Serv. **48**, 136–143 (2019). Elvesier
21. Barnes, S.: Understanding Virtual Reality in Marketing, Nature, Implications and Potential, SSRN (2016)
22. Mystakidis, S.: Metaverse. Encyclopedia 2022 **2**(1), 486–497 (2022)
23. Reis, A.B., Ashmore, M.: From video streaming to virtual reality worlds: an academic, reflective, and creative study on live theater and performance in the metaverse. Int. J. Perform. Arts Digital Media **18**(1), 7–28 (2022)
24. Weiss, C.: Fashion retailing in the metaverse, Fashion, Style & Popular Culture, vol. 9, Merchandising Technologies, p. 523–538 (2022)
25. Herz, M., Rauschnabel, P.A.: Understanding the diffusion of virtual reality glasses: the role of media, fashion and technology, Technological Forecasting and Social Change, vol. 138, pp. 228–242. Elsevier B.V., Amsterdam, Netherlands (2019)
26. The Fabric of Reality – An Immersive VR Fashion Show. https://www.fialondon.com/projects/ryot-studios-the-fabric-of-reality/. Accessed 21 Apr 2023
27. Unplanned Paths: A Metaverse Fashion Week Exhibition. https://www.thechockablock.com/exhibitions/unplanned-paths. Accessed 21 Apr 2023
28. Somnium Space Mixed Reality VR Fashion Show. https://somniumspace.medium.com/announcing-2022-somnium-space-mixed-reality-vr-fashion-show-cfd771ddfd85. Accessed 21 Apr 2023
29. Brooke, J.: SUS: a quick and dirty usability scale. Usability Eval. Ind. **189**(194), 4–10 (1996)
30. Sauro, J.: SUStisfied? Little-known System Usability Scale facts. User Experience: The Magazine of the User Experience Professionals Association (2011). http://uxpamagazine.org/sustified/. Accessed 21 Apr 2023
31. Koolhaas and AMO, Design the support for real-virtual catwalk of PRADA fashion collection, Metalocus (2021). https://www.metalocus.es/. Accessed 21 Apr 2023

Measuring the Effectiveness of Virtual Reality for Stress Reduction: Psychometric Evaluation of the ERMES Project

Giovanni D'Errico[1]📵, Maria Cristina Barba[2], Carola Gatto[2(✉)]📵,
Benito Luigi Nuzzo[2], Fabiana Nuccetelli[3], Valerio De Luca[2]📵,
and Lucio Tommaso De Paolis[2]📵

[1] Department of Applied Science and Technology,
Polytechnic University of Turin, Turin, Italy
giovanni.derrico@polito.it
[2] Department of Engineering for Innovation, University of Salento, Lecce, Italy
{cristina.barba,carola.gatto,benitoluigi.nuzzo,
valerio.deluca,lucio.depaolis}@unisalento.it
[3] Department of Health Psychology, Nursing Home Prof. Petrucciani, Lecce, Italy

Abstract. Among all the technologies that make up the Digital Psychology intervention, Virtual Reality (VR) represents a decisive paradigm of innovation since it allows to work in terms of prevention and monitoring of many psychological issues, such as stress, anxiety, depression and burnout. This paper presents ERMES project "Virtual Reality to promote the well-being of vulnerable people within Hospitals", and a preliminary psychometric assessment of the results obtained from its first experimentation. Specifically, the main goal is to provide a tool that can act on stress levels by practicing Mindfulness sessions, virtual museum exploration, and Art Therapy activities, with the possibility of safely sharing the experience with other patients. During the experimental phase, clinical interviews and psychometric tests were carried out in order to assess the impact of VR therapy after participating in the experimental protocol. This first analysis shows significant changes in the stress levels, that have to be confirmed by the biosignals data acquired during the experimentation, that still needs to be evaluated.

Keywords: Virtual Reality · Healthcare 4.0 · Stress Reduction · Psychometric · Mindfulness · Wellbeing

1 Introduction

Extended Reality technologies are frequently employed in psychological studies to enhance therapeutic methods and create a sense of being immersed in an

---

The original version of chapter 32 was revised: two authors' names were displayed incorrectly due to a tagging error. This has been corrected. The correction to this chapter is available at https://doi.org/10.1007/978-3-031-43401-3_36

L. T. De Paolis et al. (Eds.): XR Salento 2023, LNCS 14218, pp. 484–499, 2023.
https://doi.org/10.1007/978-3-031-43401-3_32

alternate setting, distinct from one's immediate surroundings [10]. Virtual Reality (VR) in particular is strongly connected with the sense of presence in a total synthetic environment, and the embodiment of the user in the virtual alter ego.

Thanks to these features, VR has demonstrated its effectiveness for acting on the psychological well-being of patients with different health issues, in situations of isolation, burnout, and high stress levels [1,30]. This paper presents the implementation of ERMES project, "Virtual Reality to promote the well-being of vulnerable people within hospitals", and a preliminary psychometric assessment of the results obtained from its first experimentation campaign.

The project stems from an interdisciplinary partnership composed by Augmented and Virtual Reality Laboratory (AVR Lab), Department of Innovation Engineering, University of Salento, and Casa Prof. Petrucciani, a private Hospital Facility accredited with the National Health Service. The project involves the creation of immersive and interactive virtual scenarios with the possibility of performing various individual and participatory therapeutic activities through the use of Virtual Reality, promoting the psychophysical well-being of patients in hospital wards. Specifically, the goal is to develop a tool that can reduce stress levels by practicing Mindfulness sessions, virtual museum exploration, and Art Therapy activities, with the possibility of safely sharing the experience with other patients [20]. As a result of the changes brought about by the Global Health Emergency of Covid-19 and with the advent of new reforms, e-Health is set to play an increasingly important role in the world of healthcare.

Among all the technologies that make up e-Health and Digital Psychology, Virtual Reality (VR) represents a decisive paradigm of innovation since it allows to work in terms of prevention and monitoring, on many psychological issues, such as stress and isolation burnout, that the most fragile people may encounter during their hospitalization in the ward and to promote, thus, the safeguarding of the patient's mental health. During the experimental phase, clinical interviews and psychometric tests were carried out in order to assess the impact of VR therapy after participating in the experimental protocol.

This first analysis shows significant changes in the stress levels, that have to be confirmed by the biosignals data acquired during the experimentation, that still needs to be evaluated. Specifically, a clinical interview preceded the experimental phase and another one followed the VR session. In particular these questionnaires were provided to each subject involved: Hospital Anxiety and Depression Scale (H.A.D.S.) and Perceived Stress Scale (P.S.S.). This contribution discusses the results coming from the assessment of these tests.

2   Related Work

The prevalence of applications and studies investigating the use of VR in the healthcare sector has significantly increased [24]. In therapeutic field, there is growing evidence supporting the effectiveness of Virtual Reality Exposure Therapy (VRET) for treating phobias [3,6], anxiety disorders, and post-traumatic stress disorder [18,21]. VR has also shown promise in the areas of physical rehabilitation [17,26] and cognitive rehabilitation, incorporating serious games as an additional approach [7,33]. Recent research [23,27,37,40] has demonstrated that Virtual Reality is an exceptionally effective and innovative method for enhancing the psychological well-being of patients with diverse mental health conditions or individuals experiencing isolation and burnout. Immersion plays a crucial role in facilitating therapeutic benefits [27]. Active engagement in the VR environment and interaction with stimuli during the immersion process are fundamental elements contributing to the positive effects of psychological interventions [2].

Virtual Reality (VR) presents potentially beneficial features for supporting mindfulness practice, specifically immersive and multisensory VR, which can enhance relaxation self-efficacy, reduce mind wandering, and preserve attentional resources [4]. Clinical studies have explored the application of VR in addressing conditions such as pain, stress, depression, anxiety, borderline personality disorder, and addictions [9,11,15]. Real-time adaptive experiences can be achieved through the utilization of bio/neurofeedback sensors. The concept of virtual mindfulness aims to minimize the occurrence of distracting thoughts and mind wandering. By transporting practitioners to a new environment free from distractions, VR enables them to engage in a multisensory experience with natural surroundings, all within the comfort of their own homes [14]. This approach helps restore attentional resources that are often depleted as a result of stress [25]. Numerous studies have utilized immersive VR to immerse users in natural settings. Blum and colleagues proposed an adaprive nature-inspired VR experience which incorporates heart rate variability (HRV) biofeedback [8], while Kosunen and colleagues employed a tropical paradise-inspired immersive VR scenario and a neurofeedback interface to module relaxation and concentration levels by monitoring peculiar EEG features [28].

Museums have acknowledged the beneficial role of art therapy in enhancing mental well-being [38], leading to increased collaboration with various sectors of the healthcare industry [39]. Art therapy within museum settings facilitates mental recuperation by addressing physical tension and mental anxiety. The combination of museum education and art therapy significantly contributes to the treatment of anxiety disorders [12,13]. Several studies have examined the utilization of VR to enhance visitor-exhibition interactions and enable visitors to create virtual content within an immersive environment [19,29]. The potential of VR-based Art Therapy has primarily been investigated as an innovative creative medium for clinical procedures [22].

3   Methodology

An interdisciplinary working group was established to carry out a pilot project aimed at this fragile target group. The project had, as its objective principally the quality of life of patients experiencing mental and physical distress and to offer, through new technologies, an engaging and stimulating alternative care protocol for the reduction or prevention of stress. To achieve this, the project acts on three levels aimed at:

- Emotionally involving and cognitively stimulating the user (reducing stress, inducing pleasant-relaxing emotional states, stimulating cognitive capacities, such as memory, attention, and learning);
- Increase socialization and opportunities of sharing, through the use of virtual activities to be shared with other users in the ward or with family members at a distance, in order to increase socialization opportunities;
- Detect the effects of the treatment on the users before and after the execution of the protocol, by monitoring the progress of physiological responses to the proposed activities through specific sensors.

The project uses VR (Fig. 1) to implement Mindfulness sessions, Museum Therapy, and Art Therapy activities, all under the guidance and ongoing mediation of trained practitioners.

Fig. 1. Mindfulness and Museum Therapy scenarios inside the Virtual Reality application.

Through virtual reality viewers equipped with controllers for interaction, such as the Meta Quest 2, a participatory and collaborative approach is provided, with the opportunity to safely share some virtual experiences with other patients or family members outside the facility. In addition, psychophysiological sensors are intended to be used as a noninvasive tool for monitoring, collecting, and analyzing the psychophysical state of patients involved in the experience. This module is intended to be preparatory to the future development of a Biofeedback tool, aimed at helping the user become more aware of his or her reactions, participate actively in the project, and learn to use his or her mental abilities to balance his or her psychophysical state.

Through VR, the user is confronted with immersive virtual stimuli that can induce the feeling of actually being inside the virtual world. The use of specific virtual environments (especially those that immerse the user in nature scenarios, in accordance with the so-called Attention Restorative Theory) can, therefore, reduce mind wandering in the form of distracting thoughts (mind wandering), because the subject's attention is drawn to specific virtual elements, promoting an experiential focus on the present moment.

Ultimately, by limiting the distractions of the real world, increasing the sense of presence and providing people with a stimulating and suitable place to practice, virtual reality can certainly facilitate the practice of mindfulness. To summarize, the scenes created for the Virtual Reality environment are:

- Opening scene: This scene guides the user to the main screen, where he or she will have access to the menu of scenes and can choose to begin the therapeutic journey from the first scenario, follow a suggested order, or select a specific scenario based on the desired practice. The visual appearance is simple and functional, with soothing colors. Interaction with the buttons is via a pointer provided by the controllers.
- Tutorial: This essential scene provides instructions on using the application through short videos and voice instructions.
- Breath awareness meditation scene: This scene introduces the user to the practice of breath awareness meditation. The virtual environment is neutral, with soft lighting and soothing color. The user is in a monotonous environment in which a balloon inflates and deflates following the rhythm of the user's breath. A guiding voice provides instructions on conducting the meditation.
- Mountain meditation scene: This scene uses visualization practice to evoke the qualities of a majestic mountain, a symbol of stability and resilience. The user is immersed in a virtual natural environment with mountains, forests and a stream. The user's vantage point is that of observing the mountain from base to summit.
- Lake meditation scene: This scene uses the practice of visualization to allow the user to confront the surface of a lake, which can be calm and clear or agitated and dark, representing the human mind. The user is immersed in a virtual natural environment with mountains, forests and a lake. The user is sitting on a pier, observing the surface of the water.
- Group meditation on pure mindfulness: This meditation, also known as unfocused mindfulness, involves practicing mindfulness without a specific object to focus on. In this scene, the user can see avatars of other participants performing the same exercise, creating a collaborative environment.
- Museum scene: In this scene, the user moves through an indoor virtual environment representing a virtual museum based on the collection of the Sigismondo Castromediano Museum. The aesthetic is characterized by muted tones and soft lighting. The user can explore and interact with some artifacts inspired by the real collection. The user has the opportunity to perform different tasks.

The technological architecture, customized for the specific need of the project, provides a comfortable and monitored environment, in order to observe and detect all the patient's behaviors. This allows to offer the doctor a therapy monitoring tool and the patient a personalized and innovative therapy service. This is possible thanks to the data collected through special devices equipped with specific sensors, worn by patients during therapy, described in the next paragraphs, in order to develop a patient profile with which to track the progress of the patient's health status. There are two main actors in the therapeutic process: the therapist and the patient. The therapist is responsible for managing and administering the therapy, the patient for enjoying the therapy. The entire project was implemented while maintaining the centrality of these figures. Collaboration with the medical staff contributed, to the design of the system, identifying some specific tasks and validating the experimental protocol also from an ethical point of view, thanks to the approval within the hospital's ethics committee.

In the next paragraphs, implementation details, architectural information and experimental protocols will be defined in order to discuss the results of the first tests conducted.

4   Implementation

4.1   Virtual Content Creation

Two main methodologies were used to create the virtual content: photogrammetry and 3D modeling. Specifically, in the context of the museotherapy scenario, a close range photogrammetry campaign was carried out using a Nikon D3500 camera.

The process began by setting up a photographic set in a controlled environment with constant temperature and uniform lighting. Two cold-light lamps were placed on the table, which was covered with a green cloth to facilitate the removal of the stand in subsequent processing. The objects were placed one at a time on the table, taking special care to choose a background that contrasted with the colors of the objects themselves. Several photos were taken for each sculpture, using fixed manual settings for ISO, zoom, aperture, and shutter speed. In addition, the photos were taken in .RAW format to preserve all image data. After capturing the photos at different angles to cover the entire surface of the object, they were imported into the Camera Raw plug-in of Adobe Photoshop 2022. Here, each parameter (such as exposure, contrast, temperature, and white balance) was manually adjusted, and the photos were exported in the .TIF format at 16 bits per channel. The .TIF files were then imported into Metashape, where they were analyzed to eliminate those with a quality below 0.5 in order to avoid overlapping errors during the subsequent process. On average, 150 images were processed for each object. Next, the photos were aligned and used to create a "Dense Cloud" of points, with high quality settings and moderate depth. This point cloud was cleaned to remove those that could have caused aberrations in the creation of the 3D mesh, including the background points on which the objects were placed. In this way, a 3D mesh was created exclusively of the sculpture itself. Finally, after completing the process of creating the high-quality mesh, texture was generated to give the objects a realistic appearance.

This process was repeated for each of the eight selected objects. After that, the 3D models were exported in the .fbx format for documentation and archival purposes. Before importing them to Unity, they were optimized to ensure proper viewing and reading. Once the creation of the 3D models of the exhibits was completed, we moved on to modeling the other environments from scratch. In particular, we created the meditative scenarios and the virtual museum, which included an exhibition hall and an antiquarium. The 3D modeling was based on archaeological sources for the Cavallino site and historical and museographic information for the virtual museum. For the Art Therapy environment, we modeled several structures, including an archaic building with interior rooms and an arcade, under which is a ceramic laboratory. This workshop is equipped with the traditional tools for pottery making, such as a potter's wheel and the necessary tools such as stylus, sponge, bowl, clay, and pigments. In the outdoor space, not far from the workshop, there is a kiln for firing pottery.

To create the scenarios, we used Blender (version 2021), an open source 3D modeling software, and Unity (version 2021.3.14.f1), a cross-platform graphics engine used for the entire application. Blender was mainly used to model interior furnishings and render structures. Unity was used for building and populating landscapes, such as through the use of the 3D object "Terrain" already present in Unity and the addition of content-rich plug-ins to reproduce main nature scenes. This allowed us to create realistic and fully explorable settings.

4.2 User Experience (UX) and Workflow

User Experience (UX) is the impact that hardware and software have on user perception and interaction. It is fundamental to design, as it determines whether the experience will be enjoyable and achieve the desired goal. UX design must consider all aspects of user-application interaction, including actions and GUI. Some general characteristics of UX include attracting and motivating the user, offering freedom in interactions, providing a sense of control, and ensuring a pleasant sensory experience. In the context of Virtual Reality, an important choice concerns the VR visor and controllers used. Visors such as the Meta Quest 2 and the HTC Vive offer good visual, audio, and computational performance, as well as hand tracking systems in virtual space.

These devices support $6°C$ of freedom, allowing the user to move freely in the virtual environment. It is important that users become familiar with the controllers or hand gestures to feel in control and focus on the application. In the case of the application described, the Meta Quest 2 viewer was chosen for its ease of use, being a stand-alone viewer without the need for connections to a PC. The graphical user interface is one of the key aspects of the UX. A basic menu allows the user to access the various modules or activities of the application. It should be visually pleasing and enhanced by visual and sound effects. It is important to simplify the experience to avoid distractions and facilitate interactions. Other important elements for space control include perspective and first-person point of view, which make interaction with virtual elements more realistic. The sitting position is recommended to promote relaxation and safety for hospitalized patients. Movement in the virtual space is through teleportation. Experience design is also based on the principles of gamification, using playability elements to enhance user engagement. The Mechanics, Dynamics, Aesthetics (MDA) framework is used to identify gameplay elements, responses to user actions, and the audiovisual aspect that evokes emotions. The game experience is structured with interactive virtual elements, clear objectives, positive responses, and audio and visual effects that create comfort and pleasure. In conclusion, it is worth specifying that before tasks within the virtual scenarios are carried out, video tutorials are provided to explain how to interact with the user.

4.3 Application Development

For the creation of the various scenarios, two main software were used: Blender, an open source 3D modeling software, and Unity 3D, a cross platform engine. Blender was mainly used for modeling interior furnishings and representing structures, while Unity was particularly useful for creating the nature scenarios. The use of Terrain, a predefined 3D object in Unity, and the addition of plugins containing a wide range of content to reproduce the naturalistic sceneries, enabled the creation of fully explorable realistic settings. This tool was instrumental in creating the first natural scenery, which depicts a picturesque mountain lake, offering the user different perspectives and meditative cues. Terrain was used to reproduce natural terrain features, while the main scenery was created in Blender. The combination of these landscapes, distinct but connected by a narrative focused on meditation and relaxation, offers the user the opportunity to gain new insights, engaging their time not only in meditative practice but also in engaging interactive experiences. At the beginning of the session, the user is immersed in a neutral scenario that allows the user to select the beginning of the therapeutic path or view a general tutorial explaining how to use the game controllers. By clicking on the button to start the experience, the user accesses the main screen of the application, where he or she can choose which session to participate in.

4.4 Virtual Environments' Features

Mindfulness Meditation. The Mindfulness meditation session includes four scenes with specific characteristics. In the Breath Awareness Meditation scene, the user starts the meditation by clicking on a button. During the meditation, the user visualizes in front of the eyes a balloon that rhythmically inflates and deflates, simulating the breathing. This method facilitates the achievement of a relaxed state. In the Mountain Meditation scene, the user experience includes a virtual environment, a guiding voice, and landscape changes synchronized with the seasons and the cycle of day and night. For example, the Skybox adapts to the weather described by the guide voice. In the Lake Meditation environment, in addition to the 3D landscape models, there is a guide voice and landscape transformations synchronized with the seasons and the cycle of day and night. During the meditation, the voice describes the transformations of the lake, which are animated in real time. In the Pure Consciousness Group Meditation scene there is the possibility to visualize other users that are participating at the same time to the session. Allo of the users are displayed as neutral avatars, creating a group experience. This innovative feature enables shared participation in virtual reality.

Museum Therapy. In this scene, users explore a virtual museum that recreates the environment of a real museum. The museum features soft lighting and welcoming tones, eliminating distracting elements. Objects from the collection are placed around the room. The narrative is based on the themes of ancient ceramics, such as myths or convivial scenes depicted on them. The user can interact via controllers to turn on or off audio tracks that include ambient sounds, musical melodies, and a narrator's voice. These audio tracks provide emotional guidance, narrating the depicted myth,s and their connection to human psychology. After the tour in the exhibition hall, the user can move to a second room called the "Antiquarium,". Here, artifacts are arranged on shelves and inside cabinets, along with other objects that are not part of the collection. The user's active task is to search for artifacts by following the sound they make, consistent with the previous narrative. The user has a virtual notebook that provides support in searching for the objects. This scene is based on a gamification strategy, involving the user in the role of a museum curator who selects objects to complete the exhibition catalog.

Art Therapy. The scene takes place in the ancient Messapian settlement of Cavallino, Apulia, Italy. An outdoor virtual scenario has been created showing some artifacts within the archaeological site, telling the social history through the objects. Users have the opportunity to explore the virtual environment and interact with the objects. They are taken to an ancient ceramic production center to observe the process of making the artifacts displayed in the museum. The chosen aesthetic reproduces a natural environment that includes the old potter's workshop. In this scene, users participate in an activity that combines learning and relaxation: Art Therapy in Virtual Reality. Using traditional ancient techniques, users learn to virtually model a vase called a Trozzella, typical of Messapian material culture. The task consists of virtually modeling and decorating this type of artifact, following the instructions of experimental archaeology. Art therapy is implemented through three modes: passive observation using controllers, a guided sequence of operations, or specific hand gestures of the user. These options are offered to adapt the "game" to different target users in terms of age and cognitive and motor abilities. The interactions take as reference the movements used in reality, simplifying the manual gestures used by the artisans. While the automatic and controller-based modes have been developed and tested, the mode based on hand tracking and gestures of the user's hand in virtual space is still in the prototyping stage. A neural network model has been trained to recognize the correct gestures, and an application has been developed to respond to each identified gesture.

5   Experimental Setup

This pilot study aims to assess the ERMES system by subjecting it to a group of participants, measuring various psychophysiological variables, and conducting a preliminary evaluation of the system's effectiveness in analyzing a series of psychometric tests. The study included 33 patients, with an average age of 68.7 years (21 males with an average age of 64.9 and 12 females with an average age of 73), who were admitted to the cardiac rehabilitation department of Prof. Petrucciani Clinic in Lecce, Italy. All participants had a cardiac condition and had previously undergone cardiac surgery, resulting in extended hospital stays (approximately one month). Ethical approval for the study was obtained from the Clinic committee.

Participants' personal data was treated with confidentiality, and informed consent was obtained from all participants. Psychometric data was collected during the experimental phase through clinical interviews and psychodiagnostic tests conducted by the project's lead psychologist. Biosignal data was collected from 7 out of the 33 patients using wearable devices capable of recording and capturing biosignals. The administered pre- and post-intervention psychometric tests included the Hospital Anxiety and Depression Scale (H.A.D.S.) [41], a 14-item tool used to assess anxiety and depression levels, and the Perceived Stress Scale (P.S.S.) [34], consisting of ten items and utilized to measure stress perception. The two devices employed for biosignal measurement were Empatica E4 [31] and Emotiv Epoc X [5]. The EMPATICA E4 device allowed for the monitoring of individuals' stress phases. This wristband included an electrodermal activity (EDA) sensor, measuring changes in specific electrical properties of the skin, as well as a photoplethysmography (PPG) sensor, used to measure Blood Volume Pulse (BVP), a three-axis accelerometer, and an optical thermometer, enabling simultaneous measurement of sympathetic nervous system activity and heart rate. Only the EDA and BVP signals were considered, as they are associated with stress reduction protocols in the literature [32]. Emotiv EPOC is an EEG headset equipped with 14 electrodes and 2 reference channels, capturing 128 samples per second for each channel.

The VR experience (experienced once by participants) consisted of three consecutive sessions with no transition periods between them: session 1 (lasting 10 min) served as an introductory phase for adapting to VR, session 2 (15 min) involved Mindfulness practice (using two standard meditation practices: the lake and mountain meditations), and session 3 (15 min) included alternating experiences of art therapy and museum therapy scenarios. Figure 2 illustrates the architecture of the experimental protocol, including the analysis of biometric data (which falls outside the scope of this pilot study). Throughout each session, participants received instructions through a pre-recorded calming voice provided by a mindfulness facilitator psychologist. During the entire duration of this step, the signals derived from the EDA, BVP, and EEG sensors were recorded for the 7 patients who completed the full protocol.

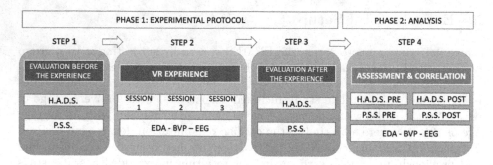

Fig. 2. ERMES experimental protocol.

6   Psychometric Assessment

The psychometric assessment was based on the evaluation of the states of Stress, Anxiety and Depression in 33 patients by administering the P.S.S. and H.A.D.S. questionnaires mentioned in the previous section. In particular, the Stress factor was derived from the P.S.S. questionnaire, while the Anxiety and Depression factors were each derived from 7 of the 14 items of the H.A.D.S. questionnaire. For each patient, variations in these factors were calculated as the differences between the scores assessed after the VR experience and the scores assessed before the experience. Percentage variations were calculated as the percentage ratios between the score variations and the scores before the experience.

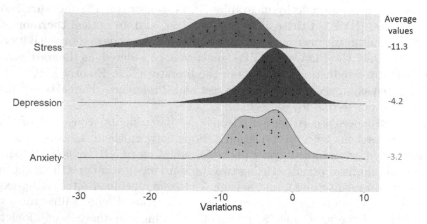

Fig. 3. Distributions of the variations in Stress, Depression and Anxiety after the VR experience

The density plot in Fig. 3 depicts the distributions of the variations in *Stress*, *Depression* and *Anxiety* after the VR experience. The average values are shown to the right of the waveforms. All three factors decreased in almost all users after the VR experience, although to a very variable extent. *Depression* has the lowest variability, while stress has the highest variability.

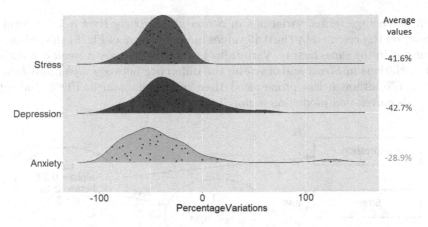

Fig. 4. Distributions of the percentage variations in Stress, Depression and Anxiety after the VR experience

The density plot in Fig. 4 depicts the distributions of the percentage variations in *Stress*, *Depression* and *Anxiety* after the VR experience: it can be seen that, in relative terms, stress reduction has the lowest variability.

Hierarchical cluster analyses, depicted in Figs. 5 and 6, were performed on variations and percentage variations using the ICLUST *R* package [36], which aims at maximizing internal consistency and homogeneity: it employs Cronbach's *alpha* [16], which is the mean of all the possible split-half reliabilities of a scale, as a measure of internal consistency and Revelle's *beta* coefficient [35], defined as the minimum value among all the possible split-half reliabilities, to assess the scale homogeneity.

Variations in *Stress* and *Anxiety* have a medium level of correlation, represented by the 0.64 values in the diagram of Fig. 5 (indicating how correlated they are with cluster *C1*): Cronbach's *alpha* and Revelle's *beta* values, which coincide in cluster *C1*, suggest that this prediction is very reliable. Variations in *Depression*, on the other hand, have a much weaker correlation with the other two, which should also be considered unreliable due to the considerable difference between *alpha* and *beta* in cluster *C2*.

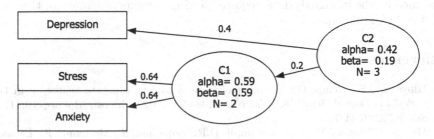

Fig. 5. Cluster analysis of the variations in Stress, Depression and Anxiety factors after the VR experience

In percentage terms, variations in *Stress* and *Anxiety* have a lower level of correlation (represented by the 0.45 values in the diagram of Fig. 6) than absolute variations in the same factors. Variations in *Depression* have a weak correlation with variations in *Stress* and *Anxiety*: the difference between *alpha* and *beta* in cluster *C2*, although less pronounced than in the diagram in Fig. 5, indicates that this correlation prediction is unreliable.

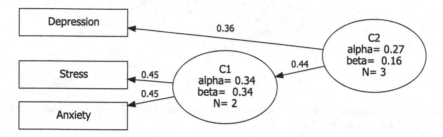

Fig. 6. Cluster analysis of the percentage variations in Stress, Depression and Anxiety factors after the VR experience

7   Conclusions and Future Work

This paper presented the ERMES project "Virtual Reality to promote the well-being of vulnerable people within Hospitals", in terms of methodology, design and development of the VR application. Specifically, the main goal was to provide a tool that can act on stress levels by practicing Mindfulness sessions, virtual museum exploration, and Art Therapy activities, with the possibility of safely sharing the experience with other patients. Additionally, we provided the first analysis of data collected from 33 patients during the experimental phase, through clinical interviews and psychodiagnostic tests (H.A.D.S. and P.S.S.). The results of the H.A.D.S. and P.S.S. questionnaires revealed that stress, depression and anxiety decreased in almost all users after the experience, although to a very variable extent. Furthermore, biosignal data was collected from 7 out of the 33 patients using wearable devices capable of recording and capturing biosignals. This first analysis shows significant changes in the stress levels, that have to be confirmed by the biosignals data acquired during the experimentation, that still needs to be evaluated.

References

1. Adhyaru, J.S., Kemp, C.: Virtual reality as a tool to promote wellbeing in the workplace. Digital Health **8**, 20552076221084470 (2022). https://doi.org/10.1177/20552076221084473
2. Alyan, E., Combe, T., Awang Rambli, D.R., Sulaiman, S., Merienne, F., Diyana, N.: The influence of virtual forest walk on physiological and psychological responses. Int. J. Environ. Res. Public Health **18**(21), 11420 (2021)

3. Apicella, A., et al.: Electroencephalography correlates of fear of heights in a virtual reality environment. Acta IMEKO **12**(2), 1–7 (2023)
4. Arpaia, P., D'Errico, G., De Paolis, L.T., Moccaldi, N., Nuccetelli, F.: A narrative review of mindfulness-based interventions using virtual reality. In: Mindfulness. pp. 1–16 (2021)
5. Badcock, N.A., Mousikou, P., Mahajan, Y., De Lissa, P., Thie, J., McArthur, G.: Validation of the emotiv epoc® EEG gaming system for measuring research quality auditory ERPS. PeerJ **1**, e38 (2013)
6. Baños, R.M., et al.: Virtual reality treatment of flying phobia. IEEE Trans. Inf Technol. Biomed. **6**(3), 206–212 (2002)
7. Barba, M.C., et al.: BRAVO: a gaming environment for the treatment of ADHD. In: De Paolis, L.T., Bourdot, P. (eds.) AVR 2019. LNCS, vol. 11613, pp. 394–407. Springer, Cham (2019). https://doi.org/10.1007/978-3-030-25965-5_30
8. Blum, J., Rockstroh, C., Göritz, A.S.: Heart rate variability biofeedback based on slow-paced breathing with immersive virtual reality nature scenery. Front. Psychol. **10**, 2172 (2019)
9. Botella, C., Garcia-Palacios, A., Vizcaíno, Y., Herrero, R., Baños, R.M., Belmonte, M.A.: Virtual reality in the treatment of fibromyalgia: a pilot study. Cyberpsychol. Behav. Soc. Netw. **16**(3), 215–223 (2013)
10. Carroll, J., Hopper, L., Farrelly, A.M., Lombard-Vance, R., Bamidis, P.D., Konstantinidis, E.I.: A scoping review of augmented/virtual reality health and well-being interventions for older adults: redefining immersive virtual reality. Front. Virtual Reality **2** (2021)
11. Chavez, L.J.: Virtual reality meditation among youth experiencing homelessness: pilot randomized controlled trial of feasibility. JMIR Mental Health **7**(9), e18244 (2020)
12. Coles, A.: What do museums mean? public perceptions of the purposes of museums and implications for their use in art therapy. Art Therapy in Museums and Galleries. Reframing Practice, pp. 44–62 (2020)
13. Coles, A., Harrison, F., Todd, S.: Flexing the frame: Therapist experiences of museum-based group art psychotherapy for adults with complex mental health difficulties. Inter. J. Art Therapy **24**(2), 56–67 (2019)
14. Costa, M.R., et al.: Nature inspired scenes for guided mindfulness training: presence, perceived restorativeness and meditation depth. In: Schmorrow, D.D., Fidopiastis, C.M. (eds.) HCII 2019. LNCS (LNAI), vol. 11580, pp. 517–532. Springer, Cham (2019). https://doi.org/10.1007/978-3-030-22419-6_37
15. Costa, M.R., Bergen-Cico, D., Hererro, R., Navarro, J., Razza, R., Wang, Q.: xR-based systems for mindfulness based training in clinical settings. In: Chen, J.Y.C., Fragomeni, G. (eds.) VAMR 2018. LNCS, vol. 10910, pp. 31–39. Springer, Cham (2018). https://doi.org/10.1007/978-3-319-91584-5_3
16. Cronbach, L.: Coefficient alpha and the internal structure of tests. Psychometrika **16**(3), 297–334 (1951). https://doi.org/10.1007/BF02310555
17. Dulau, E., Botha-Ravyse, C.R., Luimula, M.: Virtual reality for physical rehabilitation: A pilot study how will virtual reality change physical therapy? In: 2019 10th IEEE International Conference on Cognitive Infocommunications (CogInfoCom), pp. 277–282. IEEE (2019)
18. Garcia-Palacios, A., Hoffman, H., Carlin, A., Furness, T.A., III., Botella, C.: Virtual reality in the treatment of spider phobia: a controlled study. Behav. Res. Ther. **40**(9), 983–993 (2002)

19. Gatto, C., et al.: Wellbeing assessment of a museum experience in virtual reality through ucl measurement tool kit and heart rate measurement: a pilot study. In: 2022 IEEE International Conference on Metrology for Extended Reality, Artificial Intelligence and Neural Engineering (MetroXRAINE), pp. 483–488. IEEE (2022)
20. Gatto, C., et al.: A virtual reality application for stress reduction: design and first implementation of ermes project. In: De Paolis, L.T., Arpaia, P., Sacco, M. (eds.) Extended Reality, pp. 162–173. Springer International Publishing, Cham (2022). https://doi.org/10.1007/978-3-031-15546-8_15
21. Gatto, C., D'Errico, G., Nuccetelli, F., De Luca, V., Paladini, G.I., De Paolis, L.T.: XR-based mindfulness and art therapy: facing the psychological impact of Covid-19 emergency. In: De Paolis, L.T., Bourdot, P. (eds.) AVR 2020. LNCS, vol. 12243, pp. 147–155. Springer, Cham (2020). https://doi.org/10.1007/978-3-030-58468-9_11
22. Hacmun, I., Regev, D., Salomon, R.: The principles of art therapy in virtual reality. Front. Psychol. **9**, 2082 (2018)
23. Hatta, M.H., et al.: Virtual reality (vr) technology for treatment of mental health problems during Covid-19: a systematic review. Int. J. Environ. Res. Public Health **19**(9), 5389 (2022)
24. Helou, S., Khalil, N., Daou, M., El Helou, E.: Virtual reality for healthcare: A scoping review of commercially available applications for head-mounted displays. Digital health **9**, 20552076231178620 (2023)
25. Kaplan, S.: The restorative benefits of nature: toward an integrative framework. J. Environ. Psychol. **15**(3), 169–182 (1995)
26. Keshner, E.A.: Virtual reality and physical rehabilitation: a new toy or a new research and rehabilitation tool? (2004)
27. Kolbe, L., Jaywant, A., Gupta, A., Vanderlind, W.M., Jabbour, G.: Use of virtual reality in the inpatient rehabilitation of Covid-19 patients. Gen. Hosp. Psychiatry **71**, 76–81 (2021)
28. Kosunen, I., Salminen, M., Järvelä, S., Ruonala, A., Ravaja, N., Jacucci, G.: Relaworld: neuroadaptive and immersive virtual reality meditation system. In: Proceedings of the 21st International Conference on Intelligent User Interfaces, pp. 208–217 (2016)
29. Koutsabasis, P., Vosinakis, S.: Kinesthetic interactions in museums: conveying cultural heritage by making use of ancient tools and (re-) constructing artworks. Virtual Reality **22**(2), 103–118 (2018)
30. Lee, L.N., Kim, M.J., Hwang, W.J.: Potential of augmented reality and virtual reality technologies to promote wellbeing in older adults. Appli. Sci. **9**(17) (2019). https://www.mdpi.com/2076-3417/9/17/3556
31. McCarthy, C., Pradhan, N., Redpath, C., Adler, A.: Validation of the empatica e4 wristband. In: 2016 IEEE EMBS International Student Conference (ISC), pp. 1–4. IEEE (2016)
32. Nath, R.K., Thapliyal, H.: Smart wristband-based stress detection framework for older adults with cortisol as stress biomarker. IEEE Trans. Consum. Electron. **67**(1), 30–39 (2021)
33. Nunnari, F., Magliaro, S., D'Errico, G., De Luca, V., Barba, M.C., De Paolis, L.T.: Designing and assessing interactive virtual characters for children affected by ADHD. In: Bourdot, P., Interrante, V., Nedel, L., Magnenat-Thalmann, N., Zachmann, G. (eds.) EuroVR 2019. LNCS, vol. 11883, pp. 285–290. Springer, Cham (2019). https://doi.org/10.1007/978-3-030-31908-3_17
34. Reis, R.S., Hino, A., Añez, C.: Perceived stress scale. J. Health Psychol. **15**(1), 107–114 (2010)

35. Revelle, W.: Hierarchical cluster analysis and the internal structure of tests. Multivar. Behav. Res. **14**(1), 57–74 (1979). https://doi.org/10.1207/s15327906mbr1401_4
36. Revelle, W.: ICLUST: a cluster analytic approach to exploratory and confirmatory scale construction. Behav. Res. Methods Instrum. **10**(5), 739–742 (1978). https://doi.org/10.3758/bf03205389
37. Siani, A., Marley, S.A.: Impact of the recreational use of virtual reality on physical and mental wellbeing during the Covid-19 lockdown. Heal. Technol. **11**, 425–435 (2021)
38. Stickley, T., Eades, M.: Arts on prescription: a qualitative outcomes study. Public Health **127**(8), 727–734 (2013)
39. Wei, Z., Zhong, C., Gao, Y.: Art therapy practices in museum education: A mini review. Front. Psychol. **13**, 1075427 (2023)
40. Yang, T., Lai, I.K.W., Fan, Z.B., Mo, Q.M.: The impact of a 360 virtual tour on the reduction of psychological stress caused by Covid-19. Technol. Soc. **64**, 101514 (2021)
41. Zigmond, A.S., Snaith, R.P.: The hospital anxiety and depression scale. Acta Psychiatr. Scand. **67**(6), 361–370 (1983)

HRV-Based Detection of Fear of Heights in a VR Environment

Pasquale Arpaia[1,2], Simone Barbato[6], Giovanni D'Errico[3],
Giovanna Mastrati[1(✉)], Nicola Moccaldi[4], Rachele Robbio[1],
and Selina Christin Wriessenegger[5]

[1] Department of Electrical Engineering and Information Technology (DIETI),
University of Naples Federico II, Naples, Italy
giovanna.mastrati@unina.it
[2] Interdepartmental Center for Research on Management and Innovation in
Healthcare (CIRMIS), University of Naples Federico II, Naples, Italy
[3] Department of Applied Science and Technology,
Polytechnic University of Turin, Turin, Italy
[4] Department of Engineering for Innovation University of Salento, Lecce, Italy
[5] Institute of Neural Engineering, Graz University of Technology, Graz, Austria
[6] Idego Digital Psychology, Rome, Italy

Abstract. In the present study, an electrocardiographic (ECG) -based
system is proposed for the classification of three levels of fear of heights. A
virtual reality (VR) environment was employed for the gradual exposure
of the participants to the fear arousing stimuli. The VR scenario consists
of a canyon in which a wooden lift brings the subjects to three different
height levels. 20 subjects participated in the experimental activities and
carried out three experimental sessions. The use of psychometric tools
like the Acrophobia Questionnaire (AQ) and the Subjective Unit Of Distress (SUD) allowed to carry out an initial screening of the sample to
assess the severity of fear of heights and the effectiveness of the VR environment in the induction of fear. According to the AQ and SUD, three
clusters of subjects with different levels of acrophobia severity were identified. A 1-lead ECG recording was acquired during the exposure to the
eliciting VR environment. Hearth rate variability (HRV) -related features
were extracted from the ECG signal, specifically linear (statistical and
geometric) and nonlinear features. Those features were input to different classifiers for discriminating three-levels of fear. Domain adaptation
methods resulted effective in improving the generalizability of the results.
On the contrary, clustering the subjects according to their acrophobia
severity level did not impact on the classification performances. Average
accuracies of 40.9 ± 5.9 in the inter-subject setting and of 43.8 ± 7.6 in
the intra-subjects setting were achieved by employing the Linear Correlation Alignment (CORAL) DA method.

Keywords: Electrocardiography · hearth rate variability · brain
computer interfaces · fear of heights · virtual reality

© The Author(s), under exclusive license to Springer Nature Switzerland AG 2023
L. T. De Paolis et al. (Eds.): XR Salento 2023, LNCS 14218, pp. 500–513, 2023.
https://doi.org/10.1007/978-3-031-43401-3_33

1   Introduction

Among the most common anxiety disorders there are specific phobias. Specific phobias are marked by evident fear or anxiety that phobic people feel towards a particular object or situation [1]. Four different types of specific phobia can be distinguished mainly: animals (e.g. fear of spiders), blood/injection/injury (e.g. seeing blood), situational (e.g. public speaking), natural environment (e.g. fears of height) [2]. In this study, a focus was made on acrophobia due to its widespread diffusion among the population (at least 1 in 20 adults suffers from it [3]). Acrophobia refers to the irrational fear of heights and elevated places [4]. Acrophobic people avoid situations related to height, limiting them in carrying out even simple daily activities. Typical physical symptoms include panic-like symptoms, such as heart palpitations, shortness of breath, nausea, tremor, and dizziness [5]. The most common method of treating acrophobia is Cognitive Behavioral Therapy (CBT) which consists of subjective and behavioral treatments. The former assesses how fear can be affected by the individual's cognitive constructions, while the latter assesses how the patient responds to the exposure to anxiogenic stimuli [6]. In 1958, Wolpe [7] developed one of the first behavioral treatments called *systematic desensitization*. The imagination of relaxing situations along with muscle relaxation allow to suppress anxiety-provoking symptoms caused by the stimulus. Among the CBT techniques, there is the *exposure therapy* that includes in vivo exposure (the patient comes into direct contact with the stimulus), or in sensu exposure (the patient imagines the stimulus) [8]. In recent years, equally valid alternative techniques to in vivo exposure have been introduced, such as Augmented Reality Exposure Therapy (ARET) and Virtual Reality Exposure Therapy (VRET) [9]. Virtual Reality (VR) is established in the scientific literature as a unique tool for engaging subjects and providing effective training. By simulating predictive mechanisms of the brain [10], VR helps modulate dysfunctional characteristics and is suggested as an adaptive platform to support psycho-educational and psychotherapeutic therapies [11]. Additionally, it promotes wellbeing [12] and facilitates the practice of mindfulness [13]. VRET, which was first implemented and described as a clinical application for acrophobia by Rothbaum et al. [14], can be considered a form of VR training useful to modulate dysfunctional characteristics, specifically through desensitization. It uses computers and interfaces to simulate real events and situations, and it is particularly advantageous for several reasons: it can be used on patients who cannot undergo in vivo treatment because they are too anxious or on patients who have a poor imagination, it allows to vary and control the intensity of stimuli [15,16]. To estimate the level of anxiety or fear it is possible to distinguish methods that use self-assessment questionnaires and methods that record biosignals during stimulus exposure sessions. Often, both methods are used together [17]. During situations that generate fear or anxiety, the physiological responses can be observed in Electrodermal Activity (EDA), breathing, electroencephalogram (EEG) and electrocardiogram (ECG). This is due to the modulation by the Autonomic Nervous System (ANS) of the functions of the organism at rest and of the reflex reactions [9]. In particular, the ANS acts through the Sympathetic Nervous System (SNS) which intervenes in dangerous and emergency situations, and the Parasympathetic Nervous System (PNS) which prevails in relaxation situations. The regulation on the Atrial Sinus node (AS) by the ANS defines Heart Rate Variability (HRV), i.e. the variation over time of successive heart beats, caused by the variation of the sympathovagal balance in response to external and internal stimuli [18,19]. When an individual feels threatened, the SNS is activated, while the PNS is inhibited. This leads to an increase in Heart Rate (HR) and a decrease in HRV [17]. Scientific literature confirms the link between emotional states and HRV: emotional states characterized by a low level of anxiety and the lower probability of suffering from phobias can be associated to a high HRV [20]. Therefore, both the strong link between emotional states and HRV, and the ease of access of the ECG signal, make HRV-based features particularly suitable for detecting states of fear of heights. In fact, the ECG signal can be easily measured thanks to the use of non-invasive, portable and low-cost sensors. The goal of the present study is to distinguish three levels (i.e. low, medium and high) of acrophobia perceived by subjects starting from the measurement of HRV, through classification based on Machine Learning (ML). In Sect. 2 a state of art of studies dealing with acrophobia detection starting from the ECG signal is presented. In Sect. 3, the experimental sample, the psychometrics tools, the hardware, the software, the experimental protocol, the signal processing and the feature extraction pipelines, and the classification are described. In Sect. 4, the results of the present study are presented.

2   Background

Some previous studies show that it is possible to discriminate emotions, experienced during conditions that arouse fear, also through the descriptors of the HR and HRV. In [21] the eye movement (EMO), pupil, and ECG were exploited to detect the presence/absence of acrophobia in 17 healthy participants. The "Richie's plank experience" was the virtual scenario used to induce fear of heights. The HRV-related features extracted were mean, median, standard deviation of intervals between heart beats (SDNN), root mean square of successive differences between neighboring heartbeat intervals (RMSSD), proportion of differences between successive heartbeats greater than 50 ms (pNN50), Power Spectral Density (PSD) in $[0, 0.4]$ (Very Low Frequency - VLF), $[0.04, 0.15]$ (Low Frequency - LF), and $[0.15, 0.4]$ Hz (High Frequency - HF) bands, and LF/HF ratio. The ReliefF algorithm was applied to discriminate the most significant features. Relying on the only ECG, an accuracy of 77.73% was achieved with the Support Vector Machine (SVM) classifier but only considering a binary problem. In [17], a protocol for estimating anxiety levels was proposed. 7 subjects were exposed to Virtual Reality (VR) scenarios in which coins placed on the balconies of a building at three different heights had to be collected. Subjects were asked to fill in the Subjective Unit of Distress (SUD) on the perceived level of anxiety from 0 to 10. The data analyzed were: EDA and HR. In particular, the extracted features relating to the HR were: mean absolute value (MAV), standard deviation (STD), low frequency signal intensity (LFI), high frequency signal intensity (HFI), high/low frequency intensity ratio (HLR). The accuracies of anxiety classification for two levels of anxiety (high and low) were 99% for "low" anxiety and 75% for "high" anxiety. For the three levels, accuracies of 95% for "low" anxiety level, 76% for "mild" and 100% for "high" were achieved. Authors of [22] proposed a methodology for predicting fear of heights. The aim of the experiment was to distinguish people able to work at height and people who are not able, using the Richie's Plank Experience application. While subjects walked on the virtual plank, EDA and HR were acquired with a sensor wristband and the dimensional (Valence - Arousal - Dominance) model was used to evaluate the affect state. The clustering of the sample was performed using K-means and Expectation Maximization techniques. A linear multivariate regression model, namely MANOVA was used for the statistical analysis: the null hypothesis of having similar clusters was rejected (p-values < 0.05). In [23], 33 subjects were placed on a virtual plank in a VR environment and the following data were acquired during the experiments: temperature, acceleration, EDA, photoplethysmography for the inter beat interval (IBI) and HR. After the simulation, each participant expressed the levels of valence and arousal felt. The HRV descriptors selected with the SPEC algorithm were: standard deviation for HRV, range (difference between minimum and maximum values), RMSSD, SDSN, SDNN, and NN50 which are based on the IBI, the total power, high frequencies (HF) and low frequencies (LF) variance, and, finally, the triangular index (TI). A cluster analysis technique was implemented. The MANOVA test led to the rejection of the null hypothesis of having similar clusters. With regards to heart rate, it was noted that for some participants it increased sharply during the simulation, and for others it decreased smoothly. To analyze and distinguish fear, frustration, and insight in [24], respiratory, pupillary, cardiac, and EDA signals were measured during exposure to VR environments. One such scenario involved subjects walking on a virtual plank at heights of 100, 150 and 300 m to elicit fear of heights. In this scenario, perceived levels of anxiety were reported through the SUD scale. The cardiac features used in the analysis were: beats per minute (BPM), mean IBI, median absolute deviation of intervals between heart beats (MAD), SDNN, RMSSD, standard deviation of successive differences between neighboring heartbeat intervals (SDSD), proportion of differences between successive heartbeats greater than 50 ms and 20 ms (pNN50, pNN20), sd1, sd2, s, sd1/sd2. Their correlation with the SUD scores was evaluated using the Spearman's ρ coefficient, reporting a value of 0.01 for the BPM and -0.24 for the MAD. Cardiac, EDA and eyes features were input to logistic regression (LR) classifier and a micro F1 score (the harmonic mean between precision and recovery) equal to 75% was obtained in the detection of fear of heights.

3   Materials and Methods

3.1   Participants

20 healthy subjects (age 26.3 ± 7.9; 8 males and 12 females) participated in the experiments. Participants had no previous experience in virtual reality and had never participated in experiments on fear of heights. All participants signed a prior informed consent to participate.

3.2   Psychometric Tools

The Acrophobia Questionnaire (AQ) [25] and the Subjective Unit of Distress (SUD) [26] scores were combined to assess the severity of fear of heights in the experimental sample prior to the exposure to the eliciting stimuli. The AQ is a self-report scale used for the assessment of the anxiety and avoidance levels associated with 20 situations reproducing different heights conditions. The AQ is made of 20 items for each subscale, namely anxiety and avoidance. The SUD was employed during the experiments to monitor subjects' changes in fear of heights due to exposure to different heights. The scale is commonly employed to evaluate subjects' habituation to anxiety, agitation, or other distressing feelings aroused during the exposure therapy. Perceived levels of anxiety are usually rated on a Likert scale from 0 to 100 (or 0 to 10) where 0 means no distress and 100 means extreme distress. In this study, a Likert scale ranging from 0 to 10 was used. The main use of the SUD in the exposure therapy consists in the development of fear hierarchies in order to arrange fear-eliciting stimuli by order of severity. The SUD can be also employed to assess the subjects' initial level of fear.

3.3   Hardware

The wireless amplifier *LiveAmp* from Brain Products [27] (Fig. 1(a)) was used for data recording.

The LiveAmp is a wearable amplifier, with a 24-bit A/D converter and also an exchangeable memory card to store recorded data. It guarantees a recording time of up to 4 h without interruption. In addition, it allows the connection of different sensors thanks to the *Sensor & Trigger Extension* (STE) (Fig. 1(b)), that was connected to the LiveAmp. The STE consists of 8 AUX inputs to record other physiological signals. The *Bipolar-to-auxiliary (BIP2AUX) adapter* (Fig. 1(c)) was connected to the STE to perform a bipolar mounting, recording the ECG signal. The BIP2AUX adapter is an analogue differential DC amplifier to optimize the incoming signal and improve the recording quality. The ECG signal was acquired using three electrodes (one positive, one negative, and the ground).

The headset employed for the VR exposure was the *Meta Quest 2* [28], produced by Meta Platforms (Fig. 2).

Quest 2 can be implemented in combination with VR software running on a desktop computer or even as a stand-alone device. It runs an Android-based

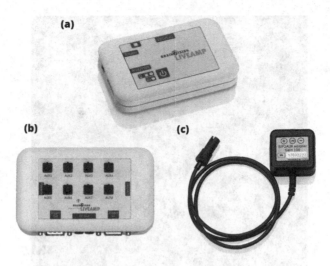

Fig. 1. Brain Vision LiveAmp (a) , Sensor & Trigger Extension (b), and Bipolar-to-auxiliary adapter (c)

Fig. 2. Meta Quest 2

operative system. It provides a 3D positional audio integration, a motion tracker with 6 °C of freedom (DOF) that allows to track the user's movements. In addition, it can store data of 128 GB or 256 GB. The headset is characterized by a fast-switch LCD display with a per-eye resolution of $1832 * 1920$. Refresh rates are 60, 72, 90 Hz.

3.4 Software

The *AKRON* application, a VR app developed by IDEGO [29] for the treatment of acrophobia, was used in the experiment [30]. The user is projected into a scenario characterized by a canyon in a rocky desert, see Fig. 3.

Thanks to the presence of a wooden lift and a platform, the subject is virtually carried from ground level up to three levels of height (15 m, 30 m, and 45 m). In this way, the subject relates to the fearful stimulus whose intensity is gradually increased. The user can feel safe with the presence of protective

Fig. 3. VR scenario

barriers surrounding him. However, these are not present in the front when the subject has reached the desired height level. The subject is allowed to look around thanks to the 6 DOF. With the C# as a programming language, an IL2CPP-type backend configuration, and the OpenGLES3 graphics library, the *AKRON* application was developed on the Android platform with the use of the Unity game engine (version 2019.4.16). By means of an ASTC compression system, it is possible to use it on virtual reality headsets (e.g. The Meta Quest 2). A refresh rate of 72 Hz was used.

3.5   Protocol

The experiments, which included three sessions for each subject, were all conducted on the same day at the Institute of Neural Engineering (BCI Lab) at the Graz University of Technology. First, there was a preparation phase to make participants aware of the purpose of the study. Subsequently, the EEG cap was mounted on the head of the subjects and the electrodes were filled with conductive gel, keeping the impedance of the electrodes below 25 kΩ. After that, participants wore the VR headset.

Before the experiment began, EEG signals were visually inspected. At this point, after showing the ground level scenario so that the subjects could familiarize themselves with the scene, they were asked to relax and restrict their movements to acquire the baseline signals. During each of the three sessions, participants were subjected to three runs for the three height levels. Each run started with a visual 5 s countdown, and then the platform started elevating. Once the desired level was reached, the participant was asked to stay in that position for 90 s. At the end of the run, a first relax phase began and the subject was teleported to the ground level. The participant was asked to report the level of discomfort on a scale from 1 to 10. Thus began the other relax phase of the duration of 60 s. The total duration of the three sessions was approximately 45 min. The experimental procedure is shown in Fig. 4.

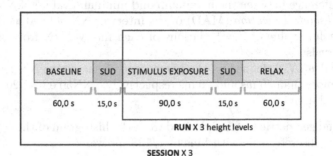

Fig. 4. Framework of the experimental sessions. After the baseline and the exposure phases, the subjective unit of distress (SUD) is provided.

3.6   Signal Processing

The biosignal processing was developed in Matlab v. R2021b. The algorithm used on the raw ECG signal was the Pan Tompkins [31]. It consists of a filtering operation and a detection operation of the QRS complexes corresponding to the ventricular depolarization. It includes the following steps:

- filtering with a digital bandpass filter ([5−12] Hz) obtained from the cascade of a high-pass and a low-pass filter, to attenuate the noise caused by interference of the 50 Hz, muscle artifact, baseline wander.
- Differentiation to obtain information on the slope of the QRS complex;
- signal amplitude squaring to enhance the high frequencies;
- moving window integration with a width window of 30 samples to obtain information on the slope of the R wave;
- adaptive thresholds method and decision rule algorithm to distinguish signal peak from noise peak and T-wave discrimination technique.

3.7   Feature Extraction and Classification

Starting from the R waves detected by the previous algorithm, the RR intervals were obtained and several features related to HRV were extracted, in particular linear statistical and geometric features, and nonlinear features [18,32]. Defining the NN interval as the Normal-to-Normal interval obtained from the signal without abnormal beats, the linear and statistical features extracted were:

- *Root Mean Square of successive differences of NN intervals* (RMSNN) that allows to estimate vagal modulation;

- *Standard Deviation of the NN Interval* (SDNN) which is an indicator of the action of both the SNS and the PNS;
- *Standard Deviation of successive differences of NN intervals* (SDSD);
- *Mean value of NN intervals*;
- *Median value of NN intervals*;
- *Range* (difference between the maximum and minimum value) of NN intervals;
- *Median Absolute Deviation* (MAD) of the intervals NN defined as the median of the absolute value of the deviations of each interval NN from the median of all intervals;
- *pNN50* and *pNN20* defined as the percentage of successive NN intervals differing by more than 50 ms and 20 ms respectively. pNN50 e pNN20 are related to the vagal activity.

The linear and geometric features derived from the histogram of the RR intervals obtained on a discrete scale with bins of 1/128 ms were:

- *Triangular Index* (TI) defined as the ratio between the total number of NN intervals and the number of NN intervals in the modal bin;
- *Triangular Interpolation of the NN Interval Histogram* (TINN) defined as the baseline width of the triangle that approximates the histogram distribution obtained from the minimum square difference.

TI and TINN are more influenced by sympathetic activity.
The nonlinear features extracted were:

- *SD1* and *SD2* obtained from the Poincaré map that represents each interval NN with respect to the previous one, and thus obtaining an ellipse. SD1 is defined as the standard deviation of the distance of each point from the identity line, while SD2 is defined as the standard deviation of each point from the line perpendicular to the identity line. SD1 is related to PNS activity, while SD2 is related to SNS activity;
- *SD1/SD2 ratio* that provides a measure of the unpredictability of NN intervals and it allows to estimate the autonomic balance;
- *Tone* that provides a measure of sympatho-vagal balance. It is defined as the average of the percentage of the change in heart period [33].

Once the features were extracted, they were used for the classification phase. The aim was to classify three intensity levels (i.e., low, medium, and high) of acrophobia. Two cases were evaluated: *inter-subject* and *intra-subject*, to deal with the variability in the ECG signal between different subjects and in the same subject, respectively. Before classification, for the inter-subject approach, the features were standardized for each subject, whereas for the intra-subject approach, the features were standardized for each session. In addition, *domain adaptation* (DA) was employed to improve the generalizability of the results. DA allows to adapt the testing dataset and training dataset that have different distributions [34,35]. The DA methods used were: *Linear Correlation Alignment* (CORAL) and *Subspace Alignment* (SA). Gaussian Naive Bayes (NB), k-Nearest Neighbor (k-NN), Random Forest (RF), Support Vector Machine (SVM), and

Multi-Layer Perceptron (MLP) were the employed classification algorithms. In the inter-subject setting, classification was carried out both considering the whole experimental sample and the three clusters (severe acrophobia, mild acrophobia, and slight acrophobia), separately.

4   Results

According to the AQ and SUD scores, the experimental sample was divided in 3 clusters which differed in the severity of fear of heights [36]. Subjects simultaneously reporting AQ scores < 20 and < 6 on the anxiety and avoidance scales, respectively, and a SUD score < 2, were considered not to suffer from fear of heights (*slight acrophobia cluster*). Subjects simultaneously reporting AQ scores [20, 40], [6, 12] and a SUD score [3, 4] were considered to suffer from a mild form of fear of heights (*mild acrophobia cluster*). Subjects simultaneously reporting AQ scores > 40 and > 12 and a SUD score > 5 were considered to suffer from a severe form of fear of heights (*severe acrophobia cluster*).

Accuracy was used to evaluate the performance of the implemented classifiers, and was defined as the ratio between the number of correct predictions and the total number of predictions. For the inter-subject study, the results obtained considering the whole experimental sample and the three clusters separately (i.e., severe, mild and slight acrophobia) are reported in Tables. 1, 2, 3, and 4, respectively.

For the intra-subject study, the results are reported in Table 5.

Table 1. Inter-subject classification accuracy (mean and standard deviation) in % of fear of heights on a 3-level intensity scale for all subjects.

All subjects	Classifier			
	NB	kNN	RF	MLP
None	35.1 ± 4.9	33.7 ± 3.9	36.1 ± 4.3	35.2 ± 4.4
CORAL	36.9 ± 6.2	36.6 ± 4.5	39.5 ± 6.8	**40.9 ± 5.9**
SA	38.1 ± 6.1	38.0 ± 6.6	39.3 ± 8.0	39.6 ± 5.6

The best performances were achieved by the RF and MLP algorithms in the case of the inter-subject approach, and by the kNN algorithm in the case of the intra-subject approach. For the inter-subject setting, an accuracy of $40.9 \pm 5.9\%$ was achieved for the whole experimental sample, of $42.2 \pm 2.9\%$ for the severe acrophobia cluster, of $44.0 \pm 6.6\%$ for the mild acrophobia cluster, of $37.7 \pm 4.6\%$ for the slight acrophobia cluster.

For the intra-subject setting, an average accuracy of $43.8 \pm 7.6\%$ was achieved. The DA technique that allowed to reach better results was CORAL. Domain adaptation methods resulted effective in improving the generalizability of the results. On the contrary, clustering the subjects according to their acrophobia severity level did not impact on the classification performances.

Table 2. Inter-subject classification accuracy (mean and standard deviation) in % of fear of heights on a 3-level intensity scale for *Severe Acrophobia* cluster.

Severe acrophobia	Classifier			
	NB	kNN	RF	MLP
None	34.6 ± 3.4	38.8 ± 2.2	33.8 ± 2.8	35.6 ± 4.0
CORAL	37.8 ± 4.0	40.5 ± 5.0	**42.2±2.9**	38.5 ± 5.0
SA	37.8 ± 2.3	40.7 ± 7.2	38.8 ± 2.3	40.5 ± 3.6

Table 3. Inter-subject classification accuracy (mean and standard deviation) in % of fear of heights on a 3-level intensity scale for *Mild Acrophobia* cluster.

Mild acrophobia	Classifier			
	NB	kNN	RF	MLP
None	36.4 ± 7.9	37.7 ± 5.3	37.7 ± 2.5	35.2 ± 3.2
CORAL	43.2 ± 6.9	38.9 ± 5.4	43.4 ± 5.5	43.2 ± 7.5
SA	40.0 ± 5.3	40.1 ± 5.1	**44.0±6.6**	43.8 ± 7.4

Table 4. Inter-subject classification accuracy (mean and standard deviation) in % of fear of heights on a 3-level intensity scale for *Slight Acrophobia* cluster.

Slight acrophobia	Classifier			
	NB	kNN	RF	MLP
None	34.0 ± 3.2	34.2 ± 4.4	**37.7±4.6**	34.6±3.4
CORAL	35.1 ± 3.6	34.0 ± 7.2	36.5 ± 4.8	37.6 ± 3.1
SA	31.9 ± 4.9	37.0 ± 1.6	35.8 ± 3.1	35.6 ± 5.7

Table 5. Intra-subject classification accuracy (mean and standard deviation) in % of fear of heights on a 3-level intensity scale for all subjects.

All subjects	Classifier			
	kNN	RF	SVM	MLP
None	40.0 ± 7.0	38.4 ± 7.3	40.7 ± 6.7	39.6 ± 5.7
CORAL	**43.8±7.6**	41.5 ± 9.4	41.4 ± 9.3	42.7 ± 8.0
SA	41.9 ± 8.1	40.9 ± 8.9	40.7 ± 9.4	41.5 ± 8.1

5   Conclusions

The current study reports an ECG-based detection of three levels of acrophobia. A VR environment was implemented to induce fear of heights in 20 participants by bringing them to three levels of height with the use of an elevating platform. To assess the acrophobia severity of the subjects, the AQ and the SUD scores were employed. The ECG signal was acquired during the exposure to the eliciting VR scenario. HRV features were exploited for the classification. The average accuracies in the inter-subject and intra-subject settings were computed for the three-classes fear classification task. Domain adaptation methods were exploited to improve the generalizability of the results. The best performing DA strategy was CORAL. On the other hand, the clustering of the subjects according to their acrophobia intensity did not affect the performances. In the case of the inter-subject setting, the RF and MLP algorithms were the best classifiers, providing accuracies of $40.9 \pm 5.9\%$ considering the whole experimental sample, $42.2 \pm 2.9\%$ considering the severe acrophobia cluster, $44.0 \pm 6.6\%$ considering the mild acrophobia cluster, and $37.7 \pm 4.6\%$ considering the slight acrophobia cluster. In the case of the intra-subject setting, an average accuracy of $43.8 \pm 7.6\%$ was achieved with the kNN algorithm. In future works, (i) a larger experimental sample, (ii) the extraction of more features or combination of features, and (iii) the use of further strategies to improve the generalizability of the results will be considered.

Acknowledgment. The authors thank the Institute of Neural Engineering (BCI Lab) at the Graz University of Technology for the support in the research activities. The authors also thank the PhD Grant "AR4ClinicSur- Augmented Reality for Clinical Surgery" (INPS - National Social Security Institution - Italy). This work was carried out as part of the "ICT for Health" project, which was financially supported by the Italian Ministry of Education, University and Research (MIUR), under the initiative 'Departments of Excellence' (Italian Budget Law no. 232/2016), through an excellence grant awarded to the Department of Information Technology and Electrical Engineering of the University of Naples Federico II, Naples, Italy.

References

1. Edition, F., et al.: Diagnostic and statistical manual of mental disorders. Am Psychiatric Assoc. **21**(21), 591–643 (2013)
2. Curtis, G., Magee, W.J., Eaton, W.W., Wittchen, H.-U., Kessler, R.C.: Specific fears and phobias: Epidemiology and classification. Br. J. Psychiatry **173**(3), 212–217 (1998)
3. Depla, M.F., Ten Have, M.L., van Balkom, A.J., de Graaf, R.: Specific fears and phobias in the general population: results from the Netherlands mental health survey and incidence study (nemesis). Soc. Psychiatry Psychiatr. Epidemiol. **43**, 200–208 (2008)
4. APA Dictionary of Psychology - Acrophobia. https://dictionary.apa.org/acrophobia (Accessed 10 July 2022)
5. Davey, G.C., Menzies, R., Gallardo, B.: Height phobia and biases in the interpretation of bodily sensations: some links between acrophobia and agoraphobia. Behav. Res. Ther. **35**(11), 997–1001 (1997)
6. Abdullah, M., Shaikh, Z.A.: An effective virtual reality based remedy for acrophobia. Inter. J. Adv. Comput. Sci. Appli. **9**(6) (2018)
7. Wolpe, J.: The systematic desensitization treatment of neuroses. J. Nerv. Ment. Dis. **132**(3), 189–203 (1961)

8. Hofmann, S.G., Smits, J.A.: Cognitive-behavioral therapy for adult anxiety disorders: a meta-analysis of randomized placebo-controlled trials. J. Clin. Psychiatry **69**(4), 621 (2008)
9. Bornas, X., Llabres, J., Noguera, M., López, A.M., Gelabert, J.M., Vila, I.: Fear induced complexity loss in the electrocardiogram of flight phobics: a multiscale entropy analysis. Biol. Psychol. **73**(3), 272–279 (2006)
10. Riva, G., Serino, S., Di Lernia, D., Pavone, E.F., Dakanalis, A.: Embodied medicine: mens sana in corpore virtuale sano. Front. Hum. Neurosci. **11**, 120 (2017)
11. Barba, M.C., et al.: BRAVO: a gaming environment for the treatment of ADHD. In: De Paolis, L.T., Bourdot, P. (eds.) AVR 2019. LNCS, vol. 11613, pp. 394–407. Springer, Cham (2019). https://doi.org/10.1007/978-3-030-25965-5_30
12. Gatto, C.: Wellbeing assessment of a museum experience in virtual reality through ucl measurement tool kit and heart rate measurement: a pilot study. In: 2022 IEEE International Conference on Metrology for Extended Reality, Artificial Intelligence and Neural Engineering (MetroXRAINE), pp. 483–488. IEEE (2022)
13. Arpaia, P., D'Errico, G., De Paolis, L.T., Moccaldi, N., Nuccetelli, F.: A narrative review of mindfulness-based interventions using virtual reality. Mindfulness, 1–16 (2021)
14. Rothbaum, B.O., Hodges, L.F., Kooper, R., Opdyke, D., Williford, J.S., North, M.: Effectiveness of computer-generated (virtual reality) graded exposure in the treatment of acrophobia. Am. J. Psych. (1995)
15. Coelho, C.M., Waters, A.M., Hine, T.J., Wallis, G.: The use of virtual reality in acrophobia research and treatment. J. Anxiety Disord. **23**(5), 563–574 (2009)
16. Arpaia, P.: Virtual reality enhances EEG-based neurofeedback for emotional self-regulation. In: Extended Reality: First International Conference, XR Salento: Lecce, Italy, 6–8 July 2022, Proceedings, Part II, 420–431. Springer (2022). https://doi.org/10.1007/978-3-031-15553-6_29
17. Petrescu, L., et al.: Integrating biosignals measurement in virtual reality environments for anxiety detection. Sensors **20**(24), 7088 (2020)
18. T. F. of The European Society of Cardiology et al., The north american society of pacing and electrophysiology (membership of the task force listed in the appendix). Heart rate variability standards of measurement, physiological interpretation, and clinical use. European Heart J. **17** 354–381 (1996)
19. Bisogni, V., Pengo, M.F., Maiolino, G., Rossi, G.P.: The sympathetic nervous system and catecholamines metabolism in obstructive sleep apnoea. J. Thorac. Dis. **8**(2), 243 (2016)
20. Chalmers, J.A., Quintana, D.S., Abbott, M.J.-A., Kemp, A.H.: Anxiety disorders are associated with reduced heart rate variability: a meta-analysis. Front. Psych. **5**, 80 (2014)
21. Zheng, R., Wang, T., Cao, J., Vidal, P.-P., Wang, D.: Multi-modal physiological signals based fear of heights analysis in virtual reality scenes. Biomed. Signal Process. Control **70**, 102988 (2021)
22. Boccignone, G., Gadia, D., Maggiorini, D., Ripamonti, L.A., Tosto, V.: Predicting real fear of heights using virtual reality. In: Proceedings of the Conference on Information Technology for Social Good, pp. 103–108 (2021)
23. Boccignone, G., Gadia, D., Maggiorini, D., Ripamonti, L.A, Tosto, V.: Wuthering heights: gauging fear at altitude in virtual reality. Multimedia Tools and Applications **82**(4) 5207–5228 (2023)
24. Luong, T., Holz, C.: Characterizing physiological responses to fear, frustration, and insight in virtual reality. IEEE Trans. Visual Comput. Graphics **28**(11), 3917–3927 (2022)

25. Cohen, D.C.: Comparison of self-report and overt-behavioral procedures for assessing acrophobia. Behav. Ther. **8**(1), 17–23 (1977)
26. McCabe, R.E.: Subjective units of distress scale. J Phobias: Psychol Irrational Fear **18**, 361 (2015)
27. Liveamp. https://www.brainproducts.com/solutions/liveamp/ (Accessed 17 Nov 2022)
28. Meta quest 2. https://www.meta.com/at/en/quest/products/quest-2/, (Accessed 17 Nov 2022)
29. Idego - Digital Psychology. https://www.idego.it/ (Accessed 12 June 2022)
30. Apicella, A., et al.: Electroencephalography correlates of fear of heights in a virtual reality environment. Acta IMEKO **12**(2), 1–7 (2023)
31. Pan, J., Tompkins, W.J.: A real-time qrs detection algorithm. IEEE Trans. Biomed. Eng. **3**, 230–236 (1985)
32. Shaffer, F., Ginsberg, J.P.: An overview of heart rate variability metrics and norms. Front. Public Health, 258 (2017)
33. Oida, E., Moritani, T., Yamori, Y.: Tone-entropy analysis on cardiac recovery after dynamic exercise. J. Appl. Physiol. **82**(6), 1794–1801 (1997)
34. Geng, B., Tao, D., Xu, C.: Daml: Domain adaptation metric learning. IEEE Trans. Image Process. **20**(10), 2980–2989 (2011)
35. Bazi, Y., Alajlan, N., AlHichri, H., Malek, S.: Domain adaptation methods for ECG classification. In: 2013 International Conference on Computer Medical Applications (ICCMA), pp. 1–4. IEEE (2013)
36. Wang, Q., Wang, H., Hu, F., Hua, C., Wang, D.: Using convolutional neural networks to decode EEG-based functional brain network with different severity of acrophobia. J. Neural Eng. **18**(1), 016007 (2021)

Role of the Motor Cortex in Virtual Reality-Based Neurofeedback for Emotional Self-regulation

Pasquale Arpaia[1,2], Giovanni D'Errico[4(✉)], Mirco Frosolone[3],
Lucio Tommaso De Paolis[5], Sabrina Grassini[4], Giovanna Mastrati[1],
and Nicola Moccaldi[1,5]

[1] Department of Electrical Engineering and Information Technology (DIETI),
University of Naples Federico II, Naples, Italy
[2] Interdepartmental Center for Research on Management and Innovation in
Healthcare (CIRMIS), University of Naples Federico II, Naples, Italy
[3] Institute of Cognitive Sciences and Technologies,
ISTC-National Research Council CNR, Rome, Italy
[4] Department of Applied Science and Technology,
Polytechnic University of Turin, Turin, Italy
giovanni.derrico@polito.it
[5] Department of Engineering for Innovation University of Salento, Lecce, Italy

Abstract. A relationship emerged between the progress in performing neurofeedback exercises for emotional regulation and the trend of the μ-band power spectral density from the bipolar channel FC4-CP4. The exploratory study involved 3 subjects. As emerged in previous studies on the analysis of the emotional response in the motor cortex, the significance of the FC4-CP4 channel is confirmed. As already demonstrated for high μ in FCz-CPz, also μ and μ in FC4-CP4 decrease during emotional regulation training within single sessions and between sessions. This is particularly confirmed if the neurofeedback is done with immersive VR compared to the one in 2D.

Keywords: brain-computer interface · EEG · extended reality · virtual reality · health 4.0 · emotion regulation · neurofeedback · motor cortex

1 Introduction

Neurofeedback is a type of biofeedback based on brain-derived signals. It represents a promising methodology to facilitate self-regulation of brain electrical activity [1]. Electroencephalography (EEG) is commonly employed to capture the electrical activity of the brain, enabling the real-time provision of brainwave information to the individual undergoing neurofeedback training [2]. Extensive

L. T. De Paolis et al. (Eds.): XR Salento 2023, LNCS 14218, pp. 514–524, 2023.
https://doi.org/10.1007/978-3-031-43401-3_34

literature supports the effectiveness of neurofeedback across a range of clinical applications, highlighting its potential as a therapeutic intervention [3–5].

Emotion regulation (ER) refers to the cognitive and behavioral processes involved in recognizing and managing emotions, including the ability to regulate the intensity and duration of emotional experiences [6]. Impairments in emotion regulation can lead to emotional vulnerability, characterized by a greater sensitivity to intense emotions that persist for extended periods of time. Extensive research in the field has identified various cognitive and behavioral strategies for effective emotion regulation. Cognitive strategies commonly employed in emotion regulation encompass attentional shifts, distancing from the emotional stimuli, and cognitive reappraisal [7]. Among these strategies, cognitive reappraisal has demonstrated considerable success in modifying emotional responses by altering perception and evaluation of emotionally salient situations [8]. Moreover, the combination of emotional acceptance and neurofeedback has also emerged as a highly promising strategy for regulating emotions [9].

Among the numerous techniques available for inducing emotional states and providing neurofeedback, Virtual Reality (VR) demonstrates considerable promise. VR presents an ecologically valid paradigm for investigating emotions due to its capacity to incorporate motivational and empathy mechanisms. The sense of presence is derived from a technological simulation that corresponds to the predictions of the brain, i.e. the body matrix [10,11].

Individuals with motor dysfunctions resulting from central nervous system damage commonly exhibit impairments in emotion processing as well. The literature agrees on the existence of a functional relationship between the neural regions involved in emotion regulation and the sensorimotor area, although further investigation is needed [12–14]. Fiess and colleagues examined emotion regulation and functional neurological symptomatology (FNS) in a sample of 20 patients with FNS and 20 healthy participants [13]. This study analyzed neuromagnetic activity and somatic sensation during an emotional regulation task. The findings revealed modulation of frontocortical alpha activity in the healthy participants, whereas the patients with FNS exhibited prominent activity modulation in the sensorimotor regions. Aybek and colleagues [14] examined patients with Conversion Disorder (CD) while they performed a functional magnetic resonance imaging (fMRI) task involving the viewing of faces displaying negative emotional expressions. The results highlighted that emotion regulation involves the frontal lobe and motor cortex.

Referring to specific EEG features, the suppression of activity in specific bands within the sensorimotor area of the right hemisphere was observed during tasks involving emotion regulation. Fabi and Leuthold demonstrated how stimuli that evoke empathy produce automatic and controlled effects on both perceptual and motor processes [15]. Specifically, they showed a suppression of μ rhythm (8–13 Hz) on the right somatosensory cortex (channel C4) during the post-response interval (700–1500 ms). The study found a positive correlation between Empathy Quotient scores and μ band activity on the right somatosensory cortex. This suggests that individuals with higher levels of dispositional empathy show greater down-regulation of their motor system when observing others in painful situations. The same study observes larger Event-related Desynchronization in the μ and β bands in the painful condition compared to the neutral condition in the time interval between 700 and 1500 ms. Other studies, also focused on the analysis of neural somatosensory responses to the pain of others, show greater suppression of oscillatory activity in the μ and β bands of the somatosensory cortex [16,17]. This empathy-linked activation increases when stimuli are presented in a way that weakens the bodily boundaries between the participant and the targets [16].

In a previous study, the authors performed experiments for emotion regulation by means of neurofeedback based on high-β-power extracted from FCz-CPz channel [18]. The present study, using the same neurofeedback system, explores the signal pattern in the sensorimotor area. The goal is to find further EEG features to improve the accuracy of the neurofeedback system in recognizing the user's current emotional state.

2 Material and Methods

2.1 VR Neurofeedback System

2D-neurofeedback system and a VR-neurofeedback system were developed. The reference theory adopted was the circumplex model of affect, which categorizes emotions along valence and arousal dimensions [19]. Therefore, in order to elicit specific emotional states in users, stimuli from the International Affective Picture System (IAPS) [20] were utilized, consisting of negatively polarized images on the valence axis with neutral arousal. These images depicted scenes related to danger, death, violence, disease, and other similar themes. To prevent habituation and familiarity, the images were presented randomly and varied across participants.

In the 2D-neurofeedback system, visual stimuli surrounded by a coloured frame were sequentially displayed on the screen.

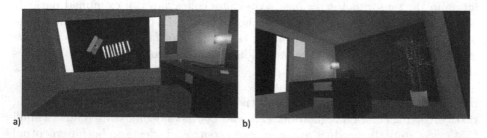

a)   b)

Fig. 1. VR neurofeedback when (a) the user is focusing the picture form IAPS dataset and (b) the user is exploring the virtual environment

The VR-neurofeedback system implemented a visual stimulation mechanism employing IAPS images to enable a direct comparison with the 2D neurofeedback scenario. Specifically, subjects were immersed in a minimalist virtual office room devoid of distractions, where stimuli were presented on a wall within the virtual environment. Feedback was provided through both a traditional thermometer displayed alongside the image and a manipulation of the room's lighting color. The color-changing image frame effectively transformed the entire virtual environment, adjusting its colors based on the subject's feedback. In Fig. 1, the VR environment is shown.

In both systems, the color bar switches from a lower position (blue) to an upper position (yellow) in accordance with the recorded cortical activation, adhering to the color scale proposed by [21]. Blue, red, and yellow corresponded to negative, neutral, and positive emotional states, respectively. The bar heights were updated every 1 s to correspond with the level of the EEG feature being regulated. The two applications were developed utilizing the Unity game engine [22] (version 2019.4.4f1, Personal 64 bit for Microsoft Windows). For the VR system, the HTC Vive Pro 2 headset [23] was employed.

EEG signal was acquired by means of FlexEEG^{TM}from Neuroconcise [24]. The basic version of FlexEEG is equipped with three bipolar channels, namely FC3-CP3, FCz-CPz, and FC4-CP4 (according to the International 10–20 Positioning System). AFZ is the reference electrode. Electrodes have to be filled in with conductive gel. FlexEEG sends data via Bluetooth 2.0 and allows an adjustable sampling rate (125 Hz–250 Hz) and an ADC resolution (16–24 bits).

The EEG signal was acquired, transmitted, and processed in real-time within the Matlab environment, specifically using version R2021b. The EEG system included a Matlab script for parameter configuration and a default Simulink model containing compiled code to operate the FlexEEG device.

Simulink was also utilized for the online processing of the acquired EEG signal. The data underwent bandpass filtering (20–34 Hz), followed by the extraction of 2 s epochs with a 1 s overlap. Each epoch then underwent Fast Fourier Transform (FFT) to derive power values within the targeted EEG frequency band.

The neurofeedback was linked to the value of high-β power in midline locations (FCz-CPz) [25]. The more the high β power decreased, the more the color of the interface veered towards yellow. Each session started with an initial calibration phase to customize the neurofeedback session for each participant. During this phase, a 2 min resting state with eyes open and a task-related baseline were recorded [26]. The mean high-β powers of the neurofeedback electrodes were calculated for both phases and associated to the upper and lower limits of the color scale, respectively.

Following the calibration phase, the neurofeedback training began. EEG data were processed in real-time, and the high-β power derived from the FCz-CPz electrode guided the visual feedback provided to the user.

Communication between Simulink and Unity was established using the UDP protocol. Unity transmitted start and end messages to Simulink for each task, while Simulink provided real-time updates of the reference feature computed during the resting state, baseline phases, and neurofeedback training. These updates informed the visual feedback presented to the user.

2.2 Participants

The pilot study included three participants. Two (one male and one female) were below 30 years old. The third was a male over 65 with an onset of neuromotor slowdowns. None of them had previous experience with emotion-related BCI experiments or VR systems. Written informed consent was obtained from all participants prior to their participation. The study protocol received ethical approval from the Ethics Committee of Psychological Research at the University of Naples Federico II, following the guidelines outlined in the Declaration of Helsinki.

2.3 Procedure

The study encompassed a total of six neurofeedback sessions, divided equally between the 2D-neurofeedback system and the VR-neurofeedback system. These sessions were conducted over the course of three days per week, with one session per day. All neurofeedback sessions took place at the Arhemlab laboratory of the University of Naples Federico II, within a controlled environment that was both dark and soundproofed to minimize distractions.

Participants received a detailed explanation of the experiment's objectives and were provided with the necessary instructions to complete the procedures. Subsequently, participants were instructed to sit on a comfortable chair, situated at a distance of approximately 70 cm from a 16-in. monitor.

Following the placement of the EEG cap on the participants, the researchers applied conductive gel to the electrodes and visually inspected the EEG signal for quality assurance. Once the EEG was properly configured, participants were instructed to focus their gaze on the screen and carefully adhere to the instructions displayed, maintaining a stationary position.

A neurofeedback experimental protocol was developed, in accordance with previous research [27,28]. The objective of the experimental task was to reduce the recorded β power values at midline scalp site, specifically when exposed to negative stimuli within a chromatic context that provided information about the distance from the target.

Each neurofeedback session consisted of two distinct phases: an initial calibration phase and a neurofeedback training (NF-training) phase. The calibration phase encompassed a 120-s period of eyes-open resting state, followed by a negative baseline phase consisting of the presentation of 21 images. Each image was displayed for 5 s and preceded by a 10-s fixation cross. During the calibration phase, participants were instructed to relax and subsequently observe the projected images passively.

The training phase comprised 22 trials, consisting of (i) 14 trials of emotion regulation (ER) with participants receiving feedback regarding their performance lasting 20 s and (ii) 7 trials of passive vision where participants solely viewed the projected images, and (iii) a final transfer run where participants were tasked with regulating their emotions without receiving feedback.

In the training phase, participants were tasked with actively regulating their experienced emotions based on the feedback provided. They were also instructed to employ the cognitive reappraisal [29], for actively altering the emotional impact of a situation through cognitive processes.

3   Results

For each participant, the average μ and β absolute power spectral densities in the right sensorimotor area (FC4-Cp4) were computed at varying the session (Figs. 2, 3, 4). The first three sessions were conducted using 2D feedback, while the last three sessions involved experiences in virtual reality (VR). A consistent decreasing trend of μ and β powers was observed in the last three sessions. The β band exhibits higher spectral density levels compared to the μ band, except for subject 2, i.e., the person over 65 years old. The typical single-trial trend of power spectral density in the μ band from FC4-CP4 is reported in Figs. 5, 6, and 7 for subjects 1, 2, and 3, respectively. An almost monotonic decrease can be observed.

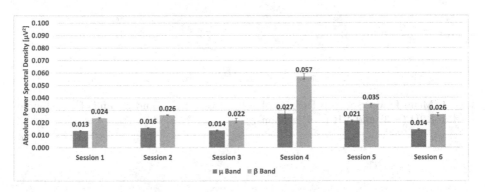

Fig. 2. Mean Power Spectral Density of subject 1 in the μ and β bands from channel FC4-CP4 for 2D (1–3) and VR (3–6) sessions.

Finally, in Table 1, Spearman's Rank correlation coefficients of the relationship between the succession of sessions and the PSD of β and μ from the Fc4-Cp4 channel are reported. A strong negative correlation emerged for all the subjects when only VR Sessions are considered. The direction and the strength of the relationship change when (i) all the Sessions or (ii) the 2D Sessions are evaluated.

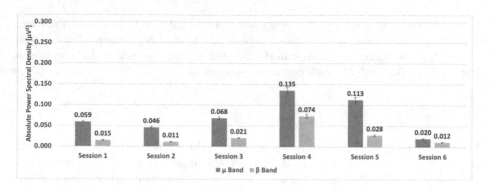

Fig. 3. Mean Power Spectral Density of subject 2 in the μ and β bands from channel FC4, for 2D (1–3) and VR (3–6) sessions.

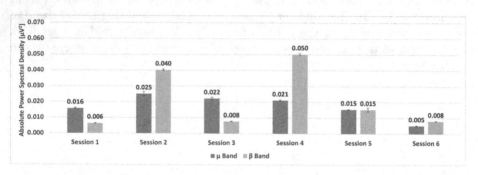

Fig. 4. Mean Power Spectral Density of subject 3 in the μ and β bands from channel FC4, for 2D (1–3) and VR (3–6) sessions.

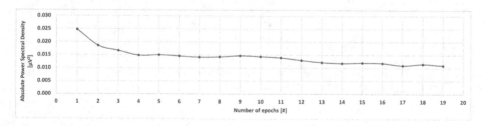

Fig. 5. Typical PSD trend in μ band from FC4-CP4 during a single trial of subject 1, during a VR session.

4 Discussion

During the VR training, a decreasing trend can be observed for the absolute spectral power density power from the Fc4-Cp4 channel in both μ and μ bands across all subjects. In contrast, the trend is not as monotonic during the 2D feedback training. VR-based neurofeedback may offer greater efficacy in eliciting emotions, making the process less susceptible to external influencing factors.

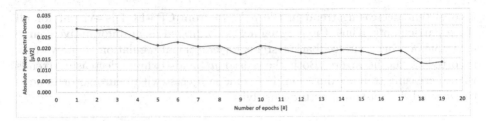

Fig. 6. Typical PSD trend in μ band from FC4-CP4 during a single trial of subject 2, during a VR session.

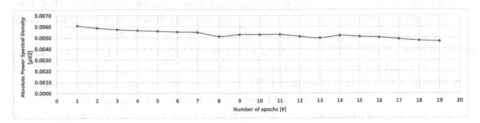

Fig. 7. Typical PSD trend in μ band from FC4-CP4 during a single trial of subject 3, during a VR session.

Table 1. Spearman's Rank correlation coefficients of the relationship between the a succession of Sessions and the PSD of β and μ from the Fc4-Cp4 channel. A strong negative correlation emerged for all the subjects when only VR Sessions are considered.

Band	Subject	Sessions		
		All	2D	VR
μ	# 1	0.41	0.50	−1.00
	# 2	0.37	1.00	−1.00
	# 3	−0.66	0.50	−1.00
β	# 1	0.41	0.50	−1.00
	# 2	0.41	0.50	−1.00
	# 3	−0.23	0.50	−1.00

Particularly for the μ band, the trend indicates progressive cortical activation. This finding differs from previous studies focused on empathy towards others' physical pain (which directly correlates with μ band suppression) [15–17]. In this case, the presumed enhanced emotional regulation ability leads to μ band desynchronization in the motor area.

Only for subject 2, the μ band exhibits higher spectral density levels compared to the μ band. Subject 2 is an elderly individual who reported neuromotor issues. This aligns with literature findings for individuals with such issues, indicating a particular involvement of the sensorimotor area (hence the μ band) during emotional regulation tasks [13,14]. Even when considering intra-trial trends, a consistent decreasing trend in the μ band from CP4-FC4 is evident for all three participants. Thus, the C4 channel is confirmed as an informative source for implementing neurofeedback systems for emotional regulation, as previously reported in the literature. Both the μ and μ bands exhibit decreasing trends with increasing training duration. For some subjects (with neuromotor issues), the μ band demonstrates better sensitivity.

5   Conclusions

The involvement of the motor cortex during emotion regulation training was experimentally investigated. Three participants were involved in neurofeedback tasks aimed at down-regulate negative emotions by reducing the midline μ power measured in FCz-CPz. Negative emotions were induced through the use of IAPS images as eliciting stimuli. Participants completed three sessions of VR-based neurofeedback and three sessions of 2D-based neurofeedback. Each training session began with a calibration phase to record the rest and baseline values specific to each participant, allowing for customization of the neurofeedback system. A relationship emerged between the progress in performing neurofeedback exercises for emotional regulation and the trend of the μ-band power spectral density from the bipolar channel FC4-CP4. As emerged in previous studies on the analysis of the emotional response in the motor cortex, the significance of the FC4-CP4 channel is confirmed. As already demonstrated for high μ in CPz, also μ and μ in FC4-CP4 decrease during emotional regulation training within single sessions and between sessions. This is particularly confirmed if the neurofeedback is done with immersive VR compared to the one in 2D. Future developments for this study include: (i) expanding the sample size ($\geq$30 subjects), (ii) increasing the number of neurofeedback sessions.

References

1. Zotev, V., Phillips, R., Yuan, H., Misaki, M., Bodurka, J.: Self-regulation of human brain activity using simultaneous real-time fMRI and EEG neurofeedback. Neuroimage **85**, 985–995 (2014)
2. Enriquez-Geppert, S., Huster, R.J., Herrmann, C.S.: EEG-neurofeedback as a tool to modulate cognition and behavior: a review tutorial. Front. Hum. Neurosci. **11**, 51 (2017)
3. Arns, M., Heinrich, H., Strehl, U.: Evaluation of neurofeedback in ADHD: the long and winding road. Biol. Psychol. **95**, 108–115 (2014)
4. Gomes, J.S., Ducos, D.V., Akiba, H., Dias, A.M.: A neurofeedback protocol to improve mild anxiety and sleep quality. Brazilian J. Psychiatry **38**, 264–265 (2016)
5. Cavazza, M., et al.: Towards emotional regulation through neurofeedback. In: Proceedings of the 5th Augmented Human International Conference, pp. 1–8 (2014)
6. Gross, J.J.: Emotion regulation: current status and future prospects. Psychol. Inq. **26**(1), 1–26 (2015)
7. Mende-Siedlecki, P., Kober, H., Ochsner, K.N.: Emotion regulation: neural bases. The Oxford Handbook of Social Neuroscience, p. 277 (2011)

8. Cutuli, D.: Cognitive reappraisal and expressive suppression strategies role in the emotion regulation: an overview on their modulatory effects and neural correlates. Front. Syst. Neurosci. **175** (2014)
9. Arpaia, P., et al.: Mindfulness-based emotional acceptance in combination with neurofeedback for improving emotion self-regulation: a pilot study. In: 2022 IEEE International Conference on Metrology for Extended Reality, Artificial Intelligence and Neural Engineering (MetroXRAINE), pp. 465–470. IEEE (2022)
10. Moradi, A., Pouladi, F., Pishva, N., Rezaei, B., Torshabi, M., Mehrjerdi, Z.A.: Treatment of anxiety disorder with neurofeedback: case study. Procedia Soc. Behav. Sci. **30**, 103–107 (2011)
11. Engelbregt, H.J., et al.: Short and long-term effects of sham-controlled prefrontal EEG-neurofeedback training in healthy subjects. Clin. Neurophysiol. **127**(4), 1931–1937 (2016)
12. Kienle, J., Rockstroh, B., Fiess, J., Schmidt, R., Popov, T., Steffen-Klatt, A.: Variation of functional neurological symptoms and emotion regulation with time. Front. Psych. **9**, 35 (2018)
13. Fiess, J., Rockstroh, B., Schmidt, R., Steffen, A.: Emotion regulation and functional neurological symptoms: does emotion processing convert into sensorimotor activity? J. Psychosom. Res. **79**(6), 477–483 (2015)
14. Aybek, S., Nicholson, T.R., O'Daly, O., Zelaya, F., Kanaan, R.A., David, A.S.: Emotion-motion interactions in conversion disorder: an fMRI study. PLoS ONE **10**(4), e0123273 (2015)
15. Fabi, S., Leuthold, H.: Empathy for pain influences perceptual and motor processing: evidence from response force, ERPS, and EEG oscillations. Soc. Neurosci. **12**(6), 701–716 (2017)
16. Riečanský, I., Lengersdorff, L.L., Pfabigan, D.M., Lamm, C.: Increasing self-other bodily overlap increases sensorimotor resonance to others' pain. Cognit. Aff. Behav. Neurosci. **20**, 19–33 (2020)
17. Riečanský, I., Lamm, C.: The role of sensorimotor processes in pain empathy. Brain Topogr. **32**(6), 965–976 (2019)
18. Arpaia, P., et al.: Virtual reality enhances EEG-based neurofeedback for emotional self-regulation. In: De Paolis, L.T., Arpaia, P., Sacco, M. (eds.) XR Salento 2022, Part II. LNCS, vol. 13446, pp. 420–431. Springer, Cham (2022). https://doi.org/10.1007/978-3-031-15553-6_29
19. Russell, J.A.: A circumplex model of affect. J. Pers. Soc. Psychol. **39**(6), 1161 (1980)
20. Lang, P.J., Bradley, M.M., Cuthbert, B.N., et al.: International affective picture system (IAPS): technical manual and affective ratings. NIMH Center Study Emot. Attenti. **1**(39–58), 3 (1997)
21. Brühl, A.B., Scherpiet, S., Sulzer, J., Stämpfli, P., Seifritz, E., Herwig, U.: Real-time neurofeedback using functional MRI could improve down-regulation of amygdala activity during emotional stimulation: a proof-of-concept study. Brain Topogr. **27**(1), 138–148 (2014)
22. Unity. https://unity.com/. Accessed 28 Apr 2022
23. HTC VIVE PRO 2. https://www.vive.com/eu/product/vive-pro/. Accessed 28 Apr 2022
24. Neuroconcise technology. https://www.neuroconcise.co.uk/. Accessed 28 Apr 2022
25. Hammond, D.C.: What is neurofeedback? J. Neurother. **10**(4), 25–36 (2007)
26. Balconi, M., Frezza, A., Vanutelli, M.E.: Emotion regulation in schizophrenia: a pilot clinical intervention as assessed by EEG and optical imaging (functional near-infrared spectroscopy). Front. Hum. Neurosci. **12**, 395 (2018)

27. Herwig, U., et al.: Training emotion regulation through real-time fMRI neurofeedback of amygdala activity. Neuroimage **184**, 687–696 (2019)
28. Lawrence, E.J., Su, L., Barker, G.J., Medford, N., Dalton, J., Williams, S.C., Birbaumer, N., Veit, R., Ranganatha, S., Bodurka, J., et al.: Self-regulation of the anterior insula: Reinforcement learning using real-time fMRI neurofeedback. Neuroimage **88**, 113–124 (2014)
29. Lazarus, R.S., Alfert, E.: Short-circuiting of threat by experimentally altering cognitive appraisal. Psychol. Sci. Public Interest **69**(2), 195 (1964)

Design and Development of an Adaptive Multisensory Virtual Reality System for Emotional Self-Regulation

Giovanni D'Errico[1]([✉]), Pasquale Arpaia[2,3], Lucio Tommaso De Paolis[4], Antonio Esposito[2], Carola Gatto[4], Sabrina Grassini[1], Giovanna Mastrati[2], Nicola Moccaldi[2], Angela Natalizio[5], and Benito Luigi Nuzzo[4]

[1] Department of Applied Science and Technology,
Polytechnic University of Turin, Turin, Italy
giovanni.derrico@polito.it
[2] Department of Electrical Engineering and Information Technology (DIETI),
University of Naples Federico II, Naples, Italy
[3] Interdepartmental Center for Research on Management and Innovation in
Healthcare (CIRMIS), University of Naples Federico II, Naples, Italy
[4] Department of Engineering for Innovation University of Salento, Lecce, Italy
[5] Department of Electronics and Telecommunications (DET),
Polytechnic of Turin, Turin, Italy

Abstract. A pilot study aimed to assess the usability of an adaptive multisensory virtual reality (VR) system for emotional self-regulation is presented. The neurofeedback relies on electroencephalography (EEG) and is proposed to participants for strengthening the anxiety regulation capacity, by following the task to down-regulate the high-beta band measured in the parietal region of the scalp (i.e., Pz). With respect to a previous version of the system, the proposed solution guarantees: (i) a better specification of the measurand, namely the anxiety regulation, within the context of emotional regulation, (ii) the implementation of a 3D fully adaptive neurofeedback in virtual reality, and (iii) a multisensory feedback combining visual and acoustic channels. Standardized auditory stimuli and abstract geometric primitives following principles of neuroaesthetics are used in order to induce emotional states. The study was conducted on three male participants, and the preliminary results demonstrate the acceptability of the proposed design, identifying it as a promising system for emotional self-regulation.

Keywords: BCI · EEG · virtual reality · emotion regulation · anxiety regulation · neurofeedback · active elicitation · multisensory

L. T. De Paolis et al. (Eds.): XR Salento 2023, LNCS 14218, pp. 525–536, 2023.
https://doi.org/10.1007/978-3-031-43401-3_35

1   Introduction

Emotional Regulation (ER) refers to the capacity to identify and effectively control one's emotional states, including the level of intensity and duration [1]. When the ability to regulate emotions is compromised, it can result in emotional susceptibility, characterized by heightened sensitivity to experiencing intense emotions over prolonged periods. In this context, Anxiety Regulation focuses on the management of anxiety as a distinct emotional state (often approximated to the construct of fear [2]) and is a field of growing interest in psychology and affective neuroscience [3]. Numerous cognitive and behavioural techniques can be used for ER, including redirecting attention, creating psychological distance, cognitive reappraisal or the use of mindfulness and emotional acceptance to regulate the anxiety response [4,5].

Neurofeedback, a type of biofeedback that relies on gathering signals emitted by the brain, is commonly facilitated through the use of electroencephalography (EEG) to measure the brain's electrical activity. Real-time brainwave data is then presented to individuals, enabling them to learn how to independently regulate their brain's electrical activity [6]. Given the link between emotions and the various patterns of brain activation [7], as well as the connections between brain damage and emotion perception and expression [8], neurofeedback holds promise as a therapeutic intervention for disorders related to emotion regulation. Successful applications of neurofeedback in the context of emotion regulation include the treatment of schizophrenia [9], depression [10], stress [11], and anxiety [12–14].

Virtual Reality (VR) has a consistent potential in eliciting emotions, providing mechanisms for motivation and empathy. VR effectively engages various sensory modalities, integrating proprioception, interoception, and sensory information [15]. The sense of presence experienced in VR results from a technological simulation that aligns with the brain's predictive mechanisms, often referred to as the "body matrix" [15]. Several studies indicate that VR utilization enhances the elicitation of valence and arousal even further [16]. The absence of standardized reference datasets and databases for VR content represents the primary challenge faced by researchers in this field to date. An important but less explored aspect pertains to the utilization of neurofeedback for ER within VR environments. In comparison to conventional passive induction mechanisms where the subject assumes a passive observational role, VR provides the opportunity for active elicitation of emotions [17]. By leveraging the immersive and interactive nature of the medium, users actively participate in the eliciting scenario and dynamically manipulate it based on their real-time reactions. This approach enhances ecological validity and facilitates the generalizability of experimental findings [18].

In a previous investigation, in accordance with literature [19], International Affective Picture System (IAPS) images [20] negatively polarised on the valence axis (and with neutral arousal) were used as visual eliciting stimuli within a virtual environment [21]. In this scenario, neurofeedback was provided through colour modulation of the room lighting: the objective was to reduce the recorded high-beta power levels in the midline regions of the scalp. Elevated levels of this feature have been linked to an escalation in state anxiety [22].

However, the study is subject to several limitations. Firstly, despite the use of VR, a passive paradigm for emotion elicitation was employed within a static and non-interactive scenario, neglecting the potential of immersive conditions and relying solely on two-dimensional and monosensory stimuli. Furthermore, while exploiting a feature associated to anxiety responses (low valence and high arousal), emotional states were induced using stimuli with negative valence and neutral arousal. In order to address anxiety response regulation, it is essential to take into account not only valence but also arousal.

In light of this background, the objective of the current study is to enhance the preceding system through: i) a more precise specification of the measurand, moving toward anxiety regulation within the realm of emotional regulation, ii) the implementation of an active paradigm for emotion elicitation, and iii) the integration of a multisensory approach in the neurofeedback, while maintaining an anchor to standardized datasets for emotional elicitation.

The self-monitoring and real-time regulation of mental states through immersive neurofeedback scenarios is particularly used in the context of supporting meditation [23–25]. These systems offer individuals a dynamic and interactive representation of their psychophysiological state, thereby motivating them to pursue their training objectives. Semertzidis and colleagues propose Neo-Noumena, a system that aims to improve interpersonal communication through dynamic emotion representation, using EEG to drive procedural content generation algorithms (specifically fractals) [26]. In line with this proposal, the current study introduces a collection of three-dimensional geometric primitives within the visual neurofeedback channel. The geometric properties of these primitives are modulated in response to the subject's emotional progression, aligning with the principles of neuroaesthetics, an interdisciplinary field focused on investigating the neural foundations of aesthetic experiences [27]. Numerous studies are currently investigating the correlation between emotions and the aesthetic attributes of geometric patterns, including fractals and primitive forms [28]. These patterns exhibit aesthetic properties that capture attention and elicit emotional responses [26,29]. Angular geometric patterns, distinguished by sharp edges and well-defined angles, are often associated with sensations of threat or danger [30]. Conversely, curvilinear shapes characterized by smooth curves are commonly linked to feelings of pleasantness or happiness.

Finally, the level of immersion offered by the VR system depends on the extent of the involved perceptual domains and the ability to combine multiple sensory channels [23,31]. The use of multisensory interfaces provides a level of immersion that can support more reliable elicitation of emotional experiences, particularly concerning negative emotions such as fear and anger [32]. Based on this premise, the present study considers not only the visual channel but also the auditory channel, leveraging the music emotion dataset proposed in [33].

In Sect. 2, the overall neurofeedback systems, the experimental campaign for the EEG signal acquisitions are presented. The usability results is reported in Sect. 3. Discussions and conclusions are illustrated in Sect. 4 and Sect. 5, respectively.

2   Material and Methods

2.1   VR Neurofeedback System

Inducing a specific emotional state in the user is achieved through a multisensory approach, utilizing both the auditory channel and the visual channel. For the auditory channel, musical tracks from the publicly available standardized dataset produced by Soleymani et al. were used [33]. The utilization of a standardized dataset ensures the preservation of a ground truth for emotional elicitation. The dataset consists entirely of Creative Commons music from the Free Music Archive, containing 1000 unpublished tracks from non-label sources (to reduce familiarity bias), each annotated by a minimum of 10 subjects. The dimensional model is employed as a reference theory, as the tracks are evaluated using Russell's circumplex model [34]. The objective is to move from a point hypothetically close to the extreme boundary of the second quadrant to its opposite extreme in the fourth quadrant, assuming that the starting point and endpoint can be likened to a high anxiety condition and a relaxation condition, respectively. This assumption was made considering that anxiety is commonly characterized by high arousal and low valence [35]. Thus, to achieve self-regulation of anxiety responses, considering the valence-arousal plane (x-axis valence, y-axis arousal), sound stimuli were selected according to their alignment with the y=-x line. However, analyzing the distribution of annotations on the Russell plane reveals that the stimuli are polarized along line y=x. Therefore, the tracks closest in terms of Euclidean distance to the extremes of the second and fourth quadrants were considered. From these samples, a more densely populated area was identified, with valence $v \in [3,6]$ and arousal $a \in [2,8]$ (the gray area in Fig. 1). Then, the anti-diagonal of this region was divided into 6 subgroups, calculating as many equidistributed centroids and considering the samples closest to these centroids according to the K-means algorithm. The sample sizes for each subgroup are shown in Fig. 1. During both the emotional elicitation (baseline) and regulation phases, subjects were presented with songs from the first 3 groups according to the following ratio: 50% from group 3, 30% from group 2, and 20% from group 1 (the group with the highest anxiety elicitation). The songs were presented randomly to avoid habituation and familiarity. In the neurofeedback phase, there is a gradual transition to songs belonging to groups 4, 5 and 6 as anxiety levels drop.

Regarding the visual channel, abstract geometric primitives were used[1], possessing aesthetic properties in accordance with the literature and capable of eliciting specific emotional responses. Following the approach taken for the auditory stimulus, six different models were created (see Fig. 2): those associated with groups 4–6 (relaxation-related area) were derived from elaborations of simple and smooth geometric shapes (such as toroids, spheres, and spirals). Those associated with groups 1–3 were modeled by an elaboration of angular and fragmented forms (such as triangles).

---

[1] "Abstract Primitives 1", freely downloadable on Sketchfab.

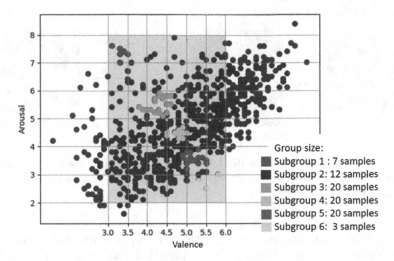

Fig. 1. Scatter plot of annotated audio samples from the dataset of Soleymani et al. [33], indicating the six selected subgroups.

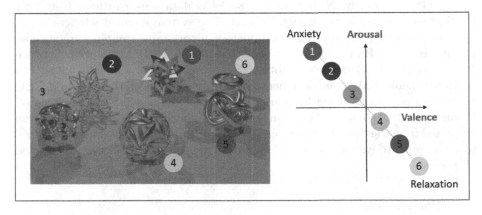

Fig. 2. Abstract geometric primitives associated with the six music subgroups.

Specifically, the application immerses the user in a neutral, relaxing, and distraction-free space, akin to a meditation room. Three-dimensional models, all in white color, appear in front of the user's perspective, undergoing a constant rotation around the y-axis of 20° per second; sound is delivered utilizing spatial audio features, with a sound source positioned corresponding to the model. In the previous study, neurofeedback was provided through the evolution of a chromatic progress bar while keeping the stimulating image static. In this upgrade, both visual and auditory stimuli evolve in harmony with the EEG feature's dynamics. The transition between tracks and primitives occurs through a fade-in/fade-out effect, triggered by new EEG scores (see Fig. 3). Every pair of stimuli has at least a duration of 3 s. The scores associated with the EEG feature values are

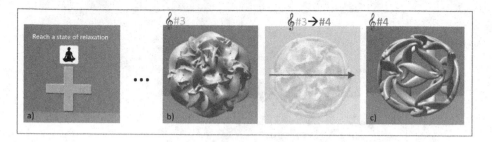

Fig. 3. Excerpt from the Neurofeedback training protocol: after the task introduction (a), a typical transition from a more anxious state (b) to a less anxious state (c) is performed by the subject.

smoothed using a moving average algorithm to avoid abrupt transitions caused by noise-induced sudden changes. The application was developed using Unity [36] (version 2019.4.4f1) as game engine, and the VR system used the HTC Vive Pro 2 [37] as the VR HMD. Signal recordings were conducted using the FlexEEG^{TM} system by Neuroconcise [38]. EEG data were captured from only Pz electrode placed in the parietal region. The system enabled wireless signal transmission using Bluetooth 2.0 and offered customizable sampling frequencies ranging from 125 Hz to 250 Hz, along with adjustable ADC resolution between 16 and 24 bits. EEG signal was obtained and processed in real-time within the Matlab version R2021b environment. Online processing of the acquired EEG signal was performed using Simulink. Following bandpass filtering with cutoff frequencies of 20 Hz and 34 Hz, consecutive 2-s epochs with a 1-s overlap were extracted from the data. Fast Fourier Transform (FFT) was subsequently applied to each epoch to extract power values within the specific EEG frequency band of interest.

2.2 Participants

The developed prototype was preliminarily tested by three male Automation Engineering students from the University of Naples Federico II (average age 26.7), aiming to evaluate its usability. All three participants were familiar with BCI technology, but had no previous experience in the context of passive BCI specifically related to emotions, nor had any prior experience with VR. Written informed consent was obtained from all participants prior to their participation. Ethical approval, in accordance with the Helsinki Declaration, was obtained from the Ethical Committee for Psychological Research at the same university.

2.3 Procedure

The present usability evaluation study comprised a single session lasting approximately 20 min, conducted within the ARHeMLab laboratory at the University of Naples Federico II. The laboratory environment was deliberately low-lit and acoustically isolated to minimize distractions and interferences. Before starting the experiment, participants were briefed on the purpose of the study. Subsequently, participants were instructed to sit on a comfortable chair and wear the EEG headset and VR visor (see Fig. 4). The researchers present prepared the EEG headset by applying conductive gel and visually checked the signal quality on the scope. Following the EEG setup, participants were asked to immerse themselves in the virtual scenario displayed in front of them, following instructions provided by a prerecorded guiding voice.

Fig. 4. Experimental setup

Table 1. Instruction script for the emotion regulation.

Neurofeedback instruction
"Please strive to achieve a state of relaxation during the neurofeedback session by progressively making the geometric shapes you see appear softer and more curvilinear. Similarly, aim to make the music you listen to become increasingly soothing and calming. Focus on allowing both the visual and auditory stimuli to contribute to a sense of tranquility and relaxation".

Neurofeedback training focused on reducing high-beta power in the parietal area (Cz), associated with down-regulation of anxious response [39]. Following the same experimental protocol as the previous study [21], the session involved an initial calibration phase consisting of 2 min of resting state with eyes open and a task-related baseline, where the subject passively listens to audio tracks and observes geometric shapes (18 in total, each lasting 15-s and preceded by 10-s 3D fixation cross) belonging to groups 1–3. Mean high-beta powers were calculated for both phases. These values were then used (increased by 25% of their absolute value) as the upper and lower limits of the neurofeedback excursion scale, with each of the six groups occupying an equal portion of this range. After the calibration phase, the neurofeedback training was introduced. It consisted of a total of 18 trials, including 12 trials of active engagement with ER feedback provided to participants regarding their performance, and 6 trials of passive exposure to stimuli, during which participants were solely tasked with observing rotating 3D objects and listening to the provided music. Participants were presented with both regulation and passive viewing trials in a randomized manner. Each neurofeedback trial comprised an initial instructional prompt, followed by a 14-s fixation cross period (including a visual reminder of the upcoming task), and concluded with a 20-s stimulus presentation. During the training phase, participants were instructed to regulate their experienced emotions based on the feedback provided. Specifically, they were guided to modulate the activity of the target region according to the instructions provided in Table 1. The usability of the proposed neurofeedback system was assessed using the System Usability Scale (SUS) [40], Italian version. The EEG data were processed online, and the high-beta power calculated from the Fz electrode was used to drive the visual feedback provided to the user. The communication between Unity and Simulink followed the same approach described in [21] (Fig. 5).

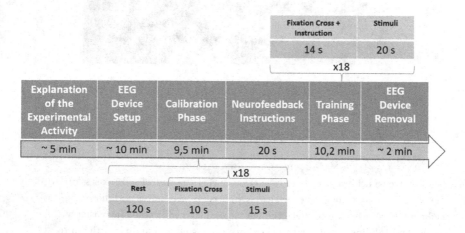

Fig. 5. Experimental protocol

3 Usability Results

Regarding the usability of the systems, the average System Usability Scale (SUS) score is 75 (SD = 6.61). As all SUS scores are greater than or equal to 70, the results indicate an acceptable level of system usability [41]. Participants tend to positively evaluate the overall usability.

4 Discussion

This pilot study aimed to provide an initial assessment of the usability of an adaptive multisensory VR system for emotional regulation. The study was conducted on a small sample of participants, therefore without claims of statistical significance. However, it lays the groundwork for future utilization of the system in an efficacy evaluation context, particularly regarding neurofeedback. Achieving a high average score on the System Usability Scale (SUS) provides preliminary and encouraging confirmation of the usability of a system that aims to actively elicit emotions in VR. The positive user feedback emphasizes the successful design of the proposed system from various perspectives.

First and foremost, in terms of multisensoriality, adaptability was ensured by effectively synchronizing stimuli across multiple channels. The synchronization between the auditory and visual channels was perceived as effective by the test participants, who did not perceive consisent discontinuities or interruptions in this integration. The impression of gradually performing a mental task that allowed for smooth transitions between stimuli was facilitated by setting a wait time parameter. This ensured minimal exposure to each individual stimulus before transitioning to the next. Without this precaution, users might have encountered continuous jumps between different stimuli, leading to fragmented experiences and hindering the development of a continuous mental engagement in regulation.

However, the proposed design also suffers from several limitations that need to be addressed in future work. Regarding the standardized auditory stimuli, which served as the ground truth in this study, a dataset [33] was used that had some regions of the Russell's plane underrepresented in its annotations. Considering stimuli from a more densely populated subset of the entire dataset may lead to a potential loss of elicitation power (e.g., for more anxiety-inducing or relaxing stimuli). Therefore, there is a need to create datasets in the future that better represent all regions of the Russell's plane. As for visual stimuli, the generation of procedural content was not offered. The transition between geometric shapes, based on theories of neuroaesthetics, was conducted based on predefined intervals. A future step could involve generating the eliciting stimuli procedurally in the regulation process, starting from subjective reactions, for both visual and auditory stimuli. Such an approach would provide greater adherence of stimuli to individual responses and potentially enhance responsiveness in the regulation process, albeit at the cost of losing anchoring to standardized data.

5   Conclusions

In this study, the design and development of an adaptive multisensory VR system for emotional self-regulation are presented. By integrating neurofeedback and VR technology, a more immersive and interactive experience for emotion elicitation and regulation was provided. The system utilizes EEG to measure brain activity and provides real-time feedback to individuals, enabling them to learn and regulate their emotional responses. The VR environment enhances the elicitation of emotions by engaging multiple sensory modalities and providing a realistic and interactive experience. The preliminary usability evaluation indicated an acceptable level of system usability, suggesting the potential of this approach for emotional self-regulation. Future research should focus on further evaluating the effectiveness of the system in larger and more diverse populations and exploring its potential applications in therapeutic interventions for disorders related to emotion regulation. Overall, this study contributes to the growing field of emotion regulation and highlights the promising role of neurofeedback and VR technology in this domain.

References

1. Gross, J.J.: Emotion regulation: current status and future prospects. Psychol. Inq. **26**(1), 1–26 (2015)
2. Cisler, J.M., Olatunji, B.O., Feldner, M.T., Forsyth, J.P.: Emotion regulation and the anxiety disorders: an integrative review. J. Psychopathol. Behav. Assess. **32**, 68–82 (2010)
3. Grecucci, A., Sığırcı, H., Lapomarda, G., Amodeo, L., Messina, I., Frederickson, J.: Anxiety regulation: from affective neuroscience to clinical practice. Brain Sci. **10**(11), 846 (2020)
4. Hamdani, S.U., Zafar, S.W., Suleman, N., Waqas, A., Rahman, A., et al.: Effectiveness of relaxation techniques 'as an active ingredient of psychological interventions' to reduce distress, anxiety and depression in adolescents: a systematic review and meta-analysis. Int. J. Ment. Heal. Syst. **16**(1), 1–17 (2022)
5. Arpaia, P., et al.: Mindfulness-based emotional acceptance in combination with neurofeedback for improving emotion self-regulation: a pilot study. In: 2022 IEEE International Conference on Metrology for Extended Reality, Artificial Intelligence and Neural Engineering (MetroXRAINE), pp. 465–470. IEEE (2022)
6. Enriquez-Geppert, S., Huster, R.J., Herrmann, C.S.: EEG-neurofeedback as a tool to modulate cognition and behavior: a review tutorial. Front. Hum. Neurosci. **11**, 51 (2017)
7. Hamann, S.: Mapping discrete and dimensional emotions onto the brain: controversies and consensus. Trends Cogn. Sci. **16**(9), 458–466 (2012)
8. Fox, N.A.: Dynamic cerebral processes underlying emotion regulation. In: Monographs of the Society for Research in Child Development, pp. 152–166 (1994)
9. Balconi, M., Frezza, A., Vanutelli, M.E.: Emotion regulation in schizophrenia: a pilot clinical intervention as assessed by EEG and optical imaging (functional near-infrared spectroscopy). Front. Hum. Neurosci. **12**, 395 (2018)
10. Davidson, R.J.: Affective style and affective disorders: perspectives from affective neuroscience. Cogn. Emot. **12**(3), 307–330 (1998)

11. Hafeez, Y., et al.: Development of enhanced stimulus content to improve the treatment efficacy of EEG-based frontal alpha asymmetry neurofeedback for stress mitigation. IEEE Access **9**, 130638–130648 (2021)
12. Al-Ezzi, A., Kamel, N., Faye, I., Ebenezer, E.G.M.: EEG frontal theta-beta ratio and frontal midline theta for the assessment of social anxiety disorder. In: 2020 10th IEEE International Conference on Control System, Computing and Engineering (ICCSCE), pp. 107–112. IEEE (2020)
13. Mennella, R., Patron, E., Palomba, D.: Frontal alpha asymmetry neurofeedback for the reduction of negative affect and anxiety. Behav. Res. Ther. **92**, 32–40 (2017)
14. Trystuła, M., Zielińska, J., Półrola, P., Góral-Półrola, J., Kropotov, J.D., Pąchalska, M.: Neuromarkers of anxiety in a patient with suspected schizophrenia and TIA: the effect of individually-tailored neurofeedback. Acta Neuropsychologica **13**(4), 395–403 (2015)
15. Riva, G., Wiederhold, B.K., Mantovani, F.: Neuroscience of virtual reality: from virtual exposure to embodied medicine. Cyberpsychol. Behav. Soc. Netw. **22**(1), 82–96 (2019)
16. Rivu, R., Jiang, R., Mäkelä, V., Hassib, M., Alt, F.: Emotion elicitation techniques in virtual reality. In: Ardito, C., et al. (eds.) INTERACT 2021. LNCS, vol. 12932, pp. 93–114. Springer, Cham (2021). https://doi.org/10.1007/978-3-030-85623-6_8
17. Meuleman, B., Rudrauf, D.: Induction and profiling of strong multi-componential emotions in virtual reality. IEEE Trans. Affect. Comput. **12**(1), 189–202 (2018)
18. Kihlstrom, J.F.: Ecological validity and "ecological validity". Perspect. Psychol. Sci. **16**(2), 466–471 (2021)
19. Bekele, E., Bian, D., Peterman, J., Park, S., Sarkar, N.: Design of a virtual reality system for affect analysis in facial expressions (VR-SAAFE); application to schizophrenia. IEEE Trans. Neural Syst. Rehabil. Eng. **25**(6), 739–749 (2016)
20. Lang, P.J., Bradley, M.M., Cuthbert, B.N., et al.: International affective picture system (IAPS): technical manual and affective ratings. NIMH Center Study Emot. Attent. **1**(39–58), 3 (1997)
21. Arpaia, P., et al.: Virtual reality enhances EEG-based neurofeedback for emotional self-regulation. In: De Paolis, L.T., Arpaia, P., Sacco, M. (eds.) XR Salento 2022, Part II. LNCS, vol. 13446, pp. 420–431. Springer, Cham (2022). https://doi.org/10.1007/978-3-031-15553-6_29
22. Hammond, D.C.: Neurofeedback with anxiety and affective disorders. Child Adolescent Psychiatric Clinics **14**(1), 105–123 (2005)
23. Arpaia, P., D'Errico, G., De Paolis, L.T., Moccaldi, N., Nuccetelli, F.: A narrative review of mindfulness-based interventions using virtual reality. Mindfulness 1–16 (2021)
24. Roo, J.S., Gervais, R., Hachet, M.: Inner garden: an augmented sandbox designed for self-reflection. In: Proceedings of the TEI 2016: Tenth International Conference on Tangible, Embedded, and Embodied Interaction, pp. 570–576 (2016)
25. Kitson, A., DiPaola, S., Riecke, B.E.: Lucid loop: a virtual deep learning biofeedback system for lucid dreaming practice. In: Extended Abstracts of the. CHI Conference on Human Factors in Computing Systems 2019, pp. 1–6 (2019)
26. Semertzidis, N., et al.: Neo-noumena: augmenting emotion communication. In: Proceedings of the 2020 CHI Conference on Human Factors in Computing Systems, pp. 1–13 (2020)
27. Zeki, S., Lamb, M.: The neurology of kinetic art. Brain **117**(3), 607–636 (1994). https://doi.org/10.1093/brain/117.3.607

28. Bies, A.J., Blanc-Goldhammer, D.R., Boydston, C.R., Taylor, R.P., Sereno, M.E.: Aesthetic responses to exact fractals driven by physical complexity. Front. Hum. Neurosci. **10** (2016). https://www.frontiersin.org/articles/10.3389/fnhum.2016.00210

29. Street, N., Forsythe, A.M., Reilly, R., Taylor, R., Helmy, M.S.: A complex story: universal preference vs. individual differences shaping aesthetic response to fractals patterns. Front. Hum. Neurosci. **10** (2016). https://www.frontiersin.org/articles/10.3389/fnhum.2016.00213

30. Larson, C., Aronoff, J., Steuer, E.: Simple geometric shapes are implicitly associated with affective value. Motiv. Emot. **36**, 09 (2011)

31. Bohil, C.J., Alicea, B., Biocca, F.A.: Virtual reality in neuroscience research and therapy. Nat. Rev. Neurosci. **12**(12), 752–762 (2011)

32. Susindar, S., Sadeghi, M., Huntington, L., Singer, A., Ferris, T.K.: The feeling is real: emotion elicitation in virtual reality. In: Proceedings of the Human Factors and Ergonomics Society Annual Meeting, Los Angeles, CA, vol. 63, no. 1, pp. 252–256. SAGE Publications, Sage (2019)

33. Soleymani, M., Caro, M.N., Schmidt, E.M., Sha, C.-Y., Yang, Y.-H.: 1000 songs for emotional analysis of music. In: Proceedings of the 2nd ACM International Workshop on Crowdsourcing for Multimedia, pp. 1–6 (2013)

34. Russell, J.A.: A circumplex model of affect. J. Pers. Soc. Psychol. **39**(6), 1161 (1980)

35. Ding, Y., Liu, J., Zhang, X., Yang, Z.: Dynamic tracking of state anxiety via multi-modal data and machine learning. Front. Psychiatry **13** (2022)

36. Unity. https://unity.com/. Accessed 28 Apr 2022

37. HTC VIVE PRO 2. https://www.vive.com/eu/product/vive-pro/. Accessed 28 Apr 2022

38. Neuroconcise technology. https://www.neuroconcise.co.uk/. Accessed 28 Apr 2022

39. Hammond, D.C.: What is neurofeedback? J. Neurother. **10**(4), 25–36 (2007)

40. Brooke, J.: SUS: a 'quick and dirty' usability. In: Usability Evaluation in Industry, vol. 189, no. 3 (1996)

41. Bangor, A., Kortum, P.T., Miller, J.T.: An empirical evaluation of the system usability scale. Int. J. Hum.-Comput. Interact. **24**(6), 574–594 (2008)

Correction to: Measuring the Effectiveness of Virtual Reality for Stress Reduction: Psychometric Evaluation of the ERMES Project

Giovanni D'Errico⊙, Maria Cristina Barba, Carola Gatto⊙,
Benito Luigi Nuzzo, Fabiana Nuccetelli, Valerio De Luca⊙,
and Lucio Tommaso De Paolis⊙

Correction to:
Chapter 32 in: L. T. De Paolis et al. (Eds.): *Extended Reality*, LNCS 14218, https://doi.org/10.1007/978-3-031-43401-3_32

In the original version of the book contained a tagging error regarding chapter 32. The first and last names of two authors (Valerio De Luca and Lucio Tommaso De Paolis) were not displayed correctly. In fact, the first name is 'Valerio', while the surname is 'De Luca', whereas on the portal it appears indexed "Valerio De" as first name and "Luca" as surname. The same problem appeared for the other author "Lucio Tommaso De Paolis": the first name is "Lucio Tommaso", and the surname is "De Paolis". This has been corrected.

The updated version of this chapter can be found at
https://doi.org/10.1007/978-3-031-43401-3_32

Author Index

L. T. De Paolis et al. (Eds.): XR Salento 2023, LNCS 14218, pp. 537–540, 2023.
https://doi.org/10.1007/978-3-031-43401-3